# ∽ Pubs of ∽
# Royal Leamington Spa

*Two Centuries of History*

For Taverns, Inns, or Grand Hotels,

Not Buxton, Bath, nor Tunbridge Wells,

Nor any Spas, Thro'out the land,

Tho' they may boast of Crescents grand,

Can shew you Larders better fill'd

Or Cooks in piquant sauce more skill'd.

As for genteel accommodation,

None beats them in the British Nation.

For civil treatment all agree,

The best way is to come and see!


*James Bisset 1816*

# Pubs of
# Royal Leamington Spa

## Two Centuries of History

Allan Jennings, Martin Ellis and Tom Lewin

BREWIN BOOKS

First published by
Brewin Books Ltd, 56 Alcester Road,
Studley, Warwickshire B80 7LG in 2014
www.brewinbooks.com

ISBN: 978-1-85858-522-2

A Cataloguing in Publication Record
for this title is available from the British Library.

Typeset in Minion Pro
Printed in Great Britain by
Cambrian Printers.

# CONTENTS

# THE AUTHORS

**Allan Jennings** is a Leamingtonian whose passion for photography, local history, nostalgia and the occasional pint of 'real ale' have combined to provide the stimulus to embark on this project. He is a member of both Sydenham and Leamington History Groups and regularly gives history presentations to local history groups, church groups, charities and schools.

**Martin Ellis** is an ex-Leamingtonian now residing in Australia. During visits to 'Leam' between 1992 and 2008 he had lamented the declining number of 'traditional' English pubs over numerous pints of 'real ale' in the ever diminishing 'old haunts'. The seeds for an independent project were sown in June 2008 when discussing this very subject with friend Tom Lewin and learning that there was no printed record of the Leamington pubs that existed in the late 1960s/early 1970s.

**Tom Lewin** is the third Leamingtonian of the group who also has an interest in local history and nostalgia as well as a 'real pint' in a 'real pub'. He also gives talks to local history groups and is old friends with Martin. After losing touch in 1971 they were firstly reunited by e-mail in 2007 and then face-to-face at the Red House on the Radford Road the following year.

Quite independently, Martin Ellis commenced his pub project in early 2009 at home in Australia. The research was primarily internet based, with the sole objective then being to compile a list of premises and identify approximate opening and closing years. He never intended to research the licensees/landlords because he didn't have access to sequential trade directories and, as he says, "it was always going to be just a list, not a book, because with my remote resources it could never have been much more". Within six months, Martin's list of 'traditional' pubs extended back 150 years, but by his own admission it was skeletal, sources were drying-up and progress was slowing.

Back in Leamington, Allan Jennings had been taking photographs around town for many years, including the local pubs, and had also collected information on the latter during the same period. He had mentioned to Nigel Briggs from the Sydenham History Group that he might publish the photos one day but that he had no particular time-frame in mind. Nigel knew Tom Lewin, another local historian, who mentioned that he had a friend in Australia that was compiling a list of Leamington pubs. Nigel suggested that the three get together, which they did – and the rest, as they say, is history....

# PREFACE

There have been numerous books written on many aspects of Leamington's history and while its pubs have been covered to some extent the information has usually been limited to part of another story, a paragraph here and there or the odd photograph. As we could find no evidence of a [Leamington] pub specific book having been written previously, we decided that filling the void would be a worthwhile project.

Our brief was to research the history of the pubs of Royal Leamington Spa covering the period 1800 until the end of 2012, albeit with the occasional reference predating 1800, which takes us back to a time when there were only two pubs in the then village of Leamington Priors. But what constitutes a pub, or a public house? Is it a Victorian ale house, beer house, a parlour bar, or is it what the three authors of this tōme remember as a 'traditional' pub from our time growing up in the 1960s and 70s? Where is the line drawn between a pub and a bar, a bar/restaurant and a wine bar, etc? Does it even have to be brick built or does a marquee called the Leamside Inn also qualify?

Initially we had intended this book to be solely about 'traditional' pubs but the word 'traditional', and that approach, was considered inappropriate as the pub has been evolving for centuries and continues to do so. Variously referred to as an inn, tavern, alehouse, beer house and public house, its evolution has certainly accelerated since the early 1970s. Until then the 'local' was most likely a brewery owned pub, selling beer from a British owned brewery and offering a choice of rooms to drink in, at prices that varied accordingly to the comfort level.[1] To use our 'old locals' as examples, and in escalating price sequence, the Jet and Whittle and Sun in Splendour once comprised a *bar* and *lounge* [saloon], while the Joiners Arms also had a *snug* [smoke room] which was a small room offering privacy to those that didn't want to be seen. If drink was required at home it was available from the pub's 'outdoor' [or 'off-sales counter'] but the advent of the supermarket in the 1970s, and their cut-price alcohol, soon made these outlets redundant. Nowadays, most of the major British breweries are owned by multi-national companies, and most of the pubs are owned by a PubCo [e.g. Wetherspoons, Punch Taverns]. Furthermore, since the 1970s many pubs have been converted to, or built as, single-room spaces ['open plan']. In summary, we suggest that the definition of a pub [versus wine bar, for example] is purely subjective, as the term 'pub' will conjure up different images to different individuals and the resultant opinion may be influenced more by one's age than anything else.

As this book was originally to be solely about pubs we hadn't intended to include hotels or hotel bars, but then we found that people fondly remembered bars such as that in the Bath Hotel, Syd's Bar at the Regent Hotel and the Tavern Bar at Guys Hotel, so in they went! Some hotels began as an inn and evolved into a hotel, examples being the Angel Inn [Regent Street], Crown Inn [High Street] and the New Inn [Bath Street] which became the Bath Hotel. Many other hotels also achieved iconic status, and a place in Leamington's history, such as the Bedford [Lower Parade], Clarendon [Parade], Great Western [High Street] and Manor House [Avenue Road], so they too earned a place in the book.

The prime sources for our research have been local history books, business directories, licensing records, licensing sessions' reporting and local press reports. In the case of the latter, all editions of the Leamington Spa Courier have been checked from the date of its first publishing in 1828 until the present day. Similarly, Morning News editions [published: 1896-1991] have also been comprehensively reviewed, although the majority of its reporting was also covered by the Courier. Where fitting, we've either quoted the respective newspaper verbatim or applied an edited version of the original report, the objective being to tell the story through the eyes of the local press as it happened. Accordingly, special thanks go to Chris Lillington, the editor of the Leamington Spa Courier, for granting us permission to use information sourced from the aforementioned newspapers – without his support there would've been no book. We are also grateful to many of Leamington's publicans, past and present, for their support and the sharing of their photos, memorabilia and memories; likewise their clientele who have done the very same. Finally, thanks go to the local historians who have also generously shared information relevant to this project.

While we have endeavoured to make the entries as comprehensive as possible we were mindful that it would be impossible to research every aspect of every pub's history, both timewise and because one doesn't know what one doesn't know. As it is, with more than 350 entries on our masterlist [including name changes], the number of research hours invested by the three of us are incalculable. Unfortunately, many of the key historical records that we sought either no longer exist or their whereabouts are unknown, thus resulting in unavoidable gaps in our research; we also came across a lot of conflicting information that had to be corroborated.

Among other obstacles to overcome were the incessant renaming and/or renumbering of streets, particularly in the 19th century, and of course the renaming of the pubs themselves; when combined, these factors made it painstakingly difficult to link some pub sites that would otherwise have been incorrectly treated as being unrelated. Although our research has been as thorough as realistically possible, occasionally we have had to consider conflicting evidence; if we have misinterpreted any information and/or drawn any incorrect conclusions along the way we apologise.

Finally, herewith a brief explanation of the 'licensee' related dates as tabled in the pub entries and some pointers on how to interpret them:

- If it is a complete date such as '5th May 1940' then that is the date that the licence was transferred and we are confident of its accuracy.
- If the licensee's first year is listed as '≤1848' [less than or equal to '1848'], then we have confirmed their presence in 1848, but the actual 'start date' could be earlier.
- If the licensee's last year is listed as '≥1849' [greater than or equal to '1849'], then we have confirmed their presence in 1849, but the actual 'end date' could be later.
- If listed as '1945-1950' then we have confirmed that the licensee's tenure spanned [at least] that period, but that he/she may also have been the licensee prior to, and/or post, that period.

*Additional Notes*

- You may notice that some of the listed pubs have a first licence date of 1869, but also have directory entries that pre-date that year. These inconsistencies emanate from the implementation of the *Wine and Beerhouse Act of 1869* which saw a return to stricter licensing controls; from that year it was a requirement that retailers of beer, cider, wine and spirits make application to the local justices for a 'certificate of permission' before they could obtain an Excise on-licence [a similar certificate was also necessary before an off-licence could be obtained].

- Furthermore, we have also found discrepancies between directory listings and licensing records. While directories are renowned for being out-of-date, any such discrepancy could simply be a timing issue due to a licensee taking-over after the annual directory had been compiled; as the subject's name is not listed in that edition it appears that he/she took over the following year. Similarly, a check of the licence register sometimes revealed that a directory was not updated to reflect that a licensee was deceased and that his wife, or another member of the family, had taken over.

The compilation of this history has been a fascinating and enjoyable experience for us and we have done our utmost to deliver a book that you will find both interesting and informative, and one that will hopefully trigger some fond memories.

Enjoy the read....

Cheers!

*Allan, Martin and Tom*

# INTRODUCTION

In 1776, Samuel Johnson wrote, "There is nothing which has yet been contrived by man, by which so much happiness is produced as by a good tavern or inn."

The 'pub' has been an important part of the British cultural fabric for centuries with its origins believed to date back to Roman times; however, it is likely that the 'pub' as we know it was in its early stages of development in Anglo-Saxon times. In his book, 'Beer has a History' [1947], F. A. King refers to wooden huts described as 'tabernae' which were built alongside the old Roman roads for the sale of liquid refreshment during the Saxon period.[2] Furthermore, in his book 'A History of the English Public House' H. A. Monckton writes, "Somewhere between 740 and 750 – the exact year is not conclusively established – Ecbright, Archbishop of York ordained 'that no priest go to eat or drink in taverns.'"[3]

Relatively speaking, Royal Leamington Spa has a very short history as a town of any consequence. Although mentioned in the circa 1086 Domesday Book [a survey record of English land properties ordered by William I] as Lamintone, it would've been nothing more than a hamlet. From early in the 12th century until the dissolution of the monasteries in the mid 1530s the land in the subject area was owned by the Priors of Kenilworth; it was during this period that the hamlet became known as Leamington Priors.

The earliest evidence we have found of any licensed premises in Leamington Priors is in 'A Complete History of Royal Leamington Spa' [1896] when T. B. Dudley informs us that in 1625 there were two inns and William Mills and Margaret Wallsgrave were the licence holders. In all probability the two inns were the Black Dog on London Road [now High Street] and the Bowling Green [Church Lane], subsequently famous in the days of Benjamin Satchwell and William Abbotts.[4] Although by then still no more than a village of less than 250 persons, the following order by the Warwickshire Court of Quarter Sessions dated 1625 has the appearance of a report from a well populated and thriving township:

"An order for the suppressing of Wm. Mills and Margrett Walsgrave, of Lemington Priors, Victualers. Forasmuch as the court was this present day informed by a certificate of dyvers of the inhabitants of Lemington Pryors, in this Countie, that William Mills and Margrett Wallsgrave, two victualers, who in the said towne keepe very ill order and rule in their houses, soe that their neighbours are offended and wronged thereby, besydes, as this Court is informed, the said Margrett selleth also without a lycense, in contempt of this court. It is, therefore, Ordered that the said William Mills and Margrett Walsgrave shall be from henceforth absolutely suppressed from offering or sellinge Ale, beare, or victuals any more, which if they, or eyther of them continue, Then the Constable there is required to apprehend them and attache the bodyes, and them, the said Wm. Mills and Margrett Walsgrave, or eyther of them, and them soe attached, to bring or cause to be brought before some justice of peace of this Countie, there to finde sufficient sureties to forbeare selling ale, beare, and victuals as aforesaid, which if they, or eyther of them refuse to doe, then to committ them soe *refusing to His Majestie's gaole of this Countie, there to remaine untill they willingly doe and perform the same. Hereof faile not, as the contrarye you will answere at your perill."*

In 1662, victualler Edward Heath of Leamington Priors was presented in front of Warwick County Court for selling less than a quart of ale for a penny, this being in breach of the statute [a short measure], and in Epiphany 1663 he was fined.

Born at Long Itchington in 1736, William Abbotts erected the first baths in Leamington Priors but from 1776 until the time of their construction in 1786 he kept the Black Dog Inn [or the 'Dog' as it was also known]; this together with the Bowling Green were the only two premises during that period that were suitable for the reception of visitors.[5]

In 1783, with a population of less than 300 and still situated primarily on the south side of the River Leam, the village of Leamington comprised, a parish church and vicarage, parish poor house, post office, manor house, three farms, water mill, 'smithy', two inns [Black Dog and Bowling Green], up to maybe 50 cottages, the village stocks, an old well, a duck pond and a fish pond.[6]

However, due to the existence of saline water springs, the medicinal properties of which had been recognised, it became increasingly fashionable to 'take the waters', and so Leamington Priors became Leamington Spa and its population growth began to accelerate....

| | | |
|---|---|---|
| 1801 | 315 | - |
| 1811 | 543 | +72% |
| 1821 | 2,183 | +302% |
| 1831 | 6,269 | +187% |
| 1841 | 12,812 | +104% |
| 1851 | 15,723 | +23% |
| 1861 | 17,402 | +11% |
| 1871 | 20,917 | +20% |
| 1881 | 22,976 | +10% |
| 1891 | 23,124 | +6% |
| 1901 | 26,888 | +16% |

As the town grew and prospered so too did the number of public houses, hotels and boarding houses also increase. In 1800 there were still just two inns in the village and by 1829 the *Moncrieff Guide* only listed fourteen *'taverns &c'* in Leamington, i.e.

| | |
|---|---|
| Angel Inn | Regent Street |
| Bedford Tap [Inn] | Bedford Street |
| Birmingham Tavern | Wise Street |
| Golden Lion | Regent Street |
| Half Moon | Satchwell Street |
| Kings Arms Inn | Warwick Street |
| Ranelagh Tavern | Ranelagh Street |

|                              |                    |
|-----------------------------:|:-------------------|
| Royal Hotel Tap              | Clemens Street     |
| Royal Oak                    | Park Street        |
| Shakespeare Inn              | Regent Street      |
| Union Inn & Commercial Hotel | Church Street      |
| Warwick Tavern               | Regent Street      |
| Wellington Tavern            | Wellington Street  |
| Woodman                      | Bedford Street     |

Our listings indicate that the Crown Inn [Kenilworth Road] and Star & Garter [Warwick Street] should also have been included in the 1829 *Moncrieff Guide* thereby making a total of sixteen, of which twelve were located in the 'new' town and four south of the river. However, these figures were about to increase enormously, totally outstripping the population growth due to other influences....

**Footnote:** Subsequent statistics referencing the growth and decline in the number of Leamington's pubs exclude premises that were primarily operated as a hotel, however these are well covered in the alphabetical listing of 'establishments' that follows this introduction.

Over the centuries *public houses* have also been variously referred to as *inns, taverns, alehouses* and *beer houses,* but in the upcoming paragraphs we have elected to use the term 'pub' as the generic reference, this no doubt being the most familiar to the majority of readers. However, by definition, each of the above did play a different role in society. While *inns* could be described as premises that provided lodging, food and drink for travellers, *taverns* differed by providing food and alcoholic drink, but no accommodation. The *alehouses,* on the other hand, were essentially for drinking only and sold all types of alcoholic liquor, while *beer houses* were restricted to selling beer and cider only [the term *alehouse* would gradually be replaced by that of *public house* from the early 19th century]. Towards the end of the 20th century, along with the changing pubscape, would come new terms such as *bar, wine bar, bistro bar, bar and restaurant* etc, but more about those later.

Although there is evidence of localised controls being exercised over *alehouses* in medieval times, from a national perspective it is considered that the selling of alcohol was loosely regulated prior to 1552. It was as this point in time that Parliament saw it necessary to enact legislation to control the growth of such establishments on a national basis. The *Alehouse Act* of 1552 [5 & 6 Edw VI c.25] prohibited the sale of ale or beer without a licence granted by the local justices. Furthermore, it was a requirement of each licensee to enter into a recognisance [bond] pledging to abide by the act and maintain good order in their *alehouse*.[7] This Act is commonly acknowledged as that which laid the foundation for subsequent and modern licensing laws.

It would be more than 250 years before there were any further significant changes to the legislation that governed the issue of licences. The *Alehouse Act 1828* [9 Geo 4 c.61] provided that the grant of licences be made at annual licensing meetings [better known as Brewster Sessions] and in Leamington Spa these sessions were held in August/September; periodic 'special sessions' were also held during each year to process the transfer of existing licences. Furthermore, it was no longer necessary for a licensee to enter into a bond or provide certification of their good character. From hereon, a full publican's licence was the only licence type that authorised the licensee to retail any class of excisable liquor.[3] Unfortunately for modern day researchers, the Act made no provision for the ongoing maintenance of licence registers, or their recognisances [as enacted in 1753], and therefore the completeness of these records is sadly deficient for the period 1828-72.[7]

The *Beerhouse Act 1830* [1 Wm IV c.64] was introduced in an attempt to reduce the excessive consumption of spirits, eradicate 'gin houses' and suppress the increasing incidence of public drunkenness and other anti-social behaviour. However, this Act also dismantled many of the controls introduced under previous Acts and, in doing so, relaxed the regulations applicable to the licensing of premises. It enacted that any householder assessed to the poor rate [a tax levied by parishes for the support of the poor] could retail beer from their premises without obtaining a licence from the local justices, simply an Excise licence costing two guineas [£2.2s.] per annum.[7] These lower tier establishments were termed *beer houses*, as they could only sell beer [and cider].

Due to the ease of obtaining a *beer house* licence and it's relatively low cost when compared to the profit potential the take-up rate proved to be overwhelming. During the first five years following the 1830 Act at least 53 *beer houses* were opened in Leamington, by 1840 the cumulative total had passed 75 and by 1850 the total number opened in the twenty year period approximated 95 [68% in the 'new' town and 32% south of the river]. However, it was soon perceived that many of the *beer house* licences had been taken out by unscrupulous operators who, with an eye for a quick profit, often provided sub-standard facilities and poor quality beer.

*"In the early 1800s the lot of the working classes was not a happy one – very low wages, intolerable housing conditions and little or no health care. The average week was almost totally occupied at work, and not much was done to cater for the needs of leisure time [little that it was] for the town's small army of working people. It is therefore understandable that the growth of taverns kept pace with the rapid increase in the numbers of male workers who were mainly employed in domestic service. The men of the long suffering working classes gladly forsook their overcrowded and squalid dwelling-places to congregate in the humble but cheery beer-houses."* [8]

The *Beer House [Amendment] Act 1834* attempted to redress the situation and for the first time a distinction was made between 'on' and 'off' retail sales. The on-licence fee was reset to three guineas [£3.3s.], an increase of one guinea, and stricter conditions were attached to its issue [good character references]; the annual off-licence fee was set at one guinea.[3] Although 18 of the 75+ *beer houses* that opened in the period 1830-1840 also closed during the same time-frame, all of the closures were in 1838-40 suggesting that their demise was more to do with market forces, or enforced closure, than the increased licence fee.

Nevertheless, by 1840 there were about 78 pubs in the town compared with just 16 on the eve of the 1830 *Beer House Act*, a fivefold increase during a period when Leamington's population doubled to circa 12,500. By 1869, the count approximated 95, bringing the total number of *beer houses* opened since the *1830 Act* to circa 120 – during the same period their attrition rate approximated 28%. Among the casualties were five from the '1829 listing' these being the Birmingham Tavern [Wise Street], Crown Inn [Kenilworth Road],

Royal Hotel Tap [Clemens Street], Union Inn & Commercial Hotel [Church Street], and Wellington Tavern [Wellington Street].

The next licensing legislation to impact significantly on the issue of licences was the *Wine & Beer House Act 1869* [32 & 33 Vic c.27] which re-introduced the stricter controls that had existed prior to the *1830 Beerhouse Act*. Until 1869 licensing justices could only grant [full] publican's licences but this Act gave them the power to control all types of retail 'on' and 'off' licences. However, they were not empowered to refuse a renewal certificate for an on-licence which was already in existence on 1st May 1869 [beer house licences] unless certain conditions were breached, i.e. the applicant's lack of good character, poor conduct or ill-conduct of the premises.[9]

One of the key features of the 1872 *Licensing Act* [35 & 36 Vict c.94] was the provisioning for a two tier licensing hierarchy; the local magistrates would hear and determine each new licence to be granted but their decision would not be valid until confirmed by the county licensing committee; the number of licensed houses, and the power to close-down any considered superfluous, was relegated to the local licensing justices. Also from 1872, it was a requirement that the clerks of the licensing justices maintain a comprehensive licence register[10] [thereby making modern day research from thereon marginally less difficult].

In Leamington, the impact of the 1869 and 1872 Acts was immediate as the prolific issue of on-licences was stemmed but although the new licensing laws prevented the opening of new *beer houses* those existing were able to continue and many applied for full on-licences. During the next three decades the number of pubs in the town would remain unchanged, with there being just 13 additions and 13 closures during the period 1870-1904. There were also two more casualties from the '1829 listing' these being the Royal Oak [Park Street] and the Shakespeare Inn [Regent Street] with the Warwick Tavern becoming a hotel in 1904. According to our research the Leamington pub count peaked at about 100 houses circa 1880 before commencing its decline from 1905.

At the end of the 19th century the government was again concerned about alcohol consumption and set-up the *Peel Commission*. Summarily the *Peel Report [1899]* recommended a reduction in the number of *beer houses* and that the standard of those remaining be improved; some of its recommendations would be implemented in the 1902 and 1904 *Licensing Acts*. The *Licensing Act 1902* [2 Edw 7 c.28] enacted that an application for a new on-licence must be accompanied by a plan of the premises for due consideration by the licensing justices. Similarly, on receiving application for an on-licence renewal the licensing justices were empowered to request a plan of the premises and order structural alterations, if deemed necessary, to secure the proper conduct of the business. Furthermore, structural alterations to existing licensed premises could not be undertaken without formal application, submission of plans and the consent of the licensing justices.[11]

The key change made by the *Licensing Act 1904* [4 Edw 7 c.23], relative to our history of the local pubs, was to restrict the power of the licensing justices when refusing licence renewal to the following statutory reasons: illconduct of premises, structurally deficient or unsuitable premises and unsatisfactory character or unfitness of the licensee. All other grounds for licence withdrawal were to be referred by the local licensing justices to the county licensing committee who had the power to refuse licences on almost any grounds [e.g. redundancy] on payment of compensation in accordance with the Act. If the value of the compensation granted was disputed then the issue was referred to the Commissioners of Inland Revenue for determination; any licence referred for 'extinction' would remain valid until the matter had been finalised. This Act brought the pre 1869 *beer houses* within the control of the local licensing justices who could now deal with them in exactly the same manner as they dealt with other licensed premises [the transfer of this authority became effective on 15th August, 1904].[12]

The impact of this Act was swift with the Albatross [Clemens Street] and the Victoria Vaults [Tavistock Street] being closed in February 1905 without compensation being paid; these were the first pubs in Leamington to have their licence renewals refused because the premises were not structurally suitable for use as a licensed house. The Warneford Arms [Charles Street] was to meet the same fate twelve months later although in that case compensation was paid.

Following the annual licensing session held on 6th February 1906, the Leamington Courier reported that Mr. Crowther Davies [clerk to the licensing justices] had stated that by the direction of the justices of the borough he was instructed to object to the renewal of certain licences. The outcome of this process was tabled at the annual licensing sessions held on 4th February 1908 when the chief constable reported that a further eight licensed premises had been closed since 1905 [with compensation] after being adjudged 'redundant' these being: Ivy Tree [Queens Street], Noahs Ark [Regent Street], Queens Cross [Livery Street], Gloucester Tavern [Gloucester Street], Rising Sun [Bedford Street], Reindeer [Clemens Street] all in 1907, and Red Lion [Park Street] and Stamford & Warrington Arms [Rugby Road] in 1908.

In 1922, there was another round of closures after more licences were adjudged 'redundant' at the annual licensing sessions in 1920, these being: Alexandra Inn [Abbotts Street], Chase Inn, Oxford Tavern [Oxford Street] and Garibaldi Inn [High Street]. Later the same decade the Guy Tavern [Guy Street] and Old White Lion [Brook Street] would also be closed and by 1930 the count had dropped to about 75 [there had been no new pubs opened since pre-1900]. During the 1930s and 1940s the status quo was maintained but with the latter decade delivering the Heathcote Inn [Tachbrook Road] – the first post war addition.

However, more change was on the way and there would be a further significant drop in numbers during the 1950s and 1960s, evidence of the redevelopment that was taking place in the town. The roll call at the end of the 1950s would identify eleven absentees: Althorpe Arms and Eagle Inn [Althorpe Street], Aylesford Arms [Bedford Street], Bell Inn [Rugby Road], Globe Inn [Park Street], Hare & Hounds [Regent Street], New Kings Arms [Warwick Street], Rob Roy [Brook Street], Star Inn [Wise Street], Volunteer Arms [Comyn Street], and Swan Inn [Clarendon & Swan Streets]. On the other side of the ledger there were just three additions, the Bulldog in St Margaret's Road [now Whitnash Tavern], Sun in Splendour in Tachbrook Road [now The Sun] and the Walnut Tree at Crown Way, Lillington [now the site of a supermarket].

Also noteworthy from this period was the increased focus on pub catering, which H. A. Monckton explains as follows, "There are good reasons for this pronounced swing towards snack and full catering. There are now more people on the road than ever before, whether on business or pleasure. Many travellers and their families simply cannot afford the high prices which have to be charged by the many excellent hotels and restaurants. There are also some who do not feel completely at ease in the rather more formal atmosphere of higher grade eating places. The less pretentious atmosphere of the pub and the lower prices associated with it seem to answer a definite need."[13]

However, there were those who were reluctant to embrace this, or any other, change to 'pub culture', hence the following article that appeared in the Leamington Spa Courier on 7th October 1960:

### Pubs not what they used to be, says Harry

*"Bit choosy what sort of pub he goes in is ol' Pete; likes a good, honest working class atmosphere. None o' this smart stuff you get so much of these days."*

*With his deep understanding of human ways, Pete had seen clearly right through the facade of middle class superficiality and was quite content with his lowly but proud position. He had few social aspirations, which was perhaps fortunate because Pete was a pretty non-descript mixed-bred dog.*

*It was Harry, his owner, who had been giving me this insight into Pete's psychological make-up as we sat in his local. Harry had taken to reflecting about the changes which had been creeping over local inns recently. The passing of the old Portobello in Warwick and the forthcoming introduction of eating facilities at the Coach & Horses were to him manifestations of a sinister revolution.*

*After all, the 'Coach' wasn't the only place to have taken this step. The Globe at Warwick had been doing a roaring trade in meals for some time while even down Bath Street the Chair & Rocket was doing steady business with its snack bar and grill.*

*In almost every pub you went into, hot steak pies, salads, cold meat and bulging sandwiches were as much in evidence as the mugs of beer. Things, he concluded, were changing. "But the changes lie not only in the move towards eating at public houses," I added, "but in the whole atmosphere. The old browns and creams have been disappearing to be replaced by bright multi-coloured decors with flowers, hanging plants and coloured lighting. Look at the Star & Garter for example. Many of the best old beer houses have to-day an almost cocktail-sipping air." Harry nodded sadly throughout my assessment of the situation. "All too true," he agreed, "but as to why...."*

*It was at this point in the conversation that George, who had till now remained silent, made his first contribution. By all reports, George was a much-travelled man – at least, he had been on the works' trip to Paris the previous year – and, bringing his wider experience to bear on the problem, he concluded that it was the increasing amount of travel abroad that had brought about the change. "People go abroad for their holidays," he explained, "and get continental ideas and atmosphere, see? Why, the Elephant & Castle in Warwick even calls two of its rooms the Spanish Lounge and the French Lounge. And all this pub and snack-bar combined is just like on the continent."*

*Harry, who had been seeking inspiration in a large frothy mug of mild, dismissed this explanation with a disdainful "Narrrr!" and with the finality of careful consideration pinpointed "television" as the sole cause. He described how the whole process of change in social life had taken place. The brewers had been forced to find some way of drawing people away from TV. Many had tried putting a set in the bar but this tended to drive away those who came for the company rather than attract the stay-at-homes. The breweries finally decided to smarten up their premises, as an incentive to people to come in.*

*Few dared to doubt the wisdom of Harry's judgement. Yes, television, that's what started the rot. But if the changes have met with the disapproval of the Harrys and the Georges, such is certainly not the reaction of all. The smarter places like the Clarendon, Regent, Crown and the Saxon Mill are busier than ever before.*

*The difference, perhaps, is the clientele. These places seem to attract a younger public not set in the old tradition of the English pub, ready and eager for something new and smart to match their new smart suit or their new smart car. It is particularly, though by no means exclusively, the younger people who listen to the Elephant & Castle band, eat at the Globe, cross over to the Regent for a beer after Saturday morning coffee or drive out to the Saxon Mill at the weekend.*

*Harry supposed it was all right if you liked that sort of thing and George, getting quite loquacious, reckoned young people should keep to coffee bars. Pete signified his sympathy for this view with a sad stare which indicated at the same time his resignation to the advances which the modern age expected.*

By the end of the 1960s the pub count had dropped to around 60 following yet another eleven closures: Brunswick Inn [Brunswick Street], Clarendon Tavern [Russell Street], Cottage Tavern [Queen Street], Gold Cup, Leamington Tavern [Tavistock Street], London Tavern [Satchwell Street], Mason's Arms [Rugby Road], Rose and Crown [Kenilworth Street], White Hart [Windsor Street], White Lion [Althorpe Street] and the Woodman Inn [Bedford Street], the latter being another casualty from our '1829 listing'. The only additions during this decade were the Jet & Whittle, Brunswick Street [replacing the Brunswick Inn], New Binswood Tavern, Rugby Road [replacing the 'old one' in Binswood Street] and the Jack & Jill [Lillington]. Additionally, although not typically classed as pubs, there were two very popular new venues added during this period; in December 1960 Syd's Bar opened at the Regent Hotel and in 1965 the Tavern Bar opened in the basement of the Guys Hotel.

During the latter part of the 1970s there began a cultural shift away from the 'traditional' pub to a new trendier format favoured by the younger generation. Some early examples of this in Leamington were Hinton's Wine Bar [Augusta Place], Regent Wine Bar [now Murphy's Bar], Regent Street; Wilde's [Parade], Winston's [Clarendon Avenue] and KA Bar [Clarendon Street], previously the Kings Arms. Conversely there were just two closures during this decade, the Holly Bush [King Street] in 1974 and the Queens Arms [Queen Street] in 1978.

Although more of the same would come on-line in the 1980s the popularity of the new format would gather even more momentum early in the following decade. In the meantime, mention should also be made of a few notable closures. After opening as the Half Moon in 1813, the Royal Priors development accounted for the Silver Jubilee [Satchwell Street] in 1985; the Golden Lion [Regent Street], one of the first buildings in the 'new' town in 1810, closed in 1988 [both the aforementioned being on our '1829 listing' of sixteen]. Others to go were the Britannia [Chandos Street] in 1980, Jolly Brewer [Guy Street] in 1981 and Leopard Inn [Court Street] in 1982.

Also in 1989 the outcome of the Monopolies and Mergers Commission was that all brewers owning more than 2,000 on-licence premises had to release one half of the number above that threshold by November 1992; if the brewers chose to retain more than the 2,000 threshold they had to offer at least one competitor brew as a 'guest' beer. The resultant release of thousands of pubs onto the national market in the early 1990s facilitated a new type of business, with the rebranding of many pubs as 'theme' pubs, bars, wine-bars or restaurants, often part of national chains.

And so to 2013 and the pubscape remains as dynamic as ever. Many of the 'traditional' pubs continue to vie for survival, and the bars, wine bars, etc, are in a perpetual state of flux, often with frequent changes of ownership and signs to match, a fact borne out by the difficulty we had compiling information on these establishments.

The summer 2012 edition of 'Pint Sides' [the magazine of the Coventry and N. Warwickshire Branch of the Campaign for Real Ale], reported that, "National research commissioned by CAMRA has found that [up until the end of March 2012] Britain's national pub closure rate stands at 12 pubs per week and behind that figure we've seen 4,500 pubs close since 2008. We blame the rate of closures on the recession, the tax on beer being too high, the extortionate rents charged by the pub companies and supermarkets selling alcohol cheaply. Going to the pub is increasingly becoming an unaffordable activity. A third of the price of every pint you buy is now taxation. Excise duty on beer has increased by 42% since 2008."14 In January 2013, the editor of 'Pint Sides', Jim Witt, informed us that the "latest CAMRA research shows a closure rate of 18 per week" [by May 2013 the latest figures revealed that the rate of net closures had shot up to 26 every week during the previous six months].

Although there were relatively few closures in Leamington during the years 2008-2011, there were some notable losses: the Debonair [originally Ranelagh Tavern], Ranelagh Street; Lock, Dock & Barrel [originally Queen's Head], Brunswick Street; Oak Inn [Radford Road] and Walnut Tree [Crown Way, Lillington]. In 2012, we lost the Venew @ The Binswood [Rugby Road] plus two with considerable pedigree, the Bedford [originally Bedford Tap/Inn] and the Red House [Radford Road].

Although the Exchange [High Street], Cask & Bottle [Lansdowne Street] and Avenue [Spencer Street] were closed mid 2013, all three premises had reopened by year end. Notwithstanding, at the end of December Leamington had approximately 60 pubs [including bars, wine bars, etc], which can be loosely categorised as follows: 50% are pre-1970 'traditional' pubs [many of which have undergone extensive refurbishment], 15% are of a contemporary format but were originally pub premises and 35% are of a contemporary format but are either new-builds or conversions from unrelated businesses. Nevertheless, we don't want to pigeon hole these establishments as we should just be grateful that Leamington offers such a plentiful choice of licensed premises of varying formats.

Finally, one more check of the '1829 listing' and specifically the five '*taverns &c*' that we have not yet accounted for....

- **Angel Inn** – Became the Angel Hotel circa 1860, and is still the Angel Hotel in 2013.
- **Bedford Tap/Inn** – Closed in the late 1990s and after a few name changes, and an extensive refit, reopened as the Envy Bar in 2010, but closed the following year; after

reopening as The Bedford in December 2011 it closed just six months later and in July 2013 it remains boarded-up.

- **Ranelagh Tavern** – Renamed the Debonair in 1988, it closed in 2008; in 2012 work commenced on converting the premises for residential use and in July 2013 the work is ongoing.
- **Warwick Tavern** – Became the Warwick Hotel 1904-84, then the Birch & Billycock and the Birch Tree for a combined period of 15 years; in 2013 it is known as the Voodoo Bar.
- **Star & Garter** – The oldest existing pub in Leamington, and still carrying its original name; it underwent an extensive refurbishment in 2012 and remains open in 2013.

*Citations:*

1. Adapted extract from 'The Vanishing Faces of the Traditional Pub' by Geoff Brandwood [from The Journal of the Brewery History Society, Number 123, Summer 2006]
2. 'Beer has a History' by F. A. King [First published by Hutchinson's Scientific & Technical Publications, 1947]
3. Adapted extract from 'A History of the English Public House' by H. A. Monckton, reprinted by permission of Peters Fraser & Dunlop [www.petersfraserdunlop.com] on behalf of the Estate of H. A. Monckton
4. Adapted extract from 'A Complete History of Royal Leamington Spa' by T. B. Dudley [Printed & published by A. Tomes, 1896]
5. Adapted extract from 'History of Royal Leamington Spa' by George Morley [written for the Leamington Spa Courier, 1887-89]
6. 'Ground Plan of Leamington [1783]'
7. Adapted extract from 'London Metropolitan Archives, Information Leaflet Number 45: Licensed Victuallers Records, A Brief History of Licensing' [First published July 1998 by London Metropolitan Archives, The City of London Corporation]
8. W.G. Gibbons [Local historian]
9. Adapted extract from 'A History of English Ale & Beer' by H. A. Monckton, reprinted by permission of Peters Fraser & Dunlop [www.petersfraserdunlop.com] on behalf of the Estate of H. A. Monckton
10. Adapted extract from the 'Licensing Act 1872' [35 & 36 Vict. c.94] / National Archives / *www.legislation.gov.uk*
11. Adapted extract from the 'Licensing Act 1902' [2 Edw. 7 c.28] / National Archives / *www.legislation.gov.uk*
12. Adapted extract from the 'Licensing Act 1904' [4 Edw. 7 c.23] University of California/ California Digital Library *www.archive.org/details/thelicensingact00greaiala*
13. Extract from 'A History of the English Public House' by H. A. Monckton, reprinted by permission of Peters Fraser & Dunlop [www.petersfraserdunlop.com] on behalf of the Estate of H. A. Monckton
14. Extract from 'Pint Sides' - Magazine of the Coventry & N. Warwickshire Branch of the Campaign for Real Ale [Summer 2012 Edition]

# PUB ENTRIES

**Alastairs** – 40 Warwick Street

Alastairs was a wine bar/bistro, the type of drinking/eating establishment that would become increasingly more popular from the late 1970s and threaten the very existence of the 'traditional' pub. It opened circa 1975 with Alastair MacBrayne running the business until 1981; Alastair was previously manager of the wine department at Burgis and Colbourne which later became Rackhams. In October 1980 plans were lodged [for the second time] with the Warwick District Council by Aldergate Ltd to change the use of the building to two shops on the ground floor and basement plus offices and a penthouse flat, but the application was again refused. Around February 1982 the owners refurbished the building and extended and restored the garden at a cost of £100,000. At this time Keith and Meidi Roper and Jeremy Pinnock managed the wine bar; it was open lunch-time and evenings Monday to Saturday and closed on Sunday. In July 1982 Alastairs was awarded the coveted Relais Routiers recommendation which allowed them to display the famous red and blue Routier sign.

Alastairs was sold in August 1984 after its parent company [S. L. Dowell Group] was placed in the hands of a receiver the previous month. However, it retained the name Alastairs until 2004 when it became Macky's Bar and Restaurant and then the Saint Bar in 2007.

In 2009, the Saint Bar was advertised as: "An ultra chic hideaway with unique design, softly lit, underground den offering luxurious seating areas, including a VIP section, with table service and a very extensive selection of premium spirits, wines and champagnes, not to mention an eclectic range of beers and cocktails." The Saint Bar remains open in

*Left: Alastairs circa 1980s courtesy of Nick Wilkins. Middle: Photo of Macky's taken on 29th August 2004 courtesy of John Hartnup. Right: The Saint Bar taken on 11th August 2011 © Allan Jennings.*

December 2013 and has the same owners as the Glasshouse next door, although they are run as separate businesses.

Circa 2006          Emma Louise Ford
25th June 2007 →      Ulief Coppor Burton

**Albatross** – 60 Clemens Street

Originally a beer house named the Three Tuns, the first reference point we have is the August 1856 licensing session when it was granted a full licence. In 1861, it was described as originally being two dwelling houses, numbers '27' and '28' Clemens Street, since converted into a single dwelling and used as a public house known by the name of the Three Tuns; it comprised a shop, smoke room, two sitting rooms, five bedrooms, kitchen, scullery, wine and beer cellars.

It was renamed the Albatross in 1879 and renumbered as 60, Clemens Street around the same time. In 1903 the ground landlords were Messrs Cobb, the lessees were Messrs Lucas and Co. Ltd and the tenant was George Salmon. During the day George worked at Gas House [gasworks] from 6.00am until

> **Three Tuns Inn,**
> CLEMENS STREET, LEAMINGTON.
>
> **R. BARNACLE,**
> **Dealer in Foreign Spirituous Liquors,**
> **HOME-BREW'D ALE, &c.**
>
> HOT COFFEE EVERY MORNING AT FIVE O'CLOCK.
>
> STEAKS, CHOPS, &c., ON THE SHORTEST NOTICE AND MOST REASONABLE TERMS.

*An advert for the Three Tuns courtesy of Jo Clark.*

5.00pm and his wife looked after the pub. In February 1905, the chief constable objected to the renewal of the Albatross licence stating that "the premises were very small, were used by comparatively poor people and that the only room for drinkers could only accommodate twelve persons." It was also said to be very dirty, in a dilapidated state and there was only one water tap and that was in the cellar kitchen; also there was no stabling. The bar was 21 ft x 12 ft and in the daytime it would not be busy but in the evening there could be more people than the premises could accommodate. Mr. Parfitt, barrister for the licensee Mr. Salmon asked the chief constable if his objection to the lack of stabling was straining a point. The chief constable replied, "No sir, at any time we might have cavalry come through the town and want to billet them." The magistrates refused to

*Photo of the site of the Three Tuns / Albatross [with the blue fascia] taken 18th July 2010 © Allan Jennings.*

renew the licence as the premises were not structurally suited for use as a licensed house. The Albatross was closed on 7th February 1905 without compensation being paid.

| | |
|---|---|
| ≤1856-Apr 1860 | Ann Letts |
| April 1860-Apr 1867 | James Letts |
| April 1867-Jul 1868 | Mrs. Letts |
| July 1868 | John Elliott |
| 1870-71 | Mrs. Cliff |
| 1871-Aug 1871 | Robert Barnacle |
| August 1871-Jul 1872 | George Pollentin |
| July 1872-Jan 1873 | Francis Wilson |
| January 1873-74 | Robert Ralph |
| 1879-Oct 1892 | James Letts *(Also a wine and spirits merchant)* |
| October 1892-Aug 1895 | James Satchwell |
| August 1895-Feb 1905 | George Salmon |
| 7th February 1905 | Closed for business |

*The 1901 census recorded George Salmon as a 29 year old publican at 60, Clemens Street with his family Lillah aged 25, 4 year old daughter Edith, 2 year old son Tom and 1 year old son George. The numbers in Clemens Street continued with 62, 64 and 66 Clemens Street. By 1933 George Salmon is listed as a tripe dresser at No. 64; in 1961 there is a Harry Feasey, a beer retailer, at No. 66.*

In 1917 during the First World War Tom Salmon, the 19 year old son of George Salmon, Private, 35647, 1st/4th Battalion, Duke of Cornwall's Light Infantry [T.F.] was drowned at sea when the S.S. Transylvania was torpedoed in the Gulf of Genoa. He is commemorated on the Savona Memorial in Italy.

**Albion Hotel** – High Street
See Great Western Hotel for details.

**Ale and Porter Vaults** – 10 Gloucester Street
In 1822 three plots of building land on the south side of Gloucester Street were sold by Nathan Izod at the Bath Hotel; this was one of them. The first directory listing we have for the Ale and Porter Vaults is in 1830 and the last in 1839. Between 1885 and 1902 James Brown is listed as the agent for the Anglo Bavarian Brewery at 118, Parade, with vaults in Bedford Street, and the stores at 10, Gloucester Street.

| | |
|---|---|
| 1830-39 | John Stafford |
| | *(Owner of the premises was William Benton)* |

**Alexandra Inn** – 1 Abbott Street
The first directory entry we have is in 1866 and the last listing is in 1922. In 1865 Mrs. Doherty applied for a spirit licence but the application was refused. The following year she

applied for what we understand to be a full on-licence for an existing beer-house; she advised the licensing sessions that the house belonged to Warwick Brewery, that she had spent nine years as a barmaid at the Anchor in Northampton, that her husband had deserted her in 1861 and that her sister had been helping out. She added that friends and customers had been asking for spirits but again the application was refused; a wine licence was granted in September 1882.

As Leamington agents for the Warwick Brewery they sold India pale and mild ales and double stouts. There were two entrances to the Alexandra, one in Abbott Street and one in Bath Place via a private yard belonging to the cottage next door. It had three rooms, a bar [12 ft 3 in x 12 ft 10 in], a smoke room [12 ft 3 in x 11 ft 2 in] and a bar parlour [11 ft x 9 ft 8 in]. It is possible that the inn was extended in 1915 as the records of [owners] Lucas and Co. Ltd show that on 27th May 1915 they approved the £500 purchase of 3, Bath Place, a cottage adjoining the Alexandra Inn from the estate of the late Mrs. Edmunds. However, on 1st March 1920 Leamington's licensing justices referred the Alexandra Inn 'for extinction', and on 28th May 1920 the county compensation authority refused the renewal of the licence. On Monday 2nd January 1922 compensation totalling £1,550 was awarded, £1,350 to the owners [Messrs Lucas and Co. Ltd] and £200 to the tenant. The compensation was paid on 25th March 1922 and the pub closed for business the same day.

| | |
|---|---|
| ≤1860-Aug 1863 | Mrs. Doherty *(Sister-in-law of Sarah Ann Doherty)* |
| August 1863-Aug 1901 | Mrs. Sarah Ann Doherty |
| August 1901-Jun 1906 | Miss Emma Broome |
| June 1906-Jun 1907 | Miss Ethel Broome *(Niece of Emma)* |
| June 1907-Mar 1922 | Thomas Miller |
| 25th March 1922 | Closed for business |

*The Leamington Spa Courier dated 23rd April 1870 carried the following sale advert: To be sold by auction by Mr. John Moore, at the Crown Hotel, on Tuesday, 3rd May, 1870, at five o'clock in the afternoon; All that freehold messuage and premises, called the Alexandra Inn, situate in Abbotts Street, Leamington Priors, containing sitting and smoke rooms, bar and bar parlour, 4 chambers, scullery and good cellaring, with other offices, hard and soft water, in the occupation of Messrs Webb and Barron, and their undertenant, Miss Doherty, at an annual rent of £19.*

### Althorpe Arms – 18 Althorpe Street

Althorpe Street was named 'in complement' to the Althorpe family. In 1814 the daughter of a Mrs. Acklom, sister of the first Earl of Brandon, married Viscount Althorpe; Mrs. Acklom resided at the Manor House Hotel until her death in 1840. The first information we have on the Althorpe Arms is a reference in the 1837 rate books relating to George Lees at a public house in Althorpe Street, and the first directory listing we have for the Althorpe Arms is in 1838. On 6th July 1887 these fully licensed premises were taken over by Hunt, Edmunds and Co. Ltd, Banbury. There were four entrances, one in Althorpe Street, two in Drummond Street and one in Buchanan Street. At the time the chief constable claimed that the pub was frequented by a lot of rough people and reported that there were sixteen cottages that had

*Althorpe Street and the Althorpe Arms taken on 10th July 1957. Photo courtesy of Peter Coulls.*

access to three narrow passages which led to the back door of the pub and that it didn't have any stabling. It comprised three rooms, a bar [12 ft 11 in x 14 ft], a smoke room [9 ft 9 in x 7 ft 10 in] and a club room [25 ft 7 in x 14 ft]. The licence was suspended on 1st October 1959 by reason of compulsory acquisition by the local authority, Section 92 [1] of the Licensing Act 1953 and a suspension certificate was issued to the owners by the Commissioners of H. M. Customs and Excise. The site later became part of the Althorpe Industrial Estate.

| | |
|---|---|
| 1837-38 | George Lees |
| 1839-Jun 1854 | Faith Wrighton |
| June 1854-66 | Ann Wrighton *(On the death of Faith)* |
| 1868-Mar 1871 | Edmund Cheeseman |
| March 1871-Nov 1871 | John Harris |
| November 1871-Feb 1875 | Peter Bradley |
| February 1875-Apr 1881 | Thomas Ledbrooke |
| April 1881-Jul 1887 | Edward Roddis |
| July 1887-Sep 1887 | Closed for renovation and repairs |
| September 1887-May 1888 | Edwin Webb |
| May 1888-Oct 1889 | Mrs. Mary Webb |
| | *(Married Richard Parsons and transferred the licence)* |
| October 1889-Jan 1892 | Richard Parsons |
| January 1892-Aug 1898 | Alfred James Butler |
| August 1898-1900 | Mrs. Sarah Ann Butler *(On the death of Alfred)* |
| 1900-1907 | Mrs. Sarah Ann Simpson *(Mrs. Butler remarried)* |
| 1907-Sept 1907 | Charles John Harris |
| September 1907-Nov 1914 | George Knight Kightley |
| | *(Died 3rd June 1930, aged 67)* |
| November 1914-Oct 1917 | William Griffin *(Killed in action)* |

| | |
|---|---|
| October 1917-Oct 1949 | Edward Reading |
| October 1949-Jul 1956 | Kate Reading |
| July 1956-May 1959 | Kenneth Austin Scott |
| May 1959-Oct 1959 | Charles Webb |
| 1st October 1959 | License suspended |

*In 1917, the First World War claimed the life of the pub's landlord William Griffin, Private, 267904, 11th [Service Battalion] Royal Warwickshire Regiment. He originally signed up as part of the Territorial Force in June 1915. He was killed in action aged 34, on Wednesday 25th of April 1917. He is commemorated on the Arras Memorial, France. He is stated as being the son of Edward and Jane Griffin, 30, Shrubland Street, Leamington Spa and the husband of Susan Griffin, the Althorpe Arms, Althorpe Street, Leamington Spa.*

The Leamington Spa Courier dated 3rd September 1943 reported: We regret to announce that 20 year old Able Seaman F. R. Dawkes, R.N; second son of Mr. and Mrs. Harry Dawkes, 64 Court Street, and grandson of Mr. E. Reading of the Althorpe Arms, has been reported missing, presumed killed on active service. He was an old boy of Clapham Terrace School.

*On Sunday 15th November 1944 George L. Deeming Private, 1778652, 5th Battalion, The Buffs, [Royal East Kent Regiment] was killed in action in Italy, aged 36. He is commemorated on the Casino Memorial in Italy. George is the son of Mr. and Mrs. Deeming, Althorpe Arms, Althorpe Street, Leamington Spa. [In 1944 the landlord was Edward Reading so we can only assume that they lived upstairs – Ed]*

The Leamington History Group produced a book called People and Places. John Smith wrote about Althorpe Street from people's memories:

"There were lots of pubs in Althorpe Street and at weekends adults went to the pub and left the children outside with a bag of crisps."

"Granny liked her beer and we had to get it from the back door of the Eagle Inn."

"Althorpe Street had two long rows of terraced houses broken up by side streets such as Buchanan Street, Drummond Street, and Neilston Street. The houses were home to families of up to twelve adults and children. The houses were demolished in the 1950s to make way for industrial generation."

"The houses fronted directly onto cobbled pavements where, until the 1930s, street lighting was by gaslight."

"The area was a self contained community with a variety of shops and small businesses with its social needs catered for by three public houses, the Eagle Inn, White Lion and Althorpe Arms."

"The Althorpe Arms had a bar at one end divided by a chimney breast. The pub was heated by lovely fires on either side. At the top end of the bar the men played cards and dominoes and at the other end was a dart board. Down the corridor was a posh smoke room where fellows brought their girls to introduce them to the neighbourhood and buy them a gin and orange. Women in their pinnies used to pop in at lunchtime into 'the donkey box' which was a small room with two settees facing one another. They usually had a Guinness and maybe placed a bet. Entertainment was provided by a piano and singing."

***The Reading Sisters*** - *Around 1974, two Reading sisters were interviewed for the first edition of the Bath Place Times:*

Q. How long have you been in the licensed trade?
A. 42 years we kept one place [Althorpe Arms] where they've made the trading estate in Althorpe Street.
Q. What happened to it?
A. They commandeered it for a trading centre and what have you, about 15 years ago. It was in 1916 we went into the pub when the war was on, when our Kitty was three. When I was younger, my mother used to say, "Kate, don't you dare argue at that bar – come out smiling even if you have been crying at the back".

My mother always used to say that there are three pubs down this street and about every twelve months they'd change the managers and we'd lose the custom and all of a sudden they'd come back – don't you dare say "Hello Stranger" and make them believe we'd missed them. You just say "Been poorly?" They'd been in the other pubs to see what they were like with the new people.

Our parents when they went into the pub, it cost them £50 lock, stock and barrel. When mother and father took it over Guinness was 2½d. My mother couldn't write but she learned by putting 4d strap [on the slate]. They had 'tick' written on cardboard which used to hang behind the bar and they came in on Fridays to pay, then on Mondays the pawnshop. They used to be black-eyed and fighting on Friday and Saturday because they got their money. We used to keep a bottle of Witch Hazel to get the bruises out the black eyes that the beauty boys had done.

**Altoria** – 45 Warwick Street
See KoKo's for details.

**Anchor Tavern** – 30 Oxford Street
Ten years prior to being the Anchor Tavern these premises were listed as a beer house named the Hope and Anchor [not to be confused with the Hope and Anchor that opened at 30, Hill Street circa 1852]. Following its brief lifespan [1838-39], there is no evidence of any licensed premises trading at this address from 1840-48, or of Oxford Street being renumbered during that period. We have therefore concluded that these premises reverted to being a private dwelling, until reopening as the Anchor Tavern which we

*This photo was taken on 27th February 2010. The entrance to Miles of Tiles used to be Melbourne Street. The house with a Miles of Tiles hanging sign was the Anchor Tavern.*

can date from 1849 until 1864. On 12th June 1861 it was listed for sale by auction and described as a freehold three-story public house called the Anchor Tavern, in the occupation of Joseph Payne.

| | |
|---|---|
| 1838-39 | W. J. Wood *(Hope and Anchor)* |
| 1840-48 | Private dwelling |
| 1849-61 | William Clifton *(Anchor Tavern)* |
| 1861-≥1861 | Joseph Payne *(Anchor Tavern)* |
| ≤1863-64 | Thomas Clarke *(Anchor Tavern)* |

## Ancient Druid – Lansdowne Street
The first directory listing we have is in 1837, with closure taking place between 1838 and 1840.

## Angel Hotel / Inn – 143 Regent Street
Now a thriving town centre hotel, the Angel is very obviously a Coaching Inn standing on the corner plot at the end of Regent Street in Leamington. The first reference point we have is an 1813 entry in the licensed victuallers' records which lists Richard Ballard at the Angel Inn. The address of these premises was originally Cross Street, New Town, which was laid out circa 1808-1814 but, circa 1827, around the time Ann Ballard took over the business, it was renamed Regent Street in honour of the Prince Regent who had visited Leamington in September 1819, and the Angel was readdressed 1, Regent Street. The death blow to coaching in Leamington was delivered by the arrival of the railways, firstly the opening of the Leamington Terminus in 1844 [later to become Milverton station] and the completion of the Avenue station in 1851.

In 1844, when James Ballard insured the Angel with the district fire office [Birmingham] for £2,300, at a premium of £2.17s.6d, it was described as: "A dwelling house known as the Angel Inn, including a stable with loft over, fronting Regent Street; ... coach house, with room above, in the yard at the rear [now used as a joiner's shop], saddle room, stabling, and room over [sometimes used as a club room], a store room for hay and straw, a dwelling house in Kenilworth Street adjoining the Angel Inn in the tenure of John Campion, near to but detached from the stable and loft."

On the death of Ann Ballard in 1843, James, William and Henry Ballard inherited the Angel [Henry sold his share to William]. William was a builder so, at first, James ran the hotel but ran into debt; too ashamed to face the court, he apparently sent his wife from a place of hiding to deliver his excuses. Declared bankrupt, James and William fell-out and the subsequent litigation lasted from 1852-58. For reasons in all likelihood relating to the bankruptcy, James Ballard was banned from keeping an inn/hotel in Leamington, or within a twenty mile radius, and in 1852 he leased the Angel to Lewis Chaffin Le Page from Bath. By then the building must have been in a dilapidated state, for Ballard agreed to mend all the broken windows in the inn, the coach house and the private dwelling next door [where he lived]. There was also a covenant to enlarge and improve the premises, "expending £150 at least", as Le Page should direct; under Le Page's management the Angel also acquired billiard rooms. Also in 1852, the Angel was described thus: "Inn or Public House known as the Angel Hotel with yard, stables, laundry, and outbuildings.... and also two tenements adjoining." By 1854 the rooms over the coach house were used as a brew house and malt room and the building in Clarendon Street, next to the stables, was used as an Inland Revenue office; James Ballard was described as "late innkeeper, but now collector of taxes."

In the late 1850s, the ownership of the Angel returned to the Ballards, firstly William in 1857 and then Henry; evidently the Angel Inn was also renamed the Angel Hotel during the period 1857-60, as it was certainly 'Hotel' in 1861. James and Annie Proctor arrived in Leamington and took over the running of the hotel in May 1866; when husband James died in the December Annie carried on managing the business

A circa 1889 advert for the Angel Hotel courtesy of Alan Griffin.

until marrying Thomas Welch and moving on to the Bath Hotel in 1870 [Annie died in 1903]. By 1876, Wellington Street had become part of Regent Street which was simultaneously renumbered from the western end, hence the change of number from '1' to '143'. On 13th July 1898, Lucas and Co. Ltd [Leamington Brewery] purchased the Angel Hotel for £6,500; it would later be owned by the Northampton Brewery Company, Northampton.

In February 1972 the Angel Hotel opened a new aperitif bar, "relax in comfortable surroundings", they said, "for that pre lunch or dinner drink, or just use the bar as a meeting place to have that quiet drink with your friends or business associates". In 1979, Ray and Betty Hinton [previously the owners of Leamington's Hinton's Wine Bar] purchased the hotel for an estimated £200,000 from Gwyn Jones, who had owned the property for the past ten years. Simultaneously, a planning application was submitted to the Warwick District Council by the new owners to refurbish the outside of the building and to carry-out alterations to the front elevation. Because of its architectural and historical merits the Angel is a listed building which probably delayed the start of the project. We have not yet been able to establish whether this refurbishment was completed during the Hinton's tenure or whether it was undertaken by subsequent owners as the property would shortly change hands again.

In 1981 the Angel was bought by Gordon Faulkner, whose plans included increasing the restaurant's seating capacity from forty-five to eighty and having a new look bar and reception area by early 1982. The 18-bedroom, two star hotel changed ownership again in

*The Angel Hotel on 7th September 2011 © Allan Jennings.*

August 1984 when it was purchased by Mike Duffy and business partner David Bundy for a reported £250,000; Duffy was previously general manager and director of the 220-room St. Johns Hotel in Solihull for sixteen years. The Angel then underwent a major refurbishment, including the addition of twenty-one new bedrooms, which was reportedly completed in the September at a cost of £400,000.

The Angel went into receivership in October 1991 with debts reported to be around £1 million and in 1992 the new owners were Dennis Clifford and Bernard Swindells who purchased the Angel for an 'undisclosed figure' said to be in the vicinity of £750,000. Following the death of Dennis Clifford circa 1997, and the departure of Bernard Swindells to follow other business interests, the Clifford family became the owners of the hotel and remain so in 2013. [See also: Counting House - Bar and Restaurant]

**Footnote:** The name 'Angel' is a reminder of the ancient link between church and inn with the earliest signs depicting an Angel appearing at the Annunciation.

| | |
|---|---|
| 1813-26 | Richard Ballard |
| 1826-43 | Mrs. Ann Ballard |
| 1843-50 | James Ballard |
| January 1852-Mar 1857 | Lewis Chaffin Le Page |
| March 1857-60 | William Ballard |
| 1860-Apr 1863 | Charles Beeke *(Angel Hotel)* |
| April 1863-≤1866 | William Ballard |
| ≤1866-May1866 | Henry Ballard |
| May 1866-Dec 1866 | James Proctor |
| December 1866-Aug 1870 | Mrs. Annie M. Proctor *(On the death of James)* |
| August 1870-Feb 1871 | Mark Howes |
| February 1871-May 1878 | Thomas Mannin |
| May 1878-May 1887 | Mrs. Prudence Mannin *(On the death of Thomas)* |
| May 1887-Jul 1887 | J. A. Locke and T. H. Nolan *(Executors on the death of Prudence)* |
| July 1887-Dec 1890 | George Lawrence *(License transferred from the executors of Mrs. Mannin)* |

| | |
|---|---|
| December 1890-Mar 1894 | Robert Cordell *(Previously at Golden Cross Hotel, Bromsgrove)* |
| March 1894-Nov 1895 | John Hopper Jeffrey |
| November 1895-May 1898 | George Henry Holder |
| May 1898-Sept 1898 | Tom Sumner *(Owner of the hotel – Miss Collins had been running the hotel since the bankruptcy)* |
| September 1898-Mar 1900 | Frederick Johnson |
| March 1900-Mar 1903 | Charles Baker |
| March 1903-Mar 1904 | Henry 'Harry' Norton Covell |
| March 1904-May 1906 | Leonard Evans Covell |
| May 1906-09 | William George Broadbridge |
| 1910-14 | John A. Berry |
| Circa 1914–Dec 1914 | Mrs. Berry |
| December 1914-Oct 1916 | Thomas 'Tom' Albert Smith |
| October 1916-21 | Miss Whitbourne *(Previously at Royal County Hotel, Durham)* |
| 1921-32 | Mrs. H. A. Broadbridge |
| 1932-Dec 1937 | Thomas Jenkins *(Tenancy agreement 14th September 1932)* |
| December 1937-Sep 1945 | John Joseph Burton |
| September 1945-Mar 1947 | Charles Rodney St. John Rich |
| March 1947-Sep 1947 | George Henry Penfold |
| September 1947-Oct 1948 | Cecil Paul Hawkins Fisher |
| October 1948-May 1950 | Arthur Cedric Baynton Forge |
| May 1950-Oct 1951 | Francis Edgar Newman |
| October 1951-Feb 1952 | William James Sauter |
| February 1952-Apr 1954 | Thomas Stapleton |
| April 1954-Jun 1962 | Travers Vinden |
| June 1962-Jul 1966 | Tom Hardman Schofield |
| July 1966-Apr 1968 | Maria Catherine Maw |
| April 1968-Apr 1969 | Hubert 'Gwynn' Winfield Jones |
| April 1969-Oct 1969 | Clifford Henry Brooks |
| October 1969-1979 | Guiseppe Schillaci |
| 1979-Sep 1981 | Ray and Louise 'Betty' Hinton |
| September 1981 | Gordon Faulkner *(Owner)* |
| September 1981 | Manuel Herranz-Aldea *(Manager)* |
| ≤1983-Jun 1983 | John Anthony Connors *(Manager)* |
| August 1984-≥Feb 1988 | Michael Duffy [and David Bundy From 1987] *(Owners)* |
| Circa 1990 | Patrick Duffy *(Owner)* |
| May 1992-1997 | Dennis Clifford and Bernard Swindells *(Owners)* |
| 1997 → | Clifford family *(Owners)* |
| May 1992 → | Simon Beesley *(Manager)* |

*The Leamington Spa Courier dated 2nd February 1884 reported that: On Saturday afternoon, thirteen members of the Leamington Harriers Club ran a distance of five miles for prizes donated by Mrs. Mannin and others. They left the Angel Hotel, their headquarters, at three o'clock and, owing to the rain, ran over rough roads through Cubbington and then home via Offchurch. The first three back were Hems, five minutes' start; Powell, five minutes' start and Franks, one minute and fifteen seconds' start. However, there was some difficulty about the trail, in consequence of which the referee has decided that the race shall be run again to-day.*

**Anglo-Bavarian Refreshment Bar** – 63 Bedford Street
This business is tied-in with the Anglo-Bavarian Brewery whose agent operated from 118, Parade, with the stores at 10, Gloucester Street.

| | |
|---|---|
| 1885-1901 | James Brown |
| 1902 | Samuel Horatio Marsden |
| 1903-1904 | Wyllie and Co. |

**Apollo Rooms and Wine Vaults** – 13 Clemens Street
See Great Western Inn for details.

**Augusta Tavern** – 6 Augusta Place
See Willoughby Arms for further details.

**Australian Arms** – Clemens Street
The first directory listing we have for the Australian Arms is in 1860 when James Letts was the licensee and as it is not listed in 1868 we initially assumed that it closed between 1865 and 1867. However, we know that James Letts was the licensee of the Three Tuns in Clemens Street between 1860 and 1864 as it is reported in the licensing sessions for that period [his tenure continued until April 1867]. We are also aware that he had a connection with Australia and have concluded that it is the same pub and that the licensing records incorrectly list it as the Three Tuns for that four year period instead of the Australian Arms. James Letts had two properties on the west side of Clemens Street numbered '27' and '28' which were on the south corner of Printers Street [now West Street]; number '27' was used as a house and bakehouse and his beer house was at number '28'. See the Albatross for further details.

| | |
|---|---|
| 1860-64 | James Letts |

**Avenue Hotel** – 15/17 Spencer Street
The conservation department at Warwick District Council describes the premises as, "a pair of houses, three storeys, now public house, circa 1832-39". The first information we have on any occupation is in April 1871 when John Andrew [a confectioner and proprietor of a restaurant at 11, Victoria Terrace], applied to the local magistrates to transfer his beer licence to premises he had bought for £2,000 [including fitting out] at 1-2 Spencer Street;

*Part of the Avenue in 1890 showing a completely different frontage including steps. Photo courtesy of the late Bill Gibbons.*

he intended to call it the Railway Refreshment Room and claimed that it now had twelve beds. This apparently simple act proved complicated as transfers were unheard of locally, and very rare nationally, so the application was adjourned to ascertain if the magistrates had the authority. This issue remained unresolved until the adjourned annual licensing session in September 1871 when, after much legal wrangling and Andrew pointing out that he had bought the premises for £2,000 and was paying "a hundred odd pounds" in rent, the licence was finally granted. It opened as the Andrews Commercial Hotel, is [directory] listed from 1872-76 as the Commercial Hotel and by 1878 it is the Avenue Hotel; the first full on-licence was granted on 26th August 1901.

Empty since the early 1980s, in August 1987 the Morning News reported that after an eleven week £95,000 refurbishment the Avenue pub had been transformed by owners Ansells into their 13th Heritage pub. The interior of the 100-year old listed building was altered to match the exterior, the building was completely redecorated and re-roofed with second-hand slate and the two previously separate rooms were knocked into one, with the bar brought all the way round. Downstairs the cellars remained as they were in 1877 with the original tiles, cooking range and washing area. According to the Morning News, the Avenue was one of fifteen pubs that Ansells specially selected to carry their Heritage Inn flag; the aim of the heritage theme was to restore customers' faith in English pubs – "traditional beers hand pulled and every pint served in the peak of condition".

Between April and June 2001 the premises were given a £200,000 facelift that included five guest rooms and a complete refit of the bar area. Jim Guiden [licensee] told the Leamington Observer, "Basically we're reverting back to a hotel. We're trying to get some extra revenue and compete with places up town especially since the Regent Hotel closed. It's going to look really great. We're also getting a new sign and doing up the front so we are trying to do our bit to improve the bottom end of town and make it more attractive for visitors." In January 2013, Kamarl Nayar sold the lease on to Babs Kandola [Green Man, Tachbrook Street] and the Avenue closed. After reopening briefly in the March it again closed and in April the premises licence was transferred from Punch Taverns to Kamaljit Singh Dhesi; it remained closed until late 2013, when it reopened following another refit.

| | |
|---|---|
| September 1871-May 1876 | John Andrew *(Andrew's Commercial Hotel)* |
| May 1876-Aug 1877 | John Hall |
| August 1877-May 1879 | Nathanial Merridew Jnr |
| May 1879-Dec 1889 | Thomas Perkins Jackson *(Retired due to ill-health)* |
| December 1889-Sep 1893 | John Thomas Hobbs *(Became bankrupt - Known as Peter, he had been a popular waiter at the Clarendon Hotel)* |
| September 1893-Oct 1893 | James Frederick Burgis *(Trustee in bankruptcy)* |
| October 1893-Jun 1895 | Henry 'Harry' Willis |
| June 1895-Jun 1901 | Miss Jane Ordish |
| June 1901-May 1905 | Thomas Groves *(Went on to Pitts Head, Coventry)* |
| May 1905-Jun 1924 | George Frederick Waters |
| June 1924-Mar 1935 | Arthur Woodland *(Proprietor – late of Notts County FC)* |
| March 1935-Feb 1936 | Clarence Proctor Wood |
| February 1936-Nov 1942 | Christopher Charles Chedham |
| November 1942-Oct 1946 | William Speed |
| October 1946-Jan 1949 | Ernest George Spong |
| January 1949-Nov 1954 | William Payne *(Glynis Jennings' grandad)* |
| November 1954-May 1958 | Arthur Samuel James |
| May 1958-Nov 1958 | Geoffrey Royson Griggs |
| November 1958-May 1960 | Albert Edward Taylor |
| May 1960-Mar 1962 | Alan George Franks |
| March 1962-Jul 1963 | Edward Alfred May |
| July 1963-Apr 1966 | Cyril Thomas Hewitt |
| April 1966-Aug 1966 | Thomas William Alderson |
| August 1966-Oct 1966 | Margaret Elsie Alderson *(On the death of Thomas)* |
| October 1966-Jun 1967 | Albert Edward Moorcroft |
| June 1967-Dec 1970 | John Alfred Howard |
| December 1967-Jan 1970 | Peter Leonard Morton |
| January 1970-May 1971 | Arthur Buller Ingram |
| May 1971-Oct 1972 | Thomas O'Shea |
| October 1972-Apr 1973 | Derrick John Watson |
| April 1973-Sep 1975 | William John Poole |
| September 1975-Mar 1976 | Douglas 'Doug' G. Stevenson *(Relief Manager - formerly head barman at the Woodland Tavern)* |
| March 1976-Nov 1976 | Douglas 'Doug' G. Stevenson |

| | |
|---|---|
| November 1976-Nov 1977 | Michael Burke and his wife Jane |
| November 1977-early 1980s | Patrick 'Pat' Dowling |
| August 1987 | Steve Van Simons *(Licensee – also owned Caesars American Restaurant, Spencer Street; the pub was run by Caroline and Kevin Wiley)* |
| 1990–1997 | John Shackleton *(Lease holder)* |
| 1990-1997 | Various managers including - Mick Briggs, Kevin and Caroline Wiley [1993], Chris Kelly, Sue English and Jim Guiden [1995] until he bought the lease. |
| ≤May 1995-Oct 2007 | James Edward 'Jim' Guiden *(Punch Taverns PLC)* |
| 5th October 2007-Jan 2013 | Kamarl Nayar |
| April 2013 → | Kamaljit Singh Dhesi |

The following article is from the Leamington Courier dated 12th May 1905 which Allan Jennings copied for part of a biography about his grandad Thomas 'Skerry' Jones. However, from a pubs point of view, it shows an interesting insight into how the Avenue was used, as well as giving an insight into journalism at that time.

**Football Club Supper**

*A*lthough in the first year of its existence, the Leamington St. John's Football Club has had a successful season and, as is not hampered financially, the committee thought fit to hold their first annual supper at the Avenue Hotel on Wednesday evening. A company numbering nearly fifty sat down to an excellent repast, over which Councillor W. Lee presided. – Apologies were received from Mr. T. H. D. Berridge, Alderman Gordon Bland, and Mr. B. S. Streeten. – The chairman proposed, "Success to St. John's Football Club", and said from what he could see, considering they were in the first year of formation, it spoke volumes for the management that they were not in debt, but had a balance in hand. – The toast was accorded musical honours. – Mr. G. Green said he had a very pleasing duty to perform. They had closed a very successful season, and as much of that success was due to the untiring energy and great ability of their worthy secretary and captain, they thought it would be only right and proper that they should give them some token in recognition of what they had done for the club. A large number of members had subscribed towards the purchase of the little presents, and he had the greatest pleasure in giving to those gentlemen a bag and pipe and pouch respectively. The recipients Mr. H. Burton [secretary] and Mr. H. Robbins [captain] suitably responded.*

*The secretary, in presenting the report, said the club was formed on September 5th, 1904, to take place of St. John's Institute F.C. [defunct] as it was thought desirable to keep up a club in connection with St. John's Parish. They had had a most successful season both from a playing and monetary point of view. Their assets when they started were nil, but with the assistance of their worthy president and other gentlemen, after meeting liabilities to the extent of £7, they were able to show a balance on the season's working of £1.18s.11½d. With regard to the matches, they had played 26, won 19, lost 3, and drawn 4. They had scored 125 goals against their opponents 26. The scorers were: H. Robbins [captain] 29, W. Watson 22,*

A. Cleaver 16, J. Saul [vice captain] 12, J. Harris 7, Savill 6, Frost 4, Maycock 4, Woodward 3 and Hubbard 3, and A. George, T. Saul, J. Compton, J. Holtom, Willoughby, Bunn, Benson, J. Dumbleton, and G. Green one each.

The team was making a bold bid for the Leamington Town Junior Cup, had reached the semi-final stage, and were looked upon as being winners when unfortunately the competition was stopped, much to their disappointment. On several occasions some of their players had played for the Leamington Town F.C. with great credit to themselves. A cricket club was being formed in connection with the football club, and they hoped it would be as great a success. – Mr. Hopper congratulated the club on its position, as also did Mr. S. Blunt who said he considered they were a clever lot of young men and there were several players who deserved to figure in a better team. – Songs, recitations, and instrumental selections were rendered during the evening, and a very enjoyable time was spent.

*This photo which is courtesy of Glynis Jennings was taken in the bar at the Avenue pub circa 1940s. It shows Flora Davies, Dick Turpin, the famous Leamington boxer, [?] , Victor Davies and to the right, just out of shot is William Payne who was the landlord. Glynis Jennings is the daughter of Vic and Flora Davies, and the grand-daughter of William Payne. Vic was friends with Dick and also worked with him. It is interesting to note that this Ansells pub has two mild pumps and only one bitter pump, and no lager pumps.*

Dick Turpin was the eldest of the three boxing brothers. Perhaps the most famous brother was Randolph who became the world middleweight champion in 1951. Jackie was the other boxing brother. Dick won the British Commonwealth title on 10th May 1948 in Coventry when he knocked out Bos Murphy of New Zealand in the first round. On 28th June 1948 he beat Vince Hawkins for the British middleweight title at Villa Park in Birmingham. Dick was born on 26th November 1920 and died aged 69 on 7th July 1990. He had 104 fights and won 77 of them, 33 by a knock out. He lost 20, drew 6 and 1 was a no contest. Dick was the trainer of his brother Randolph who beat Sugar Ray Robinson to take the world middleweight title in 1951. He was the son of Lionel Turpin who was born in British Guyana, and Beatrice Elizabeth Whitehouse. Many years later, Dick was living in Shrubland Street and used the Joiners Arms. Two of the regulars were Allan and Glynis Jennings and at some point the connection was made and I'm sure someone would have said, "It's a small world, isn't it?"

In August 1987 former taxi driver Les Simmonds, 74, visited the Avenue following a £95,000 revamp turning it into Ansell's 13th Heritage pub. Les told the Coventry Evening Telegraph he used the pub regularly in the 1930s when it was a hotel favoured by jockeys who were up for the races at Warwick. He particularly remembered the time he ferried famous jockeys Billy Nevitt and Freddie Fox to and from Warwick Racecourse – and got tips three times the size of his fare. He said, "I just wish I was 20 years younger and I could take on the pub myself." Mr. Simmonds had run the Golden Lion fifteen years earlier.

*Memories of a lucky customer... by Tom Lewin - You never know who you might meet!*
"It is the 2003 Rugby World Cup, we're at the Avenue Hotel pub and Jim Guiden, the landlord has laid on a breakfast for us privileged customers. I thought the guy I was talking to with a pronounced Welsh accent looked a little familiar, but it wasn't until Jim said, 'you know who that is? – Barry John!' Yes, the most famous of Welsh rugby legends. We watched England play one of their early group matches and Barry John sat with us to give his thoughts on the play. He was stopping at the Avenue after giving an after dinner talk at the local Leamington Rugby Club. Having shared a few drinks with us we took him for a few more bevvies at the Royal Exchange until he caught his train back to Wales. You never know who you might meet in good old Leamington Pubs!"

*This circa 1940s photo of the Avenue was used as a Christmas card.*

The conservation department at Warwick District Council describe the building as: A pair of houses, now public house; circa 1832-39 with later additions and alterations including early 20th century bay windows. Pinkish-brown brick with painted stucco front façade and Welsh slate roof; three storeys, four first-floor windows; first floor has tall 6/6 sashes, second floor has 3/6 sashes, all in plain reveals with tooled architraves and with sills; frieze, low parapet; pair of central entrances, board doors with overlights with margin lights in a pair of door cases with Doric pilasters, continuous frieze and cornice. To either side are canted bays with casement windows and cornices; tall end stacks with cornices, rebuilt to left.

### Aylesford Arms – 87 Bedford Street

The first information we have on the Aylesford Arms is in the 1856 licensing session listings. In July 1862, Wheal and Son took over from Samuel Oldham at 24, Lower Parade and advertised themselves as cooks, confectioners, wine and spirit merchants and agents for Allsopp's, Bass ales, and Guinness stout. There is a gap in the licence details from 1864 until 6th March 1879 when the licence was transferred from the late Charles Wheal to his widow Emma Wheal. However, we have evidence to suggest that Charles Wheal was the landlord for the six years prior to that and probably also since 1864. Since its opening, access to the Aylesford Arms had been via the wine and spirits business at the front of the premises [24, Lower Parade, subsequently renumbered as 146, Parade]. When Thornley and Co. [Radford Hall Brewery] took over the licence in 1899 an entrance was created at the rear of the building to provide direct access into the pub from [87] Bedford Street.

By 1906 the business at 146, Parade had changed from being a wine and spirits merchant to the Aylesford Restaurant. In later years the Aylesford Arms premises in Bedford Street would be associated with the Gaiety Café when, for a period, the owner was Gaiety Café Ltd [John Chesterfield], 'Deeping', Woodcote Road, Leamington Spa; it was later transferred to Kunzle Ltd, Five Ways, Birmingham 5. In January 1958 the licence was transferred to Morley Francis Wheeler, property manager of Sketchley Dry Cleaners, who had purchased the property. However, the term 'property' was probably an overstatement as the Aylesford Arms was by then defunct and demolished. Local magistrates were told at the time that the police would shortly be asking the brewery to surrender the licence because structural alterations had been carried out without consulting the justices. Again, considering that it had been demolished, 'structural alterations' was probably an understatement.....

The licence for the Aylesford Arms [nicknamed by some locals as the 'Hole in the Wall'] was surrendered on 11th February 1958 at the annual licensing session. These days the site of the Aylesford Arms is just an opening between two buildings.

| | |
|---|---|
| ≤1856-Jul 1862 | Samuel Oldham |
| July 1862-64 | Richard and Charles Wheal |
| ≤1873-Mar 1879 | Charles Wheal |
| March 1879-Jul 1883 | Mrs. Emma Wheal *(On the death of Charles)* |
| July 1883 | Alfred Wheal *(Son of Emma)* |
| 1895-Jun 1897 | George T. Powell |
| June 1897-Mar 1899 | Frederick May Andrews *(146, Parade - Trading as Lisseter and Miller)* |
| March 1899-Mar 1901 | H. E. Thornley and Co. |

*Happy customers in the Gaiety Café / Aylesford Arms circa 1950s. Photo courtesy of Leamington Library.*

| | |
|---|---|
| March 1901-Aug 1905 | William Wallace Seymour *(Seymour and Son)* |
| 1903-1904 | James Greenaway *(Manager)* |
| August 1905-Nov 1922 | Mark Herbert Kingston |
| November 1922-Feb 1925 | James Henry Miles |
| 1923-27 | Archibald Payne Underwood *(Manager)* |
| February 1925 | George Woolley |
| 1928-Jan 1935 | Henry 'Harry' William Weedon |
| January 1935-Aug 1942 | John Chesterfield |
| August 1942 | Change of ownership to Messrs Kunzles |
| August 1942-Dec 1942 | Stanley John William Hall |
| December 1942-Sep 1944 | Isobelle Ellanastia Ford |
| September 1944-Dec 1946 | Constance Morrell |
| December 1946-Jan 1947 | George Williams |
| January 1947-Jul 1947 | Mrs. Hilda Frost |
| July 1947-Oct 1947 | Mrs. Myra Grace Baker |
| October 1947-Nov 1949 | Miss Molly Rosina Allbutt |
| November 1949-Nov 1950 | Mrs. Ellen Emma Ryan |
| November 1950-Oct 1951 | Henry Benjamin Rees |
| October 1951-Sep 1952 | Mrs. Vivienne Bendixen |
| September 1952-Oct 1956 | Mrs. Gertrude Share |
| October 1956-Jan 1958 | Mrs. Mary Howard *(Manager – Kunzle Ltd)* |
| January 1958-Feb 1958 | Morley Francis Wheeler *(Property manager of Sketchley Dry Cleaners)* |
| 11th February 1958 | Licence surrendered |

**Aylesford Inn** – 29 Eagle Street

In August 1881, William Roberts [builder] successfully applied for a beer house licence for his premises at Eastbourne Terrace, Eagle Street, at the rear of which was a builder's yard and workshop. On 29th June 1896, an auction was held at the Crown Hotel, on instructions from the Northampton Brewing Company Ltd, to sell-off a parcel of land lately in the occupation of Mr. W. Roberts, but now let to Mr. W. J. Talbot at £20 per annum; it was

*This photograph taken on 22nd August 2011 shows 29 Eagle Street, the site of the Aylesford Inn and the Star off-licence © Allan Jennings.*

situated in the rear of the Aylesford Inn. Although the last listing we have for this pub is in 1927 it continued to be listed as a beer retailer and off-licence. However, the Morning News dated 3rd February 1960 reported that two Leamington public houses, the Leopard Inn [Court Street] and the Talbot Inn [Rushmore Street], and an Eagle Street off-licence were each granted a full on-licence at the local licensing sessions.

| | |
|---|---|
| August 1881-July 1895 | William Roberts |
| July 1895-Sept 1911 | William Henry Potter |
| September 1911-27 | Mrs. Beatrice Elizabeth Smith |

**Bakers** – 33 Regent Street
See Murphy's Bar for details.

**Bar 44** – 44 Clarendon Street [corner of Warwick Street]
See Kings Arms for details.

**Bar Citrus** – 26 Park Street
See Wig and Pen for details.

**Bar Code** – 27 Augusta Place
See Hintons for details.

**Barnies** – 75 Bedford Street
See Bedford Inn for details.

**Barons** – 4 Bedford Street
See Coach and Horses for details.

**Baroque** – Clarendon Avenue
See Fox and Vivian for details.

**Bath Hotel** – 32 Bath Street
William Abbotts was previously the landlord of the Black Dog [also known as the 'Dog'] in High Street, from 1776-93; he also built the town's first bathhouse which, according to J. C. Manning ['Glimpses of Our Local Past', 1895], was commenced in 1784 and opened in 1787. In 1790, construction of the New Inn commenced on the corner of Spencer Street and Bath Lane [Bath Street] upon freehold land left to him by his uncle. However, it would be 1793 before the New Inn opened for business, William having been twice denied a licence by the licensing justices on the grounds that the two existing licensed houses [Black Dog and Bowling Green] were more than sufficient for the small village of Leamington Priors.

On the death of William on 7th March 1805 [aged 69], Mrs. Abbotts carried on the business until April 1806 when she transferred ownership of the New Inn [and the Baths] to her son-in-law William Smith [who died in April 1808, aged 42]. Under the new management the New Inn was enlarged and a spacious mews added at the rear. It soon became a place of some importance owing to the original Baths being located next door and, in accordance with its increased status, it was renamed the Bath Hotel in 1814.

In February 1819 the Bath Hotel was still in the possession of the Abbotts family and was advertised for sale as, "a most eligible and much frequented inn, with pleasure ground, two good dwelling houses, an apothecary's shop, stabling, yards, cottages, and other out-offices thereto belonging." However the sale must have been aborted for, in May of the same year, Mrs. Elizabeth Potterton [née Mrs. Elizabeth Smith, daughter of William Abbotts] returned thanks to the public for the very liberal and distinguished support she had for so many years experienced, and informed them that the business at the Bath Hotel would in future be carried on by her family. In 1820 the Bath Hotel was acquired by John Russell [the son-in-law of Mrs. Potterton] who was the town surveyor and assessor of taxes; in 1825 he built a spacious market-place at the top of Abbott Street which existed for many years.

On 29th February, 1840 the Leamington Spa Courier advertised the forthcoming auction of the hotel [11th March], with the auction notice describing it thus:

"All that substantially built freehold inn, the Bath Hotel, most advantageously situated in Bath Street, with a frontage of fifty-two feet, which includes the portico, entrance hall, commercial and coffee rooms [the windows from which command an excellent view of the bridge and the whole of Bath Street], the old established and well-known coach office, from which coaches proceed to, and arrive from, all parts of the Kingdom. The entrance to the family hotel, in Smith Street, comprises a frontage of sixty feet, and consists of entrance hall and staircase, leading to a large and elegant dining room, drawing and sitting room, twenty capacious bedrooms and dressing rooms, servants' rooms, water and other closets. The domestic offices are well arranged, and comprise the large and convenient bar parlour and small bar, a complete cooking kitchen, scullery, larder, pantry, brew house with an extensive plant and large and capital cellars fitted up with every convenience. The out-offices are in every way suitable for so first-rate an establishment, large yard, with lock-up coach houses, and stabling for thirty horses."

Also to be auctioned as a separate lot, was the market situated in Bath Place with a large garden and extensive stabling attached – adjoining the stable yard of the Bath Hotel and approximating 2,190 square yards in total.

Although John Russell owned the hotel prior to the auction in 1840, we believe that he had died in 1838, and that his wife Elizabeth had appointed William Mash as caretaker manager, pending the 1840 auction. Evidently, the freehold was not sold at auction but retained by Elizabeth [and the Russell family for quite some years] who then leased out the hotel. On 4th October 1844, it was reported that: "This town is fortunate in regard to the excellence and respectability of its hotel accommodation and the enterprise with which these establishments are conducted. Determined not to be behind in the competition for public favour, Mr. Welch, the business-like and genial proprietor of the Bath Hotel, has just been enlarging and setting that comfortable, old-established hostelry in fresh order, and fitting it with some of the latest modern conveniences. The whole of the front of the building has been renewed and rendered uniform in appearance, and other exterior and interior alterations effected. The work has been carried out by Mr. W. Gascoyne with a result, looked at from the

*Photo of the Bath Hotel circa 1923. The man in the doorway is proprietor Francis James. Photo courtesy of Frank James.*

exterior alone, which is a great improvement to Bath Street. Internally, the alterations are such as will be largely conducive to the increased comfort of visitors as well as to the convenience of all parties on festive occasions. In connection with these alterations, the untidy piece of ground at the back of the premises, along by the wall in Avenue Road, have been enclosed within a neat iron fence and constitutes in itself no slight improvement."

In the coaching days, the Bath Hotel was a noted coach house with as many as twenty coaches departing the mews every morning; these included the London bound 'Crown Prince' and the Cambridge bound 'Tally Ho'. The death blow to coaching in Leamington was delivered by the arrival of the railways, firstly the opening of the Leamington Terminus in 1844 [later to become Milverton Station] and the completion of the Avenue station in 1851.

In October 1857 the Bath Hotel, still in the possession of the Russell family [though it had been closed for some time previously], was offered for sale by public auction; bidding started at £1,000 but stalled at £2,300 and the property was withdrawn from sale. The hotel remained closed until the first quarter of 1858 when George Russell re-opened it together with the Bath 'tap', or Bowling Green as it was then called, in Spencer Street. In 1861 the Bowling Green in Spencer Street was known as the Bath Hotel Refreshment Room but local residents were not accepting of this bar claiming that the worst of characters congregated therein. Fearful of the consequences, they tried to stop the licensing magistrates renewing the licence but were unsuccessful. Also in 1861, the adjoining stable yard was described as having an area of about 2,000 square yards and containing a groom's cottage, stabling for twenty-four horses, saddle rooms, six lock-up coach houses and piggeries, sub-let at a rental of £70 per annum.

As the premises continued to develop, it opened the Bath Hotel Lounge and Vaults Bar [with off-licence] which was accessed from Spencer Street. By 1930 the Bath Hotel had three bars, two billiard rooms, fifty-four bedrooms and five bathrooms, and by then the Spencer Street bar was known as a saloon bar [17 ft 6 in x 11 ft 9 in]. The Spencer Street entrance was to the left of the Assembly Room [built 1926] and in 2013 this redeveloped aspect of the Bath Hotel is used as the Malibu tanning studio and the Gilliland Martial Arts Academy.

During the Second World War the Bath Hotel was requisitioned, and closed to the public, until the beginning of August 1946. In 1947, it had the Green Cocktail Bar on Bath Street and the Red Cocktail Bar on Spencer Street, both of which were open from 11.00am until 2.00pm and 6.00pm until 10.00pm. The premises closed on 2nd June 1951 and the owners failed to apply for the licence renewal at the licensing sessions on 6th February 1952. By 1958 the building was owned by Lockheed who had renamed it Festival House and opened it as a staff hostel for female factory workers; according to a headline in the Morning News at the time, "the formerly impressive Bath Hotel had become an eyesore". Shortly afterwards, the former Bath Hotel building was demolished and made way for a new phenomenon – the supermarket. It opened as Burton's supermarket in 1960 before changing to the supermarket that many remember, Fine Fare; the building remains a supermarket in 2013.

| | |
|---|---|
| 1793-1805 | William Abbotts |
| 1805 | Elizabeth Abbotts |
| 1806-07 | William Smith |
| 1808-12 | Elizabeth Smith *(No pub name listed in register)* |
| 1813 | Elizabeth Smith *(New Inn)* |
| 1814-19 | Elizabeth Smith *(Bath Hotel)* |
| 1820-Sep 1838 | John Russell |
| September 1838 | William Mash |
| 1840-45 | Elizabeth Russell |
| 1849-57 | George Russell |
| 1857-Feb 1858 | Abraham Alexander |
| February 1858-61 | George Russell |
| 1861-Jan 1862 | Edmund Franklin *(From Northampton)* |
| January 1862-70 | Thomas B. Bazley |
| 1870-Oct 1906 | Thomas Welch *(Tenant)* |
| October 1906-Mar 1913 | Harry Welch *(On the death of Thomas)* *(Died 14th December 1917, aged 45)* |
| March 1913 | Robert Proctor *(Proprietors Robert and William Proctor, Harry Welch's half brothers - Temporary transfer as Harry Welch was seriously ill)* |
| 1908-20 | Thomas Welch and Co. |

*On 21st September 1920, the Bath Hotel was withdrawn from auction at the reserve price of £8,000. However, on 8th October it was reported that it had been sold to a Francis James who would take possession in March 1921.*

| | |
|---|---|
| March 1921-Oct 1923 | Francis James *(Proprietor)* |
| October 1923-Mar 1937 | Stephen M. Devis *(Proprietor)* |
| March 1937 | Charles O. Brettell *(Proprietor)* |
| March 1937 | Thomas William Mountford *(Formerly of the Golden Cross Hotel, Henley-in-Arden, on behalf of Mr. Brettell)* |

| | |
|---|---|
| September 1941-Jul 1945 | Henry Ernest Thompson |
| July 1945-Nov 1946 | Samuel Waldron Adcock *(Resident manager)* |
| May 1946 | Purchased by Messrs Overton's of Victoria, London |
| November 1946-Dec 1947 | Stanley Arthur Hollis |
| December 1947-Jun 1951 | Arthur Leonard Herbert |
| 2nd June 1951 | Closed for business |

*The Leamington Spa Courier dated 28th July 1849 advertised:* **Leamington Priors Licensed Victuallers Association** *- The fourth anniversary meeting of this association is fixed to be held at the Bath Hotel, on Tuesday, the 7th August. Dinner will take place at half past two. Dinner tickets at 2s.6d may be had at the Bath Hotel and the Angel Inn. The first anniversary celebration was also held at the Bath Hotel on Thursday 27th November 1846.*

**Bath Hotel Lounge and Vaults Bar** – Spencer Street
Also referred to as: Bath Hotel Refreshment Room, Bath Hotel Vaults and Bath Vaults. See Bath Hotel for details.

**Bedford Hotel** – 15 Lower Parade
The Bedford Hotel was built in 1811 on the west side of what was then called Union Row [latterly Union Parade and then 15, Lower Parade] and was the first hotel in the new town [since 1876 the whole length of the street from Clarendon Avenue to Dormer Place has been called simply, the Parade]. Named after the sixth Duke of Bedford, the hotel was opened on 25th October 1811 with its proprietors being John Williams and wife, formerly butler and house-keeper to Mr. B. Greatheed at Guys Cliffe House; a grand inaugural dinner, attended by 128 guests, was held on 4th December.

The Bedford Hotel extended through to Bedford Street where the Bedford Inn stood from circa 1824, this being the hotel 'tap' frequented by coachmen, footmen, grooms, stablemen and the large number of servants and domestic workers living in the area.

After 25 years of patronage by the nobility and gentry, the decline of the Bedford Hotel had begun with the 1836 financial crisis and also as a consequence of the social changes that had taken place by the 1850s. The fate of this historical hotel was decided in July 1856 when it was purchased

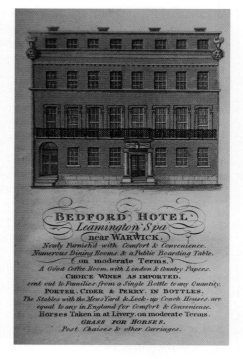

*The Bedford Hotel courtesy of Leamington Library [Moncrieff's 1824 Guide].*

by the Leamington Priors and Warwickshire Banking Company for rebuilding as their banking premises; plans were approved in November 1856, and the bank transferred from Bath Street to their newly built premises on 26th October 1857. In May 1889 the Leamington Priors and Warwickshire bank amalgamated with the Birmingham and Midland Bank Limited. Subsequent amalgamations have seen the name change to the London and Midland [1891], London City and Midland [1898], London Joint City and Midland [1918], and Midland [1923]. These days it is the HSBC Bank at 126, the Parade. See the Bedford Inn for details of licensees and landlords.

### Bedford Inn – 75 Bedford Street

Originally named Frost Street, Bedford Street was named in honour of the Duke and Duchess of Bedford after their visit to Leamington in 1808. The first directory listing we have for the Bedford Inn, or Bedford 'tap' as it was then known, is in 1824 [refer also to Bedford Hotel entry]. In July 1885 the licence was transferred from Lewis and Ridley [Leamington Brewery] to Morton Peto Lucas representing the new brewery owners, Lucas, Blackwell and Arkwright. In 1897 the ownership of the Leamington Brewery changed again and on 19th November 1898 the directors of Lucas and Co. Ltd approved the purchase of the Bedford Inn for £2,000; it would become an Ansells pub following their 1928 acquisition of the brewery and its closure in 1934.

By August 1983 Chris Willsmore was the licensee of the Bedford Inn as well as licensee of the Haunch of Venison [since 1977]. Later that year extensive building works were

undertaken to join the two pubs together which were only separated by a dividing wall and a cluster of outbuildings; the 'Haunch' being situated behind the Bedford, fronting the Parade. At the time, Chris said that, "the idea is to keep the pubs as two but have them connected by a corridor; one of the main attractions will be a patio in the centre." In December 1984 it was reported that Willsmore was proposing to call the Bedford Street pub the Seldom Inn, however there is no evidence to suggest that the Seldom Inn ever opened as such or that the sign was ever displayed; in fact the entire project proved unsuccessful and the Haunch of Venison and, most likely, the Bedford Inn closed in July 1985. Although the Haunch would remain closed for five years, the Bedford Inn was advertising in December 1985 indicating that it had a new owner, albeit maybe for a short time only [we have no licensee records for the period July 1985 to December 1990]. It was reported in September 1990 that the Haunch would reopen at Christmas

*Photo of the old Bedford Inn circa 1930 showing Mary Hobbs [née Sutton] and Ada Draper [née Hobbs]. Photo courtesy of Joyce Mary Timms.*

*Photo of the Bedford taken by Bill Bigley in 1987.*

with both pubs again having a single owner, this time Tony Hall. "I'm planning to extend the Bedford but the two pubs will not be linked as they once were," said Tony.

The pub went on to be called Pacific Rim [post 1998] and Barnies [2006] but when Barnies closed in 2008 the premises remained boarded-up for eighteen months. The Envy [bar] was opened on 28th May 2010 by Jason Bradshaw, and his parents Karl and Lyn, and advertised the cheapest pint in town at £1.85, with a bottle of house wine costing £9; a resident DJ played a variety of music on Saturdays and there was live music

*The Envy bar taken on 9th June 2010 © Allan Jennings.*

every Sunday night. However this venture lasted less than a year and Envy closed in April 2011. With the name reverting to the Bedford, the premises reopened on 9th December 2011 before closing yet again on 16th May 2012.

| | |
|---|---|
| 25th October 1811-19 | John Williams *(Bedford Hotel)* |
| 1819-28 | Thomas Hilsdon |
| 1819-24 | Mr. John Cross |
| 1824 | Thomas Howe |

| | |
|---|---|
| 1824-35 | John Gomm *(Bedford Hotel and Tap)* |
| 1832 | Broom Rogers *(Bedford Tap)* |
| 1833-34 | John Beaseley *(Bedford Tap)* |
| 1835-39 | John Cross *(Bedford Tap)* |
| 1836-40 | Thomas Bryan *(Bedford Tap)* |
| 1845-50 | Thomas Price *(Bedford Tap)* |
| July 1841-Feb 1850 | Thomas Wright *(Bedford Hotel)* |
| February 1850-Jan 1855 | Thomas Alfred Hill *(Bedford Hotel)* |
| ≤1856-Jan 1857 | Edward Reading *(Bedford Tap)* |
| January 1857-May 1876 | Humphrey Moore |
| May 1876 | Henry Goode *(Of Manchester)* |
| 1877-81 | Thomas Henry Cadby |
| 1881-83 | Josiah Croad |
| 1883 | H. A. Hatley |
| 1884-85 | T. Tompkins |
| July 1885 | Morton Peto Lucas/Leamington Brewery |
| 1885-March 1889 | Mrs. J. Simpkins |
| March 1889-Nov 1893 | William Utting |
| November 1893-Apr 1925 | William Harwood *(Died May 1925, aged 76)* |
| April 1925-Jul 1929 | Richard Hobbs and his wife Mary |
| July 1929-Jun 1940 | Richard George Sutton Hobbs and his wife Miriam *(Son of Richard Hobbs – known as George)* |
| June 1940-Mar 1954 | William Alfred Henry Astill and his wife Rose *(Previously at the Great Western, High Street)* |
| March 1954-Jul 1954 | William John Quelch *(Of Warwick)* |
| July 1954-Feb 1956 | Frederick Poole |
| February 1956-Jul 1957 | James Tynan |
| July 1957-Nov 1957 | Patrick Geraghty |
| November 1957-Mar 1961 | Leslie William Evans |
| March 1961-Jun 1962 | Charles Harry Atkins |
| June 1962-Apr 1964 | James Campbell McDonnell |
| April 1964-Aug 1964 | Cyril George Doughty |
| August 1964-Feb 1965 | Stephen Austin |
| February 1965-Jun 1965 | Joseph Gardiner |
| June 1965-Feb 1966 | Arthur James Hickman |
| February 1966-Feb 1967 | Edward George Hulm |
| February 1967-Jun 1967 | William McCaffrey |
| June 1967- circa 1983 | James Campbell McDonnell |
| Circa 1980s | David Thomas Turner |
| 1983-Jul 1985 | Christopher Willsmore |
| 1990 | Tony Hall |
| 1991 | Peter Main *(Manager)* |
| 1996 | Bedford under new management – licensee not known |

*Ada Draper [née Hobbs] serving behind the bar of the Bedford Inn circa 1930. Ada is the sister of licensee Richard Hobbs. Photo courtesy of Ada's niece, Kathleen Carter [née Hobbs].*

| | |
|---|---|
| 2006 | Andrew McCormick *(Pacific Rim)* |
| 8th September 2006-2008 | David Garvock Barnie *(Barnies)* |
| 2008 | Barnies closed |
| March 2009 | Martin Bailey |
| May 2010-Apr 2011 | Jason Bradshaw *(Envy Bar)* |
| April 2011-Dec 2011 | Envy Bar closed |
| December 2011-May 2012 | Simon Standbridge *(The Bedford)* |
| 16th May 2012 | Closed for business |

*In 1926 Richard Hobbs advertised: The Bedford Inn, Bedford Street - Richard Hobbs wishes to announce that he has taken over this old-established house, and will welcome old and new friends – Lucas' well known Ales and Stouts, Wines and Spirits. [Richard had previously been the licensee at the New Inn, Cubbington].*

In 1929 it was reported: **Late Mr. Richard Hobbs – Funeral of Leamington ex-Police Constable**. The funeral took place at Leamington Cemetery, on Wednesday afternoon, of Richard Hobbs, who passed away at his residence, 75 Bedford Street, on Sunday last. Mr. Hobbs, an ex-police constable in the local constabulary, was the licensee of the Bedford Inn. In his earlier days he was a keen sportsman and up to the time of his death he was held in high esteem by a large circle of friends. The service in All Saints' cemetery chapel was conducted by the Rev. J. A. Murray, M.A; the hymn 'Abide with me' was sung. The coffin was of polished elm with brass fittings, and bore a name tablet inscribed: 'Richard Hobbs. Died 17th November 1929, aged 66 years'.

*The Leamington Spa Courier dated 12th March 1954 reported: Retiring after 25 years in the licensed trade is Mr. William Alfred Astill, for the past 14 years licensee of the Bedford Inn, Bedford Street. Mr. Astill, who started at the White House, Bedworth, took over the Great Western Hotel, Leamington, in 1929 and moved to the Bedford Inn in 1940. The transfer of the licence of the Bedford Inn to Mr. William J. Quelch, of Warwick, was approved by Leamington licensing justices on Tuesday.*

*This photo of landlord William Alfred Henry Astill [1940-1954] is courtesy of his son Barry Astill.*

### Been – 29 Chandos Street

Been was previously the Carpenters Arms. In 2013 it is classed as a bar/restaurant but realistically it is a [Chinese] restaurant that incorporates a bar, rather than a pub. See Carpenters Arms for further details.

### Bell Inn – 69 Rugby Road [corner of Union Road]

The first information we have on the 'Bell' is in the J. C. Manning's book 'Glimpses of Our Local Past' [1895], which informs us that about the year 1828 a group of cottages were built at the north-east corner of Union Road, by John Toone. The corner house was the Bell Tavern and the first landlord was William Dosha who left around 1837 to take over a pub in Snitterfield. The first directory listing we have is in 1835 when it was addressed as Bertie Terrace.

The pub was owned by the Leamington Brewery [Lucas and Co. Ltd] but it would become an Ansells pub following their 1928 acquisition of the brewery and its closure in

*This photo of Rugby Road with the Bell on the corner of Union Road has been taken from a postcard that was posted on 11th June 1907. Courtesy of Frank James.*

1934. The licence for the Bell was transferred to the newly built Walnut Tree at Crown Way in 1958 [refer to Walnut Tree for further details] and the new Ansells pub opened on 20th May 1958. The landlord was John Alfred Charles Draper who took over the licence on 23rd June 1958, but it is possible that the ex Bell landlord Dennis McCallum filled in as interim landlord for a month. After the closure of the Bell it became 'Robins Corner', a sweet shop owned by Mr. Lemburger, and in 1996 the property was sold to Mr. P. Muddeman and became Regency Heating; the upstairs has been a hair and beauty salon since the early 1970s. In 2013, the old Bell Inn premises is a retail shop named Regency Fireplaces.

| | |
|---|---|
| ≤1835-38 | William Dosha |
| 1849 | Thomas Eaden |
| 1852-Aug 1854 | John Edwards |
| August 1854-Oct 1854 | Isaac Greves |
| October 1854-Nov 1861 | Edmund Merry |
| November 1861-66 | Thomas Nunn |
| 1868-Jan 1875 | John Jones |
| January 1875-Jun 1875 | Eliza Jones |
| June 1875-Nov 1897 | Charles Cowland |
| November 1897-Dec 1899 | Mrs. Sarah Cowland *(On the death of Charles)* |
| December 1899-1905 | John Thomas Beddington |
| 1905-Dec 1932 | Herbert Pinder |
| December 1932-May 1941 | Albert Woodman |
| May 1941-Jul 1941 | Nellie Woodman *(On the death of Albert, aged 58)* |
| July 1941-Oct 1947 | Ronald Hume |
| October 1947-Sep 1955 | Thomas Arthur Welch |
| September 1955-May 1957 | Robert Stanton Bavington |
| May 1957-Nov 1957 | John Henry Hollins |
| November 1957-1958 | Dennis McCallum |

*John Jennings tells us that the Bell was one of the pubs that he played darts in when he played for the Emscote Tavern and the Nelson Club in Warwick during the 1940s and 50s. "Once the team arrived it was very packed. When you took your throw you were in the way of the bar. If you wanted to see the score, it was easier to go outside and look through the window."*

**Benjamin Satchwells** – 112/114 Parade
Benjamin Satchwells opened on 13th August 1996, but who was Benjamin Satchwell? Although born in Stratford-upon-Avon, he figured prominently in the history of Leamington and was a man of many parts. In his account of the 'History of Royal Leamington Spa' [1887-89], George Morley informs us that in 1783 Satchwell was living in a cottage in Mill Lane [now named New Street] which was also Leamington Priors' first post office; as well as being the postmaster he was also a shoemaker and a poet. Although, at this time, Leamington Priors comprised no more than twenty thatched cottages, Satchwell was reliant upon its few inhabitants for his livelihood, supplementing the

marginal income from his boot repair service with the small fee he received for administering the basic postal service. Benjamin's rise to prominence came in 1784 when he and friend William Abbotts [landlord of the Black Dog] found Leamington's second mineral water spring; the medicinal properties of the salt baths were the fundamental reason that our once unknown 'village' developed into a prosperous spa town. As he rose to fame so too did his benevolence increase and in 1806 he founded the Leamington Spa Charity that would provide the health-giving waters and bathing facilities to the poor at no cost; Satchwell was also the local chronicler ['newsletter'] of his time. After his death on 1st December 1810, his daughter Elizabeth took on the role of postmistress. The first Leamington post office [Mill Lane] was demolished in 1871.

In December 1995 the Leamington Spa Courier reported: "A carpet shop to become a new pub – a new pub sandwiched between shops in Leamington's prime thoroughfare will be in the best possible taste, say planners. The sweeping transformation of a carpet shop and adjoining empty premises midway along the Parade will be a vast improvement on the site's current drab appearance, members of the Warwick district plans sub-committee heard on Monday. The £800,000 refurbishment is expected to begin in April, with the pub opening in August and employing around thirty full and part time staff. Planning officers were congratulated on striking the right balance of design and character to maintain the standards of the conservation area. Preservation is a key part in the scheme which members approved for developers J. D. Wetherspoon who are behind the Moon Under Water chain of bars and eateries. A doorway and hall will be retained to restore some domestic character and the existing shop-front at 112, the Parade will also be kept."

The 1995 plans for the premises included the demolition of part of the internal walls, change of use and conversion of retail units to a food and wine bar with traditional ale and the erection of a new shop front [at '114'] for J. D. Wetherspoon Plc: "The application concerns two properties which are currently separate shops. Number 112, Parade is presently a carpet shop with display areas on ground and upper floors, whilst number '114' is a vacant shop. Both properties extend a considerable distance to the rear and they both have frontages to Bedford Street. The elevations to the Parade are four storied of traditional design and number '112' is a listed building. The projecting shop-front to number '112' is old, whilst that to number '114' is modern and is recessed under a canopy. The two buildings form part of an important terrace of buildings in the conservation area and are opposite the Regent Hotel. It is proposed to demolish part of the dividing wall at ground floor between the two properties so as to form a drinking area over most of the ground floor of the site. The remaining parts would be used as kitchens, storage and toilets. The upper floors of the two buildings would provide a manager's flat and staff facilities."

Benjamin Satchwell's opened with a complete ban on all music and pool tables; it encouraged a non smoking policy and served six cask conditioned beers. The first managers were Mark Thexton and Philippa Jones. At the time John Crossling, chairman of the Heart of Warwickshire branch of CAMRA, the campaign for real ale, said, "Wetherspoons are expanding and have a better reputation than most for the range and quality of real ale they sell. They are good at promoting brews from small independent breweries, which is something we very much welcome." The 'Beer & Ragged Staff'

*Photo of Benjamin Satchwells taken on 29th April 2011 © Allan Jennings.*

magazine commented at the time, "Wetherspoons have an enlightened policy on cask conditioned beers. The regulars are Theakston Best and XB, Youngers Scotch and Courage Directors, showing the company's ties with the Scottish empire. There are usually two guest beers with the emphasis on small independent brewers, bringing some welcome choice to the town. All the real ales are sensibly priced and there is a helpful three monthly guest beer list with tasting notes. For the hungry, bar meals are available at most times from a straightforward and inexpensive menu. The pub is already proving popular, the atmosphere being generated by conversation not loud music."

Tim Martin opened his first Wetherspoon pub in Muswell Hill, North London in 1979. Thirty years later he runs a company that has around 750 pubs with annual sales of around £1 billion. The company has more pubs listed in the [CAMRA] Good Beer Guide than any other pub company. On 28th April 2010, the pub commenced opening at 7.00am to serve food and non alcoholic drinks. Benjamin Satchwell's remains open in December 2013.

| | |
|---|---|
| 1996-97 | Mark Thexton and Philippa Jones *(Managers)* |
| 1997 | Liz Herrang and Mat Reeves *(Assistant managers)* |
| Dec 2005-Jul 2007 | Tammy Selina Montgomery |
| July 2007-Apr 2008 | Kay Hayes |
| April 2008-Mar 2009 | Andrew Phelps |
| March 2009 → | Robert Browning |

**Berni Royal Hotel [Berni Inn]** – Kenilworth Road
See Guys Hotel for details.

**Binswood Tavern** – 2 Binswood Street / Rugby Road
The earliest information we have on the Binswood Tavern is a sale notice in the Leamington Spa Courier dated 15th December 1832: "To be sold by private contract by auctioneer George Carter with immediate possession. The whole of that valuable freehold messuage or dwelling house and appurtenances, called Binswood Tavern; comprising six good bed-rooms; sitting room; parlour; convenient bar; bar-parlour; tap room; club room

[29 ft x 16 ft]; four capital cellars, and excellent brew house and cooking kitchen; 2 coach houses; stabling for five horses, with lofts; a yard, with folding gates communicating with the main road, and other conveniences. The above premises are most desirably situated in the Milverton parish and, from their close proximity to Clarendon Square, enjoy all the advantages of Leamington Spa without contributing to its necessary payments; they are now a well established and daily increasing business and afford a favourable opportunity for any enterprising person to make a rapid fortune. With the purchase of the above premises, will be included a butchers shop and an adjoining dwelling house."

The first directory listing we have is in 1833, however there is a John Hanson of Binswood Street listed as a retail brewer in 1829 and 1830 and, although there is little evidence, it is possible that his brewing operations were associated with the Binswood Tavern during this period. Binswood Street, the site of an ancient wood and formerly known as Clarendon Place North, was extensively rebuilt and by 1835 the pub's address was Clarendon Place, but by the 1880s the address had reverted to 2, Binswood Street. During the early part of the 20th century the pub was owned by the Leamington Brewery [Lucas and Co. Ltd], but it would subsequently become an Ansells pub following their 1928 acquisition of the brewery and its closure in 1934.

In the late 1950s Rugby Road, Barrett Place and Binswood Street were part of a housing redevelopment scheme and the original plans included the Binswood Inn. However, the Minister of Housing excluded the pub from a compulsory purchase order. Negotiations then took place between the redevelopment committee and Ansells regarding the re-siting of the inn. A provisional order for the removal of the justices' licence from the Binswood Tavern, Binswood Street, to premises to be built on the junction of Rugby Road and Barrett Place was granted on Tuesday 14th April 1959. It was pointed out at the time that the new premises would almost adjoin the current premises.

The New Binswood Tavern opened on 26th November 1962 and the first pint was pulled by the mayor, Alderman E. H. Fryer. It had three public rooms, a lounge, a smoke room and a bar. In 1963 it cost Leamington town council £275 to have the old Binswood Tavern pulled down. Development in the area continued with new flats and a row of shops, and a plaque shows the opening of the completed redevelopment as 7th October 1968.

In 1982, under a new trading agreement with Ansells, the New Binswood was leased to Wolverhampton and Dudley [Banks] Brewery, and from 23rd August 1982 it sold Banks' traditional draught beers. Gatsby's, the new lounge bar at the New Binswood opened at 6.00pm on the 19th August 1983; Taylor Ridgeway Design of Coventry was

*Photo of the Binswood, a Lucas & Co pub. Courtesy of licensee Tommy O'Reilly.*

*Left: The New Binswood Tavern taken by Nick Wilkins. Right: Venew @ The Binswood taken on 9th June 2010 © Allan Jennings.*

responsible for the transformation. On 17th March 2010 it was renamed the Venew @ The Binswood. A planning application in the Leamington Spa Courier dated 30th March 2012 told of plans by TMK Developments Ltd to demolish the existing public house and erect three 3 bedroomed town houses and six 2 bedroomed flats. Having obtained planning permission the Venew @ The Binswood was closed for business on Sunday 27th May 2012.

| | |
|---|---|
| ≤1832 | Licensee not known |
| 1833-34 | T. Hall |
| 1835-39 | Francis Beaumont |
| 1841-79 | Robert Adkins |
| 1880-85 | Rudolph Rowell |
| 1886-1910 | J. A. Higham |
| September 1910-Nov 1915 | Edward Alexander |
| | *(Transferred from executor Anne Elizabeth Higham)* |
| November 1915-29 | Frederick Johnson |
| 1929-36 | Mrs. Sarah Johnson *(On the death of Frederick)* |
| 1936-Sep 1939 | Clarence Proctor Wood |
| September 1939-Jun 1942 | Frederick Allan Alderman |
| June 1942-Sep 1946 | Kathleen Alderman |
| September 1946-Jan 1955 | Frederick Allan Alderman |
| January 1955-Sep 1955 | Robert Stanton Bavington |
| September 1955-May 1956 | Charles Leonard Wainwright |
| May 1956-Nov 1956 | Stanley Frederick Stower |
| November 1956-Nov 1962 | William Bird |
| **26th November 1962** | **Moved to new premises** |
| 26th Nov 1962-Jan 1964 | William Bird |
| January 1964-Apr 1966 | Reginald James Colledge |

| | |
|---|---|
| April 1966-Jun 1968 | Harold William Sims |
| June 1968-Apr 1969 | Norman Alexander Thomson |
| April 1969-Aug 1970 | Leslie Day |
| August 1970-Jul 1973 | Arthur John 'Vic' and Betty Vicary |
| July 1973-Jan 1974 | Kaljo Uussalu |
| January 1974-75 | Gerald Henry Trueman |
| 1975 | David Reeve |
| 1983 | Mary and Olly Mann |
| 1983-Nov 1986 | Chris and Jeanette 'Janet' Huxtep |
| November 1986 | Keith and Jean Darby |
| 1990 | Barry and Anne Bridgett |
| | (*Previously at the Grist Mill*) |
| 1996-2001 | Kenneth 'Ken' and Ella Underhill (*Previously at the Montgomery of Alamein, Hampton Magna*) |
| Circa 2005 | Mrs. Lily Prabha Debnath [née Kandola] |
| May 2006-Jun 2008 | Simon Mackenzie |
| June 2008-Aug 2008 | Victor Broom |
| August 2008-Oct 2008 | Deborah Bennett |
| October 2008-Dec 2008 | Lee Singleton |
| December 2008-Apr 2009 | Stephen Boyle |
| April 2009 | Ken Preece |
| April 2009-Oct 2009 | Peter Law |
| October 2009-27th May 2012 | Thomas Hugh O'Reilly and his wife Treena (*Previously at the Hope Tavern*) |
| 27th May 2012 | Closed for business |

*On 17th March 1943, the chief constable granted permission for a room at the rear of the pub to be used as a gymnasium by the Ford Foundry Co Ltd boxing 'club'.*

The Leamington Spa Courier dated 19th January 1962 reported that: Leamington's new £30,000 Binswood Inn on Rugby Road is expected to be complete by the end of November. Building is in progress behind the existing inn which is managed by Mr. and Mrs. Bird. Mr. K. Donaldson, the brewery representative, said that the new licensee had not yet been chosen, but Mr. Bird was being considered. A member of Trepass, Harley-Smith and Steel, Warwick Architects, said that a feature of the new public house was the glass and Cumberland slate porch which will run the length of the frontage. Land adjoining the site is at present vacant, but it is planned to build lower flats linking the new inn to Stamford Gardens, the recently completed nine-storey block 150 yards further up the road. The present Binswood Inn, and some adjoining properties fronting Binswood Street, is due for demolition, probably within 18 months. Contractors for the new inn are Messrs Morris and Jacombs, Ltd, Birmingham.

*The following article has been taken from the Morning News of 27th September 1985: With the arrival of a Scott Fitzgerald serial on television, the lure of the twenties glamour will no doubt persuade viewers into trying it out in real life. And where better to indulge the urge than at the Binswood Tavern in Rugby Road. There, the Gatsby's lounge bar recreates temptations of twenties opulence of blue and orange, wicker and brass decor. Huge ceiling fans, luxurious settees and greenery all add to the atmosphere. And to cap it all, a library with books ranging from the Pilgrim's Progress to the Laughing Diplomat is there to browse through as you sip the pub's speciality, chilled wine. But for those who prefer the traditional English pub, there's a down-to-earth bar and a separate pool room.*

*Chris Huxtep is manager of the Binswood, owned by Banks' brewery. He said, "It's the first pub I've managed. It's been hard work but the customers I get make it very enjoyable. The range of customers adds to the pub's friendly atmosphere. Eighteen to eighty-year-olds all aim to have a good time, and get it. Some people have been drinking here for forty years and a dominoes team, still with all the same players, has been using it for 15 years."*

The Morning News of 24th October 1986 reported on the New Binswood following its redecoration and the arrival of new licensees Keith and Jean Darby. Traditional Banks' bitter is 70p a pint and Banks's mild 65p. Oversized glasses are used to avoid spillage and ensure that there is a head on the beer. Every Tuesday there is a disco featuring solely music of the 1960s and 70s, which is always well attended and where the choice of the records is made by the customers not the DJ. Previous licensees Chris and Jeanette Huxstep have moved to the Basket Maker in Quedgeley, Gloucestershire.

**Birch and Billycock** – 35 Regent Street
See Warwick Tavern for details.

**Birch Tree** – 35 Warwick Street
See Warwick Tavern for details.

**Birmingham Tavern** – Wise Street
This was the tap-house [pub] for Leamington's first brewery built in 1812 and located at the top of Wise Street, close to the Warwick and Napton canal [now part of the Grand Union canal]. As the Birmingham Tavern was incorporated on the same land title, its ownership mirrors that of the brewery. The brewery's first proprietor was William Fowler but by 1815 ownership had passed to Thomas Paris [also spelt Parris]; the first directory listing we have for the Birmingham Tavern is also in 1815. Thomas Paris retained the freehold until circa 1829, when ownership passed to Edward Woodfield. The brewery was advertised for sale by auction in November 1839 with immediate possession of all premises except the public house which we believe was closed in early 1840; all premises were demolished later that decade.

| | |
|---|---|
| 1815-18 | Thomas Paris |
| 1819 | John Hanson |
| 1821 | John Bedford |
| 1823 | Meredith Evans |
| 1824-26 | Thomas Grant |
| 1826 | Thomas Merryman |
| 1827 | Thomas Paris |

| 1828-32 | Edward Woodfield |
| 1832-35 | Henry Woodfield |
| 1835-36 | Joseph Tunnicliff |
| 1837-40 | T. Chattaway |

**Black Dog** – London Road [now High Street]

On the south side of the London Road, and about 30-40 yards from the east corner of Clemens Street, stood the Black Dog Inn, also known as the 'Dog'; although said to date from at least 1529 we have not been able to substantiate such a claim.

*Local historian Robin Taylor shared the following story that possibly explains the origin of the name Black Dog: "In every way except physical strength Edward II could hardly have been more different from his father. He might have been a goodish squire of a small estate. He was totally unfitted to be a King. When he succeeded in 1307, aged twenty-three, he had long been besotted by Piers Gaveston, a Gascon Knight of no great standing, frivolous and arrogant. Before long the country was ruled not so much by Edward nor even by the Barons who reasonably expected to have the King's ear, but by Gaveston."*

*"If Edward had been discreet; if he had been competent and responsible; if he had finished off the war against Scotland as he should have done; the scandal of the relationship might have been tolerated. But Edward's only thoughts were for Gaveston, and Gaveston was foolish enough and conceited enough to flaunt his power. He had a clever tongue and gave the most important Barons contemptuous nicknames. The mini-court he had made from his pals laughed, and the Barons were…displeased! The Earl of Warwick, who had a swarthy skin, he called the 'Black Dog of Arden'. 'And one day,' said Warwick, 'he'll find that this dog has teeth'."*

*"By 1312 the country had sunk into a squalid civil war, Edward and Gaveston against the Barons; and in the early summer that year Gaveston found himself holed up in Scarborough Castle and short of supplies. On a promise of safety, and of an appearance later in the year before Parliament, he surrendered. It was decided that the Earl of Pembroke would keep him under house arrest in his castle at Wallingford. On the journey south, at Deddington on the other side of Banbury, Pembroke rode off to see his wife and left Gaveston under guard in the rector's house. That may or may not have been a put-up job. No one knows. In the night the Earls of Warwick, Hereford, and Lancaster nabbed him, marched him to Warwick Castle, and chucked him in a dungeon. A few days later he was taken to Blacklow Hill, where two toughs removed his head."*

**Footnote:** *The sign of the Black Dog pub at Southam depicts a 'knight in armour' which would probably appear strange to anyone who hadn't heard the story [Ed].*

The first corroborated reference we have for this inn is in 1776, when William Abbotts was the landlord. In his account of 'The History of Royal Leamington Spa' [1887-89], George Morley informs us that, "William Abbotts was born in 1736 at Long Itchington. Orphaned at an early age he was adopted by his uncle, a gamekeeper at Birdingbury, who left him heir to a small property at Leamington Priors, situated on the London Road and containing an

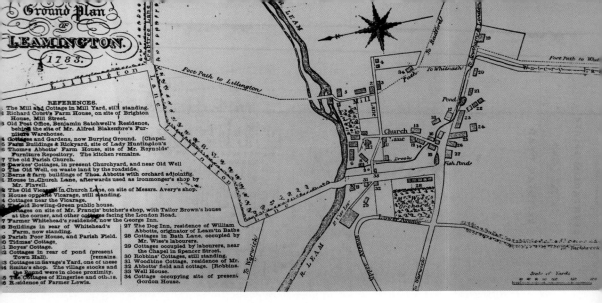

*A 1783 map of Leamington Priors showing its only two inns, the Bowling Green [no. 15] and the Black Dog, also known as the 'Dog' [no. 27].*

old roadside inn." Morley described Abbotts as, "A comparatively wealthy native, a publican, farmer and a churchwarden of All Saints."

Circa 1776, soon after the death of his uncle, Abbotts relocated to Leamington to takeover occupancy of the Black Dog, "where he and his patrons were wont to sit of an evening enjoying 'potations pottle deep' [ales in measures equal to four pints - Ed] and discussing the latest news brought down by coach".

In 'Glimpses of Our Local Past' [1895], J.C. Manning described the premises thus: "The Dog Inn must have been a curious little structure when William Abbotts first took possession of it somewhere about the year 1776. It was originally a small thatched alehouse, standing alone by the roadside, with a good sized garden and apple orchard in the rear; in front, a flower garden reaching to the gravelled footpath; a hedge and ditch on the right hand, leading continuously up the Warwick Road to the west and a hedge and ditch on the left hand leading continuously to the east towards Radford ....with a lattice on each side of a low-pitched door, and two small casements above, indicating a tiny dormitory to each."

"Two years after Abbotts came to the Dog he changed the aspect of the inn by substituting, for lattice and thatch, two smart bow windows and tile roofing, cutting down the hedge in front and clearing away the little garden, defining the frontage by placing three posts with loop-chains before each window." The Dog now began to see itself as a competitor for the more aristocratic Bowling Green and it began to encourage the favours of the growing number of visitors to the village.

"The Dog was the village alehouse in which Ben Satchwell used to hold high court as the 'oracular authority' on all local questions. Here, of an evening, in a cosy chimney corner of the quaint little kitchen, Benjamin would sit, puffing a cloud of smoke from behind a yard of clay, and moistening its dryness from a can of Will Abbotts' best home brewed ale" .... "At the time Abbotts entered upon the Dog, Satchwell was thus the stay and prop of the humble little inn as its most influential frequenter. His reason for attending is thus explained in rhyme by his own writing"....

*"Some to the Dog do go to drink,*
*But I go there to smoke and think;*
*To hear folks tell, o'er cup of ale,*
*How Leamington doth wag its tail."*

Abbotts and Satchwell became good friends and in January 1784, when out walking together on the former's land, they discovered a spring of saline water; Abbotts would erect the first bathhouse in Leamington Priors which, according to J. C. Manning, was commenced in 1784 and opened in 1787. In 1790, Abbotts commenced building the New Inn in Lillington Lane [corner Spencer and Bath Streets] upon part of the freehold land left to him by his uncle and in 1793 he took possession. At this point the 'Dog' was acquired by Thomas Sinker who re-christened it Sinker's Boarding House; according to George Morley's 1887-89 account, it would subsequently be renamed the Greyhound.

In 1812, Sinker advertised his business for sale and it was sold to Michael Copps the following year. Soon afterwards Copps purchased the adjacent Fisher's Balcony Boarding House [which briefly became the Oxford Boarding House/Hotel] and by 1816 both premises had been renamed the Copps' Royal Hotel. Manning also informs us that by 1816 there was a public coffee-room at the hotel which "was the identical old Dog Inn itself, at the east end of the hotel buildings, set apart for that special purpose".

Also according to J. C. Manning, "The old 'Dog' premises were standing in 1842 when the palatial hotel was closed and formed an annexe to the hotel building." This claim appears to be reinforced by Richard Hopper in his 1842 account, when he states, "From this period [1813] the hotel which, for a considerable period time went by the name Copps' Hotel, was much enlarged and improved. The house which was first occupied by Abbotts, and then by Sinker, retains much of its original form. The plain bow windows may at this time be seen to the east of the hotel; they retain much of the appearance of a small neat country inn." However, whether Hopper's observation described in the last sentence was made in 1842 is open to interpretation.

Copps' Royal Hotel was demolished in May 1847 to build the bridge that would facilitate the extension of the railway line to Rugby – for more information refer to [Copps'] Royal Hotel.

**Footnote:** In 1841, author J. C. Manning was apprentice to a Leamington printer, who was then engaged in printing a work entitled, 'The History Of Leamington Priors – From The Earliest Records To The Year 1842' by Richard Hopper. Manning tells of, "Being a near neighbour of Benjamin Satchwell's daughter, Mrs. Hopton, who was particularly communicative as to the state of things as they existed at Leamington as far back as she could remember." Additionally, "Hopper's history was enriched, too, I remember, with historical information given by Mrs. Potterton, a daughter of William Abbotts."

| | |
|---|---|
| 1776-93 | William Abbotts *(Black Dog)* |
| 1793-1813 | Thomas Sinker *(Sinkers Boarding House/Greyhound)* |
| 1813 | Michael Copps |
| | *(Premises became part of Copps' Royal Hotel)* |

**Black Dog** – 9 Satchwell Street

The first directory listing we have is in 1833. In September 1882, and again in August 1883, the licence renewal was refused by the local licensing justices. Judging by the subsequent gap in directory listings, it would appear that pub was closed from 1882 until circa 1890 when it briefly reopened, before finally closing in the late 1890s. The site is now part of the Royal Priors shopping centre.

| | |
|---|---|
| 1833-33 | Clarke |
| 1833-35 | Thomas Smith |
| 1835 | W. Smith |
| 1839-64 | John Howe |
| 1864-Aug 1864 | Joseph Gilbert *(Executor of the late John Howe)* |
| August 1864-65 | Charlotte Lynes |
| 1865-68 | Richard Poulton |
| April 1869-1870 | Charlotte Pullen |
| February 1870-Feb 1878 | Arthur Soden |
| February 1878-May 1878 | William Godfrey *(Executor of the late Arthur Soden)* |
| May 1878-81 | Edward John Adkins |
| 1881-Jan 1882 | Edwin Spencer |
| January 1882-82 | Elizabeth Hunt |
| 1882-Sep 1882 | Charles Satchwell |
| 1891-97 | R. Brandon and his wife Mary Ann |

*In March 1891 Ellen White [26], a respectable dressed tramp, who had been living at the Black Dog in Satchwell Street, was charged with wilfully breaking two large squares of plate glass at 92,*

Parade, the property of Messrs D. Melia and Company. The prisoner admitted the offence and said she had a row with her husband and wanted to be put out of his way. The Bench decided she was guilty of a most wanton and wilful act of destruction and fined her a guinea plus costs of 12/6d, or, in default, commit her to prison for one month's imprisonment, with hard labour. The prisoner, leaving the dock, to be conveyed to gaol, in default of payment, said, "Thank you kindly, gentlemen."

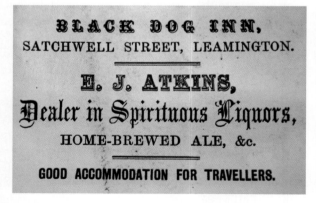

**BLACK DOG INN,**
SATCHWELL STREET, LEAMINGTON.

**E. J. ATKINS,**
**Dealer in Spirituous Liquors,**
HOME-BREWED ALE, &c.

**GOOD ACCOMMODATION FOR TRAVELLERS.**

*Black Dog business card circa 1880 courtesy of Jo Clark.*

**Black Horse** – 18 Princes Street

The Black Horse dates back to 1863 when it opened as a beer house belonging to George Hunt; it closed ≤2004. In 1869, it was stated that the business also included a grocer's shop which was in the same room as the bar. It was the only Hook Norton tied-house for miles around and was purchased by J. H. Harris and Co. in 1897, predecessors of the Hook Norton Brewery Co. Ltd which was founded in 1900. On 8th March 1949 the local licensing justices approved plans for alterations to the pub and it was modernised soon afterwards. In its latter years the premises were much altered and at some point a single storey flat roofed extension was built over the backyard to create an unusually large bar; this was in marked contrast to the cosy lounge which was tucked away where the old door on the corner used to be. Although we have not been able to establish the exact time of closure, we know that it was in the early 2000s and that it was closed by year-end

*Photo of the Black Horse taken on 17th December 2005 courtesy of David Stowell.*

2004. Plans to convert the vacant building into four houses and two flats, submitted to the Warwick District Council on 10th March 2010, were approved conditional on the development being completed within three years. In July 2013 work commenced on converting the premises to residential use.

| | |
|---|---|
| 1863-Jan 1872 | George Hunt |
| January 1872-Feb 1884 | Mrs. Elizabeth Hunt *(On the death of George)* |
| February 1884-Sep 1885 | Charles Baker |
| September 1885-Mar 1889 | William Henry Green |
| March 1889-Jan 1899 | Joseph Freeman |
| January 1899-Nov 1913 | Joseph Ward |
| November 1913-Oct 1933 | Herbert Henry Wincott |
| October 1933-Nov 1948 | Alfred Lane and his wife Gertrude |
| November 1948-Jan 1951 | Kenneth Robinson |
| January 1951-Jan 1954 | Sydney John Type |
| January 1954-Mar 1956 | Leslie John Olorenshaw Sutherland |
| March 1956-Jul 1956 | Frederick Lucas |
| July 1956-Mar 1957 | Stanley Brooks |
| March 1957-Jun 1972 | Albert Edward [Taffy'] Jenkins and his wife Marjorie |
| June 1972-Oct 1973 | Janet Mas |
| October 1973-≤Mar 1986 | Pete and Carol Elizabeth Cousins *(Carol died 21st Dec 1993, aged 52)* |
| January 1988-1993 | Roger and Julie Constable *(Roger left to take over the Cuttle in Long Itchington, and then emigrated to Spain in* |

|  |  |
|---|---|
| 1993-95 | *2007. After returning in 2009 he became the landlord of the Kings Head, Napton; in 2013 he is licensee of the Black Dog, Southam).* David 'Smudger' Smith |
| ≥1995-≤2004 | Jim Goodman *(Last licensee)* |

*The Leamington Spa Courier dated 10th October 1969 reported: Some licensees do it quietly, putting the towels on the pumps and saying, "May I have your glasses please"; others ring a discreet bell; but one Leamington landlord blasts out a bugle. Ken Jenkins tenant licensee of the Black Horse in Princes Street comes from Pontypool where he was a sheet metal roller for 18 years until 1939. He then worked in munitions factories and after the war was for eight years chauffeur mechanic to the Earl of Warwick and later to the manager of the Alvis Works in Coventry. He moved to the Black Horse from there in 1957 and has since, aided by his wife Madge, built the inn into a popular rendezvous. He was for ten years president of the North Leamington Football Club. Mr. Jenkins is a fine singer who has given many concerts, and learned to play the bugle when he was 18. He was an instructor with the Church Lads' Brigade in his native Pontypool.*

The Black Horse was referenced in the Courier on 31st March 1972, when the son of landlord Taffy Jenkins had his photo taken in the pub, with the family. Twenty two years old and six foot tall Stuart Jenkins, a Coldstream Guard, had just passed out from Pirbright Guards Depot in Surrey.

*In August 1976, landlady Carol Cousins was having a tough time with trade and went to the Morning News with her story [MN 23rd August 1976], "We're still standing, still here and still in business," she told the MN. Trade had gone flat since rows of houses in Comyn Street were demolished and people moved away. Many customers from outside of the area who used to call in for a good pint – the Black Horse was in the 'real ale' guide – weren't coming any more. "They think we were pulled down at the same time." Trade was down 50% on what it used to be, and she was only selling three or four 18 gallon barrels of bitter a week instead of seven or eight.*

**Blasted Oak** – Sydenham Farm Estate
See Fusilier for details.

**Blenheim Hotel** – Clemens Street
See Stoneleigh Arms for details.

**Blood Bucket** – 19 Russell Street
See Clarendon Tavern for an explanation of this name.

**Bohemia @ the Willoughby** – 12 Augusta Place
See Willoughby Arms for details.

**Bowling Green** – Spencer Street
This Bowling Green was the 'tap' to the Bath Hotel. See Bath Hotel for details.

**Bowling Green Inn** – Church Lane, Church Street

There were two successive Bowling Green Inns in Church Street with the earliest occupying a site between Bath and Church Streets, close to High Street [for the location, refer to 1783 map attached to the Black Dog entry]. In his book, 'A Complete History of Royal Leamington Spa' [1901], T. B. Dudley wrote, "Unfortunately, no definite details are preserved of its form and arrangements, but it may be taken for granted that it was an ordinary country way-side public house having at its back, in lieu of the customary orchard, a bowling green reaching as far as the present Regent Place ...." and, "all we know of it with certainty is that it had a low roof, that the assembly room in which the fashionable visitors were accustomed to meet and make merry, was about fifteen feet wide and that generally it was small and comfortable." The first reference we have is in 1768 when Simon Hinton was the landlord of the Bowling Green Inn, then addressed as Church Lane.

As an aside, the process of 'enclosure' was the parcelling-up of open or common land into privately owned blocks [or fields] and enclosing them with fences, hedges and ditches, etc; this translated into the reallocation of the rights that people possessed to cultivate plots and/or common grazing land. Although 'enclosure' had been gathering momentum for centuries it required the Enclosure Act of 1767 to regulate the process. According to T. B. Dudley, "In the Award of 1768 it [the inn] is referred to as the 'Bowling Green House' and Simon Hinton was then the landlord. The commissioners, as proxies of the Imperial Parliament, assembled there, parcelled out the commonable lands on the south bank of the river, and their divisions constitute the title deeds of nearly one half of the land in Leamington." The first meeting was held on 13th March, 1768. At that time there were only two inns that were suitable for the reception of visitors in the village, one being the Bowling Green and the other the Black Dog close-by in High Street.

In his account of the 'History of Royal Leamington Spa' [1887-89], George Morley wrote, "In 1810 it is recorded that the Bowling Green was shut-out from the public gaze by a thick set hedge, said to have been 10 feet to 12 feet high, intersected by tall elms. The first open market was established in 1813 on a piece of waste land on the south-east side of the Bowling Green Inn, kept by a delightful lady named Mistress Shaw. It was open every Wednesday during the season and was plentifully furnished with butter, eggs, poultry, vegetables, and various kinds of fine fruits. Fresh river fish of almost every description could be had here which must have taxed the resources of the Avon and the Leam. The butchers of Warwick and Leamington also had stalls in the market, and the other wares offered consisted of glass, china, crockery, toys and pedlar's goods." The first market comprising six stalls was held on 5th May 1813. In 1816, the Bissett Guide informs us that, "A bowling green adjoins [the inn] which was formerly much in use amongst the gentry in the neighbourhood, but is now resorted to by tradesmen of the village, and the company frequenting the inn. The house is kept by Mrs. Shaw, 350 paces from the [original] post office, and near to the Baths."

Also according to George Morley, "[In the 1820s], on the east side of Bath Street, there were no houses from High Street to Regent Place, that portion being covered with gardens belonging to the Bowling Green Inn, and skirting Bath Street with luxuriant trees."

In 1896 T. B. Dudley informs us that, "On 18th May 1824 the aeronaut Green ascended from the Bowling Green Inn in a balloon that had been used in the celebration festivities that followed the Coronation of George IV. It had been brought to Leamington and exhibited to thousands of visitors from 10th May until the day of the ascent when, from an early hour, the town was full of excitement and sightseers from all parts of the surrounding neighbourhood; the number of spectators being estimated at fourteen to fifteen thousand."

On 25th October 1828 the Leamington Spa Courier carried the following notice: "To Innkeepers and others – Old Bowling Green Inn – Mr. T. H. Atkins respectfully announces that he will offer for sale by auction, on the premises of Mr. Joseph Parsons, Old Bowling Green Inn, Leamington Priors, on Tuesday, Wednesday and Thursday, the 4th, 5th and 6th days of November 1828 under an execution from the Sheriff – All the stock of wines, spirits, upwards of 1,000 gallons of fine ale, porter, cider, &c; modern and genteel household furniture, brewing utensils, copper furnace, capital iron-bound casks, from 36 to 500 gallons each, general fixtures and other effects."

On 21st March the following year, the Courier reported that Joseph Parsons, victualler, dealer and chapman [hawker or merchant] had been declared bankrupt. He was ordered to surrender himself to the commissioners on the 27th March at the Swan Hotel, in the Borough of Warwick, where he was to make a full discovery and disclosure of his estate and effects; creditors were requested to come prepared to prove their debts.

In the lead-up to its closure and subsequent demolition, the original Bowling Green [often referred to as the 'Old' Bowling Green Inn], offered for sale by auction in March 1830, the stock, household furniture, valuable paintings and fittings etc. The catalogue also listed copper furnaces, brewing utensils and capital iron bound casks from thirty-six to five hundred gallons. At this point of proceedings we understand that the premises were in the control of Robert Bark [an administrator] and the sale was under a 'distress for rent'. We have also concluded that the original auction scheduled for November 1828 [of much the same items] was aborted, possibly because Joseph Parsons had allegedly absconded.

In April 1830 the premises were being advertised 'for let' as the Old Bowling Green and Commercial Inn. The house comprised two good sized front parlours, a large dining room, 13 bedrooms, a spacious bar, excellent kitchens and tap room, brew house and cellaring; there was also a spacious yard, with good stabling and a coach house. The next stage was to prove much more dramatic and, renamed as the Union and Commercial Inn, the premises were advertised to be urgently sold by auction on 24th August, 1830 at the Bath Hotel, by order of the assignees of Joseph Parsons, a bankrupt. It was described as a substantial, eligible, and convenient dwelling place, together with a piece of front land adjoining, calculated and intended for building one or more houses upon, approximating a total area of 931 square yards, situated in Church Street, and commanding one of the best locations in the town for a commercial inn.

In the meantime, and commencing in 1825, a 'new' Bowling Green had been built on the opposite side of the road upon land purchased from Edward Treadgold [the road was described as being part of Town Close]. This new inn consisted of five superior sitting rooms, a spacious bar, fourteen bedrooms, kitchen, cellars, stabling and coach houses; it was opened by E. Woodfield [maltster, Wise Street]. In 1827 it was licensed to George Dickenson followed by John Burridge from the early 1830s until the 1850s.

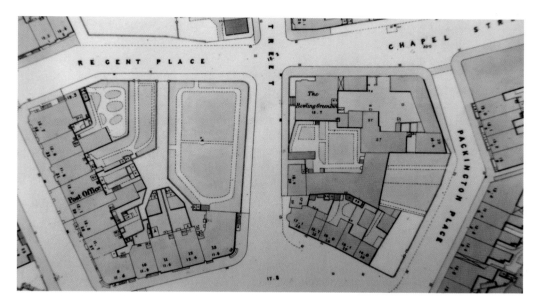

*This 1852 map courtesy of Leamington Library shows where the New [2nd] Bowling Green was situated.*

The Leamington Courier dated 7th August 1852 advertised the 'new' Bowling Green Inn 'for let'; by then it comprised a commercial room, smoking room, bar, bar parlour, tap room, two kitchens, scullery, offices, dining and drawing rooms, thirteen excellent chambers, a spacious club room, excellent cellaring, brew house, malt room, enclosed coach house, stabling for twelve horses, piggeries and a productive garden.

By 1856 the Bowling Green Inn had become the Guernsey Commercial Inn managed by Misses Eliza and Emma Ann Gill but on 24th March 1860 the premises, including stable yard and brew house, were again advertised 'to let'. The next tenant was Charles Liebenrood a son of George Christopher Liebenrood who at that time was proprietor of the Royal Leamington Spa Courier. In 1862 he opened a concert room/music hall at the hotel for the 'gentlemen of Leamington' to enjoy performances of vocal and instrumental music. Affected adversely by market competition from rival hostelries the business was unsuccessful and Mr. Liebenrood relinquished the tenancy in 1863 to a Mr. Payne. The next occupant, a Mrs. Meeks who had previously kept a second-hand furniture store in Ben Satchwell's cottage in New Street, reopened the Guernsey as a temperance hotel during the period 1866-68. In 1868 it was the Guernsey Hotel, in 1871 it was listed as the Guernsey Temperance Hotel and in 1902 it was the Guernsey Family and Commercial Hotel. Those of us 'of a certain age' will also remember the site as the Guernsey garage which opened on Saturday 31st May 1969. In 2013 the site is residential.

**Footnote:** A number of local history books refer to the Old Bowling Green as being demolished in 1825. As we have newspaper reports referencing the auctioning of the property in 1830, and no further information on the Union and Commercial Inn post 1830, we have concluded that this was the year that the building known as the 'original' Bowling Green was sold and demolished.

**1st Bowling Green**

| | |
|---|---|
| 1768 | Simon Hinton |
| 1788-1806 | Samuel Shaw *(Although Samuel is listed as a licensed victualler the name of the premises is not mentioned. As Mary Shaw was at the Bowling Green, and as there were only two licensed premises in the village, an assumption has been made that he was also there)* |
| 1807-18 | Mary Shaw |
| 1822-28 | Joseph Bowles Parsons *(Died 18th January 1848, aged 65)* |
| 1828-30 | Robert Bark |
| 1829 | Name changed to the Union and Commercial Inn |
| 1830 | Demolished |

**2nd Bowling Green**

| | |
|---|---|
| 1827-30 | George Dickenson |
| 1831 | W. Linney *(Possibly)* |
| 1832-54 | John Burridge |
| 1854 | J. Flecknoe *(Possible temporary transfer)* |
| 1854-1856 | John Burridge |

**Guernsey Commercial Inn/ Guernsey Temperance Hotel**
**[continuation of Bowling Green entry]**
Although the Guernsey became a temperance hotel we have included the occupancy details available to us:

| | |
|---|---|
| 1856-1860 | Misses Eliza and Emma Ann Gill |
| November 1860-Nov 1861 | Emma Ann Gill |
| November 1861-Oct 1863 | Charles Liebenrood |
| October 1863 | John B. Payne |
| 1864 | Not listed in annual licensing session records |
| 1866-73 | Mrs. Meeks *(Temperance Hotel)* |
| 1874-97 | C. Purser |
| 1900-14 | S. H. Fisher |
| 1931 | Mrs. A. Hayes *(Leamington Temperance Hotels Ltd)* |

**Bowling Green Inn** – 20 New Street
James Batchelor opened a beer house at 7, New Street in 1867 after ending his career with the 2nd Warwick Militia; the first directory listing we have for these premises is in 1870

when it was known as the New Bowling Green Inn. This is the third pub in Leamington with this name and the fourth if the one in Spencer Street ['tap' to the Bath Hotel] is included. Applications for a spirits licence in 1873 and 1874 were both refused but a licence to sell wine [in addition to beer] was granted in February 1928. The pub was owned by Hunt, Edmunds and Co. Ltd but on 1st May 1967, after the brewery was taken over and brewing ceased, it was acquired by Messrs Bass, Mitchells and Butlers Ltd, Cape Hill Brewery, Birmingham. As an M&B pub it sold M&B mild and Brew XI bitter. In October 1978 the Bowling Green was modernised at a cost of £15,000; Leamington's mayor, Councillor John Higgins sampled the first pint at the re-opening on 24th October. The Bowling Green reopened on 25th September 2009 having been closed earlier in the

*Photo of the Bowling Green taken on 25th October 2009 © Allan Jennings.*

year and a new sign was installed in October 2010. It closed again in mid August 2012 but in the second quarter of 2013 it was refurbished and newly signed 'The Bowling Green' before reopening in the August; in December 2013, it was being advertised 'to let' by Enterprise Inns.

| | |
|---|---|
| 1867-Mar 1877 | James Batchelor |
| March 1877-Jan 1882 | Eliza Batchelor *(On the death of James)* |
| January 1882-Apr 1890 | William Hitchman |
| April 1890-Mar 1895 | George Potter |
| March 1895-Mar 1904 | Charles Duffin |
| March 1904-May 1908 | James Glenn |
| May 1908-21 | John Henry Stevens |
| 1921-Sep 1924 | William Henry Plummer |
| September 1924-Nov 1929 | Henry Cyril Walton |
| November 1929-32 | Sydney Woodward |
| 1932-Jan 1933 | Percy Parker *(Died 14th January 1950, aged 56)* |
| January 1933 | William H. Summers |
| 1936-38 | Harold Thomas Wosket |
| 1939-Jul 1939 | William Henry Plummer *(Died 9th June 1939, aged 54)* |
| July 1939-Jan 1954 | Mrs. Lilly Jane Plummer |
| January 1954-Nov 1957 | Gerald Atherton Brown |
| November 1957-May 1959 | John Richard Prestidge |
| 11th May 1959 | Kenneth Austin Scott |
| Mid 1970s-May 1987 | Ellen English *(Died 7th May 2010)* |
| May 1987-1991 | Anny and Colin Odey-Smith |

| 1992-≥1995 | Barry Hunt *(Previously of the New Inn)* |
| 2006 | Lyndsey McDonnell |
| October 2007 | Cathie Julia Bailey |
| June 2009-Jul 2010 | Brian Hegarty and Eleanor Anne Leacroft |
| | *(Also licensee of the Lounge, the Parade)* |
| July 2010-Feb 2012 | Kulwinder Sahota |
| February 2012-Mid Aug 2012 | Andrew 'Andy' Murray |
| | *(Also licensee of the Town House)* |
| August 2013 → | Peter Griffith |

*In the 1970s and 1980s Ellen English ran the 'Bowler' with help from her son John and daughter-in-law Sue. John later took over the Bowling Green in Warwick and Sue took over the Vine, also in Warwick. Ellen was previously at the Commercial in Long Itchington [now the Harvester] and would latterly move on to the Engine in [Mill End] Kenilworth for nine years. After more than 35 years in the pub business, the last 26 years running her own Bass pub, Ellen retired in 1995.*

The Morning News dated 13th September 1985 ran the following article: In one of Leamington's village street look-alike back waters is a village-style pub. It is called the Bowling Green and has all the atmosphere and camaraderie you'd expect from a local. Clever redecoration undertaken some years ago has kept it feeling fresh and spacious with plenty of mirrors and red plush seating. Characteristically, the walls are covered with a wide selection of brasses. The tenant, Ellen English, needs no introduction. She is well known to Leamingtonians for her fund raising activities as chairperson of the Ladies Auxiliary of the Licensed Victuallers Association. Ellen has run the Bowling Green for 10 years and has spent all her life working in pubs or clubs.

The pub hosts a football team and regular gatherings take place. It is also a meeting place for the old-time regulars and the mixture of young and old helps along an extremely friendly and relaxed atmosphere. Food is served at lunch times and an impressive menu of meals all costing less than £1.55 is served. Roast beef and Yorkshire puddings, roast pork, scampi and chips or salads are just some of the selection. Another typically village feature is the television which is put on for the races. All in all, it's very much like a comfortable sitting room with drinks on tap.

Mitchells and Butlers own the pub and draught Brew XI is the standard drink, although a selection of lagers and a good variety of wines are available. There is an incentive to drink spirits with 15p off every double. The Bowling Green at New Street, Leamington, opens from 11.00am to 2.30pm at lunch-times and from 5.30pm to 11.00pm in the evenings.

*The Leamington Observer carried the following article in the 24th September 2009 edition:* **New life is being breathed into what is believed to be Leamington's oldest pub** *The Bowling Green, which is thought to have been a pub since the 1600s [in name only – Ed], will officially open its doors again tomorrow [Friday] after a major facelift. The previous owners of the New Street pub called it a day earlier this year as the growing financial pressure of running a pub became too much. But new landlord and landlady, Brian Hegarty and Ellie Leacroft, are undaunted and remain convinced they can make a success of the Bowling Green despite the hard times the industry is going through.*

*Ellie, 26, said, "It's a difficult time for the pub trade. More people are drinking at home and buying from supermarkets where drink is cheaper. But to survive it is important to understand the trade and create the right atmosphere to pull customers in. Many people come into the trade thinking of it as almost a hobby but it is hard work 24/7 and more so than ever at the moment." The couple have the experience having taken over the running of the Lounge on Leamington's Parade a year ago, where 29 year old Brian had previously spent four years as manager. And although the makeover of the Bowling Green has a modern twist, Ellie is adamant they want to keep the traditional value of the pub as the heart of the community.*

*Ellie added, "While we want to see the faces that have been coming to the pub for years, we obviously also want to attract new customers. We are also keen to hear from any sports clubs who would be interested in representing the pub." The launch evening tomorrow starts at 5 pm. There will be introductory drinks offers throughout the night and a free prize draw.*

**Brewery Tap** – Satchwell Court, Clemens Street
To the best of our knowledge the only brewery located in the vicinity during this period was the [then named] Regent Brewery. Although it was situated at the top of Wise Street, we understand that its site extended through to Clemens Street. Furthermore, all the information that we have relating to the brewery indicates that its tap-house [pub] was the Birmingham Tavern. This is the only directory listing we have for these premises and the licensee's name is uncorroborated. [See Birmingham Tavern for more information]

| | |
|---|---|
| 1829 | Caldeycutt *(Or Caldecutt)* |

**Bricklayers Arms** – 34 King Street
The first reference we have for this beer house is in April 1865 when George Walton was the licensee. In April 1866 James Allwood, keeper of this beer house, was charged with keeping his house open for the sale of beer after 11.00pm on Saturday, contrary to the statute. He pleaded guilty and was fined the full penalty of 40s, plus 10s expenses, in default 21 days imprisonment in Warwick gaol. Owned by the Burton Brewery Co. Ltd, the chief constable opposed its licence renewal in March 1913 on the grounds of 'structural unfitness' and 'redundancy' describing the pub as simply a cottage with neither stabling nor sleeping accommodation. There were two entrances to the house, one in King Street and

*Photo of the Bricklayers Arms, King Street circa 1905 courtesy of the late Bill Gibbons. The Bricklayers is on the right.*

one in Thomas Street, and it had two rooms for drinking, a smoke room [12 ft 3 in x 7 ft 2 in] and a bar [13 ft 9 in x 9 ft 7 in]. The local justices referred the Bricklayers Arms for 'extinction by compensation' and in June 1913 the county's compensation committee refused to renew the licence, ruling that it was 'not structurally adapted for use as a licensed house' and that it was also 'redundant'. It was closed on 27th January 1914 with compensation being paid.

| | |
|---|---|
| ≤April 1865 | George Walton |
| ≤April 1866-87 | James Allwood |
| 1887-Aug 1889 | William Allwood |
| August 1889-Sep 1899 | E. 'John' Blackwell |
| September 1899-Jan 1914 | Frederick John Jones |
| 27th January 1914 | Closed for business |

**Bricklayers Arms** – Tavistock Street
See Victoria Vaults for details.

**Brickmakers Arms** – Clarendon Street / Lillington Road
The only directory listing we have for the Brickmakers Arms is in 1849, addressed as Lillington Road. However, John Hewitt is listed in the 1837 church rate books as having a public house on the brickyard in Clarendon Street. He is also listed as a beer retailer [beer house] in 1841 and 1842 at Kenilworth Road, and in 1851 and 1857 at the top of Clarendon Street, this being in the vicinity of the Leamington Brickworks [in the first half of the 19th century Lillington Road was called Kenilworth Road or Old Kenilworth Road]. It is

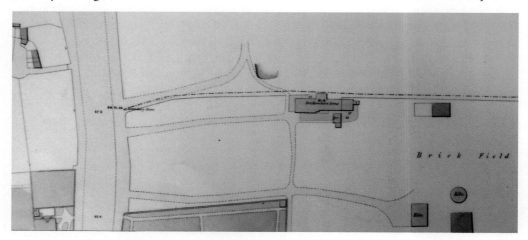

*This 1852 Board of Health map courtesy of Leamington Library shows the site of the Brickmakers Arms. These days we would say that it was on the corner of Upper Hill Street and North Villiers Street. Although it was classed as Lillington Road there weren't any streets or houses around it and Lillington Road was approximately 50 yards away.*

interesting to note that in 1841 John Hewitt is also listed as a brickmaker, obviously a hardworking man of many talents; the pub closed in the early 1860s. Another point of interest is that the wall of the Brickmakers Arms appears to have been built along the Leamington side of the parish boundary. As there was an embargo on the building of public houses on most of Lillington's land it seems that the Brickmakers Arms was built as close as possible to the boundary without actually breaking the law.

1837-62                                    John Hewitt

**Bridge** – 7 Brunswick Street
See Queens Head for details.

**Bridge End** – Clemens Street
There is only one entry and that is in 1873; we have concluded that this is in fact the Reindeer. See Reindeer for details.

**Britannia** – 7 Chandos Street
Our earliest directory entry for these premises is as the Briton in 1835 [likely an error] but by 1837 it is listed as the Britannia; however, this pub has also been variously listed in directories as the Britannia 'Inn', 'Tavern' and 'Vaults'. It was located on the upper part of Chandos Street, on the same side of the road as the Carpenters Arms. Previously owned by Lucas and Co. Ltd [Leamington Brewery], it would become an Ansells pub following their 1928 acquisition of the brewery and its closure in 1934.

The 'Brit' closed in September 1980. In May 1982 it became Gannets, a bistro, wine bar and coffee shop owned by John and Jim Sephton who had converted the old cellar into the wine bar; the ground floor became the restaurant. On Friday and Saturday nights Gannets entertainment was by Richard Lawson, the resident guitar soloist. In September 1984 it was renamed Memories Wine Bar and in May 1985 Margo Farrant briefly took over its management prior to becoming licensee of the Tavistock Inn [Tavistock Street] in the August. In 1986 a new fish bar was opened within, selling cockles, mussels, jellied eels, oysters, gambas, dressed crab and prawns; it would remain Memories Wine Bar until its closure in mid 1987.

In September 1987 the Morning News reported that the premises had reopened on 12th September, as The Gate, "a Christian run community centre and coffee shop for young people in the town, keeping them off the streets

*This photo of the Britannia was taken in 1976 and is courtesy of Peter Coulls.*

61

and away from the drug and pub scene; but the community centre is only temporary, with redevelopment plans due to be carried out in the area in the New Year." The centre was closed and demolished in 1988 to make way for a Baptist church.

| | |
|---|---|
| 1835 | Robert Harris *(Briton)* |
| 1837 | Licensee not listed |
| 1839-56 | John Treavor |
| 1854 | Thomas Brooks *(Possible temporary licensee)* |
| 1856-Feb 1860 | Thomas Blunt |
| February 1860-Sep 1862 | Jacob Findlow |
| September 1862-65 | Walter Rawlings |
| 1866 | Thomas Chetland |
| 1868 | Nathan Smith |
| 1870 | A. Smith |
| 1871-Jul 1871 | Henry Dowler |
| July 1871-Jun 1873 | Mrs. Hannah Smith |
| June 1873-Nov 1879 | Thomas Smith |
| November 1879-Jul 1891 | James and T. Hampson |
| July 1891-92 | Elizabeth Morgan *(Temporary transfer)* |
| 1892-Aug 1902 | W. H. Clements |
| August 1902-1903 | John Mason |
| 1903-Jan 1906 | Charles John Mann |
| January 1906-Mar 1912 | Charles Frank Townsend |
| March 1912-24 | Herbert Tew |
| 1924-Jun 1938 | John Thomas Standbridge |
| June 1938-Feb 1954 | Albert Edward Standbridge |
| February 1954-Feb 1956 | Agnes Venetta Standbridge |
| February 1956-Aug 1966 | Geoffrey Thomas Skelcher *(Died in 1971, aged 68)* |
| August 1966-Aug 1968 | Patricia Patterson *(Previously at the Woodman)* |
| August 1968-Oct 1968 | Patrick McGrath |
| October 1968-Aug 1970 | William Arthur Johnson |
| August 1970-Mar 1972 | Leslie George Simmonds |
| March 1972-Apr 1973 | Michael John Alcock |
| April 1973-Jun 1974 | Pamela Joyce Fearn |
| June 1974-1975 | Joan Richardson *(Of Loughborough)* |
| 1980 | David Barrett and Ian McLoughlin |
| September 1980 | Closed for business |

*Tom Thorne remembers the 'Brit': "When Geoffrey Skelcher was licensee of the Britannia in the 1950s he kept a bale of hay in the bar, hanging from the ceiling. His theory was that it absorbed cigarette smoke. I don't know whether it worked but it was a novel idea."*

The Morning News dated 22nd March 1980 ran the following article: **Rule Britannia!** That's the motto of two Leamington bachelors who have taken over at the helm of the

Britannia pub in Chandos Street. David Barrett and Ian McLoughlin, who both originally come from Leamington, have returned to the town to take on the pub after travelling all over the world. David bumped into 'Mac' in Australia, when they met through a mutual friend, and when they both arrived back in Britain they thought they'd try the pub life. They admit that since they arrived at the Britannia at the beginning of the week they have been learning as they go along. "We don't know anything about running a pub," David said. "We've even had other landlords coming in to help us tap the barrels." Both men are planning to give themselves time to settle in before they decide on any new plans for the pub. But they told the MN that the future of the building is in doubt as Ansells is considering demolition.

*The Morning News dated 12th August 1981 reported that: Plans for a 'Victorian chop house' in the old Britannia pub have been given the go ahead. Planning permission for a restaurant in the semi-derelict building, which stands by itself in the car park in Chandos Street, was given by the plans sub-committee on Monday. The prospective buyer, Mr. J. Sephton, plans to turn the building, which is on a key residential site in the Town Centre Plan, into a middle-market restaurant. He proposes to renovate the premises completely and make it an attractive building. His 'Victorian chop house' type restaurant would perhaps offer morning coffee and afternoon tea. Mr. Geoff Wilson, planning officer, said in a report to the committee that a restaurant use would be better in the planned residential area than a pub. The Britannia Inn is said to be 150 to 200 years old. It was put on the market last year [1980] at a price of £35,000. A company spokesman said the decision to sell the pub had been made because it only had a limited life. The last pint was pulled and the towel went up in the Britannia for the last time in September 1980.*

**British Bird Fancier** – Morris Street
The only directory listing we have is in 1837; it is not listed in 1838 or subsequent directories, so therefore a very short-lived business. The 1834 plan of Leamington shows Morris Street as being between Bedford Street and Windsor Street; Morris Street would later be renamed Windsor Place.

**Briton** – 18 Chandos Street
See the Britannia Tavern for details.

**Britons Boast** – Queen Street
The only information we have on the Britons Boast is two reports in the Leamington Spa Courier dated 2nd March 1861. The first mentions the landlord as John Richard Cave and the second is a sale advert for a freehold public house called the Britons Boast situated in Queen Street. It is possible that once sold the Britons Boast became the Queens Arms, a Queen Street beer house that is first referenced in August 1861, but we have no corroborating evidence.

**Brown Bear** – Regent Street
The only directory listing we have for this pub is in 1837 [without licensee's name]; as it is not listed in 1838 or subsequent directories, we have concluded that it closed in 1837-38.

**Brunswick Hotel** – [Western] Corner of Warwick Street and Clarendon Place
Although we have established that these premises were designed by William Startin and built in 1837, unfortunately there is insufficient information available in directories, registers, newspapers etc, to enable us to compile a meaningful history of this building when it was a hotel. In Pigot's 1841 directory and Slater's 1842 directory it is listed as Jarman's in Clarendon Place, and on the 1843 map it is named as Jarman's Brunswick Hotel. Jarman is also listed as the proprietor of the Brunswick Hotel in 1845 and 1846 but as there are no listings in subsequent years we have concluded that its duration spanned circa 1840-46. In later years the building was renamed Somerset House and it is still that today.

In October 1859 Somerset House was described as an excellent family mansion situated in the best part of the Royal Spa and fronting Beach Lawn, the residence of Henry Jephson, Esq, M.D. On the ground floor the house comprised a noble entrance hall and vestibule [78 ft long x 14 ft wide x 24 ft high]; dining room [41 ft 6 in x 28 ft]; drawing room [35 ft 6 in x 17 ft 6 in]; library [20 ft 6 in x 15 feet]; breakfast room [17 ft x 15 ft 6 in]. It also included ten large bedrooms and six small bedrooms, bathroom, three water closets, kitchens, servants' hall, larder and butler's pantry, housekeeper's room, steward's room and superior cellars. Also, a good walled-in garden, coach-houses with servants' rooms over and stabling for eight horses; well-suited either for the reception of a nobleman's family or for a first class hotel.

In 1962 the building was let as offices and in December 1962 Mr. M. Walden unsuccessfully applied for permission to use the building as a gambling saloon. In 2013 the building is occupied by EHB Estate Agents.

*Margaret Rushton says: "The building was designed by an architect named William Startin. He designed Dr. Jephson's house close by and I'm sure Toby Cave once said he did Somerset House and the Christadelphian Home at the other end of that terrace, intending to fill in the crescent in between, but he went bankrupt, as did a lot of land speculators, architects and builders of the time, and his design was never completed. Instead, it was filled in with those chunky Victorian villas which are now apartments and bedsits. I remember when we first came to live in Leamington in the 1960s that Somerset House was shockingly dilapidated, and looked destined for the same fate as many of the big houses at that time – demolition, and then someone took it over, did it up to a dazzling degree and was never heard of again. Roy Thompson who played cricket for Leamington and was also into insurance had an office there in the 1970s."*

**Brunswick Inn** – 67 Brunswick Street
The first evidence we have of a public house in this part of the town is a sale notice listed in the Leamington Spa Courier dated 26th March 1831: "For auction on Wednesday, the 6th day of April – A newly erected dwelling intended for a public house, being no. 53 in Brunswick Street and having a large yard, garden, and out-offices."

The first directory listing we have for the pub is in 1832 when it is listed as the Brunswick Inn; it has also been variously listed as the Brunswick, Brunswick 'Arms' and even 'Hotel'. In October 1833, the Brunswick Inn was listed in an auction sale at the Castle Inn, Brunswick Street. At that time it comprised a liquor bar, large front parlour, back parlour, large tap-room, brewhouse, bowling alley, yard, two large basement cellars, kitchen,

Above: Photo of the Brunswick taken circa 1957 courtesy of Frank James who was born at the pub when his parents ran it. The photo was taken from the top of the Radcliffe Gardens flats which were completed in 1957. The gardens on this side of the pub are the garden to the pub and a nursery. The old pub site later became the car park for the new Jet and Whittle pub; the garden became a Mobil garage and these days it is a residential block known as Brunswick Court. Below: This photo taken on 7th April 2010, © Allan Jennings, allows you to make a comparison with the one taken in 1957.

scullery and a pantry. On the first floor there were two large rooms plus two bedrooms and on the second floor there were six bedrooms.

In September 1913 an old Leamingtonian reminisced about life in the 1850s and 1860s, "I am old enough to remember when the Brunswick Inn, with land adjoining as far as the corner of Aylesford Street, was in the occupation of old Mr. Thomas Robbins, the premises at the back of the public house then being occupied for slaughtering purposes by his son Dan Robbins who at that time kept a butcher's shop in Clemens Street. On the south side of the Brunswick Inn, where now are situated the Shrubland Street Elementary Schools, were allotment gardens, adjoining which was a large meadow also in the occupation of the Robbins' family."

In August 1894, William Watts applied for a full on-licence claiming that he had once had a wine and spirits licence but it had lapsed, thereby effectively rendering the Brunswick as a beer house. This is a strange claim considering that Watts had only taken over the licence in 1893-94; the application was refused. In 1903 there was a bowling green adjoining the pub but, although access was through the pub, it was not part of the licensed premises. In February 1927, Mrs. Watts, the landlord's wife, applied for and was granted a licence to retail wine 'on' or 'off' the premises.

Having previously leased the premises, Flower and Sons Ltd [Stratford-upon-Avon] purchased the Brunswick from the South Leamington Company Ltd in 1927 for £3,000; it was tenanted by the James family until 1962 when Francis James moved to the Queen's Arms. On 8th March 1949 the licensing justices granted a full licence to Mrs. Agnes Mary James thereby also permitting the sale of spirits.

In 1964 the Jet and Whittle was erected beside the Brunswick and the latter's licence was transferred to the new pub on 14th December 1964. The 'Jet' had a cosy modern style and comprised a bar, lounge, off-sales shop, toilets and cellars on the ground floor and a compact flat on the first floor for the licensee. The old Brunswick was demolished sometime during 1965 and the site became the car park for its successor. From 1998 until 2003 the new pub was renamed the Brunswick but it was an unpopular decision with the locals and in October 2003 the name was changed again, this time to the Jet. See Jet and Whittle for further details.

| | |
|---|---|
| 1832 | J. Waring |
| 1838-39 | William Bloxham |
| 1841-72 | Thomas Robbins |
| 1872-Jun 1893 | Daniel F. Robbins |
| June 1893-Oct 1893 | Henry Phillip Gibbins |
| | *(Local Manager for Flower and Sons)* |
| October 1893-Dec 1925 | William Watts |
| December 1925-Jul 1927 | Mrs. Watts *(On the death of William)* |
| July 1927-Aug 1930 | Francis James *(Died 30th July 1930, aged 60)* |
| August 1930-Jan 1955 | Mrs. Agnes Mary James *(Died 3rd December 1954)* |
| January 1955-Jul 1962 | Francis Henry James *(On the death of his mother Agnes; Francis was born on 11th May 1905 at the Queen's Head)* |

July 1962                              John William Crabtree
                                       *(Previously at the Shakespeare Hotel, Stratford-upon-Avon*
                                       *– he went on to the Jet and Whittle)*

**Bubbles Champagne Bar & Bistro** – 29 Chandos Street
See Carpenters Arms.

**Builders Arms** – 38 Lansdowne Street
See Lansdowne Tavern for details.

**Bull and Butcher** – 77 Regent Street
The first directory listing we have for the Bull and Butcher is in 1835 when Thomas Archer
is the licensee and the address 56, Regent Street; he is still listed there in 1838 when the
address is 77, Regent Street. The Bull and Butcher was renamed circa 1838-40, as the pub
listed at this address in 1841 is the Woolpack. Neither the Woolpack [nor the address] are
listed in 1846, or thereafter, so we have concluded that it closed circa 1845.

1835-38                                Thomas Archer *(Bull and Butcher)*
1841-42                                Henry James Cooke Fenn *(The Woolpack)*
1845                                   G. Dodd *(The Woolpack)*

**Bulldog** – St. Margarets Road, Whitnash
The Bulldog opened at 6.00pm on 15th February 1956 and its first licensee was Douglas
Pickett who had been issued with his licence the day prior. It was the first new licensed
house in the Borough of Royal Leamington Spa since prior to World War II and it was
owned by Thornley-Kelsey Ltd [Radford Brewery, Leamington Spa]. A music licence was

*The Bulldog*
*Inn taken by*
*Nick Wilkins.*

*Photo of the Whitnash Tavern taken on 6th January 2010 © Allan Jennings.*

granted on 13th March 1956 and music on Sundays was limited to programmes [sound or vision] broadcast by the BBC. On the afternoon of Monday 10th February 1962 a fire raged through the cellars and two fire engines were called to deal with it; although the bar closed for a few days due to damaged beer pipes the regulars were still able to use the lounge. When Thornley-Kelsey closed their brewery in 1968 and sold-off their [tied estate] pubs, the Bulldog was acquired by Davenports Brewery who in turn would sell-out to Greenall Whitley & Co. Ltd in 1986.

In 1981 the bar was known as Mooney's bar [after landlord Austin Mooney] and the large room, which was available for private hire, was named the Victorian room. Austin would go to America on a regular basis and on these occasions barman Ray Buswell was left in charge. On Thursday 16th September 1982, Jesters was opened at the Bulldog – where the sounds of the 1980s could be heard nightly. Jesters was formerly used primarily as a pool room but Mr. Mooney transformed it into a spacious, superbly equipped private function room [including comfortable velvet covered seating] which could also be hired out for parties for up to 100 people. They advertised the Bulldog as a three in one pub; you could enjoy your drink in the Dew Drop Inn, Falklands, or the big one – Jesters. The Bulldog was renamed the Whitnash Tavern in 1994 [sometime prior to 14th June when world darts champion Eric Bristow visited for a special exhibition session] and on 23rd September it was being referred to as the newly refurbished Whitnash Tavern. It remains open in December 2013.

| | |
|---|---|
| 14th February 1956-Sep 1958 | Douglas John Pickett |
| September 1958-Nov 1959 | Illtyd Edward Toomey |
| November 1959-Apr 1961 | Ivor Neville Campbell |
| April 1961-Jul 1962 | Douglas Leslie McQueen |
| July 1962-Aug 1969 | Bernard Lewis Wilner |
| August 1969-Sep 1971 | Bernard Denis Goodby |
| September 1971-Oct 1972 | Leslie Cyril Booth |
| October 1972 | Howard Peter Watton and his wife Doreen |

| | |
|---|---|
| March 1981-≥Aug 1990 | Austin Mooney and his wife Hilary |
| 1993 | Paul and Denise *(Surname not known)* |
| Circa 2007 | Sandeep Panaich |
| October 2007-Nov 2009 | Kamaljit Singh Dhesi |
| November 2009-Mar 2010 | Allan Wareing |
| March 2010-Nov 2010 | Patrick Minihane and Sandra Chesterton |
| November 2010-May 2011 | Marion Tarver |
| May 2011-Nov 2011 | Mark Vincent Nicholls |
| November 2011-Apr 2012 | Kevin William Mooney |
| April 2012-May 2012 | Paul White |
| May 2012 → | Sandeep Panaich |

*The Leamington Spa Courier dated 17th February 1956 reported:* **Leamington's first post war public house** - *The first public house built in Leamington Spa since before the war was opened on Wednesday evening. It is just over twelve months ago that work began on 'The Bulldog' and this well built public house will now play a part in maintaining a community spirit on the rapidly growing Whitnash estate. The mayor of Leamington Spa unveiled the attractively painted 'Bulldog' sign and afterwards the guests at the opening ceremony visited the lounge to drink champagne. Those present included the Lord Mayor and Lady Mayoress of Coventry, the Mayoress of Leamington, Police Superintendent J. H. Waghorn, Mr. W. J. Webb, [chairman of the Leamington licensing justices], Councillor Eric Lucas, [Housing Committee chairman], Henry Fedeski, [the architect who designed the premises], P. G. Kelsey, [Chairman of the Directors, H. E.Thornley Ltd], and other officials of Radford Brewery. The manager of the Bulldog is Mr. D. J. Pickett, formerly licensee of 'Manor House', Fillongley, Coventry.*

On 3rd March 1967 the Bulldog was advertising that its Rendezvous Room had now re-opened with the Melody Makers Trio on Saturdays and dancing on Sundays; it was 'free and easy' and admission was free. In October the same year customers could enjoy a pleasant evening with Neville Broughton on the piano – witticism and song every Saturday and Sunday. The Whitnash Labour Party held a dance and social at the Rendezvous Room, on Friday, October 23rd 1967. In 1978, the Culpepper Country and Western Club was based at the Bulldog and customers could listen to the likes of Mike Dalton and his band [direct from the 10th International Country Music Festival at Wembley].

*The Leamington Spa Courier dated 4th October 1974 reported that: Wednesday is the Bulldog folk club's first birthday and to celebrate they are holding an evening of Lancashire folk. Guest artists are married duo Guy and Vera Aspey who come from Lancashire and perform traditional Lancashire songs and music. Also appearing will be two clog dancing teams, the Earlsdon Morris Men and the Coffers Tree Clog, as well as the resident group, Okens Feast.*

### Bunch of Grapes – Clemens Street

The only reference we have to this likely alehouse is an entry in the 1818 edition of the *Moncrieff Guide* [under public houses]. As it had not been listed in the 1816 and 1817 guide books it is possible [though not definite] that it had only recently opened, and as it is not listed in 1822 or subsequent directories it is likely that it was short lived. Unfortunately, the lack of any licensee names in the 1818 guide book precludes the possibility of establishing a 'renaming' connection with any other pub in Clemens Street circa 1818-23 [e.g. the Swan/White Swan closed during this period]. There would also be a Grapes Tavern at unnumbered premises in Clemens Street from 1849-57 but the time lapsed is too great to consider any connection.

**Butchers Arms** – 45 High Street
See Guards Inn for details.

**Caines** – 27 Augusta Place
See Hintons for details.

**Car Inn** – 30 Kenilworth Street / 7 Warwick Street
Another beer house, the Car Inn was situated on the corner of Warwick Street and Kenilworth Street, on the adjacent corner to the Prince of Wales. The first directory listing we have is in 1835 and the last one is in 1857. In 1836 the premises consisted of a large parlour and tap room, an adjoining bar and parlour, five bedrooms, two attics, kitchen, brew house, cellaring, piggeries, coach-houses capable of carrying four carriages, a three stall stable with loft over, three loose boxes and a large yard. On 16th January 1844, there was an auction of seized goods on the premises to settle unpaid rent and taxes. As well as all household furniture and effects, the auction items also comprised brewing equipment [120 gallon copper furnace, 14 bushel mash tub, rearing tub and coolers], a beer machine with piping and taps and stock of ale and beer, thus signalling a change of tenant at this point. In 1850-51 it was listed as the Car Tavern. Following the pub's closure circa 1857, the premises became Colley's Temperance Hall and in the 1860s it was used as a rehearsal room for the Royal Leamington Good Samaritans Brass Band. Its final use was as a printer's shop before it was demolished circa the 1970s to build offices for the Leamington Spa Building Society.

**Carpenters Arms** – 29 Chandos Street
The name 'Chandos' was chosen for the street in honour of Chandos Leigh [1791-1850] who would later be elevated to peerage when created as 1st Baron Leigh of Stoneleigh [1839]. The first directory listing we have is in 1835 and the last is in the 2000s. On Thursday 12th January 1837 the Carpenters Arms was one of a number of properties that were listed for public auction to be held on 1st February at the Lansdowne Hotel. The auction notice described it as including a two stall stable, a shed, a good yard, a back entrance from Oxford Row and, like many beer houses, a brew house; later it would be owned by the Leamington Brewery [Lucas and Co. Ltd] and then Ansells following its 1928 acquisition of the brewery. The occupier at that point was Richard King and as he was still there in 1856 it would appear that he wasn't successful in selling the property.

Records show that the Edgerton family ran the pub for approximately 55 years, first William [previously of the White Lion in Brook Street] who took over in 1865, followed by

*Left: The Carpenters Arms taken in July 1976 courtesy of Peter Coulls. Right: Photo of Bubbles Champagne Bar taken in 2004 by John Hartnup.*

John from 1870 until 1919; quite an innings! When the local licensing justices sanctioned the transfer of the licence to John's successor in October 1919, the chief constable commented that during the whole of the time Mr. Edgerton had been in Leamington there had never been a single complaint made against the management of his house; another significant achievement. In October 1994 the pub underwent a £50,000 refurbishment that created an open plan bar and lounge. It was reopened as Bubbles Champagne Bar and Bistro circa 2004 and by 2009 it was known as Been, a Chinese restaurant and bar.

| | |
|---|---|
| 1835 | Richard Hodgkinson |
| 1837-Sep 1856 | Richard King |
| September 1856-64 | John Hunt |
| 1864-70 | William Edgerton |
| 1870-Oct 1919 | John Edgerton |
| October 1919-Aug 1930 | Andrew Walter Philpotts |
| August 1930-32 | Alfred Victor Tuckey |
| 1932 | Mrs. E. Tuckey |
| 1936-Apr 1936 | Thomas Pointer |
| April 1936-Oct 1947 | Thomas Arthur Welch |
| October 1947-May 1957 | Walter William Tilly |
| May 1957-Jan 1959 | William Henry Robert Eckersley *(Mr. Tilly deceased)* |
| January 1959-Apr 1959 | Harry Thomas Card |
| April 1959-Jul 1960 | William Davies |
| July 1960-Jun 1961 | Patrick Keogh |
| June 1961-Apr 1962 | Henry Bates |
| April 1962-Jun 1963 | John Charles Coleman and his wife Eve |
| June 1963-Oct 1965 | Leonard Albert Care |

| | |
|---|---|
| October 1965-Apr 1966 | Michael Fitzgibbon |
| April 1966-Feb 1967 | Alan Brooks |
| February 1967-Jun 1967 | Hugh Gerard McGuire |
| June 1967-Jun 1968 | Stanley James Golding |
| June 1968-Dec 1968 | Dorothy Joan Hudson |
| December 1968-Apr 1969 | James Mullally |
| April 1969-Jan 1971 | Patrick Vincent Kelly |
| January 1971-Sep 1971 | Reginald James Colledge |
| September 1971 | Albert Ernest Green |
| 1983 | Joan and Don *[Surname not known]* |
| 1984-85 | Margaret Wilkinson |
| 1989 | 'Fozzy' *(Name unknown)* |
| 1991-Sep 1992 | Steve Evans |
| Sept 1992-Apr 1993 | John and June Williams |
| | *(Previously six years at the Cricketers Arms)* |
| 1994-95 | Peter and Margaret Zaparaniuk |

*We have historian John Ashby to thank for the research he did for one of Ansells Heritage leaflets on the Carpenters Arms – "The Edgerton family were at the Carpenters' for over fifty years, during the period which saw the hey-day of the Victorian pub. In their earlier days of residence the family would have witnessed the transition of the house from being a very basic establishment where the poor would congregate for company and warmth to a slightly more sophisticated meeting place. This was the time when the pub began to play a more vital role in the social development of the town. Various activities were held in the pubs and their gardens. Games such as bowls and quoits were popular, and flower, fruit and vegetable shows took place. Music was also a vital requirement of the patrons of a public house and most had a music or singing room."*

*"It must be remembered, though, that the Carpenters' Arms in no way compared with the superb hotels nearby that catered for the thousands of visitors to the town. The pub was certainly a 'local', but it appears that at some time it may have catered for overnight guests as there is a room/bell indicator in one of the downstairs rooms, but in its earlier years only a handful of 'toffs' would have entered through its doors to mix with the regulars from the nearby streets."*

*"Nearer to the present day, Bill Welch recalls the years between 1934 and 1947 when his father Thomas Arthur kept the pub. There were popular trips organised for the regulars, a favourite being to Cadbury's. He also remembers a serious fire at the local paint shop which necessitated nearby residents being evacuated to the safety of the Carpenters Arms. No doubt to partake of the landlords 'linctus', a necessity for smoke-affected throats."*

The Leamington Spa Courier dated 14th March 1975 reported: Cancer research is £1,350 better off thanks to the efforts of members and officials of Leamington's summer darts League. On Wednesday night at the Carpenters Arms Derek Price, the league secretary, handed over a cheque for that amount to Professor Derek Burke.

*In December 1985, it was reported that the 'Carps' reopened after a £50,000 refurbishment. To celebrate, the merry throng dressed up in Victorian gear and roasted hot* potatoes and chestnuts on an original Victorian oven. Local, Bill Welch was on hand to say how his father ran the pub between 1934 and 1947. However, information from the licence records indicates that Thomas Welch was landlord from April 1936 - October 1947.

**Cask and Bottle** – 35 Kennedy Square
See Greyhound for details.

**Cassis [Cocktail and Lounge Bar]** – 12 Augusta Place
See Willoughby Arms for details.

**Castle Inn / Hotel** – 85 Brunswick Street
In his account of the 'History of Royal Leamington Spa' [1887-89], George Morley wrote that, "About 1820 a bridge was built across the Napton Canal, and passing across [from Clemens Street into Brunswick Street] the visitor would come to the Castle Tavern on his left, which then stood at the bottom of Charlotte Street," – on the site of what is now Kilby Court/29 Brunswick Street, corner of Clarence Street.

Furthermore, "Close-by the Ranelagh Gardens and pleasure grounds were established in 1811 and in 1814 came into the occupation of John Cullis, a churchwarden and commissioner of the town, and were an attractive feature of Brunswick Street in those days. Together they were nine acres in extent, some charming houses were erected in them, the walks were laid out with exquisite taste and they were open to the public. A band played there three nights a week from 7.00pm until 9.30pm."

The first reference we have for these premises is an 1816 entry in the licensed victuallers' records that lists Joseph Baker as the landlord. Until its closure circa 1854, it would be variously listed as the Castle Inn, 'Hotel' and 'Brewery'. On 12th May 1832, the Leamington Spa Courier carried the following 'to let' notice that provides an insight to the premises: "Castle Hotel to be let on lease, with immediate possession, the present proprietor retiring from business. The house is pleasantly situated in Brunswick Street; has been established about twelve years and contains three parlours, two drawing rooms, thirteen bedrooms, bar, tap room, kitchen, brew house, and good cellaring; stable-yard with four lock-up coach houses and stabling for eleven horses, with servant's bedrooms over."

In May 1847, following the death of J.W. Baker, the premises were advertised 'to let' and in August 1848 were used to conduct an auction of houses in Springfield Street, Russell Street and Bertie Terrace. We have no further information until the annual licensing session in 1854 when Elizabeth and Ann Herbert held the licence; while it has not been established whether the hotel closed during the intervening period it would appear that the Herbert's tenure was brief.

| 1816-20 | Joseph Baker |
| Circa 1820 | Mrs. J. Baker |
| 1822-33 | William Herbert *(Listed as J. Herbert in 1824)* |
| 1833-40 | Joseph Baker |

| 1841-42 | Sarah Baker |
| 1844-47 | J. W. Baker |
| | (Castle Hotel Commercial Inn and Boarding House) |
| 1854 | Elizabeth and Ann Herbert |

*In 1820, 6,036 square yards of freehold building land, on the south side of Charlotte Street, was sold at the Castle Inn by a Mr. Booth, indicating that the premises were also used for local auction sales [this land would eventually become what is known today as Radcliffe Gardens – Ed].*

The Leamington Spa Courier dated 14th February 1846 carried the following advert: Wanted at the Castle Hotel and Brewery, a strong active man [to lodge and board on the premises] who can groom horses well, and make himself generally useful. His chief employment will be to attend a horse and cart and deliver beer in casks. To save trouble, no person need apply who cannot read writing and figures or who is afraid of hard work.

## Chair and Rocket – 43 Bath Street / 13 Bath Street

In 1813, Leamington's first theatre was erected on the site of what would become the Chair and Rocket in 1957. The theatre closed in 1831 [which contradicts many historical accounts that say 1833] and the building was sold freehold to William Ind, a wine and spirit merchant. The church rate book for 1832 confirms that Ind is at the theatre premises. He had previously been in partnership with a Mr. Poole at another address in Bath Street, trading as Ind and Poole Wine Merchants. The partnership was dissolved in 1830 and, in August of the same year, the extensive stock of wines and spirits was sold by auction. Ind continued trading, and in 1831 relocated the business to the old theatre building adjoining his dwelling house. Following his death, both premises were sold at auction in 1838.

In October 1835 William Ind was advertising his Vaults in Bath Street and that he had been appointed the Leamington agent for D'Arcy and Co's celebrated Dublin porter. "For those persons of a delicate constitution this porter is strongly recommended by the faculty. It may be had in large or small casks or in quart or pint bottles."

On Thursday 8th March 1838, the following auction notice appeared in the Leamington Courier: "Lot 1 - All that capital and elegant leasehold messuage or dwelling house, situate in Bath Street, late in the occupation of Mr. William Ind, wine merchant, deceased, and now of his widow, Mrs. Elizabeth Ind; comprising extensive wine vaults, kitchen, and back kitchen in the basement; dining, drawing, and breakfast rooms on the ground floor; three large bedrooms on the first floor; two attics, and a small garden at the back having an entrance from Church Street. These premises have an internal communication with Lot 2, and both lots were occupied by the late owner as one house, in which the wholesale and retail liquor trade has been carried on for the last seven years. This lot will be sold for the residue of an unexpired term of 96 years, from the 24th June 1830 subject to an annual ground rent of £30. Lot 2 – All that capital freehold adjoining to Lot 1, formerly used as a theatre, presenting extraordinary advantages for a linen draper, or any other trade requiring exhibition and attraction and comprising on the ground floor an area sufficient for one of the best shops in Leamington." In May 1844 the premises were

*Photo of the Chair and
Rocket courtesy of Nick
Wilkins.*

again being advertised for sale or let: "All those very desirable premises known by the sign of the Wine Vaults, wherein the wine and spirit business has been carried on for the last 14 years."

Another name that would become part of the history of 13, Bath Street [originally numbered '43'] is 'Johnson' and in 1828 a William Johnson is listed as a wine and spirit merchant at another [unnumbered] premises in Bath Street. In 1846 David Johnson [wine merchant] was the agent for Barclay and Perkins London Porter Stores at 43, Bath Street, having signed a lease dated 1st September 1844; the annual rent was £60 [Doctor Johnson's famous 'Cough Cure' was also sold on these premises]. In 1858 David Johnson stated [in an advert] that he had been in the business for upwards of 20 years; we also understand that the business was established by his father William in 1817.

We believe that the Wine Vaults and the Vaults public house co-existed for a time and that the transition to public house occurred in the 1850s as David Johnson's business was fully utilising its on-licence by 1858. Following the death of David Johnson on 25th August 1885, the licence was transferred to Alexander and Jane Johnson and in November 1892 transferred again to Alexander's son Herbert Henry Johnson. When application was made to renew the licence in February 1903 objections were raised because there was no urinal on the premises. However, Johnson assured the licensing justices that he intended to install a complete lavatory [with the best fittings] and that plans had already been submitted; the owner of the premises at that time was the Dowager Countess of Aylesford. By 1922, H. H. Johnson had decided to move away from Leamington and in the December the licence was transferred to Francis 'Frank' James. This ended an era of 100+ years that the 'Johnson' name had been prominent in Leamington's liquor trade.

Flower and Sons Ltd acquired the premises in 1944 and approval to extend the bar was granted at the licensing sessions on 1st February the same year; the licence was upgraded to a seven day licence in February 1948. The name was changed from the Vaults public house to the Chair and Rocket on Monday 16th December 1957. In 1961 the Chair and Rocket were advertising Flowers Keg and Brewmaster, snacks and bed and breakfast; also in 1961 [April], Bath Street was changed to a one-way street. In February 1979 ownership

*A photo of some of the original stone casks taken on 15th January 2010 © Allan Jennings.*

of the pub was transferred from Whitbread Flowers Ltd to the Wolverhampton and Dudley Brewery, who retained it until 1996.

At 12 noon on Tuesday 18th February 1997 the premises reopened as the Jug and Jester. Taphouse Breweries [the new owners] had spent three months and £500,000 transforming the pub, which had expanded into the adjacent premises [the old Leamington Spa Building Society building, later to become the Bradford and Bingley] to become a Banks' Strongarm Tap House. Despite the refurbishment, the building retained some of the older features including a wooden gallery of stone wine casks which date back to 1835 and are subject to a preservation order. Then landlord, John Jennings, said, "We chose the name as a bit of fun to recall its time as a theatre and later as a pub." By 2010 it was owned by Marston's Brewery but on 27th February it closed-up.

According to local historian Lyndon Cave, the adjacent premises [corner of Bath Street and Church Walk] which are incorporated in the current Jug and Jester were originally erected as a private dwelling in 1814-15 [1, Church Walk], but by the mid 19th century had been adapted for commercial use. Lyndon Cave also noted that from 1858-73 the upper floors of the building were used by the free public library and subsequently as offices for

*The Jug and Jester taken on 4th December 2009 © Allan Jennings.*

the Leamington Spa Courier; the Leamington Spa Building Society would later occupy the ground floor [as would Bradford and Bingley – Ed].

On 5th March 2010, it was announced in the Leamington Courier that the pub had been bought by the J. D. Wetherspoon chain and was likely to become a Lloyds No. 1 Bar after a £600,000 redevelopment. A new sign with a new design was installed on 22nd October 2010 and the revamped Jug and Jester reopened at 7.30am on Tuesday 9th November 2010 [under the Wetherspoon name, not Lloyds]. It was reported that the cost of the project amounted to £800,000 and that it had created forty jobs; Dean Ricketts was the licensee and manager. The Jug and Jester remains open in December 2013.

The following is what we believe the time-line of the premises to be:

| | |
|---|---|
| 26th October 1813-1831 | Leamington Theatre – 1st theatre in Leamington |
| 1831-1838 | Wine, Spirits and Ale Merchants [William Ind] |
| 1838 to circa early 1957 | Wine, Spirits and Ale Merchants and then Vaults public house |
| 16th December 1957-1997 | Chair and Rocket |
| 18th February 1997-2013 | Jug and Jester |
| | |
| 1916 | David Johnson |
| 1921-Dec 1922 | Herbert Henry Johnson |
| December 1922-Aug 1930 | Francis James *(Died 30th July 1930, aged 60)* |
| August 1930-Sep 1942 | Agnes Mary James |
| September 1942-Jun 1949 | Reginald Mytton |
| June 1949-Jun 1951 | Kenneth Arthur Hawkes |
| June 1951-May 1953 | Rigte Hilbrandie |
| May 1953-Feb 1954 | James Edward Lloyd |
| February 1954-Oct 1954 | Harry Peter Jamieson |
| October 1954-Apr 1958 | George Howard Mason |
| April 1958-Oct 1967 | Leonard Denmead Payne |
| October 1967-Feb 1979 | Lawrence 'Laurie' Bernard Sylvanas Scott |
| February 1979-1984 | Colin and Eileen Munro |
| | *(Previously at the Bridge, near Dudley)* |
| May 1984 | Tony and Anita Hollis |
| 1985-86 | Barry and Anne Bridget |
| | *(Went on to the Grist Mill)* |
| 1987 | Keith Hobbis |
| 1988 | Neil Osbourne *(Manager)* |
| 1989-90 | Pat and Tony Leahy |
| 1996-Feb 1997 | John and Mary Jennings *(Chair and Rocket)* |
| 18th February 1997 | John and Mary Jennings *(Opened as the Jug and Jester)* |
| Circa 2006 | Mark Roden |
| October 2006-Nov 2006 | Kristian John Chambers |
| November 2006-Sep 2007 | Jonathan Moreby |

| | |
|---|---|
| September 2007-Feb 2008 | Lee Bane |
| February 2008-Apr 2008 | Andrea Pacey |
| April 2008-Jul 2008 | Simon Beasley |
| July 2008-Dec 2008 | Zoe Samantha White |
| December 2008-Dec 2009 | Christopher Paul Patton |
| December 2009-Nov 2010 | Sean Victor Holmes |
| Nov 2010-Dec 2011 | Dean Ricketts *(Wetherspoon)* |
| December 2011 → | Andrew Tomkins |

*John Jennings remembers the Vaults: "I used to go in the Vaults in 1945 when I was 18. It was opposite the Bath Hotel; the hotel had the only bar where you could buy a pint of Youngers Scotch Bitter. The Vaults had a brass rail around the bar and they had a monkey on a chain attached to it. It was known by some as the monkey house."*

The following article on the Chair and Rocket building appeared in a paper at Leamington Library – the author and date are not known.

**The Chair and Rocket – Symbols of the Past and Future**
This site is bound up with the history and development of Leamington Spa, and has an historical background not possessed by any other house of refreshment in the town. In 1813, Leamington's first theatre was erected on this site and the new Playhouse was opened on Tuesday, October 26th, 1813, by Mr. J. Simms [a theatrical proprietor widely known in the dramatic world].

The following address to the public, issued by Mr. Simms was the first theatrical advertisement ever published in Leamington: "J. Simms most respectfully informs the nobility and gentry of Leamington, its vicinity and the public in general, that the new theatre should be opened during the present season. He trusts that he shall have some portion of the credit for his exertions, in preparing a more commodious place of amusement, in so short a period: he flatters himself he shall be honoured with that support and patronage a discerning public are ever ready to confer on those who endeavour to merit their favors."

The building had a composition front with the word 'Theatre' above the central window and an ornamental cover over the door forming a shelter in wet weather for the patrons in carriages while entering and leaving the building. At the time of its erection it was an architectural addition of striking prominence and importance. The interior of very limited capacity was elegant and when the decorations were completed – comprised views of Leamington, Warwick, Guy's Cliffe, etc – in 1814, it was as bright, cheerful, and comfortable, as any other theatre in the provinces. At ordinary prices it produced when full about £30 but on the occasion of the visit of Edmund Kean in 1820, the receipts amounted to £97.

The theatre opened in melodramatic form with a drama entitled 'The Earl of Warwick' and a farce called 'Fortune's Frolic'. In the early days the theatre was a great success and during its life attracted to its boards many celebrated actors and orchestras, described at the time as "stars of the first magnitude". In 1828 appeared William Charles Macready who had known Leamington from his boyhood days. Other celebrities who played here were Robert

Elliston, [a great favourite who at one period was the lessee of the Theatre Royal, Drury Lane], Joseph Shepherd Munden and Charles Matthews. Miss Jenny Lind, the famous singer, also performed here in 1828.

*The Leamington Spa Courier dated 13th December 1957 reported:* **Sputnik bar for the Spa** *– The Chair and Rocket – An offspring of Chippendale and Stephenson? – Or a comment on the Leamington of 1900 and 1957? – It is the title of a public house in Bath Street, formerly the Wine Vaults, which has been redesigned as a counter to the legend that Leamington lags behind other towns in its bars. On Monday night, 16th December, it will be officially opened by comedian Nat Jackley, currently rehearsing for pantomime at Oxford and well remembered for his show at Coventry Theatre recently. The licensee, Mr. George Mason, is trying to discover the origin of a wood carving of the god Bacchus, which he and several of his predecessors inherited with the premises. An intricate work, there is so far no indication of who did it although it is obvious that it is not the work of a contemporary craftsman.*

The Leamington Courier dated 14th April 1961 reported that: A Leamington Inn, which stands on one of the town's most historic sites, has never been allowed to hang up its sign! It is the Chair and Rocket, Bath Street, which was known as the Vaults until 1957. Its heavy metal sign depicts a fiery old gentleman being propelled towards the stars in a rocket-driven bath chair. The brewers Flower and Sons Ltd believe that it expresses the vigorous, changing character of Leamington, but they could not get planning permission to hang it outside the pub – and today it rests in the office of the licensee, 37 year-old Mr. Leonard Denmead Payne. Mr. Payne said, "It's a bit of a sore point with us, but I have hopes that we will be able to hang it up soon."

**Memories of the Chair and Rocket in 1967, by Tom Lewin** - *"I used this pub on Friday nights in 1967, with the then girlfriend. The pub had two rooms, of which we used the lounge, if that was what it was called. The sign of the Chair and Rocket showed an old man sitting in a bath chair being fired into space on a rocket! What was that all about? The distinguishing feature was that it had barrels high up on one wall; probably fake features [Note: Tom should read the press reports from 1997 – Ed]. The lounge was always quiet, even on a Friday night, although the bar looked quite busy. Today, the 'Jug and Jester', as it is now called is much larger. It acquired the old Curry's building and then the Foster Brothers clothes shop. The old room that we used to frequent now has a pool table and the pub specialises in catering. The old 'Fosters' room is more of a lounge and only seems to open when busy."*

The Leamington Courier dated 10th September 1971 reported: **Pub's plaque** - Mr. C. J. Flynn, the secretary of Father Hudson's Home for Children has presented Mr. Laurie Scott, the manager of the Chair and Rocket pub in Bath Street, Leamington, with a plaque to mark the pub's achievement of raising £500 for the charity. The money was raised by donations from pub patrons and through a local racing tote. The presentation took place at the Chair and Rocket on Friday evening.

*The Leamington Spa Courier dated 25th May 1973 reported that: Mr. Laurie Scott and his wife Iris, of the Chair and Rocket, Bath Street, have collected £1,000 to aid Father Hudson's*

*Homes and last week they were presented with a 'thank you' plaque by Canon Wilfred Smith, administrator of the homes.*

On 13th January 1999, it was reported that: Drinkers across the Midlands will be toasting a Leamington doctor who was honoured yesterday by the launch of a new ale bearing his name. Pharmacist Dr. Johnson lived in the town years ago and was renowned for his cough remedy. He was once landlord of the now Jug and Jester pub at the corner of Bath Street and Church Walk, Leamington, where Banks' 5-per-cent Dr. Johnson's brew was served for the first time yesterday. John Jennings, who runs the pub with wife Mary, said, "We feel proud that the pub's history is being celebrated with the launch of a new brew."

*On 19th August 2005 the Leamington Spa Courier were reporting that: Up and coming bands are being given a stage to perform thanks to the Abandon night at the Jug and Jester. The event, every Monday, sees the best of the town's live acts raise the roof with others from around the country. One of the highlights this month was a set from the Post War Years, a highly-rated Leamington band tipped for bigger things. Organiser Hannah Morland said, "The night got the name because it's a-band-on every Monday. The idea is to feature lots of really good up-and-coming touring bands, that wouldn't normally play in Leamington, and have the best local talent as well." Doors open at 8.00pm and entry costs £1.*

The conservation department at Warwick District Council describes the building as: Bath Street was a main street of the 18th century village of Leamington – A theatre, now a public house. 1813 with later additions and alterations including an 1833 change to public house and also late 19th century, probably by Henry Hakewill for Mr. J Simms. Brick with painted stucco façade and concealed roof; Exterior – 2 storeys, 5 first floor windows, ground floor projects approximately 2.5 metres; Entrance to canted left angle, step to part-glazed door with overlight; To right a further entrance recess, now blocked, step; Moulded plinth; 3 pairs of 6/9 casement windows in plain reveals and with sills; Moulded cornice, frieze, modillion cornice, low parapet; First floor – 4 pairs of Tuscan pilasters to ends of range and to either side of central window; 6/6 sashes throughout in plain reveals; Frieze, cornice, low parapet stepped twice to centre; Right end stack; Interior – room to right has gallery to two sides, approximately 0.75 metre high with moulded base, square columned, round-arched arcade and cherub head frieze; To each opening a stone barrel labelled for beer and spirits.

**Chanelles** – 44 Clarendon Avenue
See Jekyll and Hyde for details.

**Chase Inn / Tavern** – 35 Oxford Street
The first directory listing we have is in 1832 when, for three years, it is addressed as Kenilworth Street. Initially a beer house, its status was upgraded in June 1853 when its licensee [Robert Bonehill] was granted a new publicans on-licence. On Monday 1st March 1920 it was one of a number of pubs that were referred for 'extinction by compensation' by the local licensing justices as part of a weeding out process, or "thinning the inns", as it was reported at the time [the defence had unsuccessfully argued that the licensee Mr. Chaffey had only been the landlord for a short time and that £780 had been spent on structural alterations]. On 28th May 1920, the county's compensation authority refused the renewal

This 1852 map courtesy of Leamington Library shows where the Chase Inn was situated.

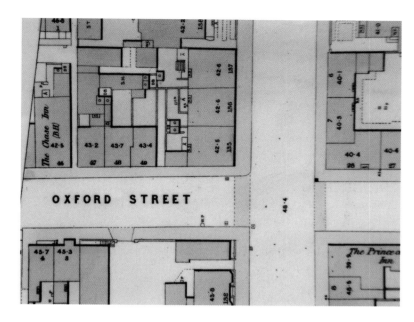

of the licence and on 2nd January 1922 it awarded £3,108, with the registered owners [Mitchells and Butlers Ltd, Cape Hill, Smethwick, Birmingham] receiving £3,058 and the manager receiving £50. The Chase was closed for business on 25th March 1922.

| | |
|---|---|
| 1832 | J. Hitchman |
| 1833-56 | Robert Bonehill |
| 1856-67 | Thomas Willoughby |
| 1867-Nov 1870 | Emma Willoughby |
| November 1870-75 | James Edward Rooker |
| 1875-Dec 1880 | Benjamin Crosby |
| December 1880-Nov 1894 | James Alfred Coles |
| November 1894-Sep 1895 | Harriett Coles *(Executor)* |
| September 1895-96 | Thomas Webb |
| 1896-Jan 1897 | Frederick Edwin Green |
| January 1897-Jan 1899 | Thomas Brooks Jones |
| January 1899-Jan 1901 | Thomas Roberts |
| January 1901-Mar 1904 | Mrs. Elizabeth 'Eliza' Roberts *(On the death of Thomas)* |
| March 1904-Dec 1906 | William Perks *(Of Birmingham)* |
| December 1906-Jun 1909 | William Thomas Pullen |
| June 1909-Jun 1911 | Thomas Hooley |
| June 1911-19 | John B Radbourne |
| 1920 | F. W. Needham |
| 1920-Mar 1922 | Alfred Augustine Chaffey |
| 25th March 1922 | Closed for business |

**Chequer** – Leamington Priors
This is the only information we have been able to uncover on this establishment:

| | |
|---|---|
| 1812 | John Knight *(Listed as a licensed victualler but the name of the establishment is not listed)* |
| 1813 | John Knight *(Listed at Chequer)* |

**Clarendon** – 44/46 Clarendon Avenue
See Jekyll and Hyde for details.

**Clarendon Hotel** – 1-3 Parade
Building work started on the Clarendon Hotel in 1830 and it opened in November 1832 on the north-east corner of what was then Lansdowne Place, Union Parade. Lansdowne Place was in Upper Parade and extended from Warwick Street to Christ Church, York Terrace being the houses on the left and Lansdowne Place being the ones to the right. The entrance was through a handsome portico, behind which lay a spacious hall which led to an elegant suite of apartments. The first proprietor was William Jarman who, on 24th June 1832, leased the property for 21 years at the yearly rent of £320. He then made two unsuccessful attempts to sell the business, in 1833 and 1840, and then in May 1842 Mrs. Hughes and her son took over and "refurnished, refitted and re-embellished throughout". The Clarendon consisted of an entrance hall, dining room, two drawing rooms, numerous sitting rooms, a parlour-bar, 17 bedrooms, dressing rooms, water closets, servants' rooms, housekeeper's room, servant's hall, butler's room, kitchens, sculleries, larders, ale, beer and wine cellars, and a garden in the back. The house was four stories high with a frontage of 19½ yards towards Lansdowne Place and a view over the pleasure gardens in the centre of Beauchamp Square. In September 1854 the lease, goodwill and possession were again being advertised for sale, this time by sealed tender.

In June 1924 a new company was registered – The Clarendon Hotel Ltd, with capital amounting to £8,000 in £1 shares – to adopt an agreement with Miss H. L. Mouflet and Miss E. C. Godley to carry on the business of hotel and boarding house proprietors, restaurant, café, tavern and beer house keepers, licensed victuallers, wine, beer and spirit merchants, brewery maltsters &c. The life directors were Helen L. Mouflet [chairperson and proprietress] and Emily C. Godley [proprietress]. A music and dancing licence was granted in August 1925.

*The Clarendon Hotel when the Hughes family owned it [1842-54]. Photo courtesy of Lyndon Cave.*

The Clarendon Hotel,

. . . High-class Family and Residential Hotel.

LEAMINGTON SPA.

Situated in the highest and best position, near but away from Trams.

Electric Light and Lift. Baths on each Floor. Sanitation Perfect. Billiard-Smoking Room. Comfortable Lounge, Corridors Heated, always Warm in Winter. Essentially a home from home hotel. Revised Tariff.

**Perfect Cuisine.**

Special terms made for a prolonged visit. *En Pension* terms can be arranged. Motor Garage.

A speciality is made of Invalid cooking. Under personal supervision of Proprietress . ..

**Mrs. MOUFLET.**

TELEPHONE NO. 0663.

*This advert was in the 1909/10 Leamington Corporation Guide Book.*

Although the Clarendon Hotel was requisitioned and closed during World War II its bar remained open with a full publican's licence; during this period the hotel was occupied by the Ministry of Works. On Monday 16th June 1947 there was a civic dinner party to celebrate the re-opening of the Clarendon Hotel.

Trust Houses Ltd bought the Clarendon Hotel early in November 1954 and took over its management shortly after New Year. In 1980 the Clarendon bar sold Manns Bitter, Samuel Smith's Bitter, Bass and Hook Norton Bitter. In April 1983 Trust House Forte closed the two star, 54 bedroom hotel and was on the verge of selling it to Warwick financier Keith Hunt when the Morning News reported his sudden and mysterious disappearance, and the sale fell through. On Tuesday 3rd May 1983 the contents of the hotel were sold by auctioneers Locke and England and in the October the listed building was purchased by Birmingham Properties, who had plans for its redevelopment. In May 1989 the Morning News reported that the building remained "empty and derelict" and that "town traders are making an urgent call for action to spur on the redevelopment of the crumbling hotel". Although plans for a four to five million pound revamp were submitted the previous December by the Dinton group [a Jersey based firm owned by Robert Morton of Wappenbury Hall], who by then owned the building, permission had not yet been given because leading conservationists were not satisfied with the scheme; the proposal included prestigious shops and office complex. The former Clarendon Hotel is now known as Clarendon Court [housing 24 luxury apartments] and the building has also been hugely extended; the new part is known as Villiers House. In 2013 the building is also being used as furnished office space.

| | |
|---|---|
| November 1832-May 1842 | William Jarman |
| May 1842 | Mrs. Hughes and son |
| 1848-1854 | Mr. Charles Cox Hughes |
| 1854-Sept 1858 | Mrs. Elizabeth Wood |

| September 1858 | Miss Elizabeth Hood |
|---|---|
| September 1858-74 | Miss Rachel Hood |
| 1874-Feb 1897 | William Edward Franklin |
| February 1897-Aug 1899 | Mrs. Franklin *(On the death of William)* |
| August 1899-Dec 1901 | Albert Abraham Kerridge |
| December 1901-Sep 1906 | Frederick Walter Smith |
| September 1906-Oct 1906 | Richard Meinhardt |
| October 1906-Jun 1910 | Mrs. Emily Ann Mouflet *(Died 10th May, aged 58)* |
| June 1910 | Transferred to the Executors of Mrs. Mouflet |
| November 1917-1924 | Mrs. Helen Louise Mouflet *(Transferred from Harry Back and Mrs. E. Hatton – Executors)* |
| June 1924-Dec 1938 | Mrs. Helen Louise Mouflet and Emily C. Godley |
| December 1938-Mar 1947 | Capt. James Blower *(Later to become Major)* |
| March 1947-Oct 1949 | Miss Amy Beatrice Vale |
| October 1949-Nov 1949 | James Blower |
| November 1949-Jan 1955 | Anne Taylor Griffiths |
| January 1955-Mar 1962 | Charles James Montague Pratt |
| March 1962 | Pierre Gilles |
| 1960s | Ibrahim *(No further date or name details known)* |
| April 1965-Apr 1966 | Charles Cyril Radford |
| April 1966-Jul 1966 | Trevor Wynne Jones |
| July 1966-Apr 1968 | Reginald James Norman |
| April 1968-Feb 1971 | David Allan Wright |
| February 1971-Jun 1973 | Anthony John Stephen Green |
| June 1973 | Michael Allen Bush |
| 1983 | Closed for business |

**Clarendon Inn** – 27 Clarendon Street

The first information we have on the Clarendon Inn is a sale notice for an auction to be held on 1st May 1837, describing it as: "A substantial well-accustomed public house, situated in Clarendon Street in the occupation of William Smith, comprising two parlours, kitchen, eight bedrooms, sculleries, malt-room, brew house, cellar, hard and soft water pumps, extensive yard, together with a valuable piece of adjoining land having a frontage of sixteen yards, and comprising a total area of 658 square yards." The first directory listing we have is also in 1837, but the above sale notice indicates that this beer house was open prior to then.

In November 1855 the Leamington Spa Courier advertised the premises 'to let' with immediate occupation [with the household furniture, brewing plant, casks, &c; to be taken at a valuation], although George Ward [landlord] didn't vacate the premises until July 1856. The Clarendon Inn closed in 1861 and on the 13th August there was a sale by auction of all the household furniture, bar fittings, a four-pull beer engine and other general effects. Shortly after the closure a Baptist church was built on the site and there was a school at the rear. In 1921 the Clarendon Street church and the Warwick Street Baptist church amalgamated [at

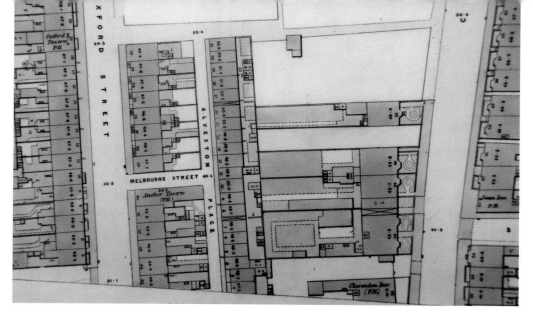

*This 1852 Board of Health map courtesy of Leamington Library shows where the Clarendon Inn was situated on the west side of Clarendon Street almost opposite Swan Street.*

Warwick Street] and the building became a Sunday school; in 1935 Clarendon church was sold. The premises later became Gor Ray, a clothing company. In 2013 it is an empty building and has been for some time.

| | |
|---|---|
| ≤1837 | William Smith |
| 1841-45 | John Seed |
| 1846-47 | William Bobby |
| 1847-≤1854 | Sarah Bobby *(On the death of William)* |
| ≤1854-Apr 1854 | Robert Harris |
| April 1854-Jul 1856 | George Ward |
| July 1856-60 | Thomas Atkins |
| 1861 | John Whately |
| 1861 | Closed for business |

*The Leamington Spa Courier dated 21st February 1846 carried the following advert: Clarendon Inn, Clarendon Street. William Bobby respectfully acquaints his friends, and the public generally, that he has taken to the above old established house, and that it will ever be his earnest desire to keep beer, wines, spirits, &c; of the purest quality, through which, together with civility and attention, he hopes to deserve a portion of their kind patronage and support. To persons travelling, either upon purposes of business or of pleasure, the Clarendon Inn presents many advantages. It is situated on the main road leading from Leamington to Kenilworth and Coventry; it affords refreshments at the cheapest rate, possesses excellent sleeping apartments, and every convenience for the comfortable accommodation of customers. Attached to the premises there is excellent stabling, and also a well-frequented skittle ground, so enclosed as to be impervious to all changes of weather. Genuine home-brewed ale supplied in casks of any size, and sent to any part of the town at the shortest notice. W. B. waits at Dinners, Balls, Routs, &c.*

**Clarendon Tavern** – 19 Russell Street
The first directory listing we have for this beer house is in 1833 when Richard Pratt was the first licensee; it would remain with the Pratt family for the next 33 years. On 2nd November 1923 the purchase of the Clarendon Tavern and adjoining house for £1,900 was approved by the directors of Lucas and Co. Ltd [Leamington Brewery]; it would become an Ansells pub following their 1928 acquisition of the brewery and its closure in 1934. The pub closed on 29th July 1968 and the licence was transferred from Helen Bird to a James Joseph Butler, but put into 'suspense'; we have found no record of Butler using this licence in Leamington.

| | |
|---|---|
| 1833-42 | Richard Pratt |
| 1845-Apr 1858 | Sarah Ann Pratt |
| April 1858-Feb 1867 | Miss Maria Pratt |
| February 1867-Mar 1871 | James Henry Haynes |
| March 1871-Jul 1872 | Joseph Pollentine |
| July 1872 -76 | Charles Barrett |
| 1877-80 | W. Arscott |
| 1880-Jun 1883 | John Dixon |
| June 1883-1905 | Romeo Bond *(Died 27th January 1905)* |
| 1905-20 | Mrs. Annie Bond *(Died 3rd January 1920)* |
| 1920-Mar 1920 | Alfred Augustine Chaffey |
| March 1920-Feb 1940 | Alfred William Collingridge |
| February 1940-Dec 1945 | Frederick Ernest Martin |
| December 1945-Aug 1964 | Ernest Wilson Priestley *(Died Jan 1964, aged 59)* *(Chairman of Licensed Victuallers Association in 1960)* |

*Photo of the Clarendon Tavern is courtesy of Leamington Spa Art Gallery & Museum [Warwick District Council] ref: LEAMG: M3781.1993.1.*

*This painting of the Clarendon Tavern was painted on 31st December 1967 by Martin Mims. It is part of the late Bill Gibbons collection and is courtesy of Jo Clark. It is interesting to see that Martin has inserted the name 'Cog and Sprocket' on his painting. This was not an official name for the pub but a nickname that some locals used, and we understand from Tom Thorne that there was a cog and sprocket behind the bar. [Also, see the earlier report dated 10th January 1964]. Bill Gibbons has inserted the name 'Blood Bucket' on the original. We understand that before the paintwork had faded to an orange colour it was blood red and assume that some locals also nicknamed it the Blood Bucket.*

| | |
|---|---|
| August 1964-Feb 1965 | Millicent Mary Priestley *(On the death of Ernest)* |
| 8th February 1965-Jul 1968 | Helen Bird |
| 29th July 1968 | Closed for business |

*On Friday 10th January 1964, it was reported that 59 year old Ernest Wilson Priestley, landlord of the Clarendon Tavern [aka 'Cog and Sprocket'] for the past 17 years, died at Warwick Hospital on Monday after an operation and prolonged illness.*

The Leamington Spa Courier dated 22nd January 1965 reported: Mr. Bill Bird, a former licensee of the Binswood Tavern who returned to Leamington after 12 months in Henley-in-Arden is 'officially retired' – but his wife holds the licence of their new public house the Clarendon Tavern. Bill, now 65, worked with the Admiralty for 30 years before becoming a publican. He left the Binswood to become manager of the Nag's Head in Henley-in-Arden.

**Coach and Horses** – 4 Bedford Street
Bedford Street was originally called Frost Street but by 1835, the year of our first directory listing, the address of the Coach and Horses was 3, Bedford Street [it would retain its

original name until 2004]. In March 1860, the Leamington Spa Courier carried an auction notice that exemplifies the pub's early life as a coaching inn; the following is an extract: "To be sold on Friday, the 13th April, 1860, upon the premises of the Coach and Horses Inn .... three capital harness horses, two phaetons [a four wheeled, two seater, open top carriage – Ed], two dog carts, two sets of double harness, five sets of single harness, four saddle-horses, two saddles, side saddle, two bridles, one suit of horse clothing, weighing machine and weights, patent chaff machine, with two knives, twenty-four wood buckets, four carriage jacks, and various other effects." From 1901, the pub was part of the tied-estate belonging to the Radford Hall Brewery [Thornley and Co].

On 1st February 1961, the Leamington Spa Courier reported the official opening of the new restaurant and grill bar, "The 32-seat restaurant has been built by Thornley's, the Radford Semele brewers [Thornley-Kelsey Ltd], at a cost

**CHARLES BARRETT,**
"Coach and Horses" Inn,
**BEDFORD STREET,**
LEAMINGTON.

CARRIAGES, DOG CARTS, AND VEHICLES
OF EVERY DESCRIPTION,
ON HIRE.
**LOOSE BOXES & LIVERY STABLES,**
**HUNTERS, HACKS,**
AND
**SADDLE HORSES,**
FOR SALE, OR HIRE.
HORSES BOUGHT AND SOLD ON COMMISSION.

C.B. has always on hand a choice selection of the best Wines and Spirits, Ale and Porter, of the best quality. A trial is respectfully solicited.

*An 1880 Stevens directory advert for the Coach and Horses.*

believed to be in the region of £10,000. It will be open during normal licensing hours for the time being, but later it may open until 11.00pm to cater for the after-the-theatre diners. Mr. George von Arx, the brewery's 37-year-old Swiss-born catering manager said that the restaurant would be the first of a chain of eating places to be established in Thornley's houses throughout the Midlands." In November 1961, the 'Coach' was one of five Leamington pubs that were granted permission under the new Licensing Act to open their off-licence premises from 8.30am. In June 1963, Thornley-Kelsey Ltd opened a new restaurant called the Silver Grill after builders and interior decorators had worked twelve hours a day for nine days to get the job done; the original restaurant had seated forty-one people and the new one could seat sixty. By November 1965 the Coach and Horses was also advertising that it had opened a cheese & wine bar as well as having a cocktail bar. When Thornley-Kelsey closed their brewery in 1968, and sold-off their [tied estate] pubs, the Coach and Horses was acquired by Davenports Brewery [who in turn would sell-out to Greenall Whitley & Co. Ltd in 1986].

In July 1982 the pub advertised that Baron's Music Bar had opened adjacent to the Coach and Horses, "a new kind of bar with a new kind of style: Great Décor! - Great Atmosphere! - Real Ale!", and it would remain open until at least May 1986. At 7.30pm on 28th July 1986 the former Baron's reopened as the Coachman's Kitchen and Loose Box lounge. It was advertised as the place to eat and drink in a relaxed and sophisticated atmosphere, serving morning coffee, lunch, afternoon tea and early evening meals from 6.00pm until 9.00pm, combined with traditional ales and quality wines; this adjoining building would later become part of an extended Coach and Horses premises.

On 4th February 1988 John and Andrea Moore opened 'Carriages', a new concept lounge with satellite TV and MTV, music mix with top DJ's every Thursday through to Saturday, a sumptuous menu, and the Mr. Baron disco. On the Wednesday evening of 24th October 1990, landlord Alan Gregory and wife Sue [who had taken over the pub seven months prior], reopened the 'new look' lounge bar after a five week 'make-over'. It was described by the Morning News as resembling a country barn with comfortable seats and soft lighting; the pub's 'new look' also extended to the pumps with an improved range of beers and lagers, including three traditional bitters and most of the leading lager brands. In April 1995, the pub underwent a £100,000 refurbishment and installed a full size pool table, a large TV screen, and a state of the art £2,000 sound system.

The Coach and Horses closed in 2004 and, following a seven week refurbishment, the premises reopened as Mumbai Bluu in the summer of the same year; the owners were Mac and Mo Kandola. In 2009, Mumbai Bluu was advertised as: "A friendly modern bar with an ethnic twist and a great atmosphere. The bar and restaurant are air conditioned and we have a beautiful patio heated garden area; the perfect venue to relax and enjoy yourself after a busy day." At 7.00pm on 11th March 2011 the business reopened under the banner of an earlier name, the Loose Box; it remains open in December 2013 after undergoing a subtle name change to Leila @ Loose Box Café Bar circa October.

*A 1987 photo of the Coach and Horses taken by Bill Bigley.*

*Above: Photo of Mumbai Bluu taken on 7th September 2010 © Allan Jennings. Below: Photo of the Loose Box taken on 29th April 2011 © Allan Jennings.*

| | |
|---|---|
| 1835-Aug 1857 | Christopher Littlewood |
| August 1857-Jul 1859 | Mrs. Ann Littlewood *(On the death of Christopher)* |
| July 1859-May 1860 | David Salter |
| May 1860-68 | John Marriott |
| ≤1870-75 | Mrs. Jane Marriott |
| 1875-Feb 1884 | Charles Barrett |
| February 1884-87 | Mrs. Barrett *(On the death of Charles)* |
| 1887-Apr 1890 | John Turner |
| April 1890-Jan 1895 | Richard Coulden |
| January 1895-Mar 1901 | Mary Ann Brown |
| March 1901-Sep 1916 | Henry Edward Thornley |
| September 1916 | Edward Richard Thornley *(On the death of Henry)* |
| 1902-52 | John Hinks *(Manager, but see below)* |

*The licence was in the name of Henry Edward Thornley and Edward Richard Thornley until it transferred to John Hinks on 23rd December 1929.*

| | |
|---|---|
| November 1952-Jan 1956 | Douglas William Froude |
| January 1956-Sep 1957 | James Edward Booden |
| September 1957-Sep 1958 | Illtyd Edward Toomey |
| September 1958-Nov 1960 | Francis Leonard Tedd |
| November 1960-Jan 1961 | William Thomas Shaw |
| January 1961-Jun 1961 | Arthur Stanley Leaman |
| June 1961-Oct 1961 | Bernard Edward Purcell |
| October 1963-Feb 1968 | Thomas Henry Wright |
| February 1968-≥1973 | John Kenrick 'Ken' Humphreys and his wife Joan |
| January 1985-Mar 90 | John and Andrea Moore *(Of Leeds)* |
| March 1990-1992 | Alan Gregory and wife Sue *(Of Nottingham)* |
| 1995 | Trevor and Suzanne Thompson |
| 1998 | Jason Lee |
| 2003 | Joseph Wilson |
| 2004 | Closed as Coach & Horses, opened as Mumbai Bluu |
| 2004 | Gareth Beddows |
| | *(Mumbai Bluu – Owners Makhan and Mohan Kandola)* |
| 2005 | Matt Crowley *(Manager – Mumbai Bluu)* |
| 11th March 2011 | Matthew Peter Shepherd *(General Manager – Loose Box)* |
| July 2012 → | David Anthony Sutcliffe |

*The Leamington Spa Courier dated 18th February 1860 reported that: David Salter, landlord of the Coach and Horses pleaded guilty to a charge of riding a horse in a furious manner, in Upper Bedford Street, on the 18th January. PC Cottrill detailed the circumstances of the case. Defendant was riding a horse at half-past two on the day in question, at the rate of about fifteen miles an hour, and afterwards in Lower Bedford Street, where he was beating the horse, at an increased rate, probably at twenty miles an hour. Salter said he was not conscious of having ridden the horse so furiously. The animal was 'showy' and 'frisky' and he had only one hand with which to manage him, having accidently injured the other, but he was not aware that there was any risk. The superintendant of police said that Salter had been reported for a similar offence. The bench considered the defendant's conduct in the matter to be inexcusable, and inflicted a penalty of £1, and costs of 10s.*

The Morning News dated 31st December 1987 said that coach drivers from the Elizabethan era would be pleasantly surprised at the changes made to their old coaching inn. Still known by the same name as it was back in the 17th century, the Coach and Horses offers the very best of traditional and modern hospitality. During the past eighteen months, while the pub has been managed by John and Andrea Moore, it has undergone many changes and now offers a large bright and airy lounge and eating area, and a new beer garden – which is certain to be a popular haunt of Leamington townsfolk in the summer months. But unlike many other pubs which have been updated and as a consequence have lost nearly all their character, the bar at the Coach and Horses has been left just as it always was, with fine oak panelling, cosy corners and welcoming open fire places. [Note: The Coach and Horses did not exist in the 17th century. Queen Elizabeth reigned from 1558 until 1603, a little early for a pub north of the river – Ed]

### Cock Public House – Park Street
The only reference we have for this beer house is a report in the Leamington Spa Courier dated 31st January 1835. Two men by the names of Jones and Clerking brought a charge of assault against Joseph Smith, the landlord of the Cock public house in Park Street. Joseph Smith brought a counter charge of riot against the two men. The bench declined to entertain either case. Not much of a history, is it?

### Cog and Sprocket – 19 Russell Street
See Clarendon Tavern for an explanation of this name.

### Colonnade – 2a Victoria Terrace
See Robbins Well for details.

### Commercial Hotel – Spencer Street
See Avenue Hotel for details.

### Coopers Arms – 2 Court Street
The first directory listing we have for this address is as the Eagle and Shamrock in 1833, a beer house run by 'McDonald'. It was renamed the Coopers Arms circa 1834 when taken over by John Pearson, a cooper by trade. We believe that the reason that it is not listed in the 1841 directory is because [circa 1840] it had been renamed the Hope Tavern, which is listed in 1841. Furthermore, when a street number was first notated against a directory listing for the Hope Tavern in 1849, it was also 2, Court Street [see also, the Hope Tavern].

| 1833-34 | McDonald *(Eagle and Shamrock)* |
|---|---|
| 1834-39 | John Pearson *(Coopers Arms)* |

**Copper Pot** – 41-43 Warwick Street
In August 1996, Whitbread Severn Inns submitted plans for the conversion of the Viceroy Carpet shop [Warwick Street] into a pub with first floor flats. It opened as the Hogshead in early March 1997 and a photograph of the Ford Rugby Club players posing with the first pint was printed in the Leamington Spa Courier dated 7th March. It was acquired by Greene King in the autumn of 2004 and renamed the Old Butchers; it was renamed the Copper Pot in October 2005 and remains open in December 2013.

*The Hogshead taken on 27th March 1999 © Allan Jennings.*

| 1997 | Phil Nathan *(Owner)* |
|---|---|
| 2005 | James Anthony Jack Davies |
| June 2007-Oct 2009 | Sandra Mayor |
| October 2009-Nov 2011 | Darren Fraser |
| November 2011 → | Sophie Ahearne |

Tom Lewin says, *"I remember the Hogshead. It has also been the Old Butchers, and is now The Copper Pot. The one thing that drew me to the Hogshead was the beer Leffe which they*

*Left: Photo of the Old Butchers taken on 28th August 2005 courtesy of Tom Lewin.*
*Right: Photo of the Copper Pot taken 26th October 2008 © Allan Jennings.*

sold alongside other Belgian specialities. I first tested this nectar whilst in Belgium and it came in two types, dark and light; I should remember the French words for that. They also served the beer in their own Leffe glasses of which I have acquired a set, enough said! I also tried a strawberry flavoured beer in Belgium, but it was not for the faint-hearted."

In 2009, they advertised the Copper Pot as, "well placed on Warwick Street serving traditional food in a modern environment. Coffee is served all day plus an extensive range of beers and wines. Offers include two meals for £10 Mon-Fri. Breakfast served daily. Curry Club on Thursday, Sunday lunch served. Sky and Setanta. DJ every Saturday night."

**Cottage Tavern** – 38 Queen Street

The first directory listing we have is in 1863 when addressed as 20, Queen Street. It was a beer house until August 1864, when Samuel Voss was granted a public house licence. Owned by the Northampton Brewery Company [Phipps Northampton Brewery Co. Ltd, from 1957], there were three rooms to drink in, a bar, a smoke room and a club-room; there were also two bedrooms available for guests or travellers. In February 1911, the chief constable objected to the renewal of the licence, stating that it was in a congested area and that within 250 yards there were seven fully licensed houses and four beer houses, but the licence was renewed.

The Cottage closed on 15th June 1961 and the licence was surrendered. The part of Queen Street closest to Lansdowne Street was demolished in August 1961, but the upper part remained until early 1978; Queen Street would form part of a major housing redevelopment.

*This Leamington Spa Courier photo of the Cottage Tavern is courtesy of Warwickshire County Record Office ref: PH(N),600/337/1.*

| | |
|---|---|
| 1863-66 | Samuel Voss |
| 1868-75 | Stephen Woodhouse |
| 1875-81 | James Skelsey |
| 1881-Jun 1888 | Thomas Phelps |
| June 1888-Mar 1897 | Thomas Samuel Meadows |
| March 1897-Oct 1898 | James Cleaver *(On the death of Thomas Meadows)* |
| October 1898-Aug 1899 | Frederick Townley *(On the death of James Cleaver)* |
| August 1899-Oct 1902 | Joseph Cook |
| October 1902-Jun 1961 | Harry and Rosetta Mary Buswell *(Rosetta died c1948)* |
| 15th June 1961 | Closed for business |

*Colin Jennings remembers drinking here: "From Campion Terrace, it was half way down Queen Street on the left. I remember that there was an old horse hair bench that had holes in it and you had to sit in the holes."*

The Morning News dated Friday 10th March 1961 reported: For the past 58 years Harry Buswell has been the licensee of the Cottage Tavern in Queen Street, but on 7th May, Mr. Buswell who has just celebrated his 90th birthday – will be serving behind the counter for the last time for the tavern is closing down. Mr. Buswell, who was born in Northampton, came to Leamington in October 1902 after fighting in the South African war. He became licensee of the Cottage Tavern, which is probably one of the smallest public houses in the town. "In those days, we were open from six o'clock in the morning until 11 o'clock at night and although very few people came in early in the morning, two or three came in to have a coffee and rum before going to work," said Mr. Buswell. "The weekends were the busiest times as we had a skittle alley at the back of the house and the beer was only 2d a pint." Since his wife died 13 years ago, his daughter, Mrs. Violet Lines, has been helping him to look after the tavern. Mr. Buswell also has two sons, both of whom live nearby, another daughter who lives in Coventry and six grandchildren.

Although he is 90 years old, Mr. Buswell still serves behind the bar every day and also does some of the cellar work with the help of his sons. "I am very lucky," he said, "I have some of the nicest customers I could possibly have. During the Second World War we tried to keep open, but alcohol was rationed and often we would have to close because we had nothing to sell. I did, however, always manage to keep some beer for the old people so that they could still have their drink," he said. As yet, Mr. Buswell is not sure what he is going to do when the tavern closes, but he thinks he will give up his job of being a publican. "I shall be very sorry to give it up, but I am getting too old now."

*The Leamington Spa Courier dated 28th July 1961 reported: – The legendary "pub with no beer" has been found – in Leamington. It's the Cottage Tavern, in Queen Street, where 90-year-old Harry Buswell still keeps the glasses polished, in spite of the fact that he will never have another customer. The licence was taken away from the tiny pub last month when Mr. Buswell finally retired, with the distinction of being Warwickshire's oldest licensee. Since then he has used the bar parlour as a sitting room. But soon the brewery will clear out the counter, beer pulls, glasses and domino club trophies and give the place a thorough face lift, so that Mr. Buswell can comfortably spend his last days in the place where he was "mine host" for 59 years. "Old customers still pop in for a chat," he says, "but unfortunately all the beer has gone."*

**Counting House** [Bar and Restaurant] – Kenilworth Street
When Gordon Faulkner purchased the Angel Hotel in 1981 his plans included increasing the existing restaurant's seating capacity from forty-five to eighty, and having a new look bar by early 1982. Faulkner was also managing director of Griffin and Steel Ltd [wholesale fruit and vegetable merchants] when it purchased the property adjacent to the hotel at 49, Kenilworth Street [from A. C. Ballinger – builder's merchants]. By August 1982 application had been made for planning permission to develop the property as part of the first stage of an extension scheme for the Angel Hotel, providing increased bedroom capacity and a nightclub at street level. Met with "a storm of protest" and "uproar over upmarket night-

club" [Morning News, 6th and 7th August], the applicants said that the night-club would cater for the "upmarket, sophisticated clientele over 25 age group [something which this town is lacking at present] and that it is also intended as an additional facility for hotel residents." While we have not been able to determine whether the district plans sub-committee approved the night-club, we know that the Madhatters wine bar subsequently opened on the same premises and was still being advertised in November 1991.

By the time new owners of the Angel took over in 1992, Madhatters wine bar was already closed; it was subsequently demolished, rebuilt as the Print Room [restaurant] and opened in 1994, again with its own side entrance in Kenilworth Street. In 2008 it underwent further refurbishment, re-opening as

*The Counting House Restaurant and Bar taken on 5th February 2009 © Allan Jennings.*

the Counting House [Bar and Restaurant]. It was so named because the building was originally used for the counting and collection of taxes [Inland Revenue]; the designer also thought it appropriate to display porcelain models of 'hands' behind the bar as symbols of counting [refer also to the Angel Hotel/Inn].

**Coventry Arms** – 2 Regent Street
See Warwick Arms for details.

**Coventry Arms** – 23 Guys Cliffe Road
The first reference point we have for this pub is in August 1843 when, named the Railroad Inn, the premises were used to auction a nearby residential property. On the 27th October 1843 the Railroad Inn was sold at auction; the premises included large parlours, bar, tap room, kitchen and a brew house. By 1845 it is listed as the Coventry Arms [New Milverton], in 1849 the address is 9, Sidney Terrace [New Milverton] and circa 1866 it is Guys Cliffe Road. In 1851, following the death of owner Henry Roberts, the Coventry Arms was sold along with his other adjoining properties in the same terrace and a cottage at the rear. The pub was described as having a double frontage, situated on the main road from Warwick to Leamington and within two or three minutes walk of the railway station.

For many years it was owned by Lucas and Co. Ltd [Leamington Brewery] but it would become an Ansells pub following their 1928 acquisition of the brewery, and its closure in 1934. In December 1987, the Morning News reported that, "[It] has recently been restored in careful consideration of its local heritage. None of its character has been lost, with quality period furnishings and not a plastic beam or fake brass in sight. Licensee, Sean McAndrew, has signed the Heritage Charter promising to keep things just the way they were with traditional beers, warm hospitality, freshly prepared food and proper traditional pub games such as dominoes, darts and crib. The Coventry Arms is Ansells 14th Heritage

*The Coventry Arms courtesy of Nick Wilkins.*

Inn [of fifteen] and the fourth in Leamington; hand pulled traditional ales include Ansells bitter and mild, and Burtons best bitter." In February 2010 the pub underwent a major refurbishment costing "tens of thousands of pounds"; the changes included a new seating plan, wooden flooring and two 50-inch televisions for sporting events. After Matthew Crowther took over in September 2012 the interior underwent further refurbishment and a change of decor, and in the summer of 2013 the Coventry Arms was renamed Fat Pug; it remains open in December 2013.

| | |
|---|---|
| 1843 | Licensee not known *(Railroad Inn)* |
| 1845-Apr 1850 | John Boyes |
| April 1850-51 | Henry Roberts *(Died in 1851)* |
| 1851 | Mrs. Roberts *(On the death of Henry)* |
| 1854-Apr 1856 | Thomas Adkins |
| April 1856 | William Davis |
| 1856-Apr 1859 | Richard Davis |
| April 1859-Jan 1861 | Anne Robinson |
| January 1861-Oct 1867 | Richard Hitchman |
| October 1867-78 | George Sewell |
| 1878-80 | Daniel Parker |
| 1880-83 | Mrs. S. Parker |
| 1883-Nov 1892 | William Harwood |
| November 1892-Oct 1931 | Fred Savage |
| October 1931-Sep 1938 | Mrs. Georgina Savage |
| September 1938-Mar 1947 | Arthur James Lown and his wife Lil |
| March 1947-May 1957 | Leonard Albert Care |
| May 1957-Jun 1959 | Herbert Charles Loxley |
| June 1959-Oct 1959 | Thomas Parnell |
| October 1959-Oct 1961 | Dorothy Smedley |
| October 1961-Apr 1962 | Sidney Thomas Taylor |

| | |
|---|---|
| April 1962-Jul 1963 | Bert Charles Edward Elmer |
| July 1963-Apr 1964 | John Barrie Kitchener Barnes |
| April 1964-Feb 1965 | Ronald Lobb |
| February 1965-Feb 1966 | Ralph James Shaw |
| February 1966-Jul 1966 | Arthur James Hickman |
| July 1966-Jun 1967 | Graham William John Boulton |
| June 1967-Feb 1973 | Daniel Harrison |
| February 1973-≥1980 | Colin Dennis Gulliver |
| 1984 | Pat Burke |
| October 1986-Aug 2009 | Sean and Teresa McAndrew |
| August 2009-2011 | Maria Parker and Keith Brison |
| 2011-Sep 2012 | Maria Parker |
| September 2012 → | Matthew Albert Crowther |

*The Leamington Spa Courier dated 14th October 1843 carried the following sale notice: Desirable freehold property, situate at Milverton, between Leamington and Warwick, and nearly contiguous to the intended railway station. To be sold by auction, on Friday, the 27th day of October inst, at 4 o'clock in the afternoon, at the Crown Hotel, by direction of the mortgagee; all that messuage or public house, known by the name of the Railroad Inn, being the corner house in Sidney Terrace, adjoining the high road from Leamington to Warwick. The house contains large parlours, bar, tap-room, kitchen, &c. There is a capital brewhouse, with pump, skittle alley, piggeries in the yard, and the whole is complete with every convenience for carrying on an extensive retail business. Also, in a separate lot, an eligible piece of freehold land, adjoining the last lot, and now let therewith as a garden, and fronting to the road from Milverton to Leamington. This lot is walled all round, and contains in width about 9 yards, by 28 yards deep.*

The Leamington Spa Courier dated 11th September 1987 reported: Taking a nostalgic trip down memory lane this week was 92 year old former landlady Lil Lown who returned to her first ever pub, the Coventry Arms, to launch Ansells latest Heritage Inn. Affectionately known by all as Auntie Lil, she was invited to pull the first official pint at their newly revamped Leamington pub, and although Lil said she had not pulled a pint for more than 20 years the sprightly pensioner proved she still had the knack.

The popular landlady, who lives in Lansdowne Crescent, ran the pub with her late husband 'Uncle Arthur' for 11 years from 1935; both of them having originally come from Coventry [refer to licensee listing for correct dates – Ed]. "I had some of the happiest times of my life here and coming back today after all these years is very exciting. I really, really am happy," said Lil, who had not visited the premises since 1946. Lil remembers days when mild ale was fourpence a pint and best bitter sixpence. And she vividly remembers a councillor refusing to pay for his whisky because it had gone up from 10d to 11d.

Lil, who went on to run another Leamington pub, the Woodland Tavern, for 11 years, recalled the comradeship of the war days with particular warmth. "They are some beautiful memories. Landladies and landlords from Coventry, friends of mine, had to leave the city when it was being blitzed so they would spend the nights here on their bed rolls," said Lil.

One Christmas, with troops of several nationalities stationed in and around Leamington, a special licence extension was granted to enable a group of Americans to have a party at the pub.

Asked how she got her affectionate title of 'Auntie', she said that "it started when my niece came to help at the pub and because she didn't know very much about it she kept saying 'Auntie Lil whats this and whats that?' and before I knew it everybody was calling me Auntie." And even today, some 40 years after the couple and their four children left the Coventry Arms, friends and old regulars continue to call her Auntie Lil.

In 1958, Lil and Arthur retired from the pub world and moved to Australia for five years to join several of their children who had set up their homes downunder. Unfortunately though, since that time, two of her children and her husband have died.

*The Coventry Arms, which is Ansell's 14th Heritage Inn and the fourth in Leamington, is now run by John 'Sean' and Theresa McAndrew [Oct. 1986-Aug. 2009]. Among Ansells many guests at the official opening, which included local councillors and landlords, were two of the pubs regulars from way back in Lil and Arthur's days. Mick Smith and Charles Wilcox, both in their 80s, have been regulars at the Coventry Arms since the Lowns took over in 1935.*

The Leamington Spa Courier dated 20th May 1988 reported the sad news that Mrs. Lilian Lown, for many years a popular Leamington pub landlady had died at the age of 93. Born in Hartshill near Nuneaton in 1894, Mrs. Lown worked in a munitions factory during the 1914-18 War, marrying Arthur Lown in 1918. The couple had five children of which only two are still surviving. In 1938, Mr. and Mrs. Lown became licensees of the Coventry Arms in Rugby Road where they stayed until 1947, becoming known throughout their ten years there as 'Arthur and Auntie Lil'. They then moved to the Woodland Tavern in Regent Street before emigrating to Australia in 1959 to join their son and daughter Brian and Elaine. Two years after emigrating Mr. Lown died from a heart attack and, within two years, Mrs. Lown returned to Leamington. For many years she lived in a flat at the home of an old friend, Alderman Wallsgrove, an ex Leamington mayor until his death many years later.

*The Leamington Spa Courier of 17th September 1993 reported that: Television sports presenter Gary Newbon was in Leamington on Monday to toast the new look Coventry Arms. He was guest of honour at the pub which has recently been refurbished by licensees Sean and Theresa McAndrew. The pub dates back to the 19th century when it was known as the Railway Inn. The old building contained a brewhouse and a piggery in the rear yard before the pub was extended.*

The conservation department at Warwick District Council describes the building as follows: House, now public house; forms the end of a longer terrace; circa 1830 with later additions and alterations including early-mid c20th ground floor; Pinkish-brown brick with painted stucco facades and Welsh slate roof, hipped to left; Three storeys, first floor: 6/6 sashes; second floor: 3/6 sashes, all in plain reveals and with sills; Ground floor: quoins surmounted by continuous frieze and cornice; Entrance to left return is a three-panel door with overlight, otherwise casement windows; All windows have flat arches and raised keystones; Blocking course; Rear and ridge stacks. Occupies a corner site and forms an architectural group with Nos. 159 and 161.

**Coventry City Arms** – 30 Clemens Street

We have not been able to find out any information on this beer house other than the following directory listings:

| | |
|---|---|
| 1842 | J. Tabberer |
| 1845 | J. Bell |
| 1849-57 | William Ashbourne |

**Cricketers Arms** – 19 Archery Road

The first reference point that we have for the Cricketers Arms is in 1854 when the licensing justices issued a new licence to Joshua Fardon [thus suggesting that its history predates 1854]. In 1855 it was advertised 'to be let' with immediate possession and described as a fully licensed and free public house, situated at the entrance to Parr and Wisden's Cricket and Archery Ground, and comprising six conveniently arranged rooms, cellaring, accommodation for brewing and a good garden. Although we have also sighted records of preceding

*This 1880s advert is from the Bill Gibbons collection and courtesy of Jo Clark.*

licensing sessions, the first directory listing we have is in 1860 when the address is given as Adelaide Road; for the next 30 years the address would also be variously listed as Archery Place, Archery Road and 1, Victoria Street.

However, the site of the original Cricketers Arms was actually at the rear of the current pub where 1, Victoria Street is situated, and the urban myth is that the site of the current pub was the changing rooms for the cricket team, the pitch being where the bowling greens are now [unfortunately, the street directories don't list any building at 19, Archery Road prior to 1889].

In June 1889, Mr. Humphries from Messrs Field and Son applied for the temporary transfer of the licence at 1, Victoria Street from Mrs. Eliza Mills to Mr. Whitacre [a farm bailiff to Mrs. Wise, Shrubland Hall, who owned the property]. He stated that Mrs. Mills had not been successful in carrying on the business and that it was proposed to close the present house and to adapt some adjacent and larger premises. When that was accomplished, the magistrates would be asked to transfer the licence of the present premises to the new and more commodious building. In September 1889 Mr. Humphries applied on behalf of Samuel Whitacre to transfer the six-day licence of the Cricketers Arms in Victoria Street, to new premises, adjacent to the old, and situated on the corner of Victoria Street and Archery Road. In reply to Alderman Wackrill, Mr. Humphries said that the old premises would be demolished. The application was granted.

On 8th March 1949 a seven day licence was granted to Leonard Ernest Brooks. In late November 1989 the Whitbread pub was closed for two weeks to undergo an £85,000 refurbishment that realised an extended back bar and the relocation of the toilets inside; it was reopened on 6th December 1989 by then Coventry City manager, John Sillett. In 2010 the local ale was Slaughterhouse and the business was being advertised as: "A busy traditional street-corner pub, opposite Royal Leamington Spa Bowling Club; family friendly with a beer garden and free WiFi; food sourced locally thro' Aubrey Allen [butchers] where possible; en-route between the station and the town centre." The Cricketers remains open in December 2013.

*Photo of the Cricketers Arms taken by Nick Wilkins.*

| | |
|---|---|
| ≤1854-Feb 1856 | Joshua Fardon |
| February 1856-Apr 1860 | Edward Wilks |
| April 1860-Jul 1860 | Emanuel Fardon |
| July 1860-Jan 1862 | Samuel Bird |
| January 1862-Jan 1875 | Cyrenius Ledbrooke |
| January 1875-78 | Samuel Rainsford |
| 1878 | Holmes |
| 1879 | Edward Henry Salmon |
| ≤1880-Apr 1880 | William Taylor |
| April 1880-Nov 1880 | Joseph Collins |
| November 1880-87 | Joseph Henry Mills |
| 1887-Aug 1889 | Mrs. Elizabeth Mills |
| August 1889-Nov 1889 | Samuel Whitacre |
| November 1889-Oct 1908 | John Sherratt |
| October 1908-May 1922 | John Henry Sherratt *(On the death of John Sherratt)* |
| May 1922-≥1932 | Cyril Charles Fell |
| 1936-Dec 1936 | John Henry Key |
| | *(Owned by Flower & Sons Ltd, Stratford-upon-Avon)* |
| December 1936-Sep 1942 | Leonard Ernest Brooks |
| September 1942-Dec 1946 | Phyllis Mary Brooks |
| December 1946-1976 | Leonard Ernest Brooks *(Died January 1976)* |
| Circa 1976-80s | Pat Boffin |
| 1982-87 | Pat Boffin and partner John Colledge |
| 1987-Jul 1992 | John and June Williams, |
| | *(Went on to the Carpenters Arms)* |
| July 1992-Sep 1992 | John and Viv Fairbrother *(Temporary management – previously at the Simple Simon, Warwick)* |

| | |
|---|---|
| Sept 1992-1996 | Greg and Heather Pacelko |
| Nov 1996-Jan 1997 | Fiona Buchanan and Charli Edmunds |
| | (*Temporary management*) |
| January 1997-1998 | Derek and Mandy Beck |
| 1998-2004 | Jon and Sue Felles |
| Autumn 2004-May 2008 | Fraser Clarke |
| May 2008-Oct 2010 | Mark Roland Docker |
| October 2010-Oct 2011 | Alan Francis 'Babs' Babbington |
| October 2011 → | Mark Roland Docker |

*The Leamington Spa Courier dated 25th September 1942 reported:* **Leamington airman is a prisoner of war** *- Reported missing from an operational flight, it has been established through the international Red Cross that Sgt.- Pilot Leonard E. Brooks [31], who before joining the R.A.F. was licensee of the Cricketers Arms, is a prisoner-of-war in German hands. S/P Brooks underwent part of his flying training in Canada under the Empire Training Scheme. An old boy of Warwick School, he was prior to the war well-known in local 'rugger' circles. His place at the Cricketers Arms is being taken by Mrs. Phyllis Brooks, a daughter of the late Mr. H. Blackham, a well-known Leamington optician.*

The Morning News of 31st January 1986 reported: It's not often that you find the splendours of a London pub outside the country's capital, but tucked away in a Leamington backwater is as good an example as you're likely to come across. The Cricketer's Arms on Archery Road, though from the outside looks like any other country town drinking place, is on the inside a celebration of the impressively grandiose Victorian era. The solid, polished wood bar and ornate array of drinks and glasses together with a vast tiled fireplace, mantelshelf and mirror could well convince customers they could step outside into the old Smoke. It's scarcely surprising then that the pub was nominated for a Leamington Society award for the preservation of its style.

For all its grandeur the 'Cricketers' remains friendly and comfortable but with a lively atmosphere and plenty of regulars to keep the conversation going. A favourite with many for its lunches, the pub attracts a wide range of customers from youngsters to businessmen. And particularly in the summer, crowds of sportsmen take a break there from their energetic games in the nearby Victoria Park. The tenants Pat Boffin and her partner John Colledge have ensured the pub is kept in top condition and have put in a new carpet and wallpaper. Determined to maintain a sociable feel to the place, they often organise pop quizzes and every fortnight they hold a jazz evening with a live band.

*In August 1986 John Colledge was again talking to the Morning News: "Tradition is obviously very important and the pub has always benefited from its unchanged appearance and atmosphere," said Mr. Colledge who has helped look after the pub for eight years. The pub has a long history in the town and Mr. Colledge believes the present building was once a vicarage. "I understand the Cricketers Arms was then situated a short distance down the road," he said.*

*The Cricketers Arms was once a popular haunt for the cricket enthusiasts – as the name suggests. However, times have changed and the pub now appeals to dozens of bowlers who play*

*In 1989 the Cricketers Arms entered the Leamington Midweek Cricket League for the first time and won the knock-out cup against Lillington Club. Back row L-R: Keith Poulter, Ted Ward, Dave O'Neill, Richard Clarke, Mike Ireland, Andy Clarke. Front row: Paul Coleman, Malc Coleman, Andy Ball [capt.], Ken Pinfold, John Williams [landlord]. Photo courtesy of Mike Ireland.*

on the nearby greens. "Whenever there is a tournament in Leamington the pub is usually overflowing with bowlers," said Mr. Colledge. "They usually pop in and out for meals and drinks. So although the pub is not a regular for cricketers any more it is still very sport orientated."

Apart from a large crowd of locals the pub also attracts tourists and has played host to visitors from as far afield as Australia and Japan. "Every year we have tourists from all over the world. A lot of visitors come into the pub after watching bowling matches on the nearby greens."

The pub also boasts an enthusiastic raft team. The locals making up the team took part in a recent race in Leamington but failed to win any major prizes. "I think the team got quite a taste for raft racing and are looking for similar challenges."

September 1991 saw landlord John Williams preparing a legal case against Warwickshire County Council. In the four years that he and his wife had run the pub, they had never had a full year of trading due to the disruption that repairs to the Adelaide Bridge had caused. It was revealed that work may not be completed until 1994 and that the road may be closed for eighteen months.

By the following June it was reported in the Leamington Observer that a Leamington landlord is being forced out of his pub because road works in the town are ruining his trade. John and June Williams are due to leave on 23rd July because plans to close Adelaide Bridge for repairs in the autumn will once again leave them devoid of custom. Mr. Williams told the Observer, "The last time the bridge closed we lost a minimum of £12,000 in five months. We lost all our lunchtime trade. We could not take on a new lease knowing the bridge would be closed." The pub will be run by a temporary landlord from July 23rd.

From September 1992 until 1996 the Cricketers Arms was run by Greg and Heather Pacelko. Greg was a New Yorker who left managing a bar at Madison Square Garden to run the pub with his Wolverhampton born wife. 1993 saw a redecoration of the pub with a new sign, wooden floor and a new colour scheme. Sue English who went on to be a landlady worked here at the time. In 1994 Greg employed 18 year old barman Nick Ford who now runs the Talbot. The old sign from the 1970s and 80s, and possibly even the 1960s, still exists and is in the possession of Mike Ireland who lives in Warwick. It is metal and very heavy.

*The landlord in 2009 obviously had a sense of humour. A poster pinned to the wall just inside the front entrance said: The grey rectangular objects on the wall which the landlord has paid £58 each for are called ashtrays. The grey concreted structure which is mainly used by motor vehicles is called a road. The landlord would greatly appreciate it if you could distinguish between the two, otherwise you might find the 5 digited bony structure covered in a steel toecap at the end of his leg coming into sharp contact with the flabby portions located on the posterior of your pelvic region. Many thanks – Smurf.*

On Thursday 7th November 2013 a plaque, in remembrance of John Wisden, was unveiled on the Cricketers Arms building by ex England cricketer Mike Smith. It states: John Wisden [1826-1884] – Cricketer and Almanack Publisher – A cricket ground was created near this spot in 1849 by John Wisden and his friend and fellow player, George Parr. Many important matches were played here to large crowds. Wisden lived in the town from 1848 to 1852. In 1850 he founded John Wisden & Co. probably selling sporting equipment. They gave up the lease of the ground in 1863. His obituary in his Almanack in the 1885 edition reads: "...A quiet, unassuming and thoroughly upright man. A fast friend and generous employer. Beloved by his intimates and employees and respected by all in whom he came in contact."

**Cross Keys** – 44 Tavistock Street
See Victoria Vaults for details.

**Cross Keys** – 128 Warwick Street
See Kings Arms for details.

**Crown Inn** – Kenilworth Road
The Kenilworth Road listed is actually the 'old' Kenilworth Road, which today is known as Lillington Road [the current Kenilworth Road wasn't laid until 1840]. In 2013, the original site of the Crown Inn is 67, Lillington Road which is a residential property. In 1895, when talking about the year 1829, J. C. Manning said, "For some years, the Crown Inn at Lillington stood alone in its rural glory. The directory of 1829 makes no mention of this well-known hostelry, but in that of 1830 I find it announced that the newly established exotic nursery gardens of Messrs James Frost and Co. are near the Crown Inn on the Kenilworth Road. We may take it, therefore, that both the Crown Inn and Frost's Nursery came simultaneously about the year 1829."

*Photo of 67 Lillington Road taken on 21st September 2010 © Allan Jennings.*

| | |
|---|---|
| Circa 1829 | Landlord not known |
| 1837 | Thomas Amos |
| November 1837-1845 | John Page |

Pubs in Lillington are few and far between because the Wise family, who owned most of the land in the area, inserted a clause into the deeds of all the land in Lillington forbidding its sale for the purpose of erecting a non-conformist chapel, a Roman Catholic church, a public house or any business that would be a nuisance; Catholics and Free Churchmen had to travel into Leamington. The 1839 Tithe Apportionment Map shows that although the Wise family owned most of the land there were small parcels owned by others; the Crown owned by William Welch and occupied by John Page was one of them. An order by the lands tribunal dated 26th November 1951 lifted the restrictive clause.

## Crown Inn / Hotel – 10 High Street
The first reference we have for the 'Crown' comes from Richard Hopper's book entitled 'The History of Leamington Priors [From the Earliest Records to the Year 1842]', who indicates that the earliest part of the building was formerly used as a school and dates from circa 1805. According to J.C. Manning ['Glimpses of Our Local Past', 1895], the first guide to Leamington was published by a Mr. Pratt in 1812 and the seminary mentioned therein "was in all probability the first established in the village" and, ".... originally forming part of what is now [in 1895] the Crown Hotel in High Street."

Early accounts of when the premises became an inn vary slightly. For example, in the 'History of Royal Leamington Spa' [1887-89], George Morley wrote, "The Crown Inn was in the same eccentric style of architecture as the Bath Hotel. It was used as a parish vicarage when the original vicar's house in Church Street became too humble for the parson's residence, and in 1812 was occupied by the Rev. J. Wise MA. Joseph Stanley, churchwarden, purchased this property and converted it into an inn which was duly opened under his management in 1814. The splendid mews in the rear made the 'Crown' an important posting house and here the coaches returning to and from London, used to call." Although there is a licensed victualler's record naming Joseph Stanley as the licensee in 1814, the authors believe that he secured the licence in 1814 and opened in 1815.

In another account, T. B. Dudley informs us in 'A Complete History of Royal Leamington Spa' [1896] that, "On 31st March 1815, Joseph Stanley advertised that he had taken and entered on the premises which is now converted into and called the Crown Inn; the 'housewarming' being the universal custom at the time when a new public house or hotel was opened [and frequently when they changed hands] took place on 26th April."

Similarly, local historians differ in their opinions of when the 'Crown' changed from being an inn to a hotel. In 1842, Richard Hopper wrote that, "In the year 1825 the Crown Hotel was completed," but we also have another account written by J.C. Manning in 1895 which states that, "The Crown Hotel was finished in 1829, and by that time the line of road on which it stands was known as Royal Parade." Many years later [February 1849], the Leamington Spa Courier would publish an article mentioning that Joseph Stanley purchased the Crown in 1814 for £5,620 and occupied it until 1829 when he leased it to

*Photo of the Crown in 1860 courtesy of the late Bill Gibbons.*

William Rogers for £565 per year; the 1829 church rate book confirms that Stanley was the owner and Rogers the tenant. Although by no means conclusive, the licensed victuallers' records and the directories list the premises as the Crown, or Crown Inn, period 1814 to 1830; the first directory listing for the Crown Hotel is also in 1830 [which probably reflects the 1829 status].

Notwithstanding, we have deduced from our research that the premises were a vicarage until 1814, that the Crown Inn opened in March 1815 and that it reopened as the Crown Hotel in 1829, but this too is conjecture.

In May 1830, William Rogers informed his customers that he had opened extensive premises attached to the hotel for the sale of wines, spirits and compounds; he was also advertising that he now had, "very superior carriages and phaetons ready at a moment's notice, with careful drivers". Also in 1830, Rogers assigned his lease to William Adams for a consideration of £1,500 and in 1832 Adams opened a repository [a horse and carriage mart] for the sale of horses, carriages and the like at the Crown. In 1837, Adams was 'cramped for means' and surrendered the property [without any payment of premium] to John Stanley [Joseph's son], who was by then 'engaged in a London business of increasing value'; reluctantly he left London to become 'superintendant' of the Crown, although he received no salary. After gaining some experience, and with his father wanting to be released from management, he agreed to take on the lease at a reduced rent of £450 per year.

The Leamington Spa Courier reported the death of Joseph Stanley on the 10th April 1847: "Another good man is removed from amongst us, and the remains of 'Honest Joseph Stanley' are laid in the grave. All who are conversant with the early days of Leamington will acknowledge his worth, and recall to their memory his unaffected simplicity of manners and kindness of heart, and his death is regretted by all who knew him. The deceased, who expired on Sunday last, was in his 68th year." On Monday 29th March 1858, the freehold of the Crown Hotel was listed for sale by auction; its owners were the Great Western Railway Company.

In November 1890, following the death of Alderman John Stanley, the Crown Hotel was sold by auction. At the time the premises comprised on the ground floor a commercial room, ladies' and gentlemen's coffee rooms, a private bar with ante room and sitting room adjoining, a large dining saloon [40 ft x 24 ft x 14 ft high] and a billiard room [42 ft 3 in x 24 ft 8 in] occupied by two full-sized tables. On the other side of a covered yard entrance were a smoke room [21 ft x 16 ft], a wine and stock room [34 ft by 13 ft 3 in]. On the main landing [first floor] approached by two staircases were ten chambers, a drawing room and four other apartments furnished as private dining and sitting rooms and a large dormitory, mangle room etc. On the same floor, in the new wing, were four chambers and on the second floor and upper wing were 24 chambers giving 40 bedrooms in all. There was extensive cellaring, stabling and a yard that comprised 10 loose boxes, 18 stalls, saddle room with living room over. The grounds included a kitchen garden and the total acreage of the property was 5,500 square yards. The Crown was sold to John Franklin of Northampton [who owned the Bath Hotel] for £8,050. In 1903 there were 35 letting-out beds and stabling for 100 horses.

In July 1936, Louis Morris of 52, Shaftesbury Avenue, London made application to the county council for a licence to erect a new cinema on the site of the Crown Hotel. The cinema was to be named the Ritz, be on a two acre site, have a capacity of 1,500 and cost £60,000. In October 1936, following a number of meetings and appeals, the committee approved the site subject to the provision of a forty feet entrance/exit from the car-park into Wise Street. However, the cinema was never built and in July 1937 the Crown Hotel was taken over by Messrs Flower and Sons, Stratford-upon-Avon. In April 1969 the Crown had 3 fully licensed bars, 25 centrally heated bedrooms accommodating 45 people, hot and cold water, radios in every room, and parking space for 20 cars.

*Circa 1893 postcard of Leamington High Street showing the Crown Hotel on the right with the Portico.*

The Crown seems to be the place for meeting wives – two of the authors, Tom Lewin and Allan Jennings both met their wives there, Tom in 1970 and Allan in 1971. In an effort to re-invent itself in 1978 the Crown was advertised as the 'New Crown Hotel', all rooms having been refurnished and redecorated. A special winter rate meant that a single room including a full breakfast cost £3.75 plus V.A.T. and a double cost £7 plus V.A.T. In 1982 the Crown Hotel was owned by Breezepalm Ltd. In August 1983 the Morning News reported that the new father and son management team of Bryan and David Rogers were determined to clean up the High Street hotel's reputation in the town. A total of £25,000 has already been spent on completely re-vamping the lounge area, with extensive work set to take place on the public bar in the near future. The run-down carpeting and furniture in the lounge was stripped wholesale and the regular discos abandoned. Eight pool tables stand where the dance floor once was and are proving extremely popular amongst the young and old. Bryan Rogers said that, "The place is unrecognisable from when we took over [and] we now have an entirely different set of clientele." By the late 1980s the owners were Quibtone who kept the premises for 18 months until April 1989, when they were negotiating a sale. The Crown Hotel closed around August 1989 and in mid 1990 it was bought by a consortium of local businessmen, Edward Carroll, John Long and Michael Coulson. At 10.00pm on Sunday 3rd February 1991 there was a massive fire at the old Crown Hotel building, flames could be seen from Radford Semele and around 100 fire fighters were required to bring it under control. At the end of October 1994 planning permission was granted to the developer Orbit Housing to transform the derelict fire damaged building into eighteen flats with a special needs unit at the rear and that is its status in 2013.

| | |
|---|---|
| 1814-1829 | Joseph Stanley |
| 1829-30 | William Rogers |
| 1830-37 | William Adams (*Opened a wine and spirits vaults at 43, Bath Street in June 1838*) |
| 1837-Feb 1876 | John Stanley |
| February 1876-Jan 1893 | John Edward Stanley (*Born 25th June 1846 – died 11th January 1894*) |
| January 1893-Jul 1898 | John Campbell Franklin |
| July 1898-May 1899 | Robert Dixon Sykes |
| May 1899-Feb 1901 | George Mellor |
| February 1901-Mar 1901 | Herbert Thomas Gould |
| March 1901-June 1906 | Arthur Phillips |
| June 1906-Nov 1921 | Thomas Edgar Phillips (*On the death of his father*) |
| November 1921-Apr 1923 | Frederick Verner Walford |
| April 1923-Mar 1925 | George R. Richards (*Previously at Bear Hotel, Esher, Surrey*) |
| March 1925-Nov 1925 | William Latham |
| November 1925-Feb 1932 | Arthur Kugler (*Proprietor – Previously manager of the Grand Hotel, Birmingham*) |

| | |
|---|---|
| February 1932-34 | Clive Maurice Clapham *(Of Stratford-upon-Avon)* |
| 1934-Mar 1935 | J. A. Cronin |
| March 1935 | Mrs. F. E. Latham |
| 1935 | J. Burton |
| 1936-Jul 1937 | S. R. Beechey *(Proprietor)* |
| July 1937 | Taken over by Flower and Sons, Stratford-upon-Avon |
| July 1937-Aug 1938 | William Arthur Jeavons |
| August 1938-Jun 1948 | William Hubert Chandler *(Proprietor)* |
| | *(Died 28th March 1948, aged 63)* |
| June 1948-Oct 1950 | Doris Ada Chandler *(On the death of William)* |
| October 1950-Feb 1953 | John Wilson |
| February 1953-Oct 1953 | Mrs. Vera Florence Stratton |
| October 1953-Jan 1956 | Leonard William Handy |
| January 1956-Sep 1958 | Ian Frederick McCall |
| September 1958-Nov 1958 | Barry Carmichael Callow |
| November 1958-≥1977 | Robert 'Bob' Sanderson Clough and his wife Nan |
| Circa 1970s-≥1972 | Lionel Henry Hiscox |
| 1976 | James Nolan *(Hotel manager)* |
| 1978 | Terry and Frances Smith *(Resident managers)* |
| 1978 | Mr. and Mrs. A. E. Summers *(Proprietors)* |
| April 1979-1982 | Alan Wells and his wife Penelope 'Penny' |
| 1982-≥1985 | Bryan and David Rogers *(Managers)* |
| November 1987-Aug 1989 | Quibtone *(Owners)* |
| May 1988-Aug 1989 | George and Patricia Ward *(Managers & licensees)* |
| 1989 | Closed |

*On Thursday 8th September 1831, the Crown organised a Coronation Ball and Supper to celebrate the ensuing Coronation of their Most Gracious Majesties William IV and Queen Adelaide at the Royal Assembly Rooms in Bath Street. Visitors and respectable inhabitants of Leamington, Warwick, and the neighbourhood were invited at a cost of 6/- for ladies and 7/6d for gentlemen.*

In March 1962 the local justices approved an application by Mr. R. Clough, of the Crown Hotel, for a music, singing and dancing licence for his dining room and grill room. The licence covered the period from 10.30pm to 2.30am. Leamington Jazz Club was based at the Crown Hotel from March 1963 until September 1964 when it was forced to wind-up as it could no longer use the hotel. The resident 'Jazz at the Crown' group consisted of Stan Rawlings [piano and vibes], John Vale [bass], Ron Rawlings [drums], Harry Bodenham [guitar], Geoff Gough [flute, clarinet and alto] and Dave Eales [tenor]. In September 1966 the Crown Hotel ran a 'Crown Club' on Monday evenings and charged 4/- admission.

*Sloopy's Club opened at the Crown Hotel on Tuesday 14th October 1969. Every Tuesday was soul music, Thursdays was blues and progressive and Friday was reggae. In January 1970, the entertainment at Sloopy's was – "Reggae in your Jeggae" with Mike Francis on Friday night from 8.00pm until 11.00pm.*

The Leamington Spa Courier dated 18th June 1971 reported: Landlords, tenants, and managers in the Leamington, Warwick, and Kenilworth area left their pubs on Tuesday evening to sample the wines of Italy. The tasting took place in Leamington's Crown Hotel where about 140 licensees and their wives had the opportunity of meeting the president of the local Licensed Victuallers Association, Mr. George Brennan. Mr. Brennan works with Hunts the soft drinks company which is a member of the Beecham group. Another member company, F. S. Matta Ltd supplied the wines. The guests included the Mayor of Warwick - Alderman John Howlett, himself the licensee of the Warwick Tavern, and his wife Kathleen.

*On 10th February 1972 the Crown Hotel opened the Diadem Room which they advertised as the new Leamington night spot. It had a cabaret, a buffet and dancing 3 nights a week. Resident group was the Tony Whittaker Sound and tickets were £1.50 which included the cabaret and buffet [special guests included Edmund Hockridge, the Kay Sisters, Bert Weedon and Ronnie Hilton].*

Teddy's Tavern opened at the Crown on 21st December 1977 with the slogan, "Every night is party night – music, dancing and fun." There was free admission for couples until 10.15pm and normal admission was 50p per person. On 25th May 1978 there was a grand opening in Teddy's Tavern for 'Country at the Crown' with admission costing £1.

*Also in 1978, the Crown ran a Solo Club [music and dancing] every Tuesday evening for widowed, divorced and separated people. There was a disco and bar every Friday and Saturday from 10.00pm until 1.30am, but from 3rd February 1978 there was a dress code; jacket and trousers were compulsory and no denims!*

The Leamington Spa Courier dated 4th May 1979 reported that: The new manager of the Crown Hotel, Alan Wells, and his beautiful model wife Penelope, arrived this week. Mr. Wells has been in the hotel and nightclub business for the last 30 years and has worked all over the world. Prior to coming to Leamington he ran a hotel and nightclub in Weston-Super-Mare. During his career he has met many famous personalities including Bernard Delfont, Freddie Starr and Ken Dodd. "Freddie Starr told me he performed at the Crown a few years ago during the early part of his career," said Mr. Wells. For a short time in 1967 Wells was engaged to the actress Jane Mansfield. "The Crown Hotel is a great challenge for me; there is a lot of future for the hotel. The 30 bedrooms have new furniture and are newly decorated and we have a good menu and reasonable prices. I want to get a nightclub atmosphere and have cabaret with people like Bernard Manning performing." Wells has raised money for various charities including the Police Dependant's Trust through which he has met former Prime Minister, Sir Harold Wilson. Penelope, who is 21 years old, has been modelling professionally for a year. She has appeared in the Sun, the Daily Mirror and readers of the Daily Star would have seen her in last Friday's issue. Last summer she took part in the Benny Hill show and has also modelled in various countries such as Portugal and the Canary Islands. Her ambition is to be a film star. [On Tuesday 24th July 1979, star comedian Bernard Manning did appear at the Crown for a charity auction in aid of the Police Dependant's Trust; the tickets were £2. The auctioneer for the evening was Roger Stuchber from Cartwright Holt and Son and the items auctioned included a holiday for two in Jersey and a donkey].

*In May 1979 the Crown opened Penelope's Disco, named after Penelope Wells the wife of the new licensee.*

The Leamington Spa Courier dated 17th August 1979 reported that: **Hotel owner is warned** - An application to incorporate the former café at the Crown Hotel into the hotel and open up the space for music, singing and dancing, was granted by the licensing magistrates on Tuesday. But the chairman of the magistrates Mr. T. K. Meredith told licensee Alan Wells to pay particular attention to his premises. "The name [Crown] often comes up on other matters when problems of young people who have had too much to drink and then do regrettable things afterwards are discussed at Juvenile court," he said.

*In 1981 there was a musicians' workshop every Monday night and live bands every Tuesday, Wednesday and Thursday. The Leamington Spa Courier dated 4th June 1982 reported that 40 residents had to be evacuated early on Wednesday morning [2nd June] as a fire gutted the television room. Eight firemen wearing breathing apparatus took 35 minutes to extinguish the fire.*

**Cuba** – 116 Warwick Street
See Prince of Wales for details.

**Debonair** – 2-4 Ranelagh Street
See Ranelagh Tavern for details.

**Desmond Hotel** – Kenilworth Road
See Guys Hotel for details.

**Dog and Duck** – Covent Garden / 6 Square Street
See Kings Head for details.

**Dog Inn** – London Road [now High Street]
See Black Dog for details.

**Duke** – Warwick Street
See Yates for details.

**Eagle Inn** – 41 Althorpe Street
The first directory listing we have for the Eagle is in 1837, when it was a beer house. It was granted a full on-licence in August 1856 and was owned by Flower and Sons Ltd of Stratford-upon-Avon. At the 1903 licensing session, the chief constable reported that the pub had three entrances, one into Althorpe Street, one into White Street and one into a passage leading from Neilston Street to White Street, and that the residents of twenty six cottages had access to the passage. In his opinion the premises were used by men and women of a very rough class. In reply, it was said that the passage had now been bricked up and also that a number of witnesses had stated that it was frequented by respectable working class people. In April 1925 the licensing justices approved plans for alterations that

included taking in an adjoining cottage for the purpose of domestic accommodation. The Eagle closed on 31st August 1959 when the licence was suspended by the local authority 'by reason of compulsory acquisition' under section 92 [1], Licensing Act 1953; following the Eagle's closure the licence was transferred to another licensee indicating that the brewery had allocated it to another of its public houses [outside of Leamington]. The site of the Eagle Inn later became part of the Althorpe Industrial Estate.

*Photo of the Eagle Inn, donated to Leamington Library by the late Mr. R. T. Lamsdale.*

| | |
|---|---|
| 1837-40 | John Shutt |
| 1840-42 | Robert Watchman |
| 1845 | G. Beasley |
| 1846-56 | William Parsons |
| | *(Owned by S. Priest, Grocer, George Street)* |
| 1856-60 | James Stephen Jenkins |
| 1860-Mar 1861 | John Gilks |
| March 1861-Mar 1864 | William Chaplin |
| March 1864-66 | Isaac Putt |
| 1868 | John Elliott |
| 1870-Jul 1874 | Charles Henry Sprenger and wife Martha |
| | *(Charles was born in Hanover, Germany in 1825)* |
| July 1874-Mar 1898 | Levi Marner |
| March 1898-May 1898 | Mrs. Sarah Marner *(On the death of Levi)* |
| May 1898-Nov 1902 | Donald Broad |
| November 1902-May 1909 | Charles Bayliss *(Previously an engine driver)* |
| May 1909-20 | William Alfred Smith |
| 1920-Sep 1924 | Albert Woodman |
| September 1924-Jul 1935 | William Henry Plummer *(Died 9th June 1939, aged 54)* |
| July 1935-36 | Arthur Henry Bell |
| 1938-Aug 1939 | John Thomas H. Derby |
| August 1939-Jul 1941 | Walter Hewitt |
| July 1941-May 1952 | Mrs. Annie Green |
| May 1952-Jun 1956 | William Thomson Imrie |
| June 1956-Mar 1957 | Dennis Frank Manners |
| March 1957-Jun 1957 | George Henry White |
| June 1957-Aug 1959 | Mrs. Marlow Donaldson |
| 31st August 1959 | Closed for business |
| 2nd February 1960 | Licence transferred to Thomas Edwin Overbury |

*Tom Lewin remembers, "The picture of the Eagle is just how I remember it; it's part of my childhood. I would sit on those steps hoping for a Vimto or a packet of crisps while my parents were inside sampling the ale. I spent most of my infant days with my grandparents in Charles Street. My sister was 4 years older than me and she was the one who would get a jug of beer for my gran and granddad; she vividly remembers fetching it in a white enamelled jug. Another of her memories is seeing all the ladies sitting outside on chairs sipping their half pints of beer while their men folk were inside. We looked forward to Saturday mornings most as all us local kids would go to Saturday morning flics. Happy days on that old estate, Althorpe Street, Court Street, White Street, Neilston Street and Charles Street."*

**Eagle and Shamrock** – 2 Court Street
See Coopers Arms for details.

**Earl Grey Arms** – 5 Gloucester Street
See Gloucester Tavern for details.

**Eight** – 8 High Street
This building on the corner of Wise Street will be remembered by many as Leamington Social Club. A premises licence was granted to Scott Rowlinson on 24th April 2012 and a D.P.S. licence [designated supervisor licence] was granted on 31st October 2012. Towards the end of 2012, building work commenced on the corner part of the ground floor. Eight, a bar and bistro, opened in January 2013 [whilst work continued on its completion] and remains open in December 2013.

*Eight bar and bistro taken on 18th January 2013 © Allan Jennings.*

**Envy Bar** – 75 Bedford Street
See Bedford Inn for details.

**Exchange** – High Street
See Royal Exchange for details.

**Falstaff** – 67 Parade
It was advertised on 11th April 1885 that the Falstaff at 67, the Parade [late Old Spanish Stores] had just opened with a wide choice of wines, spirits, ales and cigars; it had wines from the wood in dock glasses and champagne on draught at 6d per glass. "The old premises have been transformed into a most attractive and comfortable bar, with parlour, and private side entrance thereto. Excellent draught dinner ales and London stout is to be

This 1887 map courtesy of Leamington Library shows the location of the Falstaff on the Parade. It also shows the Golden Lion in Regent Street and the Half Moon which was renamed the Palace Inn and later the Silver Jubilee.

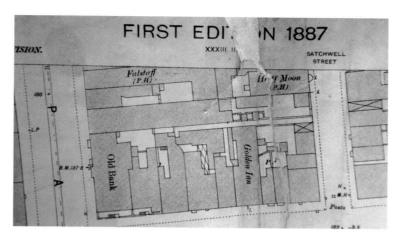

obtained at the side entrance. Visitors to the Falstaff will find a good selection of newspapers, daily and weekly." The only other reference we have to this public house is on a map dated 1887, but drawn-up in 1885. This venture proved to be shortlived and in September 1885 the licence was transferred to C. T. Pierson [official receiver] as the process of liquidating the estate commenced. In August 1886 Mr. Powell, a Birmingham solicitor, applied to the magistrates court for the transfer of said licence from Mr. E. T. Pierson to Mr. Chevasse, the lessee. The mayor pronounced that because the house had been closed for almost a year the bench was unanimously of the opinion that the licence was not needed, therefore the application would be refused. The Falstaff was 3 doors up the Parade from Lloyds Bank which is on the corner of the Parade and Regent Street.

| | |
|---|---|
| April 1885 | W. Hopekirk *(Proprietor)* |
| September 1885 | C. T. Pierson *(Official receiver)* |

**Fat Pug** – 23 Guys Cliffe Road
See Coventry Arms for details.

**Festival Inn** – Jephson Gardens
See Leamside Inn for details.

**Fewtrells** – 2a Victoria Terrace
See Robbins Well for details.

**Flanagans** – 12 Augusta Place
See Willoughby Arms for details.

**Flying Horse** – Neilston Street / White Street
The first reference we have for the Flying Horse is in a Leamington Spa Courier report dated 9th April 1831, covering a theft from the Ranelagh Tavern. The first directory listing

we have is in 1837, addressed as Neilston Street, but with no mention of the landlord's name, however the 1837 church rate book shows William Kingerley as the owner of this beer house. The Flying Horse was sold by auction without reserve on the 7th February 1838 by order of the mortgagee. It was described as: "A newly-built freehold messuage, with brew house, yard, and other appurtenances to the same belonging, situated in Neilston Street, Leamington Priors, commonly called the Flying Horse, lately occupied by William Kingerley as a beer house at the yearly rent of £30, but now untenanted. The house contains four rooms on the ground floor, three over, suitable cellaring, and brew house at the back; the whole site comprises 147 square yards."

The Leamington Courier dated 10th November 1838 reported on the following item discussed at the most recent council meeting, "Mr. Enoch has been requested to lay before the council a memorial from several inhabitants anxious to buy and pull down the Flying Horse public house. The sum of money required was £750, £500 had already been subscribed, £100 was expected to be raised from a sale of the materials and £150 was wanted to complete the requisite amount. The object was to pull down the property and convey the land to the corporation for the public good." It was resolved that the memorial would be taken into consideration at the next meeting, but we have been unable to find out what happened.

In 1839-40 the occupier was William Haynes, but as it is not listed in the 1841 or subsequent directories we had concluded that it closed circa 1840. However the 1852 Leamington Board of Health map shows the pub alongside the canal in [what was then] White Street and an 1853 court report lists the occupier of the Flying Horse tavern as being a W. Smith.

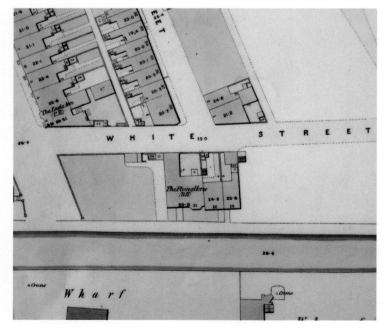

*This 1852 Board of Health map showing the site of the Flying Horse is courtesy of Leamington Library.*

The Leamington Spa Courier dated 15th September 1855 carried the following sale notice: "To be sold by auction by Henry Elvins, at the Crown Hotel on Wednesday, the 3rd day of October 1855, at four o'clock in the afternoon, by order of the mortgagee. All those superior premises, used as a public house, and known as the Flying Horse Inn, situate in Althorpe Street, Leamington Priors, late in the occupation of Mrs. Martin, but now void; containing five bedrooms, large smoke room, bar, tap-room, large cellar and good brew house, with convenient out-offices and a good supply of water." Either the premises failed to sell, or the buyer was quick to resell, as the Flying Horse was again listed for auction on 19th December 1856.

**Forty Four** – 44 Clarendon Street
See Kings Arms for details.

**Fountain** – Brook Street / 44 Warwick Street
We only have three directory listings for this beer house but, based on the two addresses that we have, we believe that it was on the corner of Brook Street and Warwick Street. As it is not listed in the 1841 or subsequent directories we have concluded that it closed circa 1840.

| | |
|---|---|
| 1835 | Thomas Sims *(Brook Street)* |
| 1837-39 | Thomas Sims *(44, Warwick Street)* |

**Fountain** – 12 Clemens Street
See Railway Inn for details.

**Fox** – 32 Clarendon Avenue
See Fox and Vivian for details.

**Fox and Vivian** – 32 South Parade East / 32 Clarendon Avenue

South Parade, as Clarendon Avenue was originally named, was completed by 1825. The first reference point we have for the Fox and Vivian is in the 1837 church rate book, when William Barnwell is listed against a pub in South Parade [it is not listed as Clarendon Avenue until 1883]; the first directory listing we have is in 1838. In 1865 it had a 6-pull beer machine and had a brew house that included a 125 gallon copper, two iron furnaces, a 16 bushel and some smaller mash tubs, one 1150 gallon and 30 smaller iron-bound casks. By 1910 the owners were Showell's Brewery Co. Ltd,

*A Fox and Vivian advert taken from the 1882 Becks Directory.*

*Left: A 1987 photo of the Fox and Vivian taken by Bill Bigley. Right: The Fox taken on 27th December 2009 © Allan Jennings.*

Oldbury, Staffordshire, [acquired by Samuel Allsopp Ltd in 1914; merged with Ind Coope & Co. Ltd in 1934].

In 1984 the pub was extensively refurbished and a grand ceremonial reopening, attended by hundreds of people, was held on 21st August. It would continue to be known as the Fox and Vivian Inn until September 1988 when, following a £100,000 refurbishment, it reopened as the Slug and Lettuce at midday on Tuesday 25th October 1988; however, by January 1989 it had been renamed the Slug and Lettuce @ The Fox and Vivian. In 1992 'The Slug' was sold to Grosvenor Inns as part of a deal for the whole 'Slug and Lettuce' chain comprising 13 premises. In 1995 it was known as The Fox.

In November 2001 it became Baroque and in 2009 it was again named The Fox. By March 2011 the signage was again being altered to the Fox and Vivian, albeit belatedly as the official date of it reverting to its original name was 1st December 2010. The Fox and Vivian remains open in December 2013.

| | |
|---|---|
| 1837-Jun 1848 | William Barnwell *(Died 7th February 1848, aged 42)* |
| June 1848-56 | Hannah Barnwell *(On the death of William)* |
| 1856-Dec 1861 | William Bradshaw |
| December 1861-Jan 1866 | Richard Taylor |
| January 1866-80 | Robert Colton |
| 1880-Apr 1897 | Mrs. Naomi Colton |
| April 1897-Jan 1899 | William Moseley |
| January 1899-Nov 1905 | Charles Frank Townsend |
| November 1905-Aug 1906 | John Thomas Handley |
| August 1906-Aug 1910 | William George Wincott |
| August 1910-Jun 1911 | Joseph Rose |
| June 1911-Mar 1920 | Frederick Standbridge |

| | |
|---|---|
| March 1920-Aug 1920 | William Joseph Dwyer |
| August 1920-Aug 1922 | John Leonard Parker |
| August 1922-Aug 1923 | A. E. Burgess |
| | *(Left without notice 4 weeks prior to license transfer)* |
| August 1923-Jun 1931 | Henry 'Harry' Wake |
| June 1931-Nov 1953 | Roy Joseph Wallace Allen |
| November 1953-Oct 1960 | Clifford Stewart Jenkins |
| October 1960-Oct 1972 | Raymond Victor Scotford |
| October 1972 | Daniel Dolan |
| 1979-1983 | Patrick Reid and his wife Joyce |
| 1983-Mar 1988 | Ray and Louise Hinton |
| March 1988 | Peter and 'Bubbles' Nielson |
| 1989 | Andrew Simpson *(Manager)* |
| 2006 | David Baker |
| 2009 | Christopher Huw Lewis Powell |
| July 2009 | Martin Brian Vickers |
| 2010 | David Barnbrook |
| June 2010-Aug 2010 | Michael Solomons |
| August 2010-Dec 2010 | Claire Elisabeth Evans |
| December 2010 → | Matthew Crowley |

*In October 1861 two coal dealers were charged with allowing their carts to stand in the street whilst they were drinking in the Fox and Vivian. As they lived some way from Leamington the defendants were not fined but had to pay the court expenses.*

From September 1972 until at least September 1974 the Fox and Vivian was the base for the local branch of the National Federation of 18 plus Groups; nationally there were almost 200 groups with 7,000 members.

*In 1983, letters of concern were being sent to the Courier because of news that landlord Ray Hinton was changing the name of the Fox & Vivian to the 'Royal Swan'. He replied in their 8th July edition to reassure them saying, "There is no decision that can't be changed. The image had to be changed and it was felt that it was best to go the whole way and change the name to the Royal Swan, the new name being simply as a kind of tribute to our lovely families of 'Cob' and 'Pen' and signets adorning and creating so much interest from people both near and far who visit, particularly, the Jephson Gardens."*

*The Editor of the Courier wrote below Ray's letter: Research in the Courier files reveals that the name 'Fox and Vivian' has associations with a Captain Brook in the Grand National. Tradition has it that the captain mounted 'Vivian' his horse, who was challenged to a five mile cross-country race by the Marquis of Waterford on his horse Cock Robin, Vivian won easily. During subsequent celebrations at the local inn the marquis referred to the captain as a sly fox. The innkeeper with an ear for an unusual phrase that would commemorate the 'wager' and with an eye for business coined 'The Fox and Vivian'.*

A slightly different take on the race was given in 1895 by George Morley: "The first course of the Leamington Steeplechases proper was laid out at Ashorne and the races were run on 14th November, 1834. There the Marquis of Waterford's celebrated horse, Jerry, beat the no less popular Vivian of Captain Lamb. Emboldened by his success, the Myton-like nobleman was eager for enterprises of greater pith and moment. He at once sent out his famous challenge to match his favourite horse, Cock Robin, against the Vivian of Captain Lamb, for the princely sum of one thousand pounds a side. The wager was accepted with alacrity. Then came the tossing as to whether the match should take place in Warwickshire or Leicestershire. The Marquis of Waterford won the toss and chose four miles of Leicestershire country – from Norton Steeple to Carlton Clump. On the 21st December this celebrated performance took place, the marquis riding his own horse, and Mr. Beecher being astride Vivian. It was a valiant and glorious race, so the chroniclers assert, but defeat followed the Waterford colours, much to the discomfiture of the marquis. Vivian won in dashing form and the church bells of Leamington actually rang out a merry peal [surely the vicar must have been a sporting parson] for the victory of the Warwickshire horse!"

*Hundreds of people attended the reopening of the Fox and Vivian pub in Leamington's Clarendon Street [Avenue] on Tuesday 21st August 1984 after its extensive refurbishment. The ceremony was performed by Councillor Michael Coker, the Chairman of Warwick District Council. Also present were Norman Parker, who was master of ceremonies for the evening, Central Television presenter Sally Jones and mine hosts, Ray and Louise Hinton.*

Chris Brown bought Baroque in 2004 and planned a substantial refurbishment for the spring of 2005 which included making the first floor suitable for business meetings and for use as a party venue.

*Baroque in August 2004 courtesy of John Hartnup.*

### Fusilier – Stanleys Court, Sydenham Drive

On 10th August 1964, a provisional licence was granted to Leslie Robert Crowder on behalf of Hunt, Edmunds Ltd for a pub to be known as the Blasted Oak on Sydenham Farm Estate; it was ratified on 14th June 1965. Also in 1964, the building of an estate had commenced on the land that had previously been Sydenham Farm. On 9th August 1965 the provisional licence was transferred to Royston James Cooper but the Blasted Oak never opened as a pub. The idea for the name Fusilier came from Alderman Tickle the farmer who had owned and farmed Sydenham Farm, the land that the pub was to be built on. The Fusilier, a Mitchells and Butlers' pub selling M&B mild and Brew XI, eventually opened in the winter of 1974 and by December 1977 the lounge had been enlarged. The Fusilier remains open in December 2013.

| | |
|---|---|
| Winter 1974-≥1983 | Keith and Denise Spicer |
| 1988-1990 | Denny and Charlie Mullin |

*Photo of the Fusilier taken on 24th March 2010 © Allan Jennings.*

| | |
|---|---|
| Circa 2000 | Jaz Uppal |
| Circa 2009 | Kevin John Murphy |
| March 2010 | Neil Brookes |
| June 2010-2013 | Donna Charmaine Rose |

*The Leamington Spa Courier dated 10th August 1973 reported:* **Call new pub after local alderman** – idea - *An alternative name for the Sydenham estate pub has been suggested by a Whitnash man who would like to see it called the Plough and Tickle. "The estate was built on Sydenham farm which belonged to Alderman Arthur Tickle," said Mr. A. M. Byth, of Heathcote Road, Whitnash. He has no children to carry his name on so I thought the pub ought to be called after him." Mr. Byth has known Alderman Tickle for 40 years and would like to see him on the pub sign dressed in his gaiters, breeches, bowler hat, and carrying his thumb stick. "He has been a very well respected man in the town for all these years and a very respected Alderman for the County," Mr. Byth said. The Mitchell and Butlers Brewery who are building the pub have decided to call it after the Royal Warwickshire Regiment. Mr. Byth said the new Hampton Magna pub built on the site of the Budbrooke barracks should have been named after the Warwicks and the Sydenham pub after Alderman Tickle. "We have a Jet and Whittle, why not a Plough and Tickle," he said. But Alderman Tickle is not too keen on the idea, "I would much rather have a square on the estate called after me. That would be nice," he said. "I would say that a good name for that pub is the Fusilier. Up in Lancashire there are lots of pubs called after Tickles but it is not right for Warwickshire," he added. Whatever the pub is called, Alderman Tickle says he will be in it as soon as it opens. Mr. Paul McMahon, the district manager of Mitchells and Butlers Brewery, said he would suggest the name to his seniors who would make a decision.*

The Coventry Evening Telegraph of 13th September 1974 reported: Work is progressing on the Fusilier, the new Mitchells and Butlers pub to serve Leamington's Sydenham estate. The name was chosen in honour of the 6th Leamington Battalion of the former Royal Warwickshire Regiment and the pub is due to open this winter. [Note: The brewery also considered the 'Saucy Sixth' as a name for the pub]

**Gardeners Arms** – 72 Regent Street

The first directory listing we have is in 1835 when it was addressed as 51, Regent Street. By 1837 the premises had been renumbered '72' but the licensee is not listed, suggesting that it may have been temporarily vacant pending a new tenancy [George Walker]. In 1840, the church rate book lists William Palmer at a public house at 72, Regent Street but as there are no subsequent listings we have concluded that it closed circa 1840.

| | |
|---|---|
| 1835 | John Hewitt *(51, Regent Street)* |
| 1837 | No licensee listed |
| | *(Owner: William Freeman – 72, Regent Street)* |
| 1838-39 | George Walker |
| 1840 | William Palmer |

**Garibaldi Inn** – 16 High Street

Previously Coopers Wine Vaults, the first reference point we have for the Garibaldi Inn is a mention in a magistrates court report dated 5th October 1861; the first directory listing we have is in 1862. Originally a beer house, it was later owned by the Northampton Brewery Company. In 1863 and 1865 the address was listed at the annual licensing sessions as Windham Terrace and in the late 1880s it was known as the Garibaldi Vaults.

There were two entrances to the premises both from High Street and in 1903 clear glass was put into the upper panels of the bagatelle room door to permit a view into the [bar] room; there was also a billiard room. On Monday 16th January 1920, the owners of the Garibaldi Inn applied to the local magistrates for approval of plans to extend the premises; they proposed to alter the smoke room and, by taking in the adjoining premises, open up

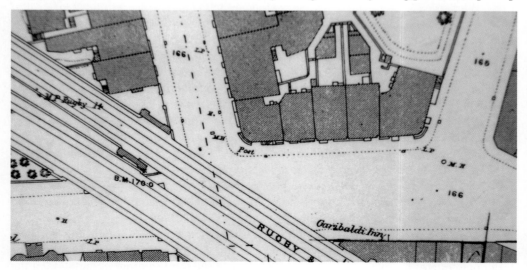

*This plan shows where the Garibaldi Inn was situated on the corner of High Street and Clemens Street next to the railway bridge.*

new rooms where refreshments of all kinds could be sold. Additionally, proposed changes to the domestic part of the premises would provide improved bedroom accommodation for the tenant and his family. The mayor responded that the bench had carefully considered the matter but, after taking into consideration the number of licensed houses in the immediate neighbourhood, had agreed that the application should be refused; the Garibaldi's days were numbered.

On Monday 1st March 1920, the pub was one of a number that were 'referred for extinction by compensation' by the local licensing justices as part of a weeding out process, or "thinning the inns" as it was reported at the time. On 28th May 1920 the county compensation authority refused the renewal of the licence and on Monday 2nd January 1922 compensation was awarded. However, its value was disputed and the case was referred to the Inland Revenue Authority the same month. Although the licence was provisionally renewed in February 1922 pending an outcome the Garibaldi Inn was closed on 30th September 1922. During World War Two it was the Garibaldi Fish Restaurant and in the 1960s it was the very well known Garibaldi fish and chip shop 'near the bridges'; in 2013 it sells Indian cuisine.

| | |
|---|---|
| 1861-Jul 1867 | John Louch |
| July 1867-Jan 1869 | William Louch *(Son of John)* |
| January 1867-Feb 1869 | Philip Allen of Northampton |
| February 1869-Jan 1874 | Richard Cooper |
| January 1874-Oct 1876 | William Ricketts |
| October 1876-Mar 1888 | William Warren |
| March 1888-Sep 1892 | Matthew Arnold |
| September 1892-Jun 1895 | Christopher Lewis |
| June 1895-Oct 1900 | Richard Coulden |
| October 1900-May 1904 | Robert Woolf |
| May 1904-Jun 1907 | Walter James Reader |
| June 1907-Jul 1914 | Thomas Orton |
| July 1914-Sep 1922 | Henry 'Harry' Inwood |
| 30th September 1922 | Closed for business |

**George and Dragon** – 21 Park Street
See Globe Inn for details.

**George Inn** – 53 High Street
An 1822 description of the George Inn reads, "Further along the London Road, beyond Copp's Hotel, was a row of small comfortable houses known in those days as Barford Buildings, and at the end of these houses appeared another cluster, this side of the old Town Hall; these were called Pain's Buildings. On the north side of the street was the George Inn with stabling to the rear." In 1879 it was a free house and a fully licensed hostelry with extensive buildings, yards, stabling, coach-houses, cottage and shop. The frontage to High Street [facing the Town Hall, now the Polish Club] was about 122 feet and it was 129 feet to George Street.

The George Inn was later renamed the George Hotel. In 1909 it was a Mitchells and Butlers pub and it was still that in the 1960s. The first directory listing we have is in 1830 and the George closed circa 2004. In 2013 the premises are a residential apartment block.

| | |
|---|---|
| 1822 | Licensee not known |
| 1830-32 | Catherine Powell |
| 1833-35 | Richard Court |
| 1835 | Brotheridge |
| 1837-1844 | Job Bloxham |
| 1845-50 | John Richards |
| 1850-Apr 1851 | Daniel Simmonds |
| April 1851 | Sarah Simmonds *(On the death of Daniel)* |
| 1854-60 | Thomas Jarrett |
| 1860-May 1870 | Miss Margaret Jarrett *(Died 28th May 1870)* |
| May 1870-72 | Rachael Jarrett |
| 1872-Aug 1874 | Mary Higham |
| August 1874-Jun 1878 | Edward Charles Whittell |
| June 1878-Dec 1901 | Mrs. Mary Whittell *(After Edward left his wife)* |
| December 1901-Nov 1910 | Charles Cooke Spraggett |
| November 1910-14 | Alfred W Burton |
| 1914-20 | James William Freeborough |
| 1920-Dec 1934 | Mrs. Eliza Jane Freeborough *(On the death of James)* |
| December 1934-Jan 1935 | Miss Gwladys Freeborough *(Daughter of Eliza – name as spelt)* |
| January 1935-Jun 1944 | Percival 'Percy' Ernest Swann |
| June 1944-Apr 1952 | Frank Harold Bryan |
| 1945-48 | *(It is understood that Sam Knightley was the landlord during these years, but not the licensee)* |
| April 1952-Apr 1958 | Albert George Hemingway |
| April 1958-Aug 1964 | John Pyatt |
| August 1964 | Edward George Silburn |
| February 1974-≥1978 | Charlie and Betty Wheeler *(Previously of the Great Western, Deppers Bridge)* |
| 1983 | Christopher Merrick *(Acting licensee)* |
| September 1984-86 | Brian and Janet Woodward |
| 1986-≥91 | Alec and Corinna Pears |
| 1993-≤c2004 | Martin and Marie McGeough *(As spelt)* |

*Bruno Eurich moved to Leamington in 1994 and says, "A few years ago, I was talking about the oldest Leamington buildings to my builder [Henry Blomfield who lived next door to the Red House on Radford Road and who tragically died early a few years ago], and he mentioned to me that he had seen the inside of the large chimney of the George, and he was convinced that it was older than most of the surrounding buildings due to its construction methods [he*

had a great knowledge of old buildings]
and even older than the 'old' cottages on
Church St. I'm not sure whether this
chimney has survived the conversion of
the George to student accommodation
though!"

*The George Hotel taken on 7th January 1996 ©
Allan Jennings.*

The Morning News dated 20th
December 1985 reported that: Brian
Woodward, who took over as tenant of
the George Inn in September 1984 had
already grown to love the pub's old
fashioned, Victorian image, having
worked there for two years as a bar man.
So, on taking the reins, he was
determined to allow its character to live
on. The pub is divided into two rooms,
the bar and the lounge, each with its
own distinct appeal. The bar is a down to earth, no nonsense area dominated by a full-size
pool table to allow plenty of space for the team competitions. But through in the lounge the
atmosphere totally changes. Subdued red lighting, red seating and heavy red curtains all
contribute to an opulent image, redolent of the turn of the century. The few touches Brian has
added to the pub include providing the new curtains and a red checked floor covering. He
said, "I didn't want to muck about with the place. If I had done I would have spoiled it. Now
everything fits in." The bar itself is old-fashioned with heavy dark wood shelving and a dark
wood clock with a steady peaceful tick hangs on the lounge wall. Deep red wallpaper, ceiling
beams and a huge beamed fireplace add the finishing touches. Owned by Mitchells and
Butlers, the pub serves Brew XI, mild, Bass, Tennants beers and Carling Black Label. Along
with pool there are crib, dominoes and darts teams. The bar has a television in the corner
which is switched on for sports viewing and there is also a well stocked juke box.

**Glasnost Vodka Bar** – 86 Regent Street
In 1958 the premises at 86, Regent Street opened
as the Il Cadore café and it was the place for
teenagers to be when it was 'cool' to frequent
coffee shops. It is difficult now to recall the
impression that coffee bars had on the local
population at the time but this one was reported
as being "a centre of controversy". It is believed
that Il Cadore was opened by Pietro di Lorenzo
but by 1960 it was run by Miss Jennet Thomas in

*The Stresa Bar taken on 29th August 2004 by
John Hartnup.*

association with two young Italians Valerio Mio and Gino Bertoletti. We have not been able to determine when it opened as the Glasnost Vodka Bar, but from circa 2001 it was the V Bar and by 2004 it was the Stresa Bar. In May 2008 it opened as La Coppola Italian Restaurant and it remains so in 2013.

| | |
|---|---|
| 2006-Apr 2008 | Marco Esposito *(Stresa Bar)* |
| 24th April 2008-Sep 2011 | Mrs. Charlotte Ahmadi *(Stresa Bar)* |
| May 2008 | Opened as La Coppola Italian Restaurant |
| 28th September 2011 | Premises licence transferred to La Coppola Ltd |

**Glass and Candle** – 31 Parade
See Lansdowne Hotel for details.

**Glasshouse** – 38-40 Warwick Street
See Slug and Lettuce for details.

**Globe Inn** – 13 Park Street
Our first reference point for the Globe is a crime case report published in the Leamington Spa Courier in April 1831. Despite frequent renumbering of Park Street in the latter half of the 19th century, we know that the Globe Inn was situated at number '21' in the 1830s. In 1833-34, a Richard Hilsdon is listed as the licensee at number '21' but the name of the pub is omitted. Ordinarily, this may not have been of any consequence but in 1835-37 the George and Dragon is listed at this address before reverting to the Globe Inn in 1838, and thereafter. At the time of going to print we have been unable to establish whether the pub was called the Globe Inn or the George and Dragon during the period 1832-34. In the 1830s the premises had a parlour and tap room in the front, a bar and kitchen at the back, a skittle alley, three bedrooms, a cellar, coach-house, a two-stall stable [with a loft and bedroom above] and a carpenter's shop.

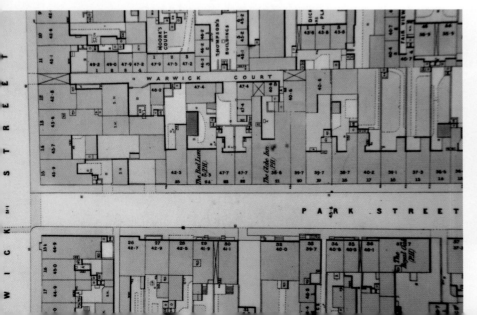

*This 1852 map courtesy of Leamington Library shows where the Globe Inn was situated in Park Street close to Warwick Street.*

In July 1885, the licence was transferred from Lewis and Ridley [Leamington Brewery] to Morton Peto Lucas representing the new brewery owners, Lucas, Blackwell and Arkwright; in 1897, ownership of the brewery would change again [Lucas and Co. Ltd]. The Globe Inn would subsequently become an Ansells pub following their 1928 acquisition of the Leamington Brewery and its closure in 1934. A music singing and dancing licence was first granted in November 1892 for the upstairs back room, which was used as a club room seating approximately 100 people. There were two entrances to the Globe, one in Park Street and the other in Atkinson's Court, and in 1906 there were four rooms for the drinkers. Local residents said that in the pub's latter days, "it had two smoke rooms and a bar; as you went through the front door the bar was on the left, the smoke room was on the right and the other smoke room was behind the bar."

The Globe Inn closed for business at 10.00pm on 2nd December 1958 and the following day the licence was transferred to The Mountford, Overgreen Drive, Kingshurst, Castle Bromwich, Birmingham. In 1976 it was a decaying building owned by Warwick District Council and used for storage and in 2013 it is a retail business.

| | |
|---|---|
| 1831 | No landlord listed *(Globe Inn)* |
| 1833-34 | Richard Hilsdon *(No pub name listed, only address)* |
| 1835-37 | Edward Smith *(George & the Dragon)* |
| 1838-56 | Edward Treen *(Globe Inn)* |
| 1856-Apr 1861 | Mrs. Elizabeth Treen |
| April 1861-Apr 1864 | James Fowler |
| April 1864-66 | Timothy French |
| 1868-74 | Washington Wallis Willes |
| 1874-Apr 1875 | William Bollans |
| April 1875-Dec 1876 | Joseph Palmer |
| December 1876-Nov 1879 | James Hampson |
| November 1879-80 | William Griffin |
| 1880-Mar 1882 | Frederick William Griffin |
| March 1882 | Messrs Lewis and Ridley/Leamington Brewery |
| 1882-83 | T. Squires |
| 1884 | J. Squires |
| 1884-85 | J. Smith |
| July 1885 | Morton Peto Lucas/Leamington Brewery |
| 1885 | A. J. Lewis |
| 1886-87 | W. and S. Warner |
| 1887-Sep 1888 | Alfred Knightly *(Manager)* |
| September 1888-Mar 1891 | Frederick Edward Taylor |
| March 1891-Oct 1898 | Frank Davis |
| October 1898-Oct 1901 | Edward Alexander |
| October 1901-Jan 1913 | William Garrett |
| January 1913-Apr 1913 | Nellie Lewis Garrett *(On the death of William)* |
| April 1913-Jan 1924 | Harry Bedding |

| | |
|---|---|
| January 1924-25 | C. H. Langston |
| 1925-40 | Charles William Miller |
| 1940-Nov 1940 | Harry Farmer |
| November 1940-May 1951 | Charles Reginald Naylor |
| May 1951-Oct 1952 | James Arthur Green |
| October 1952-Nov 1954 | James Wilkins |
| November 1954-Jan 1956 | Arthur James Warren |
| January 1956-Nov 1956 | John Talbot |
| November 1956-Nov 1957 | Joseph Edward Mills |
| November 1957-Apr 1958 | Harry Stokes |
| April 1958-Dec 1958 | Harry Thomas Card |
| 2nd December 1958 | Closed for business |

*In March 1960, it was reported that plans to redevelop the building previously known as the Globe Inn [and adjoining premises] as shops, warehouses, stores or showrooms, were being considered by the Warwick District Council.*

The Coventry Evening Telegraph, dated 21st October 1976, reported that: A former Leamington pub, the Globe Inn, has been earmarked as headquarters for the Leamington and Warwick Sub-Aqua Club. The pub in Park Street closed in the mid 1960s [1958 – Ed] and the premises have since been taken over by the district council. They are vacant and dilapidated but negotiations have started with a view to a lease being granted to the club. Arthur Wardman, the chairman, said that they had never had a home of their own and for the last seven years had used the Avenue Bowling Club's premises in Leamington. "This has been a very happy marriage, but our membership is expanding," he said. The club formed 10 years ago now have 90 members and are regarded as one of the leading diving clubs in the Midlands. They have submitted a planning application to convert the old pub premises into headquarters, providing lecture, committee and chart rooms and an equipment store.

**Gloucester Hotel** – 11 Clemens Street

Our first reference date for the Gloucester Hotel is 30th August 1828 when the following advert was placed in the Leamington Spa Courier: "Gloucester Hotel, Clemens Street – Roby and Co, wine merchants to their Royal Highnesses the Duke and Duchess of Gloucester, importers of and dealers in foreign wines and spirits, respectfully beg leave to return their sincere thanks to their friends and the public, for the very liberal support they have hitherto experienced, and to assure them that every exertion shall be used to merit a continuance of the same." As well as a range of wines and spirits, they also sold fine home brewed ale and Whitbread's London porter and brown stout. We also have a directory listing for Richard Roby as licensee of a wine vaults 1825-27 [no address given] so it appears that Roby and Co. started off as wine merchants before expanding their business and also becoming hoteliers. In 1829 they opened a spacious and elegant wine and coffee room in the 'London style' for the accommodation of gentlemen.

However, the business venture would soon prove unsuccessful and Joseph Roby would become bankrupt. The first signs were in August 1830 when the premises were advertised 'to let' [or the lease and furniture to be disposed of], they comprised: an elegant wine and coffee room [39 ft x 20 ft]; drawing room [22 ft x 16 ft]; two private sitting rooms; parlour; travellers' room; smoking room; sixteen bed chambers of good dimensions, with water closets; cooking kitchen, scullery and larder; store house; enclosed bar; and counting-house adjoining. The outside premises consisted of a brewery that included two coppers capable of holding 830 gallons; a large mash tub; stabling for ten horses with lofts over the same; excellent wine, spirit, and beer cellars with brick and stone bins that could contain thirty pipes of wine in bottles.

In February 1831, there was an extensive and unreserved sale by auction of the household furniture and fittings of the hotel and bar. This included a pewter liquor counter and drain, spirit fountain with about 109 feet of metal piping, a three motion beer machine with brass cocks and 125 feet of metal piping, painted liquor casks, 43 iron-bound casks, vats, coppers, brewing utensils, wines, spirits, compounds and London porter. In July 1831 the premises were advertised 'to be let' for a term of 7 years.

| | |
|---|---|
| ≤1828-1831 | Joseph Hewitt Roby |
| 1832 | George Adams |
| 1833 | John Hopkins |

### Gloucester Tavern – 8 Gloucester Street

Gloucester Street was named after the Duke and Duchess of Gloucester who visited Leamington in 1822 and stayed for five weeks in Cross Street, later renamed Regent Street. The first directory listing we have for this premises is in 1830 when John Stafford is listed as licensee of the Ale and Porter Vaults; he is also listed in the church rate book as the owner of the premises until at least 1840, although it appears that William Benton managed the business during this period. In 1832-34 it was known as the Earl Grey Arms before being renamed and listed as the Gloucester Tavern in 1835. Early in 1844 the small freehold public house and vaults, by then in the occupation of Mrs. Benton, was advertised for sale and, in the March, Job Bloxham advertised that he had taken over the business.

*This 1852 map courtesy of Leamington Library shows where in Gloucester Street the Gloucester Tavern was.*

During the period 1846-62 [approx], the Gloucester Tavern and the Gloucester Wine and Spirit Vaults co-existed on the same premises under the same licence. In 1851 the combined public house and wine and spirit vaults was sold by auction; on the ground floor it comprised a front retail liquor shop with a large bar, a parlour at the back, private side entrance, sitting room, kitchen, larder, china closet and offices with entrance into a public passage in the rear, plus a newly erected billiard or club-room [28 ft x 18 ft]. On the first floor there was a sitting room and bedroom and on the second floor a closet. The cellaring could accommodate a large stock of wines, spirits, ale and beer. Owned by brewers Phillips and Marriott of Coventry, the Gloucester Tavern closed on 7th September 1907, with compensation being paid.

| | |
|---|---|
| 1830 | John Stafford |
| 1832-42 | William Benton |
| 1844 | Mrs. Benton |
| 1844-45 | Job Bloxham |
| 1845-Jul 1851 | William Crockett |
| July 1851 | Henry Allen *(On the death of William Crockett)* |
| 1854-56 | James Wyatt and Henry Thomas |
| 1856-Apr 1859 | James Wyatt |
| April 1859-Jan 1872 | John Edgerton |
| January 1872-Nov 1874 | Thomas Bullock |
| November 1874-Jan 1875 | Thomas Bullock jnr |
| January 1875-78 | Richard Bullock |
| 1878-Jul 1881 | Richard Heeley |
| July 1881-Oct 1883 | Edward Forty |
| October 1883-Apr 1894 | John Dunnicliffe |
| April 1894-Oct 1894 | George Herbert Bamford |
| October 1894-Jun 1902 | John Read |
| June 1902-Sep 1907 | Clement Jesse Moody |
| 7th September 1907 | Closed for business |
| 1907-≥1934 | Thornley Brewery Stores |
| February 1928 | Transferred from F. Thornley to Edward Richard Thornley |

*The Leamington Spa Courier dated 15th March 1844 carried the following advert:* **Gloucester Tavern and Chop House** *– Job Bloxham most respectfully begs to inform his friends and the public generally, that he has entered upon the above established premises, where he hopes by perseverance, moderate charges, and careful attention to the comforts of his customers, to merit a share of public patronage. Dinners dressed on the shortest notice – soups always ready.*

### Gold Cup – 10 Tavistock Street

The first information we have on this premises is taken from the 1839 and 1840 church rate books when Charles Baker is listed against the public house, at what would've then been 21, Tavistock Street. The first directory listing we have for the Gold Cup is in 1841 [from 1850-74 it would occasionally be listed, or reported, as the Golden Cup]. In 1856 the pub

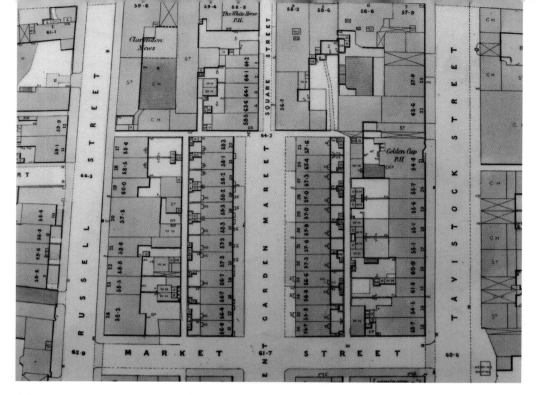

*This 1852 Leamington Board of Health Map courtesy of Leamington Library shows the location of the Golden Cup.*

consisted of two cellars, a bar, parlour, tap room, kitchen, yard, scullery. On the second floor there was a large club room [over the entry] extending from front to back and adjoining the west-end, a storeroom and five bedrooms; it also had hard and soft water supply. A condition of the licence was that the door to the passage leading from Covent Garden Market to Tavistock Street was not permitted to be open for trade purposes. By the early 20th century it was owned by the Leamington Brewery [Lucas and Co. Ltd] but would become an Ansells pub following their 1928 acquisition of the brewery and its closure in 1934. The Gold Cup closed for trading on 28th June 1968; the licence was put into suspense and on 9th December 1968 it was transferred to James Joseph Butler. The premises were demolished shortly after to make way for the Covent Garden multi-storey car park. By April 1969 workmen had begun work on the second level and in July 1969 the bridge from the car park to the east side of Tavistock Street was being built; the car park was completed in the autumn of 1969.

| | |
|---|---|
| 1839-54 | Charles Baker |
| 1854-74 | Mrs. Mary Baker *(On the death of Charles)* |
| 1874-May 1874 | John Davis |
| May 1874-May 1876 | John Hall |
| May 1876-Jul 1876 | Hannah Coole |
| July 1876-May 1887 | Charles Henry Sprenger |
| May 1887-Oct 1888 | Mrs. Harriett Barrett |
| October 1888-Dec 1888 | Herbert Robert Arkwright/Leamington Brewery |

| | |
|---|---|
| December 1888-Feb 1889 | Charles Robert Wells *(Of Oxford)* |
| February 1889-95 | Frank R. Mills |
| 1895-Nov 1898 | Mrs. Susannah Meads Mills |
| November 1898-1900 | Frederick Alderman |
| 1900-Aug 1902 | Joseph Freeman |
| August 1902-Aug 1910 | William Henry Clements |
| August 1910-Oct 1911 | William Mann |
| October 1911-13 | Lewis Hickman |
| 1913-Apr 1924 | Robert William Jeffery *(Died April 1924, aged 64)* |
| April 1924-Mar 1926 | Mrs. Fanny Jeffery *(On the death of Robert)* |
| March 1926-Apr 1930 | Thomas Andrews *(On the death of Mrs. Jeffery, aged 65)* |
| April 1930-Sept 1940 | John Leonard Parkes |
| September 1940-Jan 1946 | Donald Leslie Stewart Dewar |
| January 1946-Nov 1958 | Reginald Sidney Ward |
| November 1958-Jul 1959 | George Frederick Heritage |
| July 1959-Sep 1959 | Frederick Timms |
| September 1959-Jul 1960 | Albert James Insley |
| July 1960-Jan 1961 | Joseph Henry Barnsley |
| January 1961-Apr 1962 | Raymond William Gardner |
| April 1962-Apr 1963 | Ralph James Shaw |
| April 1963-Jan 1964 | Raymond Jeffery Collins |
| January 1964-Jun 1968 | Laura Ena Thomas |
| 28th June 1968 | Closed for business |

*It is worth pointing out that licensee Robert Jeffery, who died aged 64 years of age in April 1924, was connected with the musical life of the town for many years. He was in the Theatre Royal Orchestra and played on the opening night in 1882. In 1881 he toured the continent with George Sanger's circus as a trombone player. At the age of 13 years he joined the Warwickshire Yeomanry and had the reputation of being the youngest cavalryman in the British Yeomanry. Some time later he joined the 2nd Battalion of the Royal Warwickshire Militia. Mr. Jeffery was secretary of the local Licensed Victuallers Association from 1908 to 1913. For over 40 years Mr. Jeffery was a prominent member of the R.A.O.B [Buffs] and held the degree of Knight of the Order of Merit. For many years he had also been a brother of the Royal Spa Lodge, No. 530 of the Ancient Order of Druids.*

**Golden Cup** – 10 Tavistock Street
See Gold Cup for details.

**Golden Lion** – 91/93 Regent Street
The address of these premises was originally Cross Street [New Town] which was laid out circa 1808-1814; circa 1827 it was renamed Regent Street in honour of the Prince Regent who had visited Leamington in September 1819 [as was the Regent Hotel]. The Golden Lion was one of the first buildings in the new town when it opened in 1810. One source

tells us that, "The first stones of the new town were laid on 20th September 1808 and bell ringing could be heard" however, in Random Papers by the Leamington Society it says, "George Stanley, mason, of Warwick, laid the first brick of the first house erected at New Leamington on 8th October, 1808." On 29th June 1812 the Golden Lion was offered for sale by auction at the George Inn, Warwick, by Messrs J. & R. Loveday, Auctioneers. On 15th April 1831, a new omnibus called the Paul Pry commenced running at 8.45am each day from the Golden Lion, then on to the Green Dragon Inn, Warwick, passing through Kenilworth and on to the Red Lion Inn, Hertford Street, Coventry. It returned in the afternoon arriving in Leamington at 6.00pm.

In 1868, the Golden Lion was a freehold property consisting on the ground floor of a large entrance hall, a commercial room, smoke room, large bar, tap room, larder and kitchen; the upper floors contained a sitting room, a large club or ballroom [34 ft x 17 ft 6 in] and five bedrooms. In the basement was a partly arched cellar capable of storing 3,000 gallons of ale and outside, at the rear,

*Photo of the Golden Lion courtesy of Sheila McCarthy.*

was a brew house, a yard, stabling for seven horses [with a loft over] and a coach-house, with a frontage to Satchwell Street, then used as a butcher's shop by a Mr. White. The Golden Lion was one of a tied-estate of 35 pubs owned by the Leamington Brewery when it was purchased by Lucas, Blackwell and Arkwright in 1885 [later to become Lucas and Co. Ltd]; it would become an Ansells pub following their 1928 acquisition of the Leamington Brewery and its closure in 1934. In January 1897 Charles Baker successfully applied to the local licensing justices to take in the premises next door, which were formerly a milliner's shop but also part of the pub. There were three entrances into the pub, all of them on Regent Street; the lounge to the right, the bar to the left and the outdoor in the middle.

The Golden Lion closed in 1988 and that same year Ansells Properties Ltd sought planning permission for "the use of a public house as a bank, demolition of internal walls and the erection of a replacement shop front". In 2013 the premises are a branch of the Royal Bank of Scotland but it is heart-warming to see that the RBS values the building's heritage, for inside there is a framed print of the Golden Lion pub sign with a notice underneath which reads: "This building was one of the first to be built north of the river Leam as part of the 'new' town in 1810. The site, previously part of a farmland estate belonging to Mr. B.

*Photo of the Golden Lion sign, courtesy of Leamington Art Gallery & Museum [Warwick District Council]. The pub sign was painted by Len Shurvinton who worked for Wallsgrove Brothers, painters and decorators. They designed and painted heraldic signs as well as pub signs. Len, who is now in his 80s and lives in Whitnash, remembers painting signs for the Golden Lion, the Gold Cup, the Cottage Tavern, Queens Arms, the Stoneleigh Arms and the Somerville Arms. He says that Frank Wallsgrove used to make the designs and then provided them with a template to work from [The Golden Lion sign depicted a lion walking with right forepaw raised and all other paws on the ground.]*

B. Greathead of Guy's Cliffe, Warwick, measured 1,440 square yards and was sold for the sum of £360 to Mr. William Pratt, a local joiner and the Warwick banker Mr. John Russell. It was built as the first 'common public house' in this part of the town, the first landlord being a Mr. Miles, and it continued to be used as a public house, with its original name the Golden Lion, until 1989, a total of 179 years." [It closed in 1988 – Ed]

| | |
|---|---|
| 1810-14 | James Miles |
| 1815 | Robert Parry |
| 1822-23 | R. Whitehead |
| 1823-25 | James Powell |
| 1825-26 | Benjamin Ward |
| 1826-27 | Benjamin Collins |
| 1827-42 | John Smith |
| 1845-46 | P. Foxwell |
| 1847-48 | Charles Price |
| 1848-Jan 1854 | Thomas Rich |
| January 1854 | Edmund Williams |
| | *(Assumed name, correct name Arthur Walker)* |
| February 1855 | George Dakin |
| 1856-July 1859 | Elias Wilcox |
| July 1859-68 | Charles Price |
| 1868-Aug 1869 | G. T. Baseley |
| August 1869-Jan 1870 | Thomas Henry Wyatt *(of Banbury)* |
| January 1870-80 | Henry Keene |
| 1880-May 1895 | Henry Goode |
| May 1895-Mar 1900 | Charles Baker *(Councillor)* |
| March 1900-Oct 1900 | George Patterson *(Of Nuneaton)* |

| | |
|---|---|
| October 1900-Jul 1902 | James Thomas Gardner |
| July 1902-Dec 1902 | James Stone |
| December 1902-Aug 1906 | William Charles Bailey *(Of Gloucester)* |
| August 1906-Jul 1908 | William John Jenkinson |
| July 1908-Nov 1910 | Albert Ernest Lennon *(Or Seymour)* |
| November 1911-Jul 1913 | Cornelius Paul |
| July 1913-Aug 1915 | Robert C. Clay |
| August 1915-Jan 1917 | Mrs. S. A. Clay *(On the death of Robert)* |
| January 1917-Oct 1921 | Ralph Bell |
| October 1921-Oct 1922 | W. J. Power *(Previously, Councillor Power was a member of Warwick Town Council for 30 years)* |
| October 1922-28 | James Levi Duncan |
| 1928-May 1933 | John Henry Kerslake |
| May 1933-34 | Edward J. Price and his wife Gladys |
| 1936-37 | F. Blackham |
| 1938-39 | C. T. Rate |
| 1940 | Reginald S. Ward |
| 1940-Dec 1940 | Walter Maurice Hancock |
| December 1940-Jan 1944 | Arthur Barton |
| January 1944-Oct 1947 | Mrs. Nellie Beatrice Barton |
| October 1947-Mar 1961 | Reginald Thomas Sinnett |
| March 1961-Jun 1963 | Leonard Albert Care |
| June 1963-Aug 1964 | Thomas Edward Ford |
| August 1964-Aug 1966 | James Campbell McDonnell |
| August 1966-Dec 1967 | John James Garrigan |
| December 1967-Jun 1969 | Gerald McGann |
| June 1969-Jun 1970 | Gilbert Edward Robottom |
| June 1970-Mar 1972 | Violet 'Viv' Masters |
| March 1972 | Leslie George Simmonds |
| August 1978-82 | William 'Bill' and Sheila McCarthy *(And 'ace barman' Ron Deeming)* |
| ≤1984-1988 | Edmund 'Eddie' Francocci and his wife Mary |
| 1988 | Closed for business |

*The Leamington Spa Courier dated 6th June 1829 carried the following: J. Smith, Golden Lion Inn, Regent Street, returns sincere thanks to his friends, and the visitors and inhabitants of Leamington, and its vicinity, for the very liberal support he has already received, and begs leave to inform them that they may rely upon being supplied with genuine home-brewed ales, table beer, prime porters, cider, &c. in any quantity in barrels, and on the most moderate terms. N.B. Well-aired beds &c. Dinners served up at the shortest notice. Good stabling and coach-house.*

The Leamington Spa Courier dated 26th January 1850 published the following notice: **Burton, East India pale ale & strong ales** - T. Rich, Golden Lion Commercial Inn begs respectfully to return thanks for all past favours, and to inform the nobility, gentry, hotel and inn-keepers, and the public generally, that he is appointed sole agent to Messrs Meakin and Co. for the sale of their celebrated strong and East India pale ales, which may be had [if preferred] direct from the brewery at Burton-on-Trent, at prices and quality not to be surpassed by any other firm in the kingdom.

*At the annual licensing session in 1854, there was a good deal of discussion about the licence for the Golden Lion. It seems that there was a building accessed from Satchwell Street that was connected to the Golden Lion but "not adjoining or attached to the building for which the licence had been issued". The superintendant of police said that his attention had been called to this house, particularly 'Uncle Tom's Cabin' [the name locals gave to the building], which was without exception, the most disorderly house in the town. He said, "If there were a hell upon earth that was the place. It required more looking after than all the other seventy-two houses in the parish." At the end of February 1855 George Dakin applied for a new licence; it was granted on condition that the part of the pub called 'Uncle Tom's Cabin' was not opened.*

In 1856, the Golden Lion advertised the following with flyers printed by Brierly Printer, Eagle office, 2, Clemens Street: **Golden Lion Inn, Regent Street** – The public is respectfully informed that a ball will be held in the large room of the above inn on Monday next, 21st January, 1856. An efficient quadrille band is engaged – dancing to commence at eight o'clock in the evening – admission sixpence each – refreshments will be provided.

*In 1888 the Carpenters' and Joiners' Trade Association was based at the Golden Lion [secretary: Mr. W. Pratt] as was the Plasterers' Trade Association [secretary: Mr. A. W. Robbins of 6, Farley Street].*

The Leamington Spa Courier, dated 29th January 1904, reported that: On Thursday a horse and cab, the property of Mr. G. Pratt, was standing outside the Golden Lion Inn, Regent Street, when the horse got on to the path during the temporary absence of the driver. The animal fell down and in struggling to get up again broke one of the plate glass windows of the public house. Before he could get up another pane of glass was broken, the horse severely cutting itself around the neck and shoulders.

*The Leamington Courier dated 17th March 1961 reported that: Customers of the Golden Lion Inn, Regent Street, Leamington, toasted their host and hostess, Mr. and Mrs. Reginald T. Sinnett, who left on Monday to take over the Somerville Arms, Campion Terrace. Mr. Davis Ahern, chairman of the inn's 'B' Social Club, presented a tea-set to Mr. and Mrs. Sinnett on behalf of the all-Irish club. Mr. and Mrs. Sinnett came to the Golden Lion nearly 21 years ago with their parents after being bombed out of the Bull's Head Inn, Bishops Street, Coventry. Their mother, Mrs. Nellie Barton, who formerly held the licence, still helps to serve customers at the age of 74. They have two sons - the elder, 21 year old John, is a bank official in Lagos, West Africa.*

On Monday 28th November 1961 Leamington magistrates gave five pub landlords permission to open their off-licence premises from 8.30am, as permitted by the new Licensing Act; the change came into operation immediately. The applications were made by the Sun in Splendour, Tachbrook Road; Coach and Horses, Bedford Street; Golden Lion, Regent Street; Walnut Tree, Lillington; and the Wheatsheaf, Tachbrook Road.

*The conservation department at Warwick District Council describes the premises thus: A hotel, now bank, circa 1808-1813 with later alterations. Pinkish-brown brick with painted stucco façade and Welsh slate roof; Exterior: 3 storeys, 3 first-floor windows; End full-height pilasters; First floor has tall 1/1 sashes with margin-lights with lunettes with carved acanthus and anthemion decoration, with architrave of fluted pilasters with acanthus capitals and round-arch with acanthus and beading; Second floor has 1/1 sashes with margin-lights in tooled architraves; Console modillions support cornice; Ground floor: central entrance, double 10-panel door with overlight in pilastered doorcase with consoles and frieze supporting pediment; Continuous frieze and cornice, otherwise plate-glass shop windows; Stepped end stacks.*

**Grand Union Bar and Restaurant** – 66/68 Clemens Street
See Reindeer for details.

**Grapes Tavern** – 48 Clemens Street
This is the only information we have for this beer house. At first we considered a possible connection to the Apollo Vaults/Great Western Inn due to both premises having been numbered 48, Clemens Street. However, we subsequently concluded that the latter was renumbered from 43, Clemens Street, to number '48' sometime during the period 1857-62, therefore after the Grapes Tavern had closed.

1849-57                         John Roberts

**Great Western Hotel** – 8 High Street
This site, situated on the eastern corner of High Street and Wise Street, was originally occupied by the Albion Hotel. The building was completed in 1813 and initially used as a boarding house [Albion House]; in 1816 it was described as "a singular structure, built in a sort of Gothic style, rather more fanciful than tasteful". The 1829 church rate book names the occupier of Albion House as being Thomas Thompson and our earliest directory listing for the Albion Hotel is 1833, when Thompson is the licensee.

For the years spanning 1839 to 1860 we have no directory or licensing sessions' listings and can only draw the conclusion that it was unlicensed during that period. The 1860 church rate book shows the occupants as John Toone and George Carter and lists the property as a house and a shop. In 1861 an application for a licence for the Albion 'Inn' was refused, but at the 1862 licensing sessions the Albion is again granted a licence. In 1869 the hotel comprised a bar [with a sitting room at the back] and a smoke room; the ground floor also included a kitchen, larder with a large bottle-rack, scullery, pantry, knife and shoe house, two water closets, a storeroom and capital cellarage. The first floor consisted of a private sitting room and bedroom, coffee room, two commercial rooms and a commercial smoke room, small conservatory, and water closet. On the second floor there were two sitting rooms, four bedrooms and two water closets, and seven bedrooms and three servants rooms on the third floor; gas and town water was laid on.

After taking over the business in November 1874, Thomas Tyler changed the name to the Great Western Hotel, the reason quite simply being that he was already the licensee of the Refreshment Rooms at the Great Western Railway Station. A music and singing licence

was granted on 27th July 1959. On Sunday 27th November 1966 a Traditional ['Trad'] Jazz Club was started by Pat Self; the club met weekly at 7.30pm, the cost was 3s.6d and the first band to appear was the Crescent City Stompers from Birmingham. In August 1967 a demolition team moved in and, once the site was cleared, work began immediately on the building of the Leamington Spa Social Club, which would relocate from across the road at 15-17 High Street [and be renamed from the Trades Hall and Social Club]. Needless to say, the licence for the Great Western Hotel was not renewed at the annual licensing sessions in February 1968.

| | |
|---|---|
| 1833-39 | Thomas Thompson *(Albion Hotel)* |
| 1862-71 | John Toone |
| 1871 | Sarah Watkins |
| 1872-Nov 1874 | John Toone |
| November 1874-Apr 1875 | Thomas Tyler *(Albion Hotel, then renamed the Great Western Hotel)* |
| April 1875-Jun 1875 | Mary Ann Tyler *(On the death of Thomas)* |
| June 1875-76 | Henry Umbers |
| 1878-Oct 1878 | James Watkins and Charles Wheeler |
| October 1878-Jan 1885 | Alfred Barnes *(Previously house steward to the Earl of Glasgow, at Cupar)* |
| January 1885-Nov 1888 | Edward Knibbs |
| November 1888-Jul 1897 | Philip Owen |

| | |
|---|---|
| July 1897-Apr 1898 | Robert Jones *(Of Liverpool)* |
| April 1898-Feb 1899 | James Smith |
| February 1899-Feb 1901 | George William Spraggett |
| February 1901-Jan 1903 | Joseph Kelly |
| January 1903-May 1903 | James Smith |
| April 1903-May 1905 | Frederick Pinder |
| May 1905-Sep 1908 | Herbert Holloway *(Of Bromsgrove)* |
| September 1908-Oct 1908 | Henry Simpson Griffiths |
| | *(On the death of Herbert Holloway)* |
| October 1908-Feb 1910 | Harry Howard Knight |
| February 1910-Mar 1910 | Alfred Arthur Pickering *(Licence not confirmed)* |
| March 1910-Mar 1911 | Edmund Lilley |
| March 1911-Sep 1913 | John Henry Hinsley Astbury |
| September 1913-Sep 1916 | Henry 'Harry' Dale *(Previously at Railway Inn, Rugby)* |
| September 1916-1917 | W. T. Mathieson *(Transferred from Mrs. Emily Dale)* |
| 1919-21 | Charles Henry Gurley |
| 1921-29 | Arthur Benjamin Murcott |
| 1929-Oct 1931 | William Roberts |
| October 1931-37 | William Alfred Henry Astill and his wife Rose |
| | *(Went on to the Bedford Inn, June 1940-March 1954;* |
| | *William died 2nd July 1968 & Rose died 30th August 1997)* |
| 1937-40 | Sidney John Brodie |
| 1940-Jun 1941 | Mrs. Doris Lilian Allen |
| June 1941-Nov 1950 | Albert Frank Robinson |
| November 1950-Sep 1951 | Norman Grosvenor Harcourt |
| September 1951-Oct 1955 | Robert William Bloor *(Transferred from Madge* |
| | *Harcourt on the death of Norman)* |
| October 1955-Nov 1956 | Harry Llewellyn Jackson |
| November 1956-Feb 1958 | John James Beckley |
| February 1958-Jul 1959 | William Frederick Edwards |
| July 1959-Feb 1968 | Sidney George Cornwall |
| February 1968 | Licence not renewed |

*The Leamington Spa Courier dated 18th April 1913 carried the reminiscences of a local man:*
*"About half a century ago it was kept by a Miss Watkins, a grand daughter of the late Mr. John*
*Toone, one of the pioneer builders of the town. Mr. Toone, whom I remember as an occasional*
*visitor to the Albion Hotel, was a finely built man, over six feet high and well proportioned.*
*His daughter, Mrs. Watkins was an equally finely built woman, not quite as tall as her father,*
*but also well proportioned. When I was a boy I used to go to the Albion on business and in*
*this connection I became a favourite with Miss Watkins, so that one day she insisted upon my*
*going to have my portrait taken by a photographer. I think the Daguerreotype process was*
*then in vogue, prior to the carte-de-visite coming into popular favour. I took the portrait to*
*Miss Watkins and it hung in her private sitting room at the Albion until after I was married,*

*when she gave it back to me, jocularly remarking that as I had given my heart to another lady she felt that she had no right to have possession of the portrait any longer. The Albion Hotel was first known as Albion House and was described when first built as a singular structure, built in a sort of mock Gothic, rather more fanciful than tasteful."*

Tom Lewin remembers that around 1966 he drank in the Great Western Hotel when it had disco music playing and that the bar was always known by locals as the 'long pull'. Legend has it that the name came from the bar, which was the longest in Leamington.

**Great Western Inn** – 13 Clemens Street
In the spring of 1812, James Bisset [1760-1832] arrived in Leamington from Birmingham and took over part of the Apollo Rooms in Clemens Street [large rooms which had been built for assemblies] and opened them as a library, select news-room and picture gallery. Bisset said at the time, "There was not a house in Clemens Street beyond my gallery, which was the only building on the east side of the street," and, "there is a billiard room immediately under the picture gallery and leading from the billiard room the public can proceed to the 'show apartments' of the millinery goddess and the other premises of Mr. Palmer, the draper." In addition to the billiard room on the ground floor there was a wine vaults, both fronting Clemens Street. In 1818, James Bisset moved out of the Apollo Rooms and they, along with the wine vaults, were taken over by Mr. W. G. Parry, a printer. The first listing we have [sourced from the licensed victuallers records] is in 1825 when John Brockman is named as victualler at the Apollo, as he is in 1826.

By 1828 the wine vaults had been taken over by Jonathan Oldfield and by 1833 Apollo Vaults is listed as a wine and spirit merchants, and also a beer house. The business addition of a beer house at this time is not surprising given how easy it was to obtain a [excise] beer on-licence following the 1830 Beer House Act. However, so as not to compromise the existing wine and spirits licence there must have been separation between the two business interests. The Leamington Spa Courier dated Saturday 19th February 1848 reported the opening of the Leamington Temperance Hall: "On Monday last the friends of Temperance met in their new hall, formerly called the Apollo Rooms, Clemens Street, to celebrate its dedication to the temperance cause. About 200 persons sat down to tea on the occasion and a happier company cannot be imagined." An 1853 auction notice described the Apollo Rooms as a leasehold property, occupied by T. Naul, consisting of three large and spacious rooms on the ground floor [used for the Boys National School-room] and, in the basement, a wine and spirits vaults with extensive cellars. The site dimensions comprised a frontage to Clemens Street of 43 ft 6 in, at the rear 51 ft 6 in, a depth of 70 ft at the northern end and at the southern end 63 ft 4 in; the lease had 56 years to run on 21st June 1853.

The Apollo Rooms took up three sites that many will know as the Great Western, Union Walk and Frettons, so it was quite a building. The name of the licensed premises was changed to the Great Western in 1860 and the 1870 church rate books show the inclusion of Union Walk. On Monday 19th May 1862, Thomas Naul opened a bowling green at the rear of the premises, for which the seasonal subscription was 10s.6d. On 11th February 1863 all of the pub's fixtures and fittings, household furniture and stock-in-trade were sold by auction "under a distress for rent warrant" and there was a change of tenant. The pub was owned by the Burton Brewery Co. Ltd and later Ind Coope and Co. Ltd, Burton-on-Trent [the brewery underwent a number of name changes]; in the early days horse drawn brewer's drays would use Union Walk to access the cellars. On 25th February 1863 the leasehold ground rent was sold by auction at the Crown Hotel, having been described in the Leamington Gazette as: "A well secured improved leasehold property on which formerly stood the Apollo Rooms, now the Great Western Inn, and a shop in the occupation of Mr. John Mash, shoemaker. The whole of the property, which produces a gross rental of £74 per annum, is held under a lease for the term of 99 years, from the 24th June 1810, at the ground rent of £8.12s.3d per annum."

On Monday 1st March 1920 the pub was one of a number 'referred for extinction by compensation' by the local licensing justices as part of a weeding out process, or "thinning the inns" as it was reported, but it would survive until the 1990s. After a brief closure in 1989, due to the collapse of Classic Inns, it re-opened as an Ansells pub in 1990 with John Skett as licensee. After a short lived venture the pub closed again, and in August 1993 the

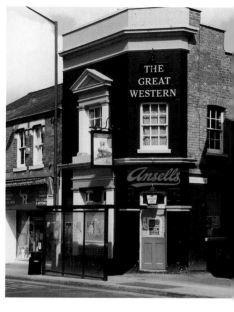

*The Great Western courtesy of Nick Wilkins.*

premises were on the market for £79,950 plus VAT. The advert described it as a two storey period property, suitable for a variety of uses including a 'take-away' or restaurant; the upstairs accommodation consisted of a lounge, kitchen, three bedrooms and a bathroom. However, there was a limiting clause that stated that the property could not be used as a public house or a wine bar. Following its sale, and after a three year delay, the building was converted into a Chinese take-away called The Jumbo. It opened on the 8th August 1996 and remains so in 2013.

**Footnote:** The Royal Leamington Spa Building Conservation Trust have affixed a plaque to, what they believe to be, the original Apollo Rooms in recognition of the restoration carried out in 2001-02. The building they have nominated is on the west side of Clemens Street [currently number '6'], not the east side as described by early owner James Bisset.

| | |
|---|---|
| 1816 | J. Broomhall *(Vaults, Apollo Rooms)* |
| 1825-26 | John Brockman *(Apollo)* |
| 1828 | W. Naul *(Apollo Vaults)* |
| 1828-37 | Jonathan Oldfield |
| 1841-42 | Robert J. Tilsley |
| 1848-49 | George Adams *(Apollo Shades)* |
| 1850 | John Farr *(Apollo Vaults)* |
| 1850-54 | Thomas Naul |

| | |
|---|---|
| 1854-Mar 1857 | William Dickinson |
| March 1857-Apr 1858 | Henry Sanderson |
| April 1858-April 1860 | Walter Martin |
| April 1860 | Thomas Naul *(Transfer of Apollo Vaults)* |
| 1860-Feb 1863 | Thomas Naul *(Renamed the Great Western)* |
| February 1863-Jan 1864 | Samuel Taylor *(Of Coventry)* |
| January 1864 | Daniel Field |
| 1864-Sep 1864 | Alfred Field |
| September 1864-69 | James Carvell |
| 1869-Apr 1872 | John Doughty |
| April 1872-Sep 1874 | Thomas Palmer |
| September 1874-Nov 1874 | John William Cooper |
| November 1874-Oct 1893 | William Watts |
| October 1893-1924 | William Dutton |
| 1924-Oct 1936 | Joseph Edward Alderman |
| October 1936-Oct 1956 | Leonard Frank Samuel Beaver |
| October 1956-Oct 1965 | John Norman Beaver *(On the death of Leonard)* |
| October 1965-May 1966 | George Matthew Moorhouse |
| May 1966-Jan 1972 | Francis Ramsey |
| January 1972-≥1977 | Kenneth Copeland |
| Mid 1980s | James Bernard Meade |
| Aug 1985-1986 | Michael 'Mick' Riches and his wife Evelyn 'Ev' |
| 1986-87 | George Patrick Alexander O'Reilly |
| ≤1989-1990 | David Twitty and his wife Sylvia |
| 1990-1993 | John Skett *(Also licensee of the Railway Inn)* |

**Great Western Railway Station Refreshment Rooms** – G. W. R. Railway Station
Firstly, we acknowledge that it wasn't a pub by any stretch of the imagination but it did hold a publican's full on-licence. It was owned by the Great Western Railway Company before being transferred to the British Transport Commission, London SW1. In July 1861 Mr. Sherwood, on behalf of G.W.R. Co, applied to the local licensing justices to grant a licence before the annual licensing session "as the rooms were useless without it, and the public were suffering". Although the magistrate refused the initial application, the licence was granted at the licensing session in August 1861 and in August 1879 it was amended from a six day to a seven day licence.

| | |
|---|---|
| July 1861 | Licence request declined |
| August 1861-Nov 1863 | Elizabeth Tyler |
| November 1863-Apr 1875 | Thomas Tyler |
| April 1875-Oct 1878 | Mary Ann Tyler *(On the death of Thomas)* |
| October 1878-May 1880 | George Parsons |
| May 1880-Jul 1891 | Thomas Hards Wesley and George Henry Browning |
| July 1891-May 1902 | George Henry Browning *(Partnership dissolved)* |

| | |
|---|---|
| May 1902 | Stanley Dunbar Buott |
| 1912 | George James Walker |
| June 1936-Dec 1947 | Robert Alfred Percy Setterfield |
| December 1947-Jun 1949 | William Paterson Keith |
| June 1949-Apr 1951 | William Henry Johnson |
| April 1951-Dec 1965 | Thomas Henry Baker |
| December 1965-Dec 1968 | Paul John Basil Long |
| December 1968-Jun 1971 | Eric Kenyon Brunt |
| June 1971 | George William Thompson |

**Green Dragon** – Leamington

The only reference we have for the Green Dragon is a record from the July 1835 licensing sessions when the local justices granted the transfer of a licence from John Smith to John Lowe Overton. We have no directory information, or address, for this establishment and we have not found any record of a J. L. Overton at any other Leamington pub. Although we do have a record of a John Smith at that time [a fairly common name] he is listed as the landlord at the Golden Lion, period 1827-42. As the licensing justices also dealt with Warwick and Kenilworth transfers, it is possible that the court reporting of proceedings was incorrectly referring to the Green Dragon in Market Place, Warwick [known in 2013 as the Tilted Wig].

**Green Man** – Grove Place / 114 Tachbrook Street

The first directory listing we have for the Green Man is in 1833 when its address was Grove Place, the location of the 'original' pub. In March 1925, a Mr. Field submitted plans to the local magistrates for the rebuilding of the Green Man on an adjacent site and asked for an indication that they would not be opposed at the next licensing session; the magistrates approved the proposal. On Tuesday 1st February 1927 Frederick Hopkins applied for, and was granted, an order authorising the removal of the licence from the premises in Grove Place to "a certain house and premises to be built at the corner of Eagle Street and Lower Tachbrook Street, and to be named the Green Man Inn". It was anticipated that the new pub would take six months to build and be open in August 1927 [the original Green Man was demolished around the same time]. Fred Hopkins was landlord at both the Grove Place and Tachbrook Street premises, his tenure extending from 1905 until 1934.

The new pub was referred to as the New Green Man by many locals [and in some directories] and was still listed as such in 1940. A lounge was added in the 1960s, most likely following the approval of plans

*The Green Man taken on 6th August 2010 © Allan Jennings.*

for structural changes on 4th January 1960 which also included provision for an off-sales shop and new lavatories; the extended licence for off-sales was granted on 1st January 1962. Once a Flowers pub, it was subsequently owned by Whitbread until 1991 when it was sold to the Bedford brewery, Charles Wells. In 1996 it also incorporated a Peking and Cantonese Restaurant which was open at lunch-time from 12.00pm until 2.00pm and in the evenings from 5.30pm until midnight.

A 'closing party' was held at the Green Man on Saturday 18th August 2012 and the pub was closed for business on Sunday 19th August 2012. On 24th September 2012, application was made to Warwick District Council for planning permission: "Proposed demolition of existing public house and habitable accommodation and the erection of five terraced houses and ancillary facilities." Following the planning application, it was thought that the Green Man would

*The Green Man in the late seventies courtesy of Tom Lewin. The pub had two distinct rooms with the bar at the front and a separate lounge at the rear. The photo depicts three locals from Waverley Road, from right to left, Mrs. Eileen Lewin, Mrs. Betty Ellis and Mrs. Tibbs. In the rear was the main feature, a tropical fish tank complete with fish.*

never re-open as a pub, however it did so on 22nd December 2012 [as a free house] under the ownership of Babs Kandola, Kul Dhesi and Kam Dhesi; Lynn Unitt remains as licensee and in-house tenant. The Green Man remains open in December 2013, albeit with [self imposed] reduced opening hours.

| | |
|---|---|
| 1833-35 | Mary Baylis *(Grove Place)* |
| 1838-39 | William Baylis |
| 1845-70 | John Edmonds |
| 1871-82 | Mrs. Ann Edmonds |
| 1882-Oct 1888 | Benjamin Jasper |
| October 1888-Jan 1889 | Sydney Herbert Jones *(Of Banbury)* |
| January 1889-1905 | Arthur Essex |
| 1905-Nov 1905 | Emma Essex *(Administratrix of the late Arthur Essex)* |
| November 1905-Jan 1934 | Frederick William Hopkins |
| January 1934-Sep 1942 | Thomas Howard Charman |
| September 1942-Dec 1946 | Frances Mildred Charman |
| December 1946-May 1956 | Thomas Howard Charman |
| May 1956-Oct 1965 | James Henry Fine |
| October 1965-Dec 1967 | John Dudley Chaffey |

| | |
|---|---|
| December 1967-1978/79 | Francis 'Frank' Martin Drinkwater-Lunn |
| 1980-81 | Michael Kerry Harrison |
| 1984-1991 | Malcolm and Megan Heydon |
| 1995 | Pat and Pam King (*Previously stewards at Flavel's Sports and Social Club*) |
| Circa 1995-96 | Andrew Richard and Christine Crosby |
| 1997 | James and Tracey Fitzpatrick |
| 2004 | Christopher Rudge |
| May 2006-19th Aug 2012 | Lynn Unitt |
| 19th August 2012 | Closed for business |
| 22nd December 2012 → | Lynn Unitt |

*Francis [Frank] Drinkwater-Lunn took over the pub in 1967 along with his wife Sally. They had two daughters, June and Angela. Prior to taking over the Green Man they were managers at Newlands Inn in Cheltenham. Afterwards they went on to manage the Double Barrel pub in Cheltenham. Daughter Angela currently runs a bed and breakfast at Dolgoch Farm in mid-Wales. [Source of info: Lynn Unitt]*

In 1978 the Morning News invited readers' letters about the origins of the Green Man, following a request from a lady in New York for information on her grandfather, James Glenn. Bill Keight, secretary of the local Licensed Victuallers Association, was the first to write saying that he had records going back to 1877; "those were the days when 1/5th gill of whisky was seven old pence."

*Clare Hogg [née Ingram] followed this up by saying, "I have every reason to remember the pub, as I still bear a scar which I knew would be permanent. Firstly, it was run by Mr. Fred Hopkins who remained there [Grove Place] until it was declared not suitable due to unsatisfactory toilet facilities. He went temporarily to the Green Man, Tachbrook Street and then he went as manager to the bar at the Crown Hotel, Leamington Spa."*

*"During the 1914-18 war my late father was home on leave [I was about 8 years old] when I went with my eldest sister to put some washing through the mangle. How well I remember Mrs. Hopkins warning me not to go near the mangle. I decided to help my sister and finished up with my fingers in the mangle, the middle finger of my left hand getting the worst of it. This during the dinner hour, my dad took me to the Warneford hospital, and I had a handkerchief over my hand with Union Jacks in each corner. Our family were living at 14, Grove Place. At the rear of the pub they had a long room built which was used by one of the local football teams [I think it was St. John's] who used it as a dressing room. The team played on the recreation ground by Flavels."*

J. H. Fine of Stalmine, near Blackburn also responded. "Having been the manager of the 'New' Green Man for 10 years I felt that I might be able to supply some information on the 'Old' Green Man. "I feel certain that Mrs. Fiddes is referring to the Green Man which did the wonderful business of dispensing the beverage known as 'ale or beer', and was situated at the end of Scotland Place near to Shrubland Street. The premises were certainly changed or torn down to build houses, but that happened long before World War II." [Note: This site information is incorrect – Ed]

"The gentleman who occupied the old Green Man was a Mr. Hopkins who was later the first tenant of the new Green Man in Tachbrook Street. I'm afraid I can't remember how long he was there, but he was followed by Mr. H. Charman who stayed there for 23 years as tenant for – of course – the famous Flowers Brewery. I followed Mr. Charman as manager for Flowers Brewery for a further 10 years until I left to go to the Antelope at Lighthorne."

*Mrs. E. A. Bowring and Mrs. E. A. Yardley of Charles Gardner Road wrote, "We are two Leamingtonians aged 83 years and we well remember the 'old' Green Man in Grove Place. It was situated in about the middle of the street and had steps up to the entrance. Fred Hopkins was the only tenant."*

The secretary of the local Licensed Victuallers Association wrote again in July 1978. He could not understand why he could not find James Glenn in records going back practically to Doomsday. He says that Mr. Glenn was landlord of the Green Man Inn – which was a converted house in Grove Place – around the turn of the century. He says that Mr. Glenn was never a member of the LVA but that he did attend a meeting in 1902 when restrictions on pub opening hours were first introduced. [Note: We have no directory information on Mr. Glenn however, he may be getting confused with either the Talbot Inn or the Holly Bush, both of which list a James Glenn – Ed]

*In November 1985, the Green Man was run by Malcolm Heydon and his wife Megan, and they had been there for about 18 months. This Whitbread pub was one of the busiest in town. They ran games teams and quizzes, had a football team, and were looking to have live entertainment. They refurbished the bar and proposed extending it to allow more space for the pool table as well as the live groups. Malcolm sold Flowers IPA and Poacher as well as mild, draught Guinness and two lagers. The juke-box had a good selection of fifties and sixties hits and sometimes Malcolm played his own stereo and encouraged people to sing along. He also persuaded people to play the bar's piano and, having been a drummer in a band for 10 years, was always ready to join in. [Morning News dated 22nd November 1985]*

The Observer of 4th May 1995 carried an article on the Green Man: If you thought things at the Green Man in Leamington couldn't get any better then why not pay it another

*Photo of the Green Man football team © Allan Jennings. They reached the Division 5 Cup Final and played Sporting Oak at the Windmill Ground, Tachbrook Road in March 1988. Unfortunately, they were beaten 2-0 after extra time.*

visit. The Tachbrook Street Pub reopens this weekend after a £70,000 refurbishment and it's better than ever. And husband and wife team Pam and Pat King who have run the pub for just over two years, promise their customers something a little different.

From Monday the Green Man will be serving a wide range of food, from simple bar snacks to traditional Sunday lunch, and all at reasonable prices. All dishes, with the exception of steak, cost under £5. Food will be served seven days a week, from 10.30am to 10.30pm, making the Green Man one of Leamington's top eating houses.

You will be able to start the day properly with a full breakfast served until 12 noon. Filled baguettes and jacket potatoes will be amongst the mouth watering snacks served from the bar. But those with more discerning tastes may prefer to try out the pub's newly built restaurant. Dishes ranging from traditional steak pies to more exotic Cajun chicken will be served along with a large vegetarian menu. A full children's menu will also be available offering such delights as turkey dinosaur and chips.

Weekends will be a busy time with a traditional roast dinner served all day Sunday. And for £3.95 for adults and £2.95 for children, for two courses, it's excellent value too. And to whet that appetite the Green Man will be offering a variety of beers including Charles Wells traditional ale, Guinness and Murphys as well as a range of other alcoholic and non-alcoholic drinks. So if it's breakfast, lunch or dinner you're after the Green Man will have it all. Isn't it time you tried it out?

*In September 2010, the local press reported that the pub would be included in CAMRA's 2011 Good Beer Guide. Lynn Unitt, landlady of the Green Man, said, "It's the first time the pub has won a listing and we're overjoyed by the news. We're a nice friendly pub with quiz nights, bingo, two pool teams, and ladies darts, but this is recognition for the way we keep our cask ales like the Charles Wells Bombardier."*

**Green Tailed Dragon** – 2 George Street
See Shakespeare Inn for details.

**Greyhound** – London Road, Leamington Priors [now High Street]
See Black Dog for details.

**Greyhound** – 17 Lansdowne Street
The first reference point we have for the Greyhound Inn is in November 1837 when the licence was transferred from Thomas Pratt to George Fathers; by 1897 the pub had a full on-licence. When in 1958 the council decided to redevelop the King Street and Queen Street area and demolish existing houses, it was announced that the Greyhound [corner of Lansdowne Street and Queen Street] would be spared. Councillor Lucas said in September 1958, "It was decided that while it may have no decorative features, it ought to be preserved – if only as a relic of the times and of its type."

The Greyhound closed during Christmas 1993 and reopened as the Cask and Bottle on 7th July 1994, following an extensive refurbishment carried out "in a traditional way" by Whitbread Pub Partnerships using builders P. Griffin and Sons of Coventry; it served six different real ales at any one time including a regularly changed guest beer. The Cask and

*Left: The Greyhound © Allan Jennings. Right: Photo of the Cask and Bottle taken on 27th July 2011 © Allan Jennings.*

Bottle closed in mid April 2013 and on 30th May the premises licence was transferred [from Mr. & Mrs. Reeve] to Enterprise Inns who, after major refurbishment, reopened the pub in September 2013.

**Greyhound Licensees**

| | |
|---|---|
| ≤1837 | Thomas Pratt |
| 1837-Feb 1859 | George Henry Fathers |
| February 1859-Jan 1883 | Mrs. Frances Fathers *(On the death of George)* |
| January 1883-Apr 1883 | George Henry Father Jnr |
| April 1883-Sep 1885 | Harry Read |
| September 1885-Jul 1886 | Henry Bartlett |
| July 1886-Mar 1889 | William Warren |
| March 1889-Jan 1890 | Alexander Wood |
| January 1890-Jan 1892 | Sarah Ann Wood *(On the death of Alexander)* |
| January 1892-Jun 1893 | Edward Pugh |
| June 1893-Apr 1895 | Edward Barnacle *(Of Stratford-upon-Avon)* |
| April 1895-Aug 1898 | Mrs. Nora Veronica Ball |
| August 1898-Jul 1914 | John Robert Ward |
| July 1914-Dec 1942 | Eric James Briggs |
| December 1942-Nov 1952 | Herbert Binns Ashworth |
| November 1952-Jul 1955 | Alfred Aitken |
| July 1955-Mar 1956 | William Edmund Quantrill |
| March 1956-Sep 1957 | Alfred James Toomes |
| Sept 1957-≥Aug 1988 | Derek Steven Judd and his wife Audrey |
| July 1992-1993 | Ian Harris |
| Christmas 1993 | Closed as the Greyhound |

**Cask and Bottle Licensees**

| | |
|---|---|
| 7th July 1994 | Opened as the Cask and Bottle |
| Circa 1994 | Neil Moffatt |
| 1994-1999 | Robert Muldowney and wife Mel |
| 23rd April 1999-Aug 2013 | Jane Anne and Alan Michael Reeve |
| | *(Previously at the Silver Jubilee)* |
| 29th August 2013 → | Benjamin Philpotts |

The Leamington Spa Courier dated 22nd October 1920 reported that: The annual supper in connection with the Greyhound Inn Air Gun Club took place on Thursday week, when about 30 members sat down. After the supper a 'free and easy' was indulged in. Mr. W. Shuff [chairman] was supported by Messrs S. Vernon and H. Smith and songs were sung by Messrs Shandley, Briggs, Newington, Jenkins, Gardner, Messinger and the Bros. Middleton. A recitation entitled 'An Enchanted Shirt' was ably rendered by Arthur Harris. Tom Standbridge [captain] said he hoped that this season the club would again have the pleasure of winning the cup and shield; they have already won them twice.

*The Morning News dated 13th June 1986 reported: This month the Greyhound Inn in Leamington's Kennedy Square celebrates its 150th anniversary. Bought from the builders by a wealthy Leamington property owner, Mrs. Annie Ball, in June, 1836, it retains a solid, early-Victorian atmosphere – but without the piggery which is detailed on an auction sheet of 1856. Towards the end of the 19th century the Greyhound was a Flowers' pub, later to be Whitbread owned.*

*Derek and Audrey Judd have been tenants of the Greyhound for almost 30 years. When they first moved in they vastly extended the place but have insisted on preserving its old-time*

*Below: This photo of the annual pub outing from the Greyhound in 1923 was sent in to the Leamington Spa Courier for their 19th September 1986 edition by 72 year old John Harris of Broadway, Cubbington. When the picture was taken, it was a highlight for the craftsmen and artisans who went on it. They had to squeeze into charabancs for the rattling journey to Goodwood, Newmarket or Epsom for the Derby. There was time for a modest flutter on their modest wages and a few local beers before they set off home. The outings were common to all pubs in Leamington at the time but went out of fashion around the time of World War II.*

*elegance. The lounge has full length deep red velvet curtains and a large ornately framed mirror over the fireplace while the bar is kept unfussy and has a bar billiards table and darts board. A concession to modern times is made with the television – used only for sport – and the fruit machine. But there is no music – and many customers are attracted in for that very reason.*

*Derek said: "One of the reasons I'm so fond of this place is that it attracts a huge variety of customers from managing directors to road sweepers and everyone gets on with one another." Drinks include Flowers Original, IPA and Best Bitter, Stella Artois and Heineken lager and draught Guinness and cider. The chilled wine is also popular – particularly during the summer. Combining the best of the past and present, the Greyhound Inn is certainly a find among men.*

### Grist Mill – Chesterton Drive, Sydenham

In April 1981, local councillors objected to plans submitted by the Wolverhampton and Dudley Breweries Ltd for a 'roadhouse style pub' on the corner of Sydenham Drive and Chesterton Drive. Councillor Byrd said that the land had been allocated for housing; Councillor Weekes said that it would be more appropriate on the ASDA side of the road and the district council duly refused planning permission. On 15th January 1982, the Leamington Spa Courier reported that, "the battle to put more beer on tap in Sydenham had been fought out the previous day in a public enquiry held at the Leamington Town Hall," this being the sequel to the district council's refusal to approve plans submitted by the brewery in 1981. Roger Hunt, estates manager for the brewery, said that the pub would provide lunchtime food and other facilities for nearby residents, workers at the industrial estate and shoppers at the ASDA superstore. The district council maintained the land should be used for housing and that a pub would be too noisy for local residents and cause traffic hazards. In February 1982, the Environment Secretary Michael Heseltine dismissed the appeal saying, "Highway objections are overriding". The inspector, Mr. R. Davies also pointed out that Sydenham Drive was an important feeder road and that access points to individual premises should only be made in exceptional circumstances. He said, "There would be an unacceptable interference to the free flow of traffic." However, he did add that the highway authority had no objection to a vehicular and pedestrian access on to Wilnecot Drive.

The pub was subsequently built on a different site to that originally proposed, it being further along Chesterton Drive and on the opposite side of the road. The Grist Mill, owned by the Wolverhampton and Dudley ['Banks'] Brewery was opened on 3rd April 1985 by Leamington mayor, Councillor Pat Robinson. It remains open under the same name in December 2013.

*A Photo of the Grist Mill taken on 30th December 2008 © Allan Jennings.*

| | |
|---|---|
| 3rd April 1985 | Opened for business |
| April 1985-Sep 1985 | Andrew and Tina Waddell |
| September 1985-May 1986 | Mark and Jacquie Wicks |
| | (*Went on to the Queen's Head*) |
| May 1986-88 | Barry and Anne Bridgett |
| | (*Previously at the Chair and Rocket*) |
| 2005 | Andrew James Hart |
| April 2006-Sep 2006 | James Silcock |
| September 2006-Nov 2010 | Mark and Sharon Roden |
| November 2010-Jul 2011 | James Edward Guiden |
| July 2011-Jul 2012 | Carla Rascheen |
| July 2012-Aug 2012 | Gugulethu Harwood |
| August 2012-Sep 2012 | Carolyn Anne Sneade |
| September 2012-Dec 2012 | Martin Cartwright |
| December 2012 → | Paul Matthews |

*The Grist Mill is a reminder of the areas rural past and is set on the site of the former Sydenham farm barn. Wherever you look there are reminders of bygone farming days with antique machinery strung up on the rafters and interesting memorabilia nestled into every available nook. The building itself is massive with a high, beamed ceiling rising above the open plan lounge bar. Seating is divided into small group gatherings with a raised area that can be hired out for private parties such as office celebrations or birthdays. [Leamington Morning News, 31st January 1986]*

The topping out ceremony for Banks' new pub, the Grist Mill was performed by the chairman and managing director of Banks' Brewery, Edwin Thompson. The architect for the project was Ray Barnett. The builders, contractors and joinery manufacturers were R. Bennett and Co. of Constitution Hill, Dudley. The contractor for the surfacing of the car park was F. G. Davis and Sons of Smestow Bridge, Wombourne, Wolverhampton. Ventilation services were provided by Ventilation Services of Kingswinford. Cellar finishings, timber treatments and damp proofing was provided by Permadry Ltd of Ferncote Drive, Four Oaks, Sutton Coldfield.

*The Coventry Evening Telegraph of 2nd April 1985 carried this advertisement: Banks' Brewery are proud to announce the opening of the Grist Mill Inn, their new public house in Chesterton Drive, Sydenham, Leamington Spa, on Wednesday, April 3, at 5.30pm.*

*For over 100 years Banks' have been perfecting the art of producing traditional draught beers to become a Black Country legend. Now, the flavour and strength of this popular local favourite will be cared for and presented by mine hosts Andrew and Tina Waddell, [aged 25 and 24]. There are ample car parking facilities, so no doubt the Grist Mill will be a popular gathering place for neighbour, traveller and shopper alike. Tina will be especially looking after the catering and serving home cooked lunches, just like mum's, so you can be sure of a hearty meal from Monday to Saturday between 12 noon and 2.00pm. Tina's summer barbeque specialities will be served in the tastefully landscaped sitting-out area, to the rear of the lounge.*

*Through a fine attention to detail, the experienced design team have created a lounge which is testament to traditional skilled craftsmanship, incorporating a subtle blend of modern creature comforts with homely surroundings, complemented by authentic antique and rustic fittings. This superbly presented single-room public house has been traditionally designed along farmhouse lines in order to create an instant atmosphere for the thirsty customer and no doubt, many an ASDA shopper will be grateful for an opportunity to enjoy a refreshing glass of Banks' in such comfortable surroundings.*

The Leamington Courier of 2nd September 1985 reported that the pub had received an extension to the opening hours. It was granted permission to open from 10.00am to midnight Monday to Thursday, from 10.00am to 1.00am on Friday and Saturday and from 11.00am to midnight on Sunday. There were conditions such as the closing of all doors and windows at 11.00pm, the closure of the pubs outdoor areas at 11.20pm, and that all music must not be intrusive to buildings next door. Councillors also stated that all doors and windows must be shut during the provision of entertainment. The Grist Mill's intention was only to use the extended hours for special occasions and for days of significant national interest. CCTV would also be installed.

*Barry and Anne Bridgett took over in May 1986. Barry said, "One of the first things I did was hang up a dart board – I was surprised there wasn't one already fastened to the wall. It has already led to a lot of interest." He also installed a juke-box and organised a disco for Wednesday evenings as he was trying to attract the younger generation. [Morning News 18th July 1986]*

Barry and Anne were still there is 1988 and had introduced traditional pub games such as pool, darts and dominoes. They even had their own football team. The Wednesday disco had become the oldies disco with music from the 1960s and 70s. Obviously, not trying to attract the youngsters anymore!

*In July 2011, following a refurbishment, the Grist Mill was taken over by former Beverley Hills executive chef Carla Rascheen. Fifty-five year old Carla said she said she was proud of her American roots and was going to incorporate flavours from the United States into her meals. As well as traditional English pub meals, there will also be dishes that are popular in the states, such as 'Chicken George'. She said, "We want to appeal to the locals but we think we can also be a 'destination pub' to which people want to travel."*

**G's Bar** – 27 Augusta Place
See Hintons for details.

**Guards Inn** – 45 High Street
High Street, laid out circa 1810-13, was first known as Warwick Row and formed part of the High Road from Warwick to London. Originally known as the Butchers Arms from 1838-57, the conservation department at the Warwickshire District Council believe that it was "probably a former shop and house". In September 1856 an auction was held by John Staite at the Butchers Arms to sell off the household furniture, fixtures and fittings, stock-in-trade, and the brewery equipment and utensils; the new landlord would be John Cox who renamed the pub the Guards Inn in 1857. In 1881 it was described as having a frontage of 31 ft 6 in to High Street with large cellars and brewhouse, stand-up bar and smoke room in front, large club room, seven bedrooms, water closet, two sitting rooms, kitchen, pantry, yard and out-houses; it was also connected to town water and gas.

*Above left: Photo of the Guards Inn courtesy of Nick Wilkins. Above middle: The Pig and Fiddle taken on 25th November 2008 © Allan Jennings. Above right: The Queen Victoria taken on 19th June 2011 © Allan Jennings.*

Circa 1994, the Guards Inn was renamed the Pig and Fiddle and we have been told that the repainted sign was previously the one that hung outside the George Hotel. The Pig and Fiddle closed for business on 11th August 2010.

By June 2011, work was underway refurbishing the premises and, after painting the exterior a vivid red, it reopened as the Queen Victoria on Friday 24th June; we understand that this time the frame of the Pig and Fiddle sign was repainted and a transfer affixed – altogether, a fine example of recycling. Following a dispute with Warwick District Council over the exterior paint colour, non compliant exterior lighting, noise and a possible fine of £20,000, the Queen Victoria was closed by Michael Drake on 15th July 2012. Shortly afterwards, Enterprise Inns sold the business to Birmingham company Get The Beers In Line Ltd which was set up by Hayley and Kevin Smith; they reopened on Thursday 9th August 2012. The Queen Victoria closed suddenly on Wednesday 27th February, 2013 but reopened with a new landlord over the weekend of 20th-21st April 2013. It would close and reopen yet again during August/September and remains open in December 2013.

| | |
|---|---|
| 1838-39 | John Baker |
| 1841-48 | John William Butler |
| 1849-54 | Margaret Baker |
| 1854 | William Bull |
| June 1855-Sep 1856 | George Herbert *(Butcher's Arms)* |
| September 1856-Nov 1861 | John Cox *(Butchers Arms then renamed the Guards Inn)* |
| November 1861-Jul 1862 | James Rose |
| July 1862-Oct 1863 | John Cox |

| | |
|---|---|
| October 1863-Jul 1864 | Margaret Baker |
| July 1864-66 | Thomas Mason |
| 1870-74 | James Hampson |
| 1874-Mar 1893 | Frederick Alderman |
| March 1893-Mar 1903 | Francis 'Frank' Charles Alderman |
| March 1903-Jun 1913 | Frederick Alderman |
| June 1913-Jul 1913 | Mr. Duncombe *(Executor of Frederick)* |
| July 1913-Sep 1931 | Frederick Alderman Jnr *(Son of Frederick – died 24th September 1931, aged 61)* |
| September 1931-Nov 1935 | Mrs. Sophia Alderman |
| November 1935-Jan 1956 | Sam Kightley *(Died 29th November 1955, aged 58)* |
| January 1956-Apr 1958 | Grace Elizabeth Kightley *(On the death of Sam – Grace died on 29th February 1984, aged 85)* |
| April 1958-Apr 1959 | Frederick Field |
| April 1959-Sep 1959 | Kenneth Leslie Stevens |
| September 1959-Jul 1960 | Hugh Llewellyn Parry |
| July 1960-Jan 1963 | Oswald Fleming |
| January 1963-Aug 1964 | William Henry Hodgekins |
| August 1964-Oct 1971 | Edward Alfred May |
| October 1971-Apr 1973 | William John Poole |
| April 1973-Nov 1973 | Thomas William Hayes |
| November 1973-May 1975 | Harry Charles Lane |
| May 1975-≥1978 | William Bernard Chinnery and Doreen Chinnery *(Of Redditch)* |
| ≤1980-≥1982 | Dave and Pat Butler |
| 1983 | Redvers Wood |
| 17th June 1983 | Paul O'Keeffe *(Previously steward at the Irish Club for six years)* |
| 1986-≥1990 | Pat O'Keeffe and his wife Lily *(No relation to Paul)* |
| 1994 | Named Pig and Fiddle |
| 1999-2004 | Pat Minihane |
| 24th January 2006 | Kevin John Murphy |
| 29th October 2009 | Sheila Bridget Taylor |
| 11th August 2010 | Closed for business as the Pig and Fiddle |
| 24th June 2011 | Reopened as the Queen Victoria |
| 24th June 2011-15th Jul 2012 | Michael Drake |
| 15th July 2012 | Closed for business |
| 9th August 2012-27th Feb 2013 | Danny Doran and Jay Rooney *(Managers)* |
| 27th February 2013 | Closed for business |
| 19th April 2013-Aug 2013 | Lee Abraham |

*In 1983, Heart of England Newspapers reported: "Learning by computer should soon be easier for pupils at a Leamington infant school, thanks to the big hearted drinkers from two of the town's public houses. Regulars at both the Joiners Arms and the Guards Inn have raised just over £100 towards the computer fund at Shrubland Street First School and the money will be used to buy 'programs' for the recently installed computer. The computer was purchased mainly with funds donated by the Warwick District Council lottery."*

The conservation department at Warwick District Council describes the Guards Inn as: a public house, probably a former shop and house, circa early to mid 19th century with later additions and alterations; Reddish-brown brick in Flemish bond, with painted stucco to ground floor; front façade, with a Welsh slate roof and a cast-iron balcony; The ground floor has a pair of off-centre entrances, part glazed doors with over lights and margin-lights in fielded-panel reveals within a common door case with fluted architrave; To the left a casement window in plain reveals and with sills; To the right a shop front with central blocked part-glazed entrance between two casements, all with fielded panels beneath and with pilaster strips between, frieze and cornice; The first floor has a Gothic balcony and central part-glazed door.

**Guernsey Commercial Inn / Guernsey Temperance Hotel** – 29 Church Street
See the 2nd Bowling Green for details.

**Guy Tavern** – 1 Guy Street
The first directory listing we have is in 1833 and the last listing is in 1931 [although it had already closed by then]. In 1906 it was owned by the Hunt, Edmunds and Co. brewery of Banbury who had acquired the pub as part of its tied estate circa 1876. Although it was described as the smallest [public] house in the area, "it was convenient for local cab drivers and stable hands".

In June 1928, Hunt Edmunds and Co. Ltd [as owners] fronted the county's compensation committee; they were there to appeal the decision by the local justices, who had referred the

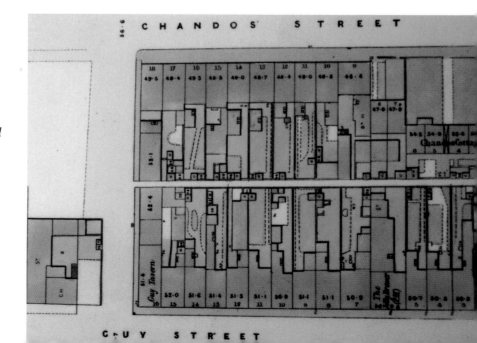

*This 1852 Board of Health map courtesy of Leamington Library shows where in Guy Street the Guy Tavern was situated.*

Guy Tavern for closure [with compensation] on the grounds of 'structural deficiency, structural unsuitability, and redundancy'. Mr. Kennan, on behalf of the chief constable, reported that the house was in a congested area, citing that the Jolly Brewer was within 60 yds; the Britannia 83 yds; Fox and Vivian 114 yds; Carpenter's Arms 146 yds; New Kings Arms 166 yds and the Prince of Wales 260 yds. He also stated that there were three entrances, one a door in a passage to which 24 cottages had access and there was no accommodation for travellers. Furthermore, it was a very small house, compared very unfavourably with the others in the area and was both structurally and decoratively poor. In reply, Mr. Fortescue [for Hunt Edmunds] acknowledged that the premises did not conform to present day requirements. However, he also advised that three adjoining cottages had been purchased in May 1925 for £500 and, when they became vacant at the end of 1928, the brewery would apply to the justices for permission to reconstruct the tavern. The committee refused to renew the licence and on 1st January 1929 awarded compensation of £1,250 for the closure; £1,172 to owners Messrs Hunt, Edmunds and Co. Ltd of Banbury and £78 to licensee George Bartlett. The compensation was paid on 19th January 1929 and the Guy Tavern closed for business on 26th January 1929.

| | |
|---|---|
| 1833-37 | Thomas Phillips |
| 1837 | John Biddle |
| November 1837 | John Noyes |
| 1841-42 | John Powell |
| 1845 | W. Hitchman |
| 1847-Feb 1853 | George and Ann Manners |
| February 1853-≥1854 | Thomas Jones |
| 1855-April 1856 | Mr. King |
| April 1856-May 1862 | David West |
| May 1862-70 | Charles Wheeler |
| 1871-Jun 1872 | George Edwards |
| June 1872-May 1874 | Edward Wheeler |
| May 1874-Nov 1880 | Edmond Meakins |
| November 1880-Mar 1909 | Harold Parrott |
| March 1909-Jun 1911 | Thomas Lawrence Kirwan |
| June 1911-Jul 1916 | Henry 'Harry' Vincent Stevens |
| | *(Called up for military service)* |
| July 1916-1917 | William H. Plummer |
| 1917-Jan 1929 | George Bartlett |
| 26th January 1929 | Closed for business |

**Guy's Hotel** – 2 & 4 Kenilworth Road
These premises were originally built as two Regency houses in 1834 and our research indicates that it didn't become a hotel until the 1920s, when it was named the Desmond Private Hotel and addressed as Beauchamp Square. In a 1931 Leamington Spa Guide, the hotel was advertised as: "First-Class, private, recently enlarged [and now has 40 bedrooms], situated in

finest position in upper Leamington, luxuriously and artistically furnished and equipped, electrically lighted throughout. The public rooms consist of drawing and dining rooms, spacious lounge and billiard room, and garage. Excellent cuisine and separate tables."

However, our main interest begins in the 1960s when it was the Guy's Hotel with the Tavern Bar downstairs. In early October 1963, the four storey, 27 bedroom, Desmond Hotel was sold for a "disappointing" £20,000 to Mr. Cyril Hewett, a Kenilworth businessman, and on 3rd January 1964 it was announced that it was to be renamed Guy's Hotel, following a £20,000 facelift. The Guy's Hotel premises were licensed on 6th April 1964, a full on-licence was granted on 14th December 1964 and the hotel was officially opened on 18th February 1965 [the Leamington Spa Courier dated 19th February reported that the conversion had cost £35,000 and that the first manager was Peter Nash, former manager of the Star and Garter at Richmond]. At this time the basement was called the Tavern Bar and by April 1969 the Blue Q Discotheque was the place to be seen on Thursday, Friday and Saturday nights. In 1970 it was advertised as, "The Tavern Bar – The Inn Within" where a "log fire folk club" was held on Sunday evenings. The Tavern Bar re-opened at 7.00pm on Monday 23rd February 1970 following a refurbishment and with a change of emphasis from teenagers to the over twenties.

The hotel was renamed the Berni Royal Hotel [aka Berni Inn], part of a restaurant-hotel chain, on 7th December 1972. Also in 1972, the basement became Guy's Bar until 24th August 1984 when it was changed to Guys and Dolls bar. On 15th June 1981 the Grape Press Wine and Dine Bar was opened. In 1986 customers could have a drink in the Edgehill bar whilst listening to the 'Spa Ramblers Quintet' playing traditional jazz and rhythm and blues. In 1987 the hotel was closed for a major refurbishment, reportedly costing £750,000. On 1st December 1990, Grand Metropolitan sold off the 31 bedroom Berni Inn at a rock-bottom price to Whitbread Plc as part of a deal involving 26 properties in the 'Berni' chain. However, apparently the Leamington Berni Inn did not fit the Whitbread portfolio and in August 1991 it was sold on to Aneesh

*A 1948 photo of the Desmond Hotel.*

*The Guys Hotel courtesy of Leamington Library.*

*Photo of the Royal on the corner of Kenilworth Road courtesy of Tom Lewin.*

Bheer of Barford; no longer part of the 'Berni' chain it was renamed the Royal Hotel. In August 1996 the basement bar was advertised as, "The Inn Within at the Royal Hotel". The building has also been known as the Guys Cliffe Hotel and in 2013 it is a residential apartment block.

| | |
|---|---|
| 6th April 1964-Apr 1965 | Ralph Clifford Edwards |
| April 1965-Apr 1969 | Peter Robert Nash |
| April 1969-Oct 1969 | Robert George West |
| October 1969-Jul 1970 | Harold William Pilkington |
| July 1970-Jan 1972 | Carl Eggington |
| January 1972-Oct 1972 | Colin Arthur Blythe |
| October 1972-Apr 1973 | Roy Greville Vincent Bridge and Brian Nixon |
| April 1973-Nov 1973 | Peter John Fagg and Roy Greville Vincent Bridge |
| November 1973-75 | Kevin Peter Byrne and Roy Greville Vincent Bridge |
| 1975-≥1978 | George Purnell and his wife Joan |
| | (*Previously at the Berni, Bristol*) |
| 1980 | Norman Tetzlaff |
| | (*Previously at the Grand Hotel, Swansea*) |
| 1981 | Kevin and Jill Byrne |
| 1983-≥1986 | Stephen and Jayne Roberts |

*In 1948 the hotel advertised that it had central heating and softened water in the bedrooms, an electric passenger lift and a fixed fire escape connected to all floors.*

The Leamington Spa Courier dated 13th September 1963 reported that: A Leamington hotel which has been owned by the same family for more than 40 years is to be put up for auction next month because of the illness of one of its owners. The Desmond Hotel, Kenilworth Road will be auctioned on October 2nd in the Masonic Rooms, Willes Road unless sold earlier by private treaty. Owned by two sisters, the Misses Kellett, the Desmond is a four storey Regency building with 27 guest bedrooms, an owner's private suite and six staff bedrooms. A spokesman for John Staite and Son, who are handling the sale, said this week that several larger hotels in the area were interested and since the sale was first advertised, a considerable number of people had requested details.

*The Leamington Spa Courier dated 19th February 1965 reported that: An on-the-spot decision by a Kenilworth businessman at a Leamington auction has led to the £35,000 conversion of the 'Dismal Desmond' into the new luxury Guy's Hotel, in Kenilworth Road. Mr. Cyril Hewett went to the auction to bid for a warehouse and came out the owner of the 30 - bedroom hotel "because it was going cheap". And on Thursday, just twelve months after he leased it to the Hereford based Welcome Inns Group, Mr. Hewett was present at the official opening of the new hotel. "The hotel was very old fashioned when I bought it and absolutely reeked of Victorians," he told me. "There was no licence and every room was covered in dark brown paper. In fact people used to call it the 'Dismal Desmond' because it was so behind the times." The transformation took almost twelve months to complete, and includes a 'Tavern Bar' - five cellars knocked into one room, and the Grill and Griddle. Manager of the Guy's is Mr. Peter Nash, former manager of the Star and Garter at Richmond.*

The same Leamington Courier carried the following article: In the heart of 'Leafy Leamington', and set at the head of the Parade, overlooking landscaped gardens is Guys Hotel. Once two Regency houses then a private hotel, Guy's has recently undergone an extensive facelift which has turned it into a most attractive hotel of its size in the town. Now fully licensed, there are three bars, the Merry Heart, the Grill and Griddle, and the Tavern Bar. The latter with its stone bar and fireplaces, bench seating and old world atmosphere, exudes homely charm rarely found in present day hotel bars. Direct access to this bar has been provided for the convenience of the clients, both from Kenilworth Road, and the car park at the rear. The Grill and Griddle with its bar, open view kitchen, restaurant and dance area should prove popular with all age groups. Here again the decor is in a quiet, restful, pseudo old world style and a feature of the room is the automatic colour change lighting over the dance area. The menu is simple, and inexpensive, as is the accompanying wine list. In strict contrast is the adjoining Merry Heart Bar, contemporary in design, with its colour scheme of black, orange, gold and peacock blue; a gay and attractive bar to set the mood of any party. The hotel is residential with thirty pleasant bedrooms and all with hot and cold basins, shaver plugs and electric gas fires. There are some pleasing, comfortable lounges for the use of residents and a passenger lift to all floors. A special call order kitchen in the residents' dining room ensures quick and efficient breakfast service. The hotel is centrally heated throughout. As in all Welcome Inns the keynote is warmth of welcome, coupled with the best of fare and top service.

*Tom Lewin remembers well the dangers of underage drinking in the 1960s: "The basement of the Guys Hotel on the corner of Clarendon Avenue and Kenilworth Road was converted into a large bar with lots of atmosphere. It was known as the Tavern and in 1966 it even had a juke-box. There were two entrances, one from the Kenilworth Road and the other from the opposite side via the Guys Hotel car park. The entrance from Kenilworth Road was down the steps to the basement. The juke-box was loud and they served a good pint of Worthington 'E'. During that time it was always regarded as the 'in' place for teenagers. The bar was well known for its underage drinking and the police often visited this venue. WPC Pembleton was the scourge of 'the underage drinker' in the 1960s. The Tavern, in the basement, was classic as there were two entrances; as the police came in one entrance the underage drinkers left via the other door. That didn't last long as the long arm of the law covered both exits - just like sending a ferret down a rabbit hole, and netting the exiters."*

In October 1966, there was dancing in candlelight to the Keith Taylor Trio every Saturday night from 8.00pm until midnight for 10/6d per couple.

**Guy's Cliffe Hotel** – Kenilworth Road
See Guy's Hotel for details.

**Half Moon** – 36 Satchwell Street
See Palace Inn for details.

**Half Nelson** – Winston Crescent, Newland Road
See Jack and Jill for details.

**Hare and Hounds** – 113 Regent Street

The first reference point we have for the Hare and Hounds is on 10th December 1831 when James Lawford placed the following advert in the Leamington Spa Courier: "James Lawford, for many years hostler at the Crown Hotel, begs to acquaint his friends, and the public generally, that he has opened the above public house, where, by civility and attention, moderate prices, and a constant supply of good brewed ales, and excellent wines and spirits, he hopes to receive a share of their patronage and support." At this time it was addressed as 12, Regent Street but, variously renumbered, it would become 113, Regent Street by 1875. The Hare and Hounds was a Banbury Brewery Company pub but following the takeover of that brewery it would have been tied to Hunt Edmunds from circa 1879. In March 1951, the licence was renewed temporarily but the local licensing justices referred the pub to the county compensation committee for closure 'with compensation' probably on the grounds of 'redundancy'. The Hare and Hounds closed on 8th March 1952.

| | |
|---|---|
| 1831-34 | James Lawford |
| 1834-38 | William Langham |
| 1838-42 | Abraham Denby |
| 1845 | R. Crowder |
| 1846-Nov 1873 | Edwin Irwin |
| November 1873-Nov 1886 | Henry Christopher Wilks |
| November 1886-Jan 1887 | Mrs. Elizabeth Wilks *(On the death of Henry)* |
| January 1887-Sep 1887 | Edward Grinstead |
| September 1887-Sep 1888 | Jonathan White |

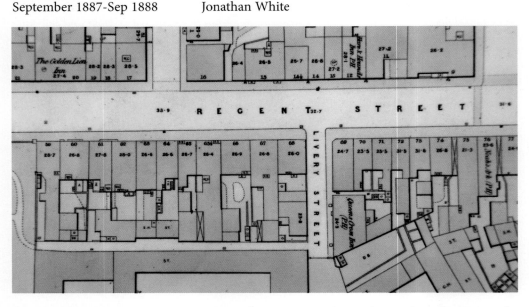

*This 1852 Board of Health map courtesy of Leamington Library shows where the Hare and Hounds was situated.*

| | |
|---|---|
| September 1888-Apr 1890 | James Matthews |
| April 1890-Jan 1894 | Richard Albert Parsons |
| January 1894-Sep 1894 | George Seymour Grey *(Of Brighton)* |
| September 1894-96 | Benjamin Hopkins |
| | *(Previously a member of the local police force)* |
| 1896-Sep 1899 | George Godfrey |
| September 1899-May 1901 | E. J. 'John' Blackwell |
| May 1901-Oct 1951 | Mrs. Emily Elizabeth Blackwell *(On the death of John)* |
| October 1951-1952 | Emily Blackwell *(On the death of her mother Emily)* |
| 8th March 1952 | Closed for business |

**Haunch of Venison** – 130, Parade

Originally addressed as 16a, Lower Parade, there is anecdotal evidence indicating that these premises date back to 1834, and were first occupied by a wine merchant. However, at the time of going to print we are yet to corroborate this claim and our first directory listing is in 1842 when it was occupied by Thomas Hilsdon, a wine and spirits merchant. The first mention we have of the Haunch of Venison [Inn] is in June 1851 when a licence in said name was transferred to James Fleming. Circa 1878 the premises was readdressed as 130, Parade. Following the death of Edwin Brown in 1883 the business was taken over by White and Hollingworth [wine and spirit merchants]; the name Haunch of Venison was not used during their tenancy.

*A pre 1936 Photo showing the premises as Lucas's Brewery town offices courtesy of Lyndon Cave.*

*A 1936 photo courtesy of Lyndon Cave showing the premises after undergoing a 'mock Tudor' makeover.*

*The Haunch of Venison taken on 2nd November 1986 © Allan Jennings.*

However, the licence was again transferred-on in said name when, in August 1889, the premises were purchased by Lucas, Blackwell and Arkwright [Leamington Brewery] for £2,100 and used as their registered office. In February 1894 it was stated in the magistrates court that the Haunch of Venison was the head office for Leamington Brewery and was "not in the nature of a public house"; [magistrate] Councillor Bright replied, "Oh yes it is, [and] to my knowledge persons go in and drink there from day to day." The first directory listing we have for the Haunch of Venison as a fully licensed house is in 1895; if there had been an inn operating on the premises prior to then it is likely that it was in parallel with a wine and spirits business, a scenario we have seen elsewhere. By July 1897 the Leamington Brewery was owned by Lucas and Co. Ltd, who would continue to use these premises as their registered office until the brewery was acquired by Ansells Brewery Ltd in 1928. In 1936 Ansells converted the building into a public house and the frontage was changed to 'mock Tudor'. Following their exit from the brewery business, Lucas and Co. Ltd retained the freehold of the Haunch of Venison until they sold it on to Christopher Albert Rookes, a Stratford based wine merchant, on 1st December 1941. Previously holding a six day licence it was upgraded to a seven day licence on 29th March, 1950.

The Haunch of Venison ceased trading on 30th April 1972 and the licence was surrendered. It remained closed until 1977 when the lease was taken over by Raymond Willsmore and his son Christopher who, following some alterations, reopened the pub in July 1977 as joint licensees. In late 1983, extensive building works were undertaken to join the Haunch of Venison with the Bedford Inn, situated behind it and fronting Bedford Street. At the time, Chris Willsmore [licensee at both] said that "the idea is to keep the pubs as two but have them connected by a corridor; one of the main attractions will be a patio in the centre." In December 1984, it was reported that Chris was proposing to call the Bedford Street pub the Seldom Inn, a name suggested by a customer who thought that it typified the landlord; the sign would portray Randolph Churchill on one side and Lord Hawke on the other. However, there is no evidence to suggest that the Seldom Inn ever opened as such, or that the sign was ever displayed, in fact the entire project proved unsuccessful and the Haunch closed again in 1985; it would remain closed for another five years.

On 21st September 1990, the Leamington Courier reported that Leamington builder Tony Hall was the new owner of the Haunch of Venison and that he was opening the pub in time for Christmas; a conflicting report in the Coventry Evening Telegraph on 29th December 1990 stated that landlord Colin Dingley "was serving festive cheer to Leamington revellers again". [Both reports follow towards the end of this entry; we have not yet been able to corroborate either]

*Photo of the Lounge taken on 20th August 2010 © Allan Jennings.*

In December 1999, following a six week refurbishment [and modernisation] reported to have cost in the vicinity of £250,000, the premises reopened as the Lounge, owned by the Leicestershire based Everards Brewery. Although the Lounge and the Bedford [once Bedford Inn] are still connected via a rear access, they are separate buildings and are run as separate businesses. The Lounge remains open in December 2013.

| | |
|---|---|
| 1834 | Wine and Spirits Merchant |
| 1842 | Thomas Hilsdon *(Wine and spirits merchant)* |
| 1851 | James Fleming |
| 1854 | Charles Chambers Hilsdon and Sarah Hilsdon |
| 1856-Oct 1861 | Sarah Hilsdon |
| October 1861-Apr 1862 | Thomas Horsfall *(Of Coventry)* |
| April 1862-Jul 1883 | Edwin Brown *(Also listed as wine and spirits merchant - died 29th May 1883)* |
| July 1883-Sep 1883 | Messrs J. Glover and H. Horncastle *(Executors)* |
| September 1883-Aug 1889 | H. W. White *(White and Hollingworth - wine and spirit merchants)* |
| August 1889-Feb 1894 | Herbert Robert Arkwright/Leamington Brewery |
| February 1894-97 | Morton Peto Lucas/Leamington Brewery |
| 1897-1928 | Lucas and Co. Ltd/Leamington Brewery |
| 1928-≤1939 | Charles Stubbs *(Owners: Lucas and Co. Ltd)* |
| May 1939-Dec 1941 | Frederick Morris James *(Owners: Lucas and Co. Ltd)* |
| December 1941-Apr 1942 | Christopher Albert Rookes |
| April 1942-Oct 1942 | Frederick Morris James *(Went on to the Oak)* |
| October 1942-Jan 1943 | Harold Thomas Thatcher |
| January 1943-Mar 1943 | Marshall Charles Bennett |
| March 1943-Jun 1943 | Christopher Albert Rookes |
| June 1943-Mar 1945 | Marshall Handyside Bennett |
| March 1945-Jul 1945 | Christopher Albert Rookes |

| | |
|---|---|
| July 1945-May 1948 | Charles Lambre Stewart |
| May 1948-Jun 1948 | Christopher Albert Rookes |
| June 1948-Jan 1956 | Harry Eustace Mills |
| January 1956-Oct 1957 | Charles Brittain Elliott |
| October 1957-Oct 1963 | Leslie John Bryan |
| October 1963-Aug 1964 | Clifford Lambert Harrison |
| August 1964-Oct 1964 | Charles William Rogers *(Died 16th September 1964)* |
| October 1964-Feb 1965 | Dorothy Rogers *(On the death of Charles)* |
| February 1965-Apr 1972 | Rudolph Edward Eden |
| April 1972-Jul 1977 | Closed by owners C. A. Rookes Ltd of Stratford |
| July 1977-Jul 1985 | Christopher Willsmore and father Raymond Willsmore |
| 1985-90 | Closed |
| December 1990 | Tony Hall *(Also owned the Bears pub, Emscote Road, Warwick)* |
| December 1990 | Colin Dingley *(See Dec 1990 article that follows)* |
| 1999 | Tony Rodia *(Previously at the Wig & Pen, Park Street)* |
| 1999 | Mark Hyatt |

## The Lounge

| | |
|---|---|
| December 1999 | Mark Hyatt |
| January 2006-Nov 2008 | John Francis Carey *(Everards Brewery Ltd)* |
| November 2008-Nov 2010 | Eleanor Anne Leacroft |
| November 2010 → | Matthew Beresford |

*Tom Thorne remembered the Haunch: – "Apparently during the 1950s and 60s only one pub in Leamington didn't have a dart board, and that was the Haunch of Venison." Tom Lewin continues the story, "I first went in the Haunch in 1966 when the pub had two rooms. The bar could be entered by two doors, one was on the Parade between the two bay windows; this has been closed for some years and now forms part of the window frontage. The other, the side door, has always been an entrance and back in 1966 we would enter this way into a passage and the bar door was on the right. The passage leading to the lounge was long and halfway along it was stairs leading to private quarters, next to the stairs was a public pay phone. The lounge was rectangular, there were tables and chairs down the left hand side and the bar was opposite on the right. Behind the tables and chairs the complete wall was adorned by full length mirrors. Having drank in both bar and lounge I would say it was hard to imagine where a dart board could have been located. I don't know what happened after the 1960s but during the late 1990s I often went into what was the old lounge to see live bands, by this time it had been considerably extended and was unrecognisable from the 60s."*

On Friday 18th September 1964, it was reported that 55 year old Charles Rogers, landlord of the Haunch of Venison, collapsed and died whilst serving behind the bar on Wednesday 16th September. Charles was from Liverpool although he had spent most of his life in Leamington and had been landlord of several Leamington pubs. During the war he volunteered for the Royal Navy and took part in the D-Day landings.

*The Morning News of 28th April 1977 reported: A father and son are to re-open the Haunch of Venison, the only public house on Leamington's Parade. It dates back to 1834, and has stood vacant for the past five years. The lease has been taken out by Mr. Raymond Willsmore and his son Christopher and they hope to be open in early June. Christopher has been in the licensed trade in Peterborough and his father is a retired engineering officer with the Royal and Merchant Navy. Christopher said they intended keeping the same name for the pub and would be serving such specialities as venison pie and haunch hot pot, "we are having some alterations carried out, and are planning a sea-food bar." Christopher said that although the Haunch had been closed for five years the building was sound and dry, "it dates back to 1834 when it was opened as a wine merchant," he said. A joint application for a licence to run the Haunch of Venison is to be made to the licensing sessions at Leamington on 17th May by Christopher and his father.*

On 26th August 1983, the Coventry Evening Telegraph reported that: Two back to back pubs in Leamington town centre – the ancient Haunch of Venison in the Parade, and the more modern Bedford Inn in Bedford Street – may be merged into one. The Parade and Bedford Street run parallel, and the two pubs are now separated only by a dividing wall and a cluster of outbuildings. The merger plan makes sense to Chris Willsmore, who for the past six years has run the Haunch of Venison as a free-house with his father, Ray Willsmore. Chris has now taken over as licensee of the Bedford Inn, an Ansells pub, and the brewery company is prepared to grant him a long lease. So father and son have put their heads together and drawn up plans to merge the two premises, creating one pub. The two pubs provide a sharp contrast in architectural styles. The Haunch of Venison is the only remaining half timbered building in the Parade, and dates back several hundred years. The Bedford Inn was rebuilt in red brick during the 1930s. [The 'mock Tudor' frontage on the Haunch of Venison was installed in 1936 and does not date back several hundred years – Ed]

*The Morning News of 14th January 1987 reported: The former Haunch of Venison pub, located in a prime spot on Leamington's Parade, and closed over two years ago, could soon be back in business under new management. Now leaseholders Skincraft UK believe they are close to ending a 12 month battle to find a new tenant for the prestige property. Alan Berry, property manager of Skincraft's parent company, Epsom based Star West, said this week, "It has been a liability. Breweries do not want to sign a lease in their own name and it seems that, for many companies, decisions on properties are taken at the highest level and given the least priority." He added, "It is quite an attractive property and somebody must make a real killing there because it is such a prime spot." The former pub has a chequered history of closure. Former landlord Mr. Willsmore called time for good in July 1985 just months after linking the 150 year old property with the Bedford pub in a neighbouring street. And in 1972 the quaint old pub was shut in a shock move by the then owners C. A. Rookes Ltd of Stratford.*

In April 1988, it was reported that the owners were London based Darwen Investments, but by February 1989 it was reported that the new owners were Cumberland Terrace Estates who wanted to convert the property into a shop with offices above.

*By 1989 there was speculation that the distinctive half timbered pub, which had now been closed for four years, may open as a shop after Warwick District Council agreed that it could be converted to office use after receiving an application to change the use of the ground floor.*

By 21st September 1990 the Leamington Courier was reporting that Leamington builder Tony Hall was the new owner of the Haunch of Venison and that he was opening the pub in time for Christmas, following its closure in July 1985. Tony Hall said, "I've lived in Leamington since I was 21 and have wanted to see the old place reopened for some time. It will be ready for early December and will be aimed at shoppers and office staff, and it is in an ideal spot for that type of customer. I'm planning to extend the Bedford but the two pubs will not be linked as they once were."

*On 29th December 1990 the Coventry Evening Telegraph was reporting that landlord Colin Dingley was serving festive cheer to Leamington revellers again. They said it took Colin nine weeks of hard work to bring the neglected building back to its former glory. Colin said, "I begged and borrowed furniture just to get it open on time. It was literally just a shell when I arrived. Everything had been ripped out and it had been standing empty." Colin was hoping to collect memorabilia about the ancient pub. He said, "It dates back a couple of hundred years and it's always been a pub. It has a lot of history and I'd like to dig it all out and put things on the wall." [We are a little confused as 3 months previously Tony Hall took over the licence and was doing the building work. We do not know whether Colin was installed by Tony as landlord, or whether Colin took over the pub – Ed]*

The Leamington Courier of 22nd October 1999 reported: One of Leamington's best known pubs is to get a £250,000 facelift as its doors closed at the weekend. Six weeks of refurbishment work got underway at the Haunch of Venison in the Parade on Monday. A new, modern bar is being created, a new menu laid on and a change of name to the Lounge is proposed. Work at the inn, owned by Leicestershire based Everards Brewery, is expected to be finished for the opening on 2nd December. Tony Rodia has taken over the pub after running the Wig and Pen in Park Street for a year and a half. He said that he and the brewery had worked together to come up with a new concept for the pub. "It's going to be a new, dynamic bar rather than a traditional pub. We are trying to come up with something different." Manager Marc Hyatt said, "The new name is trendier and more eye catching than the old one. We used to get old men and boozers who would sit nursing a pint all day. Now we attract five times as many customers and they are young, modern professionals. It was one of a few venues for live music in Leamington, but I don't think too many people really miss it."

### Heathcote Inn – Tachbrook Road
On 1st February 1939 at Kenilworth, Charles Edwin Elyard, licensee of the New Inn at Napton, made application to the licensing justices for the removal of its 'full' licence to new premises to be erected at Whitnash; the proposed pub would be known as 'The Heathcote' but like two preceding applications it was unsuccessful. However, Mr. C. W. Bourne, representing Mr. Elyard and Messrs H. E. Thornley Ltd [Radford Brewery] then made an application for a 'new' licence which was duly granted. Although the building of the Heathcote Inn was completed in 1940, it was used by the Home Guard as a base and a drill square for the duration of World War Two; it opened as the Heathcote in 1945. In 1987 a major refurbishment was undertaken with the main changes to the original layout including an extension to the bar area, to provide a roomy and well equipped games room

*The Heathcote Inn taken on 2nd March 2009 © Allan Jennings.*

with pool table, separate darts area and facilities for dominoes. The lounge was also given a new lease of life with an extension to the bar servery, a feature fireplace and patio doors to the beer garden. The Heathcote Inn was previously owned by Davenports Brewery Ltd who ceased brewing in 1989 after selling-out to Greenall-Whitley and Co Ltd in 1986. The Heathcote remains open in December 2013.

| | |
|---|---|
| 1st February 1939 | Charles Edwin Elyard |
| 1940-45 | Closed during WWII *[Used by Home Guard]* |
| 1945-46 | George English |
| Circa 1950s | Hewie [or Hughie] Cowlie |
| 1965 [circa mid 1960s] | Maurice J. Jeffs |
| 1971-1983 | Thomas and Margaret Hobbs |
| Circa 1980s | Norman and Lily Grey |
| Circa 1980s | Harvey Peake |
| January 1985-≥1987 | John and Pat Tennant |
| ≤2005-Mar 2006 | Ravinder Atwal |
| March 2006-Oct 2012 | Palminder Atwal |
| October 2012-May 2013 | Dale Stewart Ganter |
| May 2013 → | Teresa Christine 'Tracy' Shaw and husband Jim |

*The Leamington Spa Courier dated 19th March 1971 reported that: Leamington has a new, non commercial folk club at the Heathcote Inn, Whitnash. It opened under the title 'Heathcote Folk' about a month ago. So far, the performers have been floor singers, many of them playing for the first time before an audience. As soon as the organisers Shelagh Long and Pat Dollard have collected enough money, they hope to book 'name' performers every week. "Most other local folk concerns have been run primarily on a commercial basis," said Pat. "We started 'Heathcote Folk' because we like folk music and because there is a lot of talent here."*

*Membership costs only 10p and for non-members the charge is 15p. Pat and Shelagh run the club with the help of singers Lucas and Kevin Slater; it's Wednesday evenings and attracts the middle-aged as well as the young.*

### Memories of Tom and Margaret Hobbs – by Tom Lewin

Thomas [Tom] and Margaret Hobbs were landlords at the Heathcote Inn from 1971 to 1983 and went on to the Joiners from 1983 to 1986. Both were Davenports pubs.

I played dominoes for both the Heathcote and the Joiners which culminated in us winning the Cancer Cup for the Joiners around 1984. Team members included, Tom Hobbs, Stuart Aitken, Eddie Fitzpatrick, Paul Jones, 'Pop' Jones, Jeff James, Barry Whitlock and myself.

Tom and Margaret were always good friends of the football lads and the Heathcote became Whittle Wanderers F.C. Headquarters during the late seventies. Highlights were the barbecues in the Heathcote garden particularly in 1976 whilst we were in the midst of a heat wave. Whittle Wanderers would hold their meetings at the pub with the AGM in the Lounge on a Sunday Morning.

As Tom originated from Glasgow he would arrange for himself and the lads to go to Hampden Park for the bi-annually held Scotland v England home internationals. His Scottish relations always came down to England for the Wembley match. Tom would always put them up in the Heathcote and Sundays were good fun for a little banter.

Friday and Saturday evenings at the Heathcote were very popular and the pub was full most of the time. This was long before youngsters started using the town exclusively. When Tom and Margaret left the Heathcote, quite a few of the regulars followed him down to the Joiners. We always played the domino matches in the bar but used the lounge more at weekends. Robert Turpin was always in place on Sunday lunchtimes to collect the Christmas Thrift Club money.

After Tommy Hobbs left the Joiners, he spent some time on the Leamington Social Club committee until his untimely death.

*The Leamington Spa Courier dated 28th September 1987 reported that: The scaffolding has come down at the Heathcote Inn to reveal a bright new look to one of Whitnash's best loved pubs. The Heathcote is owned by Davenport's brewery, of Birmingham, and managed by John and Pat Tennant. The major part of the refurbishment has been the work of a Leamington building firm, Builtec.*

*The main changes to the 1940s pub have been to extend the bar area to provide a roomy and well equipped games room with pool table, separate darts area and facilities for dominoes. The lounge, too, has been given a new lease of life with an extension to the bar servery, a feature fireplace and patio doors to the beer garden, with brand new garden furniture from Bill Moore Products in Coventry, and children's play area with climbing frame and slide.*

*Architects Saltisford Design of Warwick have been able to keep the traditional character of the pub, but also to create a warm, friendly atmosphere by introducing autumn colours, soft lighting and oak panelling as well as new seats, carpets and beautiful stained glass screens. The new signs have been designed by Norman Hartley, of Manchester.*

*In the cellar, chilling equipment has been modernised to give an even better pint of beer, and to coincide with the re-opening, the Heathcote has launched a new premier lager of extra strength – Grunhalle Gold. Food will continue to be served as usual between 12.00pm and 2.00pm, Mondays to Saturdays.*

*There are three darts teams as well as a domino and pool team, and there is an annual fun run held in aid of heart research, which this year raised more than £2,000. Now the refurbishment is complete, the Heathcote will soon be reintroducing Friday night discos and the popular 'golden oldies' night every other Tuesday.*

**Hintons** – 27/31 Augusta Place

In early 1940, Messrs Sensicle and Son Ltd bought-up vacant factory premises in Augusta Place and converted them into a [then] state-of-the-art bakery measuring 5,000 square feet. In October 1963 the former bakery at 23-31 Augusta Place was withdrawn from an auction sale when bidding stalled at £13,000. Later, following a spell when it was used by Hewins Cash and Carry Wholesalers, Ray Hinton acquired the premises and an adjacent single storey building which ran parallel to the car park. The first Hinton's Wine Bar was opened in December 1974. In 1975, following conversion work carried out by builder Nelson Currie and architect Edward Byron, an upstairs restaurant was opened and became known as the International Friendship Room. In January 1976 permission was granted for a 'change of use' to a loading bay and part of a warehouse, thus extending the existing building to form a Bier Keller; in September 1976 councillors agreed to the proposed change of appearance with Councillor Rawnsley saying that, "this should be a delightful contribution to one of our backwaters".

Hinton's opened a new lounge bar on 1st November 1976, catering for lunches and seating 120 people. Two weeks later, on Tuesday 15th November, Ray and Louise Hinton opened that part of the building which ran parallel to the car park, calling it the Long Bar [entry was via the car park]. It was officially opened by Councillor Marshall Kerry; Harry and Mary Darby were installed as managers. This was followed around Christmas time with the addition of an adjoining small ballroom; Hinton's was a fully licensed free house.

Ray and Louise Hinton sold-out to Guzseat Ltd [set-up by local businessmen Brian Edge and Leigh Norbury] in 1979 and purchased the Angel Hotel. In November 1981 Frank and Meryl Whinyates acquired Hinton's from Guzseat Ltd, which was wound up with a total deficiency of £73,000. Ansells brewery took over Hintons in November 1984 and spent £50,000 on the premises. In June 1988 Hinton's lost its entertainments licence [except for Monday's Worldbeat events] and the licensing magistrates were informed of the committee's growing concerns with 'issues' associated with the premises. In July 1989 the Leamington Spa Courier reported that Ansells had sold the lease for Hinton's to Roger and Jane Fewtrell "for a substantial sum" on 21st July. Furthermore, "a posh wine bar and restaurant would soon be opened on the premises and work had already begun on the £¼ million transformation"; Hob Nobs opened in September 1989. In March 1992 Ansells brought in the receivers and the business was purchased by Terry Robertson and Eric Jay [Aquarius Builders]; it was reopened on 9th April 1992. Following a spate of clashes between police and drunken crowds, Hob Nobs closed in November 1993; its licence was revoked by Stratford-upon-Avon magistrates on 10th March 1994. Following the closure of Hob Nobs the building fell into disrepair, remaining vacant until at least October 1998

*Above left: Kasa taken on 10th August 2004 by John Hartnup. Above middle: Photo of Bar Code taken 26th October 2008 © Allan Jennings. Above right: Photo of Caines taken 30th March 2010 © Allan Jennings.*

when it was converted into three separate units [NB: Leeky Joe's was a bar adjacent to Hob Nobs for a short period, circa 1991-93].

When the Long Bar closed it left three units in Augusta Place, those being Kasa bar [circa 1999-≥2004] with two restaurants alongside. It then became Bar Code [27, Augusta Place, a sports bar with big screens] with Rosanna's restaurant [29, Augusta Place] and the Thai restaurant [31, Augusta Place] alongside.

On 13th March 2010, Bar Code was renamed Caines but by early December the same year Caines too was closed for business and displaying signage advertising the bar and restaurant premises to rent. G's Bar opened in September 2011 but there was an issue with the premises licence and it closed in the November; on Tuesday 31st January 2012 the local licensing authority dismissed the application for a premises licence.

| | |
|---|---|
| December 1974-1979 | Ray and Louise Hinton *(Owners)* |
| 1975-76 | Walter Hecker *(Manager – Hinton's wine bar)* |
| November 1976 | Harry and Mary Darby *(Managers – Long Bar)* |
| 1979-Nov 1981 | Guzseat Ltd *(Owners Brian Edge and Leigh Norbury)* |
| November 1981-Nov 1984 | Frank and Meryl Whinyates *(Owners – Hinton's wine bar)* |
| November 1984 | Taken over by Ansells |
| 1985 | Walter Hecker *(Manager – Hinton's wine bar)* |
| 21st July 1989 | Roger and Jane Fewtrell *(Owners – Hinton's wine bar)* |
| September 1989 | Roger and Jane Fewtrell *(Owners – Hobnobs wine bar and restaurant)* |
| 1989-91 | Bobbie de Corcey *(Manager – Hob Nobs)* |
| April 1992 | Terry Robertson and Eric Jay *(Owners)* |
| April 1992-Mar 1994 | Daryl Green *(Manager – Hob Nobs)* |

| | |
|---|---|
| Circa 2005-May 2006 | Mohammed Ifraz *(Barcode)* |
| May 2006 | Matthew John Griffiths *(Barcode)* |
| 13th March 2010 | Name change to Caines *(Licensee not known)* |
| September 2011-Nov 2011 | Miss Sigourney Ruth Gowlett *(G's Bar)* |
| November 2011 | Closed for business |

*On Friday 22nd July 1977 Hinton's held a 'Tramps Ball' in their new banqueting suite with dancing to 'Leamington's fantastic group – 'The Likely Lads'; admission was £1.50 which included supper.*

In May 1978 Hinton's advertised: If you've been to Feathers Discotheque you'll know what to expect …. And now it's Peppers. Good sounds together with dancing and drinking for the discerning over 23s, by candlelight, from 9.30pm until 2.00am – Every Friday at Hintons commencing 12th May; reasonable dress, i.e. no jeans.

*In December 1979 Hintons advertised the Long Bar, Walter's Bar, a Ballroom, accommodation and a new Roastery Restaurant. They held a grand buffet dance on New Year's Eve with music from Sweet Wine and cabaret from Mal Lynch; tickets were priced at £12.50.*

**Hob Nobs** – 27 Augusta Place
See Hintons for details.

**Hodcarrier** – 102 Coppice Road, Whitnash
The Hodcarrier was built and named by Jerry Lewitt, Graham Soden, Tony Hall [The Bear] and Mick Worrall, directors of XJS Building, Development and Leisure. This free house was opened by world professional snooker champion Steve Davis on Saturday 11th June 1983; Courage Brewery supplied the drinks with Directors bitter amongst those on offer. A large one-roomed pub [£10,000 was spent on sound-proofing the building], it also had an off-licence that sold tobacco, wines and spirits, and a large selection of sweets; it also offered a video film rental service. The spacious cellar was later converted into a function room that was available for special occasions and in January 1984 it was granted an entertainments licence. In 1986 it advertised the

*The Hodcarrier taken on 23rd October 2011 © Allan Jennings.*

Flyposters Bar for the best in live music from Thursday to Sunday. On Monday 21st April 1986, local environmental health officials closed the Hodcarrier for a couple of days after 5,000 gallons of raw sewage flooded the cellar bar, causing about £7,000 of damage; builders rubble was blamed for the blockage which caused a pumping station at Coppice Road to breakdown. The Hodcarrier remains open in December 2013.

| | |
|---|---|
| 1983-1993 | Jerry Lewitt, Graham Soden, Tony Hall and Mick Worrall *(Owners)* |
| June 1983-1993 | Andrew Williams *(Manager)* and his wife Carole *(Tony Hall – Licensee)* |
| 1985 | Pip Bartlett *(Assistant Manager)* |
| 13th March 1993-2006 | Fred Hepburn *(Owner)* |
| 2006 → | Mark Andrew Hepburn |

*The Leamington Spa Courier dated 10th June 1983 reported that: The Hodcarrier, Whitnash's plush new pub, aims to build a name for itself as an important part of the growing community. And as it develops it will be the customers who will help fashion the kind of 'local' they want. It is a place for lunchtime snacks, early evening drinks or a social night out. Soon the spacious cellar will be available for special occasions like parties and weddings. The freehouse, which specialises in a range of good beers, has opened at a time when the licensing trade is hit by the recession. Manager Andy Williams explains, "It shows the confidence we have in this expanding part of the town and in the future." Andy was running a country club in North Cornwall when he and his wife Carol married earlier this year - and decided to make their future here. "From the very beginning we have been conscious of ensuring that the Hodcarrier is an asset to the area, a place to be proud of. That is why £10,000 has been spent on soundproofing the building. We have also splashed out on the best fixtures and fittings. One great advantage of starting a brand new pub is that regular customers can chip in ideas on its development. That's why we have no pre-conceived ideas on the sort of meals we will provide. Our job is to give a first class, cheerful and efficient service, [served up with a good pint], and see how it goes from there. If there is something special people want in the way of entertainment or social events, then I hope we will be able to oblige. After all, community life flourishes around a good local pub."*

**Hogshead** – 41/43 Warwick Street
See Copper Pot for details.


**Hole in the Wall** – Bedford Street
This one puzzled us for a while as we had heard the name referenced a number of times and that it was in Bedford Street, but we couldn't find any hard evidence of its existence. Thankfully Barry Astill, who had lived in the Bedford Inn as a child, remembered it being further down the street; it turned out to be the nickname of the Aylesford Arms. [See Aylesford Arms for details]


**Holly Bush** – 89 King Street
See Holly Bush, Holly Street for details.


**Holly Bush** – Holly Street
The first information we have relating to a pub in King Street is notice of an auction to be held at the Lansdowne Hotel on 31st January 1837 when, among a number of properties to

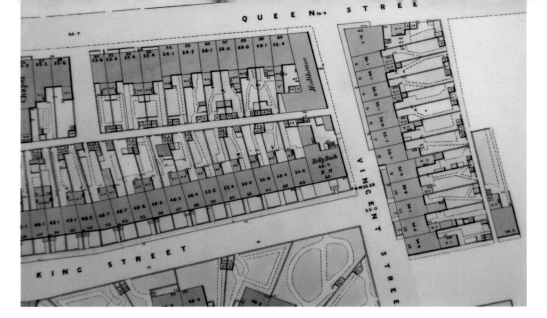

*This 1852 Board of Health map courtesy of Leamington Library shows the site of the original Holly Bush on the corner of King Street and Vincent Street.*

be sold, was a newly erected, unfinished, intended public house and cottage, situated in King Street. The first directory listing we have for the original Holly Bush is in 1842 at 45, King Street [by 1885 it had been readdressed as number '89']. Originally a beer house, it was granted a new publican's full on-licence in September 1853; it would later be owned by Marston, Thompson and Evershed Ltd, Albion Brewery, Burton-on-Trent. The original pub and the surrounding streets and houses were demolished in the mid 1970s as part of a housing redevelopment program, although the actual pub site, on the corner of King Street and Vincent Street, is just a patch of shrubs and bushes.

The original Holly Bush was a two-storey building. Downstairs there were two windows facing the street, a bay window on the left and a 3 by 4 pane window to the right; upstairs there were two 3 x 4 pane windows. At the front of the pub was a small garden surrounded by a low, wooden picket fence with a gateway and 2-3 steps leading up to a single front door entrance. Above the door, centred between the two upstairs windows, was a wooden rectangular pub sign bolted to the face of the building. Michael Coveney remembers, "Going up some steps into the pub, on the way in was the outdoor in the passage-way with a bar to the left and the lounge to the right."

An application for the removal of the licence from King Street, to premises to be constructed at the corner of Holly Street and Earl Street, was granted on 8th February 1973. The original Holly Bush [King Street] closed on 16th September

*The Holly Bush courtesy of Nick Wilkins.*

1974 and its successor [Holly Street] opened on 17th September 1974, with Councillor Peter Tombs pulling the first pint. Owned by Marston Breweries, the new premises were considered much smaller than other modern pubs, but as Joseph Harston [landlord] explained at the time "this was to preserve the traditional atmosphere and cosiness of the local pub". At 12.00 noon on Thursday 7th April 1988, the Holly Bush reopened after a six week facelift which included the conversion of the bar and lounge into a single open-plan area, new seating, carpets, curtains and flooring. The Holly Bush remains open in December 2013.

**Footnote:** The origin of the pub sign probably dates back to the Roman times. Originally, the 'sign' of the trade was a pole which jutted out from the side of the building. Where an inn/tavern/alehouse had been granted a licence to also sell wine the alestake, as it was named, carried an evergreen bush [e.g. 'holly' bush].

| | |
|---|---|
| 1842-Oct 1857 | Thomas Chamberlain |
| October 1857-64 | John Young |
| 1864-Oct 1864 | Elizabeth Young |
| October 1864-Jun 1883 | William Thomas Chamberlain |
| June 1883-Jul 1888 | James Matthews |
| July 1888-Jul 1889 | James Glenn |
| July 1889-Oct 1889 | Albert Jones |
| October 1889-Dec 1889 | Richard Bradburn Collins |
| December 1889-Nov 1896 | George Henry Birt |
| November 1896 | George Strong *(Magistrates refused to confirm transfer)* |
| November 1896-Mar 1901 | William James Roe |
| March 1901-Jan 1902 | George Godfrey |
| January 1902-Feb 1902 | Mrs. Lucy Godfrey *(On the death of George)* |
| February 1902-Sep 1902 | Richard Coulden |
| September 1902-05 | William Henry Hawkes |
| 1905- Feb 1906 | Alfred Henry Symonds |
| February 1906-Jul 1908 | Francis 'Frank' John Morgan |
| July 1908-Nov 1910 | Mrs. Alice Morgan |
| November 1910-Dec 1910 | William Bonnett |
| December 1910-Apr 1911 | Mrs. Mary Ann Bonnet *(On the death of William)* |
| April 1911-Oct 1911 | George Frederick Gilbert |
| October 1911-Mar 1912 | Walter Midwinter |
| March 1912-Aug 1930 | William George Humphries |
| August 1930-Jan 1953 | Frank Ewart Humphries *(Son of William; Frank died in August 1963)* |
| January 1953-Jul 1954 | Jeffrey Thornborough |
| July 1954-Dec 1965 | John 'Jack' Cowley and his wife May *(Retired September 1981, after 16 years at the Bowling Green, Warwick)* |
| December 1965-Apr 1970 | Alan William Moffatt Cowley |

| | |
|---|---|
| April 1970-16th Sep 1974 | Joseph and Nancie Harston |
| 17th September 1974 | New Holly Bush opened |
| 17th September 1974-1979 | Joseph and Nancie Harston |
| 1979-≥Oct 1990 | Terry and Lesley Smith |
| 1996 | Mick and Wendy Cooper |
| Circa 2006–Oct 2008 | Anthony Leahy |
| October 2008 → | Allan and Sally Wareing |

*The Leamington Spa Courier carried an advertisement for the Holly Bush on 8th April 1988:*
*A new bar, new furniture and new fittings mark the start of a new beginning for the Holly Bush*
*in Holly Street, Leamington. Over the last six weeks, the pub has been given a major facelift,*
*with the bar and lounge being knocked into one. New seating, carpets, curtains and floor have*
*added to the overall look. And the result of the hard work was finally revealed yesterday at the*
*grand re-opening. Landlord Terry Smith and his wife Lesley, who live over the pub with their*
*two children Daniel and Charlotte, hope that the pub's new lease of life is going to attract a*
*wider clientele whilst retaining the regular, but much valued, customers. According to landlord*
*Terry, the age range of the customers is from 18 to over 90, and that is how he wants it to stay.*
*One area of the pub's operation that is to be given greater prominence in the future is the selling*
*of food. Lesley Smith is responsible for the range of meals which start at 65p and go up to about*
*£2.50.*

In August 1996, The Beer and Ragged Staff, a CAMRA publication, carried this article
on the pub: The Holly Bush in Holly Street is no more than 26 years old and was purpose
built on waste land. It is a comfortable pub built in typical 1970s architectural style. It
consists of an open plan u-shaped area, mainly seating with the games area and darts and
pool at the far right hand end. Originally it was built with two rooms served from one
central bar but this was found to be difficult to manage and was soon altered. The name is
much older than the present building which is a replacement for a previous hostelry in
King Street. During the mid 1970s, there was extensive rebuilding in this area with most of
the buildings being demolished. The present landlord Mick Cooper has only been at the
pub for a few months and this is his first venture in the licensed trade. He is keeping his
Marston's bitter, Pedigree and Banks' mild in excellent condition; hopefully trade will build
up so he can reinstate the Marstons' Head Brewers Choice.

**Hope and Anchor** – 30 Oxford Street
See Anchor Tavern for details. [Not to be confused with the Hope and Anchor in Hill Street]

**Hope and Anchor** – 41 Hill Street
The first information we received on these licensed premises was courtesy of historian John
Ashby, who claims that the Hope and Anchor opened in 1853; however, the pub is clearly
shown and named on the 1852 Leamington Board of Health Map. Addressed as 30, Hill Street
in its early days, it was renumbered '41' during the 1870s. Originally a beer house, it was
granted a full licence in August 1856. On 1st May 1907 the directors of Lucas and Co. Ltd
[Leamington Brewery] approved the purchase of the Hope and Anchor from the executors of

the late Hannah Morris for £2,200; it would become an Ansells pub following their acquisition of the Leamington Brewery and its 124 licensed houses, in 1928. In 1972 Ansells Brewery offered a tenancy at the Hope and Anchor, stating that it was uneconomic to run the pub under management and that there was a trend towards tenancies. In 1986, Ansells spent £40,000 and five weeks "de-modernising" the pub and restoring the style that it boasted in its Victorian heyday, before re-launching it as an Ansells 'Heritage Inn'; it would subsequently receive an award from the Leamington Society for the restoration work. The Hope and Anchor remains open in December 2013.

*The Hope and Anchor [circa 1930] courtesy of landlord Steve Massey.*

**Footnote:** During the late 1960s, the Hope and Anchor was nicknamed the 'Swinging Tit' on account of the pub's sign featuring a mermaid with one breast exposed.

| | |
|---|---|
| 1852-68 | William Morris |
| 1870 | A. Morris |
| 1871-Jan 1907 | Mrs. Hannah Morris |
| January 1907 | Ellen Elizabeth Hewins |
| | *(On the death of Hannah Morris)* |
| 1907-Apr 1913 | George William Tubb |
| April 1913-Jul 1916 | Alfred Rose *(Called-up for military service)* |
| July 1916-Feb 1917 | Annie Rose |
| February 1917-Jun 1925 | Frederick William Smalley |
| June 1925-Dec 1926 | W. J. Arthur |
| December 1926-36 | Archibald 'Arthur' Underwood |
| | *(Went on to the Somerville Arms)* |
| 1936-39 | Mrs. Grace May Rush |
| July 1939-Feb 1949 | Geoffrey Thomas Skelcher *(Died in 1971, aged 68)* |
| February 1949-Oct 1949 | Alfred Charles Carr |
| October 1949-May 1953 | Charles Boisonnade Atkins |
| May 1953-Mar 1962 | Arthur Sidney Savage |
| March 1962-Dec 1964 | Adeline Beatrice Baillie Savage *(On the death of Arthur)* |
| December 1964-Jul 1966 | James William O'Gorman |
| July 1966-Apr 1967 | Colin Barnes |
| April 1967-Jun 1969 | James Merrick |
| June 1969-Nov 1971 | Arthur Jack Manttan |

| | |
|---|---|
| November 1971 | Derek John Manttan and his wife Sheila |
| March 1978-1979 | Arthur Taylor and his wife Francie |
| | *(Arthur was previously 11 years in the police force)* |
| 1979-1985 | Joan Richardson (and Alfred 'Alf' Smith) |
| 1985-Dec 1985 | Redver Woods |
| December 1985-Nov 2008 | Paul Patrick O'Keeffe and his wife Shirley |
| November 2008 → | Steve *(Shirley O'Keeffe's son)* and Louise Massey |

*On 30th October 1964, it was reported that landlady Mrs. Beat Savage was to retire and live in Lillington after 33 years in the licensing trade, 31 with Ansells. She had taken on the Hope and Anchor with her husband Arthur 11 years ago. Mr. Savage died nearly 3 years ago. The couple opened the new Rugby Tavern where they stayed for 20 years.*

The Leamington Spa Courier dated 17th December 1976 reported: Leamington's Hope and Anchor kept the town flag flying high in the Rothmans/Courier sports quiz on Tuesday evening. After the last of the first round matches, the Spa's Hill Street pub are the sole representatives of both Leamington and Ansells to go into the last four. The Hope and Anchor team trio are D. Mannian, W. Hewitt and G. Bunn.

*The Hope and Anchor was featured in the Leamington Spa Courier of 13th December 1985; the following is a copy of the report: Leamington's Hope and Anchor pub reopened its doors this week and received a special present from 75 year old Frank Underwood, whose father ran the establishment in the 1920s and 30s. Frank presented new landlords Paul and Shirley O'Keeffe with a framed photo of the Hope and Anchor as it was in the days when his father, Arthur, pulled the pints. And visitors to the new look 'old pub' on Tuesday found it difficult to see how time had changed the Hope and Anchor in the 50 years since Arthur Underwood called his last orders. Ansell's brewery spent £40,000 and 5 weeks 'de-modernising' the pub, restoring the style it boasted in its Victorian heyday. Space invaders, fruit machines and loud juke boxes are definitely out. Dominoes, crib and darts are in. Frank and his wife, Alice, who now live in Stuart Close, Warwick, gave the new-born Hope and Anchor their seal of approval. Said Frank, "When my father was landlord between 1924 and 1933 I was only a lad, but I can remember it was a happy place [refer 'licensee listing' for correct dates – Ed]. You could bank on regular customers coming in every night to have a pint and play dominoes or the ringboards." The Hope and Anchor originally opened in 1853 and Coventry historian John Ashby took up Ansell's offer to delve into local archives for 'heritage' that the brewery could use to re-develop the pub. Frank's memories proved particularly helpful in forming the foundations for the pub's new image. Lucas brewery, once based in Lillington Avenue, Leamington, owned the Hope and Anchor during Arthur Underwood's spell as landlord. Frank recalls there were many times when he would grab a wicker basket, and walk to the brewery to fetch fresh stocks of his father's most popular tipples. "I never go into pubs these days," said Frank. "People will soon get fed up with all the flashing lights and loud music, and traditional pubs like this will be more popular."*

The Leamington Spa Courier dated 20th December 1985 reported that: The new hosts at the Hope and Anchor are Paul and Shirley O'Keeffe who have run the Guards, another Ansells pub, in the High Street. The couple are well known figures on the Leamington pub and club scene having been stewards at a Leamington Club for over six years. A native of Leamington, Paul was born in the High Street where he was brought up above what is now a bookmakers shop. He also attended the Campion Secondary School which was situated near the Hope and Anchor in Leicester Street, "I used to be a regular at the pub about 10 years ago and was delighted to be given the opportunity to return as landlord," he said.

*The 'Beer and Ragged Staff' publication of August 1996 included the following article about the pub: According to the pub's official history it was opened in 1853; however a map in the County Records Office dated 1852 shows the pub with virtually nothing around it. The first landlord was William Morris and for a period of time he was also the licensee of the nearby Greyhound. Mr. Morris died aged 47 in 1868 and his wife Hannah carried on until she died in 1906. During the 1920s and 30s it was a lively place with regular 'charra' trips to the seaside and race meetings and weekend sing songs around the piano. Before Ansells took over, it was run by Leamington Brewery. In 1986, it was one of the first pubs to become a Heritage Inn. The Victorian character was restored using original features where possible including the stained glass windows, the door-mat and the splendid tiled fire-places. The pub has become a very popular community local, the landlord Paul O'Keeffe plays a central part in it all. Paul has described to me 'Operation Rupert' the top secret renovation of the Heritage pubs which other breweries were not aware of until the official launch. The 'Hope' has Ansells mild and bitter together with a regularly changing guest beer. This excellent local has featured in the Good Beer Guide for several years.*

### Hope Tavern – 2 Court Street

Court Street was named after Richard Court, whose farmhouse was once located at what is now the junction of Church Terrace, George Street and New Street. Court Street is built on land that Richard Court would have farmed before the village of Leamington Priors began to expand. Originally the Eagle and Shamrock [1833-34] and then the Coopers Arms [1834-39], it was renamed the Hope Tavern circa 1840, and addressed as 2, Court Street; the first directory listing we have is in 1841 when it was still a beer house. In 1888 the Hope advertised wines, ales, spirits, stouts, and cigars of the finest qualities; good beds, one shilling per night; skittle alley and every accommodation.

In October 1925, it was sold to Thornley's Brewery for £4,100. In March 1926, when Thornley's applied for a renewal of the licence, the local magistrates pronounced the Hope 'redundant' and that it would be referred for 'closure with compensation', however this decision was overturned on appeal and no further action was taken. A music licence was

*The Hope Tavern taken in 1987 by Bill Bigley.*

granted on 12th February 1957 for the bar, saloon bar, and the smoke room, and in 1985 an entertainment licence was granted that permitted music and dancing until 11.00pm Monday to Saturday and music only on Sunday until 10.30pm. When Thornley-Kelsey closed their brewery in 1968, and sold-off their [tied estate] pubs, the Hope was probably acquired by Davenports Brewery, who in turn would sell-out to Greenall Whitley & Co. Ltd in 1986. In 1996 Kevin Murphy attempted to turn the Hope into a night club named Buskers [the name of a famous Dublin pub] but it was an ill fated move and after 4-5 months [post February 1997] it reverted to the Hope Tavern. It remains open in December 2013.

| | |
|---|---|
| 1841-Aug 1865 | Joseph Underhill |
| August 1865-Jan 1868 | Sarah Underhill *(Died suddenly on the day of transfer)* |
| January 1868-81 | Mark Chatterley *(Son of the landlord at the White Lion)* |
| 1881-Aug 1886 | Lucy Chatterley |
| August 1886-Jan 1890 | William Chatterley *(On the death of Lucy)* |
| January 1890-Jan 1893 | Eliza Franklin |
| January 1893-Jun 1893 | William Hunt *(Previously at Talbot Hotel, Wellesbourne)* |
| June 1893-Jan 1895 | George Henry Sewell |
| January 1895-Nov 1895 | Mr. E. T. Pierson *(Official receiver, trustee in bankruptcy)* |
| November 1895-96 | Thomas William Smith |
| 1896-Oct 1896 | Emily Barnett |
| October 1896-Jun 1926 | Henry Russell |
| June 1926-35 | Arthur John Bradford *(Died December 1941)* |
| 1935-Jan 1937 | Charles Edwin Elyard |
| January 1937-Nov 1944 | James Frederick Cooper |
| November 1944-Jan 1946 | John Lawrence Beecroft |
| January 1946-Jul 1948 | Jack Leslie Abbott |
| July 1948-Mar 1950 | Alec Southam Clarke |
| March 1950-Feb 1951 | Frank Thomas Williams |
| February 1951-Sep 1954 | Cecil Frank Collins |
| September 1954-Mar 1955 | Alfred Herbert Lee |
| March 1955-Jul 1957 | Nigel Dunning Gough |
| July 1957-Mar 1958 | Alfred Edward Walsingham |
| March 1958-Jul 1961 | Edward Alfred May |
| July 1961-Dec 1964 | Arthur Harris |
| December 1964-Feb 1968 | Norman Herbert Lee Scott |
| February 1968-Oct 1968 | Geoffrey Derek Jones |
| October 1968-Jul 1973 | Charles 'Charlie' William Smith |
| July 1973-Aug 1976 | Arthur Harold Grant and wife Jean |
| August 1976-Jan 1979 | Ralph and Maureen Parkes |
| ≤1984-Nov 1984 | Edward 'Eddie' Walsh |
| Nov 1984-Jun 1994 | Thomas O'Reilly and his wife Treena *(Married 1987)* |
| June 1994-97 | Kevin Murphy *(Also landlord of Murphy's Bar)* |
| 1997 | Neil Geaney |

| Late 1990s | William Trevor Todd |
|---|---|
| Early 2000s | Sue Briggs |
| 2005-2011 | Donal Meaghan and Debbie Buckley |
| | *(Lease holder: Stuart Ryan)* |
| 31st January 2011 → | Patrick Minihane *(Licensee)* |
| | *(Donal Meaghan and Debbie Buckley are business partners)* |

*In April 1841 Joseph Underhill, keeper of a beer-house called the Hope Tavern was fined 40s and costs of 11s for drawing beer in his house on Sunday morning during the hours of divine worship.*

In March 1926, when Thornley's Brewery applied for a renewal of the licence, the chief constable, Mr. T. Earnshaw, objected stating that it was in a congested area and citing 23 places for the sale of intoxicating liquor, to make his point. Mr. Earnshaw confirmed that Mr. Russell, the licensee, had occupied the place since 1896 without complaint. He said that the house did not compare favourably with other houses with regard to the size of rooms and that supervision at the rear was practically impossible as a 6 foot wall separated the licensed premises from the property next door. Mr. E. R. Thornley said that his firm had purchased the Hope Tavern from Messrs Blencowe Ltd and that Mr. Russell would shortly be leaving the premises because, since the death of his wife, he had not been in the best of health. The mayor announced that the magistrates were satisfied that the house was 'redundant' and that it would be 'referred for compensation' [obviously reversed on appeal because the Hope remains open in 2013 but we have not been able to find any details of the ruling – Ed].

*The Leamington Spa Courier dated 11th January 1974 reported that: Members of the darts section of the Hope Tavern, Court Street, attended as a cheque for £20 is handed over to Mr. D. F. Sparkes of the Midland Societies for the Blind. The money was raised in spot-the-ball competitions, raffles, and in collection boxes on the bar. The pub also presented a Christmas hamper to the St. Anne's Children Home in Warwick New Road, Leamington. Among those present were Mr. Sparkes, Mrs. Jean Grant [licensee's wife], Mr. Bryan Regan, and Mr. Harry Grant [licensee], together with many of The Hope's regulars.*

### Huddy's Café Bar – 24 Victoria Terrace

The Leamington Spa Courier dated 26th April 1996 reported that self confessed soccer rebel Alan Hudson kicked off his new Leamington bar venture with a promise to introduce some old Kings Road spirit – as well as the drinks! Hudson, the former Chelsea and England star, promised customers a glimpse of old friends such as actors Dennis Waterman and Sean Connery; he achieved an early goal when the extravagant football-themed bar opened in the lower Parade on Friday night and much travelled manager and pundit Tommy Docherty put in a guest appearance. Alan Hudson advertised that Leamington's only sports bar had arrived, that there would be big screen quiz nights, full Euro '96 coverage and he also invited ladies teams to play for Huddy's LFC [It is said that local businessman Chris Willsmore, a friend of Hudson, was also involved in the project]. This bar showed football on the big screen in Leamington before it was fashionable and other pubs soon followed suit; when England games were being televised, Hudson would entertain his customers with a half-time 'talk'. Huddy's closed in 1996 after just three months. Prior to being Huddy's these premises were Caesar's American Restaurant and afterwards it became Vialli's, both of them being food outlets.

### Imperial [Public House] – Regent Street

Prior to becoming the Imperial, these premises were the [Wine] Vaults at the Royal Assembly Rooms, and the first proprietor we have listed is George Smith and Co. [1849-51]. Our next listing is in 1879 when the proprietor was Edward Collier, who had taken over the licence from William Taylor on 5th February that year. The part known as the 'Vaults' was on the south-east corner of Bedford Street and Regent Street. In 1879 the Assembly Rooms [opened 24th September 1812] underwent extensive alterations which resulted in the building being divided into, what appears to be, two properties; the licensed part of the building had a 50 foot frontage facing Bedford Street and a 24 foot frontage facing Regent Street. The licence was transferred from Edward Collier to Messrs Lewis and Ridley [Leamington Brewery] in June 1880. In November 1893, when granting a music licence for the smoke room, the local licensing justices referred to the premises as the Imperial Vaults.

In July 1885 the licence was transferred to Morton Peto Lucas, representing the new owners of the Leamington Brewery [Lucas, Blackwell and Arkwright], who would advertise the Imperial 'to be let' in October the same year. On the 5th May 1900, the Leamington Spa Courier carried a sale notice promoting the auction of the fully licensed Imperial public house, comprising a fine lofty bar, with entrances in two streets; three smoke rooms; large double billiard room; residential accommodation and cellarage. Included in the sale were the adjoining freehold premises known as 66, Regent Street, comprising a double-fronted shop and basement, with dwelling-house. The Imperial was closed by its owners on 31st

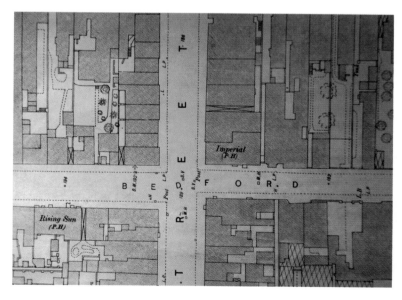

*This 1885 map courtesy of Leamington Library shows where the Imperial was on the corner of Regent Street and Bedford Street.*

January 1901 and the premises went on to become part of Woodwards' department store; Woodwards' was sold in 2006 and in 2013 the part of the building that was once the Imperial is now Castle Galleries.

| | |
|---|---|
| ≤1849-≥1851 | George Smith and Co *(Assembly Room Vaults)* |
| ≤1879-5th Feb 1879 | William Taylor *(Wine Vaults – Royal Assembly Rooms)* |
| 5th February 1879-Jun 1880 | Edward Collier *(Wine Vaults – Royal Assembly Rooms)* |
| June 1880-83 | Lewis and Ridley/Leamington Brewery |
| 1883-84 | Lewis and Ridley/Leamington Brewery *(Manager – E. P. Wright)* |
| 1884-July 1885 | Lewis and Ridley/Leamington Brewery *(Manager – W. Armishaw)* |
| July 1885-86 | Morton Peto Lucas/Leamington Brewery *(Manager – W. Armishaw)* |
| 1887-Jan 1889 | Arthur Essex |
| January 1889 | Herbert Robert Arkwright/Leamington Brewery |
| 1891-93 | H. Maycock |
| 1893 | Herbert Robert Arkwright/Leamington Brewery |
| September 1893-Apr 1894 | John Carrington Isitt |
| April 1894-Aug 1895 | Phillip George Sheldrake *(Previously Plough, St. Albans)* |
| August 1895-Jun 1900 | James Satchwell |
| June 1900-Jan 1901 | Ernest Luty |
| 31st January 1901 | Closed |

**Imperial Hotel** – Lansdowne Place

The first information we have on the Imperial Hotel is in December 1836, when Richard Hughes announced that he had left the Stoneleigh Hotel and had taken and entered upon spacious premises in Lansdowne Place, situated on the eastern side of Upper Parade in new town [approximately mid terrace]. Hughes signed a 14 year lease on 25th March 1837 at a yearly rent of £320 and the first directory listing we have is in 1838. In May 1842, the hotel was advertised 'for let' as Hughes was moving to the Clarendon Hotel and on 1st August 1842 William Webb announced his arrival; we also have a report of him being there in April 1843. In his 1988 book on Leamington, Lyndon Cave stated that it had closed by 1850.

The hotel consisted of six bedrooms in the attic; six bedrooms and a chamber maid's closet on the 3rd floor; seven bedrooms and a water closet on the 2nd floor; two drawing rooms, one very large bedroom, a bedroom and dressing room, storeroom and water closet on the 1st floor; three very large dining rooms, water closet, china closet, butler's pantry and bar parlour on the ground floor; two cooking kitchens, butler's room, larder, wine, beer and coal cellars in the basement; "a very neatly laid-out pleasure ground in the rear", with two double coach houses, a saddle house, a six-stall and three-stall stable, two loose boxes, a loft, three servant's bedrooms, and an office and stable yard opening on to Guy Street.

| | |
|---|---|
| 1836-39 | Richard Charles Hughes |
| 1841-42 | Charles Cox Hughes |
| 1842-43 | William Webb |

## Ivy Tree – 8 Queen Street

Originally a beer house, the first directory listing we have for the Ivy Tree is in 1848 when the address was 5, Queen Street. In August 1855, household furniture, effects and an extensive range of brewing utensils were auctioned off by the exiting proprietor Thomas Smith, who had "given up the house". In 1868 William Rathbone applied for a full on-licence but it was refused. In 1906 it was described as "practically a cottage house" comprising two entrances and just two rooms available for the public, a smoke room [14 ft 3 in x 7 ft] and a bar [13 ft 7 in x 12 ft 8 in]. In the early 1900s Walter Butler kept a pony which he took through the front door to the coach house. Owned by the Banbury Brewery Company, the Ivy Tree closed on 4th April 1907 with compensation being paid.

| | |
|---|---|
| 1848-55 | Richard Arnold |
| 1855 | Thomas Smith |
| 1863-64 | John Silvester |
| 1866-Oct 1870 | William Rathbone and wife Harriett |
| October 1870-May 1871 | Harriet Rathbone |
| May 1871-72 | James Mills |
| 1875 | A. Rathbone |
| 1882-Sep 1883 | Frederick Smith |
| September 1883 | George Marshall |
| 1884-May 1884 | William Webb |
| May 1884-Nov 1889 | Joseph F. Potter |
| November 1889-Oct 1892 | Joseph Copley Orange |
| October 1892-Aug 1898 | John Prime |
| August 1898-Jan 1900 | Frank Fell |
| January 1900-Jul 1901 | James Henry Boyes |
| July 1901-1907 | Walter Butler |
| 4th April 1907 | Closed for business |

## Jack and Jill – Winston Crescent, Newland Road, Lillington

On 18th October 1963, it was reported that the licensing justices had granted Ansells Brewery the removal of the licence from the demolished White Lion public house [Althorpe Street, Leamington] to a new site in Newland Road, Lillington. Building commenced in November 1965, believed to be at a cost of £60,000 - £70,000, and its full licence was confirmed on 15th August 1966. The Ansells pub was opened as the Jack and Jill by Leamington's mayor, Councillor L. L. Freeman, on 5th September 1966. As a young man growing up in Lillington Tony 'Banger' Walsh, the ex-wrestler and security firm boss, regularly drank in the Jack and Jill. Later he had the opportunity to buy it and in 1992 he renamed it the Half Nelson, secured a full entertainments licence and booked some good entertainers. In 1996 it was managed by Dave Mucklow; it closed in September the same year and the site was redeveloped as residential housing.

| | |
|---|---|
| October 1963 | James Constantine *(Provisional licence)* |
| 5th September 1966 | Jack and Jill opened for business |
| 15th August 1966-Jun 1967 | Sidney Thomas Taylor and his wife Joyce |
| | *(Previously at the Dun Cow, Stretton-on-Dunsmore)* |
| June 1967-Dec 1970 | Graham William John Boulton and his wife Joan |
| December 1970-Oct 1972 | Derrick John Watson and his wife June |
| October 1972-Apr 1973 | Thomas O'Shea |
| April 1973-Jan 1974 | Ralph Chambers |
| January 1974-Nov 1974 | David Michael Finney |
| November 1974-Aug 1978 | William 'Bill' McCarthy and his wife Sheila |
| | *(Bill died 7th April 1984)* |
| August 1978-Feb 1979 | John McCamley |
| 1980-≥1985 | Peter Campbell *(Of Edinburgh)* |
| August 1990-Sep 1991 | Michael 'Mick' and Christine Thurlbeck [in partnership with Paul O'Keeffe] |
| September 1991-1992 | Colin Vickers and Adrian Bent *(Interim licensees)* |
| 1992 | Tony 'Banger' Walsh *(Half Nelson)* |
| 1996-Sep 1996 | David Mucklow |
| September 1996 | Closed for business |

*The Leamington Spa Courier dated 9th September 1966 reported:* **Jack and Jill opens September 1966** – *Pulling the first pint was Councillor L. L. Freeman. The mayor congratulated the planning committee on their choice of site for a public house and added it was intended to build more houses nearby. Two days after the Jack and Jill opened, Lillington opened its first Free Church. Mr. Freeman commented, "I'm glad to see our priorities are right, first a spiritual uplift and then refreshment." Mr J. D. Swanson, chairman of Ansells Brewery, told the gathering that the Jack and Jill licence, so called because it is at the top of a hill, was originally held by the White Lion, in Althorpe Street. The house managers are Joyce and Sidney Taylor, who were for three and a half years at*

*Photo of the Half Nelson taken from Coventry Telegraph dated 5th October 1996.*

*The Jack and Jill circa 1974-8 courtesy of Sheila McCarthy.*

the Dun Cow, Stretton-on-Dunsmore. The two large rooms have been named the Crown Room and the Campion Room. The Crown Room carries the contemporary murals of Jack & Jill and other nursery characters. The Campion Room, a collection of old beer pumps, taps and handles. The brewery intends to decorate the room with pictures illustrating the various brewing processes.

On Saturday 3rd June 1972 the Jack and Jill started Hole in the Middle which meant good album sounds on Saturdays and Sundays from 7.00pm until 10.15pm; the admission price was 30p.

*In order to involve the local community, landlords Bill and Sheila McCarthy organised Saturday film shows for around 50 of the local children, much to the discontent of the local constabulary who considered it a breach of their licence. Up to 1974 the Jack and Jill had been plagued by 'bikers' which was putting off the local community. Bill took things into his own hands one evening by confronting the bikers with his Alsatian 'Prince' and a bicycle chain. He convinced them they would rather like to go elsewhere, and it worked, they never returned.*

The Leamington Spa Courier dated 7th March 1975 reported: **Uncle Bill, Pied Piper of the Jack and Jill** – Lillington licensee Bill McCarthy has helped to solve a problem for children living on the large local housing estates: what can we do on Saturdays? After watching children playing dangerously one Saturday morning, Mr. McCarthy, who moved to the Jack and Jill public house last November, thought back to his boyhood and decided to revive the idea of a Saturday morning cinema club for the children. Now, every Saturday morning, 'Uncle Bill' - a former professional photographer sets aside the comfortable lounge for an hour to entertain the youngsters with Woody Woodpecker, crisps and soft drinks. Some of the golden oldies, like Laurel and Hardy, prove as popular as the newer cartoons like Tom and Jerry. In only four weeks, attendances have risen from 30 to more than 100 and Mums and Dads are leaving their children while they shop in Lillington, or have a drink in another bar. All alcoholic drinks are, of course, forbidden in the lounge during film time. Ansells Brewery asked for local opinion and, although one head teacher said she would prefer the cinema sessions to be held in the community hall, another said it was a good way for the children to identify with the local community. Mr. McCarthy hopes to introduce talks and other activities during weekdays in school holidays.

*In February 1992 the stars turned out for the official opening of Tony 'Banger' Walsh's pub, the Half Nelson. They included Superintendent Bill Guest of West Midlands police, comedian Roy 'Chubby' Brown, Trevor Oaks a founder member of pop group Showaddywaddy, Olympic gold medalist Neil Adams, footballer Kirk Stevens and Chubby Brown's manager, George Foster.*

In March 1992 at 'Banger' Walsh's Half Nelson there was a range of entertainment at weekends. Friday night was the 60s music quiz and party night, Saturday morning was Uncle Sid's children's show, Saturday night was cabaret night, Cissy Stone appeared at Sunday lunch time and on Sunday night it was Peter Roberts on the Hammond organ. The entertainment continued into Monday with 60s night and family bingo night at 8.00pm.

**Jam Bar and Brasserie** – 102 Warwick Street
The premises were firstly the Toyk Bar [≤2004-≥2006] before becoming the Whale Bar and then the Jam Bar and Brasserie in 2009. The 'Jam' closed in January 2011 and was replaced on 14th February 2011 by the Âme Soeur creperie and restaurant.

| | |
|---|---|
| 2007 | Hayley Kane *(Whale Bar)* |
| 6th November 2007 | Stephen Molloy *(Whale Bar)* |
| 21st August 2009 | Alex Lovell *(Jam Bar)* |

*The Jam Bar and Brasserie taken on 10th October 2009 © Allan Jennings.*

**Jekyll and Hyde** – 44/46 Clarendon Avenue

Pre-1960 these premises were a fish and chip shop and the leaseholder was a waiter who had worked for Charles Gustavus, a restaurateur, in Oxford. When the business failed in 1960 Gustavus took over the lease and by the July had opened the Chez Gustave restaurant, which was described as having a dark, cosy atmosphere and the smell of a French bistro – Charles being a qualified chef did all of the cooking.

By April 1961 it was Gustave and Bridgette's licensed restaurant and hotel, and in December 1963 it was the Chez Gustave Casino; it was open all night every night from 9.00pm [to members over 21 years of age] and it advertised chemin-de-fer, poker and roulette. In 1964 Chez Gustave was still a licensed restaurant with the Leamington Casino adjoining it. On 21st December 1964, the address was also registered as the Travellers Club but it closed in 1965; in 1966 it was the Gustave Café. Around this time, the top of the building became the Chateaubriand [with a supper licence until 11.30pm] and the ground floor became Chanelles, a licensed premises/night club comparable with the Tavern at Guys Hotel. It was open from 9.00pm until 2.00am, six nights a week, and girls were admitted free of charge. There were two round spinning dance floors with an aluminium stage and walls, and 'cage' seating; dancing was beneath seventy coloured lights. Wednesday 19th November 1969 saw the start of a weekly disco night from 8.00pm until 11.30pm with top DJ Jonny Tee.

During the period late 1970 to March 1973, there were a number of detrimental reports in the press relating to Chanelles; these ranged from angry resident's complaining about 'late night noise' and 'disturbances' to the owners 'flaunting authority' by erecting illuminated signs without planning permission. In June 1971, the licensing justices granted an extension of the 'music, singing and dancing' licence but, in the August, an application to use the premises as a hotel and restaurant with entertainment facilities was refused outright – the main opposition being that the entertainment facilities had become the main focus and council considered this a 'change of use'. In January 1972, 'people power' won-out when the nightspot's solicitors "proposed to restore the premises to its original use; from Monday to Thursday the restaurant will be open until 11.30pm with background music only and no dancing. On Friday and Saturday there will be dinner dances finishing at midnight and on Sundays the restaurant will be open only for meals." However, on 9th March 1973 the Courier reported that the local magistrates had banned the proprietor from holding a restaurant or music licence for four years after admitting to 22 offences involving breach of licensing regulations. Chanelles was closed in March 1973 and Chateaubriand closed circa 1974.

Although a restaurant licence was granted to Winston's [upstairs] on 13th December 1973, we believe that it failed to get the simultaneously required [downstairs] drinks licence due to objections raised by local residents. In 1975 it offered a choice of the Salad Room, open for light lunches, coffee, wine etc, or Winston's Restaurant with its traditional or speciality menu. In late 1975 [or early 1976] the business became a fully licensed free house and in 1976 it was advertised as Winston's Bars and Restaurant.

In February 1978 the new owner, Balraj 'Ben' Dhesi, was advertising the premises as Winston's Wine, Dine and Beer Kellar, and in the July the emphasis was also on Winstons being a lounge and wine bar, not a pub. In September 1978, it was described as being a "modest tribute to the wartime British spirit". Local MP Dudley Smith had recently opened the restaurant as Clementine's and now there was also the Bulldog Bar and the Churchill Lounge Bar; on 26th March 1979 the downstairs bar was renamed Winnie's Victory Cellar Bar, which had a resistance theme [entrance via Oxford Street]. In October 1980 Winston's opened a new steak bar and advertised giant sized steaks. Clementine's Lounge Bar [Oxford Street entrance] opened in August 1981, advertising a long bar, intimate alcove seating, Whitbread/Flowers traditional 'real' ales and basket meals; in September 1983 [Winston's] was proudly announcing the opening of the 'new style' Winston's Bar. In 1984, Winston's was acquired by new owner Michael John Riley and renamed Top of the Town, "a superb al a carte restaurant and lounge bar".

*Photo of Winston's courtesy of Nick Wilkins.*

In October 1986 it was announced that the premises had been bought by Whitbread-Flowers Brewery and that it would be closed for 2-3 months pending a £50,000 facelift. However, on 11th December 1986, the Morning News reported that: "A new-look pub opens its doors today. The Jekyll and Hyde has been created from the old Top of the Town in Clarendon Avenue at a cost of £130,000 by Whitbread-Flowers and pub developer John Gray. It now offers darts and pool facilities in the refurbished basement bar, music and dancing in the evenings and lunchtime food on the ground floor. The ground floor has been designed as one large area, but on two levels, and entertainment will be a main feature under licensee Tom Smith, formally entertainments manager at the Mercia Sporting Club and a DJ."

*A 1987 photo of the Jekyll and Hyde taken by Bill Bigley.*

In October 1987 councillors refused to renew the entertainments licence following the receipt of complaints from local residents concerning the noise levels; it would not be renewed until May 1989. In April 1990 it again lost its entertainment licence following a breach of fire regulations [350 people admitted when the limit was 200]; this time it was not renewed until July following a change of licensee. The Jekyll and Hyde closed in May 1992, reopening as

*Photo of Oxygen taken on 21st January 2006 courtesy of David Stowell.*

Winston's on 2nd July; owned by Standard Properties Developments Ltd, it went on to be known as Oxygen [19th October 2002] and the Clarendon since February 2008. The Clarendon remains open in December 2013.

| | |
|---|---|
| 1968-1973 | Mrs. Irene Thelma Whatsize *(Chanelles)* |
| Circa 1972-73 | Peter Richard Gold *(Manager, Chanelles)* |
| 1978 | Frank and Yvonne Hannan *(Winston's)* |
| 1978-84 | Balraj Singh Dhesi *(Owner, Winston's)* |
| 1984-1986 | Michael John Riley *(Owner, Top of the Town)* |
| Dec 1986-≥Oct 1987 | Tom Smith (*Went on to the Birch and Billycock – Manageress, Mary Gillespie*) |
| 11th December 1986 | Renamed Jekyll and Hyde |
| 1989-1990 | Paul Clough |
| June 1990 | Trevor Smith and his wife Margaret |
| 1992-95 | Neil Moffatt and his wife Julie |
| 2002 | Donna Burnett *(General Manager, Oxygen)* |
| 2006-Jul 2007 | Anna Janean Craig |
| July 2007-Nov 2007 | Kevin John Murphy |
| November 2007-Feb 2008 | Rhys William Kane |
| February 2008 → | Hamish Urquhart & Benjamin J. Philpotts *(Clarendon)* |

*The Leamington Spa Courier dated 30th March 1979 reported:* **Lively cellar bar send-off** - *Winnie's Victory Cellar Bar, the latest development at Winston's Restaurant opened on Monday evening with a packed house. The Clarendon Avenue restaurant is owned by Ben Dhesi who said that the new cellar bar would be used for a private night on Mondays and would feature traditional jazz and country and western music during the other weekdays. And there would be a 'free and easy' session on Sunday lunchtime. It has taken 13 months to complete the work at Winston's which includes remodelling the kitchens at a cost of £15,000. [Balraj Singh 'Ben' Dhesi became the first Asian Mayor of Leamington Spa on 23rd May 1987 - Ed]*

The Leamington Spa Courier dated 18th December 1987 reported that: Leamington is set to become an even more dramatic place to live with the formation of a new professional theatre company based at the Jekyll and Hyde. Called 'Five and Nine', after the numbers of the basic stage make-up sticks, the company has a core of three founder members including actor and director Michael Goron. Michael said, "We will be presenting two plays that we hope will appeal to students and younger audiences." The company will be performing their productions in the cellar bar which is being converted into a theatre in the round. The first play of the season will be 'Strippers' by Peter Terson and the second play is 'La Ronde' by Arthur Schnitzler. The company is self-financed but hopes to be funded in future by West Midlands Arts.

*The Coventry Evening Telegraph dated 19th October 2002 reported that: Drinkers who need to clear their heads will be able to have a gasp of clean air at the*

*Photo of the Clarendon taken on 8th October 2009 © Allan Jennings.*

*latest pub to open in Leamington. The former Winston's in Clarendon Avenue re-opens today as the Oxygen Bar. The trend for bars where people can inhale pure oxygen is coming to the Midlands for the first time. The craze of oxygen bars across the States and the Far East, where some bars go as far as offering strawberry flavoured shots, hasn't yet peaked in the UK. There are currently four bars in London, including one in Harvey Nicholls, as well as machines in some of the capital's gyms. But this will actually be the first of its kind in the Midlands.*

**Jephson Tavern** – Jephson Gardens
See Leamside Inn for details.

**Jet** – 67 Brunswick Street
See Jet and Whittle for details.

**Jet and Whittle** – 67 Brunswick Street
The Jet and Whittle replaced the Brunswick Arms, which had occupied the adjacent site [now the 'Jet' car park] from the early 1830s until 1964. It was named in honour of Sir Frank Whittle who made a major contribution to the invention of the jet engine, and who attended Milverton School before moving on to Leamington College for Boys [1918-23].

The Brunswick's licence was transferred to the Jet and Whittle on 14th December 1964 and it opened at 6.00pm on Thursday 17th December. By the time the Morning News had been printed on Saturday 19th December, demolition of the old Brunswick Arms was already underway. A Whitbread-Flowers pub, the Jet and Whittle was built in a cosy modern style, with a bar, lounge, off sales shop, and a compact flat on the first floor. The bar had a brown and fawn tiled floor, red patterned curtains, green upholstery and red and fawn hessian covered walls with a copper canopied fireplace. The first pint at the new Jet and Whittle in December 1964 was pulled by licensee John Crabtree and Jesse Sykes, a retired coalman of 1, Aylesford Street and a regular at the Brunswick Arms for 60 years.

*Above: The Jet & Whittle courtesy of Nick Wilkins. Below: The Jet taken on 23rd October 2011 © Allan Jennings.*

Following, "a complete refit from roof to cellar" [reportedly costing £80,000], the pub reopened on 3rd October 1989 with a new lay-out comprising a large lounge, pool and darts facilities in the games area and also a beer terrace/patio; the new decor was pink, grey and blue with pinewood furniture and fittings.

During the period 1998 until 2003 the name reverted to the Brunswick but in October 2003, due to a groundswell of local[s] opinion, it was renamed The Jet. A regular in the Jet believes that the continuing problems with the car park surface are due to the movement of its foundations, the theory being that the old cellars had not been filled in properly. It remains open as the Jet in December 2013.

| | |
|---|---|
| 17th December 1964 | The Jet and Whittle opened |
| 14th Dec 1964-Oct 1967 | John William Crabtree |
| | *(Previously at the Brunswick Arms)* |
| October 1967-Aug 1972 | Horace William 'Chas' Talbot and his wife Wynn |
| August 1972-Nov 1973 | Godfrey Morgan |
| November 1973 | Alan Peter Harrison |
| September 1976-Sep 1978 | Derek Thomas Robinson |
| September 1978-Feb 1979 | Relief manager |
| February 1979-84 | Lawrence 'Laurie' Bernard Sylvanas Scott |
| 1985 | Michael and Sandra Cremin |
| 1988-89 | Richard and Rita Harrison |
| Circa 2005 | Christopher George Abbott |
| August 2006 → | Daljit Singh Gill 'Gilly' |

*The new Jet and Whittle pub was designed by Mr. K. R. B. McKnight, architect, of 48 Queen's Road, Coventry and built by Messrs W. A. Cox Ltd of Evesham. The interior design was by Mrs. David Lloyd, a director of Flower and Sons Ltd. Following a competition the pub was named by 23 year old Erik G. King of 14, Henley Road who was an ex-pupil of Leamington College for Boys, where Sir Frank Whittle, who made a major contribution to the development of the Jet Engine, received his early education. The pub sign was designed and painted by Messrs W. R. Clarke [signs] Ltd of Stratford-upon-Avon and depicted an authentic 'Gloster' Jet and a genuine blueprint of a simple jet engine.*

Sir Frank Whittle was credited alongside Dr Hans Von Ohain as the creator of the jet engine. He was a former pupil at Milverton School before going on to Leamington College from 1918-1923. Sir Frank went on to Cambridge University, became an officer in the RAF, and was knighted for his work on jet propulsion. He died aged 89 in 1996.

### Memories of the Jet and Whittle in 1968 – by Tom Lewin
*A Whitbread pub, the Jet and Whittle was duly opened in December 1964 and John Crabtree, formerly of the Brunswick, was its first landlord. The event, complete with photograph, was duly recorded by the Leamington Courier. The pub contained a Lounge and a Bar with accommodation upstairs for the proprietors.*

*My best recollections are of 1968 when I could consider myself a regular, the Bar being my favourite room. The landlords at the time were Chas and Wynn Talbot, together with their* teenage son, Gordon. Bar staff included Harry, with an 'offset eye' that sometimes made it difficult for customers; Mrs. Mac and Maureen, two lovely elderly ladies, who reminded you of Hinge and Bracket, bless them; Barmaid, Susan Pratt, who went on to marry one of the footballing customers, Pete Harris.

The Bar was reasonably spacious with the serving bar being the focal point. An unusual feature was the bar pumps which were shaped as horizontal transparent barrels with a lever attached. They were designed to pour a measured half pint with one pull of the lever; the barrel would then refill so that a second half pint measure could be poured by reversing the lever. Clever, but in later years it failed health and safety requirements.

On the bar, under glass, Wynn kept her home made ham and cheese rolls. The bar seating was supplemented with tables and stools and heating was by way of an open grate fire with a large copper chimney fender.

Entrance to both Bar and Lounge was via the side, or car park entrance. There was a small entrance hall, with toilet access for both rooms. A pay telephone was immediately inside the door. On Brunswick Street itself, the Jet sported a small off-licence or, as it was referred to, 'an outdoor'.

The Bar had its usual amenities, a dart board and a juke-box, both sited adjacent to the front window. The Lounge was very much a traditional room, ideal for the clientele who enjoyed a quiet chat and a glass of your fancy. It had a small serving bar and the room itself was arranged so that the seating was enclosed in small alcoves. Heating was similar to the Bar with a large open fire.

A notable feature of the Lounge was that it sold a strong foreign lager, known as Stella Artois, not widely known in 1968. The walls of both Lounge and Bar were decorated with photographs depicting Sir Frank Whittle's achievements.

In 1968, many of the local teenagers were frequenting the Jet and it was decided to form a local football team. After due consideration, it was obvious that the new team should be named Whittle Wanderers. Chas and Wynn were very supportive of the fledgling team and we were able to run a weekly tote to raise funds.

The team was entered into the Leamington and District Sunday Football League and over the following years posted many successful seasons. Winning a trophy would always end with a celebration at The Jet, with Chas and Wynn providing a lovely spread, washed down with umpteen bottles of Pomade.

We organised many trips to watch professional football matches, including Manchester United, Chelsea and Leeds United. Above the bar we contributed to a large number of football team rosettes and any football trophies gained were displayed behind the bar.

Midweek was usually quiet but if some of the lads met up we would pool our limited resources in an ashtray and that was our 'kitty' for the evening. Cards were often played, usually 'brag', where pennies were often lost and seemingly rarely won. Music from the juke-box kept us entertained during the winter months.

In the 1970s, the Jet and Whittle was another pub that arranged outings for the locals and Blackpool was a popular destination. Looking back, the Jet and Whittle, although a new pub at the time, captured all the old traditions and good characteristics of pubs of a bygone age, including that 'local' feel that is difficult to define.

The Morning News dated 22nd November 1985 reported that: Running the Jet and Whittle was like looking after two separate pubs, according to tenants Michael and Sandra Cremin. Walk through from the traditional basic but comfortable bar into the lounge and you're in another world never mind another atmosphere. It has been decorated in log cabin style with stained pine walls, warm muted lighting and green plants. A chimney breast divides the seating into comfortable clusters and in the corner the green and gold of the fish tank adds the finishing touch. Mike and Sandra took over the Jet about seven months ago. Sandra at 19 was probably the youngest tenant in Britain but the couple have brought a dedication and friendliness to the job which might make many a seasoned landlord look a beginner. Within three months they had started two pool teams and four darts teams, and had built up a reputation for good quality home cooking. On Tuesdays a fishmonger parks his van outside the pub and customers can choose whatever they want to have cooked. The lounge can be hired out for parties and Sandra will also make sure a full spread of food is waiting for the guests. In the bar there is a television for customers to watch maybe a boxing match while having a pint. Live music such as a one man band is sometimes laid on.

*In October 1989, the Courier, Observer and Morning News were all reporting the reopening of the Jet and Whittle following a £80,000 refurbishment. It was reopened on 3rd October by long standing regular customer George Gall who had been drinking there since its opening in 1965. Prior to that he was a regular at the Brunswick Arms which was situated on what is now the car park. There was a complete refit from roof to cellar. The new decor was pink, grey and blue with pinewood furniture and fittings. It included photographs detailing the history of the jet plane as well as having one large lounge area offering comfortable surroundings and pool and darts facilities in the games area. There was also a beer terrace/patio area. Music was provided by a juke box and a CD track system. Landlord Richard Harrison said, "The pub is now a real 1990s pub – brighter and better than ever before."*

### Joiners Arms – 63-67 Shrubland Street

The 1834 church rate book shows William Langdon as the owner of 16, Springfield Street, but there is no mention of it then being a pub [Springfield Street was so named because of its proximity to springs with an abundance of fresh water]. The first directory listing we have is in 1835 when the same premises were a beer house known as the Springfield Inn. It had been renamed by 1856 because on 17th March, at the Joiners Arms, John Staite auctioned the pub's brewing utensils. By 1886 the road had also been renamed and the Joiners Arms was readdressed as 59, Shrubland Street; it would become '59-61' in 1911 [according to library records, Springfield Street was renamed Shrubland Street in 1886 but directories

*Photo of the old Joiners M&B pub in Shrubland Street before it was demolished in the 1940s.*

191

list the Joiners Arms as Shrubland Street from 1880, as does the 1881 census]. At the annual licensing sessions on 7th February 1911, the chief constable objected to the licence renewal on the grounds that the pre 1869 beer house was structurally unsuitable and that it was difficult for the licensee to supervise the smoke room; the domestic rooms comprised a small kitchen behind the bar and two bedrooms. However, the licence was renewed on the owner's undertaking that the premises would be altered and expanded by taking in the cottage next door.

At the annual licensing sessions held in the town hall on 6th March 1939, Frederick Jesse Toseland applied for a provisional order sanctioning the removal of a licence to sell beer at the Joiners Arms, to new premises to be erected on a site bounded by Shrubland Street, St. John's Road and Scotland Place, and to be known as the Joiners Arms; previously an M&B pub the owners of the new site were H. E. Thornley Ltd of Radford Hall Brewery. The licence register shows that the move to the new Joiners Arms at 63-67, Shrubland Street took place on 9th August 1943, when James Pinnington took over as the licensee. We have concluded that the old Joiners Arms closed as the new one opened [as we don't have any information on an earlier closure], thereby making it a seamless transfer. In March 1947, the licensing justices authorised the removal of the licence from the Bull and Butcher [Napton] to the Joiners Arms; we have interpreted this as being a full on-licence permitting the sale of beer, wines and spirits.

In the 1960s Tom Hitchcox took over the old Joiners premises at 59-61 Shrubland Street converting them into a Fleur de Lys pie shop; he later combined this with a bookie's shop [turf accountants] when the law changed to allow such establishments. Prior to that Tom had run a small greengrocers on the opposite side of the road ['64'] and would allegedly take 'under the counter bets' as a sideline. When Thornley-Kelsey closed their brewery and sold-off their [tied estate] pubs in 1968 the Joiners Arms was acquired by Davenports

*The Joiners Arms taken on 5th September 2009 © Allan Jennings.*

Brewery, who in turn sold-out to Greenall Whitley & Co. Ltd in 1986. The official opening of the Joiners Arms new lounge bar took place at 7.00pm on Wednesday 12th May 1971. The Joiners closed early in 2010 but reopened on 5th June the same year with a new licensee; it remains open in December 2013 [also in 2013, the site of the old pub is just a grassed area alongside the current Joiners Arms].

**Footnote:** A friend of Allan Jennings who lived in Shrubland Street, until the family were re-housed in Christine Ledger Square, said that he saw the Springfield Inn sign in September 1968 when the builders were demolishing the bookies [turf accountants]

*This photo of the Springfield Inn sign was taken circa 1967/68 when the houses in Shrubland Street were being demolished and is courtesy of Pete Watts.*

adjacent to where the original pub stood [just around the corner from the present Joiners Arms]. This was confirmed by Barry Astill who told us that the painted sign on the gable end of the old Joiners, depicting the Springfield Inn, was discovered when 57 Shrubland Street was also demolished in the sixties. The house belonged to his grandfather Mr William Astill. See Joiners Arms for details.

| | |
|---|---|
| 1834 | William Langdon *(Owner, no mention of a beer house)* |
| 1835 | Edward Ford |
| 1837 | William Manning Langdon |
| 1838-42 | Thomas Robbins |
| 1851-57 | Joseph Sheffield |
| 1860-68 | William Langdon *(Carpenter and Innkeeper)* |
| 1869-Sept 1889 | Mrs. Mary Ann Langden *(Daughter of William Langdon; died 28th August 1889)* |
| September 1889-Dec 1889 | Mrs. Mary Ann Mason and Mr. Newsome *(Executors)* |
| December 1889-Jul 1902 | Francis Wilson Williams |
| July 1902-May 1905 | Mrs. Anne 'Annie' Williams *(On the death of Francis)* |
| May 1905-29 | Walter Henry Williams and his wife Lydia Charlotte |
| 1929-32 | Percy Parker *(Died 14th January 1950, aged 56)* |
| 1932-33 | Albert Simpson Bolam |
| 1933-Dec 1934 | Albert Marshall |
| December 1934-37 | Wilfred Burchall |
| 1937-Jun 1939 | Frederick Jesse Toseland |
| June 1939-Aug 1943 | Joseph William Ensor *(59-61 Shrubland Street)* |
| 9th August 1943 | Joiners Arms reopened in the new premises |
| August 1943-Nov 1948 | James Pinnington *(63-67 Shrubland Street)* |

| | |
|---|---|
| November 1948-Jan 1956 | Arthur Woolison |
| January 1956-Apr 1956 | Evelyn Doris Woolison *(on the death of Arthur)* |
| April 1956-Sep 1958 | Francis Leonard Tedd |
| September 1958-Jul 1960 | Hubert Leslie Groves |
| July 1960-Aug 1964 | William Robertson |
| August 1964-Oct 1964 | Ronald Poole |
| October 1964-Jun 1968 | William Arthur Cartwright |
| June 1968-Jun 1969 | Dennis Rhiwallon Williams |
| June 1969-Nov 1969 | Gordon Richard Harris |
| November 1969-Dec 1969 | Leslie Cyril Booth *(Temporary licensee)* |
| December 1969-Apr 1973 | Alan and Betty Gibson |
| April 1973-Mid 1970s | Graham David Peter Tucker |
| | *(Previously steward at Newport Golf Club)* |
| Mid 1970s | Bill and his wife Jo Green |
| January 1982 | New manager *(Name not known)* |
| 1983-1986 | Thomas and Margaret Hobbs |
| | *(Tom was born in 1941 and died in 1995)* |
| 1988-≥1990 | John and Patricia 'Pat' Bassett |
| January 2006-Nov 2008 | Mrs. Marian Tarver |
| November 2008-Dec 2009 | Gareth Beddows and Kelly Satchwell |
| 5th June 2010 → | Umbelina Costa |

### *Memories of the Joiners in Autumn 1966 – by Tom Lewin*

*The Joiners was built during the Second World War, replacing three cottages in Shrubland Street numbered 63, 65, and 67; the former Joiners was located at 59, Shrubland Street and was an M & B house.*

*Barely old enough to legally drink, I started using the Joiners as my local in the autumn of 1966. The pub had three main entrances, Shrubland Street, St. John's Road and Scotland Place and it comprised two rooms. The bar would normally be entered from the Shrubland Street door and was sizeable, but would be extended years later. The lounge/smoke room was long and spacious and could be entered via all three doors. From the Shrubland Street entrance, via two doors, you would enter what was commonly called the 'snug'. It was ideal for elderly people to sip their tipple of Guinness or Mackeson and, although open right through to the smoke room, it formed a nice contained alcove. Simplest way to be served was via a serving hatch which overlooked the bar.*

*The lounge/smoke room was served by a bar facing the St. Johns Street entrance. Entertainment was provided by a juke-box, a 'table football game' and a dart board sited over the open fireplace which backed onto Scotland Place. An upright piano divided the two rooms although I didn't see anybody wanting to tickle the ivories. Seating was mainly positioned around the perimeter of the smoke room and in leather upholstery. Toilets were sited thus, one male in the bar, one female in the Shrubland Street entrance and another one located in the Scotland Place entrance. Thornley-Kelsey provided the alcoholic beverage and if you were brave enough there was a 'yard of ale' affixed above the smoke room bar.*

*We are grateful to Doris Owen and her daughter Maureen Pierce for this photo of Shrubland Street during the 1935 Silver Jubilee celebrations for King George V and Queen Mary. At the first house on the left is Mr. Simmons with his wife peeping through the door. At the second house is Mrs. Farey. At the third house is Mr. Burchal, the landlord of the Joiners, Mrs. Smith, Gladys Smith, Dolly Reason, Mrs. Mills, Mrs. Edwards and Mrs Machin. At the right hand side of the table is Mr. Reason, Dolly Reason's father, and Mr. George from the baker's shop. At the house on the right are Mr. and Mrs. Astill. The children at the front of the photo from left to right are Barry and Tony Reason, unknown, Doris Owen and Norman and Mary Machin.*

My friends and I would meet early on a Friday evening, before venturing into the town, and there was much to discuss about the new songs that had been added to the juke-box. Amongst such favourites were the Four Tops, Ike & Tina Turner, Beach Boys, the Who and an operatic version of The Drinking Song, probably by Mario Lanza.

The 'table football game' provided great fun and John Bolitho and myself became very adept at this. A local football team at the time, Leamington Southend, would use the pub as their headquarters. Their secretary, Albert Jones, would always be in the bar on a Friday evening to collect the tote money. The 'table football game' enabled the Southend lads to organise inter pub matches to which John and I were seconded into the team.

Albert Jones of 2, Neville Close was a big mentor of mine when I started Whittle Wanderers Football Club; he was an absolute bible on football rules. Leamington Southend moved from the Joiners to the Leopard when they started a Sunday team. The Leopard provided changing rooms at the back in an old wooden barn. Albert lived to a good old age and died at 93.

The landlord of the Joiners at that time was Arthur Cartwright and was sometimes assisted by his son Michael, a big lad fresh out the army. The pub was very much a mixture *of people, mostly locals, but always a good pub to spend an evening in, whether it be with girlfriends or just the lads. Happy days spent there!*

On the 30th September 1968, the Morning News published the following article on the origins of the pub: **Springfield mystery is solved** – The origin of the sign Springfield Inn discovered by demolition workmen on the site of the old Spa Turf Accountants in Shrubland Street has been explained. Mr. Ted Goodman, a member of the Warwickshire Local History Society, has discovered that Shrubland Street was the name given to Springfield Road [should be street] in the mid 1870s when the south-east of Brunswick Street was being developed. Research by Leamington Library staff also produced the same result. Numbers 59-61 were at that time the Joiners Arms, owned by a Mrs Langden, who had previously kept a beer house in Springfield Road. In the late 1930s, houses in Shrubland Street and St. John's Road were pulled down for a new site for the Joiners Arms.

### *Memories of the Joiners – by Allan Jennings*
*The Joiners wasn't just a pub, it was part of the community. That community was basically the top half of Shrubland Street, St. Johns Road, Scotland Place and St. Georges Road. The reason was that if you went any further afield you came across other 'community' pubs such as the Wheatsheaf, Sun in Splendour, Green Man, and the Brunswick which later became the Jet and Whittle.*

*I first became aware of the Joiners as a child of the 1950s. I lived at 39, Shrubland Street and very often played in the streets and on the frontage of the Joiners with my mates. The frontage was a good place to meet; it was very central and was quite wide and off the road. It was ideal for playing marbles into the drain cover, and the slabs were brilliant for hopscotch. The wooden post office telegraph pole became the 'start and finish' point for a game of ayecki, a sort of 'hide and seek' [if that's how it's spelt]. The outdoor on the Scotland Place side was where we took the pop bottles to get the deposit back. I think it was 3d, but it was a good way to enhance any pocket money.*

*The 1970s saw me using the inside of the pub rather than the outside. By then the outdoor was closed and the beer was Davenports; I used to drink Davenports drum bitter. The pub had two rooms, the lounge and the bar. The lounge was the posh bit that had carpets and upholstered seating. It was the sort of place you could take 'other people' to for an evening out, possibly parents or the in-laws. The bar was our normal place of residence; it was the place for darts, dominoes and crib, although I only got involved in the darts side of things.*

*The Joiners catered for the different generations which was good; as I say it was part of the community. At one end of the age range were such characters as George Whittaker, Dick Turpin the famous boxer and brother to Randolph, Omer Burnell, Arthur Reynolds and Stan Green. At the other end were Pete Horley, Alan Jones, Roger Jones, Dave and Sue Hay, Colin Green, Dave and Sue Burnell, Rob Turpin, Mick Finnerty, Robert Burnell, Pete Chutte, Keith Todd, Tony Eden, Tony Griffin, John Roberts and Barry Connolly to name but a few.*

*The landlords in the mid 70s were Bill and Jo Green, and they were very involved with the social side of the pub, and supported their customers very well. Sandwiches were put on for the various matches, and if a team had won an important game or won a cup, it was not unheard of for everyone to go back after hours for a drink, and often drinks would be provided 'on the house'. They even arranged for a coach trip to a Redditch pub one evening.*

*I was in the men's darts team and my wife was in the ladies team. The men's 'A' team were good, but I wasn't in it for my prowess with the 'arrows'. I was in because I had a car and could ferry them about. I did all the secretarial side of things for the teams and collected 'subs', organised sandwiches and raffles, and I could make up the numbers when required.*

*The Joiners was a Davenports pub famous for its 'beer at home' advert although drinking at home was not what we had in mind. It sold best bitter, drum bitter, mild and lager. The older 'residents' tended to drink mild, the younger ones drank bitter and a few 'strange people' had started drinking some new tasteless cold liquid called 'lager'! However, the majority of drinkers of this strange phenomenon were the ladies and they drank it in half pints with a dash of lime, when they weren't drinking ½ pint of shandy. What they never did was drink pints, it was unheard of and not to be considered.*

*Most pubs were still the haunts of men, although there were no rules or stigma about this at this time, not like in the past. However, the Joiners was quite enlightened and many women used the pub along with the men. It was such an enlightened, community pub, that women felt that they could go in on their own and know that there would be someone there to talk to. As strange as this may seem it would have been unheard of in many pubs, even then.*

Some trivia from Tom Lewin: 'Dick' Turpin, a regular of the Joiners, was the oldest of the three boxing brothers and was actually Lionel Cecil Turpin. He obviously inherited the name 'Dick' from the notorious highwayman. Howard, Dick's eldest son became a barman at the Joiners in the late 1970s/early 1980s. Robert, one of Dick's younger sons, collected the Joiners Christmas thrift money every Sunday and Lionel Junior, Dick's second son, joined the Coldstream Guards. Dick and his family lived in Shrubland Street for some time, not far from the Joiners on the opposite side of the Street.

**Jolly Boatman** – Albion Row
See Plasterers Arms for details.

**Jolly Brewer** – 21 Guy Street
Our first directory listing for the Jolly Brewer is in 1833 when it was a beer house. By 1897 it had been granted a full on-licence and it was a freehold property at that time. In 1903 the premises underwent some improvements, the staircase was widened from its original three foot width, the upstairs clubroom was disconnected from the bedroom and a urinal was installed, as was a new water closet. Also in 1903 the building was described as having two entrances, one into Guy Street and one into a passage that connected Guy Place to Oxford Row. A Flower's pub for many years, the popular Jolly Brewer [or the 'Brewer' as it was commonly known] closed in November 1981. It was demolished in March 1982 having stood alone for some time on land assigned for car parking, and by September work had commenced on making the car park a permanent fixture. In 2013 the original site is part of [what is known as] the Chandos Street car park.

**Footnote:** During the period 1873-1940 directories occasionally listed the pub as the Jolly Brewers.

*The Jolly Brewer in 1976 courtesy of Peter Coulls.*

| | |
|---|---|
| 1833-Mar 1861 | Benjamin Hitchman |
| March 1861-Feb 1863 | Ann White *(Executrix of Benjamin Hitchman)* |
| February 1863-Aug 1864 | Samuel Watton |
| August 1864-70 | John Upton |
| 1873-Apr 1880 | William Preston |
| April 1880-May 1889 | Mary Preston |
| May 1889-Jul 1894 | William Townsend |
| July 1894-Jan 1901 | Henry Jordan |
| January 1901-Nov 1903 | Thomas Busby |
| November 1903-May 1908 | Francis Woods |
| May 1908-1913 | James Glenn |
| 1913-Oct 1915 | William Mansell |
| October 1915-1937 | David Lynch |
| 1940-Jul 1940 | William Edward Monk |
| July 1940-Aug 1950 | Francis Alfred Walker |
| August 1950-Oct 1965 | Horace Clark |
| October 1965-Nov 1981 | Fred William and Pearl Wright *(Fred was born in Long Itchington on 2nd May 1931 and died in 1995, aged 63)* |
| November 1981 | Closed for business |

During the time Fred and Pearl Wright were at the 'Brewer' they had some cards produced which said:

Free Pass and Gilt Edged Security
The "JOLLY BREWER INN"
Guy Street, Leamington Spa

Tel. Leamington Spa 28283
Fred & Pearl Wright, proprietors

Quality – Quick Service

Cleanliness – Civility

Whitbreads – Flowers Ales

Always in splendid condition

Wines – Spirits – Cigarettes

This pass is not transferable except
to another man with money

Free to sit and free to think,
Free to pay for what you drink;
Free to stop an hour or so;
When uneasy, free to go.
My beer is good, my measures just,
Forgive me please, I cannot trust;
I've trusted many to my sorrow,
So pay today and owe tomorrow.

Today I don't cash cheques,
tomorrow I may;

I have been pleasing and displeasing
the public ever since I started in
business.

I have been cussed and discussed,
robbed, lied to, held up, hung up
and knocked up.

The only reason I am staying in
business is to see what the hell will
happen next.

Life is just one damned thing after
another.

*In September 1973, Bill Keight, the landlord of the King's Head in Cubbington retired. He was replaced by his daughter Pearl Wright, the wife of Jolly Brewer landlord Fred Wright.*

The Leamington Spa Courier dated 6th December 1974 reported: **Barmaids' hopes to pull points** – Two local barmaids are hoping to pull their way into the regional final of the Whitbread/Flowers 'ideal barmaid' competition. They will be judged while working behind their own bars by a visiting panel of experts, and six finalists will be chosen to attend the regional final at Birdlip, Cheltenham; the next step is the firm's national competition held in London. Our local hopes are Moira Guest of the Jolly Brewer and Gillian Ede of the Boars Head, Hampton Lucy. Moira has worked at the Jolly Brewer for five years and agreed to enter the competition because part of the prize is a day at the races for the Whitbread Gold Cup day. The winner gets £100 to spend at the races and £100 will go to the licensee to provide a party for his customers. Moira, who works full time and usually drinks soda and lime behind the bar, says there is seldom criticism of the beer from the customers. Moira was narrowly beaten but as runner-up still came away with £15 and a bottle of champagne [Moira married Jolly Brewer licensee Fred Wright on 9th February 1995].

*The Morning News dated 14th August 1980 reported that: After an incredible 68 years supping pints together at the Jolly Brewer, Peter Price and Bob Stanley have more reason than most to regret the old Leamington pub's approaching demolition. For 88 year old Mr. Price, of Burbury Close, Lillington, and his drinking partner, 89 year old Mr. Stanley, of Clapham Terrace, it will mean an end to their regular meetings at the pub which began in 1912. "I am going to miss the pub," said Mr. Price. "It is a nice pub. It is the people here that have kept me coming all these years." Jolly Brewer veteran Mr. Price remembers the days when there was a bowling alley at the back of the pub. "Beer was cheaper and better then," he said. It was brewed locally when he started drinking. The pair drink at the pub three lunchtimes a week. They are not sure where they will go when the pub is knocked down - perhaps to their Saturday haunt, the Coach and Horses? Booze note – Our reporter calculated that at two pints each a session, the men had drunk 84,864 pints [10,608 gallons] over the 68 years.*

**Jug and Jester** – 13 Bath Street
See Chair and Rocket for details.

**K A Bar** – 44 Clarendon Street
See Kings Arms for details.

**Kasa Bar** – 27 Augusta Place
See Hintons for details.

**Kellys** – 7 Court Street
See Leopard for details.

**Kelseys** – 15/17 High Street
These premises were first listed in the 1888 street directory and from 1908 were the home of the Trades Hall and Social Club until it relocated across the road in 1968. It was also Le Can Can [1968-70] and then the Midland Red Sports and Social Club before it became Kelseys. In March 2002, Kelsey's was owned by Jasminder Satsavia who spent £350,000 on its refurbishment; at

*Kelsey's Bar taken on 6th August 2011 © Allan Jennings.*

that time he also owned the Debonair and the Leamington Spa Social Club. Kelseys remains open in December 2013.

≤2002 →                                    Jasminder Satsavia

### Kings Arms – 44 Clarendon Street

Warwick Street was laid out between 1822 and 1826. The original site of the Kings Arms was 1, Warwick Street and located on the south western corner of Warwick and Clarendon Streets, although the actual corner block was 'building free'. The first references we have for the Kings Arms are entries in the licensed victuallers' records dated 1825-27, naming Richard Dee as licensee but no address; our first directory listing is in 1828 when the address is just given as Warwick Street. In 1834 the Kings Arms consisted of two cellars, three parlours, a bar, a tap-room, kitchen, seven bed-chambers, a water closet, brew house, scullery, its own water pump, piggery, sheds for carriages and stabling for five or six horses. Circa 1868, the Kings Arms vacated the Warwick Street premises in favour of one on the Clarendon Street side of the 'building free' corner; and it would be directory listed as 44, Clarendon Street from the early 1880s [the 'building free' corner block would become an extension of number '44' towards the end of the 20th century]. The vacated premises at 1, Warwick Street were then occupied by Devis and Co. [wine, spirit, ale & stout merchants] and by 1879, they also housed Burton & Banbury Brewery Stores – also by 1879, it had been renumbered 128, Warwick Street. In 1880 the pub was sold to Hunt, Edmunds and Co. of Banbury. A full off-licence was granted in March 1955. During the era of licensee William Spriggs [1930-64], the Kings Arms was the only pub in Leamington Spa that had a six day licence; it didn't open on Sundays. Later as an M&B pub, also selling Bass bitter, the Kings Arms underwent a refurbishment in 1981 reopening in the new year of 1982.

Apart from the Kings Arms, the pub had also been variously known as the Kings Arms 'Vaults', 'Inn' and the 'Old' Kings Arms [to differentiate it from the New Kings Arms then situated at 69, Warwick Street]. After the Kings Arms it became the K A Bar in 1984 [until 1986], the Kings Arms again [1986-94] and Bar 44 [until 2010]. In March 2010 it underwent another transformation to the Three Graces, a name that references Leamington's past – local man Samuel Lockhart [1851-1933] kept elephants which he would wash in the River Leam and parade up and down the Parade as part of the circus. He called his elephants Wilhemina, Trilby and Haddie, and collectively they were known as the 'Three Graces'. Haddie was named after his wife Harriet who was known as Hattie. The Three Graces opened on the 19th March 2010 but closed in April 2011 and the signage was removed.

*Photo of the Three Graces taken 30th March 2010 © Allan Jennings.*

By May 2011 it had reopened as a wine bar named Forty Four but in early January 2012 this too had closed. On Friday 13th January 2012 it opened as the Cross Keys, addressed as 128, Warwick Street and advertised as a "traditional style pub with a pool table, quiz and fruit machines and a retro 90s style CD jukebox". The Cross Keys remains open in December 2013.

**Footnote:** The original Kings Arms premises would become the well remembered 'Thrift Shop' in the 1950s/60s/70s; in 2013 it is 'Love Vintage' [a clothing retailers], addressed as 128 Warwick Street as is the Cross Keys.

| | |
|---|---|
| 1825-40 | Richard Dee |
| March 1841-Circa 1855 | William Bicknell |
| 1858-Nov 1859 | Thomas Smith |
| November 1859-Sep 1860 | Miss Hannah Caddick |
| September 1860-May 1861 | William Davenport |
| May 1861-Feb 1862 | John Dean |
| February 1862-Oct 1862 | John Summers Gill |
| October 1862-Mar 1863 | John Dean |
| March 1863-64 | Thomas Willis |
| 1866-Jul 1870 | Samuel Sibley |
| July 1870-73 | Thomas Ward |
| 1873-74 | John Bolton Raybold |
| 1875-78 | T. Shepherd |
| 1878-Jul 1879 | G. Judd |
| July 1879-Nov 1883 | Joseph Moore |
| November 1883-Mar 1887 | William Richardson |
| March 1887-Jan 1897 | Henry Hall |
| January 1897-Sep 1910 | George Walton |
| September 1910-1910 | H. G. Hawkes |
| 1910-25 | Mrs. Annie Walton *(Died in September 1942, aged 79)* |
| 1925-32 | Edwin Charles Carter |
| 1932-Apr 1933 | Thomas Edward Mosely |
| April 1933-Jul 1930 | Albert Ernest Collett |
| July 1930-Jun 1964 | William Noel Hill Spriggs |
| June 1967-Feb 1969 | Mrs. Mary Darby |
| February 1969-Dec 1970 | Doris Gwendoline Harley |
| December 1970 | Harry George Garton |
| 1985-1986 | Neil MacPherson *(K A Bar)* |
| 1986 | Peter Ogden Jones *(Kings Arms from October 1986)* |
| April 1994 | Mark Hobbs *(Renamed Bar 44)* |
| 1995 | Sharon Carvell? |
| 1999-2003 | Rachael Harris |
| Circa 2006 | Rachael Anne Hill |
| January 2008-Aug 2008 | Thomas Paul Fitzgerald |

*This photo of a circus procession outside Hunt Edmunds Ale and Spirit Stores was inherited by Gordon Collett of Kenilworth. It was printed in the Leamington Spa Courier dated 28th May 2010. He believes that it was taken by his Uncle Albert Collett around 1912 just before he went off to fight in the First World War. Both his uncle and his father worked as general managers at the brewery stores, but not at the same time. His father, Septimus Octavius Collett ended up working for the same company for 54 years. The job came with in-house accommodation and Gordon lived there with his parents for a short time when he was 16 years old.*

| August 2008-Jan 2009 | Andrew John Potts |
|---|---|
| January 2009-Mar 2009 | Hamid Guerna |
| March 2009-Nov 2009 | Christopher Alan Lewis |
| November 2009 | Gary Summers |
| 2011 | Rachael Anne Hill *(Forty Four)* |
| January 2012 → | Rob Skinner *(Licensee - Cross Keys)* |
| January 2012 → | Tom Warwick *(Manager - Cross Keys)* |

*The Leamington Spa Courier dated 21st March 1840 carried the following sale notice: "All those very desirable freehold premises, comprising the Kings Arms public house, with the yard, brewhouse, stabling, also with the adjoining house No. 16 in Clarendon Street. There has been a good trade carried on by Mr. Dee, the present occupier for many years past.*

On 13th October 1855, the following sale notice appeared in the Leamington Spa Courier: To publicans and others – To be sold by auction on Thursday, the 18th October, 1855, upon the premises of Mr. Wm. Bicknell, Kings Arms, Warwick Street: All the household furniture comprising seven feather beds, four-post, tent, and French bedsteads; bedding, carpet, mahogany, cane seat and Windsor chairs; mahogany and painted chests of drawers; other tables; four-pull ale machine; gas and trade fittings; brewing plant, 15 sweet iron-bound casks from 300 gallons, 300 gallons of ale; 130-gallon iron furnace and setting; 18-strike mash tub; rearing, mash and general brewing tubs; culinary requisites and chamber appendages – Sale to commence at eleven o'clock.

*Above left: Bill Bigley took this photo of the K A Bar. Above right: Photo of Bar 44 courtesy of Jo Clark.*

The Leamington Spa Courier dated 4th October 1968 reported: There were drinks all round at the King's Arms, Clarendon Street on Wednesday night when the pub played its first league game of dominoes for more than 60 years. They played North Leamington rivals the Royal Naval Association – and lost 4-3. "My old man let us down," laughed licensee Mrs. Mary Darby.

*The Leamington Spa Courier of 29th April 1988 carried an article about the 'original' Kings Arms: Plans to demolish a 19th century shop in Leamington's Warwick Street – a conservation area – have angered a local pressure group. Brewers Mitchells and Butlers want to knock down the former Thrift Shop and the next door Kings Arms to build a new café-bar; an M&B spokesman said, "subject to planning permission, work would start in August with a view to opening the bar in the summer of 1989." The Central Leamington Residents' Association has no objection to demolishing the pub but feel the shop is a good, simple Leamington building dating back to the 1820s and should be preserved. "If we allow these unpretentious buildings to be whittled away, as so many have been, the character of Leamington will be destroyed," said Mr. Robert Gill CLARA committee member. The association's research has found that the shop was the original King's Arms until it became the Burton and Banbury Brewery stores in 1868. It remained as a store for almost a century until the 1950s when it became a second-hand shop known as the Thrift shop. However, on 8th September 1988, the Morning News published the following outcome: A proposal to demolish a Leamington listed building and replace it with a modern café-bar was rejected at the plans sub-committee meeting. Councillor Tony Davison said, "I think with a bit of care and thought the listed building could be adapted to be made into quite a good pub as it has been for many, many years. The plan we have seen is totally amazing and totally out of character with this part of Leamington."*

On 20th April 1990, the Leamington Courier reported that moves were underway to reopen two disused pubs, the Haunch of Venison on the Parade and the K A Bar. Kenilworth based Leycester Securities submitted planning proposals for the neglected K A Bar which would include a wine bar and restaurant for the basement with six offices, a brasserie, and conservatory on the ground floor.

*In September 2003, Bar 44 was given permission to open until midnight on Thursdays, Fridays and Saturdays. In 2009 Bar 44 advertised: "Paradise is whatever you want it to be; whatever you want to eat; whatever you want to drink; whatever occasion you are celebrating; Bar 44 can cater for your every need."*

Tom Lewin says, "I knew the Thrift Shop and the owner George Draper very well; it was on the site of the original Kings Arms. It had a courtyard at the side that the present pub uses for tables and chairs in the summer. George Draper is the brother of Bill who was at the Le Can Can club. He owned the Thrift Shop during the 1970s and 80s and lived in the house opposite the Newbold Arms. I did a bit of work for him at both properties. The Kings Arms I remember is the one on the actual corner of Clarendon Street. George sold the Warwick Street property and moved to smaller premises in Regent Street, opposite 'Murphys'. He also sold his house and moved to Northumberland Road. Later, he sold his business to John Harris and these days he is living in Brighton. John Harris sold the Warwick Street Thrift Shop when his assistant Ian Claridge sadly died suddenly."

*The conservation department at the Warwick District Council describe the Kings Arms as: "Circa 1826 with later additions and alterations, including late 19th century single-storey range to left return; reddish-brown brick, partly whitewashed and rendered, with ashlar dressings; Welsh slate and plain-tile roofs; main range of three storeys, three first-floor windows with lean-to to right and end and rear ranges; plinth; first and second floors have blind central windows, otherwise first floor has 6/6 sashes and second floor has 3/6 sashes; ground floor: central entrance a part-glazed and panelled door, in plain reveals, door case has Tuscan pilasters supporting frieze and hood; all windows in plain reveals; end stacks with cornices; range to left; two boarded and bricked-in basket-arched openings with Tuscan column between supporting hollow-chamfered arch with keystone and imposts; full height pilaster to left; modillion cornice; hipped roof has raised centre; Clarendon Street façade has double-chamfered, moulded plinth, end pilasters; centre projects; two outer similar recessed entrances 6 panel double-doors with basket-arched overlights, now boarded over, reveals have Tuscan pilaster strips; cambered arch with central keystone and imposts; between are tall, basket-arched window openings, now boarded in and with Tuscan pilasters between; moulded cornice."*

**Kings Head** – Square Street, Covent Garden Market

We understand that the Covent Garden Market was established in 1828. The first reference we have for these premises is in 1833 when it is listed as the Dog and Duck and William Carey is the licensee. The 1834 church rate book lists William Carey as having a public house, brew house and barbers at the premises. In 1834 he changed the name to the Ship and in 1835 it was renamed the Kings

KING'S HEAD INN,
COVENT GARDEN, LEAMINGTON.

A HARMONIC MEETING
HELD EVERY TUESDAY EVENING,
Commencing at 8 o'Clock.

Chairman, Mr. PALMER.   Piano, Mr. CHAMBERLAIN.

ON FRIDAY EVENINGS,
A SELECT QUADRILLE PARTY,
AT EIGHT O'CLOCK.

*An advert for the Kings Head Inn courtesy of Jo Clark.*

Head, which it remained until its closure in 1871-72. On 1st July 1872 the British Workmen Coffee Shop was opened on the premises.

| | |
|---|---|
| 1833-34 | William Carey *(Dog and Duck)* |
| 1834-35 | William Carey *(The Ship)* |
| 1835-37 | William Carey *(Kings Head)* |
| 1838-48 | Charles Bartlett *(Kings Head)* |
| June 1848-54 | Robert Weston |
| 1854-April 1865 | William Barnwell |
| April 1865-May 1866 | Mrs. Ann Treaddell |
| May 1866 | Edward Apps |
| 1870-January 1871 | William Copp |
| January 1871-≥Aug1871 | Thomas Banks |

*Historian Alan Griffin has been helping collate residents' memories of some of the old streets. He said, "In the mid 19th century most of the worst housing was in the courts between Regent Street and Clarendon Square and some of these remained until the mid 1930s. Covent Garden Market was one of these. Its name has been preserved at the multi-storey car park but the area was once one of the most densely populated parts of Leamington. The market itself was established in 1828, but by the mid 19th century the area was a badly drained and overcrowded slum. The market had fallen into disuse by 1947 and the terraced houses, which had characteristic porches extending across the pavement, were demolished in the mid 1960s."*

**KoKo's Bar** – 45 Warwick Street
In 2004 the bar operating on these premises was known as Zest. In 2009 KoKo's was advertised as: "A thrilling party and entertainments venue in the heart of Leamington Spa with a bar, restaurant, dance-floor and an open air roof terrace." However on 12th January

*Above left: Zest taken on 13th August 2004 courtesy of John Hartnup. Above right: KoKo's taken on 29th April 2011 © Allan Jennings.*

2012, the future of KoKo's became uncertain when Mood Bars [UK] Ltd, who owned KoKo's, TJs [Bath Street] and the Shakespeare [Tavistock Street], entered into administration and the holder of the premises licence became Licensed Solutions Ltd; by mid-year KoKo's had closed.

On 18th September 2012 a premises licence was granted to newly formed company Warneford Bars Ltd, who renamed the venue Altoria; it would also incorporate the space previously known as the Shakespeare in Tavistock Street. September also saw substantial work commence on the building as the company invested £1.5 million on its transformation into a bar, restaurant and club. Over four floors there is a boutique VIP lounge with table service, a semi glazed roof terrace called the Observatory, and a club room Uba, in which DJs use the latest technology to mix the soundtrack to the evening. An 'invitation only' night was held on Thursday 25th October 2012 and the premises opened to the public on Friday 26th. Altoria remains open in December 2013.

| | |
|---|---|
| 2009-Jan 2012 | Gurcharan Singh Atwal |
| January 2012-Oct 2012 | Andrew David Merricks |
| October 2012-Mar 2013 | Zoltan Branch |
| March 2013-Apr 2013 | Steven Philip Hay |
| April 2013 → | Narinder Singh Gill |

**Lamb** – 33 Park Street

The first directory listing we have for the Lamb is in 1832, the last is in 1834 and Mr. G. Bird was the licensee for the duration. However, it is apparent that the next tenant [William Dixon Davis] renamed the pub as we have a listing for the Union Tavern at 33, Park Street in 1835 [an 1837 entry in *Moncrieff's New Guide* lists the pub but no licensee]. Furthermore, on Friday 31st July 1835, the Union Tavern was utilised to auction the private dwelling of the local boot and shoemaker who resided at 25, Park Street. On May 30th and 31st 1836, an auction took place at the Union Tavern to sell off its household furniture and effects, which included painted liquor casks, a variety of pewter measures and an assortment of glass and earthenware suitable for public houses. We believe that these premises ceased to be a pub at this point in 1836, and either reverted to a private dwelling or remained empty pending its sale. In February 1838 the premises were listed for auction by order of the mortgagee and were described as: "A well built house known by the name or sign of The Lamb; now untenanted this house is calculated for a private house." We could only speculate on why the auction notice referenced the Lamb and not the Union Tavern, and we chose not to.

| | |
|---|---|
| 1832-34 | G. Bird *(Lamb)* |
| 1835-36 | William Dixon Davis *(Union Tavern)* |

**Lansdowne** – 31 Parade

See Lansdowne Hotel for details.

**Lansdowne Hotel** – 31 Parade

Built in the 1830s, and opened in 1834, the Lansdowne Hotel was situated on the corner of 31, Parade and 61, Warwick Street. However, until the 1870s the address of these premises was actually 36, Lansdowne Place, which was on the right-hand side of Upper Parade running from Warwick Street to Christ Church; York Terrace was the left-hand side of Upper Parade. In 1851, the premises were described in a sale notice as comprising on the ground floor, a coffee room, two sitting rooms, spacious bar, parlour, tap room, smoke room, kitchens, other offices; upstairs there were several suites of private apartments and many spacious bedrooms. It also had excellent wine and ale cellars, together with stabling and a coach-house. The same sale notice also promoted the premises as: "Fitted-out by the late proprietor [Thomas Buckingham] in 1848, regardless of expense, as a house of fashionable resort in the rapidly increasing and improving watering place of Leamington. It commands a first-rate situation in the healthiest part of the Royal Spa, and is replete in the accommodation of noblemen and families of the first distinction by whom it is usually frequented."

We have no record of the Lansdowne being open as a hotel post 1860 but we do know that William Rigby Magrath [a wine merchant] acquired its licence from John Chester in 1860. Furthermore, the licence was renewed in the name of: – "W. R. Magrath – Lansdowne Hotel" – at the 1860 licensing session and in 1861 Magrath opened a wine store at 36, Lansdowne Place. The new owner of the business in 1916 was a Mrs. Burgess [and probably was in 1914 when Magrath's licence was transferred to William McGuffie]. Therefore, although Magrath and Co. continued to be [directory] listed as wine and spirits merchants post 1940, it is likely that the name Magrath and Co. was retained thereafter due to its long standing reputation [refer licensee listing].

The police licence register shows that a certificate was granted on 27th November 1961 stating that the premises could only be used for off-sales, pending alterations; this proviso was still valid on 5th December 1969. A subsequent entry states that the licence was renewed on 12th March 1970 although it is not clear whether this is the off-licence or the original on-licence. Curiously, the name on the entry has been amended to the Glass and Candle, but there is no entry in the licence register to indicate the date of any change/transfer [and we have not been able to uncover any further information on the Glass and Candle]. The same page in the licence register has been annotated: "Premises due for demolition, off-licence granted in respect of 68, Warwick Street 12.8.71; licence in respect of 31 the Parade will be surrendered," and the

*The Lansdowne Hotel taken by the Leamington Spa Courier courtesy of Leamington Spa Library & Lyndon Cave.*

name of the owner has been amended to "Waters of Coventry". We have concluded that there were never licensed premises in Leamington Spa named the Glass and Candle.

| | |
|---|---|
| October 1834-48 | William Smith |
| July 1848-May 1851 | Thomas Buckingham *(Died 17th May 1851)* |
| May 1851-Sep 1856 | Ambrose Buckingham *(On the death of Thomas)* |
| September 1856-Mar 1858 | Mrs. Mary Ann Buckingham *(On the death of Ambrose)* |
| 15th March 1858 | Sale by auction of all the hotel's contents |
| ≤1860 | John Chester |
| February 1860-Feb 1914 | William Rigby Magrath *(W. R. Magrath and Co – est. 1859)* |
| February 1914-Nov 1957 | William Blair McGuffie |
| November 1957-Dec 1965 | Richard Caldicott *(Managing director of new owners Messrs Waters, of Coventry)* |
| December 1965-Aug 1971 | Robert Gordon Woodruff Caldicott |

### Lansdowne Tavern – 38 Lansdowne Street

Lansdowne Street was named after the Marquis of Lansdowne. The first directory listing we have for the Lansdowne Tavern is in 1866 when John Wickes was listed as a beer retailer [beer house] at what was then 1, Lansdowne Street; he made an application for a full on-licence in 1868 but it was refused. In 1903 there were three entrances, one in Lansdowne Street, one in Lansdowne Road and one in Swan Street. At the 1911 licensing sessions, the chief constable objected to the licence renewal on the grounds of 'redundancy', also reporting that the Lansdowne was the worst constructed public house in Leamington and that to get to the urinal it was necessary to go through one of the rooms of the dwelling house. A similar course was also taken in 1913, when the structural suitability of the premises was referred to, but with the same outcome. In June 1913, the licensing magistrates approved plans by Lucas and Co. Ltd [Leamington Brewery] to alter the property, which included taking in two neighbouring cottages; in 1930 the pub was owned by Ansells who had acquired the Leamington Brewery in 1928. In February 1938, the police again objected to the licence renewal on the grounds of 'redundancy' and this time the local justices decided to refer the licence to the county compensation authority for extinction. However, in July it was good news again when the compensation authority overruled the local justices and the licence was renewed. A full on-licence was finally granted at the annual licensing sessions on 6th February 1952 and confirmed on 2nd April.

In early 1980, Jerry Lewitt, Graham Soden, Tony Hall ['The Bear'], and Mick Worrall bought the freehold on the then closed Lansdowne Tavern, and also bought the premises next door at 36, Lansdowne Street, formerly a butchers. The pub then underwent a complete refurbishment with the main contractors being Hall and Worrall; others included Roy Gatfield Ltd [bar fittings and decoration], Justin Claire Ltd of Knowle [interior designers], Keith Griffin [electrical contractor] and Dave Sumner [carpenter]. On completion, it was renamed the Builders Arms and opened in March 1980, although work on the extension was not completed before the end of the year.

*Above left: The Builders Arms circa 1980 courtesy of Liz Soden. The driver is licensee Mick Cowlishaw. Above right: Photo of the Builders Arms by Nick Wilkins.*

In 1986, as a 'free house' it was serving Ansells mild and bitter, Courage Directors, John Smith's bitter, draught Guinness and various lagers and ciders. On 30th May 1989 the Builder's Arms was advertising that it had reopened following the completion of a major refurbishment [although its 'official reopening' would not be reported until the 17th June]; it had been totally redesigned, extended and a catering kitchen had been created to facilitate the offering of pub snacks at lunch time and during the early evening. The Builders Arms remains open in December 2013.

| | |
|---|---|
| 1866-70 | John Wickes |
| 1870-71 | Thomas Griffiths |
| 1871-72 | F. Griffiths |
| 1872-Nov 1872 | Samuel Griffiths |
| November 1872-Dec 1872 | William Barton |
| December 1872-Oct 1875 | Isaac Priest |
| October 1875-Sep 1877 | Sarah Waite |
| September 1877-≤Jun 1878 | Thomas Godfrey |
| ≤June 1878-Mar 1891 | John Sparrow |
| March 1891-Aug 1893 | Alfred Edward Gibbons |
| August 1893-Mar 1894 | Zacharias Boote *(Previously at the Victoria Vaults)* |
| March 1894-Apr 1895 | Mrs. Fanny Clarke *(Previously at Avon Tavern, Emscote)* |
| April 1895-May 1898 | George Smith *(On his marriage to Fanny Clarke)* |
| May 1898-Nov 1899 | Mrs. Fanny Smith *(On the death of George)* |
| November 1899-Nov 1911 | Henry 'Harry' E. Sparrow |
| November 1911-12 | Henry 'Harry' Walters |
| 1912-Sep 1926 | Samuel Vincent |
| September 1926-Oct 1940 | Walter Alfred Robinson |
| October 1940-Nov 1954 | Joseph William Timms |

| | |
|---|---|
| November 1954-Mar 1958 | Roy Fenn |
| March 1958-Jun 1960 | Albert Kinston |
| June 1960-Mar 1962 | Leslie John Harwood |
| March 1962-Sep 1962 | William Arthur Farmer |
| September 1962-Mar 1963 | John Cossar |
| March 1963-Aug 1964 | Harold Joseph Bradshaw |
| August 1964-Feb 1966 | Norman Frank Pritchard |
| February 1966-Jun 1967 | Michael Frederick Stewart |
| June 1967-Oct 1967 | George Frederick Trinder |
| October 1967-Apr 1969 | Michael John Alcock |
| April 1969-Jul 1969 | Michael Harold Stokes |
| July 1969-Nov 1969 | William Alfred Blythe |
| November 1969-Aug 1970 | Leslie Peter Berry |
| August 1970-Nov 1971 | Derek John Manttan *(Derek was aged 21 when he took over and his wife Sheila was aged 18)* |
| November 1971-Mar 1972 | Peter Joseph Moore |
| March 1972 | Violet Masters *(The Lansdowne Tavern closed after Violet left)* |
| March 1980-99 | Graham Soden, Jerry Lewitt, Tony Hall and Mick Worrall *(Proprietors - name changed to the Builders Arms)* |
| 1980-1999 | Graham Soden *(Licensee of the newly named Builders Arms, but he employed a number of managers)* |
| March 1980-Jul 1984 | Michael Cowlishaw |
| July 1984-1987 | Trevor 'Toetapper' Muckley and his wife Carolyn *(Previously bar staff at the Builders)* |
| 1987-90 | Kevin John Murphy |
| 1990 | Dave Smith |
| 1992 | Paul Shurvington |
| 1992-99 | Russell Soden |
| 1999-Dec 2011 | William 'Bill' Jones *(Previously barman)* |
| December 2011 → | Chao Jiang *(Licensee)* |
| December 2011 → | John and Karen Shinkwin *(Managers)* |

*The Leamington Spa Courier dated 4th March 1938 reported:* **Lansdowne Tavern licence referred** *– At Leamington adjourned licensing sessions on Monday, the justices decided to refer for extinction the licence of the Lansdowne Tavern, Lansdowne Street, the renewal of which had been objected to by the police on the grounds that it was not required to meet the needs of the neighbourhood. Mr. W. A. Coleman applied for the renewal of the licence on behalf of the licensee [Mr. W. A. Robinson] and the owners, Messrs Lucas and Co. The licence is for an 'all beer house'. Evidence given by Mr. Philip C. Smart, deputy borough surveyor, indicated that the domestic accommodation of the tavern was restricted. Within a 250-yards' radius there were 14 licensed premises. Of these 11 were fully licensed and 3 were off-licences. Some were as near as 60 - 70 yards "as the crow flies".*

*The chief constable said he first objected to the renewal of this licence in 1911 on the ground of redundancy. It was renewed, however, without the case being heard. A similar course was taken in 1913, when the structural suitability of the premises was referred to. In 1936 plans for the alteration of the premises were submitted but not approved. Mr. Earnshaw said the house was in a congested area and did not compare favourably with other licensed premises in the vicinity. No inconvenience would be experienced if the licence were taken away. It was a well conducted house, which did a good trade, and he had nothing against the licensee. The domestic accommodation is bad, as is the sleeping accommodation. In the case of fire the occupants would be trapped in a narrow wooden staircase. The clubroom would also be cut off. The chief constable agreed that there had been a good deal of building development in the Campion Hills area and at Lillington. He agreed that under the Waller covenant there can be no licensed premises at Lillington.*

*Mr. Robinson said he had held a licence for eleven and a half years. Most of the customers came from the immediate neighbourhood and from Pound Lane. There were 88 members of the sick and dividend club and 36 members of the Thrift Club. The witness produced a petition containing 204 signatures urging the justices to renew the licence. Mr. Coleman, addressing the justices, said the improvement plans were still in existence and could be carried out tomorrow if required. After a retirement, the mayor, [Alderman C. Davis], said the justices considered the licence redundant, and the question would be referred to the compensation authority.*

On 1st July 1938 the Leamington Spa Courier reported the sequel to the saga – **Lansdowne Tavern not to close** – The Lansdowne Tavern, Lansdowne Street, is not to be closed as suggested by the local licensing justices. At the meeting of county compensation authority, held at the shire hall on Monday, presided over by Lord Ilkeston and following a review of all of the arguments again, it was decided that the licence be renewed.

*The Leamington Spa Courier dated 14th August 1970 reported:* **No objections to landlord, 21** *– Britain's youngest landlord took over the Lansdowne Tavern in Lansdowne Street, Leamington, yesterday, after receiving his licence from Leamington magistrates. Derek Manttan, the new licensee, is only 21 making him probably the youngest ever, even though he has been working in public houses since he was 18. Pulling his first pint as a licensee, Derek said yesterday, "I'm really pleased about getting my licence. It's a bit of an achievement; I was worried that there might be some objections."*

The Leamington Spa Courier dated 28th January 1972 reported: **Big changes in some pubs** – The managers of six "uneconomic" Leamington public houses are being offered tenancies by Ansells Brewery Ltd. A spokesman at the brewery's offices in Birmingham confirmed that tenancies were being offered at the Hope and Anchor, Lansdowne Tavern, Railway Inn, Ranelagh Tavern, Warwick Arms and the Queen's Head, Leamington. The spokesman added, "The reason is quite simply that licensing expenses, including wages, at the pubs make them uneconomic to run under management, and tenancies are to be offered." Asked if the move involved a major policy change at Ansells, the spokesman said, "I would not go as far as that, but it is fair to say that there is an undoubted trend towards tenancies in the Ansells region, but this is not just particularly in the Leamington area."

*The Leamington Spa Courier dated 13th February 1981 reported that: Top wrestlers from ITV's World of Sport programme took part in a less strenuous sport on Sunday when they competed against a darts team from the Builders Arms. The wrestlers won by four games to three in a charity match organised by Leamington's own wrestling star Tony Walsh and about £150 raised by raffles and souvenir programmes will go to the National Children's Home at Longford and to the local Lions Club.*

The Morning News dated 11th October 1985 carried this article on the Builders: The Builders Arms is a solid, old fashioned English pub. Prints of old time street entertainers hang on the walls and a large clock ticks away in quiet moments. Simply laid out with just one large room and a long curving bar it offers comfort in the form of plush covered settees and, in one corner, a huge fireplace. Trevor Muckley and his wife, Carolyn, took over as managers of the Builder's about 15 months ago but they had long been familiar with the place, Trevor having worked there under the previous manager. It's a busy pub, not surprising with the wide range of beers on offer. Ansells bitter and mild, Directors, Kronenbourg 1664, and Guinness are just some of the free house favourites. They have even thought to supply some near alcohol free rum and whisky flavoured drinks in preparation for Christmas drivers.

Upstairs is another bar used for functions and darts. It is usually available for 21st birthday parties or weddings. Next year a patio will be opened outside. Entertainment is provided by the juke box which plays a variety of chart hits and oldies, and fruit machines. The pub is so popular that live entertainment just wouldn't fit in. The Builder's is a regular for a wide variety of people. One 88 year old woman never lets a day go by without a visit although in the evenings it's usually packed with 18 to 30 year olds. The Builder's Arms, on Lansdowne Street, Leamington, opens from 10.30am to 2.30pm at lunchtimes and from 5.30pm to 11.00pm.

**Leaf** [Tearooms and Piano Bar] – 116 Warwick Street
See the Prince of Wales Inn for details.

**Leamington Mews** – 4 Russell Street
See Royal Leamington Repository Inn for details.

**Leamington Tavern** – 28 / 30 Tavistock Street
The first licensee we have listed for these premises is a William Lewis in 1830. During the early part of his twenty-six year tenure Lewis was also listed as a retail brewer and latterly he would also become a rate collector. Originally addressed as 13, Tavistock Street, this pub was on the corner of Tavistock and Market streets, the Newmarket Inn [later the Tavistock] was just 53 yards down the road and the Bricklayers Arms was between the two.

As well as being the licensee of the Leamington Tavern period 1868-88, George Warren also opened a large newly built malthouse in 1871; situated in William Street, the building is still standing in 2013 and is currently occupied by SRF Advertising, Design and Marketing. The premises comprised a covered entrance to a yard laid with bricks, a two-stall stable, two coach houses, a kiln hole and drying room, an eight-quarter wetting pit, malting floor with drying kiln and extensive store rooms over. Gas and town water were laid on. Following his death in December 1887, the malthouse was put up for sale by auction as was 2,100 bushels

*Leamington Tavern. Photo courtesy of Leamington Spa Art Gallery & Museum [Warwick District Council] Ref: LEAMG:M3781.1993.21(69/19138).*

of new malt and barley, malt dust, tail barley, peas, 9 pockets of hops, general implements, 150 sacks, tools, van, waggonette, a grey half-bred mare, harness and saddlery and poultry.

In a May 1891 auction notice the Leamington Tavern is described as having, "important frontages to Tavistock and Market Streets of 30 ft 9 in and 55 ft 6 in respectively, and of 31 ft to passage in the rear, containing in the whole 190 square yards or thereabouts". At that point the fully licenced, freehold premises were let to Hopcraft and Norris [Brackley Brewery, Northamptonshire] but the pub would later be owned by Hunt, Edmunds and Co, possibly after the aforementioned auction. In 1903 there were four entrances to the pub, two in Tavistock Street, one in Covent Garden and one in a rear passage leading from Tavistock Street to Covent Garden [in 1928, thirteen cottages and a bakery had access to the rear passage]. The bar was 32 ft x 14½ ft part of which had been partitioned for use as a 'snug'; two or three bedrooms were available for letting and provision was made to supply meals to travellers.

On 5th March 1928, the local licensing justices decided to refer the Leamington Tavern to the county compensation authority for 'extinction by compensation' on the grounds of 'redundancy' as they considered the premises to be structurally deficient and in a congested area [within a radius of 225 yards from the junction of Warwick Street and the Parade there were 32 licensed premises]. However, the authority overturned the decision and the licence was renewed on 25th June 1928. The Leamington Tavern closed for business on 4th October 1966 and was demolished shortly afterwards. It was replaced by the Covent Garden multi-storey car park which was completed in the autumn of 1969.

| | |
|---|---|
| 1830-56 | William Lewis |
| 1856-66 | Charles Chambers Hilsdon |
| 1868-Feb 1888 | George Warren *(Died 2nd December 1887, aged 65)* |
| February 1888-Jan 1889 | Harriett Warren *(On the death of George)* |
| January 1889-Sep 1889 | George Clarke |
| September 1889-Aug 1890 | Charles Edward Margetts |
| August 1890-91 | Mrs. Harriett Barratt |
| 1891-May 1892 | James Cockerill |
| May 1892-Sep 1893 | John William Glover |
| September 1893-Dec 1893 | Charles Howard |
| December 1893-May 1894 | Stanley Harry Tyack *(Of Shelford, Alcester)* |
| May 1894-Aug 1895 | William Henry Wardall |
| August 1895-Feb 1898 | Christopher Lewis |
| February 1898-Oct 1899 | Alfred Edward Taplin |
| October 1899-Jun 1904 | George John Walton |
| June 1904-Aug 1910 | Robert William Jeffrey |
| August 1910-Sep 1926 | William Blackwell |
| September 1926-Aug 1930 | Charles Purkiss |
| August 1930-41 | A. W. B. Newton *(Of Coventry)* |
| Circa 1941 | Edward Hezzell |
| April 1941-Oct 1954 | Bertie Hawtin |
| October 1954-Jan 1956 | Harry Peter Jamieson |
| January 1956-Feb 1961 | Robert Alfred Ayres |
| February 1961-Jan 1963 | Nigel Dunning Gough |
| January 1963-Oct 1966 | Dorothy Jane Giles |
| 4th October 1966 | Closed for business |

**Leamside Inn** – Jephson Gardens

The first Lights of Leamington were the town's contribution to the Festival of Britain in 1951 and due to its success the event continued to be held each summer until 1961 [July to October]. A bar was provided in a marquee at the Jephson Gardens and in 1951 it was called the Festival Inn; in subsequent years it was also named the Jephson Tavern and the Leamside Inn.

Initially, it was a moot point between organisers and the licensing justices as to whether alcohol should be permitted and, if so, what time the bar should close. It wasn't until 1953 that it was acknowledged that the bar was an integral part of the illuminations

*The Jephson Tavern during the 'Lights of Leamington' taken by Maurice Mead and courtesy of Leamington Spa Art Gallery & Museum [Warwick District Council] Ref: LeamG:M3755.1933.16(69/18859).*

*Photo © Blinkhorns of Banbury. Courtesy of Tom Blinkhorn and Leamington Spa Art Gallery & Museum [Warwick District Council] Ref: LEAMG:M3755.1993.140(69/18874).*

programme and the justices duly extended the licence so that it could remain open until 10.30pm. In 1960 the 'Lights' licence was held by Allan William Ramsey, the landlord of the Sun in Splendour pub.

**Leeky Joes** – 29 Augusta Place
See Hintons for details.

**Leicester Tavern** – 1 Leicester Street
The first reference point we have for the Leicester Tavern is an entry in the 1837 church rate book when Charles Wright is listed as the tenant, and William Wright is the owner of the property. Situated on the corner of Leicester and Clarendon Streets, it closed in the early 1860s.

| | |
|---|---|
| 1837-57 | Charles Wright |
| 1862 | Mary Wright |

*This photo taken on 27th February 2010 shows the corner building that was the Leicester Tavern in the 19th century © Allan Jennings.*

**Leif** [Tearooms and Piano Bar] – 116 Warwick Street
See Prince of Wales Inn for details.

**Leila @ Loose Box Café Bar** – 4 Bedford Street
See Coach and Horses for details.

**Leopard Inn** – 7 Court Street

The first directory listing we have for this beer house is in 1849 although James Griffin is mentioned in a Leamington Spa Courier report dated 29th April 1848. In 1889, the pub was sold to Hunt, Edmunds and Co. Ltd by Mr. J. W. Hassell [the executor of Thomas Houghton]. In March 1925, the licensing magistrates approved plans for alterations to the Leopard which included taking in a cottage at the rear and adapting it for domestic purposes. A beer and wine licence ['on' and 'off'] was granted on 8th March 1955 [effective 19th April] and a full on-licence was granted on 2nd February 1960 [effective 5th April]. In July 1962, the Leamington Spa Courier reported that, "Alterations to provide a lounge for customers of the Leopard Inn were approved by Leamington licensing justices on 23rd July 1962. It was explained that the inn already had a bar and smokeroom and there was now sufficient need for a third room."

On 1st May 1967 the new owners were Bass, Mitchell and Butlers Ltd, Cape Hill Brewery, Birmingham. In 1982, by then known as Bass Plc, the brewery put the fully licensed Leopard Inn up for sale at £45,000, with a proviso that any new owner continued to sell the M&B product for five years. However, there would be no sale as a going concern and, on Monday 4th October 1982, the Leopard closed and the windows were boarded-up. The name was changed to Kellys in April 1983 after John O'Neil took over; the owners at that time being

Elaine Chapman and John White. It subsequently became a renowned live music venue; the bar had a stone flagged floor and the crazy brickwork along the walls was off-set by a red telephone box, butter churns, an old pram and other bric-a-brac. Kellys was sadly missed when it closed its doors in 2007.

In 2009 it was known as the Jam Jam club and by March 2010 it had become the Spayce Bar, a short lived venture that terminated on 30th May 2010. On the final evening a couple of lads put on an impromptu guitar session and after a couple of hours the bar staff gave away the drinks for free; needless to say Tom Lewin was on hand to capture the moment. In 2011, the premises were opened as Amara nightclub. However, between 6.00pm on 31st March and 10.00pm on 1st April 2013 the premises were trashed causing tens of thousands of pounds worth of damage.

*Kellys courtesy of Nick Wilkins.*

| | |
|---|---|
| ≤1848-55 | James Griffin |
| 1862 | Sarah Griffin |
| 1866 | Samuel Rathbone |
| 1868 | Possibly: Edward Hillyer *(Listed as Court Street - No pub name or street number given)* |
| 1870-Oct 1875 | Thomas Jeffs |
| October 1875-May 1876 | William Johnson |

| | |
|---|---|
| May 1876-Oct 1879 | Robert Culley |
| October 1879-May 1889 | Thomas Houghton |
| May 1889-Sept 1889 | J. W. Hassell *(Executor – on the death of Thomas)* |
| September 1889-May 1891 | Charles Bastin |
| May 1891-Mar 1914 | Alfred William Price |
| March 1914-Apr 1926 | Joseph Marshall |
| April 1926-Jun 1941 | Henry 'Harry' Charles Smith |
| June 1941-Jun 1953 | George Arthur Aitken |
| June 1953-≥1973 | George Henry Young |
| 1979-1982 | John and Shirley Miller |
| 1982 | David Humphrey *(Temporary landlord)* |
| Monday 4th Oct 1982 | Closed as the Leopard |
| 1982-84 | John O'Neil *(Kelly's from April 1983)* |
| 1984-85 | Robert 'Bob' Lidell |
| 1985 | Kevin Murphy |
| 1986 | Vincent Paul 'Winky' Berry |
| 1986 | Barry Sullivan |
| 1987-89 | Liam Fitzgerald |
| 1990-92 | Alison Shear |
| Circa 2002 | Tracy Harvey |
| August 2002 | Kelly's sold by Everards Brewery to Balvinder Singh |
| 2003-2005 | John Skinner and David Webb *(Joint licensees)* |
| 2003-2007 | David Webb and A.N. Other *(Joint licensees)* |
| 2007 | Closed as Kelly's |
| August 2008-Nov 2008 | Graham Rose |
| November 2008-Nov 2009 | Jason Giles |
| November 2009 | Douglas Hawkins |

*The Leamington Spa Courier dated 24th November 1855 reported that James Griffin, an alehouse keeper and stableman, late of the Leopard public house, Court Street, Leamington Priors, had been declared an insolvent debtor but had taken out an interim order for protection against the judicial process. However Griffin, a stableman of Clemens Street, was ordered to appear before a county court judge, at the shire hall Warwick, on the 12th December, for the first examination of his debts, estate and effects. All those indebted to Griffin were requested to make payment to the assistant clerk of the court.*

The Leamington Spa Courier dated 18th April 1941 reported that: A well-known publican collapsed and died in his chair on Sunday night. He was Mr. Harry Charles Smith [59], licensee of the Leopard Inn, Court Street. Mrs. Nellie D. Aitken, wife of the licensee of the Volunteer Arms, Comyn Street, and daughter of the deceased, said her father had a fall and broke his leg twelve months ago. He had never fully recovered, although he had been certified as fit enough to join the Home Guard. He had occasional attacks of asthma. Dr. D. F. L. Croft said that his death was due to fatty degeneration of the heart and the coroner recorded a verdict accordingly.

*The Leamington Spa Courier dated 14th February 1958 reported: Mr. George Young of the Leopard Inn, Court Street, Leamington Spa applied for a full on-licence, the existing licence only authorising the sale of beer and wines. He said, "There was a terrific demand for spirits," and produced a petition signed by 337 people. He added that when he had to refuse customers, "they look at you as if you were crackers. They think that you are refusing them a drink." The police opposed the application on the grounds that the premises were not structurally appropriate and that the district was already well served. Superintendent Waghorn commented that the application was premature, in view of the fact that the house was on the fringe of the Althorpe Street clearance area. The application was refused.*

The Morning News dated 3rd February 1960 reported that two Leamington public houses, the Leopard Inn [Court Street] and the Talbot Inn [Rushmore Street], and an Eagle Street off-licence were granted full on-licences at Leamington's licensing sessions.

*Mike Golding and Tom Thorne remember the Leopard: "The Leopard had many activities including a sports and social club, which included football, rugby and cricket teams. The main protagonists of the club were George Deely and Neville Parsons. Strange as it may seem for a pub it also boasted a choir which was ably run by Freddy Cox and John Taylor. Back in the sixties the pub was divided into three rooms the smallest, the snug, was known as Doll's Bar after a former Landlady."*

Tom Lewin remembers the Salvation Army and their publication the 'War Cry'. He says, "David Condon, a 'Sally Army' man, would come into the Leopard and shout 'War Cry!' to which the locals would retort 'Geronimo!' – how cruel!" He also remembers the Leopard day-trips [or as they say in Only Fools and Horses – "the jolly boys outings"] to Blackpool in the 1970s and has provided this photo which was taken in 1976.

The Leamington Courier dated 3rd September 1971 reported: **Leopard roars to sixes triumph** – As expected, Sunday's pub six-a-side tournament in aid of the charity 'Shelter' resulted in victory for one of the six Leopard squads, but the winners, Ivor and Roger

*Back row: Eric Canning, Ian Walker, Len King, Dave 'Bullet' Friend, Brian Smith, Graham Hawtin, Bob Marshall, Keith Jones, Jeff James, John Bolitho, Colin May. Top middle: Paul Smyth and Neville Billington. Middle row: George Morris, Alan 'Budgie' Smith, Tommy O'Reilly, Donie Shanahan, Keith Billington, Billy Shanahan, Dar Gill, Sean McFarland, Danny Connor, Wiggy Brooks. Front row: Ian Montgomery, Pete Allington and Pepe Gill.*

Talbot, Keith Jones, Paddy Caden, Julio Rives and Phil Lloyd, had to pull out all the stops in the final against a talented young Bedworth Rangers side, before edging home by four goals to nil. Their clinching goal was a beauty, Rives cleared to Ivor Talbot, who somehow found the energy for one last dash down the right. He in turn fed Jones and the Lockheed winger skipped round the Bedworth keeper to seal a richly deserved triumph. In the semi-final, two Ivor Talbot goals saw the winners at home against Jet & Whittle 'B' while Bedworth accounted for another Leopard team lead by Ian Walker, the Westlea Wanderers skipper. The competition was keenly contested and entertaining and the organisers are anticipating a profit in the region of £150. One disappointment was the non appearance of Coventry City manager Noel Cantwell, who was to have presented the prizes. He was in Hull completing the transfer of big money centre forward, Chris Chilton.

*The Leamington Spa Courier dated 14th September 1973 reported:* **Publicans' wives have a day out** – *Most mid-Warwickshire pub landlords were without their key bar staff last week, their wives. The women members of the Leamington and District Licensed Victuallers Ladies Auxiliary spent a day at the Babycham manufacturing plant at Shepton Mallet. Among them were the chairman, Mrs. Mary Burman [Highfield Terrace off-licence]; the treasurer, Mrs. Mary Cowley [New Bowling Green Warwick]; the secretary, Mrs. Marjorie Inglefield of Hanworth Road, Warwick, and assistant secretary Mrs. Doll Young [Leopard Inn, Leamington].*

The Leamington Spa Courier dated 4th January 1974 reported that: More than 80 Leamington pensioners ended 1973 with hampers paid for by the fund-raising efforts of the regulars at the Leopard Inn. The fund-raising is organised by the Leopard All Stars, the pub's committee, who organise the raffles, a walk, and a bottle to collect coins in. Names of pensioners were put to the six member committee who arranged for the hampers to be made up by Mr. and Mrs. D. E. Southwick, of the general stores, New Street. "They are regulars at the Leopard, and knock a little off the price of the tinned groceries," said George Young the licensee. Mr. Young said the cost of this year's 82 parcels was £164 and there is still some money left for a float for next year. He said the committee would like to express their thanks to G. and G. Coaches of Althorpe Street, for providing a coach on Saturday for the distribution of the hampers. Last year the pub also treated 50 pensioners to a coach outing in the summer.

*The Leamington Spa Courier dated 15th November 2002 reported that: Fans of live music say that they are disappointed to see Leamington pub Kelly's boarded up – and they do not expect it will ever be re-opened. The Court Street venue, sold by Everards Brewery at the end of August, was the only bar in Leamington dedicated to local bands. It could not make enough money to keep going. It is now owned by Balvinder Singh, who has several other businesses in the town. Mr. Singh put the venue on the market immediately after the purchase; it is believed he has no plans to redevelop it. Former landlady Tracy Harvey, now working for another Everards pub in Nottingham, said she could not think of any way to keep the pub going. The 33-year-old said, "Kelly's had a character of its own and there is no other place in Leamington geared up to do music in the same way. The location was a disadvantage – if you didn't make a special trip or know it was there you just wouldn't find it. On the other hand, it was good to be out of the way because no-one was bothered by the noise. It's a difficult balance. People say it's a shame it closed but they didn't used to come in very often. It's always the same, you don't realise what you've got until it's gone." Miss Harvey, who was assistant manager for two and a half years before taking over at Kelly's was not surprised when she was given notice of sale. She said, "The figures had been falling for a long time."*

**Lock, Dock and Barrel** – 7 Brunswick Street
See Queens Head for details.

**Loft Theatre [Bar]** – Victoria Colonnade
While this bar doesn't really meet our qualifying criteria we consider the following article, reported in the Morning News dated 10th July 1981, sufficiently interesting and worthy of inclusion, "Mac has pulled his last pint at the Loft Theatre bar – and it was a well-earned last act. For 82 year old Mac – his full name is Mr. Andrew Scott McGuire – has retired after 13 years as bar manager. He was called to the bar in the 1960s when he worked in the Angel Hotel, Regent Street, then used by Loft members as a meeting place. But when the new Loft Theatre was opened in 1968, after the old one had been destroyed by fire, they had a bar of their own for the first time – and called in trusty Mac to run it. Mac was a career soldier and reached the rank of major before retiring in the 1950s."

**London Tavern** – High Street
The only listing we have is in 1837, although these premises may have previously been the London Coffee House, Leamington Priors [listed in the licensed victuallers' records 1817-26].

**London Tavern** – 12 Satchwell Street
The first directory listing we have for these premises is in 1832 when it opened as the Paul Pry at 26, Satchwell Street. There was a lodging house attached to the building [part of the licensed premises] and by 1848 there was also a covered-in bowling alley and a club room. Originally a beer house, a publican's on-licence was granted to Joseph Lewis in April 1854 and in 1856 he renamed the pub the London Tavern, as confirmed in the report of the annual licensing sessions. In 1861 the pub consisted of a bar, a smoke room, a tap room, six bedrooms, a brew house, and skittle yard; water and gas was also laid on. In 1899 there was just the one entrance and it was also a lodging house with two bedrooms and eleven beds. Owned by Hunt, Edmunds and Co. [Banbury] the London Tavern closed permanently at 10.00pm on 21st March 1961. In the early hours of Monday 28th August 1961 a fire broke out in the then derelict building, but firemen prevented it from spreading

*Photo of the London Tavern courtesy of Joe Claydon.*

and no one was injured. The pub was demolished in the 1980s to make way for the Royal Priors shopping centre.

*So, who was Paul Pry? Well, a quick check of Wikipedia, the free internet encyclopaedia, informs us that: "Paul Pry was a farcical comedy in three acts, and was the most notable play written by 19th century English playwright John Poole. It premiered in London on 13th September 1825 at the Haymarket Theatre and ran for 114 performances. The play continued to be popular until the 1870s. The storyline is centred on a comical, idle, meddlesome and mischievous fellow consumed with curiosity. Unable to mind his own business, he's an interfering busybody who conveniently leaves behind an umbrella everywhere he goes in order to have an excuse to return and eavesdrop. At the end, however, Pry becomes a hero for rescuing papers from a well that incriminate more serious troublemakers."*

| | |
|---|---|
| 1832-39 | William Loader Meyrick |
| 1841-42 | John Toone |
| 1846 | W. Underhill |
| 1847-Jan 1851 | John Nicks |
| January 1851 | William Maycock |
| ≤1853-January 1854 | William Houghton |
| January 1854-Mar 1854 | George Charman |
| March 1854-Nov 1859 | Joseph Lewis |
| November 1859-65 | John Joseph Gilliver |
| 1865 | Ellen Mansfield |
| 1868-69 | Thomas Pullen |
| 1872-75 | Thomas Bagshaw |
| 1873-75 | Mrs. P. Bagshaw *(Mrs. Bagshaw managed the pub while Thomas was in America)* |
| 1875-Mar 1893 | John Burke |
| March 1893-Oct 1894 | John McParland |
| October 1894-Mar 1902 | Mrs. Ellen McParland *(On the death of John)* |
| March 1902-Jun 1902 | Harry William Soden *(Licence transfer not confirmed)* |
| June 1902-1907 | John Turner |
| August 1907-1908 | Robert Cooke *(Licence transferred from Mrs. Turner)* |
| 1908-June 1911 | John Betterton Radbourne *(An ex-police constable)* |
| June 1911-17 | James Marks |
| 1919-27 | Mrs. Maria Marks |
| 1927-34 | Albert William Marks |
| 1934-Feb 1940 | Albert Ernest Collett |
| February 1940-Jun 1943 | Herbert Johnson *(Died on 10th May 1943, aged 59)* |
| June 1943-Feb 1950 | Mrs. Susanna Johnson *(On the death of Herbert)* |
| February 1950-Jul 1950 | William James Waring |
| July 1950-Jul 1956 | James 'Jim' Percy Young *(Licence transferred from Rebecca Waring on the death of William; James went to the Red Lion, Kineton in 1956)* |

| July 1956-May 1958 | Frank Richard Nott |
| May 1958-Oct 1959 | Keith Witney Launchbury |
| October 1959-Jan 1960 | *(The pub may have been closed or run by a relief manager)* |
| January 1960-Mar 1961 | Frank Thomas Lacey |
| 21st March 1961 | Closed for business *(Frank Lacey transferred to the Dun Cow at Hornton, Oxfordshire, on 22nd March)* |

*The Leamington Spa Courier dated 12th February 1960 reported:* **Juke-box pub told 'danger to youth'** *- Leamington Boys Club leader Derek Tickner yesterday condemned the action of a Leamington publican, who has installed a juke-box "to liven up the place a bit". He said, "This is a very dangerous move, it is clearly calculated to encourage youngsters to drink alcohol." Leamington Youth Leaders' Council - a body representing more than 20 clubs in the area is likely to discuss the matter on March 9th. The juke-box was introduced to the bar of the London Tavern, Satchwell Street by the licensee Mr. Frank Lacey nine days ago - the first one to appear on licensed premises in the town. Says Mr. Tickner, whose club has a membership of about a hundred, "Youth leaders already have a problem discouraging under-age boys from visiting public houses. It is obvious that when a 'pub' puts in a juke-box, it is trying to increase business by drawing in young people, but how is a landlord going to tell whether a boy has reached 18?"*

*Mr. Tickner says he does not object to juke-boxes in coffee bars, because "they at least get young people off the streets". But he feels that the introduction of juke-boxes on licensed premises would be likely to entice boys from 15 to 18. "This is the sort of trend that will have to be watched very carefully. I do not begrudge the public house its business, but there is moderation in all things," says Mr. Tickner. "It is a shocking development." He is of the opinion that 80 percent of the people who frequent bars are adults "who want a bit of peace and quiet, not blaring music". Juke-boxes in public houses are covered by comprehensive music licences. Comments Mrs. Lacey, "All kinds of people like the machine. Our clients asked for some kind of entertainment, and now they have it. They don't like coming in and just looking at one another. We have one old man of 70 who is delighted by the box, but the boys are quite harmless and they have caused no trouble," she adds. "We hope that in the summer we might get even more people in." Last week the Banbury police chief, Supt. R. H. Smith, criticised teenagers who hung around juke boxes in the town's public houses. It was becoming difficult to control them, he said, and it was invariably found that juke boxes were installed in premises which were the subject of disturbances.*

Tom Lewin remembers that when he started his apprenticeship in 1964 the London Tavern was a derelict building, although the rear of the premises had been taken over by Jimmy Simms, the scrap dealer.

**Loose Box** – 4 Bedford Street
See Coach and Horses for details.

**Lounge** – 130 Parade
See Haunch of Venison for details.

**Macky's Bar and Restaurant** – 40 Warwick Street
See Alastairs for details.

**Madhatters Wine Bar** – 49 Kenilworth Street
See Counting House [Bar and Restaurant] for details.

**Manor House Hotel** – Avenue Road
The core of the Manor House Hotel building was the old manor house, which was built for Thomas Prew in 1740. Thomas died on 27th April 1747 and was buried in the chancel of Leamington church; his widow survived until April 1763 when Matthew Wise, a major landowner, succeeded to the estate. The two so called 'dovecotes' at the foot of the garden also belonged to the earliest days of the manor house. It is also noteworthy that the old manor house was approached by two avenues from the Warwick Old Road, one of those being the present Lower Avenue.

When the premises were first opened as a hotel by Isaac Curtis in 1847, the Leamington Spa Courier dated 6th November 1847 published the following, "Isaac Curtis, late of the Baths, High Street, proprietor of the above hotel, in announcing the opening of the same for the reception of visitors, has much pleasure in informing them that the house has undergone a thorough repair, with every regard to convenience and comfort, so as to ensure to his friends and patrons the advantages of a hotel, and, at the same time, the quiet of a private boarding establishment." In October 1848, Isaac Curtis advertised that "his annual tripe suppers will commence on 3rd November and will continue on each Friday evening during the season." Isaac became bankrupt in 1850 and in March 1851 a dividend of one shilling and eight pence in the pound was paid to his creditors. For twenty years the building became a school under the management of a Mr. Andrews. However, at the annual licensing session in August 1871 Thomas Radclyffe applied for a new licence for the Manor House Hotel, advising the justices that £7,000 had been spent on alterations, furnishings and embellishments for this first class hotel which had been opened 10 weeks earlier, that it had 24 beds and that it had already been frequented by 400 families; the licence was granted. The new banqueting room, situated in the new wing of the hotel and measuring 50 ft x 28 ft, was first used in May 1881 when the Leamington Licensed Victuallers' Society held their annual dinner.

The Leamington Spa Courier dated 25th November 1932 added more snippets of information to the history of the hotel [albeit some of them contradictory, but not necessarily incorrect], "It was early in 1885 that the present tenant's father, the late Robert Lamplough, took possession of the premises, which in the seventies had been used for educational purposes – as the Manor House Academy, the principal being the late Mr. Webb. At a still earlier period [from 1826 onward] the older portion of the building had been occupied as a hotel; this was when the Wise family ceased to reside there [in 1825], having erected Shrubland Hall as their abode." The article went on to describe how the enlargement of the hotel, from its original manor house configuration, had been done during a number of periods; the west wing was built at the instance of Mr. Robert Lamplough's predecessor; a second wing and a large ballroom and dining-room were added in the early 1880s; the late Mr. Lamplough erected the billiard room and smoke room in 1889, and some 15 years ago [circa 1915] the present garage accommodation was provided [Mr. Robert Lamplough died in 1903, and the management of the hotel passed to his sons, Messrs J. W. and R. Lamplough]. The same Courier article also stated that, "The hotel occupies three acres of land, and it is interesting to recall that the first lawn tennis matches played in England were played there in 1872, when Major T. H. 'Harry' Gem, a Birmingham solicitor and sportsman, and Mr. J. B. A. Pereira [a Spanish merchant then living in Avenue Road] founded a 'Pelota' Club in Leamington in conjunction with Dr. F. H. Haynes and the late Dr. A. W. Tomkins. 'Pelota' was the name originally given to lawn tennis." [The courts were where the Manor Court apartment block is at the rear of the old hotel building – Ed]

Also in November 1932, the Manor House Hotel was purchased by a syndicate of local businessmen under the chairmanship of Alderman K. R. England. The directors were Alderman A. Ashton, Mr. H. Dawson, Mr. H. Bishop, Councillor R. Salt and Alderman C. Southorn. "They transformed it from an old fashioned hotel to a hotel that was up-to-date and comparable with the most modern hotels in the country. The visitor enters the lounge hall through a revolving door made of oak. The lounge itself is a pleasant room, the woodwork is of oak. The shades of the electric lights, both in the centre and in the wall-sconces, are faintly pink, - a charming effect. By the reception desk is an attractive showcase, lit from within. On the left-hand side of the lounge is a suite of intercommunicating public rooms, admirably fitted for use in receptions. On the right, leading from the lounge by doors in which specially reflecting glass has been used, is the spacious and beautiful dining-room. The garden is useful as well as ornamental and fruit and vegetables are grown therein so that visitors can enjoy really fresh food. Near the river is a shady lawn leading to an old-fashioned sunken rose garden and next to that is a putting course and outfit for clock golf. A tennis court reminds one that it was in this very garden that lawn tennis [then called 'pelota'] was first played in England; a bowling green completes the selection of outdoor games but indoor is a fine billiard table. Every provision has been made in this forty bedroom hotel: a new fire escape, a new central heating apparatus, a hot water system which supplies soft water to the basins but keeps natural water for drinking, and a lounge bar with a separate side entrance."

The Manor House Hotel was requisitioned and closed on the outbreak of hostilities in 1939. Following the end of the Second World War, Messrs Flower and Sons Ltd of Stratford-upon-Avon acquired ownership; the contract was signed on Tuesday 20th November 1945. A new licence was granted on Monday 21st October 1946 and the Manor House Hotel re-opened on Tuesday 29th October 1946. A music licence was granted on 4th September 1950. In February 1957, Charles McCoy was the new resident managing director of the company that had purchased the property from Flower and Sons Ltd but in 1959 the hotel was purchased by Grand Hotel, Eastbourne, Ltd. In 1960, almost two acres of the hotel grounds were sold-off for residential development [luxury flats], now known as Manor Court.

In early 1962, the Grand Restaurant was completely redesigned and luxuriously redecorated; it was then capable of seating 180 people. By August the same year, a new enlarged cocktail bar had also been completed [at a cost of £5,500] and all rooms had been

*Manor House Hotel circa 1930, courtesy of the late Bill Gibbons collection.*

redecorated and fitted with upgraded central heating; the managing director Mr. Beattie ordered that the first people to use the new bar would be the people that built it. The following year a new three storey 22 bedroom wing was built in time for the Royal Show at a cost of around £40,000. In June 1963 the Morning News reported that, "In the four years since they purchased the hotel, Grand Hotel, Eastbourne, Ltd had spent close on £100,000 modernising the hotel, including £50,000 on a new wing which was officially opened this month by the mayor, Councillor F. Eaton. The hotel now has 54 bedrooms with 32 having their own bathrooms and lavatories. All have telephones, radios and shaver points and are centrally heated." It is understood that the Manor closed its doors in January 2004; it was later converted into apartments.

| | |
|---|---|
| 1847-≥1857 | Isaac Curtis *(Formerly keeper of Wise's Baths)* |
| August 1871-Jan 1873 | Thomas Radclyffe |
| January 1873-Dec 1878 | Mrs. Elizabeth Wise |
| February 1873-Dec 1878 | William Walsh *(Manager)* |
| December 1878-84 | Emanuel Duret |
| 1884-Jan 1885 | Jesse Percival |
| January 1885-Jul 1903 | Robert Lamplough *(Died in 1903)* |
| July 1903-1904 | James William and Robert Lamplough *(Executors and sons of Robert. Robert jnr died in Bournemouth in July 1936, aged 72)* |
| 1905-Nov 1932 | Robert Lamplough and Sons *(As per directories)* |
| November 1932 | Purchased by a syndicate of local businessmen |
| January 1933-Feb 1936 | Frederick Moore *(Manager)* |
| February 1936-Feb 1937 | John Littler *(Of Manchester)* |
| February 1937-Oct 1946 | Jack Hornsby *(Previously, Golden Lion Hotel, Stirling)* |
| October 1946-Dec 1946 | Thomas Fitzgerald Norbury |
| December 1946-Apr 1947 | William Grenville Kinsman |
| April 1947-Oct 1948 | Christopher McIver |
| October 1948-Sep 1951 | Richard Kendall-Tobias |

| | |
|---|---|
| September 1951-Jan 1957 | Alan Brian Muir |
| January 1957-Feb 1957 | Margaret Amy Muir |
| February 1957-Apr 1957 | Samuel Henry Alfred Lapidus |
| April 1957-Jun 1957 | Harry 'Charles' McCoy *(Resident managing director)* |
| June 1957-Nov 1957 | Joseph Alphonse John Goossens |
| November 1957-Jan 1958 | Samuel Henry Alfred Lapidus |
| January 1958-Apr 1959 | Michael Newton Baker |
| April 1959-Nov 1959 | John Howard Mills |
| November 1959-Aug 1967 | David Anthony Selby |
| August 1967-Feb 1969 | Reginald Cyrus Constable and Barry Marshall |
| February 1969-Nov 1970 | Raymond Peter Newton and Reginald Cyrus Constable |
| November 1970 | Reginald Cyrus Constable and Wyndham G. A. Heyring |
| 1971-2004 | Not available |
| January 2004 | Closed for business |

*Although Isaac Curtis is listed at the Manor Hotel in 1857 the following notice in the Leamington Spa Courier, dated 30th November 1850, indicates that he went bankrupt in 1850: Notice is hereby given that by an indenture bearing the date the 15th day of November 1850, Isaac Curtis, of Leamington Priors, Hotel Keeper, hath assigned all his stock in trade, personal estate, and effects whatsoever, unto George Sewell, of the City of London, distiller, Robert Nunn, of Emscote in the County of Warwick, miller, and Thomas Read, of Leamington Priors, coach builder, as trustees for the benefit of all the creditors of the said Isaac Curtis.*

On the 31st May 1884, the Leamington Spa Courier published the following auction notice: In bankruptcy, by order of the trustee, the lease, goodwill, and entire contents of the Manor House Hotel, comprising the furniture [much of it nearly new] of 35 bedrooms, ballroom, four sitting rooms, reading room, coffee room, smoking room, a large quantity of plate, linen, and numerous effects, 400 dozen of choice wines, carriages, horse, two prize smooth-coated St. Bernard dogs, 100 head of gold and silver pencilled Hamburg fowls – Messrs Ventom, Bull, and Cooper are directed by the trustee to sell by auction on the premises [unless previously sold privately], on Thursday, June 12, 1884, at three o'clock in the afternoon, the whole, in one lot, as a going concern, and failing selling in one lot on that day, then on the Tuesday and following days, at twelve o'clock punctually each day, in lots. The whole of the valuable furniture, in and out door effects of the hotel, principally consisting of modern bedroom suites, in polished wood, and mahogany, including wardrobes, chests of drawers, marble top and other washstands, dressing tables and glasses, brass, French, and other bedsteads, bedding, sitting room suites, in walnut and mahogany, including dining and other tables, sideboards, Cheffonnieres, easy and other chairs, chimney glasses, two cottage pianofortes, oil painting and engravings, Brussels and other carpets, a very large quantity of china and glass, linen, kitchen requisites, cellar of choice wines, carriages, and miscellaneous effects.

*The Leamington Spa Courier dated 12th September 1941 carried a sad story: News has just been received of the death, on active service in the Middle East of Sgt. J. Littler, R.A.F; formerly manager of the Manor House Hotel. He was 32 years of age and joined the R.A.F.*

*twelve months ago – at which time he was in charge of the new Glenburn Hotel in Rothesay, N.B. He leaves a widow [the daughter of Mr. J. J. Hewlett, managing director of the Palace Hotel, Buxton] and a four-year-old daughter. Since the beginning of the war, Mrs. Littler has held a responsible position in a munitions factory and was recently featured anonymously in a broadcast to America.*

**Marlborough Hotel** – 48 Brandon Parade
The premises were first licensed on 4th February 1947; however, we understand that the licence carried a number of restrictions, a key one being that there could be no public bar. The licence was surrendered in November 1963.

**Masons Arms** – 31 Rugby Road
The first directory listing we have for this beer house is in 1837, when its address is listed as New Milverton. Located just 48 yards from the Stamford and Warrington Arms, it was 144 yards from the Binswood Tavern and 285 yards from the Bell Inn. The premises also included stables and, like many beer houses, a brew house; it would later be owned by Lucas and Co. Ltd [Leamington Brewery] and then Ansells, following their 1928 acquisition of the brewery and its closure in 1934. In 1885 the tenant [William Hemming] was paying rent of £24 per annum and remarkably, according to the brewery records, the annual rent in 1930 was the same at £6 per quarter [either good negotiating skills or zero inflation?]. In August 1960 the Masons Arms stood alone, marooned in a wasteland of rubble, following the demolition of the surrounding houses in Rugby Road to enable residential redevelopment. Then licensee, Mrs. Dorothy Green said, "This is the grandest pub you could ever be in. The customers are as good as gold, like one big happy family. The close-down is very sad." The Masons Arms, latterly addressed as 31, Rugby Road, ceased trading on 20th September 1960 and the licence was transferred to New House, Kingshurst, Castle Bromwich, Birmingham. [For a photo of the Masons Arms premises – refer to the Stamford & Warrington Arms entry]

| | |
|---|---|
| 1837 | Licensee not listed in directory |
| 1838-51 | William Smith |
| June 1851-Oct 1851 | Charles Robert Sidney |
| October 1851-Nov 1854 | John Lambert |
| November 1854-Jan 1856 | Charles Dyke |
| January 1856-Dec 1861 | Richard Taylor |
| December 1861-Feb 1867 | John Mills |
| February 1867-May 1869 | Ellen Mills |
| May 1869-Jan 1870 | John Jeacock |
| January 1870-Nov 1873 | Mrs. Hannah Jeacock *(On the death of John)* |
| November 1873-May 1879 | Mrs. George Sutton |
| May 1879-83 | Frederick Fortnum |
| 1883-84 | John Henry Rose |
| 1884-87 | William Hemming |

| | |
|---|---|
| 1887-Nov 1900 | Henry Woodhouse |
| November 1900-08 | Albert Williams |
| 1908-Mar 1925 | Tom Wilkins Morgan *(Died 18th February 1925)* |
| March 1925-Sep 1925 | Miss Rose Anne Morgan *(Sister of Tom Morgan)* |
| September 1925-Jun 1939 | Frederick William Wilkins *(Died 9th June 1939)* |
| June 1939-Dec 1939 | Mrs. Grace May Rush |
| December 1939-Apr 1945 | Arthur Reddall |
| April 1945-Jan 1948 | Lancelot Taylor *(Died 20th November 1947)* |
| January 1948-Feb 1959 | Mrs. Elsie Taylor *(On the death of Lancelot)* |
| February 1959-Sep 1960 | Dorothy Hilda Green *(On the death of Mrs. Taylor; Mrs. Green was previously at Lillington Men's Club)* |
| 20th September 1960 | Closed for business |

**Merrie Lion** – 11 Brook Street
See Old White Lion for details.

**Moo** – 24 Russell Street
The Moo Bar was opened by Si Long on 16th March 2001 following a £300,000 investment. Moo Bar is still open in December 2013 under the ownership of Steven Alexander Smith.

| | |
|---|---|
| 2001-≤circa 2006 | Si Long |
| Circa 2006 | Christopher Charles Johnson |
| 1st December 2008 | David Michael O'Callaghan |
| 2011 → | Michael Browne *(Manager)* |

*The Moo Bar taken on 1st April 2010 © Allan Jennings.*

**Moon Under Water** – Parade
See Benjamin Satchwell's for details.

**Moorings** – Myton Road
On 12th October 1993, John William Fiddler [area manager - Banks' Brewery] applied for a provisional licence for premises to be constructed at the junction of Myton Road and Europa Way; the land was owned by British Waterways and the King Henry VIII charity. On 17th August 1995, a topping-out ceremony was performed by Leamington mayor, Councillor Terri Bayliss and Warwick District Council chairman, Councillor Bob Wooller. Situated alongside the Grand Union canal, the Moorings opened in October 1995; it comprised a ground floor bar

*Photo of the Moorings taken on 20th September 2008 © Allan Jennings.*

with a 94 seat restaurant above and represented an investment of £1.5 million. It received an award from the Leamington Society and Warwick District Council in August 1997 for making "a significant contribution to the quality of Leamington". In December 2010, "the canal side pub and kitchen" was reopened following an "imaginative and stylish £250k makeover" that took approximately 4 months to complete; in October 2010, the Leamington Spa Courier reported that the new owners, Charles Harris and Nigel Brown, had taken on a 15 year lease from Charles Wells Brewery. The Moorings remains open in December 2013.

| | |
|---|---|
| October 1995 | Patricia and Robert Isaacs |
| ≤2007-Oct 2007 | Joseph Heanen |
| October 2007-Jun 2010 | Andrew Webb |
| June 2010-Sep 2010 | James Christopher Treherne |
| September 2010 | Aubrey Taylor |
| October 2010 → | Charles Harris and Nigel Brown *(Owners)* |

*In January 1995 the brewery's plan for a towering mock factory chimney to top the pub was thrown out. Planners ordered Black Country brewery Banks' to lop 10 foot off the design after protests. Banks' wanted to present an industrial look but objectors complained about 'instant heritage'.*

The Leamington Spa Courier dated 29th October 2010 reported that: Around 50 full-time and part-time jobs will be created with the £250,000 refurbishment of the Moorings. Award winning chefs Charles Harris, 26, and Nigel Brown, 33, plan to have the business open by the end of November after taking on a 15 year lease from Charles Wells Brewery. Charles and Nigel already run the Stag at Offchurch. The two worked under famous chef Raymond

Blanc and have run the Stag for 2 years. They have won the Publican's Best Food Pub of the Year award. Mr. Harris said they will create a "maritime New England-style atmosphere reflecting the Anglo-French cuisine that has reaped the award-winning success of the Stag".

*The Leamington Spa Observer dated 3rd February 2011 reported: Leamington could not be further away from the sea but that has not stopped an historic anchor finding a new home in the town. A former 19th century Royal Navy anchor, claimed to have been used by one of the first iron war ships in England, has been put on display at its new home outside the Moorings pub. Weighing a half ton the anchor, which dates from 1880, was purchased and shipped to the Myton Road pub at a four figure cost from a reclamation salvage yard in North Devon. The unique naval sculpture mirrors the logo and maritime theme of the newly refurbished canal side pub.*

**Mor Bar** – 116 Warwick Street
See Prince of Wales for details.

**Mumbai Bluu** – 4 Bedford Street
See Coach and Horses for details.

**Murphy's Bar** – 33 Regent Street
The first two paragraphs of this entry include material researched by Jean Innes for 'People and Places', a book produced by the Leamington History Group; it provides a brief insight into the origins and development of the site now occupied by Murphy's Bar, and also Regent Street. In 1818, the road that we know as Regent Street was called Cross Street [laid out circa 1808-1814]; it stretched from Windsor Street/Augusta Place in the west to the Angel Inn in the east, and the subject site was a portion of undeveloped land owned by Edward Willes. Wellington Street was laid out in 1826 and named after the Duke of Wellington who visited the town in April 1827. Also circa 1827, Cross Street was renamed Regent Street [in honour of the Prince Regent who had visited Leamington in September 1819] and Wellington Street was extended eastwards [to Windsor Street/Augusta Place] due to Willes' land having been built upon.

In 1835, and now addressed as 56, Wellington Street, the building that would become Murphy's Bar was a grocer's shop owned by a Graham Collins. By 1876, Wellington Street had become part of Regent Street, which was simultaneously renumbered from the [opposite] western end and the subject site was addressed as 33, Regent Street, a family grocer/wine and spirits merchant owned by Edwin Smith. The business, which held a beer, wine and spirits off-licence, was transferred from Sydney Smith to Edwin Harris on 11th July 1910 and the then grocer's shop traded as Harris and Son until sold in 1968. Following the 1968 sale the premises became Morris Wine Stores until the early 1970s, when its off-licence would be exchanged for an on-licence.

Opening circa the mid 1970s, the Regent Wine Bar [along with Alastairs] was another pioneer of the new 'wine bar format' that was to become increasingly more popular from the late 70s; it remained open until 1983 when it was replaced by Rick's Bar, a short lived venture that closed the following year. In 1984 the premises were reopened as Bakers, a Café Bar and Cellar Bar, owned by Jerry Lewitt and Graham Soden [who also had the

*Above left: Bakers courtesy of Kevin Murphy. Above right: Photo of Murphy's courtesy of Nick Wilkins.*

Builders Arms]; it was operated by [Jerry's brother] Dave Lewitt plus a manager. In 1987, Kevin Murphy was briefly the manager of Bakers, before moving on to manage the Builders Arms from 1987 until 1990.

Kevin had always had a burning ambition to run his own licensed premises so when the opportunity arose in 1991 he purchased the lease of Bakers and renamed it Murphy's Bar. On 5th September 1991, the Leamington Observer reported that, "Murphy's on Regent Street will be opening tonight, under the new management of Kevin and Kate Murphy. Kevin, previously manager at the pub four years ago, hopes to recreate the pub atmosphere by putting in a pool table and darts boards. He has moved from the Builder's Arms in Leamington to take over as leaseholder at Murphy's, formerly Bakers; the bar would be open for food from 11.00am to 6.00pm." Apart from the Builder's Arms, Kevin has also been involved with the Pig and Fiddle, the Fusilier and other Leamington pubs; he would purchase the freehold of Murphy's Bar in November 1992. In October 2011, Kevin reopened the fully fitted-out cellar bar and advertised it as: "The Cavern - The Coolest Cellar Bar" – previously without bar facilities, it had primarily been utilised at the weekends by students. Murphy's Bar remains open in December 2013.

| | |
|---|---|
| 1876 | Edwin Smith *(Family grocer/wine & spirit merchant)* |
| Date unknown | Sydney Hubert Smith *(Wine & spirits off-licence)* |
| July 1910-Dec 1948 | Edwin Alfred Harris |
| December 1948-Nov 1962 | Oscar Rees |
| November 1962-Dec 1964 | Charles Reginald Fardon |
| December 1964-Apr 1970 | Dawn Ellen Fell |
| April 1970-≥1971 | Helen Maureen Cronin *(Morris Wine Stores)* |
| Circa mid 1970s | Opened as Regent Wine Bar |
| 1980 | Josephine Bullock *(Regent Wine Bar)* |
| 1984-91 | David 'Dave' Lewitt *(Bakers)* |

| | |
|---|---|
| 1987 | Kevin John Murphy *(Manager)* |
| 1988 | Andy Poole *(Manager)* |
| 1990-91 | Melissa 'Mel' Heppenstall *(Manager – Bakers; Dean Hornsby, assistant manager)* |
| 5th September 1991-2010 | Kevin John Murphy *(Murphy's Bar)* |
| 5th August 2010 → | Lisa Jill Murphy |

*The Regent Wine Bar was frequented by Aileen Riddett and her friends: "Back in the 70s, the current Murphy's Bar was a very popular wine bar, frequented at night by teenagers [like myself]… but during the day, ladies who lunch [like my mother], felt very comfortable meeting there. The salad bar downstairs was amazing and typical 70s with 'new' fashionable food like quiche and cheesecake… I think they used to have the odd band downstairs too. It was always packed at the weekends. There were arches/alcoves with tables in [probably still are] where we would sit all night with two bottles of cheap wine – bliss. Murphy's Bar has become a friendly and popular venue for many men and women and plays an important part in the life of the community."*

Allan Jennings says, "At Christmas 1978 the Regent Wine Bar was selling Kronenbourg and Tuborg lagers. Wine was available by the glass, goblet, bottle, or litre bottle. The cellar bar and bistro had just been refurbished and Christmas lunch including Christmas pudding or mince pies was £1.50. In February 1979, the Regent Wine Bar and Bistro were advertising – Make it an occasion on Valentines Day, enjoy an intimate evening out. Wine and dine in the friendly atmosphere of the Wine Bar. Free glass of Valentine punch to all couples arriving before 9 o'clock."

*In 2007, Kevin reflected on the success of Murphy's, "I think the most important thing in a pub is a friendly landlord, friendly staff, and friendly people. I'd say we're about 80 per cent regulars but we welcome everyone regardless of age, class, marital status, anything. We want a pub where you'll find solicitors talking to bin men. There's a real community feel to the pub and we go on a lot of trips with our regulars – this year there are 12 of us going to Thailand and every year we take about 50 people down to the seaside for the day."*

Kevin Murphy had a different idea later on in 2009. He was advertising in the local press for all people named Kevin. He was trying to get in as many Kevins as possible on the evening of 10th November in order to set a bizarre new world record. Kevin offered each Kevin a free drink from 5.30pm onwards on the day, although they would be invited to donate the cost of the drink to charity. Only people called Kevin were to be allowed in and evidence of identity would be required. They have a capacity of 80 or 90 and Kevin was looking forward to a fun night. Funds raised were to go to a special needs centre for children in Ghana. He had already raised more than £1,000 to buy appliances for the centre and paid it a visit earlier in the year as a new cooker and fridge-freezer were delivered.

**Muswells Wine Bar** – 9 Parade
The first reference we have for Muswells appeared in the Morning News on 23rd March 1989, when it was reported that, "This week, licensing magistrates rejected an application for a full licence at Muswells, soon to take the place of Pizzaland in The Parade. Area manager of the Allied Lyons owned chain of café-bars, Peter Borg-Neal, applied for the

licence that would enable customers to use the premises as a bar for drinking, rather than a restaurant. Muswells also applied for the transfer of the licence from the derelict Golden Lion pub in Regent Street, once owned by Allied Lyons, to the Pizzaland site, but the application was turned down. Muswells are appealing the decisions." We have not been able to establish whether the appeal was successful and a full licence granted. Notwithstanding, Muswells closed circa 1994 and in 2013 it is the Oriental Star Buffet Chinese restaurant.

**Negro** – Brook Street
We only have two directory listings for this pub. Although the 1840 church rate book also shows a William Brown at a public house in Clarence Terrace, we have not been able to find any information on it.

| | |
|---|---|
| 1838-39 | W. Brown |

**Nelson Inn** – 42/44 Brunswick Street
The first directory listing we have is in 1832 and, as the Nelson Inn is not listed in the 1835 or subsequent directories, we initially concluded that it closed in 1833-34. From a pub perspective this is probably true, as the premises were purchased in 1834 by William Ind, a wine, spirits and ale merchant. Ind already owned a like business that he had relocated to the old Theatre Royal building [43, Bath Street] when he purchased same in 1831. It is therefore possible that the premises previously known as the Nelson Inn became an additional outlet for this business. Notwithstanding, the Nelson Inn was sold by auction on Friday 16th June 1837 and was described as: "A dwelling house lately used as a public house, and called the Nelson Inn, now or late in the tenure or occupation of Mr. William Ind. These premises comprise 577 square yards of ground and are held for a term of 90 years, 8 months and 21 days, commencing from 25th December 1826, and will be sold subject to a ground rent of £22.10s.5d and to an agreement for a lease to Mr. Ind for 10 years from 25th March 1832." We have established that William Ind died in 1837-38 but not whether his death triggered the sale of these premises [Elizabeth, his widow, sold-off the Bath Street business in March 1838].

| | |
|---|---|
| ≤1832-34 | J. Bernard *(Henry Butler – landlord)* |
| 1834-1837 | William Ind *(Owner)* |

**New Binswood Tavern** – Rugby Road
See Binswood Tavern for details.

**New Inn** – Bath Lane [now Bath Street]
The New Inn later became the Bath Hotel. See Bath Hotel for details.

**New Inn** – Chandos Street
The only directory listing we have is in 1837 and there is no mention of the landlord's name. As it is not listed in the 1841 or subsequent directories we have concluded that it either closed between 1837 and 1840, or that it is an invalid listing.

**New Inn** – Radford Road

Listed below is the only information available on this New Inn. A possible connection to three other pubs in the vicinity was also checked-out, but to no avail. Firstly, the New Inn [Leam Terrace] opened as the Railway Tavern in 1849 and wasn't renamed the New Inn until circa 1860. Secondly, the Red House [Radford Road] didn't open until the early 1850s. Lastly, we eliminated the [Royal] Oak, also in Radford Road, because it was already open, listed in the same 1838-39 directories, but with a different licensee. We have therefore concluded that the New Inn [Radford Road] was simply another beer house with a very short lifespan.

1838-39                          John Horniblow

**New Inn** – 195/197 Leam Terrace

From circa 1849 until circa 1860 the only pub in this part of Leam Terrace [then addressed as Leam Terrace East] was a beer house named the Railway Tavern; it was located at what is now 187, Leam Terrace [see Railway Tavern entry for an 1852 map of its location and a 2010 photo of the building]. Charles Pearson was the licensee of the Railway Tavern from circa 1849 until at least 1857, but strangely in 1851 and 1857 the beer house is listed at Myrtle Place, an address we have been unable to substantiate on any maps from the period.

Circa 1860, the Railway Tavern closed and the New Inn opened just a few yards along the road at 109, Leam Terrace East, which it would continue to be named until circa 1914 when it was readdressed as 197, Leam Terrace. On 13th March 1879, the New Inn was sold at auction, with the sale notice describing the premises as comprising a front bar, smoke room, bar parlour, tap room, kitchen and scullery on the ground floor; four bedrooms and three attics upstairs; good cellaring and out-offices with a yard approached by a side entrance from Mews Road. There was also a cottage which had a frontage onto the side road and outbuildings which included stabling, cow houses, lofts, a slaughter house and an extensive yard. There was a main road frontage of 36 ft [including the Mews Road of 9 ft], a depth of 122 ft 10 in and the area of the whole premises amounted to 491 square yards. The property was sold at this auction to Messrs Flower and Son for £1,160.

In 1903 there were two entrances, one from Leam Terrace and another via a side entrance leading to Smith's livery stables. A full licence was granted on 8th February 1950 and confirmed on 29th March however, it was a condition of the licence that the side entrance leading to the livery stables was not to be used for trade purposes. On 27th July 1962, the Leamington Spa Courier

*Photo of the New Inn taken 7th January 1996 ©
Allan Jennings.*

235

reported that the local magistrates had approved an application for an enlargement of the bar by extending it into the smoke room.

In early 1986, Louise Hinton submitted plans to the district council's planning committee, her proposal being to acquire the shop next door and extend the New Inn, thus doubling its size. In early 1988, the pub was closed for two months while the refurbishment was undertaken, at a cost of £110,000. The New Inn remains open in December 2013.

| | |
|---|---|
| 1849-51 | Charles Pearson *(Railway Tavern)* |
| 1851-≥1857 | Charles Pearson |
| ≤1863-66 | James Tabberer *(New Inn)* |
| 1868-72 | Charles Brown |
| 1873-Jul 1889 | Mary Brown |
| July 1889-Aug 1889 | H. P. Gibbons |
| August 1889-Mar 1901 | John Chamberlain *(Ex marine, born in Honington)* |
| March 1901-Oct 1909 | Mrs. Ann Chamberlain *(On the death John)* |
| October 1909-29 | Albert Edward Robinson |
| 1910-Apr 1934 | Mrs. Lucy Ann Robinson |
| April 1934-Sep 1949 | Cyril C. Fell |
| September 1949-Apr 1953 | Mrs. Maria Fell *(On the death of Cyril)* |
| April 1953-Jul 1955 | William Edmund Quantrill |
| July 1955-Sep 1957 | Edwin Joseph Homer |
| September 1957-Jul 1958 | William James Bridgewater |
| July 1958-Jul 1959 | William Ashworth Sutton |
| July 1959-1984 | Kathleen Joan Sutton |
| 1984-Mar 1988 | Ray and Louise Hinton *(Leaseholders and licensees; various managers, e.g. Eric Brown, Bob Dixon)* |
| March 1988-92 | Barry and Eileen Hunt *(Went on to the Bowling Green)* |
| 1992-95 | Brian Love |
| September 1995-Sep 1996 | Marcus Easterlow *(Lease holder)* |
| September 1995-Sep 1996 | Sandy Reed and Lisa Bentley |
| September 1996-2002 | John and Linda Franks |
| 2002-May 2006 | Patrick and Geraldine Ryan |
| May 2006 → | Catherine Wilde |

*On 2nd March 1988 it was reported that the first pint at the refurbished New Inn pub had been pulled by a woman well known to regulars. Former licensee Joan Sutton, who ruled the roost for 27 years until her retirement three years before, showed she hadn't forgotten how to serve a drink. The pub had closed for two months for a refurbishment costing £110,000. The pub almost doubled its space by extending into a derelict shop next door. New tenants Barry and Eileen Hunt [1st March 1988] were determined it wouldn't lose its old character. Eileen said, "All the decorations and fittings are in keeping with the Victorian flavour of the building. We are a local pub, right in the heart of the community with four darts teams, and we will continue to cater for our regulars."*

**New Kings Arms** – 69 Warwick Street

The first directory listing we have for this beer house is in 1872. However, our first reference point is in September 1870 when application was made to the local licensing justices to also hold a wine licence; the application was refused. As the licensing sessions were held annually this is an indicator that the New Kings Arms was already open by 1869 [although the application for a wine licence was refused it would subsequently be granted in September 1880]. In 1897 the owners were the Northampton Brewery Co. Ltd, by 1903 it was owned by Lucas and Co. Ltd [Leamington Brewery] and latterly, certainly by 1931, the lessees were again the Northampton Brewery Co. Ltd [which merged with Phipps Brewery Ltd in 1957]. In February 1931 Samuel Exworthy was granted a licence to sell wine 'on' or 'off' the premises to go with the beer on-licence already held. With the lease on the premises set to expire on 29th September 1959, the licensee [Cecil William Morgan] ceased trading and closed the pub the day prior; there was no application made to renew the licence at the licensing meeting on 2nd February 1960. During 1959-60 the premises were converted into two shop units with two shop fronts, one for John Neville Cameras and the other for W. Locke Motor Cycles.

| | |
|---|---|
| ≤1870 | Mr. Sibley |
| 1872 | J. Ward |
| 1872-Mar 1873 | Thomas Ward |
| March 1873 | John Bilton Rabone |
| ≤1876-Sept 1876 | Thomas Shepherd |
| September 1876-Mar 1877 | William Henry Taylor |
| March 1877 | George Judd |

*Photo of the New Kings Arms post 1932 courtesy of Leamington Library.*

| | |
|---|---|
| 1879-April 1883 | Joseph Moore |
| April 1883-Aug 1890 | John Thomas Richardson |
| August 1890-May 1894 | Henry Pratt |
| May 1894-Nov 1894 | James Wood |
| November 1894-Apr 1895 | Charles E. Elkington |
| April 1895-Oct 1897 | Mrs. Eliza Wood |
| October 1897-Dec 1898 | Mrs. Emma Clarke |
| December 1898-May 1900 | George Leglere |
| 15th May 1900-Mar 1901 | George Collier |
| March 1901-Mar 1902 | James Cooper |
| March 1902-Sep 1912 | Henry 'Harry' Andrew Wickes |
| September 1912-Jan 1914 | William Samuel Hughes |
| January 1914-Apr 1946 | Samuel Exworthy |
| April 1946-Sep 1946 | Alfred William Ward |
| September 1946-Apr 1950 | Frederick Samuel Addy |
| April 1950-Feb 1951 | Albert Lloyd Hopkins |
| February 1951-Feb 1952 | Neville Alfred Snow |
| February 1952-Jan 1955 | Herbert Grant |
| January 1955-Sep 1959 | Cecil William Morgan |
| 28th September 1959 | Closed for business |

**Newbold Comyn Arms** – Newbold Terrace East, Newbold Comyn

The Newbold Comyn Arms, a converted farmhouse and stable, is a grade two listed building situated on a 300 acre park; it is said that some of the beams date back to the time of Queen Anne. The pub opened in two stages with the bar being part of stage one in 1984. Stage two,

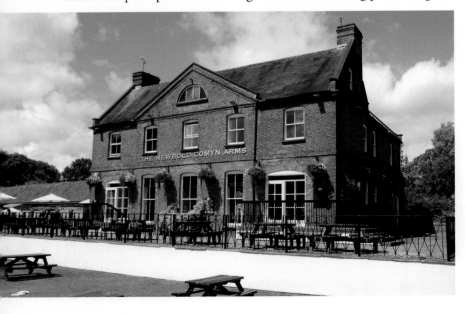

*Photo of the Newbold Comyn Arms taken on 16th July 2011 © Allan Jennings.*

*The Stables Bar taken on 6th January 2010 © Allan Jennings.*

being the new Stables Bar and partner's restaurant, was opened by retired Warwick District Council amenities officer, Alan Pedley, at 7.00pm on Friday 17th November 1989. It offered customers a childrens room, complete with toys and games, a skittle alley, traditional games and a self-service counter. The Stables Bar, situated alongside the main building, was described at the time as having "a cosy atmosphere with real fires during the winter months".

In December 2012 the Stables Bar was renamed the Newbold Comyn Arms and the existing Newbold Comyn Arms became the Manor House; a venue for conferences, banquets and weddings. The Newbold Comyn Arms remains open in December 2013.

| | |
|---|---|
| 1984-≥1997 | John Harrison and wife Maggie |
| Circa 2005-Oct 2009 | Nicholas Arthur Surtees Wormald |
| October 2009 → | Sarah Ann Miller |

*In September 1987, Leamington celebrated its third annual beer festival at the Newbold Comyn Arms. The event was opened by the town mayor, Councillor Ben Dhesi. The organisers said that 2,176 pints of real ale such as Tanglefoot, Head Banger, Old Thumper and Tally Ho would be on offer.*

### Newbold Inn / Tavern / Newbold – 18 Newbold Street

According to the conservation department at Warwick District Council, Newbold Street was laid-out in 1826; it describes these premises as "a public house circa 1826-1830". The first directory listing we have for the Newbold Inn is in 1835; in its early days it was addressed as 1, Newbold Street but by 1900 it had been renumbered '18'. In 1838 it consisted of two parlours, a large tap room, bar, a club room [30 ft x 15 ft], kitchen, pantry, eight bedrooms, two arched cellars, brewhouse, loose boxes with lofts over and stables for twelve horses. Circa the early 20th century, the pub was owned by P. Phipps and Co. [Northampton], who by 1957 had become Phipps Northampton Brewery Co. Ltd; in 1960, they would be taken over by the London based Watney Mann Ltd, Phipps Brewery, Bridge Street, Northampton.

From the late 1960s until 1999 it was known as the Newbold Tavern. In 1999, Randolph Turpin Jnr, son of the Leamington boxing legend, sold the pub he had run for 21 years to the Castle Taverns and Hotels Group. After being closed for more than two years it was reported in October 2001 that "the historic Newbold Tavern, now called the Newbold Bar and Brasserie, in Newbold Street, has undergone a £1.6 million refit". In 2009 it was closed briefly before reopening under new management as the Newbold. However, by the first week in October 2010 it was closed again with a notice on the door stating that it would re-open on 8th October under new management [Andrew White, who also owns the Vine at Warwick]. The Newbold ceased trading in March 2012 and the freehold premises remained closed-up and 'for sale' for more than twelve months. Following a major mid year refurbishment it reopened on Friday 23rd August, 2013 as the Regency Arms, a traditional pub/restaurant.

*Photo of the Newbold Tavern taken on 9th March 1980 courtesy of Leamington Library.*

| | |
|---|---|
| 1835 | Catherine and Elizabeth Lawford |
| 1837 | George Lees |
| 1837-39 | G. H. Ward |
| 1840-42 | Samuel Edward Kettle Nicklin |
| 1845 | Mrs. M. A. Clarke |
| 1846 | W. Underhill |
| 1848-62 | Henry Greves |
| 1849-51 | Job Genders |
| 1852 | G. Collins |
| 1854-56 | John Wells |
| 1856-62 | Job Genders |
| 1857-Jan 1865 | Thomas Brooks |
| January 1865-May 1891 | Mrs. Ann Elkington Brooks *(Died 1891)* |
| May 1891-Jul 1892 | Mary Catherine Elkington Bromwich |
| July 1892-Jan 1899 | Mrs. Sam Kightley |
| January 1899-May 1899 | Mrs. Annie Kightley *(On the death of Sam)* |
| May 1899-Mar 1904 | Henry Ludlow |
| March 1904-10 | John Keartland |
| 1910-May 1922 | Harry Ashby |
| May 1922-28 | Mrs. E. Ashby *(On the death of Harry)* |
| 1928-35 | George Deeming |
| 1930s-Mar 1937 | Ellen Edith Deeming |
| March 1937-Aug 1973 | Sidney Claude Deeming *(Died 25th May 1973)* |

| | |
|---|---|
| August 1973 | Doris Edith Grace Deeming *(On the death of Sidney)* |
| Circa 1976 | Malcolm and Megan Heydon |
| 1978-1999 | Randolph Turpin *(Landlord after serving as manager)* |
| 1999-2001 | Closed |
| 2001 | Toby Goddard |
| Circa 2006 | David John William Barnbrook |
| May 2006 | Melissa Price |
| June 2009 | Gaynor Lynne and Anton Thorpe |
| 2009 | Matt Hyde *(Manager)* |
| 2010 | Miss Hayley Perks |
| October 2010-Mar 2012 | Andrew White *(Owner of the Vine, Warwick)* |
| October 2010-Mar 2012 | Bill Doherty *(Manager)* |
| August 2013 → | David Myron Aller *(General Manager)* |

*The conservation department at Warwick District Council describes the building as: A public house circa 1826-1830. Newbold Street was laid out in 1826. Pinkish-brown brick with painted stucco façade and slate roof; Parapeted gable end to front and rear; Double-depth rectangular plan with central entrance and two front rooms; 3 storeys with attic, 3 first floor windows; first and second floors have 6/6 sashes; 3/6 sash to attic in gable. Ground floor: tripartite sashes. Central entrance with panelled door within porch, with Tuscan columns, entablature canopy. Left (south-east) return has sashes on left and doorway on right. Rear: 6/6 sashes to second floor and 3/6 sash to attic. End stacks, truncated to left.*

The following advert for the Newbold Inn appeared in the Leamington Spa Courier dated 19th May 1849:

**Shooting Gallery at the Newbold Inn, Newbold Street**
*Mr. Job Genders, on the advice of his friends, has opened the above shooting gallery for the nobility, gentry, and public of Royal Leamington Spa. J. Genders, having been a sergeant major in the 7th Dragoon Guards, for 28 years, is fully capable of giving instruction in rifle and pistol practices, will be given gratis, merely by payment of the shots, 1s. per dozen or 1d. each. At this gallery will be found the best fitted up harlequin target for amusement, ever yet seen, with changeable figures, which will be produced by striking the bull's eye. Open from 8.00 in the morning till 10.00 at night.*

In January 1935 there were seven pubs in the Warwick & Leamington Licensed Victuallers' Air Gun League. Top of the league was the Newbold, followed by the White Lion, the Eagle, Holly Bush, Leopard, Green Man and the Willoughby.

*The Leamington Spa Courier dated 1st June 1973 reported:* **Well - known licensee Mr. Sid Deeming dies** - *The funeral took place yesterday at All Saints Parish Church, Leamington, of Mr. Sid Deeming, one of Leamington's best known licensees, who died on Friday aged 68. Mr. Deeming was landlord of the Newbold Inn, Newbold Street, for many years, taking over as licensee from his father. In 1937 he joined the Licensed Victuallers' Association, and was one of its oldest serving members in the Leamington, Warwick and Kenilworth branch. He became a committee member in 1964 and was branch treasurer from 1970 to his death. He* *leaves a widow, Mrs. Doris Deeming, and three children, Sid, Dorothy and Pauline. "He was a very hard-working man for the Association," said the local LVA secretary Mr. Bill Knight. "He will be missed by everybody."*

The Coventry Evening Telegraph dated 26th March 1999 reported that: **Randolph Turpin jnr sells pub after 21 years** - The son of Leamington boxing legend Randolph Turpin has sold the pub he had run for 21 years. The former world middleweight champion's son, also called Randolph, was landlord of the Newbold Tavern, in Newbold Street. But he has now sold it to the Castle Taverns and Hotels group which runs pubs including the Anchor in Leek Wootton and the Clarendon Arms in Kenilworth. Mr. Turpin, aged 51, said he and his wife, Bernadette, had enjoyed their time at the pub and would miss all the regulars. "It's a nice pub in a nice area but with a different person behind the bar I feel it could be a great going concern. I have a lot of good memories of the place and have received some very nice telegrams and cards from customers. We plan to stop in this area and will take a week or two to decide what we do next." Pat McCosker, a partner in Castle Taverns and hotels, said the company planned to spend £200,000 renovating the pub. It would reopen in May, creating 20 jobs.

*The Coventry Evening Telegraph dated 6th October 2001 reported that: A newly-refurbished Leamington pub is hoping to establish a reputation for its tasty food as well as its traditional ales. The historic Newbold Tavern now called the Newbold Bar and Brasserie, in Newbold Street, has undergone a £1.6 million refit. The 150 year old pub, formerly in the hands of the family of Leamington boxer Randolph Turpin, has been closed for more than two years for the rebuild. It has 15 staff, which is expected to rise to 25 when the brasserie opens. That will allow audiences from the neighbouring Royal Spa Centre to have a meal until 11.15pm, with the premises open until 1.00am. Toby Goddard, manager and licensee, said, "We have a London chef who has hand-picked his own team. We are selling food and cask beers seven days a week and will appeal to both former drinkers of the new pub and new customers."*

### Newmarket Inn – 50 Tavistock Street

On 2nd December 1826, Richard Jones sold some parcels of land to a Theophilus Taylor, and it included the block of land upon which the Newmarket Inn would stand. Purchased by James Coult [paperhanger] on 25th September 1827 for £465, this particular block extended from Warwick Street, 40 yards up Tavistock Street to a passageway and 15½ yards back along Warwick Street, covering a total area of 620 square yards. On 9th October 1827, Coult borrowed £600 from John Campbell of Stoneleigh; the front of the deeds state, "Abstract of the title of Mr. James Coult to a freehold house in Tavistock Street, Leamington called the Newmarket Inn, in mortgage by a deposit of the title deeds to Mr. Wm. Ryley for securing £650 plus interest."

The first directory listing for this beer house is in 1830, when James Coult is listed as the licensee and also separately as a retail brewer. In its early days the Newmarket was addressed as 2, Tavistock Street and sometimes known as the Newmarket Tavern; it was renumbered as 50, Tavistock Street during the 1870s. In February 1882 application was made to the local justices to rename the Newmarket Inn, but the applicant was instructed to resubmit the application at the next annual licensing session. In 1883, it was renamed the

*Photo of the Tavistock Inn taken on 13th April 1986 © Allan Jennings.*

Tavistock Inn and was owned by H. E. Thornley Ltd. When Thornley-Kelsey closed their brewery and sold-off their [tied estate] pubs in 1968 the Tavistock was acquired by Davenports Brewery, who in turn sold-out to Greenall Whitley & Co. Ltd in 1986. The Tavistock Inn remains open in December 2013.

### Newmarket Inn

| | |
|---|---|
| 1830-44 | James Coult |
| 1844-49 | Elias Wilcox |
| 1849-Aug 1854 | John Chandler |
| August 1854-66 | Abraham Jennings |
| 1866 | George Smith |
| September 1866-1868 | Henry Parsonage (*Of Newhall Street, Birmingham – also listed as a brewer and a wine & spirits merchant*) |
| 1869 | Thomas Parsons Dafforn |
| December 1869-Oct 1870 | William Skelton |
| October 1870-Mar 1871 | Robert Hammond |
| March 1871-Jun 1872 | William Skelton |
| June 1872-May 1874 | James Daily |
| May 1874 | H. Taylor |
| 1875-Jan 1877 | James Ballard |
| January 1877 | Thomas Jordan Gibbins |
| 1877-78 | Abraham Jennings |

| | |
|---|---|
| 1878-Jul 1880 | William Leese |
| July 1880-February 1882 | Mrs. Mary Ann Ford |
| February 1882 | John Holmes |

**Tavistock Inn**

| | |
|---|---|
| 1883-May 1883 | John Holmes |
| May 1883-Oct 1886 | George Ludlow |
| October 1886-May 1887 | James Parris |
| May 1887-Feb 1893 | Thomas William Pearson |
| February 1893-May 1893 | Martin Attwood |
| May 1893-Jul 1905 | John Lee *(Died 1905, aged 42)* |
| July 1905-1928 | Mrs. Elizabeth Mary Lee *(On the death of John)* |
| 1932-Oct 1938 | Edward Checkley |
| October 1938-Apr 1942 | William Bernard Steane |
| April 1942-Jan 1953 | Leonard Ernest Knighton |
| January 1953-Sep 1957 | Thomas Lakin |
| September 1957-Apr 1958 | Howard Slott |
| April 1958-Apr 1964 | Harry Romney |
| April 1964-Jun 1967 | Alfred Hewitt |
| June 1967-Jun 1968 | Margaret Mary North |
| June 1968-Jan 1974 | Patrick 'Paddy' Joseph McCarthy and wife Nancy |
| January 1974 | David Walker |
| January 1974-Apr 1975 | Michael 'Mick' and Ann Thurlbeck *(Resident manager, rented from David Walker – went on to the Red Lion, Warwick)* |
| 1975-Aug 1985 | Michael 'Mick' Barry Brown *(In 1986 he became the landlord of the Nelson, Emscote Road, Warwick, for 25 years; Mick died 23rd August 2011).* |
| August 1985-86 | Margo Farrant |
| 1986-≥1992 | Colin Lloyd |
| December 1995-Jun 1996 | Closed |
| June 1996 | Peter, Margaret and Steven *(Surnames not known)* |
| 1998 | Steve Zaparaniuk |
| Circa 2000-Aug 2005 | Richard Modrich and Warren Blaydon |
| August 2005 → | Kamarl Nayar |

*The Leamington Spa Courier dated 11th January 1845 carried the following notice: The Newmarket Inn, Tavistock Street, Royal Leamington. E. Willcox acknowledges with gratitude the extensive support he has met with, since entering upon the above old established inn; and respectfully informs his kind friends and patrons, that his housewarming dinner will take place on Tuesday next, the 14th instant, when their attendance will be esteemed a favour. Dinner on the table at three o'clock – Tickets 3s.6d each – Tavistock Street, Leamington, Jan 8th, 1845.*

The following advert appeared in the Leamington Spa Courier dated 31st March 1849:

Newmarket Inn
Tavistock Street, Leamington Spa
J. Chandler

Having taken to the old established inn, respectfully solicits that patronage and support which has hitherto been bestowed upon his predecessors. Families supplied with genuine home-brewed ale, table beer, &c, on the shortest notice, and on moderate terms; foreign wines and spirits of the best quality.

*The sixth annual meeting of the Leamington Priors Licensed Victuallers Association took place on 2nd December 1851 at the Newmarket Inn.*

In June 1866 George Smith, landlord of the Newmarket Inn, was charged with permitting prostitutes to assemble in his house. Inspector Waters said he visited the house at half past ten on the 6th inst and he saw a number of persons in the bar including six prostitutes. He said to the landlord that it looked bad for him to have such characters in his house and left. He visited again at eleven o'clock the same evening, when he saw seven prostitutes – three of them the same as before. He visited a third time at half past eleven and there were eight prostitutes. Mr. Smith, who had already been cautioned the previous week, was fined £3 and 11s costs.

*The Rugby Advertiser dated Saturday 30th November 1869 reported that: On Tuesday morning a fire was discovered at the Newmarket Inn, Tavistock Street. About half past four o'clock when the barman went into the bar, he found the place full of smoke and the floor and counter smouldering. It is supposed that a piece of lighted paper had been dropped overnight and had ignited the sawdust on the floor, and thus the fire extended to the counter and the floor. A considerable amount of damage was done.*

The Morning News dated 1st August 1986 reported that: A warm hearted Leamington pub licensee has ambitious plans for charity fund raising events at the Tavistock Inn. Margo Farrant, who has been in charge of the recently renovated pub for almost a year, has already helped to raise hundreds of pounds for charity such as leukaemia research. The latest charity event ended last week when actor Paul Henry, who appears as Benny in the popular soap 'Crossroads', was invited to push over a huge stack of pennies collected during the past couple of months. "We managed to raise almost £150 for Leamington's blind people. The pile of pennies was huge – it was a shame to see it crumble," said Margo.

When Margo first moved into the pub in August last year it had fallen into a bad state of disrepair. It took months of renovation work to restore it to its former glory. "I was looking forward to running my first pub, but when I saw the state it was in, I thought again," said Margo. "However, after a lot of hard work it is now nicely decorated and has received a complete transformation." The pub has been nick-named the 'Pink Palace' by locals because of its pink decor.

Margo was also concerned about the pub's 'men only' image. "It was very much a man's bar and it took a long time to change this, although I am definitely making headway now," she said. "I now have a large selection of customers ranging from the local rugby team to couples, young and old." Margo has recently launched coffee mornings in a bid to encourage shoppers to visit the pub. "I want to promote a friendly, chatty atmosphere and I'm fairly confident it will take off."

### Noah's Ark – 106 Regent Street

The first directory listing we have is in 1832 when it was opened as a beer house. In its early days it was addressed as 55, Regent Street, but Regent Street was renumbered frequently to keep pace with the rapid expansion of the new town and by 1880 the Noah's Ark would be 106, Regent Street [in the meantime it would also be numbered '76' and '87']. On Wednesday 10th June 1846 the Noah's Ark was advertised for auction, with the sale notice describing it thus: "The house, number 76, is an old-established public house, known as the Noah's Ark, occupied by Mr. John Wells, a yearly tenant, at £40 per annum, and comprises a front parlour, bar, kitchen, good cellaring, six bedrooms, brew house, malt room, stabling and piggeries."

In January 1854 the premises were upgraded from a beer house when a publican's licence was granted to Leonard London. At the annual licensing sessions in February 1905 the chief constable objected to the licence renewal, stating that there were just two small rooms, a bar and a smoke room [in 1903 he had commented that to get to the smoke room one had to go behind the bar counter and then down three steps]. The licensing justices refused to renew the licence on the grounds of 'structural unsuitability and inconvenience of police supervision'. The owner of the premises was Councillor J. Smith of Warwick who

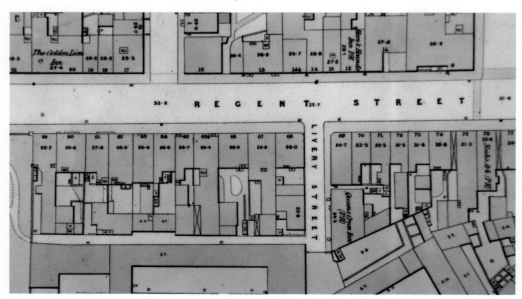

*This 1852 map courtesy of Leamington Library shows that the Noah's Ark was situated on Regent Street at the bottom of Park Street.*

had purchased the premises in 1892 and the lessees were Phillips and Marriott of Coventry. The Noahs Ark was closed on 4th April 1907 with compensation being paid.

| | |
|---|---|
| 1832-34 | Thomas Archer |
| 1835-Nov 1851 | John Wells |
| November 1851-54 | William Rogers |
| 1854-Jul 1857 | Leonard London |
| July 1857-Sep 1857 | Ann Gardner |
| September 1857-Dec 1857 | Leonard London |
| December 1857-Aug 1858 | James Hardman |
| August 1858-Oct 1861 | Richard Hardman |
| October 1861-Jan 1866 | Robert Colton |
| January 1866-Oct 1867 | Robert Rose |
| October 1867-68 | George Wilkins |
| 1868-Oct 1870 | John Lester |
| October 1870-72 | John Ife |
| 1872-76 | Thomas Mann |
| 1877 | J. Mann |
| 1877-Apr 1877 | T. B. Parsons |
| April 1877-Nov 1878 | William Wilcox |
| November 1878 | William George Wilcox *(Son of William)* |
| 1880-83 | James Wilkins |
| 1883 | Mrs. L. Wilkins |
| Circa 1883 | John Brewer |
| Feb 1884-Jul 1884 | Messrs Green and Hacker |
| July 1884-87 | John Bayliss *(Listed as William in 1885)* |
| 1887-Aug 1889 | Henry John Davis |
| August 1889-Oct 1889 | Mrs. Alice Walters *(Executor, on Henry Davis' death)* |
| October 1889-Mar 1892 | James Phillips *(Of Barford)* |
| March 1892-Jun 1892 | John Rush |
| June 1892-Apr 1893 | Frederick Bonham |
| April 1893-Oct 1894 | Richard William Sheldon |
| October 1894-Mar 1895 | James Murrall *(Magistrates refused to confirm license)* |
| March 1895-Aug 1895 | Annie Hammerton Mander *(Of Kenilworth)* |
| August 1895-May 1897 | William Henry Shakeshaft |
| May 1897-Apr 1900 | William John Read |
| April 1900-Apr 1907 | Frederick Charles Townsend |
| 4th April 1907 | Closed for business |

**Oak Inn / Hotel** – 89 Radford Road

The first information we have is in 1837, when the church rate book shows William Lovell running a public house on the Radford Road, and a directory lists the Oak Inn [Radford Road] without a landlord. Circa 1840 a Mr. McGregor arrived in Leamington from

*This photo of the Oak Inn circa 1890 shows landlord Mr. W. Smith. It was donated to Leamington Library by Mr. Savage, the grandson of Mr. Smith.*

Scotland and opened up stables at the rear of the Oak; he later started the first public transport between Warwick and Leamington – a horse bus. In April 1846 W. Staite announced his retirement from the malting business at Radford Semele, stating that the business was to be taken over by sons W. and J. [John] Staite.

On 15th August 1849 the Oak Inn [then in the occupation of William Lovell] was sold by auction to John Staite, a name that would remain prominent in Leamington for many years. The sale notice that appeared in the Leamington Spa Courier on 28th July described it thus: "The property has three fronts, and is delightfully situated, commanding a long interrupted view of the London Road [later to be Radford Road], leading into Royal Leamington Spa, and a short distance from the town hall. The premises consists of two front parlours with folding doors, bar, parlour, kitchens, brew house, three underground cellars, six chambers, large coach house, stabling for fourteen horses, lofts, large yard and garden, piggeries and pump of excellent water."

On his arrival at the Oak Inn, John Staite started to diversify his business interests; apart from being a publican he is also variously listed as a brewer, maltster, hop and seed merchant, farmer, agricultural auctioneer, valuer and estate agent. Situated close to the cattle market, Staite used to give metal discs to those that had bought livestock at the market thus entitling them to cheap beer in the bar of his public house. In 1886 he ceased to be a publican and

*An 1897 Spennels directory advert courtesy of Leamington Library.*

*The Oak Inn taken on 18th September 2008 © Allan Jennings.*

brewer to concentrate on his estate agency business. A music singing and dancing licence was granted in November 1892 for the club room measuring 25 ft x 13 ft; concerts were held on Monday and Saturday evenings until 10.30pm. Between 1894 and 1926-27 the Oak is listed primarily as the Oak Hotel.

John Staite and Sons continued to own the Oak until 30th November 1910 when the directors of Lucas and Co. Ltd [Leamington Brewery], who had been leasing the pub for £125 per annum, approved its purchase for £3,400. It became an Ansells pub following their 1928 acquisition of the Leamington Brewery and its closure in 1934. During World War Two the Oak premises were used as a mortuary. In November 1984 the Leamington Courier reported, "A major facelift for the Oak Inn, by owners Ansells Brewery, in order to bring it up to standards expected of a 20th century pub, [including] a new roof, exterior repairs, redecoration and re-signing, interior re-wiring, redecoration and refurbishment and a new food preparation area." It was described thus: "A two roomed pub – the bar, has facilities for pub games, and the lounge is of a traditional style, a comfortable room predominantly red with tapestry upholstered fixed seating and maroon velvet curtains which create a warm relaxing atmosphere." The Oak Inn continued to trade as an Ansells pub until June 2010. Previously earmarked for residential development, in June 2012 Sainsbury's submitted a proposal to convert the former pub site into a convenience store, but on 16th October 2012 this was rejected by Warwick District Council's planning committee. However, approval was subsequently granted and by December 2013 the 'conversion' was underway.

| | |
|---|---|
| 1837-Nov 1849 | William Lovell |
| August 1849-Apr 1886 | John Staite |
| November 1849 | James Scott |
| April 1886-Jan 1892 | Alfred Tertius Nichols |
| January 1892-Oct 1892 | William Godfrey Willis |

| | |
|---|---|
| October 1892-Jun 1900 | William Smith |
| June 1900-Aug 1911 | James Satchwell |
| August 1911-Jul 1923 | Frank Leary |
| July 1923-Dec 1923 | James Stanford |
| December 1923-Sep 1942 | Arthur Levi Randle |
| September 1942-Nov 1951 | Frederick Morris James |
| | *(Previously at the Haunch of Venison)* |
| November 1951-Apr 1956 | Eric James Fox |
| April 1956-Mar 1957 | Kenneth Joseph Toy |
| March 1957-Apr 1962 | Leslie James Cudworth |
| April 1962-Jul 1963 | Raymond William Gardener |
| July 1963-Aug 1964 | Edward Alfred May |
| August 1964-Jun 1965 | Harold Joseph Bradshaw |
| June 1965-Apr 1966 | Alwyn James Gibbs |
| April 1966-Feb 1967 | Joshua Paul Bell |
| February 1967-Apr 1968 | Edward George Hulm |
| April 1968-Jul 1969 | Eric George Blackmore |
| July 1969-Dec 1970 | Derek John Watson |
| December 1970-Feb 1973 | John Arnold Roberts |
| February 1973 | Philip James Skidmore *(Previously at the Stoneleigh)* |
| Circa late 1970s | Dennis Hinton |
| 1981-circa early 1990s | Vic and Pauline Walsh |
| | *(Previously at the Oak in Warwick)* |
| March 1993-≥1996 | John and Linda Fox |
| 2006-2010 | Donna Charmaine Rose |
| June 2010 | Closed for business. |

*On Sunday 22nd February 1970, 'Arthur', a new club was opened with an evening of progressive blues and folk music, plus one or two impromptu poetry recitals at the Oak Inn. About 30 people gave a warm reception to guest folk singers Roger Williamson and Paul Martin, and the resident band 'Chair'. Membership costs 2s per year and admission is 4s on the door. Organiser Scott Clements said, "We're hoping to stage jazz and poetry concerts, and are thinking of screening underground films."*

**Oak Tavern** – Court Street
The first directory listing we have is in 1880 and the Oak Tavern closed in the early 1890s.

| | |
|---|---|
| 1880 | Mrs. Chatterley |
| 1890-91 | E. Franklyn |

**Ocean Bar / Ocean Reef** – 44 Oxford Street
These premises were previously occupied, and owned, by wallpaper suppliers S. J. Dixon [Holdings] Ltd. However, when the business outgrew the building, permission was obtained

for a 'change of use' so that it could be converted into an upmarket tapas bar. Although we have not been able to establish exactly when the Ocean Bar, or Ocean Reef [as it was signed] actually opened, we know that it was operating as the Ocean Bar and Restaurant in 1998. The restaurant side of the business, "Warwickshire's premier seafood restaurant", was positioned above the bar and comprised two galleries connected by a bridge; the menu was 70% seafood and the style of cooking was described as "modern British with a hint of European influence". Steven Smith was then the owner of both Ocean Bar and Sugar [the nightclub] in Tavistock Street.

*Photo of the closed Ocean Reef taken on 10th October 2009 © Allan Jennings.*

In 2008, the lessee sold the operating licence to Lylemere Ltd, and in August 2011 Dixon's regained control over the building. The Ocean Bar closed at the end of May 2011 and the licence was surrendered in the August. It was reported in January 2012 that a new, but strictly regulated and limited, alcohol and entertainments licence had been granted to the former Ocean Bar/Reef [entertainment to cease at 11.00pm and no drinks to be served after midnight] however, there is no evidence to suggest that it ever reopened. In February 2013 the premises remain closed and appear deserted, despite the Ocean Reef signage still being displayed.

| | |
|---|---|
| January 2006 | Glenn Celestine Patrick Gamblin |
| August 2008 | Douglas Hawkins |

**Oddfellows Hall Inn** – 22 Kenilworth Street
See Rose and Crown for details.

**Old Butchers** – 41/43 Warwick Street
See Copper Pot for details.

**Old White Lion** – 26 Brook Street
Originally listed as the Merrie Lion in 1833-34, it was renamed and listed as the White Lion from 1835 and addressed as 11, Brook Street [it would later be renamed the Old White Lion]. Based on the annual licensing sessions, the date range we have for the White Lion is 1835-1863 [although there are intermittent directory listings through to 1888-95] and for the Old White Lion 1863-1925. In 1869 the premises consisted of a bar-parlour, sitting room, four bedrooms, kitchen, scullery, brew house, yard, coach-house and a three stall stable; by the 1880s it had been renumbered as 26, Brook Street.

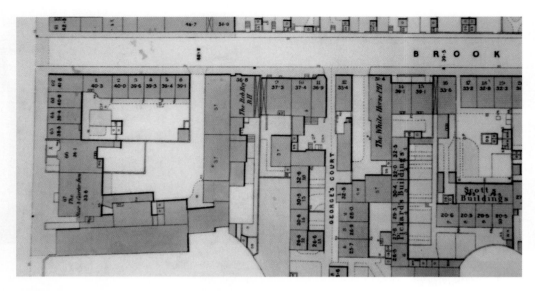

*Although incorrectly named the White Horse, this 1852 Board of Health map courtesy of
Leamington Library shows where the Old White Lion/White Lion was situated.*

On 3rd March, 1924 it was referred by the local licensing justices to the county
compensation authority for extinction; the chief constable stated that the pub had been
referred for compensation on the grounds of 'redundancy' in 1906 and 1907 but on both
occasions the licence had been renewed. The pub was owned by Lucas and Co. Ltd
[Leamington Brewery] and tenanted by Edward Paskett, who responded by saying that,
"although the premises were just a cottage it was a good cottage with eight rooms, beer used
to be brewed there and three or four people had food there during the week."
Notwithstanding, in June 1924 the authority decided to withdraw the licence and the Old
White Lion was closed for business on 28th March 1925 [with compensation having been
paid]. The premises reverted to residential until 1929 when it was vacated and sold by
Lucas and Co. Ltd to a Mr. B. Sharp for £425.

**Footnote:** The Old White Lion in Brook Street co-existed with the White Lion in Althorpe
Street.

| | |
|---|---|
| 1833-34 | J. Knibb *(1833 – No pub name listed, only landlord)* |
| 1835-37 | William Knibb |
| Circa 1837-Nov 1837 | Sarah Knibb |
| November 1837-45 | Thomas Spencer |
| Circa 1848 | William Powers |
| ≤1848-July 1848 | William Metcalf |
| July 1848-1852 | Peter Eaton |
| 1854-62 | William Edgerton |

| | |
|---|---|
| 1862 | James Parsons |
| 1866 | William Bradley |
| 1868-76 | Thomas 'John' Wilkins |
| 1876-77 | E. J. Atkins |
| 1877-Nov 1879 | Richard H. Bartlett |
| November 1879-Aug 1880 | James Collins |
| August 1880-83 | James Skelsey |
| 1883-Apr 1885 | Thomas Palmer |
| April 1885-Aug 1890 | Mrs. Lucy Palmer *(On the death of Thomas)* |
| August 1890 | William Bedding |
| 1891 | Mrs. Sarah Beddington *(As spelt)* |
| 1892-Jan 1903 | John Wickes |
| January 1903-1925 | Edward Paskett *(Son-in-law of John Wickes)* |
| 28th March 1925 | Closed for business |

**Orange Hotel** – Clemens Street
According to J. C. Manning ['Glimpses of Our Local Past', 1895] this hotel was opened in 1812. In 1814 it is listed in Bisset's 'Descriptive Guide to Leamington Priors' as Probett's Orange Hotel, comprising 30 rooms and having hunting and livery stables. However, it would appear to have closed by 1817, and undergone a 'change of use' [possibly residential], as J. C. Manning states that "adjoining this house [Crown Inn – High Street] in 1817 were the gates of an extensive mews or hunting stables, known as Probett's. These subsequently formed part of the Crown premises, being taken in when the building was enlarged"; this also indicates that the Orange Hotel was once located on the lower west side of Clemens Street.

**Other Place** – 116 Warwick Street
See Prince of Wales for details.

**Oxford Hotel** – High Street
See [Copps'] Royal Hotel for details.

**Oxford Tavern** – 10 Oxford Street
The first directory listing we have is in 1835 when the licensee was William Olorenshaw and it was addressed as 19, Oxford Street [it would be renumbered '10' by the mid 1880s]. From the time it opened until the turn of the century there was virtually nothing of any significance reported on the Oxford Tavern. However in February 1916 the landlord was prosecuted for a serious licensing infringement, and on 10th April 1916 the pub was closed by order of the Central Control Board for Liquor Traffic, under the Defence of the Realm Act [see press report following licensee listing]. It remained closed for more than two years before reopening sometime in 1918.

On Monday 1st March 1920 the pub was one of a number that were 'referred for extinction by compensation' by the local licensing justices as part of a weeding out process, or "thinning the inns" as it was reported. On 28th May 1920, the county compensation

*Photo of the Oxford Tavern during World War One [circa 1914] courtesy of licensee Stephen Clarke's great granddaughter Teresa Byrne.*

authority refused the renewal of the licence and on Monday 2nd January 1922 it awarded compensation of £2,000, apportioning £1,875 to the owners [Messrs Flower and Sons Ltd] and £125 to the tenant [Stephen Clarke]. The Oxford Tavern was closed for business on 25th March 1922. Stephen Clarke, the last licensee, continued to live on the premises until his death in 1966. The house has since been demolished and is now the site of the Baptist church.

| | |
|---|---|
| 1835-36 | William Olorenshaw |
| 1836-37 | William Boyes |
| 1837-38 | Thomas Phillips *(Previously at the Guy Tavern)* |
| 1838-39 | William Olorenshaw |
| 1841-42 | George Whiting |
| 1845 | A. Clark |
| 1846 | T. Poole |
| 1847 | Henry Lee |
| March 1847-Dec 1848 | William Clifton |
| December 1848-May 1862 | Henry Mills |
| May 1862-Oct 1867 | James Beilby |
| October 1867-68 | George Smith |
| 1870-August 1874 | Richard Hitchman |
| August 1874-Jan 1896 | Thomas Spicer |
| January 1896-Nov 1897 | Mrs. Jane Spicer *(On the death of Thomas)* |
| November 1897-Dec 1899 | Archibald William Peyman |
| December 1899-1906 | William Tranter |
| 1906-Mar 1909 | Thomas Johnson |

| | |
|---|---|
| March 1909-Jul 1910 | Arthur Richard Spicer |
| July 1910-Sep 1911 | George Henry Hancock |
| September 1911-Jun 1914 | William Brimfield |
| June 1914-Mar 1922 | Stephen Clarke |
| 25th March 1922 | Closed for business |

*The Leamington Spa Courier dated 18th February 1916 reported:* **Important licensing prosecution – beer offered to military patients** *– Stephen Clarke, licensee of the Oxford Tavern, was summoned for permitting military hospital patients to be on his licensed premises, and also for offering to supply intoxicating liquor to the patients. The three wounded soldiers were patients at 'The Warren' V.A.D. Hospital. The bench convicted Mr. Clarke being of the opinion that he did not discharge the onus which under the regulations was imposed on him. The mayor said the bench had decided to impose a fine of £10 for offering to supply intoxicating liquor to wounded soldiers, and of £5 for allowing wounded soldiers in hospital uniform to be on his licensed premises. He reminded the defendant that he had rendered himself liable to a £100 fine and six months imprisonment.*

**Oxygen** – 44/46 Clarendon Avenue
See Jekyll and Hyde for details.

**Pacific Rim** – 75 Bedford Street
See Bedford Inn for details.

**Palace Inn** – 36 Satchwell Street
Originally the Half Moon, the first listing we have for these premises is in 1813 when John Barnwell is the licensee [ex licensed victuallers' records]; although John relinquished the licence to Richard Barnwell circa 1818 he retained ownership of the premises until his death. Accordingly, the freehold property was auctioned in 1844, "By order of the trustees of the sale, under the will of the late Mr. John Barnwell, deceased," and was purchased by Thomas Barnwell. In 1845 he enlarged the pub ensuring that "it had every convenience, including a billiard room with a first class billiard table by Burroughes and Watts"; it was also renamed the Turf Inn in 1845. In 1858 it comprised, a parlour and smoke room with folding doors to make one room, tap room, eight sleeping apartments, billiard room, kitchen, brew house, a large cellar capable of containing upwards of 3,000 gallons of ale and beer and a skittle alley at the back with a malt room and loft over. In July 1859 the Turf Inn reverted to the Half Moon and Elias Wilcox returned as licensee after 2-3 years at the Golden Lion. Previously 42, Satchwell Street, it was readdressed as number '36' from circa 1880. In 1887 the Half Moon was owned by the Leamington Brewery [Lucas and Co. Ltd]. In August 1898 application was made to change the pub's name and, when the local licensing justices advised that they didn't have the power to prevent it, the Half Moon was promptly renamed the Palace Inn.

At the 1903 licensing sessions it was described as having three entrances, one onto Satchwell Street, one into Palace Yard and one into a passage that led to the Parade. The chief constable opposed the licence renewal stating that there were four cottages in Palace

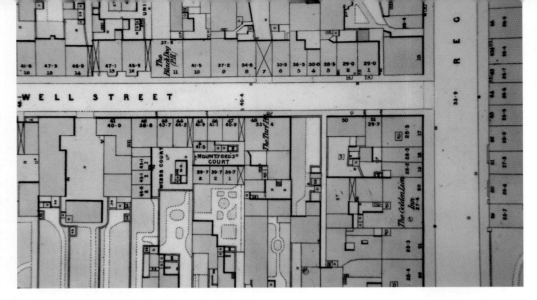

*This 1852 Board of Health map courtesy of Leamington Library shows where the Turf Inn was situated.*

Yard and two cottages in Satchwell Street that also had access to the pub's yard; he added that the side entrance entering into the yard should not be used for trade purposes as it rendered police supervision impossible. Furthermore, he believed that the pub was frequented by a "rough class of people" and did not think the house "necessary for the requirements of the neighbourhood". The defence gave an undertaking that the door leading into Palace Yard would only be used by the tenant and his family for residential purposes, adding that, "although the house, it was true, was used by what the chief constable described as a 'rough class of people' one could not condemn the house on account of that". Then owned by Flower and Son Ltd, its licence was renewed.

*Above left: Photo of the Palace Inn taken in 1976 courtesy of Peter Coulls. Above right: The Silver Jubilee taken in 1977 courtesy of Peter Coulls.*

The Palace closed in 1976, but nine months later [in July 1977] it had been refurbished, two rooms had been knocked into one and it had reopened as the Silver Jubilee [thus named to commemorate Queen Elizabeth II's Silver Jubilee in 1977]. Fred Wright [Jolly Brewer] had been installed as the caretaker manager during its transition from the Palace to the Silver Jubilee, until Ray and Jean Hobley took over. The Silver Jubilee was due to be closed under a compulsory closure order on 13th June 1985 however, the last pint was actually pulled on Sunday 30th June 1985; it was demolished the following month to make way for the Royal Priors shopping centre.

| | |
|---|---|
| 1813-18 | John Barnwell *(Owner until 1844)* |
| 1819 | Richard Barnwell |
| 1822-30 | Thomas Pearce |
| 1831-33 | George Finney |
| 1833-34 | Thomas Pearce |
| 1835 | Broom Rogers |
| 1837-56 | Elias Wilcox *(Went to the Golden Lion)* |
| 1839-44 | John Barnwell *(Owner, died 1844)* |
| 1844-Jul 1859 | Thomas Barnwell |
| July 1859-Sep 1862 | Elias Wilcox *(Transferred as the Turf Inn, then reverted to the Half Moon)* |
| September 1862-74 | John Slater |
| 1874-May 1874 | Edward Haynes |
| May 1874-Nov 1876 | Anthony Canavan |
| November 1876-78 | J. Kible |
| 1878-Oct 1883 | William [or John] Lee |
| October 1883-Dec 1883 | Edward Haynes |
| December 1883-Jan 1887 | David Wells *(Of Birmingham)* |
| January 1887-Oct 1887 | William Hyde |
| October 1887-Feb 1889 | Morton Peto Lucas/Leamington Brewery |
| February 1889-Jul 1890 | Mrs. Harriett Barrett |
| July 1890-Mar 1894 | John Turner |
| March 1894-Nov 1897 | William Sutton and his wife Jane |
| Nov 1897-May 1900 | Ernest Luty |
| May 1900-Jun 1901 | William Wilson |
| June 1901-May 1904 | John Hall |
| May 1904-May 1906 | George Clews |
| May 1906-Nov 1907 | Frederick Charles Taylor |
| November 1907-Dec 1910 | George Clews |
| December 1910-Feb 1911 | Sidney George |
| February 1911-Nov 1915 | James Creelman *(Transferred from Emma George, widow of Sidney)* |
| November 1915-32 | Arthur James Nunn |
| 1932-Feb 1937 | William Joseph Bell |

| | |
|---|---|
| February 1937-Dec 1945 | Richard John William Duckett |
| December 1945-Apr 1960 | Frederick John Clarke |
| April 1960-Jan 1964 | Joseph Marshall |
| January 1964-Aug 1964 | Philip Percy Vaughan |
| August 1964-Oct 1964 | Harold Joseph Macdonald |
| October 1964-Jun 1965 | Alfred John Roberts |
| June 1965-Jun 1968 | Frank Potts |
| June 1968-Dec 1968 | Norman Wainer Thorpe |
| December 1968-Feb 1969 | Mary Anne Evans |
| February 1969-1976 | Harold Joseph Macdonald *(Licensee; employed managers that included George Webb and Alfred 'Alf' Henry Smith)* |
| 1976 | Closed as the Palace |

**Silver Jubilee**

| | |
|---|---|
| 1977-Jul 1977 | Fred Wright *(Licensee of Jolly Brewer; caretaker managed during the transition from the Palace to the Silver Jubilee)* |
| July 1977-Feb 1979 | Ray and Jean Hobley *(Opened as the Silver Jubilee)* |
| February 1979-Apr 1983 | Paul and Eileen Wade |
| April 1983-1985 | Alan and Jane Reeve |
| Sunday 30th June 1985 | Closed for business |

*In 1844, the Leamington Spa Courier posted the following sale notice for the Half Moon: Desirable freehold property, Leamington Spa, to be sold by auction, by George Carter, early in the ensuing month. By order of the trustees of the sale, under the will of the late Mr. John Barnwell, deceased; at the Half Moon public house, Satchwell Street, Leamington. All that capital and substantially built and well accustomed public house and premises, known by the sign of the Half Moon, situate in Satchwell Street, Leamington, and now in the occupation of Mr. Elias Wilcox, as tenant at will.*

On Wednesday 28th November 1850, the Licensed Victuallers Protection Society of Leamington Priors held their fifth anniversary at the Turf Inn and an excellent dinner was provided on the occasion by Mr. Wilcox, to which about 50 sat down. After the cloth had been removed the chairman proposed a toast to "The Queen" and spoke in appropriate terms of the loyalty of the licensed victuallers. The toast was received with the warmest enthusiasm and was followed by the national anthem; the next toast was to, "Prince Albert, Albert Prince of Wales, and the rest of the royal family".

*Kenneth Owen remembers the Palace: "As a member of the Royal Leamington Spa Silver Band we used to rehearse in the upstairs room between 1955 and 1957 when it was known as the Palace Inn and Fred Clarke was the publican. When the older members of the band had a meeting, we youngsters were sent downstairs with a bottle of Vimto until the meeting was over."*

The Leamington Spa Courier dated 19th February 1960 reported: On Tuesday 16th February 1960, Mr. Reginald Pugh, a 64 year old would-be 'king' of Leamington's back street public houses acquired the tenancy of the Palace Inn, Satchwell Street. He immediately hired decorators and fitters – and asked them to work day and night until the run-down century old pub is transformed. The Palace is the second small back street inn to be acquired by Mr. Pugh in a month. Yesterday he said, "I hope to take over about another six pubs in the Leamington area and turn them into continental-style bistros. The Palace is near the corporation's new car park. I shall probably convert it into an exclusive kind of chop-house in order to cater for the tourists and shoppers who will use the park. My plans are not yet compete – but in any case I shall spend more than £500 on brightening the place up and making it a credit and an example to this rather dreary street." A month ago, Mr. Pugh, a specialist valuer to the hotel and licensed trade, who lives in St. Mary's Crescent, Leamington, took over the White Hart in Windsor Street. It was then drab and short of custom. Today it is thriving. Mr. Pugh has redecorated it and introduced a cosy club atmosphere. "I shall do the same with the Palace. In recent years it has become almost derelict and I was told that some days there was not a single customer. Come round in a few weeks time and you will find a very exciting addition to Leamington's night life."

*The Leamington Spa Courier dated 15th April 1960, reported that: Licensees from many parts of Mid-Warwickshire went on Monday night to the tiny Palace Inn, Satchwell Street, Leamington, at the invitation of its owner, Mr. L. R. Pugh - self styled 'king' of the town's back street pubs. Mr. Pugh threw a party to celebrate the completion of large-scale redecorations and the taking over of the licence by Mr. and Mrs. Joseph Marshall. The century old Palace - at one time the most notorious inn in Leamington - has been transformed in furtherance of Mr. Pugh's campaign to bring a new lease of life to Leamington's back street public houses. "When I took over there were hardly any customers," he said, "Now I think we will capture a great deal of tourist trade. One of our gimmicks is that beer is drawn in the old fashioned style - straight from the barrel." The licensees' quarters have also been decorated in contemporary style. "This is a big point in my campaign," said Mr. Pugh. "Many licensees and staff are expected to live in dilapidated rooms."*

In February 1983 there was much discussion about the redevelopment of the area and of course, what would happen to the Silver Jubilee? Warwick District Council had a display of the three short listed 'models' showing the proposed redevelopment of Satchwell Street and its surrounds, which they moved to the town hall assembly rooms. One of the bidders, Arrowcroft, would have retained the Silver Jubilee as well as Toytown on the other side of the street.

*Mid November 1984 saw landlord Alan Reeve fighting for his livelihood with articles in the Courier and the Morning News as well as a petition with around 400 signatures. The pub faces demolition next year but, by the end of October, he knew that his last minute appeals to save the pub from demolition had failed and that he had lost the battle. The Whitbread owned pub faces demolition and Alan and his wife will have to go. Plans for the redevelopment of the site as a huge shopping mall meant that the pub would come down in the spring. Satchwell Street was to have been closed-off at the Regent Street end and a temporary building erected to house the National Westminster bank. However, a new proposal to be considered by the district council's plans sub-committee will mean that the pub will have to be demolished early in the New Year so that the bank can be housed on that site instead. Mr. Reeve said, "I've worked here for five years. It's a popular pub and we thought we would be able to stay for some time. But now we are threatened with losing our livelihoods and our home to make way for a temporary bank." The* council and the developers, MEPC, decided against blocking up Satchwell Street for various reasons. The plans sub-committee backed the early demolition of the pub.

The regulars inserted the following in the Morning News of 1st July 1985: **Today heralds the end of the Silver Jubilee** – Probably the best pub in Leamington. I am sure most regulars will agree that there is no other place like it. Where else could you go to drink, and get insulted 'free', get totally worthless twaddle from Alan, then console yourself with the fact that there was always Jane to hold an intelligent conversation with. The 'powers that be' have obviously not thought of the consequences of Alan leaving the confines of 'his bar' to run amok on Leamington, being rude and cheeky, willy nilly – also the job Jane will have trying to restrain him. So it only remains for us to say bye for now, you two, and the Jubilee. But they can't keep good things down. Here's to a new watering hole with you two at the bar. Love you both to death, good luck – All the regulars.

*Work began on the Royal Priors during October 1985 after Christopher Benson, the vice-chairman of MEPC [who were partners with Warwick District Council], signed the £9.5 million deal with construction firm Lovell on Friday 20th September 1985.*

**Paul Pry** – 12 Satchwell Street
See London Tavern for details.

**Phoenix** – 12 Augusta Place
See Willoughby Arms for details.

**Pig and Fiddle** – 45 High Street
See Guards Inn for details.

**Plasterers Arms** – 1 Albion Row
The first directory listing we have for these premises is in 1835 when it was known as the Jolly Boatman. It was renamed the Plasterers Arms circa 1836, during the tenancy of John Watts. Albion Row was at the end of Wise Street facing the canal. Behind the row of houses was a power station [Midland Electric Light and Power Company] and running parallel to it was Brewery Terrace, named after Leamington's first brewery that stood in Wise Street from 1812 until it closed circa 1839 [it was demolished in the 1840s]. The latest information we have for the Plasterers Arms is the report from the 1871 licensing session and, as the licence was not renewed in 1872, we have concluded that it closed in the meantime. Albion Row was demolished circa 1957.

| | |
|---|---|
| 1835-1836 | John Watts *(Jolly Boatman)* |
| 1836-Jul 1854 | John Watts *(Plasterers Arms)* |
| July 1854 | Edward Lenton |
| April 1855-Sep 1859 | Francis Hanson |
| November 1859-Jul 1860 | Thomas Adams *(Previously at the Rugby Tavern)* |
| July 1860-Jan 1865 | Charles Houghton |
| January 1865-May 1866 | Abraham Putt |

| | |
|---|---|
| May 1866-Feb 1870 | Clarissa Bullivant |
| February 1870-Aug 1870 | William Henry Eborall |
| August 1870-≥Sep 1871 | Henry Watts |

**Plough and Harrow** – Whitnash Road, Whitnash

We understand that parts of the Plough and Harrow date back to the 1600s, but unfortunately we have not been able to corroborate this. Furthermore, historical data on this pub is scarce as it is excluded from many of the available resources due to its location; as a result our somewhat sparse coverage doesn't commence until 1845.

Between 1811 and 1861 the population of Whitnash almost doubled from 203 to 393 and during this period the Plough was the only pub in Whitnash [until the opening of the Windmill Tavern circa 1861]. When the Plough and Harrow was sold by auction at the Crown Hotel on 6th February 1854, it was advertised as having excellent farm buildings, yards, garden, orchard, two enclosures of very fertile meadow, pasture, and arable land. In 1863 it consisted of a bar, smoke and dining room, two kitchens, larder, dairy, brew house, cellar, five bedrooms, two attics, store room, excellent stables, barn, cow-pens, piggeries and other buildings, yard, garden and orchard.

*Above: This advert for a supper and dancing party in 1872 is courtesy of Jo Clark. Below: Photo of the Plough and Harrow taken on 19th November 2008 © Allan Jennings.*

For many years owned by Lucas and Co. Ltd, who had paid £3,750 for the pub and 25 acres of land, it became an Ansells pub following their 1928 acquisition of the brewery and its closure in 1934.

Following the acquisition of the Plough and Harrow in June 2012 by family members Sigourney, Paul and Caroline Gowlett, the pub was extensively refurbished by Punch Taverns; this included the installation of a new sign. It officially reopened on Saturday 20th October. The Plough & Harrow remains open in December 2013.

| | |
|---|---|
| 1845-≥1849 | A. Pratt |
| ≤1851-Sep 1851 | Charles Priest |
| September 1851-Apr 1854 | William Keyte |
| April 1854-May 1855 | William Wright |
| May 1855-Apr 1859 | Richard Reading |
| April 1859-Oct 1863 | John Whitehead |
| October 1863-Nov 1864 | William Richard Davis |
| November 1864-65 | William Burton *(Or Burgiss)* |
| ≤1871-Apr 1871 | Richard Kearsall |
| April 1871-Nov 1873 | James Tongue |
| November 1873-74 | Samuel Rainsford |
| ≤October 1874-Jan 1875 | Samuel Pegg |
| January 1875-Sep 1875 | William Daniel Thomas |
| September 1875-May 1900 | Henry Holt |
| May 1900-Oct 1905 | Archelaus Day Woolf |
| October 1905-Apr 1910 | Herbert Lewis *(Farmer & Innkeeper)* |
| April 1910-May 1915 | James Gordon Alcock |
| May 1915-Nov 1922 | John Farr |
| November 1922-Apr 1934 | Thomas Jeffs |
| April 1934-Jul 1935 | Albert Henry Porter |
| July 1935-Sep 1938 | William Harrod |
| September 1938-Mar 1955 | William Henry Marlow |
| March 1955-Mar 1956 | Sidney Towe |
| March 1956-Mar 1957 | Arthur John Gibbins |
| March 1957-Apr 1973 | John Minet |
| April 1973 | Kenneth Jones |
| November 1977-Aug 1978 | John McCamley |
| Aug 1978-Jan 1980 | Edward Townsend |
| April 1980 | Elizabeth Evans |
| 1986 | Pauline and Stan Sayers |
| Circa 1989 | Margaret and Neil McCormick |
| 1997 | Richard and Kath *(Surname not known)* |
| Circa 2005 | Anthony and Josephine O'Reilly |
| June 2009-Jul 2011 | Simon Jeremy Green and his wife Sue |
| July 2011-Jan 2012 | Jason Giles *(Manager)* |

October 2011-May 2012      Jon Bateson and Ali Bonner-Evans
May 2012-Jun 2012        Aaron Murphy *(Caretaker manager)*
June 2012 →              Sigourney Gowlett

*The Leamington Spa Courier dated 28th July 1849 carried the following notice:* **Inn and farm to let, at Whitnash** *- The Plough and Harrow Inn, in the pleasant village of Whitnash, within a mile of Leamington, and about sixty acres of arable and meadow land adjoining, of good quality, and very improvable, now in the occupation of Mr. Pratt, 'to let' on lease, from Michaelmas next, at a moderate rent. For further details, apply personally, or by letter to Messrs Welchman and Spraggett, solicitors, Southam.*

The Leamington News dated Saturday 28th June 1884, reported that: The village wake at Whitnash was celebrated with the customary boisterousness and hilarity last Sunday, Monday and Thursday, and attracted many hundreds of persons from Leamington, Warwick and the surrounding district. On Sunday afternoon and evening there were many visitors to the solitary inn of the village, which opened an additional bar for the occasion. Leap frog and other amusements were vigorously pursued. The Free Methodists made a counter demonstration, by holding an open air service in front of their chapel, but their efforts were not very successful. On Monday the swinging boats, show booths and stalls were fitted in the orchard adjoining the Plough and Harrow, and here dancing was the popular amusement, after which the exhausted couples refreshed themselves with potations obtained from the adjoining barn.

*We are grateful to the late Jean Field for her kind permission to include the following from her book, Beneath the Great Elms. "For centuries the Plough and Harrow was the only inn in Whitnash. The oldest part of the building dates from the seventeenth century. In the past the Innkeeper was also a farmer in possession of several fields and Fred Meades, George Billington and others remembered that until around 1930, a fair was sometimes held behind the inn. Younger readers may not appreciate the relief and happiness expressed at the end of the Second World War and Richard Hassan and others told me of the wonderful celebrations which took place near 'The Plough' on V.E. night – 8th May 1945. Walter Hassan rigged up some lights, a piano was transported there on Ernie Masters' cart and George Billington took along his drum kit. Jack Cotterill at one time feared for the thatch of his nearby cottage as a huge bonfire showered sparks into the night sky. At that party, as at numerous others in Whitnash, the singing and dancing went on well after midnight."*

In the 1950s, teams competed for the Plough and Harrow Darts Cup to raise money for the Guide Dog Association, Sunshine Home for Blind Babies, the Mayor of Leamington's Christmas Fund and the old people of Whitnash. In January 1952 the final was played at the new hall in Whitnash when the Liberal Club beat the Dog Inn, Harbury by six games to one.

*The Leamington Spa Courier dated 2nd June 1978 reported that: A Whitnash pub had to close its doors this week - and others in the area were either out of beer or running short - because of an Ansells dispute. The brewery workers had refused to work over the bank holiday period and pubs began to run short towards the end of the holiday, with the heat wave making customers even thirstier. On Wednesday the Plough and Harrow at Whitnash had to close, although they were hoping for a delivery of bottled beer yesterday. The pub's draught beer supply dried up on Sunday and by Tuesday night all the bottled beer had gone as well. The Wheatsheaf in Tachbrook Road ran out of draught bitter, Double Diamond and lager over the holiday and on Wednesday were on their last barrel of mild. They were restricting opening hours to noon until 2.00pm and 7.00pm to 10.00pm. Other Ansells houses in Leamington said they were running short but, with the return to work on Wednesday, were hoping to survive the beer drought.*

**Post Office Commercial Hotel** – 27/28 Bath Street
John Stiff had occupied the house at 27/28 Bath Street since 1848. In 1864 it was said that he had held a beer house licence for a considerable number of years, but our first directory listing is in 1860. At the annual licensing session in August 1864 John Stiff was granted a full licence, however on 2nd October 1867 the lease [which had 57 years to run] was up for sale by auction.

≤1860-≥1865                           John Stiff

**Prince of Wales** – 116 Warwick Street
Warwick Street was laid out during the period 1822-26 and according to the conservation department at Warwick District Council this building was a "public house circa 1826". However, the earliest reference we have for this pub is on 29th December 1849 when the Leamington Spa Courier advertised that John Lewis had taken possession [our first directory listing is 1850]; it is therefore likely that the premises were initially residential. In its early days it was addressed as 8, Warwick Street and renumbered as '116' in the 1870s.

In the late 19th century it was owned by Northampton Brewery Ltd but in 1960, after a couple of brewery takeovers, ownership passed to Watney Mann Ltd [Phipps Brewery,

*Above left: The Prince of Wales taken on 16th December 1989 © Allan Jennings. Above right: The Mor Bar taken on 23rd March 2009 courtesy of David Stowell.*

*Leaf taken on 14th July 2012 © Allan Jennings.*

Bridge Street, Northampton]. A new lounge bar was opened on 17th May 1978 and all draught beer was half price until 9.00pm [Jay Jay Weaver provided the 'live' entertainment]. On 2nd April 1987 the pub reopened following a refurbishment costing in excess of £100,000, this being the latest Mann's pub to benefit from the company's multi-million pound development program.

This pub has undergone a number of name and format changes since closing circa 1994, but it retains the name Prince of Wales on the outside wall as it is heritage listed. Its successors have been the Other Place, [February 1998 until 2001], Cuba, [June 2001 until 2006], Sweeney's, [2006-07], Mor Bar [2009] and Tryst [2009-10].

After Tryst closed in July 2010 the building underwent another refurbishment before opening once again as the Prince of Wales, on 1st December 2010. Its focus was on music and "entertaining customers with live bands", but it was to prove another short-term venture and in January 2012 the Prince of Wales was closed and the signage removed. On 30th June 2012 it reopened as Leaf [Tearooms & Piano Bar], describing itself as, "tea rooms by day and piano bar by night"; by August 2013 there had been a subtle name change to Leif [Tearooms & Piano Bar], which remains open in December 2013.

| | |
|---|---|
| 1849-Sep 1858 | John Lewis |
| September 1858-Nov 1862 | John Grainge |
| November 1862-66 | Peter Couling |
| 1870 | John Lewis |
| 1871-May 1871 | Joseph Fenna |
| May 1871-Nov 1885 | Mrs. Catherine Fenna *(On the death of Joseph)* |
| November 1885-Dec 1890 | Charles Edward Poole |
| December 1890-≤1892 | Richard Lambert |
| ≤1892-Jul 1892 | Rebecca Lambert |
| July 1892-96 | Henry Harper |

| | |
|---|---|
| 1896-Aug 1897 | James Meredith |
| August 1897-Sep 1897 | Joseph Porter Clarke |
| September 1897-Jul 1899 | Thomas Underhill |
| July 1899-Sep 1901 | Benjamin Haynes |
| September 1901-Nov 1902 | George Davis |
| November 1902-Nov 1903 | Charles Frederick Bird |
| November 1903-May1904 | Thomas Adnitt |
| May 1904-Nov 1904 | Thomas George Standing |
| November 1904-Oct 1906 | Francis Begley |
| October 1906-Mar 1908 | Sidney Lawrence Jones |
| March 1908-21 | Amos Bertie Statham |
| 1921-Aug 1932 | Herbert Thompson |
| August 1932 | Frank Henry Gollings |
| 1935 | Robert Errinton |
| 1936 | Albert Rogers |
| 1937-38 | Domenico C Gatti |
| 1938-Oct 1939 | Walter Charles Drage |
| October 1939-Sep 1946 | Richard George Earles |
| September 1946-Jun 1948 | Alfred William Ward |
| June 1948-Sep 1949 | Sydney George Mutton |
| September 1949-Aug 1950 | Ernest Walter Fawkes |
| August 1950-Oct 1951 | Thomas Edwards |
| October 1951-May 1958 | Walter William Reed |
| May 1958-Sep 1958 | Bernard Edwin Maxwell |
| September 1958-Sep 1960 | Arthur Edward Westwood |
| September 1960-Nov 1961 | Harold Widdowson |
| November 1961-Jun 1964 | Leonard Albert Slocombe |
| June 1964-Apr 1965 | Joseph William Honey |
| April 1965-Oct 1965 | Bernard Max Hayman |
| October 1965-Jun 1970 | Frank Edmund Godfrey |
| June 1970 | Michael Benedict Dillon and his wife Vivienne |
| 1977-1978 | John Alfred Collicutt and his wife Sheila |
| ≤1984-May 1986 | Gary and Marian Donnelly |
| May 1986-≥May 1987 | Joseph Roy Springate and his wife Teresa *(Prince of Wales)* |
| 1997-98 | Richard Sharp |
| 1998 | Brenda Noon *(Other Place)* |
| 2001 | Kristy McCready *(Cuba)* |
| 2006 | Makhan Singh Kandola *(Cuba)* |
| September 2006-Jan 2007 | Courtney Antonio Sweeney *(Sweeneys)* |
| January 2007-Jul 2009 | Mustafa Serdar Necar |
| July 2009-Sep 2009 | Palvinder Singh |
| September 2009-Mar 2010 | Andrew Spencer Richardson |

| | |
|---|---|
| March 2010-Jul 2010 | Lisa Spare *(Tryst)* |
| July 2010-Dec 2010 | Closed for refurbishment |
| 1st Dec 2010-Jan 2012 | Lee Bishop *(Reopened as the Prince of Wales)* |
| Jan 2012 | Closed as the Prince of Wales |
| 30th June 2012 | Reopened as the Leaf Tearooms & Piano Bar |
| 30th June 2012 → | Jack Atwal *[licensee]* Gurcharn Atwal *[manager]* |

*The following is a copy of an article from the Leamington Spa Courier dated 27th March 1987: Anyone who knew the old Prince of Wales public house in Warwick Street, Leamington Spa, will find it difficult to recognise now. From the elegant lamps and smart new paint on the exterior, to the completely remodelled Regency style interior, it has been all change.*

*Joe and Terry Springate, who took over the Prince of Wales in May have many years experience of running public houses, this plus a lot of hard work and planning have gone into this transformation. The front lounge with its new mahogany panelling, period light fittings and prints of old Leamington, is much more spacious now due to repositioning of the bar. Touches like the specially commissioned carpet incorporating the pub name, and the decorated fireplace add to this room's individual charm.*

*At the back, even more drastic changes have taken place. All that is left of the old yard are the attractive flagstones. The whole area has been covered in with a translucent roof giving a charming conservatory style area, very light and airy. The old 'toilets across the yard' have been given the luxury treatment too, and would do credit to the smartest home. No features have been overlooked. There is an area with a pool table and darts, and also a separate family room where parents and children will be welcome. A sitting out area is also planned for the warmer weather, with tables, chairs and hanging baskets to make a patio style addition to the accommodation.*

*However attractive the surroundings, good drinking has to be an important part of any successful public house and this Manns' house takes pride in its extensive draught selection with Ruddles, Wilson's Original, and Webster Yorkshire bitters, Guinness, Fosters, Carling and Holsten lagers and cider too. Food has not been forgotten either, from sandwiches and bar snacks, pies and rolls to steaks and all the trimmings.*

*The grand re-opening of this 'new' public house is planned for April 2 and is going to be carried out in some style. The staff are going to don Regency costumes and they are also inviting customers to join in the fun, with prizes for the best fancy dress in keeping with the period atmosphere. So if you ever fancied yourself as Beau Brummell here's your big chance.*

*Conveniently situated right at the heart of town, the Prince of Wales is perfectly placed for businessmen, families wanting a lunch break from a shopping expedition, or a relaxing evening in elegant surroundings. Why not try the new style Prince of Wales for yourself, you'll find good food and drink and a friendly welcome.*

The Coventry Evening Telegraph dated 17th February 1998 reported that: The owners of a new Leamington pub promise fun and games when they open the doors of the Other Place on Friday. The former Prince of Wales pub has been revamped to include giant size games such as Downfall, Jenga and Connect Four. The pub will also have a large screen especially for the forthcoming sports events. It will also become the first pub in the

Midlands to serve a new line in Indian cuisine – Putoori, a pizza base filled with dishes such as Keema, tandoori or vegetable flavours. For just £4.95, you get a complete balti meal, with rice, chapati and a pint of beer or a glass of wine. However, a little trouble was around the corner when workmen tore out the Prince of Wales ornate stone letters from the Warwick Street side while refurbishing the grade II listed building. The fragments of the old sign were consigned to a skip leaving owner Mo Kandola facing a bill for more than £15,000 after council conservation officials demanded the return of the historic lettering, even if it meant commissioning exact replicas.

*The Coventry Evening Telegraph dated 24th January 2001 reported that: A popular pub is to undergo another transformation – this time to become Leamington's first Cuban bar. The Warwick Street bar is to have a £250,000 refurbishment to transform it into a Cuban-themed inn. Staff will be dressed in a Latin American style and have holsters carrying shots and tequila for customers. A conservatory which is to be built on to the back will increase the bar's capacity to 300.*

The Coventry Evening Telegraph dated 9th June 2001 reported: The manager of a newly opened bar and restaurant named Cuba is so keen to make sure the food, drink and music are as genuine as possible she spent two weeks on the island. Kristy McCready spent a fortnight in the capital of Havana to give a genuine Cuban feel to the new venue, which opened to the public yesterday in Warwick Street, Leamington. Among the drinks on offer are popular Cuban cocktails Mogito and Cuba Libre, while people dropping in for lunch or dinner can sample Cuban food. Miss McCready said, "We opened last night and it went very well indeed. We are considering having salsa nights and we may be having live music." The pub now boasts a conservatory after an extensive re-fit from its previous incarnation as the Other Place, and before that the Prince of Wales. [Cuba was under the same management as Voodoo in Regent Street; part owner was Makhan Kandola].

*Cuba taken on 13th August 2004 courtesy of John Hartnup.*

*The Leamington Spa Courier dated 15th April 2011 reported that: A stylish new Leamington bar is slowly gaining a reputation among up and coming new bands around the country. 36 year old Lee Bishop has already attracted a number of acts to play at the venue. The bar's renovation has been a labour of love for Lee, who has done much of the iconic pop art himself. He even turned his hand to a re-design of the Prince of Wales sign, basing it on a controversial Sex Pistols album cover from the 1970s. Along with groups from in and around Leamington, bands from the USA, Northampton, and Southend have all played at this intimate venue; among them Thousandaires, Fourth Wave, 44 Magnum, Tesla's Last Secret, Fly by Night, This Happy Breed and the Feral Cats. Lee has plans to turn one or two of the building's upstairs rooms into recording studios. He's keen on diversity too, having held northern soul, ska, folk and other specialist music nights. He is also considering showing old classic movies, and maybe having a mini cinema in the back room.*

The conservation department at Warwick District Council describes the building as: Public house, circa 1826, with later additions and alterations; Pinkish-brown brick with painted stucco façade and concealed roof; The exterior has 3 storeys; 2 first floor windows; Horizontal rustication to ground floor; Quoins to first floor; First Floor, moulded band, 8/8 sashes; Second Floor: 4/8 sashes, all in plain reveals and with sills; Off-centre entrance, a part-glazed, panelled door with overlight in tooled surround, with extensive remains of probable original frontage. Plate-glass windows with aprons to either side of door, with 3-pane overlights and with pilaster strips between, and consoles with lion masks surmounted by frieze and cornice; Otherwise, large plate-glass window with side lights, apron and 5-pane overlight and narrower plate-glass window with apron and overlight; continuous frieze and small central pediment; Frieze, cornice, low parapet, copings, end stacks; Left return: Quoins, horizontal rustication to ground floor; First-floor band, 4 openings, alternately 6/6 and blind; second floor has blind openings. End and off-centre entrances are part-glazed doors, off-centre between side-lights and with overlight, tooled surround and cornice, frieze, low parapet, copings.

**Priory Cottage Inn** – Address not known
See Priory Tavern for details.

**Priory Tavern / Arms** – 10 Priory Street
Although we are well aware of these premises being a beer retailer and an off-licence, we have precious little information for the period that they were named the Priory Tavern et al. Another beer house that opened after the 1830 Beer House Act, the first listing we have is in 1838 when the licensee is Ann Knibb. On 25th January 1840 the Leamington Spa Courier carried the following sale notice: "All that substantially built dwelling house, known by the sign of the Priory Arms, and being 1, Priory Street, lately in the occupation of – Patteson, at 6s.9d per week, comprising two good bedrooms on the first floor and a parlour, tap-room, large front shop, entrance hall and pantry on the ground floor."

Circa the beginning of the 20th century the [beer house] on-licence was changed to a beer off-licence; we know it was post 1897 as in the same year James Essex was operating a shop and a beer house from the premises. In 1911, the district valuer advised the licensing magistrates that the property at 10, Priory Street had five rooms which included two bedrooms and a box room; he stated the property was worth £16 per annum rent, or £14.6s without the licence. The records of Lucas and Co. Ltd list a Priory Cottage Inn in the early 1930s having a rent of £6.2s.6d per quarter and although we cannot confirm that they are one and the same premises, it does seem likely as Priory Street is a very small street. On 9th April 1974 the beer off-licence was changed to a full off-licence. In 2013 the building is a private dwelling.

| | |
|---|---|
| 1838-39 | Ann Knibb |
| 1839-40 | Patteson (*As spelt*) |
| 1841-42 | David Morris |
| 1851-57 | Daniel Morris |
| 1866-72 | David Morris |
| 1876 | Mrs. M. A. Morris |
| ≤1879-Jul 1879 | George Payne |
| July 1879-Jun 1885 | James Cousins |
| June 1885-Apr 1886 | John Holmes |
| April 1886-Feb 1888 | Eleanor Holmes (*On the death of John*) |
| February 1888-Aug 1889 | John Blackwell |
| August 1889-Jul 1890 | William Beddington (*Priory Street beer house*) |
| July 1890-May 1894 | William Townsend |
| May 1894-Jun 1906 | James Essex |
| June 1906-Aug 1915 | Daniel Hall (*On the death of James Essex*) |
| August 1915-19 | Mrs. Hall (*On the death of Daniel*) |
| 1919-32 | W. Boucher |
| 1936-Feb 1937 | Ann 'Annie' Elizabeth Boucher |
| February 1937 | Ada Linney |
| June 1958 | Rose Astill |

*Kirth Boalch remembers, "The building's still there, but it's been converted into a private dwelling, and is now called Priory Cottage. My memory of it is more from the nineteen fifties, before the block of terraced houses at the back of 33 Tachbrook Road were demolished, and the gas works was still in full swing. In those days, it was run by a little old lady, could she have been Barry Astill's or his wife's granny? As you know, it's against the law to consume alcohol in an off-licence, but she had a loud bell on the front door that rang like the bells of doom when you opened it. Once inside, there was a door on the right that led to a room where the counter was, this was kept closed or just slightly ajar.*

*On the odd evening that I popped in for a bag of crisps, there was usually one or two of the locals leaning on the bar chatting, but no beer in sight. She used to pull pints for the favoured few who could be trusted, but when the door bell rang, she slipped the pints under the counter where they stayed until the customer had been served and left. Also, there was a door at the side of the building, behind which she used to leave a jug of beer. At ten or eleven o'clock at night, one of the night shift from the gas works could be heard clomping along Priory Street in their clogs, the side door would creak, and off they clomped with the beer."*

**Priory Way Wine Bar** – 26 Park Street
See Wig and Pen for details.

**Queen Victoria** – 45 High Street
See Guards Inn for details.

**Queens Arms** – 82 Queen Street
Originally a beer house, the first reference point we have is the annual licensing session in August 1861 when James Child's application for a public house licence was refused. The first directory listing we have for the Queens Arms is in 1863 when it is addressed as 40, Queen Street; by 1868 it would be renumbered '42' and by 1885 it would be '82' [running from Lansdowne Street through to Campion Terrace, the street was numbered: 2-78 to Vincent Street, and 80-102 from Vincent Street to Earl Street]. A music, singing and dancing licence was granted in November 1892; the music and singing took place on Monday, Wednesday and Fridays from 7.00pm until 10.30pm in the tap room [18 ft x 13 ft], and the dancing took place in the same room that housed the skittle alley [50 ft x 13 ft]. However, in September 1893 the licensing justices stated that they strongly objected to dancing in public houses and refused to renew that particular licence. By 1897 the pub had a [full] publican's licence and the freehold was owned by Flower and Sons Ltd, Stratford-upon-Avon.

*Above: Photo of landlady Win James with long standing customer Miss Elsie Phillips on 23rd December 1977. Photo courtesy of son Frank James. Right: Photo of the Queens Arms, circa 1901, courtesy of the late Bill Gibbons family. The small boy is John Newstead who was born in 1900; he is seen with his 'nanny'. John's grandad was also named John Newstead and was the licensee.*

In October 1976, the Evening Mail reported that pub regulars had organised a petition in response to the Warwick District Council's plans to demolish the pub, along with the surrounding area, as part of a housing redevelopment scheme. The petition was doomed to failure and on Friday 23rd December 1977, the Morning News reported that, "Landlady Mrs. Win James will be calling 'time gentlemen please' for the very last time on 3rd January, after which the Queens Arms will be demolished. The pub, once the heart of a busy residential area, stands amid doomed Queen Street 'ghost houses' where bulldozers are waiting to clear the land for council redevelopment." As reported, the Queens Arms closed on 3rd January 1978 – Queen Street, Earl Street and Vincent Street still exist but all formed part of the housing development scheme.

**Footnote:** It is possible that prior to being the Queens Arms these premises could have been Britons Boast, a Queen Street beer house that was for sale in March 1861, but we have no corroborating evidence.

| | |
|---|---|
| ≤1861-Jan 1865 | James Joseph Child |
| January 1865-May 1866 | Edward Heath |
| May 1866-Apr 1867 | James Barnes |
| April 1867-68 | Francis Gibbs |
| 1870-Nov 1874 | Henry Johnson |
| November 1874-75 | Edwin Poole |
| 1875-Apr 1878 | James Adland Loughton |
| April 1878-Mar 1883 | William Coles |
| March 1883-Sep 1887 | Joseph Hobbs |
| September 1887-88 | John Knight |
| 1888-Mar 1889 | Richard Tinsley |
| March 1889-Dec 1891 | Mrs. Jane Simkins |
| December 1891-Jul 1893 | George Crisford |
| July 1893-Mar 1894 | Edward Beech |
| March 1894-May 1894 | Phillip Henry Gibbins |
| May 1894-96 | Alfred Prue Woodward |
| 1896-Feb 1899 | William Mann |
| February 1899-Jun 1907 | John Andrew Newstead |
| June 1907-≥1907 | Mrs. Newstead *(On the death of John)* |
| ≥1907-19 | Mr. and Mrs. Alec Fielding Palmer |
| | *(It is likely that Mrs. Palmer is the daughter of John Newstead)* |
| 1919-Oct 1933 | Charles Joseph Davies |
| October 1933-Jul 1962 | George Henry Clifford |
| July 1962-Jan 1971 | Francis 'Frank' Henry James |
| January 1971-Jan 1978 | Winifred James |
| 3rd January 1978 | Closed for business |

The Evening Mail of 6th October 1976 reported that the regulars were fighting to keep their 150 year old pub open. They organised a petition to answer Warwick District Council's plans to demolish the pub along with the surrounding area under a redevelopment scheme. Locals explained why they used the pub. Gilbert Maull: "It's the old fashioned atmosphere that I come here for. Where can I go if they close this down? I wouldn't know what do if I didn't come here." Heather Lee: "I come here for the company. Everyone helps one another and if you've got a problem you can bring it here. We're like one big happy family." John Quinn: "It's a nice homely pub where everyone is very friendly." Leslie Winwood: "There is always a nice atmosphere with none of the plastic surroundings and flash lighting. There is nowhere else around like this," and Ken Brown: "You get a good group of people in here and always a good pint of beer. You know you can bring your wife here because we never get any trouble."

*For 73 year old Mrs. James, probably the town's oldest licensee, the Queens Arms has been her life for 15 years. "It's sad to think that it's going to be pulled down," she said, "but I think I am ready to retire now. I'm getting on a bit for this sort of life." Mrs. James won't be leaving her hundreds of friends far behind when she pulls her last pint, "I'm going to live in a flat quite close to Queen Street. I didn't want to go too far away. I know so many people in the area and want to stay among them," she said.*

*The closing of the Queens Arms marks the end of a long career in the licensed trade for her. "I started as a licensee with my husband in 1930 when we ran the Brunswick Arms and came here 15 years ago." During the years at the Queens Arms, Mrs. James said she got to know her regulars very well. "I knew some of them so well that I could tell them just by the sound of their walk. And I could always recognise one chap just by the way he wiped his feet as he came in."*

*One of Mrs. James' regulars, Miss Elsie Phillips said she had been calling at the Queens Arms since she was 15. "I used to think I was so grown up in those days coming across the road for my mother's half pint. I'm 76 now, and I've been coming in regularly for all those years," said Miss Phillips. With retirement just over a week away, Mrs. James is looking forward to taking things easy and finding herself a nice, friendly little pub where she can sit on the other side of the bar for a change.*

**Queens Cross Inn** – 1 Livery Street

The first information we have is dated 1845 when the following advert appeared in the Leamington Spa Courier and Warwickshire Standard: "Queens Cross, to be let, and may be entered immediately; this old established public house is situated in Livery Street, adjoining Regent Street; rent under £20 per annum. Apply on the premises or to Mr. George Finney, Royal Oak, Park Street." However, we do have an 1835 listing for an unnamed beer retailer [beer house] in Livery Street, which would explain why the sale advert mentions "this old established public house". This pub appears to have an impeccable record as any mention in the local newspapers is almost exclusively restricted to licence renewals at annual licensing sessions. In 1888, the Queens Cross was the headquarters of the Masons Society, not the Masons Arms as might have been expected.

At the March 1906 licensing session the chief constable opposed the renewal of the full licence, his objections being that the house was situated in a congested area, that there were three entrances to the house and that there were six fully licensed houses within a distance of 156 yards. In response the tenant stated that there had been no complaint made against the house, that alterations previously suggested by the licensing justices had been addressed and that the clientele were trades people in the immediate neighbourhood. Notwithstanding, the licensing justices referred the Queens Cross to the county compensation authority for closure on the grounds of 'redundancy'. The Queens Cross Inn closed on 4th April 1907 with compensation being paid and on 10th May it was advertised for sale by auction under instructions from Samuel Allsopp and Sons Ltd, Burton-on-Trent. See the Noah's Ark entry for an 1852 map showing where the Queens Cross Inn was situated.

| | |
|---|---|
| 1835-≥Dec 1837 | John Miles |
| 1845 | No licensee listed |
| 1846-1857 | Richard Haynes |
| 1850 | Joseph Haynes |
| 1852-59 | Mrs. Sarah Haynes |
| April 1859-Feb 1867 | James Henry Haynes |
| February 1867-Jun 1872 | Edward Haynes |
| June 1872-Apr 1873 | Frank Price |
| April 1873-May 1874 | John Watson |
| May 1874-Jun 1875 | Ann Watson *(On the death of John)* |
| June 1875-Jan 1876 | Thomas Alexander Pinner |
| January 1876-Apr 1884 | Frederick Heap *(Of Lichfield)* |
| April 1884-Aug 1884 | Henry Broad |
| August 1884-Oct 1889 | John Wickes |
| October 1889-Oct 1890 | Clement Smallwood |
| October 1890-May 1892 | Charles Burroughs and his wife Sarah |
| May 1892-Oct 1893 | Elizabeth Morgan |
| October 1893-Nov 1895 | Jessie Aske |
| November 1895-96 | Henry Wilding |
| 1896-Apr 1907 | Richard Henry Turland |
| 4th April 1907 | Closed for business |

*The Leamington Spa Courier dated 10th May 1907 advertised: Locke and Son are instructed to sell by auction, on Thursday, May 23rd, 1907, at the Crown Hotel, at 6.30 in the evening prompt, subject to conditions then to be produced and read, the following property – Under instructions from Messrs Samuel Allsopp and Sons, Limited; All those centrally situated freehold premises, formerly known as the 'Queens Cross', Livery Street [off Regent Street], now closed as a public house by the licensing committee.*

**Queens Head** – 7 Brunswick Street

On 30th March 1830, the following leasehold premises were auctioned at the Castle Inn, Brunswick Street in Leamington Priors: "A piece of land, containing 754 square yards, having a frontage to Brunswick Street of 42 feet, with a dwelling house erected thereon intended for a public house, in an unfinished state, and which may be altered at a trifling expense for a family residence. Late belonging to John Frazer, a bankrupt, 87 years of the term will be unexpired at Lady-Day next, ground rent £14.13s.7d." These premises would soon become the Queens Head and the first directory listing we have is in 1832, when the address would've been 94, Brunswick Street – from the 1850s it was renumbered '95' and by 1880 it was numbered '7'.

In 1909 there were four entrances to the Queens Head, three on Brunswick Street and one on Ranelagh Street. The drinking facilities comprised four rooms on the ground floor, including a bar [11 ft x 11 ft], a smoke room [10 ft 8 in x 9 ft 9 in], and a tap room [15 ft x 13 ft 8 in] plus an upstairs club room situated over the outhouses in the back yard. In January 1914 Francis James, who had recently purchased the freehold of this 'free house' from Messrs Cobb, sought approval from the licensing justices to make structural alterations to the premises. The final plans made provision for converting the four small rooms on the ground floor into two large rooms to provide larger 'smoke' and 'refreshment' rooms. Although the total floor area would increase from 1033 to 1417 square feet, the size of the drinking facilities would not be increased, just the domestic space; the licensing justices consented. In October 1920 it was reported that licensee Frank James had sold the Queens Head to Lucas and Co. Ltd [Leamington Brewery]; it would become an Ansells pub following their 1928 acquisition of the brewery and its closure in 1934. In 1972 Ansells offered a tenancy at the Queens Head, stating that it was uneconomic to run the pub under management and that there was a trend towards tenancies.

In January 1990 work commenced on the renovation and remodelling of the pub's interior and exterior to provide an open plan lay-out and a

*Photo of the Queens Head circa 1912 courtesy of Frank James.*

*Photo of the Bridge courtesy of Nick Wilkins.*

*The Lock, Dock and Barrel taken on 2nd November 2008 © Allan Jennings.*

canal-side garden. Renamed the Bridge, it was reopened on Wednesday 21st February 1990 when Coventry City players David Speedie, Brian Kilkline and Cyrille Regis joined landlord Brian Meacock to pull the first pint.

On the 4th October 2000, and following a refurbishment costing £176,000, it reopened as the Lock, Dock & Barrel. On 15th July 2005 the Leamington Spa Courier reported, "That more than a century of history was set to end under a plan to turn an historic 'old town' pub into flats. The canal side Lock, Dock and Barrel, which has been a pub for more than 100 years, has been earmarked for a development comprising thirteen apartments." Although this particular redevelopment project did not go ahead another would, and in April 2010 the Lock, Dock and Barrel closed. By the end of the year most of the rear of the premises and been demolished and work had commenced on significantly extending the size of the building's footprint. In 2013 the premises are residential apartments.

| | |
|---|---|
| 1832 | T. Allard |
| 1832-35 | Ann Allard |
| 1835-42 | Sarah Allard |
| 1845 | Mrs. M. A. Allard |
| 1846-Oct 1863 | Jabez Pettit *(Died 23rd June 1863, aged 50)* |
| October 1863-66 | Mary Ann Pettit *(Died 28th March 1884, aged 68)* |
| 1868-Nov 1873 | George Leonard Sanson |
| November 1873-82 | John Hunt |
| 1882-July 1885 | William Jones |
| July 1885-Dec 1888 | Henry Dobbs |
| December 1888-Apr 1904 | Henry 'Harry' Malings and wife Eliza |
| April 1904-Mar 1921 | Francis 'Frank' James |
| March 1921-Nov 1922 | Charles Stubbs |
| November 1922-Sep 1926 | Henry 'Harry' Inwood |
| September 1926-29 | Frederick C. Standen |
| 1930-31 | C. E. Wager |
| 1932-34 | Bertie Millard *(Ex Leamington F.C. player)* |
| 1934-Mar 1935 | C. Proctor Wood |
| March 1935-Jun 1941 | Ernest Wilson Priestley |
| June 1941-Jun 1944 | John William Lovridge |
| June 1944-Nov 1951 | Alfred Horace Lead |
| November 1951-Jul 1953 | Charles Bertram Henry Groves |
| July 1953-Sep 1955 | William Arthur Warren |
| September 1955-Jun 1957 | Maurice Jones |
| June 1957-Jun 1958 | Robert Charles Hynam |
| June 1958-Sep 1959 | Alfred David Bromley |
| September 1959-Jan 1964 | Sidney Joseph Cash |
| January 1964-82 | Geoffrey Tew |
| 1982-Jan 1985 | Abdel Majid 'Ben' Ghaffar |
| January 1985-May 1986 | Swarn Singh Sahota |

| | |
|---|---|
| May 1986-Feb 1989 | Mark and Jacquie Wicks *(Previously at the Grist Mill)* |
| March 1989-1990 | Paul O'Keeffe *(Renamed the Bridge, 1989)* |
| 1990-1993 | Brian 'Moose' Meacock *(Following a twelve month partnership with Paul O'Keeffe, Brian took over as sole licensee)* |
| 2004 | Keith Harwood |
| 2005 | Shaminder Singh Kang *(Lock, Dock and Barrel)* |
| 9th January 2009-Apr 2010 | Helder Filipe Dos Santos Goncalves |
| April 2010 | Closed for business |

*In the early 1900s the pub was owned by Francis James, whose grandson of the same name still lives in Leamington Spa in 2013. He said, "The pub would open at 6.00am and there would be a queue outside. My grandmother and grandfather took it in turns to open up. They used to say ale was drunk because it was cleaner than water and gave you less trouble. A lot of the regulars worked at Flavel's across the road and started work around 7.00am. On the day the Titanic sunk someone shouted up the stairs to my grandmother, 'Missus, Missus, the Titanic's sunk'!"*

The Coventry Evening Telegraph dated 1st March 1989 reported that: A landlord aims to breathe new life into a run down south Leamington pub which closed its doors only a few weeks ago, and one of the first changes will be a new name. Plans are underway to turn the Queens Head, in Brunswick Street, into a canal-side watering hole for all age groups. It will be called the Bridge. Paul O'Keeffe, the landlord of the Hope and Anchor at the junction of Hill Street and Leicester Street, has applied for a temporary tenancy. He said, "By early summer I hope to change the pub a lot. It has great potential, especially being next to the canal." Mr. O'Keeffe and his wife Shirley are well known in the town. Before they took over the Hope and Anchor they had spells at the Guards in High Street and were in charge of the town's Irish Club in Hamilton Terrace.

*In the summer of 2004 the Lock, Dock & Barrel pub was packed with revellers for a Jamaican Independence Day celebration with reggae DJs from Leamington.*

**Railroad Inn** – Sidney Terrace, Rugby Road
See Coventry Arms for details.

**Railway Inn** – 12 Clemens Street
The first directory listing we have for these premises is in 1841 when it is listed as the Fountain Inn and addressed as 5, Clemens Street. It remained the Fountain until July 1859 when Thomas Temple, the recently arrived licensee, renamed it the Railway Inn. During the late 1870s the Railway Inn was renumbered 12, Clemens Street, which it still is in 2013. In 1903, landlord George Kightley opened at 7.00am and also provided tea and coffee if required. In the same year, the pub was used by the Mechanics Band for rehearsals; John Pinfold a confectioner of 21, Clemens Street was the bandmaster.

Part of the Leamington Brewery's tied estate from the early 1900s, the Railway Inn would become an Ansells pub following their 1928 acquisition of the Leamington Brewery and its

*Above left: This photo was taken in February 1915 during the First World War when the soldiers were staying at the Railway Inn. Among the attractions that Mr. Hartopp could offer were the bowling saloon and the bagatelle table. Photo donated by Bert Usher to Leamington Library. Above right: Photo of the Railway Inn taken 31st March 1985 © Allan Jennings.*

closure in 1934. In 1972 Ansells brewery offered a tenancy, stating that it was uneconomic to run the pub under management and that there was a trend towards tenancies; latterly it would become a Banks' pub. On Friday 25th May 1990 there was a large fire at the Railway in which the landlord's two-year-old pet dog 'Harry' was killed. Thousands of pounds worth of damage was done to John Skett's bedroom, bathroom and living room by the fire which was started by an electrical fault in the immersion heater. The pub was not damaged and business continued as usual. In the summer of 2011 the pub's exterior was painted and a new sign installed. The Railway Inn remains open in December 2013.

| | |
|---|---|
| 1841-45 | Joseph Parsons *(Fountain Inn)* |
| 1846 | Edwin Denby |
| 1847-48 | Joseph Parsons |
| 1848-49 | Edwin Denby |
| 1849-Apr 1858 | Frederick Wilmin |
| April 1858-Feb 1859 | Thomas Hutton |
| February 1859 | Thomas Temple *(Transfer of Fountain Inn)* |

| | |
|---|---|
| July 1859-79 | Thomas Temple *(Railway Inn)* |
| 1879-80 | Charles B. Taberer |
| 1880-May 1880 | Messrs Lewis and Ridley/Leamington Brewery |
| May 1880-90 | William James Angus |
| 1890-Feb 1890 | Betsy Angus *(Executrix of William)* |
| February 1890-Dec 1891 | Roderick Henry Angus |
| December 1891-Mar 1893 | Thomas Watson |
| March 1893-Oct 1897 | Frederick Alderman Snr |
| October 1897-Oct 1907 | George Knight Kightley *(Died 3rd June 1930, aged 67)* |
| October 1907-Sep 1910 | William Bolton |
| September 1910-Sep 1911 | Robert Woolf |
| September 1911-Sep 1918 | Joseph Hartopp |
| September 1918-May 1919 | Ada Hartopp *(Temporary licensee until end of WWI)* |
| May 1919-Jan 1953 | Joseph Hartopp |
| January 1953-Oct 1955 | George Frederick Rollason |
| October 1955-Apr 1963 | Leslie John Paxford |
| April 1963-Jun 1964 | Harry Patrick Bembridge Kelland |
| June 1964-Aug 1965 | Reginald Robert Hancock |
| August 1965-Feb 1966 | Thomas Henry Power |
| February 1966-Apr 1967 | James Merrick |
| April 1967-Jun 1968 | Norman Alexander Thomson |
| June 1968-Apr 1969 | Elfred John Owen |
| April 1969-Sep 1970 | George Arthur Ellis |
| September 1970-Jan 1971 | Roger Holmes |
| 18th January 1971 | W. S. Wardle *(Temporary licensee)* |
| January 1971-Jun 1975 | William Henry Laird McKean and his wife June |
| June 1975-78 | Augustine 'Gus' Stapleton and his wife Joyce |
| Circa late 1970s | Alf Macari |
| Nov 1983 | Closed for 10 months |
| Aug 1984 | Michael Cowlishaw |
| ≤December 1987-1988 | Helen Clark |
| 1988-1989 | Jeanette and Andrew Canning |
| 1990 | John Skett *(Also licensee of the Great Western)* |
| 1998-2005 | Lon Anthony Mallin |
| 2005 → | Lon Anthony Mallin/Liam Anthony Mallin |

*On 28th January 1920, the Railway Inn was used for a mass meeting of strikers: – Flavel's workers were in dispute with Flavel Imperial Stove Company [Sidney Flavel & Co – Ed] over the dismissal of a male employee belonging to the National Union of Stove, Grate, and General Metal Workers. We don't know how many strikers constituted the mass meeting, or how many of them were able to fit into the Railway Inn, but we do know that it was presided over by Mr. H. Farmer, president of the local branch of the Heating and Domestic Engineers' Union. Then managing director, Percival William Flavel, refused to discuss the subject with reporters.*

**Railway Tavern** – 10 Clemens Street
The Railway Tavern was a beer house open from circa 1848 to circa 1857; the licensee was George Parsons. Following its closure, the nearby Fountain Inn [5, Clemens Street] changed its name to the Railway Inn in 1859.

**Railway Tavern** – Leam Terrace East
This beer house existed from 1849 until circa 1860 and was addressed as Leam Terrace East. Nowadays, these premises are residential and addressed as 187, Leam Terrace. In 2010 it was occupied by a Mr. Callaghan who informed us that the building was erected in 1827 [a 2010 photo of the building is inserted opposite; it is the one with the bike chained to the railings]. The Railway Tavern was replaced by the New Inn at 197, Leam Terrace circa 1860; it remains open in 2013. See the New Inn for details.

*Photo of 187, Leam Terrace taken 9th February 2010 © Allan Jennings.*

**Ranelagh Tavern** – 2/4 Ranelagh Street
The first directory listing we have is in 1827 when it consisted of three parlours, a drawing room, two kitchens, seven good bedrooms, a brew house, malt-room, and cellaring. However, if an 1844 'to let' notice, stating that the Ranelagh had been open for 18 years, is accurate then it dates from 1826. In a report presented to the annual licensing sessions in 1903, the chief constable stated that there were four entrances, one in Ranelagh Street, one in a passage leading to Brunswick Street and two doors in a passage leading to the private yard of a pork butcher at 13, Brunswick Street. He also made mention that the premises were used by respectable workmen [like foundry workers] who went to the house a great deal. The pub was owned by Lucas and Co. Ltd [Leamington Brewery] from circa the early 1900s, but it would become an Ansells pub following their 1928 acquisition of the brewery and its closure in 1934. In 1972 Ansells brewery were offering a tenancy at the Ranelagh Tavern, stating that it was uneconomic to run the pub under management and that there was a trend towards tenancies.

Following a total refurbishment, new licensee Tom Palmer reopened the pub as the Debonair in April 1988; it was named after the hugely successful Flavel's room heater launched in August 1961 and built

*The Ranelagh Tavern taken in 1987 by Bill Bigley.*

in the factory at the end of the street. Advertising in the Observer on Thursday 20th April 1995, the Debonair announced that on the upcoming weekend it was "celebrating a milestone in its history of seven successful years in business – with a party night to remember". A week earlier, the Debonair's management had launched a brand new bar on the same premises, but as a separate venue. Upstairs from the Debonair, and accessed via the same Ranelagh Street entrance, Tin-Tins boasts four pool tables and a football table; there are also plans afoot to put it all to music and have a DJ playing everyone's favourite tunes on Friday and Saturday nights. The Debonair closed in 2008 and remained boarded-up until early 2012 when work commenced on converting the premises for residential use, a project that was not completed until the latter half of 2013.

*The Debonair courtesy of Nick Wilkins.*

| | |
|---|---|
| 1826-28 | William Langham |
| 1828-31 | John Davis |
| 1832-42 | John Lees |
| 1842-43 | J. M. Mills |
| 1845 | W. Pickering |
| 1846 | G. Powell |
| 1849-Dec 1868 | William Stephenson |
| December 1868-79 | Henry Grisold |
| 1879-Feb 1880 | Charles Beacham Parsons |
| February 1880-Dec 1895 | John King and wife Emma |
| December 1895-Dec 1897 | Frederick Alderman Jnr |
| December 1897-Sep 1933 | George Harry Timms |
| September 1933-39 | William H. Summers |
| 1939-Jun 1941 | George Henry Green *(aka 'Daddy' - Leamington's most famous footballer. He played 8 times for England and over 400 times for Sheffield United)* |
| June 1941-Dec 1964 | Cyril Arthur Jarred |
| December 1964-Aug 1965 | Winifred Mary Jarred |
| August 1965-Apr 1966 | John O'Gara |
| April 1966-Dec 1966 | Peter Heale |

| | |
|---|---|
| December 1966-Jun 1967 | George William Tiplady |
| June 1967-Aug 1968 | Brian Thomas Raymond Fox |
| August 1968-Jun 1970 | Alfred Henry Smith |
| June 1970-1977 | George Arnold Roberts |
| April 1988 | Opened as the Debonair |
| April 1988-96 | Tom Palmer |
| 2008 | Closed for business |

*The Leamington Spa Courier dated 18th December 1830 reported:* **One hundred and eighty pounds stolen – Twenty pounds reward** *– Whereas, on Saturday night last, the 11th December instant, £170, in sovereigns, together with two five-pound notes of Messrs Tomes and Russell's Bank, a mahogany polished tea-chest, [in which the same were deposited], two pearl brooches, a common drinking horn, and some other articles, were stolen from the dwelling house of Mr. John Davis, known by the name of the Ranelagh Tavern, Leamington Priors. Notice is hereby given that the sum of twenty pounds will be paid by the said John Davis, to any person who will give such information as shall lead to the apprehension and conviction of the perpetrators of the above robbery. Anyone concerned in the above robbery, impeaching his accomplice or accomplices, shall be entitled to the above reward on their conviction, and also every means taken to obtain a free pardon.*

In the Leamington Spa Courier dated 4th July 1913 a local man reminisced: "Mr. Stevenson, book-keeper at the Ranelagh Wharf, was the landlord of the Ranelagh Tavern – a very stout, short man of Scottish extraction. He was a lover of porridge, but, contrary to most Scots, instead of taking oatflake for breakfast he took it for a night-cap. At the period to which this refers the Ranelagh was noted for its excellent home-brewed ales, a special brewing for Christmas being called 'redneck' but in the consumption of which customers were limited."

### Red House – 113 Radford Road

This pub was a beer house until August 1856 when William Lovell, previously of the nearby Oak Inn, was granted a full on-licence at the annual licensing sessions [the date it opened as a beer house is still to be determined]. Variously addressed prior to 1900 [including, New Radford Road and 45, Radford Road], it has been consistently numbered 113, Radford Road since circa 1890. On 24th October 1901, the "freehold and fully licensed inn" was sold at auction; a pre-sale notice in the local press described the premises as: "Substantially built and comprising, four bedrooms and water closet [first floor]; bar, bar-parlour, smoke room, kitchen and scullery [ground floor]; yard, with entrance gates from Radford Road and Leam Terrace East; brew house, with plant complete; working cellar and store cellars; coach house with loft over; stabling for three horses, with loft over; skittle alley [63 ft x 12 ft] with slated roof and well lighted; walled-in garden, planted with prolific fruit trees; fowl run and pens." In its early years the Red House was owned by Phillips and Marriot Ltd [Midland Brewery, Coventry] but when the latter were acquired by Bass, Ratcliff and Gretton Ltd [Burton-on-Trent] in 1924, it started its long tenure as a Bass house.

In 1974 it was the only Leamington pub to be listed in the Good Beer Guide. In July 1992 permission was granted to erect a balustrade over the bay windows at the front of the

*Photo of the Red House taken on 18th September 2008 © Allan Jennings.*

building. In June 2010, Punch Taverns refurbished and redecorated the Red House inside and out; this included the installation of new signage [and removal of the landmark 'Bass on Draught' sign] and the removal of the balustrade from the frontage. Sadly, the Red House closed on Saturday 14th July, 2012 and has been sold by Punch Taverns; in December 2013 its future remains uncertain.

| | |
|---|---|
| ≤1856-Nov 1865 | William Lovell |
| November 1865 | John Lovell |
| 1868-Oct 1882 | Walter Watson |
| October 1882-Feb 1898 | John Hunt |
| February 1898-Dec 1901 | Miss Ellen Owen (*Sister-in-law and executor of John Hunt*) |
| December 1901-May 1903 | William Starling |
| May 1903-Jun 1904 | John Savage |
| June 1904-Apr 1910 | Vernon James Ward |
| April 1910-14 | Arthur G. Willis |
| 1914-Aug 1914 | Samuel George Sharpe |
| August 1914-Jun 1946 | Mrs. Emma Jane Mackenzie |
| June 1946-Mar 1960 | Allan Cameron Mackenzie (*On the death of Emma*) |
| March 1960-Oct 1978 | Bernard Edwin Frayling |
| 1979-1999 | Annie Butler (*Pub converted to open plan during that period*) |
| 1999-2002 | Micky Bull |
| 2002-2011 | Julie and Jeffrey Francis James |
| April 2011-Jul 2011 | Jason Giles (*Licensee – ex White Lion, Radford Semele*) |
| April 2011-Jan 2012 | Edward 'Eddie' and Barbara Spoor (*Owners - from Gateshead*) |
| January 2012-14th July 2012 | Allan Wareing (*Also of the Holly Bush*) |

*The Leamington Spa Courier dated 12th February 1943 reported that: Flight-Sergeant A. Mackenzie, R.A.F; elder son of Mr. and Mrs. A. Mackenzie, of the Red House Inn is reported missing following an operational flight. He is an old boy of Leamington College. His father was a warrant officer in the 1914-18 war and is now a member of the Borough Special Constabulary. A younger brother is serving in the Royal Navy.*

The Leamington Spa Courier dated 4th March 1960 reported that: Leamington's most colourful licensee, 75 year old Allan Cameron Mackenzie ['Mack' to all], has pulled his last pint. And at a final farewell ceremony tonight, many dozens of regulars will assemble at the Red House Inn, Radford Road, to toast the health of the hearty scotsman who has managed the affairs of the premises for almost a quarter of a century – a period during which he has drawn more than three million pints of 'the best'.

It was in 1918 that Inverness born Mr. Mackenzie took over the business with his wife Emma, who died in February, although it had been in the family since 1909. "It doesn't seem so long ago," he told the Courier this week. "I came down here during the Great War, and when the fighting had finished I had the choice of a commission in the Palestine police or a job in the 'pub'. I tossed a coin – and the Royal Spa won. It just wasn't the thing in those days for a lady to be seen in a public house," he recalls. "They had a job to get enough money to keep the house," and the beer? – "it's not what it used to be. It tends to be quite a bit weaker than in my younger days."

One of the biggest changes noticed during the latter part of his long 'reign' was the astonishing popularity of "fruit juices, soft drinks and all those other weird concoctions". Draught beer, he regrets, has been forced to surrender an enormous amount of ground to bottled ale, the sale of which has gone up "hundreds of times over". He has just one disappointment about tonight's celebrations. Because of deteriorating health, he's forbidden to drink himself. So he's obliged to say his formal goodbye with a glass of lemonade! [Note: some of the dates do not quite fit with those that we have established – Ed]

*The Leamington Spa Courier dated 13th October 1978 reported:* **Time gentlemen please!** *Mr. Bernard Frayling, the well known tenant of the Red House public house in Radford Road, Leamington, will be giving his last shout at the end of the month for he is retiring after 18 years. During this time, Mr. Frayling has gathered a large number of regulars at the pub and for them things will never be the same again. Mr. Frayling, who is now seventy years old, came to Leamington from Coventry. He worked at the motor car firm, Alvis, based in Birmingham for 31 years before going into the pub business. It was his own decision to retire, saying he thought at the age of seventy it was time enough. Born in Guernsey, Mr. Frayling has been a member of the Licensed Victuallers Association ever since he came to Leamington and has been on the committee for a number of years. Mr. Frayling said it will be difficult to retire because he has enjoyed his time at the pub very much. He said that he does not yet know how he is going to spend his retirement, but he does plan to stay in Leamington.*

A typical British tradition is the November 5th 'bonfire night' and in recent times the Red House always celebrated in style. During her tenancy, a superb fireworks display was held every year under the guidance of landlady Julie James, who also supplied food and drink for the local families. The event was held in the spacious garden where an enjoyable evening was spent by all. Some of the more hardy drinkers, however, watched from the bar window.

**Red Lion** – 7 Park Street

The first references we have to a Red Lion are in 1817-18, 1822 and 1824, but all are unaddressed; it is not directory listed in 1816 or 1823 and directories for the intervening years [1819-21] were not available, likewise those for 1825-27. Based on the information available we have concluded that it opened circa 1817 for a brief period, closed circa 1824 and reopened in the 1830s. The next directory listing is in 1835 when this beer house is addressed as 24, Park Street and Robert Smith is the licensee. Due to a lack of street numbering in its early days, we were unsure of its exact location until we obtained a copy of the 1852 Leamington Board of Health map. Periodically numbered '23' or '24' from 1835, it was renumbered as 7, Park Street circa 1880. A music, singing and dancing licence was granted in November 1892 for the smoke room, which measured 23 ft x 12 ft. On 1st July 1842 the freehold was sold by auction; it was described at the time as comprising a bar, tap room, scullery, four comfortable chambers over, together with a large yard, brew house, workshop and cellaring.

In the second half of the 19th century it would be owned by the Northampton Brewery Company [Phoenix Brewery, Northampton]. In 1907 it had a bathing club, an air-gun club and a sick and dividend club. After being adjudged 'redundant' by the local licensing justices, and referred to the county compensation authority, the Red Lion was closed on 25th January 1908 [with compensation being paid].

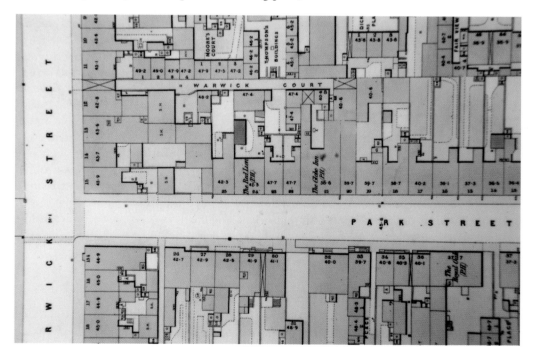

*This 1852 Board of Health map courtesy of Leamington library shows where in Park Street the Red Lion was situated.*

| | |
|---|---|
| 1835 | Robert Smith |
| 1837-42 | Silas Keen |
| 1845 | S. Keen *(Silas or Sarah)* |
| 1846-70 | Mrs. Sarah Keen |
| February 1870-Mar 1882 | William Flemming |
| March 1882-Dec 1883 | Henry Sabin Linnell |
| December 1883-Aug 1890 | Henry Pratt |
| August 1890-Jun 1893 | Charles Vallance |
| June 1893-Jul 1894 | Henry Jordan |
| July 1894-Jan 1895 | Ernest Benjamin Smith |
| January 1895-Nov 1895 | James Maycock |
| November 1895-May 1904 | William Henry Brend |
| May 1904-Jan 1908 | Edgar William Lloyd |
| 25th January 1908 | Closed for business |

*The Leamington Spa Courier dated 9th December 1871 reported that: Early yesterday morning a fire occurred at the Red Lion, Park Street. It appears that Mr. Flemming, the landlord, and the domestic arose at five o'clock. A fire was then lighted in the kitchen. The chimney runs under the floor of the bedroom over the kitchen and a side passage, an arrangement, which, as the result proves, is a most dangerous one. A stone had been placed to protect the joists of the bedroom, but in the course of time, the house being a very old one, the stone was broken. The present occupier was unaware of the mode in which the chimney was built, or the existence of the broken stone. Sometime after the lighting of the fire, the chimney caught fire, and this fact was not at first noticed. The first intimation of any danger arising from this cause was given when, at about seven o'clock, one of the inmates entered the room for the purpose of fetching a parcel. This person observed fumes of smoke, and at once raised an alarm. In the room were three beds, in which four persons were sleeping, but neither of these persons observed any signs of fire. They were, of course, immediately aroused, and every effort made to extinguish the fire, which by this time was destroying portions of the joists and floor boards. A quantity of water was thrown on the burning wood, and information was sent to the fire brigade. A hose was speedily obtained and fixed to a stand-pipe, and a plentiful supply of water thus obtained. The deputy captain of the brigade, Mr. Greet, Lieut. Eyres, Sergeant Staite, and others were speedily on the spot, and the fire was got under control before much damage was done.*

**Regency Arms** – 18 Newbold Street
See Newbold Inn / Tavern / Newbold for details.

**Regent Hotel [incl. Syd's Bar]** – 77 Parade
On 18th July 1818, the hotel's foundation stone was laid on the east side of Union Parade by Miss Greathead of Guys Cliffe. It was opened as the Williams Hotel by Mr. B. B. Greathead on Thursday 19th August 1819 and the inaugural dinner, held that evening, catered for 300 people who dined on turtle and venison. The local press reported the cost

*Photos courtesy of Leamington History Group.*

of the hotel to be around £15,000 but it is understood that the final figure was closer to £80,000. At the time it was supposedly the largest hotel in Europe, with 100 rooms [but only one bath], although the population of the town still only approximated 2,000; its first proprietor was John Williams, the former landlord of the Bedford Hotel. At the back of the hotel had been built an extensive Mews leading into Regent Street and in its yard was the Regent 'tap'. On Friday 10th September 1819 the Prince Regent, who later became King George IV, visited the town on his way to Warwick Castle and granted permission for the Williams Hotel to be renamed Regent Hotel.

The Duchess of Kent brought her daughter, the then Princess Victoria [aged 11], to Leamington on 3rd August 1830. They chose to stay in the lavish Regent Hotel which was illuminated for the visit and also decorated with three royal arches. It is said that Victoria never forgot the welcome she received, and in 1838 cheering crowds greeted the news that Leamington had been awarded a charter by Queen Victoria and could call itself Royal Leamington Spa; it was widely seen as a thankyou from the queen for the reception she had received eight years previously.

The Parade entrance to the hotel was installed in 1852 for the Warwickshire Hunt Club however, the general public still had to use the original entrance on the south side. In 1853 visitors could book a private apartment or a suite of apartments; a large drawing room and three bedrooms cost 12s.6d per day; a drawing room and two bedrooms cost 9/- per day; a sitting room fire cost 1s.6d per day and a bedroom fire cost 6d per evening. A breakfast with cold meat or eggs cost 1s.9d, 2/- with broiled ham and 2s.6d with chop or fish. Board and lodging [incl. table d'hote] was £2.2s per week and bedrooms for servants, on the third floor, cost 1/- per day. In May 1880 Lyas Bishop registered the hotel as a limited liability company - The Regent Hotel Company Ltd – with a capital of £44,000 in shares of £10 each. In 1891 the Regent Hotel advertised spacious well ventilated public rooms, extensive stabling with loose boxes, separate saddle rooms and every convenience for hunting and an omnibus that meets all trains.

In June 1904 the hotel was bought at auction by Frank J. Cridlan and John Joseph Cridlan of London for £8,000; it later being transferred to Regent Properties [Leamington] Ltd, Leamington Spa. However, it was reported to have cost as much again to modernise the building which [still] only had one bathroom, sagging ceilings and electricity on the ground floor only. The hotel was reported as having a frontage of 282 ft to the Parade and 98 ft to Regent Street, and comprised, 72 bedchambers, 7 private sitting rooms, a smoking room, banqueting hall, billiard room, large and small drawing rooms and writing and coffee rooms. In addition there was stabling accommodation for 90 horses, the Regent 'tap', the North Western Railway Company's parcel office and the 'beginnings' of a garage. It reopened the following year when journalists came from far and wide to write about the luxurious accommodation provided. Previously the 'tap' [pub] had opened into the stable yard but architects Brown and Barrow relocated its access to the thoroughfare leading into the yard [but outside the archway] so that the stablemen could not access the pub directly from their work area. Regent Hotel owner John Joseph Cridlan died in 1938; he had lived at Maisemore Park, Gloucestershire and was a breeder of Angus cattle who exhibited at Smithfield for fifty-nine years.

From 1905 until 1939 the resident manager of the Regent was Herbert Wingfield Sherry [previously of Rhode Island]. Following the death of John Joseph Cridlan, Herbert also became the hotel's licensee but died just five years later, aged 69; it is said that he died brokenhearted because his hotel was requisitioned by the Ministry of Transport at the outbreak of the war, and occupied by camouflage experts who reputedly mixed paint in the baths. During the conflict a bomb demolished the servants quarters. In October 1947 the hotel was released from the 'requisition' order and reopened by the mayor on Saturday 1st May 1948 with Mr. Sherry's son, Herbert Sydney Sherry, as manager. During the early part of the war [14th November 1940] when a stick of eight bombs hit the town, one of the explosions had smashed three stained glass windows on the main staircase; they were replaced in April 1955 with the cost being mostly met by the War Damage Commission. Mr. Sherry's assistant manager was Vernon May who stayed on to become a well known figure in the town, both as manager of the hotel and host to thousands at civic and other functions at the hub of Leamington's social life. Tragically, Mr. May died in November 1994 having officially retired the previous year. The tragedy was compounded when, on the day of his funeral, Frank Cridlan [the owner and son of John Joseph] himself a great ambassador for Leamington, collapsed and died. His widow Mary, a former Mayor of Bath, then shared ownership with Frank's two daughters, Anthea Cridlan and Jeryl Wheeldon, and ran the hotel with [former deputy] John Biesok as manager until it closed in 1998.

Syd's Bar was opened on Tuesday 20th December 1960 and D. J. Gibson was its first manager; Austin McHale, an Irishman from County Mayo, was the popular barman from the date of opening until Wednesday 9th October 1963 when he died in his hotel room. The bar was named after Leamington's well known swing pianist Syd Kirkness, who had played piano in many leading British hotels and was the leader of the orchestra onboard the liner Queen Elizabeth. Syd played in the bar nightly for six years and calculated that during that time he had played almost 70,000 numbers – the majority being requested by customers. In April 1966 he handed over to Brian Hazelby who, following his demob from the army in 1958 had played at the Pump Room tea rooms. For several months he too had played in an orchestra aboard an ocean liner, before joining top instrumental group the John Barry Seven. When Brian took over from Syd, he also played a newly installed electric organ as well as the piano.

In 1970 the hotel was the 20th to join a newly formed consortium of privately owned hotels called Interchange, and in 1978 the group was the first in Europe to join Best Western Hotels which, at the time, was the second largest hotel group in the United Kingdom, and the largest in the world with over 3,000 independently owned hotels. The hotel garden between the north side of the hotel and Regent Street was removed in 1972 to enable the redevelopment of that part of the site. The new Phoenix Bar opened in 1973 and in 1977 there was also the International Bar where snacks were available from noon until 2.00pm. In November 1980 the Cork and Fork food bar was opened, the entrance being on the south side between the hotel and the Town Hall. In the summer of 1962 the hotel's banqueting room had been enlarged to cater for 270 diners and, measuring 92 feet in length, it had opened in the September. In September 1986 the Morning News reported that the historic hotel's ballroom/banquet room had undergone a £40,000 transformation and boasts two 90-year old crystal chandeliers, new air ventilation system, new velvet curtains, new carpet and a new enlarged sprung maple wood dance floor. Known as the Stoneleigh Suite, work had begun on the ballroom in July and it was officially opened at a charity dinner and dance on Friday 12th September. In August 1993, a printed guests' guide to the Phoenix Bar explained the origin of the bar's name – when the trustees of Lyas Bishop [who died in 1893] put the hotel up for auction in 1904, our respected 'Courier' had said, "From the all but dead old Regent must spring Phoenix like a new Regent fit to lead". In its day, many important people stayed at the Regent Hotel, including Princess Victoria before she became the queen, the Duke of Wellington, Sir Winston Churchill, Isambard Kingdom Brunel, Charles Dickens, Henry Wadsworth Longfellow, Mrs. Sarah Siddons, Sir Robert Peel, Sarah Bernhardt and Prince Louis Napoleon. In 1984, two heritage panels listing many of the distinguished guests were unveiled by Earl Spencer.

The Regent Hotel was sold on 8th January 1998 to Regent Estates Ltd, which included the United Bank of Kuwait and developers Barwood, and was formerly handed over later in the month. Mary Cridlan [wife of the late Frank] said that the Cridlan family had owned the hotel since 1904 and that she didn't want to sell it, however her two stepdaughters did and they were the major shareholders in Regent Properties Ltd; the Regent Hotel closed on 27th December 1998. After being closed-up for many years it became a Travelodge Hotel, with the front ground floor of the building being the Leamington Bar and Grill. In early 2010 the latter was closed and boarded-up for a makeover and in July of the same year it reopened as a 150 seat buffet restaurant and bar, specialising in Thai, Chinese and Italian food. This too proved a short lived venture and by July 2011 it was reported that Wagamama [a British noodle restaurant chain] had signed a nineteen year lease for the ground floor, although Travelodge would remain the prime leaseholder of the Regent building. On Saturday 23rd June 2012, Wagamama opened its largest UK restaurant to date and the first to include a bar.

| | |
|---|---|
| 18th August 1819-Jun 1834 | John Williams |
| June 1834-circa 1840 | Abraham Alexander |
| March 1841-1st Oct 1854 | Breach and Thomas Bath Jeffery |

*T. B. Jeffery announced in September 1853 that his lease expired on 1st October 1854 and that he would relinquish the business in favour of a proprietary, who have selected Mr. and Mrs. Smith to run the Regent Hotel and mews. The proprietary announced that they would be refitting and embellishing almost the whole interior to match the luxury and elegance of many of the continental establishments. By July 1854 the actual managers appointed were Mr. and Mrs. Wallace.*

| | |
|---|---|
| 1850 | Charles Edwards *(Regent Tap)* |
| July 1854-Nov 1857 | Mr. and Mrs. Joseph Scott Wallace |
| November 1857-Nov 1886 | Lyas Bishop *(Of Sheffield - Died 1893)* |
| November 1886-Aug 1893 | Thomas Higgs *(Previously at the Charing Cross Hotel, London)* |
| August 1893-1904 | Henry Consett Passman |
| 1904-1938 | John Joseph Cridlan *(Owner – died in 1938)* |
| 1905-Feb 1939 | Herbert Wingfield Sherry *(Resident manager)* |
| 1938-Feb 1939 | Executors of John Joseph Cridlan |
| February 1939-1944 | Herbert Wingfield Sherry *(Died in 1944)* |
| 7th Sep 1939-25th Oct 1947 | Hotel requisitioned for war service |
| 1944-Apr 1948 | Mrs. Caroline Ethel Sherry *(On the death of Herbert)* |
| 1st May 1948 | Reopened following the Second World War |
| 26th April 1948-Apr 1955 | Herbert Sidney Sherry |
| April 1955-Oct 1963 | Stanley Wood |
| August 1959-Jun 1961 | David J. Gibson *(Of Aberdeen – manager)* |
| October 1963-Mar 1991 | Vernon May *(Commenced employment on 1st April 1954)* |
| March 1991-Dec 1998 | John Biesok |
| 27th December 1998 | Closed for business [The Cridlan family retained ownership until the very end] |

*The Leamington Courier dated 16th December 1960 reported:* **Regent's luxury bar to open next Tuesday** *- What is claimed to be the biggest and most luxurious drinking haunt in Leamington will open at the Regent Hotel on Tuesday. For more than two months a small army of craftsmen have been creating Syd's Cocktail Bar at the southern end of the 140 year old hotel. The 66 foot long room will boast a resident evening pianist, floor service, and according to one member of the staff – "the swankiest furnishings in all Warwickshire". It represents the first major piece of reconstruction work in the hotel's history. The old, high-ceilinged public bar, a stewards' room and a storeroom have been swept away in order to accommodate it. Customers will be able to enter the bar from the side door of the hotel, or from the interior. The 31 foot long counter is fronted with panels covered with real calf hide in black and white.*

*Another unusual feature is a huge stained glass window, filled with scores of oblong panes in many colours; this is at the east end, near the pianist's platform. The polished beechwood ceiling of the bar has scores of flush lights which give out an 'orangey' glow. The decor, by Magpies of London, is designed to retain the dignity and splendour of older parts of the hotel, at the same time introducing a touch of gaiety in keeping with modern trends.*

*Customers will be able to get snacks from a 'pop-dog' machine which is capable of producing a hot sausage roll in five seconds. Mr. D. J. Gibson, the manager, said on Tuesday that the bar is only the first of a series of projected major alterations. "We felt that a really first-class bar, with music and floor service, was very necessary in the town centre," he said. "We have spared no cost to provide it, and I believe that it will be the best for miles around, and a great attraction for tourists. It is in the real grand tradition of the Regent, and at the same time it shows that we are moving with the times."*

In November 1963, manager Vernon May had to deny rumours that the Beatles were staying at the hotel following a concert they gave at Coventry Theatre. He said, "If they had stayed at the Regent I would certainly have known about it. It is definitely untrue."

*The Morning News dated 24th February 1966 reported: Believed to be the first of its kind in Warwickshire, an idea to revive the Spa's night life with a 'late-night eat and dance session' will start at Syd's Bar, at the Regent Hotel, on 3rd March. The session, which will begin at 11.00pm and end at 1.00pm, is to be held on Thursdays and Fridays for a trial period of four weeks. To be called the 'Eleven-2-One', it is intended to fill the "rather deep gap for people who have been to a theatre or cinema and don't know what to do to round off the evening," said Mr. Vernon May, the manager of the hotel. The inclusive charge of 10s.6d will allow patrons to enjoy dancing to the Mike Pearse Trio and eat chicken-in-the-basket, and hot soup. "It is rather reminiscent of days when the night life of Leamington and the Regent Hotel was renowned for its quiet distinction and gaiety," said Mr. May. He hopes that the 'Eleven-2-One' sessions will cater for people within a 15 mile radius of Leamington and will accommodate 75 people each night.*

The Morning News dated 29th April 1966 reported that: Because of public demand, the Regent Hotel's 'Eleven-2-One' supper-dance sessions on Thursday and Friday evenings have now been extended to include Saturdays. Mr. V. May, general manager of the hotel, applied to the local licensing justices this week and was granted an extension for Saturday nights; the same extension had been granted for Thursdays and Fridays some weeks ago. "The police had no objections because the 'Eleven-2-One' club is well run and there has been no trouble at all," Mr. May said. The supper dances are held in Syd's Bar at the Regent. [By October 1967 the supper-dance sessions would be extended to become the 'Nine-2-One' club – Ed]

*The Leamington Spa Courier dated 27th April 1973 reported that: A new champagne fountain record of eight glasses is being claimed by the Regent Hotel and it is offering a prize to anyone who can make a higher one. The record fountain was established by head cocktail barman Anthony Crosset in front of independent witnesses. Commenting on the successful attempt, manager Vernon May said that the whole thing had been treated as a bit of fun. He read that someone had managed a fountain with seven glasses. "We are certain that there is a record to be broken, but we have checked with the Guinness Book of Records who stated that they do not know of any record, and if this is the case we have established one. We would like to make the event an annual affair and establish a competition spirit, and we are prepared to donate a magnum of champagne to anyone who produces photographic evidence of a higher champagne fountain." Mr. May said that if a competitive spirit was established the Regent would donate a cup to be presented annually. He added that in one episode of the Avengers television programme he saw a fountain of around 13 glasses but he thinks they must have been glued together.*

The Leamington Spa Courier dated 23rd November 1973 reported: **Magicians' own record** - A record number of 200 guests attended the silver jubilee of the Leamington and Warwick Magic Society at the Regent Hotel on Tuesday. Proposing the toast to the society, the mayor of Leamington, Councillor Reg Hopkins, congratulated the president, Mr. Stewart Williams, who is the only remaining founder member. The society, he said, was to be praised because it brought joy to people of all ages and did wonderful work at local hospitals. In reply, Mr. Williams said the society understood the mayor's building trade because, like it, a handful of men had laid its foundations very firmly. It was also similar because it relied on various craftsmen for its continued success. The toast to the ladies and visitors was proposed by Goodliffe, editor of Abracadabra, and the response was given by Alfred Gabriel, president of the British Ring of the International Brotherhood of Magicians, who described magic as "possibly the finest hobby in the world".

*The Leamington Spa Courier dated 18th November 1977 reported that: A coloured reproduction of Gainsborough's famous painting of Sarah Siddons wearing a wide brimmed hat has been stolen from the Regent Hotel. Sarah Siddons was present when the foundation stone of the Regent Hotel was laid in 1818. "There are probably marks where the brass plate has been removed by the thief at the bottom of the frame," said the hotel manager Mr. Vernon May. "The numerals 29/69 were pencilled in red at the bottom right hand corner on the back of the picture and if this has been erased it will show," he added. A reward has been offered by the hotel to anyone who has any information which will lead to the recovery of the picture, which is of great sentimental value to them.*

In March 1979 the hotel advertised the Vaults restaurant, which was constructed in the original wine cellars of the Regent Hotel, "It's unique, it's superb, it's air conditioned". Tom Lewin says, "I was the electrician that first wired the restaurant in the basement; I remember it well because it flooded just prior to opening. The flood was caused by the ancient sewer situation on the Parade. The weight of storm water was too much for the sewers to cope with and flooded the Vaults restaurant. The builder J. T. Rhodes of Althorpe Street had to incorporate pumps to avoid a similar situation happening again. If memory serves me right the pumps were from Walwyn Pumps, of Millers Road, Warwick."

**Regent Wine Bar** – 33 Regent Street
See Murphy's Bar for details.

**Reindeer** – 66 Clemens Street
According to Warwick District Council [conservation department] this building was originally residential and built circa 1818. The first reference point we have for the Reindeer is in August 1865, when Robert East applied for a full licence but was refused; he is also

*The Reindeer Inn courtesy of Leamington Library [Barry Hickman collection].*

listed at these premises in 1866 as a beer retailer [beer house]. During the period January 1882 until December 1883 the licence was held by John Curley of Lewis, Ridley and Co. who owned the Leamington Brewery, but by the time of the pub's closure it was owned by the Northampton Brewery Company Ltd. After being adjudged 'redundant' by the local licensing justices and referred to the county compensation authority, the Reindeer was closed on 7th September 1907 [with compensation being paid]. In July 1913 the local press reported that the premises were occupied as a saddler's shop. The Reindeer was situated at the very top of Clemens Street on the right hand side, where the Grand Union Bar and Restaurant is in 2013; the address now being 66-68, Clemens Street.

In January 1977, Eric Shadbolt [interior designer] told of making his dream of opening a canal side restaurant and bar, on the corner of Clemens Street and Ranelagh Terrace, come true at last. The origins of Eric's efforts to build on the site date back to when he bought 69, Ranelagh Terrace in 1967. Initially the town council refused permission for a restaurant alongside the canal because there were no car parks nearby, and because it would cause a nuisance to neighbours. Not to be thwarted, he gradually purchased all the nearby properties whose residents were likely to object or be inconvenienced, and then extended and fitted-out his own house to such a high standard that it won an award from the Leamington Society. In 1972 the council granted Eric permission to convert his home into a restaurant however, he was now reluctant to do so because it had proved to be such a comfortable residence. After a year of negotiations he bought 66, Clemens Street and started converting it. He said, "I hope my restaurant and wine bar will encourage all the holiday boats that pass through the town to stop and buy from the shops in the area and use the restaurant." His plan included a street level café for tea, coffee and light refreshments, and a wine bar with English food in the basement, plus an open terrace onto the canal side where he hoped boats would moor. Eric did most of the work himself and used recycled bricks and materials, collected over the years from some of the county's lovely old buildings.

In April 1977, following objections from the Licensed Victuallers Association, the local magistrates deferred granting a licence for the selling of wine, beer and cider in the basement [which was to cater mainly for the canal users]. Although the licence for the canal side wine bar was granted in May 1977, the project would be further delayed before opening in three phases during 1980. In the January Eric opened a [small scale] boutique hotel comprising just four double bedrooms. Phase two was the canal side Coffee Parlour which won a Leamington Society award in July 1980 and phase three was the Grand Union Restaurant which opened on the 13th October 1980.

By October 1981 the luncheon bar was known as the Reunion and in the December application was made for a full drinks licence so that customers could partake of more than just wine or beer while watching the boats go by, but it was refused. In July 1982 Eric was advertising that the Grand Union restaurant, now known as Shadbolt's Reunion, was opening on 12th July. The following month he announced that the business had been expanded to include an additional restaurant that incorporated the ground floor wine bar. He also trialled a 'ladies only' wine bar, that opened on Tuesday 19th July 1983, but that doesn't appear to have been very successful. Eric Shadbolt remained at the Grand Union

*The Grand Union Bar and Restaurant taken on 30th July 2011 © Allan Jennings.*

until July 1997 when the business was sold to Jaz Johal. In 2010 it was advertised as the Grand Union Bar and Restaurant and there was also canal side advertising to promote the bar and lunches to the boating fraternity. The Grand Union remains open in December 2013 with Holly Wild as the licensee.

| | |
|---|---|
| ≤1865-66 | Robert East |
| ≤1869-Nov 1870 | William Benton *(Reindeer)* |
| 1871-72 | Job Whitehead and wife Elizabeth |
| 1873 | John Peck *(Listed as 'Bridge End' Clemens Street)* |
| August 1873-81 | James Smith *(Previously at the Warwick Arms)* |
| 1881-Jan 1882 | James Lumley |
| January 1882-Dec 1883 | John Curley/Leamington Brewery |
| December 1883 | John Cunningham Isaacs |
| 1885-92 | John McParland |
| 1892-May 1893 | Roderick Henry Angus |
| May 1893-March 1894 | Mrs. Annie Elizabeth Hoskins |
| March 1894-May 1894 | Edwin John Shilton |
| May 1894-Aug 1899 | Henry Burgess |
| August 1899-Dec 1902 | Harry Clarkson Fessey |
| December 1902-Apr 1905 | Francis Jacques |
| April 1905-Sept 1907 | William Bolton |
| 7th September 1907 | Reindeer closed for business |

*The conservation department at Warwick District Council describes it as: A house now wine bar circa 1818 with later additions and alterations; Pinkish-brown brick in Flemish bond with Welsh slate roof and cast iron balconies; Exterior has 3 storeys; Three first floor 8 pane French windows; Second floor 4/8 sashes, all in plain reveals and with sills, with blind boxes and flat channelled arches with keystones; Eaves band; Ground floor has entrance to left, a part glazed 6 panel door with overlight, and gothic glazing bars within pilastered surround with frieze and hood; round carriage arch to right with inposts and keystone, has double plank doors and overlight. Off centre shop-front has central glazed entrance between plate glass windows with aprons and pilaster strips between all, with overlights with glazing bars; To left of this a 6/6 sash with flat channelled arch with raised keystone and sill; Individual balconies with stick balusters to first-floor windows.*

**Rick's Bar** – 33 Regent Street
See Murphy's Bar for details.

**Rising Sun** – 34 Bedford Street
The first directory listing we have for this beer house is in 1833 when it is addressed as 17, Bedford Street [it would also be listed as '15' and '36' before being renumbered 34, Bedford Street circa 1880]. The pub was part of Leamington Brewery's tied estate during the latter part of the 19th century through until its closure in 1907. During that period the brewery

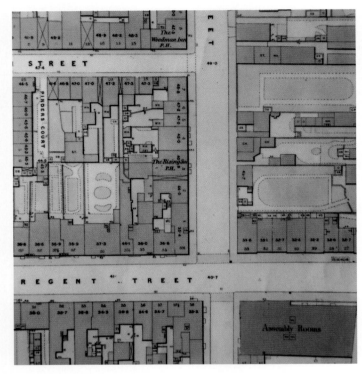

This 1852 Board of
Health map, courtesy of
Leamington Library,
shows where in Bedford
Street the Rising Sun was
situated.

was owned by Lewis and Ridley [until 1885], Lucas, Blackwell and Arkwright [until 1897]
and latterly Lucas and Co Ltd. Following the 1904 Licensing Act, which extended the
justices' powers to extinguish licences, the Rising Sun was one of eight pubs closed between
January 1905 and February 1908. After being adjudged 'redundant' by the local licensing
justices, and referred to the county compensation authority, the Rising Sun was closed on
7th September 1907 [with compensation being paid]. There is also an entry in the Lucas
and Co. Ltd records, dated 7th December 1907, stating that, "the forfeiture of any claim for
compensation in favour of the owners Taylors Trustees on cancelling the terms of the lease
on the date of closing the house was approved".

| | |
|---|---|
| 1833-39 | John Davis |
| 1841-50 | Thomas Savage |
| 1850-Nov 1871 | William Green |
| November 1871-77 | William Green Restall *(On the death of William Green)* |
| 1877-Aug 1877 | Mrs. Restall |
| August 1877-Jun 1880 | William Adderley |
| June 1880-Jul 1882 | George Collins |
| July 1882-Nov 1882 | Henry Rose |
| November 1882-83 | Messrs Lewis and Ridley/Leamington Brewery |
| 1883-Jul 1885 | John Pugh |

| | |
|---|---|
| July 1885-Sep 1887 | Morton Peto Lucas/Leamington Brewery |
| September 1887-1907 | Charles Turner |
| 7th September 1907 | Closed for business |

### Rob Roy – 16 Brook Street

The first information we have on these premises is for a proposed pub at 7, Brook Street [its original address]; the following auction notice appeared in the Leamington Spa Courier dated 11th August 1832: "On Friday 24th August inst, at six o'clock in the evening, upon the premises; all that well and substantially built freehold messuage or dwelling house, situate and being No. 7, Brook Street, consisting of two good parlours, four bedrooms, two kitchens, scullery, pantry, brew house, together with a garden at the back, well planted with choice fruit trees, bounded by a running brook at the bottom. The property was built and is calculated for a public house, and as there is no house of that description in the immediate neighbourhood, which is very much increasing, the present is a favourable opening for any person desirous of embarking in that line of business." However, the first directory listing we have for the Rob Roy is not until 1841 when Ambrose Hewitt is listed as a beer retailer [beer house] at 7, Brook Street [the address is listed as 16, Brook Street from 1885].

In 1885, the pub was part of the Leamington Brewery's tied estate that was sold to Lucas, Blackwell and Arkwright for £75,000 and in 1897 the new owners of the brewery were Lucas and Co. Ltd [it would become an Ansells pub following their 1928 acquisition of the brewery and its closure in 1934]. In 1903 there were three entrances to the pub from Brook Street. In January 1957, Ansells notified the licensing magistrates of their intention to surrender the Rob Roy's licence, which they duly did on 19th May 1958. Brook Street was part of a housing redevelopment scheme that was given the go ahead in 1955 and had already commenced prior to the closure of the Rob Roy. Around April 1957, two blocks of

*This photo from the Peter Coulls collection was taken on 17th August 1953. Although it is not specifically of the Rob Roy it does just include the left hand side of the pub and the house next door shows the nature of the buildings in the street at the time.*

three-storey flats were completed and after the pub closed the rest of Brook Street was rebuilt. The pub site became part of the frontage and entrance to a block of flats, and Brook Street went on to be renamed New Brook Street.

| | |
|---|---|
| 1841-62 | Ambrose Hewitt |
| 1863-76 | Thomas Smith |
| 1877-78 | F. Smith |
| 1878-Jul 1882 | Thomas William Smith |
| July 1882-Jan 1887 | Joseph Ernest Trussell |
| January 1887-May 1888 | Mrs. Emily Maria Trussell *(Joseph went to America)* |
| May 1888-Dec 1888 | James Haigh Turner |
| December 1888-May 1909 | William Henry Burton |
| May 1909-Aug 1915 | Henry 'Harry' Charles Smith |
| 30th August 1915-Sep 1941 | William Allibon *(Died on 11th August 1941, aged 76)* |
| 1st Sept 1941-May 1952 | Sylvia Jane Morris |
| 26th May 1952-Jun 1954 | Edith Frances Watts |
| 21st June 1954-Mar 1957 | Walter Owen Thomas Searle |
| 12th March 1957-May 1958 | Frederick Harry Watts |
| 19th May 1958 | Licence surrendered |

**Robbins Well** – 2a Victoria Terrace

Robbins Well was named after the fourth well to be found in Leamington. Mr. F. Robbins sunk his well to a depth of 25 feet on the south side of the bridge in 1804 and opened his baths on Monday 5th July 1806. First known as Bridge Well and then as Robbins Well, it was subsequently renamed Victoria Baths in honour of the then Princess Victoria. Victoria Terrace, including Victoria Colonnade, was built 1836-38; the architect was William Thomas.

In August 1962 local photographer Michael Walden attempted to open a gambling club at 2, Victoria Colonnade but was refused permission by the owners. In mid 1977, Victoria Colonnade was extensively renovated with the scope of the project including reinstatement of the original façade which fronts the river, renewal of the roof and redecoration of the entire area. On 9th December the same year, the Leamington Spa Courier reported that, "The district plans sub-committee had, subject to further design and construction drawings, given approval for a £40,000 plan to convert the building into a café, restaurant, and fashion and fancy goods store. It is to be a three storey, 10,000 sq ft building." In 1978, plans by owner James Groat, a civil engineer, were approved for a bazaar in the basement and a café and restaurant above. Evidently neither of the aforementioned proposals was implemented.

However, in March 1980 Michael Warburton and Anthony Shaw had formed Colonnade [Leamington] Ltd, and Mr. Warburton was requesting that the district plans sub-committee amend the plans for this unused building to provide for a wine bar in the basement, a café on the ground floor and a restaurant on the first and second floors. Although the company collapsed mid-project, the builders [O. H. Deacon] formed a new company [Larknight Ltd] with the same directors and completed the prescribed work; the wine bar was opened in July 1981.

Towards the end of 1982 the cellar had opened as the Colonnade Cellar Bar [open until midnight every night except Sundays] and the ground floor had opened as the Bridge Wine Bar [normal licensing hours]. On 15th November, the same year, the licensing magistrates granted a licence for a small night club on the first and second floors accommodating 100 patrons [conditional on certain building works being carried out]; it was subsequently named Nite Owl. In November 1983 David Owen was granted a provisional licence which would be made permanent once works had been carried out; he said he was looking for a more mature type of customer in the cellar bar than had previously been the case. The Bridge Bar, Colonnade and Nite Owl all closed in June 1986 with the licence for the latter expiring in the November. In November the same year the Morning News reported that, James Groat, who owns the freehold to the site in Victoria Terrace, which includes the Colonnade Wine Bar and the Bridge Bar, was applying for a renewal of the [Nite Owl] 2.00am licence. Mr. Groat, a civil engineer and property developer, who repossessed the property from its former owners, David Hall and David Owen, told the [environmental health] committee that he was presently negotiating the sale of the entire site to Jestbread – a company experienced in running public houses. But the committee held the view that it was being used as a 'bargaining counter' to clinch the sale of the property and deferred its decision until it could meet with the new owners.

In May 1987, following refurbishment and under new ownership, Tommy Fewtrell reopened the former Colonnade Cellar Bar and Bridge Wine Bar as the Fun Bar and Wine Bar, and gave his name to the premises; this was followed on 20th June 1987 by the reopening of the first floor night club [formerly Nite Owl] which Tommy renamed

*Robbins Well taken on 27th July 2011 © Allan Jennings.*

'Fewtrells – The Club' [open Thursday, Friday, Saturday – 10.00pm to 2.00am]. On 12th May 1988, the environmental health and control committee refused an application by the licensee Mr. Poole for the renewal of the premises' entertainments licence. An appeal against the decision failed and the Bridge Bar, Colonnade and Fewtrells all closed, and by mid August the premises were boarded-up. In April 1989 the Morning News reported that the Rugby based Cenprime Ltd had applied for permission to reopen the premises as a bank; the proposal was for a bank on the ground floor, offices on the first floor, while retaining a wine bar in the basement. However, the project never went ahead and the building remained boarded-up for eight years. In November 1996 Jim Groat, the [freehold] owner of the building and principal of Cenprime, stated that never again would a night club be opened on the premises, adding that the building had been deliberately kept closed until the future of the Pump Room was known.

In December 1997 it was reported that Bass Taverns had bought the defunct Grade II listed building and had plans to transform it into a bar and restaurant, thus creating about forty jobs. Robbins Well, with bars on the basement and ground levels, opened on 3rd September 1998 and targeted the student population that frequent bars south of the river. Robbins Well remains open in December 2013.

| | |
|---|---|
| July 1981-Jun 1982 | Peter and Annice Jones *(Manager – Colonnade)* |
| November 1983-Jun 1986 | David James Owen *(Of Lighthorne Heath)* and David Hall |
| 1986 | Anthony Sanders |
| 1987-88 | Tommy Fewtrell |
| Circa 1988 | Mr. Poole |
| ≤2006 | Andrew Hollier |
| February 2008-Mar 2008 | Ben Fairhurst |
| March 2008-Mar 2009 | Jennifer Aitken |
| March 2009-Jun 2009 | Ben Fairhurst |
| June 2009-Oct 2012 | Wayne Hudson |
| October 2012-Apr 2013 | James Allen |
| April 2013-Jun 2013 | Andrew Holdnall |
| June 2013 | Anthony Byrne |

**Rose and Crown** – 22 Kenilworth Street
Evidently these premises were built circa 1830. Our first reference for this beer house is a mention in a Leamington Spa Courier crime report dated 9th April 1831, relating to a theft, albeit from the Ranelagh Tavern. In 1832 the premises were owned by a Mr. Liebenrood and addressed as 41, Kenilworth Street [numbered '32' and '39' during the 1860s, it would be 1880 before it was addressed as 22, Kenilworth Street]. At this time, the Rose and Crown was the district office for the Manchester Unity Friendly Society [Oddfellows] and was the meeting venue for two of the lodges.

During the tenancy of John Warwick [1880-88], the pub was renamed the Oddfellows Hall Inn but reverted to the Rose and Crown in 1889. Owned by Hunt, Edmunds and Co. Ltd [Banbury], the Rose and Crown was one of a number of pubs referred by the licensing justices

*This photo of the Rose & Crown taken during the Silver Jubilee celebrations of King George V on 6th May 1935 shows licensee Mr. Goodman Henry Clark who was known as Val. Pictured from left to right are: Rita Harwood, Dorothy, Rover the dog, 'Val' Clark and Joy. Photo donated to Leamington Library by Joy Savage [Barry Hickman collection].*

to the county compensation authority in March 1920 for closure on the grounds of 'redundancy' – part of a weeding out process or "thinning the inns" as it was reported at the time. However, on this occasion the earlier decision was overturned and the licence was renewed.

Apparently, in the early 1900s one of the rooms at the Rose and Crown was used by the Leamington Spa Band for rehearsals; it is also interesting to note [from Jackie Turpin's biography 'Battling Jack'] that a room at the Rose and Crown was subsequently used by the town's famous Turpin brothers for training purposes, and that Sydney Graves ran a boxing gymnasium upstairs until 1961. The pub remained open until 1963 when its licence was not renewed; it closed on 5th April 1963 – with owners Hunt, Edmunds and Co. Ltd [Banbury] stating that "it is part of our policy to have fewer and better pubs". In October the same year the Rose and Crown was withdrawn from an auction sale when bidding stalled at £3,500. After the pub's closure the premises at 22, Kenilworth Street became a café [it was listed as the Tavern café in 1965].

| | |
|---|---|
| 1831-Feb 1858 | William Smith |
| February 1858-Feb 1871 | Joseph Smith |
| February 1871-Sep 1873 | George Nash |
| September 1873-Oct 1880 | Joseph Mallard |
| October 1880-Nov 1888 | John Warwick |
| November 1888-Jan 1889 | Richard Hall Bartlett |
| January 1889-Jul 1890 | Charles Baker |
| July 1890-Oct 1890 | William Wilks |

| | |
|---|---|
| October 1890-Jan 1892 | John James Richard Pearson |
| January 1892-Aug 1892 | William Henry Hulbert |
| August 1892-Jun 1894 | William Bradford |
| June 1894-Apr 1900 | William Henry Hulbert |
| April 1900-Mar 1902 | Henry Keen |
| March 1902-Dec 1906 | William Kilpack |
| December 1906-Jun 1908 | Francis Begley |
| June 1908-28 | James Paskett |
| 1928-Aug 1932 | Walter Atkins |
| August 1932-May 1933 | William Mason |
| May 1933-Feb 1938 | Goodman Henry 'Val' Clark |
| February 1938-Sep 1947 | William James Waring |
| September 1947-Apr 1963 | Sidney Robert Graves |
| 5th April 1963 | Licence not renewed - Closed for business |

*In 1878, the first steps were taken in Leamington to impart conservative principles to the working classes. Early in 1879, a banquet was held by the Leamington Conservative Working Men's Club at the Rose and Crown Inn. The reason for the venue is clear – Mr. Joseph Mallard one of the original members was the landlord.*

In 1888 the headquarters of the Carpenters and Joiners Society was surprisingly not the Joiners Arms or the Carpenters Arms, but the Rose and Crown.

*The Leamington Spa Courier dated 18th March 1893 reported the following: William Bradford, the landlord of the Rose and Crown Inn, Kenilworth Street, and Edward Thomas Bellamy of 12, Oxford Street were summoned for furious driving on March 2nd. John Wright stated that about quarter past seven he was coming out of his garden gate on the Lillington Road, carrying a bag of potatoes, when he saw two traps driven abreast coming past at a very rapid rate. He thought the drivers were racing, and he had a narrow escape from being run over. He had to jump out of the way to avoid being run over. He thought the horses were going at the rate of 13 or 14 miles per hour. Robert Summers said he was standing with a policeman at the corner of Lillington Avenue when two traps rushed past, going at a pace of 12 or 14 miles an hour. The officer sprang forward to stop them, and one of the drivers slackened his horse, but the other continued at the same rapid pace. The policeman gave his statement, the defendant's gave their defence and the bench decided to dismiss both cases, but ordered Bradford to pay the costs of 4s.6d.*

The Leamington Spa Courier date 8th February 1963 reported that: A man, who had his first drink in the Rose and Crown, Kenilworth Street, will pull his last pint there on 5th April when it closes. He is Sydney Graves who has been the licensee there for 15 years [since Mr. William Waring left]. The Rose and Crown is believed to have been a coaching inn more than 100 years ago. Up until two years ago, Mr. Graves used to run a boxing gymnasium upstairs and before that there was a skittle alley. Mr. Graves is undecided about his future, but he may go back to engineering when the Rose and Crown closes its doors for good.

**Royal** – Kenilworth Road
See Guys Hotel for details.

**Royal Exchange** – 2 High Street
In 1837, James Tennant moved into 2, High Street as a resident and in 1865 he opened his home as a beer house and named it the Royal Exchange. In June 1869 James was granted a 'foreign wine' licence. Following an application by owners Bass, Ratcliff and Gretton Ltd [Burton-on-Trent], a full licence was granted on 8th February 1950 and confirmed on 23rd March. In 1972 one of the bars was fitted-out to resemble the interior of a steam train carriage and was named the Great Western lounge. The décor included luggage racks over the seats and railway themed paintings by Terence Cuneo; the first pint was pulled by railway guard Jack Cowperthwaite.

In 1996 the Royal Exchange underwent an extensive refurbishment, reopening at 5.00pm on Saturday 20th July. However, in 2008 the pub was closed and boarded-up for what would be almost two years; it reopened as the Exchange on Saturday 6th February 2010. The Exchange closed for business again in March 2013 and, almost immediately, work started on gutting the bar of its fixtures and fittings. In the October new signage was installed and the newly named Under Graduate, a bar/bistro, opened on 10th October, 2013, seemingly to attract the occupants of the student accommodation recently built nearby.

*Above left: The Royal Exchange in 1987 taken by Bill Bigley. Above right: The Exchange taken on 20th August 2010 © Allan Jennings.*

| | |
|---|---|
| 1865-87 | James Tennant |
| 1887-Mar 1897 | Mrs. Diolatta Tennant |
| March 1897-Feb 1899 | James Syme McGregor |
| February 1899-Dec 1905 | William Mann |
| December 1905-Apr 1909 | Walter Bratt |
| April 1909-29 | Mrs. Annie Maria Purser |

| | |
|---|---|
| 1929-Sep 1936 | Alfred and Alice Tutchings *(Alfred died 23rd February 1936, aged 48)* |
| September 1936-Sep 1949 | Frank Green |
| September 1949-Jul 1951 | Harold Leslie Ward |
| July 1951-May 1955 | Cyril Charles Bicknell |
| May 1955-Oct 1960 | John Clement Sims |
| October 1960-Oct 1963 | George Reginald Perce Hamerton |
| October 1963-Apr 1964 | Alfred James Roberts |
| April 1964-Jun 1965 | Graham William Knibbs |
| June 1965-Jun 1967 | John O'Donnell |
| June 1967-Apr 1970 | David William Jones |
| April 1970-Jul 1970 | Patrick John Blake |
| July 1970-Sep 1971 | Harvey Perch |
| September 1971-Jul 1973 | Raymond Anthony Hoare |
| July 1973-Dec 1975 | Andrew 'Andy' Paul Dominic Kinsella |
| December 1975-Nov 1992 | Richard 'Dick' Power *(Died 14th June 1982)* and his wife Cissie *(Previously at the Sun in Splendour)* |
| November 1992 | John *(Of Oxford – surname not known)* |
| Circa July 1995 | Closed and 'For Sale' |
| 20th July 1996 | Reopened |
| July 1996-97 | Daniel Meagham and Debbie Buckley *(neé Cleary) (Daniel, known as Donal, originally from Cork City)* |
| April 2001 | Chris Kelly |
| September 2005-Mar 2006 | Deborah Dixon |
| March 2006-Sep 2007 | Tamara Jane Byrne |
| September 2007-2008 | Rebecca Raven |
| 2008 | Royal Exchange was closed |
| 6th February 2010 | Reopened as the Exchange |
| 6th Feb 2010-Dec 2011 | Stuart Ryan |
| December 2011-Mar 2013 | Kyle Byrne |

Courtesy of Terry Gardner, we have a photocopy of what looks to be a small flyer that would have been handed out to customers circa 1955-60; unfortunately there is no date on it. On the back are two poems:

> The ancients of old
> drank water so cold,
> soon perished and faded away;
> The locals round here
> drink Bass' beer
> and flourish like flowers in May.

**THE PICKLED FEW**
The horse and mule live 30 years,
and know nothing of wines and beers.
The goat and sheep at 20 die,
and never taste of scotch or rye.
The cow drinks water by the ton,
and at 18 years is mostly done.
The dog at 15 cashes in,
without the aid of rum and gin.
The cat on milk and water soaks,
and then in 12 short years he croaks.
The modest, sober, bone-dry hen,
lays eggs for nogs, then dies at ten.
All animals are strictly dry,
they sinless live, and swiftly die.
But sinful, ginful, rum-soaked men,
survive for three score years and ten.
And some of us, the mighty few,
stay pickled 'till we're ninety-two.
So visit – the Royal Exchange every day,
And Drink Old Age and Cares Away.

### *Memories of an Amused Customer - by Tom Lewin*

*The motto of a pub landlord is 'always be prepared', but he wasn't in this case. The pub in question was the Royal Exchange in High Street. The year approx 2003 and it is a usual Sunday lunch time with some 20 or so regulars. Chris Kelly the then landlord decided to pop out for some shopping, leaving the pub in the capable hands of one of the customers, Richard Gibbs, who did have some bar experience.*

*Arriving at platform 2 at Leamington Spa station was a trainspotter's special who had an hour to spend before moving onward. Some 40 avid thirsty trainspotters decided on the Royal Exchange for a swift pint to the sheer horror of Richard. He coped manfully until exhausted, and all but collapsed behind the bar. The trainspotters went on their way only for Chris Kelly to arrive back at the pub and wonder what all the fuss had been about.*

### Royal Horse – Poseidon Way, Warwick

The Royal Horse pub at Heathcote opened at 11.00am on Monday 6th May 2013. However, as its official postal address is Poseidon Way, Warwick, CV34 6SW it does not qualify for an entry in this book.

## [Copps'] Royal Hotel – High Street

This imposing hotel was located on the eastern corner of the London Road [High Street] and Clemens Street. From the corner, the hotel extended along High Street to Court Street and, on the Clemens Street side, it extended from the corner to the entrance of Colledge's blacksmith shop, the latter being next door to the Apollo Rooms situated on the corner of Union Walk from 1825 [and renamed the Great Western Inn in 1860].

In 1793 Thomas Sinker acquired the old Dog Inn on the London Road [High Street] from William Abbotts, who had moved to the newly built New Inn in Lillington Lane [corner of Spencer and Bath Streets]. Sinker renamed the inn Sinker's Boarding House and, according to George Morley's account of 'The History of Royal Leamington Spa' [1887-89], it was later renamed the Greyhound; notwithstanding, many locals [and historians] continued to refer to the ancient inn as the Dog Inn or the 'Dog'. In 1812 Sinkers Boarding House/Greyhound was for sale and in

*Copps' Royal Hotel High Street courtesy of Leamington Spa Art Gallery & Museum [Warwick District Council] Ref: LEAMG:M3732.1993.2(69/18735).*

*Copps Royal Hotel High Street courtesy of Leamington Spa Art Gallery & Museum [Warwick District Council] Ref: LEAMG:A677.1979(64/24169).*

1813 it was purchased by Michael Copps. In 'Glimpses of Our Local Past' [1895] J. C. Manning references Pratt's 1813 guide and notes that "the long established hotel of Sinker, in the Old Town, is being enlarged, beautified and improved by Mr. Copps, who now carries it on, with Fisher's house adjoining". In 1814 Copps purchased the adjacent Fisher's Balcony Boarding House [which briefly became the Oxford Boarding House/Hotel] and by 1816 both premises had been renamed the Copps' Royal Hotel.

Manning describes Copps' Royal Hotel as it was in 1817: "On the opposite corner [of Clemens Street] was Copps' Boarding House – an extensive range, most irregular and with no uniformity. This extensive range was, indeed, a motley group of architectural as well as historical incongruities. At one extremity – the eastern – was the old Dog Inn, modernised a little, but still retaining its quaint, old world characteristics. Over the door was inscribed 'Coffee Room'. Next to this – going westerly – was a more recent erection, with balcony and bow window, towering high and aggressively above the ancient inn, with the legendary 'Copps' over its hospitable portico; and then followed what looked like a stretch of glorified stables – long, low-pitched and mean looking – with skylights in the roof, small lattices, and one little bow-window at the end. Beyond this was a block of two houses, four or five stories high; modern balconies ran along the front. The range of buildings altogether extended from Clemens Street to what was afterwards known as Court Street."

Demand was such that the hotel was rebuilt in 1827 [to an 1825 design by Peter Frederick Robinson] and, according to T. B. Dudley in his book 'A Complete History of Royal Leamington Spa' [1901], the foundation stone was laid on 13th November 1826 by Miss Maria Copps, daughter of the proprietor. Erected at the west end of the ancient Dog Inn, with one hundred beds and stabling for fifty horses and forty carriages, it was reputedly one of the largest hotels in Europe at the time.

In the book 'Royal Leamington Spa – A Century's Growth and Development' H. G. Clarke informs us that: "The hotel front, cased in Roman cement, was of the Grecian order of architecture and 111 feet in length. It stood four storeys high and had fifty windows facing High Street, the entrance being particularly imposing as it formed a complete centre-piece from the ground to the roof, upon which was embellished the words Royal Hotel. Level with the second floor, an ornamental balcony ran the entire length of the edifice and the wings, which were slightly projected, and were adorned with handsome pilasters. These extended to the base of the four storeys and supported an entablature which ran from end to end of the frontage."

Meanwhile, *Moncrieff's Guide* of 1829 enlightens us on some of the internal features: "The entrance hall, which is 44 ft long x 14 ft wide, is lighted by a beautiful window of coloured glass, in the centre of which, on a fawn coloured mosaic ground, are the Royal Arms, richly emblazoned and surrounded by an ornamental gold scroll on a purple ground, containing medallions representing the principal views in the vicinity; the sideboards are supported and adorned by appropriate Grecian ornaments. On the right is the public dining room, upwards of 50 ft x 24 ft, the ceiling being supported by pillars and pilasters of the ionic order. A geometrical staircase of 21 steps conducts you to the public drawing room of the same noble dimensions as the dining room; on the same floor are a number of private sitting rooms, papered with rich French paper of vivid colouring, representing subjects classical, mythological, etc. The bedrooms are fitted up with every attention to comfort and convenience. Detached are extensive lock-up coach-houses, stabling, etc."

The Royal Hotel 'tap' [pub] was in Clemens Street and is listed as such from 1829 until 1841, although it quite possibly dates from the time of the Royal's rebuild in 1827. The hotel was also one of the locations in Leamington where coaches would arrive from/depart to, various towns and cities throughout country; in 1839 the schedule lists these as being Birmingham, Cheltenham, Coventry, Derby, Oxford, Rugby, Shrewsbury and Worcester.

The first indication that the 'Royal' was in financial trouble was when it was advertised for sale by auction in the Leamington Courier on 13th February 1841 and, although it was still being advertised 'for sale or let' in December 1842, it had certainly closed by June 1841. The hotel's effects were sold at the largest auction of its kind ever known in Leamington, beginning on Tuesday 8th June 1841 and lasting for twenty nine weekdays; the auctioneers were Messrs White and Son, 166, Parade. In August 1841 Michael's son, Thomas Michael Copps, announced that he had resigned from the Royal [High Street] and had opened a new hotel in Lansdowne Crescent, called the Copps' Hotel.

On 13th April 1844 the Leamington Spa Courier printed the following: "Philip Foxwell, Royal Hotel, Leamington, most respectfully begs to announce to the nobility, clergy, gentry, and public in general, that the above hotel is now opened for the reception of visitors, and solicits a share of their patronage and recommendation"; by May of the same year he was advertising as Foxwell's Royal Hotel. Meanwhile, on Wednesday 26th June 1844, the freehold property comprising the east wing of the Royal Hotel, together with the outbuildings, stabling and land attached, fronting to High Street was peremptorily sold pursuant to a decree of the High Court of Chancery.

Unfortunately, Philip Foxwell's venture at the 'Royal' was also unsuccessful for on 9th December 1845 there was a public auction on the premises to sell-off the household furniture and other effects. This was followed on Monday 15th December by another auction, this one by direction of the mortgagees under a power of sale: "The truly valuable and commodious leasehold hotel and premises, late in the occupation of Mr. Foxwell. This desirable property comprises the centre part of that noble building known as the Copps' Royal Hotel, and has a frontage of 70 feet or thereabouts to High Street, with a Grecian portico entrance into a splendid hall 30 feet in length and 13 feet in width, with a handsome stone staircase, stained window, and enriched ceiling. On the right is a noble dining room, 49 feet 4 inches in length, by 24 feet in breadth, with a drawing room the same size over. Also bar, coffee and smoke rooms, 4 sitting rooms, 17 chambers, water closets, capital cellaring, and culinary offices and pleasure gardens walled in, and fenced with iron palisades, with back entrance. Also two shops with a warehouse over fronting Clemens Street, and two tenements and a blacksmith's shop. The property is held under lease for the term of 99 years from Christmas 1810, subject to an annual ground rent of £33.13s."

Copps' Royal Hotel was demolished in May 1847 to build the bridge that would facilitate the extension of the railway line to Rugby. In his account of the 'History of Royal Leamington Spa' George Morley wrote, "The bridge was propelled over on Saturday 23rd September 1850; it comprised two wooden girders of 150 feet in length, 17 feet in depth, and 23 feet in width. The girders rested upon two massive piers of Derbyshire stone, of 25 feet in elevation, the buttresses being 139 feet 9 inches – a span then reportedly considered greater than any similar construction in the kingdom."

Michael Copps died in Guernsey on 3rd August 1849, aged 70.

**Footnote:** The plaque installed under the railway bridge at the bottom of Clemens Street states that it was originally the Balcony Boarding House in 1810, and that it was renamed the Copps' Royal Hotel in 1819. [This information is considered incorrect as the Copps' Royal Hotel is advertised in the 1816 edition of the Bisset Guide – Ed]

| | |
|---|---|
| 1813-41 | Michael Copps |
| 1844-45 | Philip Foxwell |

*In October 1835 the following appeared in the Leamington Courier:* **A foreigner's notion of injustice** *- A person, with a tremendous pair of ugly looking moustachios, and whiskers of the same fiery colour, who made frequent application to a snuff-box which he carried in his hand, complained to the magistrates that his luggage had been detained at Copps' coach-office because he would not pay a charge made upon him as a passenger, for the carriage of it to Leamington, from Birmingham. Col. Steward asked Mr. Copp's porter how much the luggage was charged upon the waybill? The porter answered half-a-crown, and that it weighed one hundred and twelve pounds. Col. Steward then informed the applicant that it was a strictly legal charge, and that he must pay it. The applicant, in broken English, complained that it was a great injustice that his baggage should be charged to that amount, as he had travelled from Dover to London, with the same quantity, without being charged. The applicant then retired.*

**Royal Hotel Tap** – Clemens Street
See Royal Hotel for details.

| | |
|---|---|
| 1829-30 | Alexander |
| 1830 | Alex Clements |
| 1834 | Name not listed |
| 1835 | Name not listed |
| 1838 | Clark |

**Royal Leamington Repository Inn** – 4 Russell Street
The first directory listing we have for this business is as the Leamington Mews in 1835 and, as it is not listed in the 1837 directory, we initially concluded that it closed in 1836. However, the Leamington Mews was included on the 1854 licensing session's list of publicans, with Robert Coates as the licensee. The only information we have found on the Royal Leamington Repository Inn is a sale notice that appeared in the Leamington Spa Courier in 1845, indicating that these premises were used for auction purposes; the sale notice, dated 5th April, states: "Freehold houses in Dale Street, Leamington, to be sold by auction, by Messrs White and Son, on Wednesday, the 9th day of April next, at Mr. Robert

Coates, Royal Leamington Repository Inn, Russell Street, Leamington, at three o'clock in the afternoon, by order of the trustee for sale...."

| 1835 | John Willson *(Or possibly Willison)* |
|------|---------------------------------------|
| 1845 | Robert Coates *(Royal Leamington Repository Inn)* |
| 1854 | Robert Coates *(Leamington Mews)* |

### Royal Oak – 37 Park Street

The first directory listing we have for the Royal Oak is in 1825. It was an 'alehouse' rather than a 'beer house' as the latter did not come into being until the Beer House Act of 1830; furthermore, it did not hold a spirits licence until one was granted at the annual licensing session in August 1878. When the pub was auctioned on 17th November 1831 the presale notice that appeared in the Leamington Spa Courier stated that: "The house is recently and substantially built, with good cellaring, kitchens, pantries, &c; a parlour and bar in the front; three excellent lodging rooms upstairs; a dining room [22 ft x 14 ft]; a large dining room [55 ft x 14 ft] over the kitchen at the back; three good attics; three good newly-built lock-up coach-houses, stabling for eight horses and a large and convenient yard. In total, it comprises a frontage of 13 yards by 35 yards." The Royal Oak closed in 1884 and was sold to the Salvation Army, after which the following items were auctioned, the brewing plant, bar fittings, furniture, malting plant, bar counter [13 ft 6 in] with mahogany top and panel front, six-pull beer machine, sign and lamp.

The Salvation Army, persecuted by the authorities as soon as it marched into Leamington on 6th April 1879, held services initially in the Public Hall, then in a large room in Packington Place and subsequently at the Victoria Pavilion [a circus building]; the founder of the Leamington corps, Captain Maycock, preached a farewell sermon there in 1880. Some sources say that the 'Circus' was the army's headquarters for a while and this seems likely from 1883, when it was reported to be bitterly divided over money. Apparently there was £5,000 available, mostly from a bequest made expressly for purchasing the 'Circus' or, alternatively for erecting a chapel or meeting house. Evidently members must have agreed that the 'Circus' was not a good long-term investment for in January 1884 they bought the Royal Oak, demolished it, and built an imposing new barracks. Known as the 'Citadel', it cost £3,370 [including the cost of

*This sketch of the Royal Oak originated in the Salvation Army publication 'War Cry'. It was sourced from the Salvation Army International Heritage Centre and provided by Leanne Wallis and Ray Oakley [Salvation Army].*

the site], was designed by Edmund Sherwood and opened on 25th June 1885. It was demolished in November 1984, ahead of the Royal Priors shopping centre development. [Courtesy of Robin Stott – Leamington History Group and Leanne Wallis & Ray Oakley – Salvation Army]

| | |
|---|---|
| 1825-32 | John Mills |
| 1833 | T. Pearce |
| 1833-Jun 1848 | George Finney |
| June 1848-Jul 1855 | John Robinson |
| July 1855-Oct 1863 | William Bull |
| October 1863-66 | Henry Haynes *(Also listed as an auctioneer, valuer, and wine and spirit merchant)* |
| 1866-January 1868 | Alfred Haynes |
| January 1868-Oct 1869 | John Astill *(John died on 9th October 1869 and his wife Emma married Joseph Ballard in 1870. Both John and Emma were born in Wolvey, Warwickshire. Emma died in 1874)* |
| November 1869-Nov 1870 | Emma Astill |
| November 1870-74 | Joseph James Ballard |
| 1874-Jul 1874 | Alfred Haynes |
| July 1874-Jul 1876 | Charles Henry Sprenger |
| July 1876 | Alfred Haynes |
| August 1876-Jan 1880 | James Green |
| January 1880-Sep 1880 | Frederick George Hillier |
| September 1880-Mid Oct | George Carter *(Managed by William Pegg)* |
| Mid October 1880 | Closed *(Licence not renewed by magistrates)* |
| August 1881-82 | Alfred Haynes |
| 1882-September 1883 | Patrick James McDonnell |
| September 1883-1884 | Alfred Haynes |
| 1884 | Closed for business |

**Rugby Arms** – Guys Cliffe Road
The first directory listing is in 1875. As it is listed in 1879 but not in 1880, or later directories, we have concluded that it closed in 1879-80.

| | |
|---|---|
| 1875-79 | G. Sewell |

**Rugby Tavern** – 43 Rugby Road, Cubbington
Unfortunately, early historical data for this pub is somewhat sporadic as, due to its location, it is not listed in many of the resources available for research [the first directory listing is not until 1860]. However, our first reference point is in 1839 when an auction of properties and land was held at the Rugby Tavern. Circa 1900 it was addressed as 51, Rugby Road and owned by Lucas and Co. Ltd [Leamington Brewery]; it would become an Ansells pub

following their 1928 acquisition of the brewery and its closure in 1934.

The 'old' Rugby Tavern closed for business on 3rd July 1935 and on the following day the 'new' Rugby Tavern opened on its current site at 43, Rugby Road. On Friday 3rd November 1967, Ansells opened its new Steak Bar with its "Tudor décor, soft lights and sweet music". The Tap Room, which was phase one of a new bar development program, opened on 20th December 1986; out went the video machine and juke-box and in came the Ansells traditional mild and bitter on hand pumps. Phase two saw Ansells spend £190,000 on the carvery pub restaurant that could cater for up to seventy people; it opened in March 1987. On 2nd December 1988 the Leamington Spa Courier reported that, "In November 1988 the Rugby Tavern underwent a £65,000 refurbishment and reopened as one of the Porterhouse national chain restaurants, which is part of Allied Breweries; the re-fit saw an expansion of the Tavern's carvery into a 96 seat restaurant."

In August 1998 permission was granted to extend and convert the premises into a 'Big Steak Pub' which would have capacity for almost 200 diners. By November 2002 the Leamington Courier was reporting that the pub was about to re-open as an "all-day family feast pub" following a £250,000 refit, and that "there are some totally new concepts including a chill-out zone for

*The original Rugby Tavern circa early 1900s.*

*Above: This photo was taken in 1935 at the time of the Silver Jubilee of King George V. The man in the photo is likely to be the landlord Arthur Sydney Savage, and the car is a 1935 Ascot 12 HP. Photo courtesy of Terry Gardner. Below: Photo of the Rugby Tavern courtesy of Nick Wilkins.*

teenage children complete with squashy sofas and games consoles; there will be a separate bar for those who fancy a quiet drink and there will be barbeques and pot roasts". In 2010 the Rugby Tavern was owned by the Punch Pub Co. Burton-on-Trent, Staffordshire. On 13th June 2011 it closed for yet another refurbishment, this one costing £300,000, and reopened as a Flaming Grill food pub on Friday 15th July. The Rugby Tavern remains open in December 2013.

| | |
|---|---|
| ≤1839 | William Eales |
| 1841-Feb 1851 | Joseph Soden |
| February 1851-Aug 1854 | Maria Soden *(On the death of Joseph)* |
| August 1854-Sep 1857 | William Henry Hawkins |
| September 1857-Oct 1859 | Thomas Adams |
| October 1859-May 1864 | Thomas Dunn |
| May 1864-68 | John Wootton |
| 1868-Jun 1879 | Samuel Ward |
| June 1879-Dec 1885 | Henry Townsend |
| December 1885-Sep 1888 | John Baker *(Of Long Itchington)* |
| September 1888-90 | John Kimberley |
| 1890-June 1890 | Morton Peto Lucas/Leamington Brewery |
| June 1890-Jan 1892 | Joseph Archer |
| January 1892-Oct 1893 | George William Tubb |
| October 1893-Dec 1912 | William King |
| Dec 1912-Feb 1934 | Levi Ernest Russell *(Proprietor)* |
| February 1934-Mar 1935 | George Sparkes |
| March 1935-May 1953 | Arthur Sydney Savage *(Went on to the Hope and Anchor)* |
| May 1953-Mar 1955 | Charles Bissonnade Atkins |
| March 1955-Sep 1956 | William Arthur Cecil West |
| September 1956-Feb 1962 | Aubrey Harding Thomas |
| February 1962-Sep 1963 | James Arthur Green |
| September 1963-Oct 1966 | Alan George Franks |
| October 1966-Oct 1968 | Pero Felice Cavagnetto |
| October 1968-Dec 1970 | Walter Victor Hartley Teare |
| December 1970-Jan 1974 | Martin Roger Glassy |
| January 1974-75 | Terence John 'Ted' and Joyce Collins *(Went on to the Wheatsheaf)* |
| 1975-Sep 1977 | Eric William Brassey and his wife Ruby *(Previously at the Woodland; Eric died 21st Sept 1977, aged 54)* |
| September 1977-≥1978 | Ruby Brassey *(On the death of Eric)* |
| Circa 1978-≥Oct 1984 | Ruby and Dennis Simons |
| 1987 | David and Anne Parkes |
| 1988 | Keith Wall *(General manager)* and his wife Cathy Wall *(manageress - Allied Breweries)* |

| 1991-92 | Chris and Ann Green |
|---|---|
| 2002 | Gail Haynes |
| November 2002 | Frank and Irene Ennis |
| ≤2006 | Michelle Finney |
| January 2007-Nov 2008 | Sally Anne Hammond |
| November 2008-Jan 2010 | Kevin Damion O'Reilly |
| Jan 2010-May 2012 | David and Claire Lonsdale *(General managers)* |
| May 2012-Sep 2012 | Amanda Jane Peters |
| September 2012 → | David Richard Hurcombe |

*In 1972-73, the Rugby Tavern was one of fifty Ansells steak bars in the Midlands that changed their name to Cavalier Steak Bars. From 31st January until 3rd February 1975 an eight ton, 28 foot long Hurricane locomotive from the Romney, Hythe and Dymchurch light railway could be seen in the car-park. It was there as part of a 500 mile event sponsored by Ind Coope and Ansells.*

The Leamington Courier dated 8th October 1976 advertised jazz on Sunday evenings at 8.00pm at the Rugby Tavern. Admission was free and the regular musicians included Johnny Morrison, trombone; Stan Rawlings, piano; Frank Racebrook, trumpet; Alan Grimley, guitar; Ray Evans, string bass and Ralph Patterson, drums.

*The Leamington Spa Courier dated 23rd September 1977 reported: Local landlords were shocked by the death this week of Mr. Eric Brassey, licensee of the Rugby Tavern, Cubbington. Fifty-four-year-old Mr. Brassey died on Wednesday in the Warneford Hospital; it is believed the cause of death to have been a brain haemorrhage. Mr. Bill McCarthy, landlord of the Jack and Jill, and chairman of the Leamington branch of the National Association of Licensed House Managers, said yesterday, "He was a very respected member of our union and of the trade locally." Mr. McCarthy knew his colleague well and often stood in at the Rugby Tavern in Mr. Brassey's absence. Mr. Brassey leaves a widow and three children.*

On 7th July 1978 Ansells announced the opening of their new Arnold Lounge at the Rugby Tavern which complemented the Tom Brown Lounge which had been open since at least January 1976. The connection is the well known novel Tom Brown's Schooldays and the Arnold Lounge was named after the school's famous headmaster.

*On 18th April 2002, eight fire engines and 40-50 fire-fighters tackled a blaze at the Rugby Tavern which caused £400,000 of damage. The fire, which was caused by an upstairs electrical fault, broke out in the roof just before 9.00am. The two storey building was badly damaged but nobody was in at the time; about 70% of the roof was destroyed. The bedrooms and living quarters, built into the roof space, were severely damaged and the bar was badly affected by smoke and water. Divisional Fire Safety Officer Steve Haynes is the husband of landlady Gail Haynes. He said, "This proves that fire has no discrimination about who you are, it can affect anybody at any time." [Sourced from local press reports of the time]*

**Saint Bar** – 40 Warwick Street
See Alastairs for details.

**Sausage** – 141 Regent Street
See Warwick Arms for details.

**Sawyers Arms** – Milverton
The only directory listing we have is in 1837. As it is not listed in the 1835 directory, or post 1837, we have concluded that it was yet another short-lived beer house and that it closed circa 1838.

**Shadbolts** – 66 Clemens Street
See Reindeer for information.

**Shakespeare** – Tavistock Street
It was good to see a new pub opening in the town, albeit during a period when many were struggling for survival; it opened in mid March 2010 and was just three doors down from the Tavistock [towards Warwick Street]. However on 12th January 2012 its future became uncertain when Mood Bars [UK] Ltd who own the Shakespeare, TJ's [Bath Street] and KoKo's Bar [Warwick Street], entered into administration. By mid-year the Shakespeare was closed and, following a substantial rework of the corner premises that included KoKo's, the space was incorporated into the new venue Altoria, which opened in October 2012.

*The Shakespeare taken on 3rd April 2010 © Allan Jennings.*

March 2010-Jan 2012       Gurcharn 'Gursh' Singh Atwal
January 2012              Katherine Kiernan

**Shakespeare Inn** – 2 George Street
In August 1881, Mrs. Jane Franklin applied for a wine licence to compliment the beer house licence that she had apparently held since 1853; the application was refused but it establishes our earliest reference point as 1853. The first directory listing we have is in 1874 when it was addressed as 1, George Street. We have concluded that these premises were a beer house/ale and porter stores from 1853 until circa 1912, when William Creelman is listed as licensee of the Shakespeare at 2, George Street [the Shakespeare would intermittently also be listed as ale and porter stores until 1919]. On application in March 1926 the licensee, Mrs. Jane Creelman, was granted a wine licence; the Shakespeare Inn was granted a full on-licence in February 1948.

It was owned by Flower and Sons Ltd [Stratford-upon-Avon] who were taken over by J. W. Green Ltd and renamed Flowers Breweries Ltd in 1954, before being absorbed by Whitbread and Co. Ltd in 1962. On 17th January 1969 the Shakespeare was acquired by

*Above left: Photo of the Shakespeare Inn courtesy of Nick Wilkins. Above right: The Town House taken on the 11th August 2004 by John Hartnup.*

Ansells Brewery Ltd but it would subsequently revert to a Whitbread-Flowers pub. When, in June 1986, the Shakespeare's lounge was gutted by fire, Whitbread-Flowers and tenants Bill and Ada Robertson took the opportunity to refurbish and upgrade the facilities at a cost exceeding £24,000; the lounge reopened on Friday 28th August and as a thank you for their customers' patience Flowers Original bitter was sold for just 50p a pint. On 1st October 1992 there was a grand reopening following an internal and external refurbishment. A satellite TV had been installed in the back room [to go with the already present dart board, gaming machine and quiz machine] and there was a beer garden; on tap there was Flowers Original, Flowers IPA, Boddingtons, Guinness, three lagers and cider, and there was live music on Sunday nights.

In September 1995, it was reported that, "A traditional atmosphere is on offer at Leamington's newest [renamed] pub, the Town House. Situated in George Street, the pub's interior is reminiscent of a Victorian town house with bric-a-brac and old pictures lining the walls, creating the feel of Leamington's 'old town'. The Town House is tied to the Whitbread Pub Partnership and offers a range of cask ales including Flowers, Boddingtons and Marston Pedigree." From 1999 it was known as the Green Tailed Dragon and in 2001 it became the Town House Tavern, which it still is in December 2013.

| | |
|---|---|
| 1853-1881 | Mrs. Jane Franklin *(Beer house)* |
| 1874-93 | James Franklin *(Ale and Porter Stores)* |
| 1877-95 | H. Franklin *(Ale and Porter Stores)* |
| 1895 | George J. Franklin *(Ale and Porter Stores)* |
| 1898-Feb 1911 | Mrs. M. Wilks *(Ale and Porter Stores)* |
| February 1911-Jan 1912 | Robert Jeffrey *(Ale and Porter Stores)* |
| January 1912-22 | James and William Creelman |

| | |
|---|---|
| 1924-Aug 1935 | Mrs. Jane Creelman |
| August 1935-Feb 1944 | Eric Joseph Francis Flynn |
| February 1944-Feb 1955 | Ivor Morgan Davies |
| February 1955-Jun 1959 | Gordon Frederick Wilson |
| June 1959-Jun 1960 | Alexander Wilson Dawson |
| June 1960-Oct 1966 | Peter Philip Horne |
| October 1966-Dec 1967 | William Barron |
| December 1967-Feb 1968 | James Thomas Byram |
| February 1968-Jun 1968 | David T. Wolton |
| June 1968-Apr 1969 | Clive Granville Jones |
| April 1969-Oct 1969 | John Philip Coppin |
| October 1969-Mar 1972 | Francis James Bromwich |
| March 1972-Jul 1973 | George Albert Cotterill |
| July 1973-Mar 1977 | Abdel Majid Ghaffar |
| March 1977 | Dennis Frogatt |
| 1984 | Winston 'Win' Cleaver and his wife Valerie ['Val'] |
| | (*Went on to the Great Western, Warwick*) |
| 1984-≥1989 | William 'Bill' Robertson and his wife Ada |
| January 1992 | Roy Scarrett |
| 1992 | Jackie and David Reynolds |
| 1994 | Graham and Clare Humphrey |
| 1995 | Lee Holden |
| January 1999 | Town House closed |
| 2004 | Manjit Chima |
| 2005-Aug 2007 | Kevin John Gallagher |
| August 2007-Sep 2007 | Andrew Mark Junakos |
| September 2007-Dec 2007 | Christopher John Wade |
| December 2007-Nov 2008 | Lesley Jayne Rogerson |
| November 2008-Dec 2008 | Susan Maindonald |
| December 2008-Mar 2010 | Stuart Ryan |
| March 2010-Sep 2012 | Andrew Murray |
| September 2012 → | Matthew Meaney |

*The Leamington Spa Courier dated 19th October 1973 reported:* **Buffaloes raise £130 for charity – A familiar face pulls a pint** *– Maurice Parsons, better known as Wilf Harvey in the ITV series, Crossroads, visited Leamington last Friday to appear at a charity concert at the meeting hall of Mid-Avon Buffaloes, George Street, Leamington. The concert, which also featured Albert Shepherd [Don Rodgers in Crossroads], was organised by the United Artists charity organisation, of which Maurice Parsons is the honorary president. Mr. D. Stanford, the Buffaloes' entertainments secretary, said that the evening raised £130 towards a £3,000 mini-coach for the Earl Shilton home in Leicestershire - a home for the crippled elderly. For readers who think they would recognise a television personality in the street, a point of interest, Maurice Parsons sat in the Shakespeare Inn, George Street, for 45 minutes, unrecognised, before his surprise appearance at the concert.*

In January 1999, Peter Ogden-Jones of the Warwick, Leamington and Kenilworth Licensed Victuallers Association told the Coventry Evening Telegraph that the Town House had closed. He added that, "The Christmas and New Year trade was pretty good but running a pub is a 24 hours a day, seven days a week job and many landlords I know are facing a squeeze. Breweries have only themselves to blame, leases are over-priced and many people they were tempting into the trade had little or no experience."

### Shakespeare Inn / Tavern – 12 Regent Street
The address of these premises was originally Cross Street [New Town] which was laid out circa 1808-1814; circa 1827 it was renamed Regent Street in honour of the Prince Regent who had visited Leamington in September 1819 [as was the Regent Hotel]. The first reference we have to the Shakespeare [sometimes spelt Shakspeare or Shakspere] is an 1827 entry in the licensed victuallers' records, which lists Robert Evans as the licensee. The same source in 1828 lists it as the Shakespeare Tavern [it has also been known as the Shakespeare Commercial Inn and the Shakespeare Inn and Commercial Hotel]; at this time it would've been termed an alehouse.

An auction notice listed in the Leamington Spa Courier dated 27th March 1830, described the Shakespeare Tavern thus: "The premises are all brick-built and are exceedingly commodious, and well calculated for carrying on a considerable trade. They consist of ten bed chambers, and patent water-closet; drawing room on the first floor, with sitting room adjoining; a large dining room sufficient for forty persons; a good sitting room on the ground floor, used as a commercial room; an enclosed bar where a considerable retail trade may be carried on without interfering with the other parts of the house; a private sitting room near adjoining; a smoking parlour and a large well-frequented tap room, with entrance from the yard. The kitchen, larder, &c. are in the basement, and are very commodious. The wine cellar is capable of holding twenty pipes of wine and there are large spirit and beer cellars adjoining. There is a paved yard with separate entrance thereto from the street. In the rear are an excellent brick-built four-stall stable and store room, and a brew house with 140 gallon copper. It is

*A circa 1827 advert for the Shakspeare Commercial Inn.*

presumed that the premises are of the annual value of £150 at the least." On 7th September 1845, the licensee Samuel Johnson opened a new club room for use by the Loyal Shakespeare Lodge, M.U. of Oddfellows. A new publican's full on-licence was granted in June 1853 and it closed circa 1870.

**Footnote:** There is no evidence to suggest any business connection between 12, Regent Street [Shakespeare] and 10, Regent Street. However, from 1883 until 1919 there is either a beer retailer or the West End Ale Stores listed at number '10'.

| | |
|---|---|
| 1827-30 | Robert Evans |
| 1830-32 | Richard Reading |
| 1832 | Mrs. Newman |
| 1832-33 | John Davis |
| 1833-34 | John Berry |
| 1834-35 | Abraham Denby |
| 1838 | Richard Russell Smith |
| 1839 | Hughes and Co. |
| 1841-Sep 1848 | Samuel Welton Johnson |
| September 1848-Apr 1853 | Charles Wharton Dodd (*Of London*) |
| April 1853-Apr 1854 | John Matthews |
| April 1854 | George Millard |
| 1868-70 | Robert Rose |
| 1870 | William Roadknight |

*In 1828 the Shakespeare Tavern was the venue for the annual meeting and dinner of the Leamington Priors Association for the Prosecution of Felons.*

By 10th July 1830 the new licensee was advertising: Shakespeare Inn, House-Warming Dinner. Richard Reading respectfully informs his friends, and the public generally, that his house-warming will take place on Thursday, the 29th inst; on which occasion he earnestly solicits their support; tickets, one guinea each. Those gentlemen who intend honouring R. R. with their company are requested to leave word of their intention at the bar of the inn, on the Saturday previous. Dinner will be on the table at four o'clock precisely.

*The Leamington Spa Courier dated 8th April 1870 reported:* **The first local case under the new [1869] Beerhouse Act** *– William Roadknight, landlord of the Shakespeare beerhouse, Regent Street, was summoned for permitting drinking in his house after eleven o'clock at night, on the 30th ult. Inspector Waters visited the house at a quarter past eleven on the night in question and found two men sitting in the bar playing at dominoes and drinking ale. Superintendent Lund said that they'd had a great deal of trouble with the house since it had been transferred to Roadknight, who did not live at the house, worked at Rugby, and left the management of the house to a barmaid. He had been repeatedly cautioned. The defendant did not appear but was represented by his barmaid, a very smart young woman. The bench expressed an opinion that it was a very bad case and fined the defendant 40s. – This was the first case under the 1869 Beerhouse Act [32 and 33 Vic], the 15th sec. of which enacts, "If any* *person suffer beer or cider to be drunk in his house at any time during which the house ought by law to be closed, he shall be liable, on summary conviction, to a penalty not exceeding 40s for each offence."*

**Ship** – 14 Covent Garden Market
See Kings Head for details.

**Silver Jubilee** – 36 Satchwell Street
See Palace Inn for details.

**Sinker's Boarding House** – High Street
See Black Dog [High Street] and [Copps'] Royal Hotel for details.

**Sip Bar** – 56a Regent Street
The only information that we have on this bar is a photograph that was taken by John Hartnup in 2004 and its inclusion on a list of 'town centre pubs' from the same year. In 2013 the premises are a bakery and café.

*The Sip Bar taken by John Hartnup on 29th August 2004.*

**Slug and Lettuce** – 32 Clarendon Avenue
See Fox and Vivian for details.

**Slug and Lettuce** – 38-40 Warwick Street
According to a dated website review and a photograph, this Slug and Lettuce opened circa 2003 although planning application for illuminated signage was not submitted until 2005. It closed for business on Thursday 14th October 2010. On 17th August 2011, the premises licence was transferred from the Slug and Lettuce Co. Ltd to Stonegate Pub Co. Ltd and on 21st October 2011 it was transferred again to Gastro Inns Ltd.

*Above left: Photo of the Slug and Lettuce taken on 8th November 2008 © Allan Jennings.*
*Above right: The Glasshouse taken on 14th December 2011 © Allan Jennings.*

Following work by RDG Carpentry [specialists in refurbishments of bars and night clubs] these premises were reopened as the Glasshouse on 1st December 2011. In addition to the bar on the ground floor the building also contains 24 apartments. The current owners also have the Saint Bar next door although they are run as separate businesses. The Glasshouse remains open in December 2013.

**Footnote:** This Slug and Lettuce is not connected to, and should not be confused with, the Slug and Lettuce @ The Fox and Vivian [Clarendon Avenue].

| | |
|---|---|
| Circa 2003 | Opened |
| 2006 | Tariq Ricketts |
| April 2006-Aug 2007 | Timothy Paul Gibbins |
| 14th-22nd Aug 2007 | Lewis Allington |
| August 2007-Sep 2007 | Timothy Paul Gibbins |
| September 2007-Feb 2008 | Bruce Pullen |
| February 2008-Apr 2008 | Annabel Sara Goddard |
| April 2008-Jul 2010 | Timothy Sanders |
| July 2010-Aug 2010 | Emma Pugh |
| Aug 2010-Oct 2010 | Carl Hoggarth |
| 14th October 2010 | The Slug and Lettuce closed for business |
| 1st December 2011 | Reopened as the Glasshouse |
| 1st December 2011 → | George Marshall *(Licensee)* |

**Slug and Lettuce @ The Fox and Vivian** – 32 Clarendon Avenue
See Fox and Vivian for details.

**Somerville Arms** – 4 Campion Terrace
It is believed that the Somerville Arms was named after a Captain Somerville, a local magistrate, whose wife Lady Somerville laid the foundation stone for the Jephson Temple on 13th May 1848 [later opened on 29th May 1849]. Although we believe that this pub may have opened beforehand as a beer house, the first reference point we have is when Richard Luscombe was granted a 'new' licence at the annual licensing session in August 1864; the first directory listing we have is in 1866. Primarily listed as Queen Street until the 1890s, the pub is located on the corner of Campion Terrace and Queen Street. In 1885 the Somerville was part of the Leamington Brewery's tied estate when Lucas, Blackwell and Arkwright purchased the brewery for £75,000. By 1897 the new owners of the Leamington Brewery [and pub] were Lucas and Co. Ltd, but it would become an Ansells pub following their acquisition of the brewery in 1928, and its closure in 1934. A check of the pub's website revealed that "the pub at one time had a glass canopy at the front, which explains why it is now set back from the main building line", and, "its railings only survived the war because they were necessary to prevent people falling down the cellar drop".

In March 1954 the licensing justices agreed to extensive alterations in order "to improve the amenities for both the public and the licensee" and, "in 1956, two of the three rooms were knocked together to form a large front bar; the smoke room [lounge] was redesigned in 1973". In 1988, it was listed in the CAMRA Good Beer Guide and advertised as an Ansells pub selling traditional ales: Burton Ale, Ansells Best Bitter, Ansells Mild and Tetley Bitter – "Real ales for your health, you'll get no better". In 1995, it won the Campaign for Real Ale [CAMRA] 'Pub of the Year' award [Heart of Warwickshire branch] and in 1996 also celebrated its 19th consecutive year in the Good Beer Guide. In July 2009, the Somerville Arms became part of the Everards Brewery Estate and sold seven traditional hand-pulled cask conditioned ales, Everards Tiger Bitter, Everards Original Bitter, Everards Sunchaser, Everards Beacon Bitter and Adnams Bitter. The seasonal cask ale was Adnams Broadside and their guest cask ale Greene King IPA.

*The Somerville Arms taken on 8th January 2009 © Allan Jennings.*

At the end of September 2010 it underwent an £80,000 refurbishment, both inside and out; the work included the refit of the cellar, the installation of an oak floor and restoration of fireplaces and the bar in order to revitalise the Somerville's Victorian charm; although it never actually closed there was a 'reopening' on 4th October. It was the only Leamington pub included in the 2010 edition of the Good Beer Guide. In 2012 the Somerville Arms was the CAMRA 'Pub of the Year' for the second consecutive year and in December 2013 its website describes the pub as "a friendly Victorian local with a busy bar at the front and a cosy lounge at the back [each bar has its own drinking motto, *Real ale for your health* and *Abound in hops all ye who enter here*]". For more information, visit: www.somervillearms.co.uk/

| | |
|---|---|
| 1864-Jan 1871 | Richard Luscombe |
| January 1871-Mar 1872 | Edward Tomblin |
| March 1872-81 | Henry Dadley |
| 1881-Dec 1882 | Alfred Shepherd |
| December 1882-May 1883 | George Keene |
| May 1883-Jul 1883 | Messrs Lewis and Ridley/Leamington Brewery |
| July 1883-1912 | James Fletcher *(Died 13th May 1916)* |
| 1912-Jun 1933 | Charles Tew |
| June 1933-Nov 1937 | Walter John Arthur |
| November 1937-Jul 1953 | Archibald Payne Underwood *(Previously at the Hope and Anchor and Aylesford Arms)* |
| July 1953-Nov 1953 | Arthur Henry Swann |
| November 1953-Mar 1954 | Frank Tew |
| March 1954-Feb 1956 | Geoffrey Thomas Skelcher *(Died in 1971, aged 68)* |
| February 1956-May 1958 | John Alfred Charles Draper *(Went to the Walnut Tree)* |
| May 1958-Jun 1960 | Frederick Harry Watts |
| June 1960-Mar 1961 | Alfred John Bounds |
| March 1961-Feb 1966 | Reginald Thomas Sinnett |
| February 1966-Dec 1966 | Ralph James Shaw |
| December 1966-Jun 1968 | Raymond Edgar King |
| June 1968-Oct 1968 | Hugh Gerrard McGuire |
| October 1968-Jun 1969 | Thomas Alexander Green |
| June 1969-1999 | John Calloway Chater and wife Barbara *(An ex-police officer in Rugby)* |
| 1999-Apr 2003 | Andy Sabin |
| April 2003 → | Paul Blatchly |

*The Leamington Spa Courier dated 31st July 1953 reported that: Mr. Archibald P. Underwood, licensee of the Somerville Arms, Campion Terrace, Leamington, for the past 16 years, retired on Monday. Mr. Underwood was formerly licensee of the Hope and Anchor Inn, Hill Street, for ten years and prior to that was manager of the Aylesford Arms, Bedford Street, popularly known as the 'Hole in the Wall', for four years. In recent months Mr. Underwood has not been in good health. He hopes to spend his retirement quietly in Willes Road. His successor at the Somerville Arms is Mr. Arthur Henry Swan, a former groundsman at Stoneleigh Abbey. The transfer was approved by Leamington magistrates on Monday.*

In May 1974 a five strong team from the Somerville Arms won the final of the Ansells Pentathlon competition against the Gladiator pub from Kings Norton, Birmingham. They took part in ladies' and gents' darts, dominoes, crib and 1001 darts.

*The Leamington Spa Courier dated 28th October 1983 published the following letter: "Little protection for landlords - What other job requires the production of six personal references, a searching character examination by the police, and a bench of magistrates to be satisfied before an applicant is successful? The licensee then becomes subject to further examination by Customs and Excise, Weights and Measures, Health Department, Performing Rights Society, magistrates, police, etc, etc. All for what? To be treated as time wasting complainers who bring upon themselves violent personal abuse or verbal invective. Being the holder of a justices' on-licence is a matter of pride to me and my colleagues. My public house is a safe and pleasant place to be. My customers know they are under my protection. It is not the people who serve the drunks who get the problem. It is the licensee who refuses who gets the trouble. If we are considered worthy of a licence by the court, then we should be worthy of protection of the court. A stern look, a rebuke and a few hours community service is not going to prove anything. Any assault occasioning bodily harm or intended must receive a custodial sentence. Then perhaps licensees might feel that the law is on their side, and they are not abandoned to do alone what really is the duty of us all. [John Chater, Somerville Arms, Campion Terrace, Leamington]."*

### Memories of the Somerville Arms by Brenda Norris of Coventry
### 26th September 2011

"In June 1933 my grandfather, Walter Arthur was the licensee of the Somerville Arms. He and my grandmother Clara ran the pub until November 1937. It was very primitive when they first moved in. There was a bar, for men only, which had sawdust on the floor and spittoon! Then there was the smoke room where women were allowed as long as they were accompanied by a man. There was also a tap room which was for women only. My grandmother explained that the occupants were either widows, or in some cases women who had never married because of the great losses from the 1914/18 war. When I was visiting on a Friday or Saturday evening I would recite sentimental poetry to the ladies, and they would give me pocket money.

"The living quarters were equally old fashioned. In their living and dining room there was a huge black leaded range, with an oven at the side of the fire. Grandma made lovely cakes and tasty meals for us. Then there was the scullery which had a large sink, but no taps! Water was drawn up by a big hand pump, which my brother and I loved to work. Laundry was done in a big open heated water tub, and there was a heavy mangle with wooden rollers. Outside in the courtyard there were some outbuildings and toilets which my mother would not let me use. There was a bathroom upstairs in the house for our use. There was also a cellar which I only went down once; it was dark, damp and very scary. My brother loved to go down with our grand-dad. I loved helping him count the money before banking. This was pre-decimal coins of course and it was my job to pile up all the different coins - ½d; 1d [pennies], 3d and 6d pieces [joeys and tanners], 1 shilling pieces [a bob], Florins [two bob], and ½ crowns. Grandad dealt with the notes, then he would put the coins into separate paper bags and we would go to the bank, and afterwards enjoy a walk in the Jephson Gardens.

"Gradually of course everything was modernised. The sawdust and spittoons went, and the living quarters became very comfortable. The range went, making a nice sized dining-sitting room, and the scullery became a pleasant kitchen with a modern gas cooker, cupboards and a sink unit with taps! My brother was sad about that change - he loved to use the pump but it was so much easier for grandma.

"They retired in 1938 and moved to a small, new modern house in Yardley, Birmingham. This was on a direct Midland Red bus route from Coventry, so I was able to visit regularly. Grandad died before I was married, but grandma lived to be 96 and knew all of my four children. I am now 85, I live on my own, but 3 of my children and 4 grandchildren are not far away."

**Sozzled Sausage** – 141 Regent Street
See Warwick Arms for details.

**Spa Hotel** – Holly Walk
This hotel was granted a full licence on 2nd February 1943. We have not listed any further details as the licence carried a number of restrictions, a key one being that there could be no public bar.

**Spayce** – 7 Court Street
See Leopard Inn for details.

**Springfield Arms** – Springfield Street
See the Joiners Arms for details.

**St. Georges Road** [54]
A beer off-licence for these premises was granted to William Gurley in November 1875, but as it was reported that he already had a beer on-licence, it follows that a beer house was operating at this address prior to 1875 [it appears that the on-licence was terminated circa 1889]. A lease document dated 27th June 1906 shows that Gurley leased the premises to Mitchells and Butlers Ltd for 21 years, commencing 24th June 1908, at an annual rent of £25. The tenancy expired on 24th June 1929 and on 9th May 1930 the premises were sold to Thomas Henry Bishop for £1,225.

L. E. Taylor is listed as a beer retailer at number '54' in 1961, but in June 1962 the council approved a 'change of use to strictly residential' and in 1963 Taylor is just listed as the occupier. Allan and Tom remember these premises having an off-licence in the early 1960s, the exterior of the building was painted a light cream or pale yellow and the sign was a bright yellow. Circa 1964 these premises were a Radford Brewery 'staff house'. Most of St. Georges Road still exists in 2013 but, being on the corner, the small house at number '54' was consumed by the redevelopment of St. John's Road. The 'housing redevelopment scheme' commenced in August 1968 with Shrubland Street being the first phase, however the east side of St. John's Road and Scotland Place had already been demolished by then. Allan remembers playing in the derelict houses in St. John's Road around 1964 and his friend Dave Burnell remembers watching the new houses being built sometime after September 1968.

| | |
|---|---|
| ≤1875-Sep 1887 | William Gurley *(Beer house, gardener & grocer)* |
| September 1887-Dec 1889 | Ann Taylor *(Beer retailer)* |
| December 1889-Jul 1893 | William Davis *(Ale and Porter Store)* |
| July 1893-Jun 1908 | Mrs. Ellen Payne *(Ale and Porter Store)* |
| June 1908-Jul 1924 | Mrs. Harriett Harrison |
| July 1924-Apr 1930 | Mrs. Daisy M James *(Transferred from Mr. E. Harrison, executor of Mrs. Harrison)* |
| April 1930-36 | William Adkins |
| 1940 | England Arthur Wellesley |
| 1961 | L. E. Taylor |

**Stables Bar** – Newbold Terrace East, Newbold Comyn
See Newbold Comyn Arms for details.

**Stag and Pheasant** – 138 Warwick Street
The only information we have on this beer house are the directory entries listed below; we have concluded that it closed in the late 1850s.

| | |
|---|---|
| 1838-39 | George Rix |
| 1842-57 | Robert Hewitt |

*This 1852 map courtesy of Leamington Library shows where the Stag and Pheasant was situated on Warwick Street near to Clarendon Street.*

**Stamford and Warrington Arms** – 20 Rugby Road

The first directory listing we have is in 1833 when John Hanson is the licensee and the address is given as 'Binswood' [its address is listed as 20, Rugby Road from the early 1880s]. In June 1844 a 'to let' notice claimed that it was the oldest licensed house in New Milverton, describing it as "spacious, convenient and that it had recently been fitted out in the best manner for business; the house stands near the terminus of the new railway and may calculate upon having a fair share of public patronage when the same is opened". After being referred to the county compensation authority for closure the Stamford and Warrington Arms was closed on 25th January 1908, with compensation being paid. In 1910, these premises are listed as being occupied by a greengrocer [Charles Gibbs], and in April 1912 they are occupied by Mrs. Watkin, a fruiterer and greengrocer [by then addressed as 39, Rugby Road]. We understand that the premises subsequently became the Milverton Coffee House, probably immediately after the premises were auctioned in April 1912.

Following the pub's closure in 1908, and prior to the 1912 auction, the premises would've been modified to suit the change of business. However, the following extract from the auction notice [Leamington Spa Courier dated 19th April, 1912] serves to provide an insight into the make-up of the premises, which are described as comprising: "A sitting room with double doors dividing into two rooms, living room, kitchen and store room with

*This photograph which was taken in 1955 shows both the sites of the Stamford and Warrington Arms and the Masons Arms buildings. The Masons Arms was the small white building. The Stamford and Warrington Arms was the large white building with the lorry parked outside. Photo courtesy of Ron Ransford.*

entrance to spacious cellars and larder. On the first floor are four bedrooms and a water closet and on the attic floor are four other good bedrooms. The stabling and outbuildings are approached from the Rugby Road through double doors and are located in a large yard; they include a two-stall stable, blacksmith's forge, coach house with double doors and a large room over the foregoing, now occupied as a laundry and a water closet. At the rear of the property, and approached by a passage from the Rugby Road, are three brick built and slated cottages known as 1, 2, and 3 Jackson's buildings, each containing two living rooms and three bedrooms. The cottages stand on a large piece of ground, having gardens in front and at back with two wash-houses, water closets etc. The property has a frontage of 42 ft to Rugby Road, an average depth of 249 ft and comprises in whole, an area of 1,163 square yards or thereabouts."

**Footnote:** The Leamington Spa Courier dated 23rd October 2009 reported that Leamingtonian Nick Nichols believes that the Stamford and Warrington Arms went on to become a coffee tavern run by the temperance movement. He also believes that it remained open until circa 1959 and, apart from the beer kegs and pumps, retained most of its former trappings, even down to the metal bracket for the sign. "It was just like a pub inside. It had a pub counter and iron tables and a bench round the side. If you had put beer behind the bar it would have looked like a pub."

| | |
|---|---|
| 1833-38 | John Hanson |
| 1842-44 | James Boughey |
| 1845 | J. Heritage |
| 1849-Jun 1862 | William Townsend |
| June 1862-Jan 1875 | Thomas Ledbrooke |
| January 1875-86 | Thomas Kirby |
| 1886-Jun 1892 | Mrs. Eleanor Kirby |
| June 1892-Jul 1892 | Messrs Ind Coope and Co. |
| July 1892-Mar 1893 | Richard Lambert |
| March 1893-Dec 1893 | John Rush |
| December 1893-Jun 1894 | Charles Kemp *(Of Barford)* |
| June 1894-Aug 1895 | Alexander Arthur Leitzer |
| August 1895-Sep 1896 | Frederick Vincent Rowe *(Died 9th August, 1896)* |
| September 1896-Oct 1896 | Mrs. Frances Mary Rowe *(On the death of Frederick)* |
| October 1896-Jan 1897 | John Nutting |
| January 1897-Aug 1898 | Thomas Atkins |
| August 1898-Dec 1898 | Thomas Reeves |
| December 1898-Jul 1902 | George William Tubb |
| July 1902 | Charles Steane |
| 1903-Jan 1907 | Charles Steane and Joseph Freeman |
| January 1907-Jan 1908 | Frederick Hoggins |
| 25th January 1908 | Closed for business |

**Star and Garter** – 4-6 Warwick Street

According to local historian Lyndon Cave, the Star and Garter was established on the bank of the Binsbrook before the New Town was laid out in 1808. This is of particular significance because it not only makes it the oldest existing pub/hotel in Leamington but also the town's fourth earliest overall, after the original Black Dog Inn [London Road], original Bowling Green [Church Street], and original New Inn [Bath Street]. Cave then goes on to say that "in 1817 the inn was run by Tom Oliver a well known retired jockey and as a result it was frequented by the racing fraternity. When the new road and bridge over the brook were built in 1821 access to the racecourse in Warwick became easier."

The first reference we have to the Star and Garter is on 17th September 1831 when William Dixon Davis placed an advert in the Leamington Spa Courier, "respectfully informing his friends and the public that his house-warming dinner would take place on Thursday 22nd September". At that time the premises included a public dining room [29 ft x 14 ft] that was capable of seating 250 people, three parlours, two kitchens, bar, nine bedrooms, a brew house, stables, coach-houses and a malt house capable of wetting ten quarters of barley. Following the bankruptcies of the first two listed licensees, it was taken over by W. Hughes in 1836-37 who advertised the business as the Star Hotel; it would continue to be listed as a hotel until 1850. In its early years the address was listed as 49, Warwick Street and it would be the early 1890s before it was listed as number '4'. On 21st April 1952 a music licence was granted for the bar and the smoke room. Then owned by Marston, Thompson and Evershed Ltd [Albion Brewery, Burton-on-Trent], who were bought by Wolverhampton and Dudley Breweries Ltd in 1999, the pub was sold to Greene King in 2001.

In 1988 it was being reported that Marston's had bought Wheels, the property next door [a railway shop and steam train themed restaurant], with the intention of extending and potentially doubling the size of the pub. On 20th December 1989 the Advertiser reported that, "The entirely restructured Star and Garter was re-opened on Wednesday 20th December 1989. The work was managed by John Pass Associates of Warwick. The interior was designed by Marston's own Gill Kirby and the building work was carried out by Andrew Wong of Builtec Developments. The whole project cost over £200,000 and included an enlarged catering area and the construction of an open plan split level interior. Iron balustrades complement wood panelling and brick walls, offset by antique oak settles, leather upholstery and old tables with traditional solid stained floorboards. The Victorian flavour is further emphasised by stained glass partition screens and a bar of polished mahogany." On 12th January 1990, the Morning News reported that the official reopening had been attended by Tony Marten the director of Inns and Taverns for Marston's Brewery, who had spent £500,000 on the purchase of the adjacent property ['Wheels'] to enable the expansion of the pub, trebling its size but still retaining a true pub atmosphere.

In March 2012 the new owner [Peach Pubs] made application for planning permission to erect a two storey rear extension, a balustrade to the front elevation at first floor level and make alterations to the front windows; accordingly, it closed for a major refurbishment on Sunday 15th July 2012. On 21st September 2012 the Leamington Spa Courier, reporting on progress, wrote that, "The pub is retaining its original fixtures and fittings, but both the inside and outside of the building is being re-fitted. It will have an open view into the

*Above left: This 1987 photo was taken by Bill Bigley before the Star & Garter was extended.*
*Above right: Photo of the Star & Garter taken 8th November 2008 © Allan Jennings.*

kitchen, that Peach describes as a stylish new look in-keeping with the age and character of the property, while there will be more relaxed style seating and Victorian style lighting. The upstairs area will be converted into a private dining room seating twenty-four with its own balcony overlooking the park opposite." The Star and Garter reopened on Saturday 29th September 2012 and remains open in December 2013.

| | |
|---|---|
| 1817 | Tom Oliver |
| 1831-33 | William Dixon Davis |
| 1834-36 | John Solloway |
| 1836-37 | W. Hughes |
| 1838 | William Bagshawe |
| 1841-43 | Thomas Olliver *(As spelt)* |
| 1846 | E. Bloor |
| June 1848-56 | John Gilks |
| 1856-Mar 1860 | Robert Henry Tayton |
| March 1860-Nov 1863 | Charles Whitworth |
| November 1863-Nov 1868 | William Ewart |
| November 1868-Mar 1869 | Harriet Ewart *(On the death of William)* |
| March 1869-70 | William Isaacs |
| 1870-Jan 1872 | Edward Wyatt |
| January 1872-73 | William Webb |
| 1873-Nov 1874 | Sarah Webb *(On the death of William))* |
| November 1874-May 1877 | Henry Widner *(Transferred from Sarah's executor)* |
| May 1877-May 1894 | William Green |
| May 1894-May 1895 | Charles Baker |
| May 1895-Jan 1897 | John Duckett |
| January 1897-Feb 1901 | Mrs. Emily Duckett |

| | |
|---|---|
| February 1901-Aug 1902 | Henry Earp |
| August 1902-Nov 1903 | Herbert Arthur Freeman (*Of Coventry*) |
| November 1903-Jul 1904 | Walter White |
| July 1904-Dec 1905 | John Perks |
| December 1905-May 1908 | Arthur Murray Bartlett |
| May 1908-09 | Benjamin Lane |
| 1909-Apr 1911 | John Barnsby |
| April 1911-17 | Harry Hooper Ellis |
| 1919-Nov 1933 | Thomas Phipps |
| November 1933-Feb 1950 | Percy Parker (*Died 14th January 1950, age 56*) |
| February 1950-Feb 1954 | Janet Elizabeth Parker (*On the death of Percy*) |
| February 1954-Jan 1959 | Joyce Kathleen Hawes (*Then Morgan when Joyce re-married*) |
| January 1959-≥1963 | Rupert Douglas Rose |
| Late 1970s-1988 | Bruce and Teresa Hunt |
| 1989-90 | Mike Holgate and Christine Guppy |
| 1990-≥1994 | Pat Shinkwin |
| January 1998-Jun 2011 | Karen Robinson |
| June 2011-Jul 2012 | Matthew 'Matt' Beresford |
| 15th July 2012 | Closed for refurbishment |
| 29th September 2012 → | Jeremy 'Jez' Kynaston |

*The Leamington Spa Courier dated 11th December 2009 reported that: Drinkers in Leamington will be able to raise their glasses – and their voices – at a night of beer and carols on Thursday evening. St. Mark's church will be holding the event at the Star and Garter pub in Warwick Street from 8.00pm. Mulled wine and mince pies will be available and carol sheets will be handed out so drinkers can join in with festivities. It is also hoped to raise money for charity. St. Mark's curate the Rev. Ellie Clack said the idea was to take carol singing to a different level. "I was thinking about who does Christmas best and I figure pubs and churches do quite a good job between us. The main point of it is for a good night out for people."*

### Star Inn – 10 Wise Street

The first listing we have is in 1832 when Robert Burges is the licensee. On 2nd June 1900 the Leamington Spa Courier included an auction notice that described the premises as: "The very valuable freehold property, with possession, known as the Star Inn, fully licensed .... the premises are in good order and repair, and comprise bar; bar parlour; smoke room; tap room; kitchen and scullery; sitting room; three bedrooms; large club room; two water closets; brew house; malt room [side entrance from same street]; three cellars and a yard. The house occupies a good position, situated near the G.W. and L. and N.W. railway stations." In 1903, the pub was mainly used by cabmen and railway servants. In 1905 new licensee Maurice Richards paid £2,900 for the tenancy; the rent was £110 per annum.

In 1920 the chief constable objected to the renewal of the licence, but the defence claimed that the Star did a considerable trade among manual workers, especially men from the gas works; the licence was renewed. On 4th March 1938 the justices again renewed the Star's licence for one year, despite police objections. However, on 4th March 1940, application was made on behalf of licensee Christopher Shakespeare and Messrs Mitchells and Butlers for the removal of the licence to premises to be erected at the junction of Tachbrook Road and the Kingsway estate; although successful the order was suspended for the duration of the war. In the meantime, the provisional grant was renewed annually until 26th November 1956 when the final order was made. Owned by Mitchells and Butlers Ltd, the Star Inn duly closed in December 1956 and the licence was transferred to the Sun in Splendour, as was the then landlord of the Star, Christopher Shakespeare, who was caretaker licensee of the Sun for a month; it opened on 10th December, 1956.

Dick Fisk remembers the old Star as he worked for Hessings, the radio and TV shop on Gas Hill [Tachbrook Road], "Around 1958/59, Hessings took over the old Star Inn building as it was at the back of Hessings premises. In 1959/60 they added on to it and converted the building into workshops and storerooms. The footprint of the old Star is now the Khalsa Hockey Club and you wouldn't recognise any of it as the Star Inn."

| | |
|---|---|
| 1832-35 | Robert Burges |
| 1839 | James Layton |
| 1841-42 | George Page |
| 1849-56 | George Arnold |
| 1856-Jul 1856 | Joseph Atkins |
| July 1856-Jan 1865 | John Field Dolphin |
| January 1865-Apr 1866 | Charles Houghton |
| April 1866-68 | Mrs. Ann Houghton |
| 1870-76 | Thomas Beachim Parsons |
| 1876-May 1894 | John Heale |
| May 1894-Jul 1895 | Theophilus Jones *(Of Wrexham)* |
| July 1895-Jul 1899 | Mrs. Hannah Jones *(On the death of Theophilus)* |
| July 1899-Aug 1900 | John Heale |
| August 1900-Jun 1901 | Albert William Woskett |
| June 1901-Aug 1903 | Frank Edward Willoughby *(Previously Warwickshire Imperial Yeomanry and late of Post Office)* |
| August 1903-Jun 1904 | Francis James |
| June 1904-Nov 1904 | George John Walton |
| November 1904-1905 | Arthur Wade Edge |
| 1905-Jun 1915 | Maurice Richards |
| June 1915-Feb 1935 | Mrs. Fanny Richards *(On the death of Maurice)* |
| February 1935-Dec 1956 | Christopher Charles Shakespeare |
| 10th December 1956 | License transferred to the Sun in Splendour |

*John Jennings tells us that he used the pub in the 1940s and 50s. "We used to go in the Star on a Friday or Saturday night. Most people went out about 8 o'clock, and of course the pubs had to close at 10 o'clock. Pubs were the only place you could get a drink, unless you took a jug to the*

*The Star cricket team circa early 1950s courtesy of Martin McKean and Phyllis Hunt. Back Row L-R: Fred Bryson, Chris Shakespeare, Jock Bryson, Mick Hunt, Ken Bryson, John Boucher, Alf Woodward, Jack Houghton, Tony Horley, ?, ? Cooksley, Percy (Tink) Evetts, Pete Devis, John Bryson. Front row L-R: Bill Bryson, John Evetts, ?, ? Checkley, Bob Bryson, Walter Osborne, Bill McKean, Reg Handy, ? Shurvington, Ken Bryson.*

pub, and then took it home. I lived in Emscote as did my mates Doug Allsopp and Graham 'Sugar' Greenway. We would catch a bus from Emscote and have a drink in the Star. It was usually only one and then we would go somewhere else, it wasn't the sort of pub that you wanted to stay in all night. It was just up Wise Street on the right, probably just past the night club that's there now. You walked into a passageway and the bar was on the left, and the lounge or smoke room was on the right. Most pubs seemed to have a passageway that you walked into. Even though we lived in Emscote we mainly came to Leamington, although we would go into the Emscote Tavern to play darts, as well as drinking in the Dragon and the Woolpack in Warwick. Going in the pub was all there was to do, although they shut at 10 o'clock, and rang the bell for last orders at 5 minutes to. Sometimes, we would stand under the bridges and chat, but within minutes the local policemen who we called 'happy Gelfs' would come along and say, 'C'mon lads, let's be 'aving you, it's about time you were off home'. That was our cue to start walking back to Emscote."

### Station Inn – Milverton

The only information we have for this pub is a 'to let' notice listed in the Leamington Spa Courier dated 22nd March 1845: "Station Inn, Milverton, 'to be let' and may be entered upon immediately. This house is nearly opposite the station of the railway from Leamington and Warwick to Coventry. It is doing a good business but the proprietor is wanting to leave it on account of the continued illness of his wife. For terms, apply on the premises, or to Mr. J. W. Baker, Castle Hotel, Leamington. Respectable parties will be liberally dealt with."

**Footnote**: The station referenced is the 'original' Milverton railway station which was located on the other side of the Rugby Road, between Old Milverton Lane and what is now Highfield Terrace; it is not the Milverton station, or the location, that many of us remember. An 1853 map shows the area to be almost rural, with only a single building close to the station.

**Stoneleigh Arms** – 31 Clemens Street [**Incl. Stoneleigh Hotel**]
Clemens Street was the first 'modern day' street in Leamington; its construction was commenced in 1808 and completed in 1816 and the first house built thereon was situated on the north-west corner. Clemens Street was named after Samuel Clemens, a Presbyterian minister from Warwick, who owned a large quantity of land in this area of Leamington Priors [an 1818 map erroneously shows it as Clement Street].

According to 'Glimpses of Our Local Past' [J. C. Manning, 1895], the Blenheim Hotel was the first building to occupy this site [1812] and the third building to be erected in Clemens Street, at that time the most fashionable street in the town. The first reference point we have for the Blenheim is an 1816 entry in the licensed victuallers' records when a Thomas Rackstrow held the licence, thus disproving other writings that the premises were renamed the Blenheim Hotel immediately after being honoured by a visit from the Duke of Marlborough in 1822. Furthermore, in his book 'A Complete History of Royal Leamington Spa', T. B. Dudley wrote that, "In 1816, Thomas Rackstrow became tenant of the new hotel in Clemens Street, which he opened at Michaelmas, under the name of the Blenheim Hotel" [and which he 'improved' in 1818]. At the end of 1831, following the death of both parents, the Blenheim was taken over by Rackstrow's daughters who had previously been in the baby linen, haberdashery and toy business; they held a house-warming dinner on 12th January 1832.

Previously at the Elephant and Castle in Shrewsbury, Richard Hughes took over the Blenheim in 1833 and renamed it the Stoneleigh Hotel, although it was initially advertised as the Stoneleigh Family Hotel, Boarding and Commercial House; he held a house-warming dinner on Tuesday 13th August 1833 with tickets costing one guinea each. The 'tap' house for the hotel, named the Stoneleigh Tap/Arms, was situated on the adjacent site [southern side] with the two premises being divided by a mews-road. Although our first directory listing is not until 1838, when Thomas Ford is listed as the licensee, there is evidence to suggest that the same premises were also the 'tap' house for the Blenheim Hotel

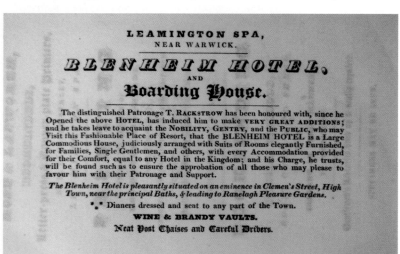

*This is an 1824 advert courtesy of Leamington Library for the 'rather posh' Blenheim Hotel and Boarding House.*

but that it was not named separately. In his account of 'The History of Royal Leamington Spa' [1887-89], George Morley informs us that, "in 1834 Mr. R. C. Hughes, in conjunction with some other gentlemen, published the Leamington Free Press from a shop in Clemens Street adjacent to the hotel"; but evidently it was an unsuccessful venture. In all likeliness this outcome was connected to Hughes being declared bankrupt in 1835, and the Stoneleigh Hotel being closed and subsequently sold; there is no licensee listed for the hotel post 1834 and the 1839 timetable lists the pick-up point for the Birmingham coach as the Stoneleigh Arms, not 'Hotel'. [Richard Hughes would reappear at the Imperial Hotel, Lansdowne Place, in 1836]

In February 1840 the Leamington Spa Courier advertised the Blenheim Hotel as being for sale by auction and in March 1840 it carried the same advert again excepting the name had been corrected to the Stoneleigh Hotel; irrespective, the premises failed to sell. In September 1840 the auction date for the Stoneleigh Hotel and Tap ['Arms'] was set for 13th October with the sale notice describing it thus: "The hotel contains in the whole thirty rooms, many of them large dimensions, forming suites of apartments very little inferior to any in Leamington. The principal staircase is wide and elegant, and by a slight attention – which would much improve the general appearance of the house – may be connected with the entrance from Clemens Street, and rendered particularly imposing. The bar is very commodious and well placed. The kitchens, servants' halls and other servants' offices, which are spacious and convenient, are at the back and on the ground floor. The cellars are large and excellent. The 'Tap' opens into Clemens Street, and also into the yard, and attached to it are a large brewhouse and other useful buildings, with three excellent sleeping rooms over. Besides the offices enumerated, are butler's pantries, water closets and other requisite offices. The stables will accommodate thirty horses and the open and lock-up coach houses will contain fifteen carriages; the yard is very spacious and well supplied with water and the whole premises occupy an area of upwards of 1,700 square yards. The premises are leasehold, that portion of them on which the house and offices stand being held for the remainder of a term of 99 years from 24th June 1810 [subject to an annual ground rent of £14.18s], and the remainder for a term of 99 years from 24th September 1811 [subject to an annual ground rent of £6.8s.4d]." Ultimately the old Blenheim/Stoneleigh Hotel would be converted into a private house, then into a coffee tavern and eating house, but the Stoneleigh Arms remained.

In 2001, when reporting on its closure, the Leamington Spa Courier stated that "the Stoneleigh Arms was built in the 1880s but stands on the site of a much older village pub". Although we have not been able to corroborate the timing, when comparing a picture of the building that stood on the site adjacent to the Blenheim Hotel circa 1820, with a recent picture of the Stoneleigh Arms, it is clear that they are not the same building. In the late 19th/early 20th century, the lessees of the Stoneleigh Arms were Lucas and Co. Ltd [Leamington Brewery], but it would subsequently become an Ansells pub following their 1928 acquisition of the brewery and its closure in 1934. In March 1986 an article in the Morning News described the Stoneleigh Arms as, "Above all a regulars' and old timers' pub. The lounge is a small, cosy room with an old-fashioned serving hatch as a bar. The bar is an extremely spacious room with a pool table and darts board, and itself is straight out of the Victorian era; the Ansells owned pub serves a wide range of drinks including the brewery's own mild and bitter, Skol lager, Guinness and draught cider."

The Stoneleigh Arms closed in February 2001 and in May of the same year was bought by the German supermarket chain Aldi. On 20th September 2001, the Coventry Evening Telegraph reported that, "A supermarket chain has been blocked from demolishing a disused Leamington pub to create access for a proposed store. Councillors at a Warwick District Council planning meeting last night refused to allow German discount supermarket chain Aldi to demolish the crumbling Stoneleigh Arms in Clemens Street." In 2010 it remained closed,

*Photo of the Stoneleigh courtesy of Allan Jennings.*

boarded-up and under a preservation order. On Friday 19th March 2010 the sad looking Stoneleigh was set on fire for the fourth time in seven months and it required two fire engines to extinguish the fire. Following the successful lodgement of a planning application on 9th April 2010 to demolish the rear of the building the work was carried out in the July. In 2013 the building remains in the same condition.

**Footnote:** Although there is a Blenheim Commercial Hotel listed at 25, Clemens Street in 1932, 1936 and 1940, there is no evidence to suggest that there is any connection with the Stoneleigh Arms, more likely just coincidence.

| | |
|---|---|
| 1816-28 | Thomas Rackstrow *(Blenheim Hotel)* |
| 1828-29 | William Jarman *(Blenheim Hotel)* |
| 1830-31 | M. Jarman *(Went on to the Clarendon Hotel)* |
| 1831-33 | Misses Rackstrow *(Blenheim Hotel)* |
| 1833-35 | Richard Charles Hughes *(Stoneleigh Hotel)* |
| 1834 | William Smith *(Stoneleigh Tap)* |
| 1837 | William Ford *(Stoneleigh Tap)* |
| 1838-40 | Thomas Ford *(Stoneleigh Tap)* |
| 1837-40 | Thomas Morris *(Stoneleigh Hotel)* |
| 1845-Nov 1850 | William Bloxham *(Stoneleigh Arms)* |
| November 1850-66 | Thomas Neale *(Licence refused in September 1866)* |
| 1868-Aug 1874 | Ellis Lynes |
| August 1874-80 | James Sargeant |
| 1881-83 | S. Chamberlain |
| 1883-Dec 1886 | W. Frederick Gossage |
| December 1886-Aug 1895 | Charles Duke |

| | |
|---|---|
| August 1895-Oct 1902 | Mrs. Emma Duke *(On the death of Charles)* |
| October 1902-Sep 1911 | Charles Clement |
| September 1911-Feb 1912 | George Harris |
| February 1912-Sep 1946 | Henry Laird McKean *(Died 9th August 1946, aged 76)* |
| September 1946-Sep 1955 | Henry Laird McKean Jnr. *(Died 11th July 1955, aged 54)* |
| September 1955-Aug 1964 | Mrs. Amy McKean *(Died 11th May 1982, aged 80)* |
| August 1964-Jun 1967 | Arnold David Hatfield |
| June 1967-Dec 1968 | John Ernest Bridges |
| December 1968-Nov 1969 | Baden Robert Neild |
| November 1969-Jun 1971 | Joseph Hartnett |
| June 1971-May 1972 | William Ernest Gray |
| May 1972-Feb 1973 | Philip James Skidmore *(Went on to the Oak Inn)* |
| February 1973-Nov 1973 | John Brady |
| November 1973-Aug 1974 | Dennis Hinton |
| August 1974-Nov 1976 | Herbert F. K. Guest |
| November 1976-Dec 1982 | Nirmal 'Nick' Chandra Dikshit and his wife Pauline *(Previously at the Winson Green Tavern, Birmingham)* |
| January 1983-≥1990 | Swarn Singh Sahota |
| Circa 1990–Feb 2001 | Sukdev Khela |
| February 2001 | Closed for business |

*Monday 22nd October 1917 was a sad day for landlord Henry Laird McKean and his family. Their 20 year old son, William, Private, 202195, 8th [Service] Battalion, Norfolk Regiment was killed in action. He is buried in the Perth Cemetery [China Wall], Belgium.*

*Photo of Amy and landlord Henry McKean circa early 1950s courtesy of their grandson Martin McKean. Their son William was the landlord of the Railway Inn from 8th April 1971 until around 1975.*

On 17th July 1964 the Leamington Spa Courier reported that: On Sunday, Mrs. Amy McKean pulled pints behind the bar of the Stoneleigh, Clemens Street, Leamington, for the last time and brought to an end a 52 year family association with the pub. It was in 1912 that the grandfather, Harry McKean, came down from the Isle of Cumbrae and became tenant of the house. The Stoneleigh is one of the oldest pubs in Leamington. Its history goes back to the early nineteenth century when it was once the tap room of the old Blenheim Hotel. In 1946, Mr. McKean's son Harry took over and when he died in 1955 Mrs. McKean took the job on, "I've enjoyed it, even when I have retired I shall still come along for a drink now and again with the regulars." On Sunday regulars presented her with a gold watch and a bouquet.

*On 2nd June 2000 the Leamington Spa Courier reported that: Strange writing has appeared on the wall of a Leamington pub. The scrawling was discovered when landlord Sukdev Khela decided to spruce up the Stoneleigh Arms in Clemens Street. Stripping the old paint away, Mr. Khela found part of the writing advertising carriages for hire. He said, "Nobody knew it was there but it probably dates back to when the pub was first built."*

On 29th June 2001 the Leamington Spa Courier reported that: Residents in Old Town are being urged to join a campaign to save the former Stoneleigh Arms from being knocked down. Janet Alty, a member of the board of directors at Regenesis and the Old Town Traders association for more than 30 years, said that Aldi had taken advantage of a recent arson attack to seek demolition of the building. It bought the building five weeks ago and "within days they had ripped the roof off without permission. Then the building was gutted by fire, which they used as an excuse to justify demolition." The Stoneleigh Arms, which closed in February, was built in the 1880s but stands on the site of a much older village pub.

**Stresa Bar** – 86 Warwick Street
See Glasnost Vodka Bar for details.

**Styles Apart** – 12 Augusta Place
See Willoughby Arms for details.

**Sugar Loaf** – Leamington Priors
The only information we have for the Sugar Loaf are three entries sourced from the licensed victuallers' records and unfortunately, in each case, there is no address listed. It is probable that the William Johnson listed here is the same one that is listed at a wine vaults in 1828 [same source] and directory listed as wine and spirit merchant at 39, Bath Street, 1830-35. That being so, then he founded his business in 1817 and was the father of the David Johnson who would later move the business to the old Theatre Royal building at 13, Bath Street. [See Chair and Rocket for more information]

| | |
|---|---|
| 1817 | Jesse Johnson |
| 1824-25 | William Johnson |

**Sun** – Tachbrook Road
See Sun in Splendour for details.

**Sun in Splendour** – Tachbrook Road

The site of the Sun in Splendour pub was previously on the edge of Shrubland Hall, the imposing home of local major landowner Matthew Wise, which we understand he had built in 1818. The 'Hall' was demolished in 1948 to facilitate the building of the Kingsway housing estate.

The Sun in Splendour opened on 10th December 1956 and on the 14th December the Leamington Spa Courier reported, "Mitchells and Butlers' Sun in Splendour, the second public house to be built in Leamington since the war [the Bulldog was the first], was opened on Monday. The licence for this new, contemporary-designed building at the junction of

Tachbrook Road and Kingsway has been transferred from the Star, Wise Street, which was closed last week. At the opening ceremony, Mr. C. Stanley Best, an executive director of the brewery, said application for the licence was first made in 1940. The excellent arrangements made for hygiene and the fine colour schemes used in the new building were commented upon by Mr. W. J. Webb, chairman of the licensing justices. It has a bar, a smoke room and an off-licence and was built by Atkins and Shaw Ltd, of Daventry. Architects were Messrs Quick and Lee, of Waterloo Place, Leamington. The licensee is Mr. Claude Woonton, manager of the Binley Oak, Coventry, for the last two

*Above: Photo by kind permission of Dar Gill. This photo was taken on the opening of the Sun in Splendour. Three people can be identified, George Ellard on the left, Alfie Crompton in the centre, and Carter Gill on the right. Below: Photo of the Sun taken on 12th June 2010 © Allan Jennings.*

years." The same issue of the Courier also carried the following advert: "A new M&B House for Leamington, the Sun in Splendour, Tachbrook Road, Kingsway, Leamington, where in pleasant modern surroundings you can relax in congenial company, make new friends and enjoy M&B beers, wines and spirits in the atmosphere of true hospitality. Now open - Mitchells & Butlers."

On 28th November 1961, and effective immediately, the licensee [along with four other local landlords] was granted permission to open the off-licence premises from 8.30am, as permitted by the new Licensing Act. The pub underwent a major refurbishment in 2006, became a free house and was renamed The Sun. In August 2011 there was a notice posted outside stating that it was closed for refurbishment and conversion to a bar, Italian restaurant, pizzeria and takeaway. By early October it had reopened and was advertising Sunday lunch of roast chicken or roast beef, but no mention of an Italian restaurant, etc. The Sun remains open in December 2013.

| | |
|---|---|
| 10th Dec 1956-Jan 1957 | Christopher Charles Shakespeare *(Transferred from the Star)* |
| January 1957-Sep 1957 | Claude Woonton |
| September 1957-Jun 1960 | Lewis Edward Hallard |
| June 1960-Feb 1961 | Allan William Ramsey |
| February 1961-Mar 1962 | William James Burke |
| March 1962-Jun 1965 | Martin Brennan |
| June 1965-Feb 1967 | Graham William Knibbs |
| February 1967-Jun 1970 | Paschal Alphonsus Doyle |
| June 1970-Dec 1975 | Richard and Cissie Power *(Previously at the Fox and Vivian, Coventry)* |
| Dec 1975-≥1976 | Tony Roberts |
| ≤March 1977 | David McCamley *(Relief manager)* |
| 1985-88 | Tony Peasland and his wife Jayne |
| 1988-91 | Keith 'Dick' and Jennifer Rheams |
| Circa 2005 | Malcolm Ernest Lewis |
| August 2006-Oct 2006 | Paul Blatchly |
| Oct 2006 | Gareth Beddows and Kelly Satchwell |
| August 2008-Jun 2009 | John Morgan Bell |
| June 2009-Mar 2010 | Zorovar Singh Atwal |
| March 2010-Mar 2012 | Gareth Beddows and Kelly Satchwell |
| March 2012 → | Liam Anthony Mallin |

**Swan** – Clemens Street, Leamington Priors

The Swan in Clemens Street was also known as the White Swan, and the combined dates for both, span the years 1810 until circa 1823. The source of the 1810-15 Swan entries are the licensed victuallers' records which do not list the pub's address, only that it is in Leamington Priors and that the licensee is Thomas Olorenshaw. In 1813, the same source lists the same licensee at the White Swan, but again with no address. Prior to 1813 these records do not list the address or the name of the pub, so we have made the connection using the licensed victualler's name ['Olorenshaw']. Pigot's 1822/23 directory lists the White Swan in Clemens Street but no mention of the landlord's name.

| | |
|---|---|
| 1810 | William Olorenshaw |
| 1810-15 | Thomas Olorenshaw |
| 1817-18 | No licensee listed |
| 1822-23 | No licensee listed |

**Swan Inn** – Kenilworth Street
This particular Swan is not listed in the 1835, or subsequent directories, so we have therefore concluded that it closed circa 1833-34. However, it is possible that it was renamed the Wheelers Arms in 1834-35, but we have no corroborating evidence.

| | |
|---|---|
| 1833-34 | William Myatt |

**Swan Inn** – 73 Clarendon Street [corner of Clarendon and Swan Streets]
The first directory listing we have for this pub is in 1835 when it was named the White Swan and John Brown was the licensee; situated on the corner of Clarendon and Swan Streets, and infrequently numbered in its early years, it would not be listed as 73, Clarendon Street until 1880. On 16th June 1849, a 'to be let' notice listed in the Leamington Spa Courier described the premises: "The house consists of bar, parlour, smoke room, tap room, seven good bedrooms, a large club room capable of dining 100 persons, a store room, two coach houses and stabling for seventeen horses." A spirits licence was granted to licensee Mrs. Bews in August 1865.

At the annual licensing meeting held at Warwick on 10th February 1959, a provisional grant was issued for the removal of the licence to premises to be erected on a site situated at the corner of Greville Road and All Saints Road, Warwick; this decision was ratified on 23rd March 1959 [when built the new premises would be known as Hobsons Choice]. Owned by Phipps, Northampton Brewery Co. Ltd, the Swan closed on 2nd November 1959. In October 1985, a proposal to open a new pub at the premises of the former Swan Inn failed to materialise following objections from local residents and councillors.

*The site of the Swan Inn taken on 3rd July 2011 © Allan Jennings.*

| | |
|---|---|
| 1835-42 | John Brown |
| 1844 | Ann Lambert |
| 1845 | J. Labram |
| 1846-57 | John Seed |
| 1851 | John Boyes *(Possibly a temporary licensee)* |
| 1865-Jan 1879 | Caroline Bews |
| January 1879-Aug 1912 | Francis Kightley *(Transferred from the executor of Caroline Bews)* |
| August 1912-Jun 1913 | Alfred Bradley |
| June 1913-Nov 1914 | Thomas Watts |
| November 1914-29 | Frederick John Jones |
| 1929-Aug 1929 | Mrs. Annie Maria Jones |
| August 1929-34 | Frederick 'Joe' Joseph Quenell |
| 1935 | Arthur L. Fowler |
| 1935-Nov 1936 | Albert G. J. Beeby *(Of Northampton – died 26th November 1936, aged 50)* |
| November 1936-Sep 1939 | Rose Beeby |
| September 1939-Dec 1945 | Ernest Felton |
| December 1945-May 1952 | Roger Thomas Lewis |
| May 1952-Nov 1959 | Geoffrey Maxwell Taylor |
| 2nd November 1959 | Closed for business |
| 30th November 1959 | Licence transferred to Thomas Arthur Beeby |

*The Leamington Spa Courier dated 8th March 1845 carried the following sale notice: To be sold by auction by George Carter on Monday, the 10th day of March 1845, at No. 53 Clarendon Street, next door to the White Swan from which place they have been removed; a quantity of brewing utensils, household furniture, about 10 or 12 gallons of fine old sherry in casks, and other effects, the property of Mrs. Ann Lambert, comprising 2 capital copper furnaces, one 50 and the other 80 gallons, with large brass tap, 2 strong square coolers, a capital 14 bushel mash tub, a large iron bound rearing tub, and several other brewing tubs, 2 capital 280 gallon iron bound casks, 100 gal. cask, and several of a smaller size, a handsome mahogany 4 motion beer machine, with piping, &c.; a 3 motion liquor fountain with counter covered in lead, a quantity of gas pendants, and piping and 2 large sign boards. Sale to begin at eleven in the morning.*

**Swan Inn** – Althorpe Street
Yet another Swan and this one also has an air of mystery about it. The listings are straightforward enough and indicate that it had a lifespan of approximately five years and closed circa 1888-89. However, although E. Roddis is listed as licensee of the Swan in 1885-87, E. Roddis is also listed as licensee of the Althorpe Arms [also in Althorpe Street] in 1882-87 inclusive; we have not yet been able to determine the connection.

| | |
|---|---|
| 1884 | E. Cully |
| 1885-87 | E. Roddis |
| 1888-89 | No licensee listed |

**Sweeney's** – 116 Warwick Street
See Prince of Wales for details.

**Syd's Bar** – 77 The Parade [part of Regent Hotel]
See Regent Hotel for details.

**Talbot Inn** – 34 Rushmore Street
A Talbot is an extinct white hunting dog with a keen sense of smell. In September 1880, James Glenn of Eastnor Cottage/Rushmore Street was granted a beer on-licence and a beer off-licence. By the early 1900s the Talbot was owned by Lucas and Co. Ltd [Leamington Brewery], but it would become an Ansells pub following their 1928 acquisition of the brewery and its closure in 1934. During the time that Mick Fathers ran the pub [1919-51] it became known locally as 'Mickies'. On 9th February 1954, the pub's licence was upgraded when a beer and wine 'on' and off-licence was granted to licensee Alfred Cross; it was ratified on 30th March. A full licence was granted on 2nd February 1960 and confirmed on 5th April 1960. Since the late 1970s it has been known by locals as 'Hectors House' so named after landlord Hector Ashwood [1977-2007]. In 1980, after being the tenant for three years, Hector bought the freehold from Ansells for £32,000. In Hector's time the pub had a bar and smoke room with an upstairs flat that included three bedrooms and a living room. The Talbot Inn remains open in December 2013.

**Footnote:** The Talbot Inn boasts by far the lowest turnover of licensees in Leamington relative to its longevity. During its 130+ years, only eight publicans have preceded Nic Ford, the current incumbent.

| | |
|---|---|
| 1880-Aug 1888 | James Glenn |
| August 1888-May 1895 | Charles Henry Summers |
| May 1895-Sep 1919 | Charles William Glenn |
| September 1919-Nov 1951 | Frederick 'Mick' Fathers *(Father of Gwendoline Cross)* |
| November 1951-Feb 1966 | Alfred James Cross *(On the death of Frederick, his father-in-law)* |
| February 1966-Feb 1975 | Gwendoline Gertrude Cross *(On death of Alfred)* |
| February 1975-Jun 1977 | Mrs. Janet Turner *(On the retirement of Mrs. Cross)* |
| June 1977-Aug 2007 | Hector George Ashwood and his wife Barbara |
| August 2007 → | Nicholas Ford |

*The Coventry Evening Telegraph dated 11th February 1975 reported that: A Leamington woman who followed her father and husband as licensee of one of the town's oldest public houses has retired. Mrs. Gwendoline Cross has been associated with the Talbot Inn, Rushmore*

*This photo of Rushmore Street, courtesy of Michael Willes and Vivienne Owen, shows a party celebrating the 1937 Coronation of King George VI and Queen Elizabeth. It was taken from the upstairs window of the Talbot Inn. Gwen Cross is at the piano and her father Micky Fathers is to the right wearing a tie.*

Street, Leamington, for more than 55 years. She spent the last working day at the pub yesterday, and plans to live in retirement a couple of doors away. Mrs. Hilda Singleton, who has helped out behind the bar of the Talbot for 48 years, also retired yesterday.

Mrs. Cross's retirement was marked at a lunch-time gathering when Mr. D. Marshall, a director of Ansell's Brewery, presented her with a tea-making machine on behalf of the company. She also received gifts from customers. "I have extremely happy memories of my many years at the Talbot," said Mrs. Cross. "I have no doubt that it is the friendliest pub in the area."

Although serving drinks has been a full time job, Mrs. Cross was once a swimming instructress. In between her duties behind the bar she regularly used to make the short trip to the Pump Room baths to teach children to swim. She gave her first lessons in 1925, and until 1973 taught thousands of children.

Mrs. Cross was 14 when her late father, Mr. Frederick 'Mick' Fathers, became licensee in 1919, and it was the shortest of moves for the family as their home was in nearby Clapham Terrace. After her marriage, Mrs. Cross stayed on at the Talbot. When her father died in 1951 her husband took over the licence. Nine years ago, following the death of her husband, Mrs. Cross became licensee. The new tenant is another woman, Mrs. Janet Turner, who has moved from Saltley, Birmingham.

In August 1983, the local press were reporting on the mural that was being painted on the outside side wall of the Talbot: A colourful giant mural is blooming among the terraced houses in a depressed area of Leamington. Local people have chosen the design with the help of volunteers from the Bath Place community arts workshop. It shows a fantasy fairground with an elephant, a hot air balloon and all kinds of Edwardian side shows. In the foreground a canal boat is passing with a parish outing of fair-goers aboard relaxing in the shade of an awning. At the end of the project local children will add animals, water birds and butterflies.

Artist Rob Mooney has been working with fourteen volunteers on the mural for three weeks and they hope to finish in another three if the weather stays fine. He said, "The whole scene has taken on an Edwardian feeling as this fits in with the subject matter and character of the area. The aim of the project is not just to add an attractive and enterprising feature to the nearby playground and canal area, but to build on the sense of community identity." The Clapham Terrace area is the latest to be given a facelift under the Warwick District Council general improvement scheme.

*The Morning News dated 27th November 1985 featured the following article: "If you didn't know it was there it would be easy to miss Hector's House. Head down on a dark, damp November night, one could stride through Rushmore Street without noticing the Talbot. Obscurity might be no bad thing in an age when so many licensed hostelries are about as inconspicuous as the lights on Piccadilly."*

*"Hector thinks there could have been a pub on the premises since the 1870s. He hasn't been there that long. Twas Jubilee year, when he arrived – Queen Elizabeth II's 25th year since accession, not Victoria's 60th. He wears a 1977 Jubilee crested tie to mark that memorable occasion."*

*"Apart from the juke-box and the new fangled electric light, the Talbot's two bars would not appear to have altered substantially since the end of the 'Widow of Windsors' long reign. No sawdust on the floors any longer, no spittoons - but a 'front room' public and a proper little 'snug' through the glass door."*

*"There was even a 'granfer' [grandad] in the corner – the latest undoubtedly, in a continuous line of sages who have discussed – and created – the 20th century history of Rushmore Street, and of Leamington Spa."*

*"A terraced house pub in a terraced street. From such humble surroundings came the lifeblood of Great Britain and its Empire. Victorian, Edwardian, and Georgian community resolution, which has sadly faded within the ruling span of our second Elizabethan age."*

*"Small wonder that tower blocks have been such monumental disasters. Hector's House on the sixth floor of such a monstrosity would never have had the same warmth and appeal as it has half way down Rushmore Street. May that appeal live on way beyond our present monarch's reign, and on through the Charlesian (he'll have to change his 'andle – that doesn't have the right ring about it); and Williamian (nor does that!) successions."*

*"Here endeth the spiel, but worth getting off the chest, if only to inform those who are not informed, that the Talbot is a smashing little town pub in the best tradition of little English town pubs."*

In December 2003 the mural on the side of the Talbot was back in the news: A mural in Leamington's old town has finally

*The Talbot taken on 11th August 2004 by John Hartnup.*

had a face-lift after 20 years. The mural now depicts a coastal scene with sunset. It took eight volunteers plus artists Dave Male and Rich Inwood from the Community Arts workshop eight weeks to complete the work, and was funded from a number of sources including a grant from Regenesis. The volunteers were Josh Myers, Kate Cliffe, [who in 2013 is the manager of the Sydni Centre], Steve, Pat and Bronia Sawyer, Marisa Montaldi, Sinead and Denny Reader.

*The Leamington Spa Courier dated 5th August 2005 reported that: Samba rhythms and Caribbean food will mark Jamaican Independence Day tomorrow Saturday. For the 23rd year running, the party will be at Rushmore Street Park and the neighbouring Talbot Inn pub in Leamington.*

*Though the island's community in the town has declined in numbers, the event has lived on. Talbot Inn landlord and organiser Hector Ashwood said, "These days 90 per cent of people who come along are English, Irish and other nationalities. Some of the older members of the West Indian community have died and others have gone back home. There are just a small number left, even though there are a lot of black people from other countries. But the celebration has survived because it has become a multi-cultural event." Jamaica became independent on August 6, 1962 but retains bonds with Britain stretching back more than 300 years.*

The Leamington Spa Courier of 30th March 2007 reported the end of an era under the heading: **Town's first West Indian landlord to pull last pint** – To some he is an old town institution and to many the name of his pub is the same as his own. Hector Ashwood was the first West Indian landlord in Leamington, and is the man behind the town's Jamaican Independence Day festival. But after 30 years the unthinkable is happening – Hector is calling time at the Talbot Inn.

Now aged 74 and recovering from poor health, the Jamaican born landlord feels it is time to move on from a life of barrels, taps, bottles and glasses. He said, "Everything has changed – the customers have changed and the trade has changed but we have no regrets. I have enjoyed the 30 years I have been at the Talbot Inn. We have had no problems and we have had some really good customers."

Mr. Ashwood first came to the UK in 1961, aged 24. A former Jamaican iron and copper worker, he spent 16 years at British Rail and the Ford foundry before noticing a gap in the market and taking on the Rushmore Street premises. He said, "There weren't any West Indian pubs in the area at the time and there were quite a few of us, so I decided to try it."

"I was the first black or West Indian landlord in Leamington, Warwick or Stratford. As time went on, there were more ethnic people opening pubs. It became normal to see a West Indian landlord." The Talbot also became the venue for the annual Jamaican Independence Day festival on August 6, and Mr. Ashwood believes the pub has become a landmark for the celebration.

Prospect Road resident Don Sykes is a regular at the pub and helped behind the bar during the landlord's early years. He recalls the relaxed atmosphere which made the pub popular in the 1980s, when there was a resident DJ and a chance for young bands to play their first gig. Mr. Sykes said, "Hector's has been an institution in this town for a long time. You didn't have to make an effort. You could just drop in. It is his charisma that made the whole thing. He created the atmosphere. If you could play dominoes, you were invited to join in and if you heard the reggae music you could come in and sit at a table."

Today, Leamington's West Indian community has shrunk greatly, and you are more likely to see a game of darts than dominoes in the Talbot, but there are still many people happy to sip cans of Red Stripe and sample a slightly wider rum selection than the average pub.

Another thing that has not changed is the decor. While other pubs have replaced comfy chairs and cosy corners for blond wood and modern design, Hector decided the Talbot would remain unaltered. He said, "It is a backstreet pub and it has its own character because it is near the side of the canal and there is a children's playground next door. It is like a country pub really."

"When I first bought it, we did a little bit of changes, like we brought the toilets inside and we moved the kitchen upstairs – at the beginning there was no kitchen. We chose to keep it basic, but it is different from all the other pubs in town."

**Tavern** – 2/6 Kenilworth Road [basement of Guys Hotel]
See Guys Hotel for details.

**Tavistock Inn** – 50 Tavistock Street
See Newmarket Inn for details.

**Three Graces** – 44 Clarendon Street
See Kings Arms for details.

**Three Tuns** – 28 Clemens Street
See Albatross for details.

**Tiller Pin** – Queensway
This site was originally owned by Warwick District Council, its location then being referenced as Europa Way. In November 1988, the council's land and buildings sub-committee agreed to seek outline planning permission for the site; this was approved in January 1989 and in the March this two acre site was advertised for sale. Although Greenhall Whitley and Co. Ltd [Warrington, Cheshire] was successful with their bid they withdrew their interest late in proceedings; Bass Plc took up the opportunity and in July 1993 applied for a provisional licence. The £1 million Tiller Pin was opened on Monday 16th May 1994 by the Mayor of Leamington, John Higgins; the ribbon was cut at 11.30am and the doors opened to the public at 12

*Photo of the Tiller Pin taken on 2nd November 2008 © Allan Jennings.*

noon. Situated on the banks of the Grand Union canal, this [Bass Plc owned] Mitchells and Butlers pub was then addressed as Centurian Way, now Queensway. The Tiller Pin remains open in December 2013.

**Footnote:** A 'tiller pin' is an ornamental pin used to secure the tiller of a canal boat [a competition held to name the pub was won by Mrs. G. Sweeney of Leamington Spa].

| | |
|---|---|
| 16th May 1994 | The Tiller Pin opened |
| 16th May 1994 | Nigel and Christine Lake |
| | *(Previously at the Wig and Pen, Nuneaton)* |
| 2006-May 2006 | Edward Christopher Binns |
| May 2006-Feb 2010 | Rose Ottaway |
| February 2010 → | Sharon Haymes |

## TJ's – 45/47 Bath Street

In the early 1960s the building addressed as 45, Bath Street was a Wimpy Bar [at street level] selling burger style meals and non-alcoholic drinks; it subsequently became the Beefy Bar which was of a similar format.

Suzannes, a licensed night club for the over 23's [wine, dine and dance], opened on 25th August 1976. Open from 8.00pm until 2.00am, the first floor restaurant was licensed until 11.30pm [and subject to normal licensing restrictions] and the ground floor was covered by a music and dance licence allowing patrons to buy alcoholic drinks after 11.30pm; "the premises had a restaurant licence for both floors but [the club] was not able to sell intoxicating liquor to patrons not taking table meals" [Morning News: 2nd June, 1977]. On 5th July 1977, the licensing justices granted the chief constable's application for a revocation of the late supper licence applicable to the ground floor; this followed the imposition of fines on the proprietors in June 1977 for breaching licensing conditions. By September 1977 the dance floor had been enlarged to twice its original size and a steak bar had been opened upstairs. However, in November 1977 following an unsuccessful appeal against the fines, the Leamington Spa Courier reported that "the revocation of [the] Leamington night-spot's late supper licence had caused a dramatic change in the fortunes of its proprietors [Warwick Crown Court was told]"; the proprietor's legal representation adding that "these premises were converted at a cost of some £16,000 but without the licence are worth very much less. I understand they are being sold for £5,000" [Morning News: 25th November, 1977]. Suzannes closed shortly afterwards.

In September 1979 council officials approved plans by Kewal Dhut [who ran a drapers shop in High Street] to open an Asian social club on the premises; this he did later the same year, combining the social club with a restaurant selling specialist Asian dishes. In 1981 45, Bath Street was being advertised as the Milaap Social Club, with the entrance at the rear of the premises via the car park in Regent Place. Jack Atwal acquired the Milaap Club in March 1985 and when Jack's son Gursh [Gurcharn] Atwal took over the business in 2002 it became TJ's, named after his son Thomas James. In 2004, Gursh bought the adjoining premises at 47, Bath Street which was formerly Breens [clothes outfitter], then Pots and Pans and latterly Bath

Street Furniture. The additional premises enabled Gursh to expand the business by extending TJ's Bar and Bistro and opening an eighteen bedroom hotel upstairs, the Thomas James Hotel, which comprised three bars, one at street level. In 2011, it was serving Butty Bach bitter [Wye Valley Brewery] and other Real Ales! On 12th January 2012, its future became uncertain when Mood Bars [UK] Ltd, then owners of TJ's, the Shakespeare [Tavistock Street] and KoKo's Bar [Warwick Street], entered into administration, an arrangement that would continue until September. Following a brief closure, the newly refurbished TJ's Bar & Grill reopened under new ownership at 5.00pm on Saturday 29th September 2012. TJ's remains open in December 2013.

*A snowy day outside TJ's taken on 6th January 2010 © Allan Jennings.*

| 1976-78 | Dorothy Joan Bailey *(Licensee - Suzanne's)* |
| 1976-78 | Dudley Charles Bailey *(Manager – Suzanne's)* |
| 1979-Mar 1985 | Kewal Dhut *(Milaap Social Club)* |
| March 1985-2002 | Jack Atwal *(Milaap Club)* |
| 2002-Jan 2012 | Gurcharn "Gursh" Singh Atwal *(TJ's Owner - son of Jack)* |
| Circa 2011 | Clint Barnett *(Manager)* |
| September 2011 | Dave Shaw *(Manager)* |
| January 2012 | Andrew David Merricks |
| February 2012 | Clinton David Barnett |

**Top of the Town** – 44/46 Clarendon Avenue
See Jekyll and Hyde for details.

**Town House / Town House Tavern** – 2 George Street
See Shakespeare Inn for details.

**Toyk Bar** – 102 Warwick Street
See Jam Bar and Brasserie for details.

**Tryst** – 116 Warwick Street
See Prince of Wales for details.

**Turf Inn** – 36 Satchwell Street
See Palace Inn for details.

**Turtle Inn** – 71 Parade
The first reference we have for the Turtle is when the wine and spirits licence belonging to Benjamin Andrews [wine and spirits merchant] is renewed at the annual licensing session in 1854. At this point the address was 42, Upper Parade; it would be readdressed 71, Parade in the late 1870s. By 1880 Andrews is only listed as a confectioner/caterer but in March 1882 the wine and spirits licence was transferred to John Powell. After trading briefly as Andrews and Powell, the former departed and the business continued in the name of the Powell Bros, becoming Bloomfield and Powell in 1900. In 1902 the business expanded and was again [also] listed as a wine and spirit merchant, and in 1906 the business mix changed again when the Turtle was listed under Hotels, Inns, &c. However, Mr. J. W. Bloomfield [owner and landlord] did not apply to renew the licence for the Turtle Inn at the annual licensing session on 5th February 1915 and the licence was considered lapsed from that date. By 1917 Bloomfield and Powell were no longer listed as wine and spirit merchants or as occupants of 71, Parade but the Turtle continued to be listed under Hotels, Inns, &c until the early 1920s.

| | |
|---|---|
| ≤1854-≥1875 | Benjamin Andrews |
| ≤1880–March 1882 | Benjamin Andrews |
| March 1882-Nov 1886 | John Powell Snr. *(Turtle)* |
| November 1886-99 | John Powell Jnr. and George Tungate Powell *(Powell Bros – Turtle Catering)* |
| 1899-February 1899 | Mrs. Powell |
| February 1899 | J. M. Bloomfield *(Transferred as the Turtle)* |
| 1900-01 | Bloomfield and Powell *(Catering)* |
| 1902-05 | Bloomfield and Powell *(Wine and Spirits Merchants & Catering)* |
| 1906-15 | Bloomfield and Powell *(Turtle, Wine and Spirits Merchants & Catering)* |

**Under Graduate** – 2 High Street
See Royal Exchange for details

**Unicorn Inn** – New Bath Street / Leam Terrace East
The first information we have for the Unicorn Inn is a sale notice dated 12th August 1846, referencing a forthcoming auction at the Crown Hotel and describing it as: "A newly erected and well built messuage or dwelling house, called or known as the Unicorn Inn, situate in New Bath Street or Leam Terrace East, comprising two parlours, four good bedrooms, underground kitchen, cellars, and other domestic offices, together with a spacious back yard; now in the occupation of Mr. George Podmore." We have no record of New Bath Street ever existing and the only two pubs we have recorded in Leam Terrace East are the Railway Tavern [1849 to circa 1860] and the New Inn [circa 1860 to present day]. While it is possible that the Unicorn Inn is an earlier name for the Railway Tavern, that is pure speculation. Furthermore, we have no listing for a George Podmore at any licensed premises in Leamington, suggesting that the premises reverted to a private residence prior to the 1846 auction.

**Union and Commercial Inn** – Church Street
See Bowling Green [Church Street] for details.

**Union Tavern** – 33 Park Street
See Lamb for details.

**Vaults** – 13 Bath Street
See Chair and Rocket for details.

**V Bar** – 86 Regent Street
See Glasnost Vodka Bar for details.

**Venew @ The Binswood** – Rugby Road
See Binswood Tavern for details.

**Victoria Arms** – Queen Street
The first piece of information we have for the Victoria Arms is an auction notice dated 12th August 1841: "All that substantially built freehold messuage or tenement, known by the sign of the Victoria Arms, with the outbuildings thereto belonging, now in the occupation of Mr. Robert Hewitt; also the freehold house adjoining, on the west side thereof, both situate in and fronting Queen Street." There is also a directory listing that places Robert Hewitt at a Queen Street beer house at the same time.

1841                                    Robert Hewitt

**Victoria Vaults** – 44 Tavistock Street
The Victoria Vaults had previously been known as the Bricklayers Arms and the Cross Keys. The first directory listing we have for these premises is in 1832 when a J. Clark is the licensee of the Bricklayers Arms. On 30th September and 1st of October 1834, the

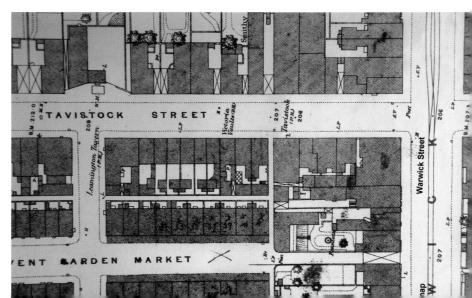

*This 1886 map courtesy of Leamington Library shows the site of the Victoria Vaults.*

following property belonging to licensee Edward Raven [who is leaving the premises] is sold by auction under a distress for rent and execution from the Sheriff: "Household furniture, linen, china and glass, brewing utensils, coolers, large copper furnace, casks and upwards of 1000 gallons of fine ale, stouts, &c. &c." By 1835, following Raven's departure, the premises [listed as 5, Tavistock Street] had been renamed the Cross Keys and comprised two parlours, a bar and tap-room, club-room, five sleeping rooms, cellar and a two stall stable. The year that the Cross Keys was renamed the Victoria Vaults is the subject of some conjecture because during the period 1868-76 both are listed with the same licensee; in the late 1870s it was renumbered 44, Tavistock Street.

In March 1903, the Victoria Vaults was one of four properties auctioned by Messrs Cookes and Southorn at the Crown Hotel, but it did not sell; at the time it was fully licensed and leased to the Northampton Brewery Co. Ltd for another fifteen years. At the licensing sessions on 10th February 1905 the chief constable objected to the renewal of the licence stating that "the premises were small; the rooms were totally unfit for a number of persons to assemble in; the bar was the smallest for a public house; the smoke room was very small; there was no sleeping accommodation and no stabling." The licensing justices refused to renew the licence as they considered the premises to be 'structurally unsuitable and deficient' for use as a public house; it therefore did not qualify for payment of compensation. The Victoria Vaults closed on 7th February 1905. In 2013 the site is now a night club.

| | |
|---|---|
| 1832 | Clark (*Bricklayers Arms*) |
| 1832-33 | J. Lowe |
| 1833-34 | Edward Raven |
| 1835 | John Pruce |
| 1835 | Jones and Elliott (*Cross Keys*) |
| 1837 | (*Bricklayers Arms & Cross Keys listed*) |
| 1838-42 | George Elliot (*Cross Keys*) |
| 1845-46 | William Jones |
| 1848 | G. Ashmore |
| June 1848-Nov 1851 | John Pratt |
| November 1851-≤1853 | Esther Pratt (*On the death of John*) |
| ≤1853-Oct 1853 | William Clifton |
| October 1853-May 1855 | John Hewitt |
| May 1855-Apr 1856 | John Muddiman |
| April 1856-Oct 1857 | Edward William Chattaway |
| October 1857-Sep 1860 | Charles Le Foss Lemon |
| September 1860-Dec 1868 | William Smith |
| December 1868-Nov 1870 | William Powell (*Cross Keys & Victoria Vaults listed*) |
| November 1870-76 | Emma Smith (*Cross Keys & Victoria Vaults listed*) |
| 1876-Jul 1879 | Emma Smith (*Victoria Vaults*) |
| July 1879-May 1883 | Alfred Kightley (*On the death of Emma Smith*) |
| May 1883-84 | Alfred Edward Rose |

| | |
|---|---|
| 1884-86 | A. Essex |
| 1886-Jun 1887 | Mark Pratt |
| June 1887-Aug 1893 | Zacharias Boote *(Went to the Lansdowne Tavern)* |
| August 1893-Mar 1894 | George Godfrey |
| March 1894-Dec 1897 | Zacharias Boote |
| December 1897-Jul 1898 | Charles Skelswell |
| July 1898-Jun 1899 | Frederick John Fisher |
| June 1899-Aug 1900 | Alfred Teague |
| August 1900-Dec 1901 | Mrs. Elizabeth Welch |
| December 1901-Mar 1902 | Hannah Hobbs |
| March 1902-Nov 1902 | Ernest Charles Lee |
| November 1902-Sep 1903 | James Alexander Weatherburn |
| September 1903-Sep 1904 | John Read |
| September 1904-Feb 1905 | William Bolton |
| 7th February 1905 | Closed for business |

**Volunteer Arms** – 46 Comyn Street

The first reference we have to a public house in Comyn Street is a court report dated 10th June 1865, when John Jones was the licensee [by 1868 Jones had moved to the Bell on Rugby Road]. The first reference we have to the Volunteer Arms is in August 1869 when Alfred Bird applied to the licensing justices for the renewal of his beer house licence. It comprised three rooms, two smoke rooms measuring approximately 12 ft x 12 ft and a club room measuring 12 ft x 10 ft. At the annual licensing sessions in March 1909, the justices objected to the renewal of the Volunteer's licence on the grounds that it was 'structurally unfit for a licensed premises' describing it as, "a small cottage style house that had mainly outdoor sales". However, the decision was overturned and the licence renewed; owned by Hunt, Edmunds and Co. Ltd [Banbury], it sold Banbury ales and stouts.

At the February 1950 licensing session the licence renewal was objected to on the grounds that "the premises were structurally unsuitable and that having regard to the character and necessities of the neighbourhood, and the number of licensed premises in the immediate vicinity, the licence which is now held in respect

*This circa 1950s Leamington Spa Courier photo of the Volunteer Arms in Comyn Street is by kind permission of Warwickshire County Record Office. Ref: PH(N),600/336/1.*

of the said premises is unnecessary". The objection was upheld and in March only a temporary licence was granted and the pub was referred to the compensation authority for closure. The Volunteer Arms closed for business on 28th October 1950.

| | |
|---|---|
| ≤1865 | John Jones |
| 1868 | James Jones |
| ≤1869 | Alfred Bird |
| 1872-Feb 1884 | Charles Grossey |
| February 1884-Jul 1884 | Hannah Grossey *(On the death of Charles)* |
| July 1884-Nov 1894 | Thomas Massey Hewitt and wife Frances |
| November 1894-1896 | James Prentice |
| 1896-Dec 1904 | William Knight |
| December 1904-Aug 1932 | Arthur Wright |
| August 1932-35 | James Edward Houghton |
| 1936-Jun 1941 | George Arthur Aitken and his wife Nellie *(George then went on to the Leopard)* |
| June 1941-Oct 1950 | James Edward Houghton |
| 28th October 1950 | Closed for business |

**Voodoo Bar** – 35 Regent Street
See Warwick Tavern for details.

**Walnut Tree** – Crown Way, Lillington
The land that the Walnut Tree sits on was originally Village Farm owned by Sidney Macgregor. The Crown Way site was not Ansells first choice when they applied for the transfer of the Bell Inn licence on its closure. In 1948, a provisional licence was granted to Ansells Brewery Ltd for a new pub to be erected in Cromer Road and it was confirmed on Friday 23rd April 1948. However, by March 1951 the licensing justices had approved a new application to change the site from Cromer Road to an area on the Stud Farm Estate. In December 1954, a deputation led by Lillington's vicar, the Rev. J. A. Carter together with churchwarden, G. E. Troth, the Rev. D. V. Gibbon [Lillington Free Church] and Mr. A. Pratt met with the chairman of the Housing Committee, Councillor E. A. Baxter and the town clerk, Mr. J. N. Stothert; they were objecting to the Leamington Corporation allowing the erection of a public house on the corner of Cubbington Road and the new Crown Way.

Notwithstanding, at the annual licensing session held on 14th February 1956, an order sanctioning the provisional removal of the licence from the Bell Inn [69, Rugby Road] to premises to be erected at the corner of Crown Way and Cubbington Road was granted; it was ratified on 19th May 1958. The pub was officially opened on 20th May 1958 by Leamington's mayor, Councillor Eric Lucas, and became known by the sign of the Walnut Tree [many years earlier the land had been owned by the Waller family and a large walnut tree grew in a cottage garden]. Owned by Ansells Brewery Ltd [Park Road, Aston, Birmingham], it was reported to have cost £50,000. Much of the housing in Lillington dates to the 1950s however, as the old Lillington parish stretched across North Leamington as far as Milverton school, it has its fair

*Photo of the Walnut Tree taken 8th January 2009 © Allan Jennings.*

share of late Victorian grandeur. Lillington is light on pubs due to a building restriction imposed by the Wise family when they owned most of the land in the area; the restriction was lifted in the early 1950s and the Walnut Tree was the first pub built in Lillington.

In July 1960, the Leamington Spa Courier reported that, "The licensing justices had approved a scheme for bigger and better off-licence facilities at the Walnut Tree, Lillington - the town's largest public house. The present 'outdoor' will be used for storage and a completely new department will be erected in an attractive layout with entrance and exit doors." Mr. C. A. Pinnell, district supervisor for Ansells Brewery, told the Courier that the extensions were designed to cater for the increased demand and the changing trends on the vast Lillington housing estate. On 28th November 1961, and effective immediately, the licensee [along with four other local landlords] was granted permission, in accordance with the new Licensing Act, to open the off-licence premises from 8.30am. In 1984, the Walnut Tree advertised, "Spend an enjoyable evening in our Nutters Bar" [not the ideal strategy for encouraging the right type of clientele – Ed]. The Leamington Spa Courier dated 12th May 1989 carried a full page advert for the Walnut Tree: "Visit the new-look Walnut Tree and see why people are now calling it one of Leamington's finest traditional pubs. Ansells has invested £180,000 in refurbishing the pub in Crown Way. Features include new seating areas combined with elegant fireplaces to remind people of the qualities of bygone days. The bar and lounge have been extensively refurbished with an area in the lounge set aside for diners as well as those just enjoying a drink. Ansells have appointed new managers Kevin Edwards and Karen Burrows to oversee the new-look Walnut Tree."

On 7th January 2005, the Courier/Weekly News reported: "Lillington pub – The Walnut Tree has been saved from demolition – for the time being – Developers Barratt Mercia want to demolish the 50 year old pub, which stands on the corner of Crown Way and Cubbington Road, and replace it with flats. In December, planning officers told the Courier little could be done to save the pub, as the owners did not need planning permission to knock it down.

But members of Warwick District Council planning committee unanimously refused planning permission for the two and three-storey flats on Tuesday. They attacked the design for being too high and imposing, and said it would result in a loss of open space and amenity space." Unfortunately, this stay of proceedings would prove to be only temporary and in May 2009 the premises were closed and boarded-up. Despite a vigorous campaign, and a 2,500 signature petition, Lillington residents were unable to prevent supermarket chain Tesco acquiring the premises, and opening an 'Express' store on Friday 19th March 2010.

| | |
|---|---|
| 20th May 1958-Nov 1980 | John 'Jack' Alfred Charles Draper and his wife Joan *(Previously at the Somerville Arms)* |
| 20th May 1958-Nov 1980 | Lou Gallagher *(Part-time barman – 22 years service)* |
| November 1980-Sep 1983 | Colin Dennis Gulliver *(Previously at the Coventry Arms)* |
| October 1983-Mar 1984 | Ruby and Dennis Simons *(Jointly with the Rugby Tavern)* |
| March 1984 | Michael 'Mike' Bush |
| 1989 | Kevin Edwards and Karen Burrows *(Managers)* |
| Circa 1994-circa 1999 | Fred and Linda Miller |
| Circa 2000s | Bob Anderson |
| Circa 2000s | Kam *(Full name not known)* |
| October 2003-May 2009 | John Morgan Bell and Deborah Bell |
| May 2009 | Closed for business |

*The Lillington History Society printed the following in the Lillington Community News booklet dated July 2010: The recent closure of the Walnut Tree public house brought to mind an item in the Courier in 2004 suggesting that a large walnut tree grew on the site, the timber of which was used in the building of the Waldorf Astoria Hotel in New York. This seemed worth further investigation, so, with the help of the United States Embassy, we contacted the New York Historical Society, who advised that the former Waldorf Astoria was replaced by the Empire State Building and the new hotel was opened on its present site in 1931 – about the time Lillington's walnut tree might have been used. The claim is plausible since the hotel spared no expense in obtaining the finest materials. Certainly, the New York Times described the gallery of mirrors outside the ballroom where the glass alternated with 'broad walnut pilasters', though, in the hotel's own brochure; the wood is described as harewood. The coffered ceiling outside the checkroom was walnut. Though most of the wood used was American in origin, the Historical Society says there is no particular reason to disbelieve the story! [Note: There was certainly a walnut tree on the Cubbington Road and in October 1933 a number of lads were summoned for "throwing missiles to the danger of passengers in the Cubbington Road on 28th September." [It turned out that the missiles were stones and they were throwing at the tree. The case was dismissed – Ed]*

**Warneford Arms** – 36 Charles Street
The first directory listing we have for the Warneford Arms is in 1871. In 1905 the licensing justices refused to renew its licence as they considered that 'the premises were not structurally adapted for use as a public house'. The case was referred to the county compensation authority

*Photo of the Warneford Arms circa 1890 courtesy of Bill Gibbons collection.*

and the Warneford Arms was closed on 6th January, 1906 [with compensation being paid]. Charles Street was subsequently demolished and the pub site is now part of the Althorpe Industrial Estate.

| | |
|---|---|
| 1871-Apr 1872 | A. Bird |
| April 1872-Nov 1874 | Edward Hillyer |
| November 1874-Jun 1875 | William Ward |
| June 1875-Jul 1876 | Benjamin Mallard |
| July 1876-Sep 1879 | Amos Morgan |
| September 1879-Feb 1890 | Mrs. Elizabeth Morgan *(On the death of Amos)* |
| February 1890-Jul 1899 | William Charles Capper |
| July 1899-Jan 1906 | Mrs. Ann Capper |
| 6th January 1906 | Closed for business |

**Warwick Arms** – 141 Regent Street

The address of these premises was originally Cross Street [New Town], which was laid out circa 1808-1814 and renamed Regent Street circa 1827 in honour of the Prince Regent who had visited Leamington in September 1819 [as was the Regent Hotel]. Originally called the Coventry Arms in 1830 [not to be confused with the Coventry Arms in Guys Cliffe Road], and addressed as 2, Regent Street, it is believed that George Dakin renamed it the Warwick Arms in 1844 [there are also 1822 and 1824 directory listings which, we have concluded from licensee records, were mistakenly and coincidentally attributed to the Warwick Arms, instead of the Warwick Tavern].

On 25th June 1834 the Coventry Arms was sold at auction and the presale notice in the Leamington Spa Courier described the freehold property as: "All that capital and substantially built messuage or tenement and premises, part of which have been lately used as an inn and called the Coventry Arms, situate in Regent Street, Leamington Priors; being a corner house, and having frontages of twenty four yards next to Regent Street and Kenilworth Street; comprising an excellent shop that fronts Regent Street [17 ft x 14 ft], fitted up with all the necessary counters, drawers, and shelves; a good parlour and room adjoining conveniently fitted up for a bar; kitchen; back kitchen; brew house with hard and soft water pumps; an excellent drawing room [19 ft x 14 ft]; dining room [16 ft x 14 ft] and seven convenient bedrooms with water and other closets."

*Outside the Warwick Arms in 1937. The photo is by kind permission of Tom Lewin whose father Robert is playing the accordion on the left and Robert's brother William is playing on the right.*

In January 1893 Robert Scurr applied for a music licence for his club room, stating that it was 50 feet in length and fifteen feet wide, that there were two doors both opening inwards and that there were never more than fifty people in the room. Alderman Wackrill granted the licence on payment of five shillings, conditional on the doors being modified to open outwards. In September 1887 the pub was owned by the Leamington Brewery [Lucas, Blackwell and Arkwright], then Lucas and Co. Ltd [1897], before it became an Ansells pub following their 1928 acquisition of the brewery and its closure in 1934.

In 1972, Ansells offered a tenancy at the Warwick Arms claiming that it was uneconomical to run the pub 'under management' and that there was a trend towards tenancies. In 1997, the Warwick Arms was taken over by Nigel Langstone who renamed it the Sozzled Sausage, claiming that it was the first bar/ restaurant in Leamington. In 2005 the name was changed to the Sausage and then, in 2008, it was changed back to the Sozzled Sausage. In the summer of 2013 the Sozzled Sausage reverted to the Warwick Arms, the name it had carried for 150+ years [1844-1997]; it closed for refurbishment in the October but had reopened by December 2013.

*Photo of the Warwick Arms taken by Bill Bigley in 1987.*

| | |
|---|---|
| 1830-34 | J. Hickling *(Coventry Arms)* |
| 1837-39 | John Price |
| 1839-42 | Thomas Mann |
| 1844-Apr 1847 | George Dakin *(Warwick Arms)* |
| April 1847-Dec 1848 | William Dickison |
| December 1848-Apr 1851 | Thomas Cummins |
| April 1851-54 | Edward Franklin |
| April 1858-Jul 1860 | William Dickison |
| July 1860-Sep 1861 | William Francis Wheeler |
| September 1861-Jul 1865 | James Hardman |
| July 1865-72 | Robert Ward |
| 1872 | John Ward |
| 1872-76 | George Thompson |
| 1876 | A. Thompson |
| ≤May 1878-Sep 1887 | Ives Lesey |
| September 1887-Dec 1887 | Morton Peto Lucas/Leamington Brewery |
| December 1887-91 | William Grant Jnr. |
| 1891-Jan 1892 | Robert Beauclerc Aldridge |
| January 1892-Sep 1892 | William Robert Scurr *(Of Barford)* |
| September 1892-Jan 1899 | Robert Scurr |
| January 1899-Jun 1930 | Frank Mackinder *(Died 29th April 1930, aged 57)* |
| June 1930-Sep 1939 | Mrs. Marie Mackinder *(On the death of Frank)* |
| September 1939-Apr 1942 | Albert Edward Bonser |
| April 1942-Feb 1956 | Druscilla Bonser *(On the death of Albert)* |
| February 1956-Mar 1959 | Peter Bennett |
| March 1959-May 1961 | Charles William Rogers |
| May 1961-Oct 1961 | Alan John Godfree |
| October 1961-Apr 1962 | Bernard Charles Edward Elmer |
| April 1962-Jun 1962 | Raymond Alfred Clay |
| June 1962-Jan 1963 | Joseph William Slater |
| January 1963-Apr 1964 | Ronald Lobb |
| April 1964-Feb 1965 | Leslie Wilfred Warwick |
| February 1965-Dec 1965 | Norman Harold Beard |
| December 1965-Feb 1967 | Maurice de Sadeleer |
| February 1967-Jun 1967 | Ralph Millard |
| June 1967-Dec 1967 | Anthony John Bannister |
| December 1967-Aug 1968 | Arthur John Vicary |
| August 1968-Apr 1969 | Donald David Ellis |
| April 1969-Oct 1969 | James McDougall Copland Nairn |
| October 1969-Jun 1971 | Hugh Desmond Quinn |
| June 1971-Apr 1972 | Brian Trevor Clark |
| April 1972-Apr 1973 | David Noel Clubbe |
| April 1973-≥1983 | Thomas O'Shea and his wife Maura |

| | |
|---|---|
| 1996 | Graham Sanders |
| 1997 | Nigel Langstone |
| 2005 | David Michael Callaghan |
| November 2008-Oct 2009 | Mark Henderson |
| October 2009-Apr 2010 | Amjad Sawobar |
| April 2010 → | David Hayto |

*In May 1896, the first anniversary dinner of the Loyal Leamington Lodge of the R.A.O.B. was held at the Warwick Arms when about 60 members and friends partook of a capital repast. The evening was pleasantly passed in toast and song.*

In 2009, it advertised: "Becky welcomes you to the Sausage, a family friendly bar in the heart of our town. Why not come and play poker on a Sunday, or take to the mike on a Tuesday with acoustic night or perhaps you just want to enjoy great food in a chilled atmosphere."

*The conservation department at Warwick District Council describes the building as: Public house circa 1820, with later additions and alterations. Reddish-brown brick with Welsh slate roof and painted stucco front façade. Exterior: 3 storeys, 3 first-floor windows, central entrance plan. First floor: 6/6 sashes. Second floor: 3/3 sashes, all with sills and in plain reveals. Ground floor: 2 steps to central entrance, double part-glazed doors with overlight within surround of pilasters with incised decoration, continuos frieze and hood. To either side are tripartite windows with pilasters to ends in plain reveals and with sills, c20 glazing; wide eaves. Tall left stack and centre and rear stacks with cornices. To right return: first floor has 3 openings, outer 6/6 sashes and central blocked opening. Second floor: to right a 3/3 sash, otherwise blocked openings. All in plain reveals with sills and flat channelled arches with raised keystones. Ground floor: central entrance a 6-panelled door in Tuscan pilastered surround with frieze and hood which continues to left; otherwise c20 windows, that to right has plain reveals with sill and flat channelled arch with raised keystone.*

*Above left: The Sausage taken on 6th January 2010 © Allan Jennings. Above right: The Sozzled Sausage taken on 20th August 2010 © Allan Jennings.*

**Warwick Hotel** – 35 Regent Street
See Warwick Tavern for details.

**Warwick Tavern** – 35 Regent Street
The address of these premises was originally Cross Street [New Town] which was laid out circa 1808-1814; it was renamed Regent Street circa 1827 in honour of the Prince Regent who had visited Leamington in September 1819 [as was the Regent Hotel]. The first credible reference we have for the Warwick Tavern is an 1823 entry in the licensed victuallers' records, when John Rainbow is listed as the licensee. However, there is also an 1822 directory listing for the Warwick Arms [which would not be named as such until 1844 and then at another location]; we have concluded from licensee records that the naming is a coincidence and that the entry should be for the Warwick Tavern. During the period circa 1827-80, it would be variously numbered '45' '52' and '53' before being readdressed as 35, Regent Street, around 1880. Circa 1890, the pub was bought by the Leamington Brewery [Lucas, Blackwell and Arkwright] and in 1897 the brewery and the pub would be acquired by Lucas and Co. Ltd. The Warwick Tavern was renamed the Warwick Hotel in 1904. On 11th September 1969, the Leamington Spa Courier reported that, "the new rooms at the Warwick Hotel were christened on Friday. A small smoke room, three small inter-connecting bars and a kitchen were knocked down. And as a result.... a fine smoke room and a lounge is glorious Victoriana."

In March 1984 and September 1985, the Morning News published articles on these premises which are summarised as follows: In 1982, Chris Miles took over as licensee of the Warwick Hotel, leasing it from Allied Breweries. Once planning permission had been granted he started work on transforming the pub, and its image, at a cost of almost £100,000. The two former bars had been converted into one large lounge served by a new circular bar in the centre of the room, and the conversion was set-off by new carpets, curtains and wallpaper. Another new feature was the brick fireplace in one corner of the lounge. The pub remained open throughout the refurbishment closing only for 3-4 weeks at the end of the project while the 'finishing touches' were applied. On completion in 1984 it reopened as the Birch and Billycock. The name of the pub was contrived by Chris with the aid of a crossword puzzle clue – with sign writers pressing him to come up with a new name, he came across the word Billycock [a type of old bowler hat] and coupled it with the birch tree which stood outside.

In 1990, Tom Smith made a number of changes to the Birch and Billycock, converting the car park into an attractive garden where people could sit and enjoy their drinks, changing one end of the long bar into a non-smoking area and also introducing a separate

*The Birch and Billycock taken in 1987 by Bill Bigley.*

*Photo of the Birch Tree taken 27th March 1999 © Allan Jennings.*

wine and champagne bar. Furthermore, he banished the TV saying, "it ruins the art of conversation, and that to me is what a pub is all about". In 1994, it was renamed the Birch Tree. In December 1999 the premises were renamed Voodoo [part owned by Mr. Makhan Kandola] and it remains open in December 2013.

| | |
|---|---|
| 1823-24 | John Rainbow |
| 1824-Aug 1845 | William Batchelor *(Retired in August 1845 and licence transferred to his son)* |
| August 1845-79 | William Batchelor Jnr |
| 1879-Dec 1882 | Mrs. Sarah Batchelor |
| December 1882-Feb 1886 | Alfred Shepherd |
| February 1886-May 1886 | Herbert Robert Arkwright/Leamington Brewery |
| May 1886-≤1891 | Alfred Womersley |
| ≤1891-May 1891 | Sarah Ann Womersley |
| May 1891-Mar 1899 | Job Boyes *(Of Stratford-upon-Avon)* |
| March 1899-May 1903 | Mrs. Sarah Boyes *(On the death of Job)* |
| May 1903-Apr 1904 | John Henry Beecroft |
| April 1904-Dec 1905 | John MacDonald *(Warwick Hotel)* |
| December 1904-1905 | John Charles Welch |
| 1905-21 | Charles Hugh Broadbridge |
| 1921 | Mrs. M. A. Broadbridge |
| 1924-Feb 1937 | Joseph Edward William Lenton *(Died February 1937, aged 57)* |
| February 1937-Feb 1940 | Mary Anne 'Annie' Lenton *(On the death of Joseph)* |
| February 1940-Jul 1963 | George Duncan Chaplin *(Ex Coventry City and Bradford City footballer)* |
| July 1963-Oct 1968 | William Arthur Johnson *(On the death of George Chaplin)* |
| October 1968-Dec 1971 | Malcolm John Stephen Hall |
| December 1971-Mar 1973 | Ralph Chambers |

| | |
|---|---|
| March 1973-Aug 1976 | Terence Harold Ward |
| August 1976-Mar 1980 | Derek John Watson and his wife June |
| | *(Previously at the King Charles, Evesham)* |
| March 1980 | Brian Carr and his wife Doreen |
| ≤April 1982-Oct 1982 | George Gallagher *(Relief manager)* |
| October 1982-≥1990 | Christopher Miles *(Warwick Hotel from 1982-84;* |
| | *renamed Birch and Billycock in March 1984)* |
| 1984/1985 | Adam 'Foz' Lees *(Bar manager)* |
| 1988 | Geoff Bingham *(Licensee)* |
| 1990-91 | Tommy Smith *(Previously manager of Jekyll and Hyde)* |
| December 1992-95 | Derek Williamson *(Renamed Birch Tree 1994)* |
| 1999 | Kristine McCready *(Bar Manager – Voodoo)* |
| 2003 | Mark Vaughan *(Bar Manager – Voodoo)* |
| 1999-Mar 2011 | Makhan Singh Kandola |
| March 2011-Jun 2011 | Eleanor Anne Leacroft |
| June 2011 → | Brian Heggerty |

*The Leamington Courier dated 10th August 1973 reported that: It has been a dry summer for beer drinkers in Leamington lately, due to shortages of some of their favourite brews. But Ansells Brewery, Birmingham says, "There is no plot to deprive Leamington drinkers of their beer." "Last week we had no draught beer at all for four days," said Mrs. Golding, wife of the licensee of the Greyhound in Emscote Road. "Its just goes on and on, whatever you order they always say the matter is in hand, but we really ought to be told what is happening." The Warwick Hotel, in Regent Street and other Leamington pubs have also had problems especially with lager. "This all stems from our pre-Easter production difficulties," said Ansells spokesman Mr. Don Wilson. "We couldn't catch up before the hot spell started. Demand is right up, and it's a question of sending out beer as fast as we can, our delivery crews are working almost 24 hours a day." He confirmed that the brewery is still having delivery problems. "If people are getting less than they ordered it's because we are trying to be fair to everyone. We hope our licensees and customers will continue to be patient and understanding as they have been so far." However, one cheering note, on Monday the price of Ansells bitter goes down by one new penny.*

The Coventry Evening Telegraph dated 15th December 1999 reported that: A piece of Africa has arrived in the heart of Leamington. Shields and chairs with animal-skin designs are among the unusual fittings revellers can enjoy at the new Voodoo bar, in Warwick Street. The former Birch Tree pub

*Photo of Voodoo taken on 26th October 2008 © Allan Jennings.*

was completely gutted as part of a £160,000 revamp and re-opened its doors last week. Mo Kandola, director of MGM Enterprises which is behind the project, stated that "it's going absolutely brilliantly and we've been packed out during the evenings. Customers have told us they love the decor and style and we're looking forward to establishing ourselves".

*On 11th September 2003, the Coventry Evening Telegraph reported that: A blaze has sucked the glass from top floor windows and sent plumes of black smoke swirling through the centre of town. The fire at Voodoo started just before 2.00pm yesterday. Police officers redirected the traffic while two fire appliances blocked the road. Six people had earlier been evacuated. Fire station officer Steve West said, "It turned out to be a store-room. There's a lot of severe damage. The fire had taken so fast because there was a lot of combustible material in there, like paper and cardboard boxes."*

The conservation department at Warwick District Council describes the building as: A hotel, now public house circa 1855 [pre 1823 – Ed] with later alterations; Pinkish-brown brick in Flemish bond with Welsh slate roof and cast-iron lamp bracket; Three storeys, 3 first-floor windows; Central entrance, 3 steps to a plate glass door within tooled architrave and consoles supporting pediment; Ground and first floor have 6/6 sashes, second floor has 3/3 sashes, all with sills, in plain reveals and with flat rusticated arches with central keystones; Hipped roof, end and ridge stacks; Left façade has two ground floor canted bay windows with 6/6 sashes between 2/2 sides with pilasters, otherwise fenestration as front façade; Above door a decorative lamp that curves outwards.

### Wellington Tavern – 9 Wellington Street

Wellington Street was laid out in 1826, and named after the Duke of Wellington [who visited the town in April 1827]. Our first reference to the Wellington Tavern is an 1828 entry in the licensed victuallers' records, when Robert Budd is listed as licensee. The Wellington changed licensees [and evidently owners] numerous times during its relatively short life, as is evidenced by the number of auction notices that we have sighted.

In April 1829 an auction was held on the premises to sell-off household furniture, stock of ale, porter and spirits, a capital four-motion beer machine and liquor fountain [and two

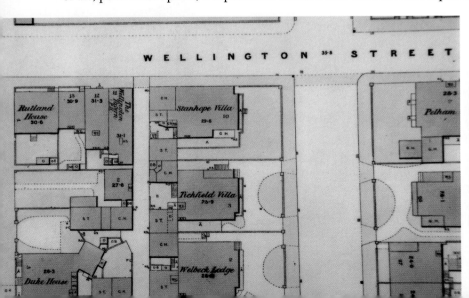

*This 1852 Board of Health map shows the Wellington Tavern situated on what we know as Regent Street, between Dale Street and Grove Street.*

excellent milking cows]; in August 1830 the pub was advertised for sale by auction, "under a deed of assignment for the benefit of creditors", and in April 1851 it was sold for £770 [including an adjoining dwelling house]. A little more than twelve months later, it was advertised to be sold by auction at the Crown Hotel on Tuesday 31st August 1852, by order of the mortgagee; at the time the licensee was Edward Lewis, an annual tenant who had established a respectable and increasing trade. The auction notice described the premises as comprising a spacious sitting room, a suitable number of bedrooms, two bars, parlour, smoke room, brew house and malt house.

Whether or not the Wellington Tavern was sold has not been determined, but Edward Lewis was still the landlord when the licence was renewed at the annual licensing session in 1856. However, the end was near and, although the licence was renewed in 1860, this fully licensed public house was auctioned on 5th April 1860. As the Wellington Tavern was not referenced at the 1861 licensing session, we have concluded that the premises had been sold at auction the previous year, and that there had been a 'change of usage', either to another business type or residential. By 1876, Wellington Street had been renamed Regent Street, which had simultaneously been renumbered [commencing at the western end].

| | |
|---|---|
| 1828 | Robert Budd |
| 1830 | Bailey |
| 1835-39 | Catherine Aston |
| 1841-42 | John Richards |
| 1846-51 | Emma Booth |
| 1851-Jul 1857 | Edward Lewis |
| July 1857-Jan 1858 | Benjamin Dickinson |
| January 1858-Aug 1858 | Richard Steeden |
| August 1858-Nov 1859 | Joseph Bolton |
| November 1859-60 | John Musson |
| 1860 | Closed for business |

**Whale Bar** – 102 Warwick Street
See Jam Bar and Brasserie for details.

**Wheatsheaf Inn** – 163 Tachbrook Road
The first reference we have to this inn is an auction notice that appeared in the local press on 28th June 1834, giving its address as Springfield Street [renamed Shrubland Street in the early 1880s and since circa 1971 its top end has been called Charles Gardner Road]. Notwithstanding, since 1835 directories have listed the pub at its current address and circa 1920 it was renumbered from '117' to 163, Tachbrook Road.

In 1856, then described as being near the Arboretum Gardens, the pub comprised a bar, parlour, kitchen, dining and drawing rooms, six bedrooms, large cellaring, stable, yard, large garden, and bowling green. On 18th February 1905, the directors of Lucas and Co. Ltd [Leamington Brewery] approved the purchase of the Wheatsheaf Inn from a Mrs. Durrant, for £3,200; it would become an Ansells pub following their 1928 acquisition of the

*The Wheatsheaf taken in 1987 by Bill Bigley.*

brewery and its closure in 1934. Although we knew that the current premises is not the original building, for three years we had been unable to determine precisely when the rebuild took place. However, in March 1940, the Leamington Courier reported on the licensing justices' decision to grant an application for a provisional order for the removal of the licence from the Star Inn [Wise Street] to premises proposed to be erected on the corner of Tachbrook Road and Kingsway [Sun in Splendour]. This application was unsuccessfully contested by the licensee of the Wheatsheaf, who claimed that "the project was premature of the neighbourhood's development", and that, "in 1936 the Wheatsheaf was rebuilt at a big cost to meet the needs of the neighbourhood, and he contended that the development since that date did not warrant the new house". A check of the Morning News for that year revealed that the new premises were opened on Friday 30th October 1936.

On 28th November 1961, and effective immediately, the licensee [along with four other local landlords] was granted permission to open the off-licence premises from 8.30am as permitted by the new Licensing Act. In May 1973, a £15,000 refurbishment was completed that included the addition of a dining room and a Victorian style lounge; the first pint was pulled by 77 year old Harry Walton who had been using the Wheatsheaf since 1912. On Friday 15th February 1974, a new Steak Room was opened, offering, "good beer, good food and good service from Tuesday to Sunday". Still owned by Ansells, the Wheatsheaf was leased to Wolverhampton and Dudley Breweries Ltd [Banks] in 1982 and from 23rd August it sold Banks' traditional draught beers. The Wheatsheaf Inn remains open in December 2013.

| | |
|---|---|
| 1834 | Sarah Clark |
| ≤1835 | John Baseley |
| 1837-39 | Leonard Clifford |
| 1839-Sep 1856 | Robert East |

| | |
|---|---|
| September 1856-Jun 1861 | William Edward Sheasby |
| June 1861-77 | William Smith |
| 1877-Jun 1877 | Hannah Smith |
| June 1877 | John Clulee |
| 1878 | MaChille *(As spelt)* |
| 1879-Aug 1887 | Mark B. Durrant |
| August 1887-May 1905 | Mary Ann Durrant *(On the death of Mark)* |
| May 1905-Mar 1915 | James Henry Clulee |
| March 1915-32 | Thomas Gulliman |
| 1932-Feb 1936 | Christopher Charles Chedham |
| February 1936-37 | C. R. Naylor |
| 1938-Feb 1941 | Harold Joseph Feeney *(Called-up for military service)* |
| February 1941-Nov 1949 | Walter Cyril Dale |
| November 1949-Jan 1950 | Nancy Marie Dale *(On the death of Walter)* |
| January 1950-May 1957 | William Thomas Henry Beetlestone |
| May 1957-April 1961 | Leonard Albert Care |
| April 1961-Dec 1965 | Alfred John Bounds |
| December 1965-Aug 1966 | Clifford Roy Bounds |
| August 1966-June 1967 | James Campbell McDonnell |
| June 1967-June 1969 | Ralph Millard |
| June 1969-Nov 1973 | William Stanley 'Stan' Wardle and his wife Jean |
| November 1973-Feb 1974 | John Brady |
| February 1974-85 | Terence John 'Ted' and Joyce Collins *(Previously at the Rugby Tavern)* |
| ≤1986-≥1987 | Alan Chamberlain |
| August 1988-1998 | Ann and Jim Miller |
| 1998-January 2006 | Ravinder Singh Khela |
| January 2006 → | Surjit Mann |

*The Leamington Spa Courier dated 3rd December 1853 carried the following sale by auction notice: To be sold by John Staite [auctioneer] at the Wheatsheaf Inn, Tachbrook Road, on Tuesday, the 20th December 1853 at five o'clock in the afternoon – All the above mentioned old-established public house, called the Wheatsheaf Inn, now in the occupation of Mr. Robert East; and also the conveniently arranged dwelling house adjoining, in the occupation of Mr. Raymond Moore, together with a paddock and garden in the rear, the same having a considerable frontage to the Tachbrook Road and to Springfield Street, the whole now producing the low rental of £50 per annum.*

This article from the Leamington Courier dated 18th May 1906 was used by Allan Jennings in a biography about his granddad, Thomas 'Skerry' Jones:

**Leamington St. John's F.C.**
A successful smoking concert* was held in connection with the above club at the Wheatsheaf Hotel on Saturday evening. Councillor W. Lee presided. On opening the proceedings, the

chairman congratulated the club on winning the league championship, wished them still further success in the future and promised to do all he possibly could for the welfare of the club. During the evening several pleasing presentations were made, consisting of silver and gold centred medal to Mr. F. Watson [trainer], and Mr. W. Griffin [reserve], a photograph of the team to Councillor Lee and a framed photograph of the team to the hon. secretary, Mr. J.H. Burton [subscribed for by the members of the club]. The secretary very suitably acknowledged the gift, promising to do all he could in the interest of Leamington St. John's FC. At the conclusion, Mr. W. Watson proposed a very hearty vote of thanks to Councillor Lee for the deep interest he had always taken in the club, and also to those who had contributed to the evening's enjoyment. Mr. A. Cleaver seconded and it was carried with marked enthusiasm; the proceedings terminated with the members all joining in the singing of "For he's a jolly good fellow". [*Smoking concerts, popular during the Victorian era, were exclusively men only functions featuring live music performances and the opportunity discuss the topics of the day, be it politics or football – Ed]

*Thomas Gulliman came to Leamington from Weston-on-Avon, near Stratford-upon-Avon, in 1851 and died at Wharf Cottage in Leamington on 27th December 1901. He married the 2nd daughter of a family from Southam. They set up home at Wharf Cottage on the canal on what is now part of Sydenham housing estate. Thomas started up a business at the wharf supplying lime to farmers around the district and coal to the merchants in Leamington. He had about 6 barges, 3 would go to the Black Country to pick up the coal and 3 would go east and south to fetch the lime from the quarries. Thomas was a sidesman at St. Marys Church for 43 years. He had 5 children, 2 boys and 3 girls and he named his second son Thomas Gulliman.*

*Thomas junior was born at Wharf Cottage. On leaving School he worked for Leamington Brick Co. and stayed there for about 15 years. He started work as a clerk in the office and finished up as the pay clerk giving out the wages each week. He then went to work in a shop in Leamington and learned the commercial side of things. He married Ada and in 1901 when he was in his late thirties he went to the Windmill Inn on the Tachbrook Road as the licensee and*

*The Wheatsheaf and licensee Thomas Gulliman in 1916 courtesy of Tony Gulliman.*

*stayed until 1915. Thomas and Ada had 3 children and they were all born at the Windmill, Dennis in 1906, Edward (Ted) in 1908 and Norman in 1911.*

*On leaving the Windmill in 1915 they moved a little way down the road to the Wheatsheaf. This was when it was the old Wheatsheaf building. The photo on the previous page shows the Wheatsheaf Hotel as it used to look. This particular photo was taken in 1916 and shows licensee Thomas Gulliman. The photo is courtesy of Thomas Gulliman's grandson Tony who lives in Bishops Tachbrook.*

*The sign on the wall to the right of the picture is thought to be a timetable for a steam-powered bus service. It is interesting to see that the pub is level with the main road and not set back, and the gas lamp is another interesting feature as I remember them around Shrubland Street in the 1950s. The pub is supplied by Ansells of Aston, Birmingham. As a square, unpainted three storey building it is quite different from the building we see today.*

*Thomas retired from the Wheatsheaf in 1932 and went to live at Rose Lawn in Lillington Road. For at least 10 years of his retirement he was chairman of the local Licensed Victuallers Association. He died in 1955 and he is buried in Leamington cemetery.*

*Thomas Gulliman took over from James Clulee and his wife Kate. The Clulee's had a son Horace who was a private in the Tank Corps during the First World War. He was killed in a training accident when another tank failed to see his hand signals at Bovington Camp on Tuesday 13th of May 1919 when he was only 21 years old. Horace had given his address as the Wheatsheaf.*

Vera Belton [née Walmesley] remembers the Wheatsheaf: "I was chatting with my sister about your Pubs project and we have many memories of various pubs in the Leamington area. I left Leamington in 1949 when our mother died but continued at school until 1951 travelling in from Solihull. Our dad's local was the Wheatsheaf, we lived in Claremont Road, and our mother would go with him for a drink on Saturday evenings. On their return I would be presented with the War Cry, a publication issued by the Salvation Army and sold to them by a 'soldier' in full regalia who visited the pubs in turn; presumably to convert the drinkers to becoming tee-total. Mother I believe drank Guinness believing it to be good for her. In fact stout and milk was considered excellent for building up one's strength! I also remember the Windmill because we had an allotment behind there where we 'dug for victory' and afterwards restored our energy. In the summer we would walk to Radford Road and sit in the garden of the Red House pub there, and I was allowed a Vimto which was the fore-runner of Coca-Cola. Another drink the women would have, they never went themselves to the bar, was port and lemon[ade]. It was not until later, after the war, that St. Clements, a mixture of orange juice and lemonade, became popular."

*The Leamington Spa Courier 27th January 1950 reported:* **Vicar of St. John's finds help at 'the local'** *- Admiring the struggle of the vicar of St. John's, Rev. J. W. Crank, the members of the Sports and Social Committee at the Wheatsheaf Inn decided to have a collecting box for his church heating fund. The idea caught on and a box, a model of a church, was packed with coins. The vicar was asked to collect on the Wednesday night. Rev. Crank was promised more to follow and he thanked the collectors, Messrs G. Wilshire and B. Neal, together with the committee, Messrs Rogers, Stacey, Fletcher, Walters, Yardley and Reynolds.*

The Morning News dated 10th March 1960 reported that: A cheque for £30 "the largest we have ever received" was presented on behalf of the Wheatsheaf Indian Social Club, by

Mr. Tara Singh, in the mayor's parlour to Mrs. R. Churches, woman commandant of the local unit of the British Red Cross Society.

*The Leamington Spa Courier dated 7th September 1979 reported:* **Cheers.... to Ted's 100 years** *- The Leamington Spa Courier was at the Wheatsheaf, Tachbrook Road, to record centurion Ted Norman celebrate his 100th birthday. To be exact, he was a week premature as he will spend that day with his family. Friends gathered at the pub where he has been a customer since 1915 and his drinks were on the house all evening. His favourite tipple is a pint of best bitter. Ted was a veteran of the First World War, joining the Royal Army Service Corp. He worked as a driver hauling ammunition to the guns on the French and Belgium fronts. "They told us they were going to make homes for heroes to live in, but when I got home hundreds were standing under bridges for shelter. Times were hard in the 20s and 30s," said Ted. He was employed as a driver for Warwickshire County Council during this time. When the Second World War started he joined Nelsons of Warwick as a driver. "I can remember the night Coventry was bombed," said Ted. "The sky looked as if it was on fire. A few incendiary bombs were dropped on Leamington." After the war Ted got a job with Flavels in Leamington and nine years later, he became a lollipop man helping children across the road. He finally retired when he was 86 years old. Lily, Ted's wife, died in 1969 and Ted went to live with his son and daughter. He has six children, six grand-children and nine great grand-children. Ted keeps himself busy reading and cooking. "I've worked hard, that's what kept me going," said Ted with a smile.*

The Leamington Spa Courier dated 1st July 1983 reported that: Banks' Brewery has built a ramp at the front door of the Wheatsheaf to aid disabled people. Mr. Ted Collins, landlord says the ramp cost about £200 to build and it will mean residents confined to wheelchairs from the nearby Royal Counties home can visit the pub unaided. The brewery agreed to build the ramp after Mr. George Gall, from Whitnash, described the difficulties his step-daughter, Ann Richards, had in negotiating the steps into the pub. Ann like other residents in the home enjoys getting out for an odd drink, but is often frustrated by the shortage of pushers to help them up the pub steps. When the ramp is finished at the Wheatsheaf they can nip in when they please after going through the second obstacle - the swing doors.

### Wheelers Arms – Kenilworth Street
It is possible that this pub was previously named the Swan Inn [Kenilworth Street] in 1833-34, but we have no corroborating evidence. The first directory listing we have for the Wheelers Arms is in 1835 and the last is in 1839 [although it is misnamed as the Weavers Arms]. As it is not listed in the 1841 or subsequent directories we have concluded that it closed 1839-40.

1835-39                                    Richard Mills

### White Hart Inn – 7 Windsor Street
The site of the former White Hart Inn is now occupied by the telephone exchange. In 1849 this beer house was recorded as being on the southern junction of Windsor Street and

*Photo of the White Hart in 1956 courtesy of the late Bill Gibbons.*

Morris Street [which would later be renamed Windsor Place]. Our first directory listing is also in 1849 when John Barker was the licensee [there is also a John Baker listed at a beer retailer/beer house in Windsor Street in 1841-42; maybe a misspelling, but more likely the John Baker that had been at the Butchers Arms, 1838-39]. The White Hart was a beer house until August 1858 when application for a publican's full on-licence was granted; it was latterly owned by Flower and Sons Ltd. In 1903 there were three entrances, two in Windsor Street and one in a passage leading from Windsor Street to Windsor Place. In October 1904, the local justices granted permission to make an additional door in Windsor Place for a bottle and jug department [only]. The White Hart was closed for business on 1st September 1966 and by February 1969 the old terraced houses that had once surrounded it had been demolished. The existing telephone exchange was extended onto the former pub site to provide an additional 4,700 lines; the building extension, and its fit-out, cost a reported £615,000.

| | |
|---|---|
| 1849-58 | John Barker |
| 1858-May 1860 | John Marriott |
| May 1860-Mar 1865 | William Bews |
| March 1865-66 | Arthur Edmund Owen |
| 1868-Jun 1869 | John Short |
| June 1869-72 | James Haynes |
| 1872-Nov 1872 | William Cooper |
| November 1872-75 | John Ife |
| 1875-Feb 1880 | Edwin Pitman |

| | |
|---|---|
| February 1880-Jul 1885 | William Griffiths |
| July 1885-Feb 1899 | Charles Hyatt |
| February 1899-Nov 1902 | Betsy Hyatt *(On the death of Charles)* |
| November 1902-Apr 1907 | Thomas Joseph Kelly |
| April 1907-Aug 1915 | Charles Henry Langston |
| August 1915-Sep 1939 | Councillor James 'Jack' Blackwell |
| September 1939-Feb 1960 | William John Hopkins |
| February 1960-Apr 1963 | Lewis Reginald Pugh *(On the death of William)* |
| 29th April 1963 | Harold J. McDonald |
| Circa 1963 | Percy Mallier *(Manager – probably working for Mr. McDonald)* |
| 1st September 1966 | Closed for business |

*The Leamington Spa Courier dated 8th January 1960 reported that: The new licensee of the White Hart Inn, Leamington, was on Monday night urged to spend as much time as possible on the premises. The request came from Mr. W. J. Webb, chairman of the Leamington justices, who had been told that the licensee, Mr. L. R. Pugh, would not be sleeping at the Inn. Mr. A. J. Lord, who successfully applied for a protection order in favour of Mr. Pugh, said he would be putting in a manageress-barmaid, who would live at the Inn with her daughter, and that he would also be on the premises for most of the day. Chief Inspector Thomas Everitt said there were no police objections to the arrangement as long as Mr. Pugh was on the premises during licensed hours. Mr. E. W. Backman [clerk] said that some areas in town required "quite a strong person" as resident innkeeper.*

The Leamington Spa Courier dated 12th February 1960 reported: **The little back-street bistro trebled trade just by being different** – Not long ago, the White Hart Inn, Windsor Street, Leamington, was typical of many back street pubs which have been fighting a rearguard action against changing social conditions - and in some cases almost surrendered. It was drab and uninviting and custom had dwindled. Then came a Leamington man who has a theory about pubs, a theory built on nearly half a century of "inside knowledge" as a specialist valuer to the hotel and licensed trade. Today, under the wing of 64 year-old Mr. Lewis Reginald Pugh, the White Hart is a different kind of place, "you'd hardly believe such a transformation possible", an astonished customer told me. Mr. Pugh has achieved this metamorphosis - trade has trebled in less than a month - by plugging a basic idea that pubs should be nicer than a man's home in order to make him leave his home to go to them.

This little, rotund, jovial man, has given the White Hart a new lease of life at a cost of less than £500. Publicans from many parts of the town have been visiting his tiny bar and smokeroom to see how he does it. "I don't use any gimmicks" he told me, "I have made the place bright and cosy with paint, gay curtains, good lighting. I have engaged a good manager – Mrs. Joan Lant, who has had twenty years experience in 'west end' and other big hotels. That counts for a lot. All too often, barmaids are grumpy and untidy. When you come in here you find dishes of crisps and biscuits on the counter and pretty well any drink you like to mention. There are plenty of little pubs that have become so run down they can't afford to buy a good variety of stock. There is no TV, no darts or dominoes; just quiet background music and encouragement for friendly talk. I often come in to chat with the customers. It is important that publicans should be able to talk about something more intelligent that what is going to win the big race."

"At one time," said Mr Pugh, "Only working men went into the White Hart. They did not bother too much how they were dressed. Now they still come in, together with shopkeepers and business men. And most look well dressed citizens enjoying a night out." The White Hart is probably the only pub of its type in Leamington which boasts its own visiting card. It gives the name of the brew and the sub-title, "Joan's Bar - Joan Lant, late Kenilworth and Balsall Common". This epitomises Mr. Pugh's belief that the small back-street pubs are an important part of community life and an indispensable adjunct of the town's tourist trade. "Make them cosy and comfortable, like smart bistros - a bit of 'west end' in Leamington - and the tourists will never forget the town," he declared. "The modern tendency of the brewers to erect vast new 'gin-palaces' is all wrong. The little inn of old England is the lifeblood of the trade because it gives customers the club atmosphere of intimacy and comfort. The brewers would be better occupied in cleaning up some of the wretched little hovels that could easily be made bright and profitable." Having proved his point at the White Hart, Mr. Pugh plans to take over other small pubs in the area with the object of 'rejuvenating' them. "I would be proud to be known as King of the Back Street Pubs," he chuckled.

*In June 1964, landlord of the White Hart in Windsor Street J. H. "Mac" Macdonald was saying if you want entertainment do not come to Leamington. He has been promoting bands for nearly 40 years and thinks the entertainment scene could do with a good shake-up. Bradford born some fifty odd years ago, he began his career in the promotion business in Coventry and can reel off a string of famous bands he has engaged for one dance hall or another.*

*He has spent over £1,000 on renovation since he took over the lease on the White Hart about 15 months ago. He also has the Palace in Satchwell Street. "I've never come across a place as bad as this, it's supposed to be a holiday resort but it's absolutely dead. There's nothing here for the young, no real dance hall, the Pump Rooms aren't big enough and as for the Town Hall, it's a monstrosity; it shouldn't be pulled down, it should be blown-up. They used to run special trains here from Birmingham and Coventry, the town was a proper rendezvous. I've seen the Jephson Gardens crammed full of people listening to the music on a Sunday, but the days of the bath-chair have gone. People want entertainment and I don't mean the "twist 'n' twang" groups. They're all right, but the trend these days seems to be to have something for twelve months. Let's face it, even the Beatles are on the way out."*

**White Horse** – 4-6 Clarendon Avenue
The first directory listing we have is in 1833 when it was addressed as South Parade, Clarendon Square [it is listed as 3, South Parade from the 1840s; then 6, Clarendon Avenue from the 1880s and finally 4-6, Clarendon Avenue from circa 1900]. When the White Horse was sold by auction on 12th June 1837 it was described as being: "All that newly-erected and substantially built commodious freehold inn, messuage and dwelling house,

with the stabling and appurtenances thereto belonging, called the White Horse Inn, and occupied by Mr. Joseph Harvey at an annual rent of £40; comprising excellent cellaring, brew house with pump of capital water, good stable and granary, large yard, &c. Also, immediately adjoining is a conveniently sized butcher's shop, with sitting room behind, newly built, in the occupation of Mr. James Ward, at a rent of £13 per annum."

On 6th March 1890 these premises were auctioned at the Crown Hotel; the sale notice published in the Leamington Spa Courier a week prior described the freehold property thus: "All that block of freehold property, Nos. 4 and 6, Clarendon Avenue, and consisting of the free and fully licensed public house known as the White Horse Inn. The accommodation of the public house consists of entrance hall, comfortable bar, smoke room, tap room and kitchen, four bedrooms, spacious cellaring with barrel slide. In the yard at the rear, with entrance from Covent Garden Market, is a capital brew house, with plant in working order, a washhouse, two closets, two-stall stable, and loft over. Gas and town water is laid on." The property also included an adjoining dwelling house with front shop [4, Clarendon Avenue] comprising a kitchen, water closet and small yard; a scullery and coalhouse in the basement and a sitting room, three bedrooms and a box room upstairs. In total, the property had a frontage to Clarendon Avenue of 44 ft 2 in and to Covent Garden Market 45 ft 7 in. In 1895, the pub was owned by Messrs Henry Mitchell and Co, who in 1898 would merge with William Butler and Co. to form Mitchells & Butlers. By 1961, it was owned by Bass, Mitchells & Butlers Ltd [later to become Bass Plc] and sold Brew XI and M&B mild.

In March 1986, the pub was extended and refurbished at a cost of £300,000 and on its re-opening the chairman of Warwick District Council, Councillor Agnes Leddy, pulled the first pint. On Thursday 8th March 1990, The Observer reported that, "The White Horse opens its doors today after a complete refurbishment. On the one hand there is the traditionally furnished bar with its original wood and mirrored back fittings like a glimpse into Leamington's past; at the other end the beautifully furnished lounge provides the perfect place for lunch or dinner as well as providing a lively atmosphere for people to

*Photo of the White Horse courtesy of Nick Wilkins.*

meet in the evenings. The White Horse also keeps up its reputation for good beer serving draught Bass and Brew XI." At the beginning of September 1998, it closed for five weeks for another make-over which included extending the lounge, improving the kitchen and toilet facilities, refurbishing the bar area and enhancing the courtyard; Bass Taverns [the owners] estimated the cost to be around £600,000. In September 2003 permission was granted to open until 1.00am on Fridays and Saturdays. The White Horse remains open in December 2013.

| | |
|---|---|
| 1833-35 | William Reading |
| 1837-39 | Joseph Harvey |
| 1839-46 | James Harvey |
| 1849-78 | Mrs. Elizabeth Harvey |
| 1878-May 1890 | James Whitehead |
| May 1890-Jun 1890 | Walter 'John' Brooks |
| June 1890-Oct 1894 | George Mason |
| October 1894-May 1898 | Lewis Allen |
| May 1898-Mar 1900 | George James Dunn Pollard |
| March 1900-May 1901 | Alfred Smith |
| May 1901-Apr 1907 | Simeon Hill |
| April 1907-Jan 1908 | John Miller |
| January 1908-Nov 1909 | Herbert William Chattaway |
| November 1909-Aug 1910 | Ernest Stephenson |
| August 1910-Feb 1915 | William George Wincott |
| February 1915-Jun 1916 | Ernest Harry Doherty *(Called-up for military service)* |
| June 1916-Jun 1920 | Mrs. Annie Maggie Doherty |
| June 1920-Jun 1951 | Ernest Harry Doherty *(Transferred back after WWI)* |
| June 1951-Jan 1954 | Charles Corley |
| January 1954-Nov 1954 | William George Deakin |
| November 1954-Jan 1955 | William George Foster |
| June 1955-Jan 1956 | Robert Frame |
| January 1956-May 1957 | Stanley Lloyd |
| May 1957-Sep 1973 | Christopher Charles Shakespeare |
| September 1973 | Christopher Ralph Shakespeare |
| 1986 | Christopher Atkins and his wife Jeanette |
| 1988 | Rod Pointon |
| 1990 | Pete Zaparaniuk |
| 1993-94 | Matthew Beresford |
| 1994-95 | John Kearney *(Assistant manager)* |
| 1997 | Darren Whittington *(Assistant manager)* |
| 2005 | Richard John Hillier |
| 2006-May 2013 | Mark Thorndycroft |
| May 2013 → | Rachael Langley |

*On 4th April 1985, the Morning News reported that: District planners have approved a scheme to extend the White Horse pub in Clarendon Avenue, to make room for a continental-style café. Brewers Bass, Mitchell and Butlers, lodged the application and they plan to build an additional lounge bar, erect a single and two-storey extension for a restaurant and build toilets and a bottle store at the rear of the site. A courtyard backing onto Covent Garden car park is to be used as a patio area for people using the pub, and the brewers plan to serve snacks and light refreshments throughout the day outside of normal pub hours.*

### White Lion – 5 Althorpe Street

The White Lion was owned by the Birmingham and Oxford Junction Railway Company until 1853 when it was taken over by a new company called Great Western Railways [GWR]; it stood on the corner of Althorpe Street and, what was then, Mathy Street. The first directory listing we have for the pub is in 1838 when Daniel Simmonds was the licensee. When these premises were auctioned at the Crown Hotel on 11th March 1846, the sale notice published in the Leamington Spa Courier described the freehold property thus: "All that substantially built and well-accustomed public house known as the White Lion in Althorpe Street, Leamington Priors, now in the occupation of Daniel Simmonds. The house contains parlour, bar, butcher's shop, kitchen, and tap room on the entrance floor; several [three] good sleeping apartments, brew house, malt room, a small stable in the yard and spacious under-ground cellaring; the whole comprising an area of 162 square yards" –

*Photo of the White Lion taken on 31st August 1961 courtesy of R. J. Blenkinsop. The train is the No.6007 King William III 16.10 Paddington to Birkenhead.*

in the 1850s it also had a covered bowling alley. After a brief closure GWR sold the pub to Edward Chatterley in 1858; in the same year it also sported a club room and a room over the stables [27 ft x 12 ft 7in] that was sometimes used for air-gun shooting.

In 1888, the White Lion was bought by the Burton Brewery Co. Ltd and in 1928 it was transferred to Ind Coope and Co. Ltd [Burton-on-Trent]. In 1850 it is first listed as 22, Althorpe Street and that is also Edward Chatterley's address on the 1861 and 1871 census records. Due to the enforcement of a demolition order, and the scheduled development of the new Althorpe Industrial Estate, the White Lion closed on 31st August 1961 and demolition of the building started the following week. The pub's licence was then suspended and, in order that it would be preserved, was transferred to Bernard Hable [or Noble] on 27th November 1961 and then on to James Constantine on 3rd September 1962. In October 1963, the Leamington Spa Courier reported that, "Ansells Brewery of Birmingham were granted a removal licence by Leamington magistrates on Monday [14th October] from the demolished White Lion public house, Althorpe Street, Leamington, to a new site in Newland Road, Lillington." When built the new public house would be named the Jack and Jill.

**Footnote:** To find the site of the former White Lion go up Althorpe Street on the left hand side, passing the plumbing supplies outlet and then the entrance to Kirkdales the builders. As the old LMS [London, Midland & Scottish] railway bridge has been removed, pass under the GWR [Great Western Railway] railway bridge and the pub was immediately on the left hand side.

| | |
|---|---|
| 1838-circa 1850 | Daniel Simmonds |
| ≤1850-Apr 1850 | Thomas Huckfield |
| April 1850-Apr 1851 | John Boyes |
| April 1851 | Charles Pearson |
| ≤1853-Jun 1853 | William Batchelor |
| June 1853-Aug 1854 | Joseph Gardner |
| August 1854 | Joseph Bolton |
| May 1858-Nov 1874 | Edward Chatterley |
| November 1874-Feb 1880 | Edward Hillier |
| February 1880-Jul 1882 | Robert Culley |
| July 1882-Sep 1885 | John Woodward |
| September 1885-Nov 1888 | Charles Baker |
| November 1888-90 | William Slack |
| 1890-Mar 1896 | George Branson (*Of Leicester*) |
| March 1896-96 | Frederick John Jones |
| 1896-Oct 1904 | George Hartley |
| October 1904-Jan 1910 | Frederick Lucas Smart |
| January 1910-Apr 1910 | Charles Duffin |
| April 1910-Apr 1911 | Frederick Andrews |
| April 1911-20 | Charles Brookes |

| | |
|---|---|
| 1921-29 | Sydney Timms Griffin |
| 1930 | L. Betteridge |
| 1931-32 | H. Underwood |
| 1932-35 | Sidney Rayment |
| 1936 | Thomas Austin |
| 1936-38 | Frank Moore Pritchard |
| 1939 | W. H. Dicken |
| 1940-Aug 1940 | Harry Weston |
| August 1940-May 1942 | Charles William Miller *(Died on 27th September 1942, aged 70)* |
| May 1942-Dec 1945 | Frederick John Clark |
| December 1945-Jun 1946 | John Boland |
| June 1946-Sep 1947 | Bernard Bednell |
| September 1947-Jan 1949 | Sidney Albert Cavanagh |
| January 1949-Feb 1953 | Leslie Vincent Dewis |
| February 1953-Nov 1957 | Reginald Alfred Hodges |
| November 1957-Sep 1961 | Ada Margaret Martina Richardson and husband Harry |
| 31st August 1961 | Closed for business |

*Landlord Edward Chatterley [1858-74] was born in Bearley, Stratford-upon-Avon circa 1812. On retirement he lived with his married sister at 15, Union Walk. Edward died in the workhouse in 1892 at 80 years of age.*

The Leamington Spa Courier dated 25th August 1961 reported that: The White Lion in Althorpe Street, Leamington's oldest remaining public house, closes its doors for the last time on Thursday with the enforcement of a demolition order. The 'Lion', which has stood for well over 100 years, is scheduled for demolition to facilitate the scheduled development of the new Althorpe Industrial Estate. Mr. and Mrs. Harry Richardson, the present licensee and his wife, have been at the pub four years, and in that time become extremely popular with the locals. When the door closes behind them they are bidding fond farewell to Leamington and going to Leicester where they will take charge of a new pub, the Scarlet Pimpernel. "We do not mind going, but we don't like leaving the old customers. It's been one big happy family," said Harry. [The statement that it was then Leamington's oldest remaining pub is incorrect – Ed]

**White Lion** – 26 Brook Street
See Old White Lion for details.

**White Swan** – Clarendon Street
See Swan Inn [Clarendon Street] for details.

**White Swan** – Clemens Street, Leamington Priors
See Swan [Clemens Street] for details.

**Whitnash Tavern** – St. Margarets Road, Whitnash
See Bulldog for details.

**Wig and Pen** – 26 Park Street

In May 1988, local justices rejected an application by Worcester based County Wine Bars for a full on-licence for Priory Way Wine Bar. However, on 12th July the magistrates had a change of mind and by Christmas the Priory Way Wine Bar had opened at the above address. In August 1996 it reopened as the Wig and Pen, one of a small chain spread around the country with the same name, retaining the café-bar styling of the previous business. In July 2001, it was reported that Bar Citrus is the latest in a series of new drinks outlets in the town centre. A spokesman for Charles Wells' brewery, which owns the former Wig and Pen premises, said, "Bar Citrus will attract a discerning drinking customer base. It's the only bar in Leamington which will have the stylish Japanese lager, Kirin, on draught." It would later become a shop selling fine ware, and in 2013 it is the Le Bistrot Pierre Restaurant.

*Although we don't have any photos of the Wig and Pen or Bar Citrus, this is the building taken on 28th August 2011 © Allan Jennings.*

| | |
|---|---|
| 1996 | Alison Turner |
| 1998-99 | Tony Rodia *(Went on to the Haunch of Venison)* |

*Tom Lewin used to use this wine bar in Park Street, "They did good food during the day and the evenings were an attraction for the younger element. It was £2 on the door and then the drinks were £1 after that; it also had 'live' bands, usually on a Sunday. There was a large downstairs area with wrought iron steps up to a small balcony, with about 6 tables and chairs, overlooking the main area. It is now a French restaurant and part of the Royal Priors; previously it had been a shop along similar lines to CASA FINA in Regent Street, for those that remember it."*

**Wilde's Wine Bar** – 7 Parade

Wilde's opened on 6th October 1976 and is located in the basement of this 1830s building. It has been family-run since its inception and offers an unfussy Gallic-style, coupled with an old-world focus and a wine list of more than sixty varieties. In the 1980s Wilde's also sold Hook Norton Best Bitter and Samuel Smith's Old Brewery Bitter. In 2009, Waitrose Food Magazine termed it: "A local hero – the place to go in Leamington. It's an experience not to be missed." Others praised the basement bar and restaurant for its French inspired

*Photo of Wildes taken on 16th July 2011 © Allan Jennings.*

international menu and fine wine. Since 1976, Wilde's has been about good food, good wine and good company. In 2011, the bar was named 29th best in the UK by national newspaper The Independent; the head chef and managing director was Christophe Charpentier, who hails from Tours in France and the co-owner is Max Smith. Christophe relocated to Warwick in August 2012 and took full control of Christophe's at Castles Bar and Kitchen, in Castle Street. Wilde's remains open in December 2013.

| | |
|---|---|
| 6th October 1976 | Wildes opened |
| 1989 | Richard Draper *(Manager)* |
| November 2005 | Geoffrey Maxwell Smith |
| 2011 → | Julie Spencer *(Joint bar manager)* |

**William the Fourth** – Queen Street
The only directory listing we have is in 1837 and unfortunately the landlord is not listed. However, we are also aware of an auction that took place in early June 1837, one of the properties for sale being described as: "A licensed and well arranged public house called William the Fourth, being on the south side of Queen Street, with two substantially erected dwelling houses and premises adjoining thereto [on its west side], comfortable cottage at the back and a frontage on to Queen Street of 45 ft 7 in." Furthermore, the church rate books show that there was a Matthew Boswell occupying a public house in Queen Street in 1837, 1839 and 1840; although the pub is unnamed, the William the Fourth is the only one we have recorded that ties in with these dates. Notwithstanding, as it is not listed in the 1841 or subsequent directories we have concluded that it closed between 1838 and 1840.

**Williams Hotel** – Union Parade
See Regent Hotel for details.

**Willoughby Arms** – 12 Augusta Place

The first directory listing we have is in 1850 when it was named the Augusta Tavern and addressed as 6, Augusta Place. Initially a beer house, the licensing justices issued a full publican's licence to Thomas Masters in 1854. We believe that it was renamed the Willoughby Arms when Charles Knibb became the licensee in 1875; it was also around this time that the building was renumbered 12, Augusta Place. The pub was initially owned by P. Phipps and Co. Ltd, and later by Watney Mann Ltd, Bridge Street Brewery, Northampton.

The Willoughby Arms has also been known as Cassis [April 1983-90], Styles Apart [December 1990-94], the Phoenix and then Flanagans, both for short periods. It then reopened as The Willoughby, was known as Bohemia @ the Willoughby for a couple of years and then reverted to The Willoughby in August 2011.

In February 2013, application was made to Warwick District Council for planning permission: "Change of use from A4 public house to Sui Generis [unique] 16 bedroom house in multi occupation. This involves the demolition/removal of parts of the building [including single storey rear extension, external rear staircases, and front balcony] and the erection of a second floor extension, part first floor side extension and rear first floor extension; together with internal and external alterations." The plans were approved, the applicant was notified on 23rd May and the Willoughby Arms closed mid year; by July 2013 work was underway converting the premises to student accommodation.

| | |
|---|---|
| 1850-Apr 1864 | Thomas Masters (*Augusta Tavern*) |
| April 1864-Dec 1865 | Samuel Seeley Hawkes Oldham |
| December 1865-Jan 1872 | William Webb |
| January 1872-73 | William Slater |
| 1873-Dec 1873 | Charles Wright |
| December 1873-Jul 1874 | James Richardson |
| July 1874-Nov 1874 | Richard Cooper |

*Above left: Photo of the Willoughby taken on 26th October 2008 © Allan Jennings. Above right: Bohemia @ the Willoughby taken on 17th February 2011 © Allan Jennings.*

| | |
|---|---|
| November 1874-May 1875 | James Richardson |
| May 1875-Jul 1875 | John Dicks |
| July 1875-Nov 1878 | Charles T. Knibb *(Willoughby Arms)* |
| November 1878-Jan 1890 | William Abbotts |
| January 1890-May 1890 | George Robinson *(Of Northampton)* |
| May 1890-Mar 1891 | Joseph Marriott |
| March 1891-Aug 1906 | William Robert Branson |
| August 1906-Nov 1906 | George K. Kightley and Thomas Henry Archer *(Executors of William Branson)* |
| November 1906-Apr 1911 | Mary Ann Branson *(Wife of William Branson)* |
| April 1911-Oct 1914 | Henry Robert Franks |
| October 1914 | John Watts |
| 1915-Sept 1926 | Mrs. Bessie Watts |
| September 1926-Sep 1946 | Harry Inwood |
| September 1946-Jun 1963 | Arthur Edward 'Ben' Cox *(Treasurer of the Licensed Victuallers Association in 1960)* |
| June 1963-Feb 1967 | Rosa Elizabeth Amy Cox *(On the death of Arthur)* |
| February 1967-Oct 1968 | Alfred Joseph Pinfold |
| October 1968-Oct 1970 | Horace Clark |
| October 1970-1980 | David Arvon Davies and his wife Dot |
| 1980-87 | Chris Donnachie *(Cassis from April 1983)* |
| 1987-≥May 1988 | Leo Dolan |
| October 1990-92 | Joan Soame *(Styles Apart)* |
| 1993 | Linda Gibson and Mick Griffiths *(Styles Apart)* |
| 2003 | Andrew Liddington *(Willoughby)* |
| December 2005-Oct 2006 | Jonathon Moreby |
| October 2006-Apr 2009 | Andrew Bernard Pyatt |
| April 2009-Aug 2011 | Victoria Peach |
| August 2011-Mid 2013 | Arthur Lucy and John O'Sullivan *(Owners)* |
| August 2011-Mid 2013 | Patrick O'Sullivan *(Licensee and John's brother)* |

The Leamington Spa Courier dated 7th May 1971 reported that: A christening party at Dave Davies' pub on Sunday went with a bang when the ceiling collapsed onto the bar. Mr. Davies, landlord of the Willoughby Arms, went downstairs from the party to get a few bottles from the bar and "the whole ceiling had collapsed", he told the Courier. "There was plaster and rafters all over the place. The cause was probably old age, but no one at the christening party heard anything. If it had been an hour earlier, there would have been about ten people right under it."

*The Leamington Spa Courier dated 7th July 1972 reported that: Local people interested in forming a branch of the Poetry Society of Great Britain will have a chance to meet and discuss plans at an informal get together at the Willoughby Arms, on Tuesday. The branch, which would be only the fourth of its kind in the country, is the 'brainchild' of Leamington poet Mrs. Marion Mallorie, of 149 Leam Terrace. Since she first talked about the scheme some weeks ago*

Marion has been inundated with requests for information and offers of help. "I thought that the first couple of meetings should be fairly casual get-togethers so that people can get to know each other." Membership of the Poetry Society is £3 a year, but this also buys members the quarterly *Poetry Review*, and the society would help the branch with information about poetry events and with booking well known writers for readings in Leamington.

These four beer mats are included courtesy of Mrs. Mary Cambray. They were taken from The Willoughby in 1968 by Mary who was working as a bar maid. She has kept them as a keepsake for all these years. Mary recalls, "I worked as a bar maid at the Willoughby during the late sixties. I remember the pub had two rooms with an adjoining passage. Across to the right of the passage was a garage where Paul and Clive Pinfold would tinker with their racing bikes, mainly side car machines, as they entered motor cycling scramble events up and down the Country. There was a small function room upstairs for private occasions. The Pinfolds were related to the then landlady."

The Leamington Spa Courier dated 4th February 1977 reported that: Publicans dressed in Victorian clothes – and hopefully drinking beer at Victorian prices – will re-enact the first meeting of their local association as part of its centenary celebrations this year. The Royal Leamington Spa, Warwick, Kenilworth and District Licensed Victuallers Association's history began with a meeting on 1st March 1877, in the Willoughby Arms, which will be the scene of this year's annual meeting on 29th March when the centenary charade will take place. On 29th March the 100th annual meeting will hear Mr. Keight, the current secretary, read the minutes of the first meeting that set-up what was then called the Royal Leamington Spa, Warwick and District Licensed Victuallers' and Beer Retailers' Benevolent and Protection Fund. At that meeting 21 members attended and they elected Mr. James Devis, president; Mr. James Tennant, treasurer; and Mr. W. G. Restall, secretary. It was agreed that new members should pay an entrance fee of ten shillings and the same again as their annual subscription.

*Cassis opened in April 1983 and was named after the French for blackcurrant, the juice of which is a common cocktail ingredient, and with its attractive lilac coloured exterior, Cassis cocktail and lounge bar was easy to locate in Augusta Place. An advert in the Weekly News dated 16th November 1983, read, "Recent years have seen a dramatic change in the type of bars many customers prefer to drink in. The rough, often uncomfortable, almost always male dominated type of establishment is gradually declining in popularity. It is slowly being replaced by something plusher and more sophisticated. Cassis cocktail and lounge bar in Augusta Place,*

*Leamington Spa provides a good example of this shift. What was previously the Willoughby Arms has been greatly transformed and now caters for the growing number of drinkers demanding improved and more stylish surroundings. Since its opening, Cassis has become popular with couples interested in a drink in relaxing surroundings. It has also become a favourite haunt of groups of girls pleased to be in a bar not packed with 'over attentive' males."* As well as cocktails with strange sounding names, wines, champagne and a selection of lagers mainly from America, Cassis also sold Stag and Manns bitter and Fosters lager.

The Leamington Spa Courier dated 18th January 1991 reported that: Everything that is best from America and Britain has been blended to create the recently opened Styles Apart in Augusta Place, Leamington. Joan Soame took over the premises in October, and

*Photo of Styles Apart courtesy of Nick Wilkins.*

since then it has undergone complete renovation. The downstairs Victorian bar opened in December just in time for Christmas, and Joan is hoping to create the American bar upstairs. There is a choice of American, Mexican or traditional dishes all home cooked by Joan in the newly refurbished kitchens. Joan said, "We got off to a bad start when we opened in December. Our opening party was held on the weekend of the very heavy snowfall."

*By August 1993, further changes had taken place to give a genuine sensation of the sixties stateside. Upstairs, a new eatery called Fat Sam's is open and selling imported American food. Customers can choose from Red Snapper, clam Chowder, t-bone steaks and gulf shrimps, all prepared the American way and at an average cost of £8 per head. All tables must be reserved. Live music will feature on advertised nights. Downstairs, the bar has been jazzed up, with bright new red, white and blue decor, memorabilia on the walls, a Wurlitzer juke box, popcorn machine, pinball and new pool table. The bar serves a wide selection of beers including the top American lager, Coors.*

### Windmill Inn – 209 Tachbrook Road

The windmill, from whence the Windmill Inn got its name, apparently has its origins in the 16th century but our first reference point is not until the late 18th century. In the 1767 Enclosure Act, the lands to be 'enclosed' within Leamington Priors approximated 990 acres and were situated south and west of the River Leam, extending to the Whitnash and Radford

*Allotment holders and regulars of the Windmill Inn gather for a photograph in 1917. Photo courtesy of Alan Griffin.*

The Windmill, Tachbrook Road, Leamington, Spa.

*Photo courtesy of Jo Clark.*

boundaries; part of Richard Lyndon's allocation was the windmill that once stood near the Tachbrook Road, described as being south of the canal. Our next reference is the 1829 church rate book which lists the tenant's named as Page, and it is also directory listed in 1850 when the miller's name is shown as Samuel Ingram [who would become the pub's first licensee].

The windmill was unique in that it was the only known example in the county of a tower mill to be winded by a tailpole. It also displayed many other interesting features: the three storey mill was topped with a thatched cap and had four common sails, two pairs of

*Photo of the Windmill taken 2nd March 2009 © Allan Jennings.*

stones, a magnificent oak vertical shaft [thirteen inches in diameter], ten bays, iron journals and a six foot diameter oak brake wheel with 60 wooden teeth; it was 33 feet from the ground to the top of the cap. Although new gearing, sails, steam driven shaft and engine house have been noted in an 1880s advert, it was reported to have ceased working in 1883 [and also that its sails were sold in 1894]. In the early 20th century the dome cap was replaced [or refurbished] and new sails fitted but, in 1943 the latter were again removed after being bomb damaged during a raid on the Lockheed factory, and the windmill fell into disrepair. By the 1960s the brewery, on whose ground the windmill stood, had declared it to be, "structurally unsafe... the roof, in part, is a hazard - it disintegrates in high winds!" – The derelict tower was demolished in December 1968 and the site is now the car park for the Windmill Inn.

The first reference point we have for the Windmill Inn is a report in the Leamington Spa Courier dated 6th July 1861, mentioning that landlord Samuel Ingram had been there for one month. Originally a beer house, the first directory listing we have is in 1872 when Sam Ingram is still the licensee. However, our first directory listing for the Windmill Inn is not until 1885 – like a few others in the then outlying parts of Leamington, early historical data on this pub is limited as it is excluded from many of the resources available to us, due to its location. When in August 1895 application was made for a wine licence, it was stated that the Windmill had been rebuilt and that it was situated on the borders of the borough and was the last house on the Tachbrook Road before going into the country; the application was refused. A full licence would not be granted until 2nd March 1948; it was ratified on 24th March. In May 1893, William Gurley was granted a music and dancing licence for an attached room and the garden, but in the September the local justices said, "they strongly objected to dancing in public houses" and refused to renew the licence; a new music licence was eventually granted on 5th September 1949. Originally owned by P. Phipps and Co, then Phipps Northampton Brewery Co. Ltd, in 1960 it was acquired by Watney Mann Ltd and in 1964 it was owned by Phipps Brewery Ltd [Bridge Street, Northampton].

On 31st December 1987, the Morning News reported that "the winds of change have been blowing at the Windmill pub and the results are very pleasing indeed. An extension built in Leamington brick, and an internal refurbishment programme, means that the pub now boasts a public bar and a lounge and dining room. The public bar, in the old part of the pub, provides entertainment such as pool and darts, while the new lounge and dining room provide a plush and relaxed atmosphere for drinkers and diners alike. The lounge is spacious and airy with comfortable furnishings and soft, warm lighting, which is carried through into the adjoining dining room." In October 1997, Tammy Montgomery [a former England darts international] and her mother Nina changed the name of the restaurant part of the business to Jack Sprats. The Windmill Inn remains open in December 2013.

| | |
|---|---|
| June 1861-Nov 1886 | Samuel Ingram |
| November 1886-Sep 1887 | James Gurley |
| September 1887-Jun 1894 | William Gurley |
| June 1894-Sep 1897 | George Knight Keightley |

| | |
|---|---|
| September 1897-Feb 1899 | George Robbins |
| February 1899-Jan 1900 | Mrs. Elizabeth (or Ellen) Robbins |
| January 1900-Oct 1900 | John Charles Bromwich |
| October 1900-Jan 1915 | Thomas Gulliman Jnr and his wife Ada |
| | *(Also refer Wheatsheaf Inn)* |
| January 1915-Oct 1915 | Edwin (or Edward) Bliss |
| October 1915-Jul 1916 | William Davis *(Called-up for military service)* |
| July 1916-Aug 1925 | Mrs. Davis |
| August 1925-Apr 1929 | Bertram Sidney Rhodes and Anne Margaret Rhodes |
| April 1929-Apr 1943 | William Page |
| April 1943-Apr 1957 | Robert Thomas Clarke |
| April 1957-Aug 1970 | William Branston |
| August 1970 | Stanley George Smith |
| ≤1983-Aug 1986 | Pat and Betty Brannigan |
| August 1986-Sep 1987 | Joanne Broom and Simon Wilkes |
| September 1987-Sep 1989 | Keith and Sally Grant |
| September 1989-91 | Keith Day and Stephen "Steve" Neal *(Owners/ licensees)* |
| 1990-91 | Sarah Watts and Steve Miles *(Managers)* |
| 1991-93 | Fred Hepburn and Barney McGarvey *(Fred Hepburn left on 13th March 1993 to take over the Hodcarrier)* |
| 1993-95 | Barney McGarvey |
| 1997-2000 | Tammy Montgomery |
| 2000-July 2012 | Danielle Ronata Montgomery |
| July 2012 → | Michelle Ramsay *(Licensee)* and Helen Willoughby |

*On the 31st May 1866, Samuel Ingram, keeper of the Windmill Tavern was charged with opening his house for the sale of beer during the hours of Divine Service on Sunday last. It was stated that he had been doing a great deal of Sunday trading, and sometimes as many as 50 or 60 people would be seen there on a Sunday. Prosecuting, Mr. Lund stated that he had adopted all the plans he could think of in endeavouring to detect him, but up to last Sunday without success. On going to the house himself he had frequently seen people run away from the back. Men were placed some distance from the house, in order to give signals on the approach of a constable. Mr. Lund had repeatedly put men to watch, and on Sunday last they succeeded. The constable saw beer being served, and saw 23 or 24 men in the house at the time. The defendant was fined £5 with costs of 10s.*

The Leamington Courier dated 21st August 1970 pictured Bill Branston of the Windmill Inn, receiving a Victorian paraffin lamp from friend Harry O'Toole, presented to him by regulars at his farewell party on Wednesday night. Mr. Branston took over the Windmill 14 years ago. He served there as a tenant as well as doing his full-time job as a machine shop foreman. He was well known in the 1950s as a professional footballer with Port Vale and Aston Villa.

*The Leamington Spa Courier dated 12th December 1986 reported that: Crossroads star Stan Stennett – alias Sid Hooper – popped in for a pint at the Windmill in Tachbrook Road last week. Making a special guest appearance, actor Stan joined proprietors Joanne Broom and Simon Wilkes in celebrating the pub's reopening following its extensive modernisation. Since the couple took over the Windmill, it has more than doubled its size. A lively pub with a ladies' darts team and a men's dominoes team, the Windmill offers live entertainment on the evening of the first and third Sunday of every month. A Mann's pub, the Windmill serves two traditional bitters, Mann's mild, draught Guinness, Fosters and Carlsberg lager.*

Tom Lewin remembers the Windmill: "As a big fan of 'live' music, I would often be found in some local pub where music was playing. Live bands were most popular in the nineteen eighties and nineties playing at many local pub haunts. It can be said that many a band can relate their early beginnings to playing for modest money at some local pub. Bands like the Beatles and Oasis can trace their early beginnings to playing in licensed premises to hone their skills. Leamington pubs offered many an opportunity for an up and coming local band to demonstrate if they had what it takes to succeed.

My first taste of this was on a Sunday night at the Windmill where I came across a group calling themselves Ten Feet Tall playing for all their worth. I was not only impressed by the band but also the atmosphere it generated by the on looking crowd. I subsequently found out that the Windmill had a regular Sunday evening spot for local musical talent so I became a Sunday visitor.

Names such as Subterranean, Official Receivers and A 2 Z to name but a few became very familiar to me. Ten Feet Tall, which I considered the cream of the crop, were playing at many different public houses across Leamington and I began to show up at their gigs. I was surprised to find they played at such venues as the Heathcote Inn, Bedford, Tavistock, Wig & Pen, Hope, Haunch of Venison and the Tiller Pin, as did many of the local bands.

At the end of the nineties things began to get tight for proprietors – beer prices, rents and a declining number of customers all added to the demise of the bands. Sadly, of all those venues, only the Windmill still offers regular live entertainment. Most town pubs like to have a very loud disco without the atmosphere that the 'live' music created. Ah well, we must move with the times!"

*In 2010 Danielle Montgomery was serving Wells Bombardier and John Smiths. She catered for such events as the Shrubland Street School reunions when about 100 school friends came together for their 7th reunion on 17th April.*

**Wine Vaults** – 13 Bath Street
See Chair and Rocket for details.

**Wine Vaults** – 25/27 Bedford Street
Kingston Brett opened his wine and spirits business on 15th December 1832 at 7, Upper Union Parade. In January 1858 he advertised that his business had relocated from 7, Upper Parade to Upper Bedford Street; the new premises are listed as having a publican's full licence. From 1926, the business was known as Brett's Wine Vaults. In March 1951 the licence was renewed only temporarily while the Wine Vaults was referred to the compensation authority for closure. The Bedford Street premises were closed on 8th March 1952.

| 15th Dec 1832-Jun 1870 | Kingston Brett |
| June 1870-Jan 1901 | Kingston Brett and Sons *(Robert and Charles)* |
| January 1901-Aug 1915 | Tom Sumner *(Transferred from Charles Brett)* |
| August 1915-Oct 1923 | Charles Baker *(Executor of Tom Sumner)* |
| October 1923-Mar 1924 | Samuel Rollason *(Of Coventry)* |
| March 1924-1952 | Mary Gertrude Claridge |
| 8th March 1952 | Closed for business |

**Wine Vaults** – 56 Bedford Street

On 3rd February 1929, 'Manns' wine and spirits vaults business was relocated from 158, Parade to 56, Bedford Street. Following an application made on behalf of Lewis Pemberton Walsh, who had purchased the Parade business carried on by Messrs Mann and Co. for nearly 100 years, the licence was granted on 5th February. The full beer, wine and spirits off-licence issued to the Bedford Street premises not only prohibited the sale of intoxicating liquor for consumption on the premises, but it was also conditional on there being no beer engine or pump installed [the Parade business had been fully licensed to sell liquor for consumption 'on' or 'off' the premises and included a small smoke room where customers could partake of drinks on the premises]. At the time of publishing we had not been able to ascertain when this business closed.

| ≤1851-≥1864 | William Mann *(Lower Parade)* |
| ≤1873-≥1878 | E. & W. R. Mann *(Lower Parade/158, Parade)* |
| ≤1889-1929 | W. R. Mann *(158, Parade)* |
| 1929-Mar 1940 | Peter Riland Bedford *(56, Bedford Street)* |
| March 1940-Dec 1945 | Martin James Mowat |
| December 1945-Jan 1971 | Peter Riland Bedford |
| January 1971-Jan 1974 | Terence Martin Connolly |
| January 1974 | Neil Kevin Lloyd |

**Wine Vaults / The Vaults** – 58 Warwick Street

These premises are listed in the police licence register as having a publican's full licence. The owners were the executors of a Thomas Lane, and the lessees were Flower and Sons Ltd. There were two entrances on Warwick Street but the door in the rear passage to Bedford Street was not to be used for trade purposes. In October 1946, numbers '52' '54' and 56, Warwick Street, 1 Bedford Street and The Vaults, a fully licensed public house at 58, Warwick Street, were sold to Banbury Co-operative Society. Mr. R. Chambers, the general manager of the Co-op, said that The Vaults was a 'free house' and would continue to be run as such. The premises were closed on 24th June 1961.

| ≤1893-Jan1893 | John Lee |
| January 1893-94 | Richard Henry Gardner |
| 1895-1903 | C. F. Carroll |
| 1905-19 | D. B. Evans |

| 1920-29 | Mrs. Helen Evans |
| Circa 1930s | Walter John Sturgeon |
| May 1939-Oct 1945 | Charles Purkiss |
| October 1945-Feb 1947 | Percy Payment |
| February 1947-Oct 1950 | James Frederick Cooper |
| October 1950-Mar 1961 | Doris Ada Chandler |
| March 1961-Jun 1961 | Thelma Ann Johnstone |
| 24th June 1961 | Closed for business |

**Wine Vaults** [Assembly Room Vaults] – Regent Street
See Imperial [Public House] for details.

**Winstons** – 44 Clarendon Avenue
See Jekyll and Hyde for details.

**Woodland Tavern** – 3 Regent Street
Wellington Street was laid out in 1826 and named after the Duke of Wellington [who subsequently visited the town in April 1827]. The first directory listing we have is in 1833 when the address was 11, Wellington Street and the licensee was John Mills [and in 1841 it was 16, Wellington Street]. By 1876, Wellington Street had been renamed Regent Street, which had simultaneously been renumbered [starting at the western end], and the Woodland's new address was 3, Regent Street. From 1880 it was variously listed as the

*The Woodland Tavern courtesy of Nick Wilkins.*

Woodland, 'Tavern' and 'Inn'. Previously owned by Lucas and Co. Ltd [Leamington Brewery], it would become an Ansells pub following their 1928 acquisition of the brewery and its closure in 1934.

In 1994, the Woodland closed for a refurbishment and reopened on 9th December 1994, with Mayor Sarah Boad pulling the first pint. The conservation department at Warwick District Council describes the building as "a mid circa 19th century public house with later additions and alterations". The Woodland Tavern remains open in December 2013 and among the selection of beers available are those brewed by the Slaughterhouse Brewery Ltd [Bridge Street, Warwick].

| | |
|---|---|
| 1833-57 | John Mills |
| June 1857-May 1862 | Mrs. Elizabeth Mills *(Transferred from late husband's executor)* |
| May 1862-67 | Henry Mills *(On the death of Elizabeth)* |
| 1867 | John Tims |
| 1868-72 | William Coombe |
| 1872 | Daniel Hunt |
| 1874-Feb 1884 | William Slater |
| February 1884-Oct 1884 | George Sturgess |
| October 1884-Jan 1886 | Herbert Henry Mills |
| January 1886-Jan 1893 | Samuel Summers |
| January 1893-1896 | George Nash |
| 1896-May 1906 | William George Broadbridge |
| May 1906-May 1914 | Ronald Henry Turland |
| May 1914-30 | Herbert William Chattaway |
| 1931-Jul 1938 | Frederick Morris James |
| July 1938-Sep 1941 | Charles Douglas Hughes |
| September 1941-May 1942 | James Frederick Hooper |
| May 1942-Mar 1947 | John Richard Bishop |
| March 1947-Jul 1959 | Arthur James Lown and his wife Lil *(Previously at the Coventry Arms)* |
| July 1959-Feb 1960 | Kenneth Arthur Francis |
| February 1960-Oct 1962 | Thomas Bernard Mulvaney |
| October 1962-Dec 1964 | James William O'Gorman |
| December 1964-Dec 1965 | Clifford Roy Bounds |
| December 1965-Jul 1966 | Reginald Barry Jones |
| July 1966-Apr 1967 | Alfred Cyril Adams |
| April 1967-Oct 1968 | Leon Stone |
| October 1968-Feb 1969 | Robert David Stokes |
| February 1969-Nov 1970 | Leonard Terence Coates |
| November 1970 | Eric William Frank Brassey |
| Circa March 1974-Nov 1977 | Maurice William Green |
| November 1977-1978 | Paul and Veronica White *(Of Solihull)* |

| | |
|---|---|
| Nov 1979-1981 | Arthur and Flora McCormick |
| 1981-Sep 1983 | Dennis Cleary |
| November 1983-Jul 1984 | Augustine 'Gus' Stapleton and his wife Joyce *(Previously at the Railway, Leamington Spa, and later the Railway, Warwick)* |
| July 1984-Dec 1994 | Michael 'Mick' Cowlishaw and his wife Thelma *(Previously at the Builders Arms)* |
| December 1994-1999 | Phil and Sue Hogan |
| August 1999 → | Josephine Anne James *(Josie took over the lease on 10th December, 2002)* |

*The Leamington Spa Courier dated 7th August 1959 reported that: Two of Leamington's best known licensed trade personalities, Mr. and Mrs. Arthur Lown, who have been hosts at the Woodland Tavern, Regent Street, for the last 12 years, are sailing to Australia in eight days' time. They plan to spend their retirement in New South Wales with their married son and daughter, whom they have not seen for seven years. Three young grand children will welcome them there. Mr. and Mrs. Lown previously managed the Coventry Arms in Guys Cliffe Road for nine years. Mr. Lown has been Warwickshire delegate on the Midlands branch of the National Trade Development Association, and his wife - they have been married 41 years - is a former chairman of the Leamington Women's Auxiliary of the Licensed Victuallers Association. At Leamington magistrates court last week, Mr. Lown was congratulated by the justices on his extremely good record over a number of years in the division. They wished him well in his new life.*

In 1986, the Woodland was owned by Ansells Brewery and served their traditional bitter and mild as well as Tetleys drum bitter, Skol, Castlemaine XXXX, Lowenbrau lager, draught Guinness and cider. The bar is packed with regulars, and some have been frequenting the Woodland for 50 years. Tenant Mick Cowlishaw is constantly raising money for different charity events including raising £1,000 for a guide dog. The pub also has a serious games side with darts, cribbage and dominoes taking over the bar from Monday until Thursday. [Morning News dated 16th May 1986]

The Courier of 17th July 2009 reported on a 'tongue in cheek' notice at the Woodland Tavern:

> **POLICE NOTICE**
>
> A NUMBER OF WOODLAND TAVERN
> CUSTOMERS HAVE ALLEGEDLY GONE MISSING.
>
> THIS AREA IS NOW UNDER FORENSIC INVESTIGATION
> IN A SEARCH FOR THEIR MORTAL REMAINS.
>
> ANYONE WITH INFORMATION OF THE '*MISPERS*'
> PLEASE ADVISE THE BAR STAFF.

Some top detectives and a local bobby are investigating the case of the 'missing customers' in a Leamington pub.

Visitors to the Woodland Tavern in Regent Street may be surprised to see a hole in the wall of a corridor with a mural of some well-known policemen around it.

The painting, featuring Inspector Goldsmith [of Touch Radio FM fame] – Inspector Jack Frost – Chief Inspector Morse – Sergeant Lewis and a police constable who drinks at the pub, were commissioned by publican Josie James after the hole appeared.

Tavern regular John Airey, who runs Mortimer's Curios in Grove Street, explained how the idea for the mural came about, "I saw the hole in the wall and we were discussing the fact that so many pubs are closing and why customers are missing from pubs."

"There were quite a few missing when I was there and I pinned up a notice on the wall next to the hole and put up some police tape for a joke; and when Josie saw it she decided to make it a permanent feature."

Local artist Chris Willsmore [former licensee of the Haunch of Venison], who painted the mural on the Nelson in Warwick, was called in to do the picture.

*The conservation department at Warwick District Council describes the building as: A mid circa 19th century public house with later additions and alterations. Brick with painted stucco facades and Welsh slate roof; Two storeys, 6 first-floor windows, those 2 to the right are at a lower level; Windows: 2/2 cambered-arched sashes throughout, taller to 3 left on first floor, all in plain reveals with moulded architraves and sills. Ground floor: Off-centre right entrance, 4 panel door with overlight in surround with horizontal rustication to pilasters, frieze, cornice surmounted by acroteria; To left an elliptical carriage arch with plank doors. Roof hipped to right; Right return: First floor has 2 similar windows; ground floor has 3 similar windows and left entrance a board door with cambered overlight in plain reveals; Rear right stack with cornice.*

### Woodman Inn – 24 Bedford Street

The earliest reference we have is an 1828 entry in the licensed victuallers' records when the landlord was a Walter Aston and the first directory listing is in 1829. In 1837 an advertisement in the local press stated that the Woodman offered stabling and that "phaetons, gigs, hunters, hacks, and ladies saddle nags" were available for hire. It predated the 1830 Beer House Act and, as an 'alehouse' [with a justices' licence], it was able to sell all types of alcoholic liquor. However, like many of the beer houses that would follow it brewed its own ale for a while and in 1862 it is recorded as using a 180 gallon copper furnace, an 18 bushel mash tub and Kent hops; at that time the stock on the premises approximated 700 gallons of ale, 8 dozen bottles of old port and 16 gallons of fine old sherry.

Until circa 1880 it is addressed as Upper Bedford Street [and predominantly number '12'], but from thereon it would be listed as 24, Bedford Street. The directors of Lucas and Co. Ltd [Leamington Brewery] approved the £2,500 purchase of the Woodman on 17th May 1898 but didn't take ownership until 1902; it would become an Ansells pub following their 1928 acquisition of the brewery and its closure in 1934. The Woodman closed on 16th August 1966 to make way for the Marks and Spencer car park.

| | |
|---|---|
| 1828-1830 | Walter Aston *(Also listed as Walter Alston)* |
| 1832-35 | William Beamish |
| 1838-39 | Ann Beamish |
| 1841-Aug 1854 | John Mountford |
| August 1854-Jul 1855 | John Woodward |
| July 1855-Jan 1863 | John Robinson |
| January 1863-Oct 1863 | Alfred Mountford |
| October 1863-Feb 1879 | Mark Blakeman |
| February 1879-May 1883 | Mrs. Charlotte Blakeman *(On the death of Mark)* |
| May 1883-Jan 1889 | Edward Mountford |

*Photo of the Woodman during the occupation of licensee Sidney Hickman, circa 1942-57; courtesy of his daughter Delma Grant who lives in Canada.*

| | |
|---|---|
| January 1889-Oct 1889 | William Davis *(Previously at the Great Western Inn, Warwick)* |
| October 1889-Nov 1889 | J. F. Burgiss *(Under a deed of assignment)* |
| November 1889-Oct 1896 | Joseph Potter |
| October 1896-May 1898 | William Henry Green *(Of Cubbington)* |
| May 1898-Oct 1898 | Daniel Barrett |
| October 1898-Aug 1907 | Lewis Allen |
| August 1907-1908 | Mrs. Ada Allen *(On the death of Lewis)* |
| 1908-Mar 1912 | Mrs. Ada Emily Farrant *(Died 1912)* |
| March 1912-22 | Joseph Henry Alderman |
| 1922-Jul 1923 | H. J. Salisbury |
| July 1923-Jul 1926 | Frank Leary |
| July 1926-34 | Archibald Horace Crisp |
| 1934-Sep 1935 | Leo Ratcliffe |
| September 1935-Nov 1942 | William Francis Jones |
| November 1942-Apr 1957 | Sidney Hickman |
| April 1957-Nov 1959 | Ernest Albert Upton |
| November 1959-Aug 1966 | Patricia Patterson *(Went on to the Britannia)* |
| 16th August 1966 | Closed for business |

*The Leamington Spa Courier dated 12th March 1887 reported that: Early on Sunday morning, a somewhat serious fire occurred at the Woodman Tavern, Regent Street. It appears that shortly after six o'clock Miss Slater, who was in charge of the premises, and whose bedroom was immediately over the bar, was aroused out of her sleep by a noise which at first she thought was rain. On descending into the bar she found the premises were on fire and the place filled with smoke. She raised an alarm and P.C. Butlin, who was on duty in the neighbourhood, called up Captain Orton, Lieutenant Stoney, and other members of the Volunteer Fire Brigade. Inspector Glenn, who was at the police station, was soon on the scene with the hose reel and other fire appliances, but in the meantime and before the Brigade could arrive, some neighbours obtained a good supply of water, prevented the fire extending and eventually extinguished it. An examination of the place showed that considerable damage had been done. All the woodwork was scorched, the leaden pipes attached to the beer engines had been partially melted, a large quantity of glass had been broken, and the counter had been consumed. The fire is believed to have originated from a lighted match dropped into the sawdust in the trough which ran along in front of the counter. The discovery was a timely one, for in a short time the fire would have extended and the damage would have been serious. The damage is estimated at £50. The building was insured. [The Woodman Tavern was in Bedford Street, the Woodland Tavern is in Regent Street, so which pub was it? – Ed]*

John Jennings tells us that he used this pub in the early 1950s: "You walked into a passage where there was a hatch that you could order your drinks from and then stand and drink in the passage with your friends; you could see the bar area through the hatch. As you walked into the passage there was a room on the left which was the bar, and if you walked down the passage, past the hatch, there was another room on the left which was the smoke room.

There was also a room on the right of the passage. I used to drink Ansells mild as most men did at that time."

*Delma Grant is the daughter of Sidney and Marie Hickman. Sidney was the landlord of the Woodman Inn in Bedford Street from November 1942 until April 1957. Delma now lives in Canada but recalls living at the Woodman: "We had a yard at the side of the pub where there was a stable; Carey's, the greengrocers used to bring their horse and cart there for the night. There were two double doors onto Bedford Street. During the war we had a pig, and mum kept a few chickens for eggs. We had what was called a concert room above the pub that was used for meetings and when I married Bill we had our wedding reception there. On the same floor were the bedrooms and bathroom and above that were attic rooms but they were never used. I guess they were originally used as inn rooms but not in our time. There was a big old piano in the smoke room. Every weekend Dot Purser would play by ear anything you asked for. The room was always packed and everybody sang along. Albert Evetts was another great piano player who played too. Darts and dominoes were very popular in the bar. The 'snug' seemed to be taken up by Irish men, there were lots of Irish songs and it was always crowded, although English were not welcome! The 'outdoor' was around the corner in John Street. It was very popular with elderly ladies who brought their china jugs to be filled. Pints and half pints had to carefully measured, not a drop short! The 'passage' entrance from the front door, right through to the back of the pub, was old wood block flooring – and it had to be scrubbed white every day. I remember it well when it was my turn on my knees! Some days at lunchtime mum would cook sausages and sell them in a batch; they were very popular."*

The Leamington Spa Courier dated 20th November 1959 reported: **Licensee gives up after 36 years** - One of the Midlands' best known innkeepers, 65 year old Mr. Ernest Upton, said good-bye to customers at the Woodman Inn, Bedford Street, Leamington, on Sunday, when he retired after 36 years in the licensed trade. Prior to coming to Leamington two-and-a-half years ago, Mr. Upton was for 26 years licensee of the New Inn, Four Oaks, Sutton Coldfield. A former chairman of the Greater Birmingham, Solihull and District Licensed Victuallers Association, he was for 25 years Midlands delegate to the National Licensed Victuallers Defence League, and for six years served as a council member of the league. He is a senior Past Master of the Masonic Lodge of Sincerity, Birmingham, and holds a provisional rank. In his younger days he was a keen sportsman, playing rugby for Aston Old Edwardians and water polo in the Birmingham and District League. During the 1914-18 war he joined the Royal Warwickshires and later served in France as a captain in the King's Liverpool Regiment. He and his wife Mabel are to live in New Milton, Hampshire.

*Tom Lewin remembers: "Mild was the cheaper of the two draught beers available back in 1966. My recollection of going into the Woodman was that Bitter was one and fourpence halfpenny and Mild was a penny cheaper. Most of us prefered a beer mixture e.g. Brown and Mild or a pint of mixed [Bitter and Mild]. I do remember the coming of Lager, I would put it at around 1967, and most of us would prefer a dash of lime, men with pints, and girls with halves. Beer glasses in those days were a choice of 'handled' glasses and straight glasses but I rarely see 'handled' glasses these days. The finest of all Mild's was Phipps Special Mild, very near to a Brown Ale, sadly its demise was when Watneys bought out Phipps. As for the Bitters, Flowers Keg, Brew XI, Ansells, and Worthington's all stood out, but few could stomach Courage, the southern beer, I guess it was what you were used to."*

**Woolpack** – 77 Regent Street
See Bull and Butcher for details.

**Yates Wine Lodge** – 44/46 Warwick Street
Peter Yates, a Lancashire wine merchant, established Yates Brothers and Co. with his brother and sister in 1884, and set-up the first Yates Wine Lodge in Oldham. Following the granting of a provisional licence on 9th May 1995, the former Woodward's furnishing store reopened as Yates Wine Lodge on Wednesday 24th April 1996 [to become the 57th of its type and name in the country]; it cost £1 million and created 35 new jobs. In 1997, following complaints of excessive noise by local residents, triple glazing was installed. In June 2003, Yates Wine Lodge were granted permission to open until midnight on Fridays and Saturdays, for a six month trial period, conditional on the doors being kept closed, no admittance after 10.45pm and a noise limiter being installed.

Leamington's Yates Wine Lodge, later renamed just Yates, was closed circa 2007. It briefly became a Spanish restaurant [La Tasca], before reopening in November 2009 as the Duke [bar and restaurant]. The Duke remains open in December 2013.

| | |
|---|---|
| 24th April 1996 | Opened as Yates Wine Lodge |
| 24th April 1996 | Rhod Jones *(Manager – Yates)* |
| 1998 | Ian Shaw *(Manager)* |
| 2005 | Gareth Nigel Cotton |
| August 2007-Oct 2007 | Daniel Howell-Jones *(La Tasca)* |
| October 2007-Mar 2008 | Andrew Ronald Alan Hodgkinson |

*Above left: Photo of Yates taken on 29th March 1999 © Allan Jennings. Above right: The Duke bar taken on 27th February 2010 © Allan Jennings.*

| | |
|---|---|
| March 2008-Dec 2008 | James Crawford Brooks |
| December 2008-Dec 2008 | Mrs. Stephanie Murphy |
| December 2008-Jun 2009 | Victoria Peach |
| June 2009-Nov 2009 | Scott Smith |
| 16th Nov 2009-May 2012 | Scott Smith *(Duke)* |
| May 2012 → | David O'Callaghan *(Manager)* |

**York House** – Leamington Priors

The only information we have is a single entry in the licensed victuallers' records and the only address referenced is Leamington Priors.

| | |
|---|---|
| 1828 | John Fallowfield |

**Zest** – 45 Warwick Street
See KoKo's for details.

# ACKNOWLEDGEMENTS

We are very conscious of copyright and have endeavoured to establish ownership of, and gain permission to use, all such material quoted and/or reproduced herein. If there are any omissions, please contact us, and we will correct the error at the earliest opportunity. In the meantime we would like to thank the following:

John Ashby, Vera Belton [née Walmesley], Roberta Boalch, Anthony Collins, Bruno Eurich, Jean Field, Dick Fisk, John French – Inn Sign Society *www.innsignsociety.com*, Esne Goldingay, Mike Ireland, Glynis Jennings, Alan Orton, Tom Thorne, Dennis McWilliams, Wendy Pedley [née Young] and Veronica Collins [née Aitken], Edna Pettipher – 'Public Houses in Leamington and their Publicans' [typed listing], Dale Sutton, Robin Taylor, Margaret Watkins

**Local Newspapers**
Heart of England Newspapers, Leamington Spa Courier & Morning News [Robert Collins, Simon Steele, Barbara Goulden, Chris Lillington and Peter Gawthorpe], Leamington Observer, Royal Leamington Spa Pictorial, Leamington Gazette, Bath Place Times, BPM Media [Alun Thorne]

**Leamington History Group**
Lyndon F. 'Toby' Cave, Jo Clark, Michael Cullen, Terry Gardner, Alan Griffin, Jean Innes, Frank James, Michael Jeffs, Colin Jennings, Richard King, Stanislaw 'Stas' Librowski, Pat McGarrell, Kenneth Owen, Michael Pearson, John Smith, Robin Stott

**Lillington History Group**
Peter Coulls, Chris Rhodes

**Landlords, landladies and ex-landlords and landladies, but special thanks to:**
Simon Beesley – Angel Hotel [Manager], Paul Blatchly – Somerville Arms, Ian Guest [stepson of Fred Wright Ex Jolly Brewer], Josie James – Woodland Tavern, Julie James – Ex Red House, Chris Kelly – Ex Royal Exchange, Sheila McCarthy – Ex Jack and Jill and the Golden Lion, Lon Mallin – Railway Inn, Steve and Louise Massey – Hope & Anchor, Danielle Montgomery – Ex Windmill Inn, Trevor Muckley – Ex Builders Arms, Kevin Murphy – Murphy's, Paul O'Keeffe – Ex Hope & Anchor & Guards, Tommy O'Reilly – Ex The Venew @ the Binswood, Alan Reeve – Ex Cask and Bottle, Joyce Stapleton – Ex Railway Inn, Pete Wilde – Ex New Inn

**Libraries and Warwickshire County Record Office**
Judith Harridge and the staff at Leamington Library, Margaret Wilson, Warwickshire County Record Office

**Warwick District Council**
David Davies – Licensing Services Manager, Alan Mayes – Conservation Manager

**Photographs courtesy of:**
Barry Astill, Bill Bigley *(deceased)*, Coventry Evening Telegraph, R. J. 'Dick' Blenkinsop, Teresa Byrne, Mrs. Mary Cambray, Susan Campbell [née Barrett], Kathleen Carter [née Hobbs], Lyndon F. Cave, Jo Clark, Joe Claydon, Gordon Collett, Eric Corbett, Peter Coulls, Coventry Telegraph, Alan Crossan, Eva Elliott, Terry Gardner, Bill Gibbons *(deceased)*, June Gibson, Dar Gill, Delma Grant, Alan Griffin, Tony Gulliman, John Harris, John Hartnup, Barry Hickman, Sandy Hunter, Mike Ireland, Frank James, Allan Jennings, Glynis Jennings, Leamington Spa Art Gallery & Museum, Leamington Spa Library, Tom Lewin, Sheila McCarthy, Jim McDonnell, Martin McKean, Steve Massey, Kevin Murphy, Tommy O'Reilly, Vivienne Owen, Maureen Pierce, Ron Ransford, Alan Reeve, Kate Rourke, Salvation Army [Leanne Wallis & Ray Oakley], Bob Saunders, Paul Shakespeare, Simon Shaw, Liz Soden, David Stowell, Joyce Mary Timms and Chris Arrowsmith, Sheila Turner [née Roddis], Peter Watts, Warwickshire County Record Office, Nick Wilkins, Michael Willes

**Leamington Art Gallery and Museum**
Victoria Slade

\*    \*    \*    \*    \*

We were overwhelmed by the volume of photographs kindly lent or donated to us but as there were restrictions governing the book's size there too were limitations on the number of photographs that could be included. However, we are considering a sequel that would focus on the people rather than the premises and draw on the vast collection of photos we are holding.

# BIBLIOGRAPHY

**Newspapers**
Leamington Spa Courier: 1828–2013
Morning News: 1896–1991

**Books**
'The History Of Leamington Priors: From The Earliest Records To The Year 1842', Richard Hopper, Published by an unnamed party, 1842
'Glimpses of our Local Past', J. C. Manning, Published by Frank Glover, at the Courier Office, Leamington Spa, 1895
'A Complete History of Royal Leamington Spa', T. B. Dudley, Printed & published by A. Tomes, Bedford Street, Royal Leamington Spa, 1896
'The History of Royal Leamington Spa', George Morley, [Compiled especially for the Leamington Spa Courier, & Warwickshire Standard, 1887-89]
'Royal Leamington Spa – A Century's Growth and Development 1800-1900', H. G. Clarke, Published by Courier Press 1947
'A History of English Ale & Beer', H. A. Monckton, First published by The Bodley Head Ltd, 1966
'A History of the English Public House', H. A. Monckton, ISBN 370 00450 7, First published by The Bodley Head Ltd, 1969
'Graciously Pleased – Royal Leamington Spa – 150 years', [Pages 54 & 55] Chapter by Lyndon F. Cave Dipl.Arch. [Liverpool], ISBN 0-9513594-0-1, Published by Mayneset Limited, 148-150 Parade, Leamington Spa 1988
'Royal Leamington Spa – It's History & Development', Lyndon F. Cave, ISBN 0-85033 520-5, Published by Phillimore & Co Ltd, Shopwyke Hall, Chichester, Sussex, 1988
'Beneath The Great Elms', Jean Field, ISBN 1 85858 012 9, First published by Brewin Books Ltd, Studley, Warwickshire, May 1993
'Royal Leamington Spa – Images From The Past', W. G. [Bill] Gibbons, ISBN 0-947764-86-0, First published in Great Britain by Jones-Sands Publishing, 1995
'People & Places', Produced by the Leamington History Group
'Royal Leamington Spa – Exploring with a Sketchbook', Michael Jeffs, ISBN: 978-0-9562773-1-2, Published by Shay Books, 2, Belmont Drive, Leamington Spa, CV32 6LS, 2011
'A Century of British Brewers – Plus: 1890 to 2004', Norman Barber, ISBN 1-873966-11-3, A Brewery History Society Publication, 2005

**Directories**
Beck's, Bisset's, Fairfax, Kelly's, Moncrieff's, Pigot's, Sharpe's & Spennell's

**Other Publications**

'The Vanishing Faces of the Traditional Pub', Geoff Brandwood, The Journal of the Brewery History Society, [Number 123, Summer 2006]

'Beer & Ragged Staff' [Ian Bayliss, Editor], CAMRA [Magazine of the Heart of Warwickshire Branch of the Campaign for Real Ale] – Various editions

'Pint Sides' [Jim Witt, Editor] CAMRA [Magazine of the Coventry & N. Warwickshire Branch of the Campaign For Real Ale] – Summer 2012 Edition [Page 1]

'London Metropolitan Archives, Information Leaflet Number 45: Licensed Victuallers Records, A Brief History of Licensing' [First published July 1998 by London Metropolitan Archives, The City of London Corporation]

**Websites**

Historic UK [*www.historic-uk.com*]

Licensing Acts: 1872 & 1902 [National Archives / *www.legislation.gov.uk*]

Licensing Act: 1904 [University of California / California Digital Library / *www.archive.org*]

Midland Pubs [Kieron McMahon] *www.midlandspubs.co.uk*

Angel Hotel / *www.angelhotel.net/history*

Somerville Arms / *www.somervillearms.co.uk*

# APPENDIX: QUICK REFERENCE GUIDE

| NAME | ST. No. | STREET NAME | FROM | TO |
|------|---------|-------------|------|-----|
| ALASTAIR'S | 40 | WARWICK STREET | c1975 | 2004 |
| ALBATROSS | 60 | CLEMENS STREET | 1879 | 1905 |
| ALBION HOTEL | 8 | HIGH STREET [CNR WISE ST] | 1833 | 1874 |
| ALE & PORTER VAULTS | 10 | GLOUCESTER STREET | 1830 | ≥1839 |
| ALEXANDRA INN | 1 | ABBOTTS STREET | ≤1861 | 1922 |
| ALTHORPE ARMS | 18 | ALTHORPE STREET | 1837 | 1959 |
| ALTORIA | 45 | WARWICK STREET | 2012 | OPEN |
| ANCHOR TAVERN | 30 | OXFORD STREET | 1849 | 1864 |
| ANCIENT DRUID | | LANSDOWNE STREET | 1837 | 1838-40 |
| ANGEL HOTEL / INN | 143 | REGENT STREET | 1813 | OPEN |
| ANGLO BAVARIAN REFRESHMENT BAR | 63 | BEDFORD STREET | 1885 | 1904 |
| APOLLO ROOMS & WINE VAULTS | 13 | CLEMENS STREET | 1825 | 1860 |
| AUGUSTA TAVERN | 6 | AUGUSTA PLACE | 1850 | 1875 |
| AVENUE HOTEL | 15-17 | SPENCER STREET | ≤1878 | OPEN |
| AYLESFORD ARMS | 87 | BEDFORD STREET / PARADE | ≤1856 | 1958 |
| AYLESFORD INN | 29 | EAGLE STREET | 1881 | c1927 |
| BAKERS | 33 | REGENT STREET | 1984 | 1991 |
| BAR 44 | 44 | CLARENDON STREET | 1994 | 2010 |
| BAR CITRUS | 26 | PARK STREET | 2001 | N/A |
| BAR CODE | 27 | AUGUSTA PLACE | ≥2004 | 2010 |
| BARNIES | 75 | BEDFORD STREET | 2006 | 2008 |
| BAROQUE | 32 | CLARENDON AVENUE | 2001 | 2009 |
| BATH HOTEL | 32 | BATH STREET | 1814 | 1951 |
| BATH HOTEL LOUNGE & VAULTS BAR | | SPENCER STREET | c1860 | ≥1907 |
| BEDFORD | 75 | BEDFORD STREET | 2011 | 2012 |

| RENAMED FROM | RENAMED TO | CURRENT BUSINESS |
|---|---|---|
| ------ | MACKY'S BAR & RESTAURANT | SAINT BAR |
| THREE TUNS | ------ | RETAIL |
| ------ | GREAT WESTERN HOTEL | EIGHT [BAR & BISTRO] |
| ------ | ------ | SITE REDEVELOPED - RETAIL |
| ------ | ------ | RETAIL |
| ------ | ------ | ALTHORPE INDUSTRIAL EST. |
| KO KO's | ------ | ALTORIA |
| HOPE & ANCHOR [1] | ------ | RESIDENTIAL |
| ------ | ------ | EXACT LOCATION UNKNOWN |
| ------ | ------ | ANGEL HOTEL |
| ------ | ------ | SITE REDEVELOPED - RETAIL |
| ------ | GREAT WESTERN | TAKEAWAY FOOD OUTLET |
| ------ | WILLOUGHBY ARMS | SITE REDEVELOPED - RESIDENTIAL |
| COMMERCIAL HOTEL | ------ | AVENUE [HOTEL] |
| ------ | ------ | GARAGE ENTRANCE |
| ------ | ------ | RESIDENTIAL |
| RICK'S BAR | MURPHY'S BAR | MURPHY'S BAR |
| KINGS ARMS [CONTIN] | THREE GRACES | MAD HATTERS |
| WIG & PEN | ------ | RESTAURANT |
| KASA BAR | CAINES | VACANT & 'TO LET' [END 2013] |
| PACIFIC RIM | ENVY BAR | PART OF 'LOUNGE' [130, PARADE] |
| FOX | FOX | FOX & VIVIAN |
| NEW INN | ------ | SITE REDEVELOPED - RETAIL |
| BOWLING GREEN | ------ | SITE REDEVELOPED - RETAIL |
| ENVY BAR | ------ | PART OF 'LOUNGE' [130, PARADE] |

| NAME | ST. No. | STREET NAME | FROM | TO |
|---|---|---|---|---|
| BEDFORD HOTEL | 15 | LOWER PARADE | 1811 | 1856 |
| BEDFORD INN | 75 | BEDFORD STREET | 1824 | ≥1998 |
| BELL INN | 69 | RUGBY ROAD | ≤1835 | 1958 |
| BENJAMIN SATCHWELLS | 112-114 | PARADE | 1996 | OPEN |
| BERNI ROYAL HOTEL | 2-4 | KENILWORTH ROAD | 1972 | 1991 |
| BINSWOOD TAVERN | 2 | BINSWOOD STREET | ≤1832 | 1962 |
| BIRCH & BILLYCOCK | 35 | REGENT STREET | 1984 | 1994 |
| BIRCH TREE | 35 | REGENT STREET | 1994 | 1999 |
| BIRMINGHAM TAVERN | | WISE STREET | 1815 | 1840 |
| BLACK DOG [1] | | LONDON ROAD [HIGH STREET] | <1776 | 1793 |
| BLACK DOG [2] | 9 | SATCHWELL STREET | 1833 | c1897 |
| BLACK HORSE | 18 | PRINCES STREET | 1863 | ≤2004 |
| BLENHEIM HOTEL | | CLEMENS STREET | 1816 | 1833 |
| BOHEMIA @ THE WILLOUGHBY | 12 | AUGUSTA PLACE | c2009 | 2011 |
| BOWLING GREEN | | SPENCER STREET | 1858 | c1860 |
| BOWLING GREEN INN [1] | | CHURCH LANE / CHURCH STREET | <1768 | 1829 |
| BOWLING GREEN INN [2] | | CHURCH STREET / CHAPEL STREET | c1827 | 1856 |
| BOWLING GREEN INN [3] | 20 | NEW STREET | 1867 | OPEN |
| BRICKLAYERS ARMS | 34 | KING STREET | ≤1865 | 1914 |
| BRICKLAYERS ARMS | 5 | TAVISTOCK STREET | 1832 | 1835 |
| BRICKMAKERS ARMS | | CLARENDON ST / LILLINGTON RD | 1837 | c1862 |
| BRIDGE | 7 | BRUNSWICK STREET | 1990 | 2000 |
| BRITANNIA | 7 | CHANDOS STREET | 1836 | 1980 |
| BRITISH BIRD FANCIER | | MORRIS STREET | 1837 | 1837 |
| BRITON | 18 | CHANDOS STREET | 1835 | 1836 |
| BRITONS BOAST | | QUEEN STREET | ≤1861 | 1861 |
| BROWN BEAR | | REGENT STREET | 1837 | 1837-38 |
| BRUNSWICK | 67 | BRUNSWICK STREET | 1998 | 2003 |
| BRUNSWICK HOTEL | | CORNER WARWICK STREET & CLARENDON PLACE | c1841 | 1845-46 |

| RENAMED FROM | RENAMED TO | CURRENT BUSINESS |
|---|---|---|
| ------ | ------ | BANK [HSBC] |
| ------ | PACIFIC RIM | PART OF 'LOUNGE' [130, PARADE] |
| ------ | ------ | RETAIL |
| ------ | ------ | BENJAMIN SATCHWELLS |
| GUY'S HOTEL | ROYAL | RESIDENTIAL |
| ------ | NEW BINSWOOD TAVERN | RESIDENTIAL [COMPLETION LATE 2014] |
| WARWICK HOTEL | BIRCH TREE | VOODOO BAR |
| BIRCH & BILLYCOCK | VOODOO BAR | VOODOO BAR |
| ------ | ------ | EXACT LOCATION UNKNOWN |
| ------ | SINKER'S BOARDING HOUSE | SITE REDEVELOPED - RETAIL |
| ------ | ------ | ROYAL PRIORS |
| ------ | ------ | RESIDENTIAL |
| ------ | STONELEIGH HOTEL | RETAIL |
| FLANAGAN'S | WILLOUGHBY | SITE REDEVELOPED - RESIDENTIAL |
| ------ | BATH HOTEL LOUNGE/ VAULTS BAR | SITE REDEVELOPED - RETAIL |
| ------ | UNION & COMMERCIAL INN | SITE REDEVELOPED - RESIDENTIAL |
| ------ | GUERNSEY COMMERCIAL INN | RESIDENTIAL |
| ------ | THE BOWLING GREEN | THE BOWLING GREEN |
| ------ | ------ | SITE REDEVELOPED - RESIDENTIAL |
| ------ | CROSS KEYS [1] | NIGHT CLUB |
| ------ | ------ | RESIDENTIAL |
| QUEENS HEAD | LOCK, DOCK & BARREL | RESIDENTIAL |
| BRITON | ------ | BAPTIST CHURCH |
| ------ | ------ | EXACT LOCATION UNKNOWN |
| ------ | BRITANNIA | BAPTIST CHURCH |
| ------ | ------ | EXACT LOCATION UNKNOWN |
| ------ | ------ | EXACT LOCATION UNKNOWN |
| JET & WHITTLE | JET | JET |
| ------ | ------ | ESTATE AGENT |

| NAME | ST. No. | STREET NAME | FROM | TO |
|---|---|---|---|---|
| BRUNSWICK INN | 67 | BRUNSWICK STREET | 1832 | 1964 |
| BUBBLES CHAMPAGNE BAR & BISTRO | 29 | CHANDOS STREET | c2004 | ≤2009 |
| BUILDERS ARMS | 38 | LANSDOWNE STREET | 1980 | OPEN |
| BULL & BUTCHER | 77 | REGENT STREET | 1835 | 1838-40 |
| BULLDOG | | ST. MARGARETS ROAD, WHITNASH | 1956 | 1994 |
| BUNCH OF GRAPES | | CLEMENS STREET | ≤1818 | ≥1818 |
| BUTCHERS ARMS | 45 | HIGH STREET | 1838 | 1857 |
| CAINES | 27 | AUGUSTA PLACE | 2010 | 2010 |
| CAR INN | | CNR WARWICK & KENILWORTH STS | 1835 | 1857 |
| CARPENTERS ARMS | 29 | CHANDOS STREET | 1835 | c2004 |
| CASK & BOTTLE | 17 | KENNEDY SQUARE | 1994 | OPEN |
| CASSIS COCKTAIL & LOUNGE BAR | 12 | AUGUSTA PLACE | 1983 | 1990 |
| CASTLE INN / HOTEL | 85 | BRUNSWICK STREET | 1816 | 1847 |
| CHAIR & ROCKET | 13 | BATH STREET | 1957 | 1997 |
| CHASE INN / TAVERN | 35 | OXFORD STREET | 1832 | 1922 |
| CLARENDON | 44-46 | CLARENDON AVENUE | 2008 | OPEN |
| CLARENDON HOTEL | 1-3 | PARADE | 1832 | 1983 |
| CLARENDON INN | 27 | CLARENDON STREET | ≤1837 | 1861 |
| CLARENDON TAVERN | 19 | RUSSELL STREET | 1833 | 1968 |
| COACH & HORSES | 4 | BEDFORD STREET | 1835 | 2004 |
| COLONNADE | 2A | VICTORIA TERRACE | 1982 | 1988 |
| COMMERCIAL HOTEL | 15-17 | SPENCER STREET | 1871 | ≤1878 |
| COOPERS ARMS | 2 | COURT STREET | c1834 | c1840 |
| COPPER POT | 41-43 | WARWICK STREET | 2005 | OPEN |
| COTTAGE TAVERN | 38 | QUEEN STREET | 1863 | 1961 |
| COVENTRY ARMS [1] | 2 | REGENT STREET | 1830 | 1844 |
| COVENTRY ARMS [2] | 23 | GUYS CLIFFE ROAD | 1844 | 2013 |
| COVENTRY CITY ARMS | 30 | CLEMENS STREET | 1842 | 1857 |
| CRICKETERS ARMS [1] | 1 | VICTORIA STREET | ≤1854 | 1889 |

| RENAMED FROM | RENAMED TO | CURRENT BUSINESS |
|---|---|---|
| ------ | ------ | THE 'JET' CAR PARK |
| CARPENTERS ARMS | BEEN | RESTAURANT |
| LANSDOWNE TAVERN | ------ | BUILDERS ARMS |
| ------ | WOOLPACK | EXACT LOCATION UNKNOWN |
| ------ | WHITNASH TAVERN | WHITNASH TAVERN |
| ------ | ------ | LOCATION UNKNOWN |
| ------ | GUARDS INN | QUEEN VICTORIA |
| BAR CODE | G's BAR | VACANT & 'TO LET' [END 2013] |
| ------ | ------ | SITE REDEVELOPED - RETAIL |
| ------ | BUBBLES | RESTAURANT |
| GREYHOUND | ------ | CASK & BOTTLE |
| WILLOUGHBY ARMS | STYLES APART | SITE REDEVELOPED - RESIDENTIAL |
| ------ | ------ | SITE REDEVELOPED - RESIDENTIAL |
| VAULTS [PH] | JUG & JESTER | JUG & JESTER |
| ------ | ------ | RESIDENTIAL |
| OXYGEN | ------ | CLARENDON |
| ------ | ------ | COMMERCIAL - OFFICE SPACE |
| ------ | ------ | SITE REDEVELOPED - VACANT: END 2013 |
| ------ | ------ | EDGE OF COVENT GARDEN CAR PARK |
| ------ | MUMBAI BLUU | LOOSE BOX |
| ------ | ROBBIN'S WELL | ROBBIN'S WELL |
| ------ | AVENUE HOTEL | AVENUE [HOTEL] |
| EAGLE & SHAMROCK | HOPE TAVERN | HOPE TAVERN |
| OLD BUTCHERS | ------ | COPPER POT |
| ------ | ------ | RESIDENTIAL |
| ------ | WARWICK ARMS | WARWICK ARMS |
| RAILROAD INN | FAT PUG | FAT PUG |
| ------ | ------ | RETAIL |
| ------ | ------ | RESIDENTIAL |

| NAME | ST. No. | STREET NAME | FROM | TO |
|---|---|---|---|---|
| CRICKETERS ARMS [2] | 19 | ARCHERY ROAD | 1889 | OPEN |
| CROSS KEYS [1] | 44 | TAVISTOCK STREET | 1835 | c1870 |
| CROSS KEYS [2] | 128 | WARWICK STREET | 2012 | 2013 |
| CROWN INN | 67 | KENILWORTH ROAD, LILLINGTON | c1829 | ≥1845 |
| CROWN INN / HOTEL | 10 | HIGH STREET | 1815 | 1989 |
| CUBA | 116 | WARWICK STREET | 2001 | 2006 |
| DEBONAIR | 2-4 | RANELAGH STREET | 1988 | 2008 |
| DESMOND HOTEL | 2-4 | KENILWORTH ROAD | c1920s | 1964 |
| DOG & DUCK | | SQUARE ST, COVENT GARDEN MKT | 1833 | 1834 |
| DUKE | 44-46 | WARWICK STREET | 2009 | OPEN |
| EAGLE & SHAMROCK | 2 | COURT STREET | 1833 | c1834 |
| EAGLE INN | 41 | ALTHORPE STREET | 1837 | 1959 |
| EARL GREY ARMS | 8 | GLOUCESTER STREET | 1832 | 1834 |
| EIGHT | 8 | HIGH STREET | 2013 | OPEN |
| ENVY BAR | 75 | BEDFORD STREET | 2010 | 2011 |
| EXCHANGE | 2 | HIGH STREET | 2010 | 2013 |
| FALSTAFF | 67 | PARADE | 1885 | 1885 |
| FAT PUG | 23 | GUYS CLIFFE ROAD | 2013 | OPEN |
| FLANAGANS | 12 | AUGUSTA PLACE | ≤1997 | ≥1997 |
| FLYING HORSE | | NEILSTON STREET / WHITE STREET | 1831 | c1840 |
| FORTY FOUR | 44 | CLARENDON STREET | 2011 | 2012 |
| FOUNTAIN | | CNR WARWICK & BROOK STREETS | 1835 | c1840 |
| FOUNTAIN | 12 | CLEMENS STREET | 1841 | 1859 |
| FOX | 32 | CLARENDON AVENUE | 1995 | 2001 |
| FOX [CONTIN] | 32 | CLARENDON AVENUE | 2009 | 2010 |
| FOX & VIVIAN | 32 | CLARENDON AVENUE | 1837 | 1988 |
| FOX & VIVIAN [CONTIN] | 32 | CLARENDON AVE | 2010 | OPEN |
| FUSILIER | | STANLEYS CRT, SYDENHAM DRIVE | 1974 | OPEN |
| GARDENERS ARMS | 72 | REGENT STREET | 1835 | c1840 |

| RENAMED FROM | RENAMED TO | CURRENT BUSINESS |
|---|---|---|
| ------ | ------ | CRICKETERS ARMS |
| BRICKLAYERS ARMS | VICTORIA VAULTS | NIGHT CLUB |
| FORTY FOUR | MAD HATTERS | MAD HATTERS |
| ------ | ------ | RESIDENTIAL |
| ------ | ------ | RESIDENTIAL |
| OTHER PLACE | SWEENEYS | LEIF [TEAROOMS & PIANO BAR] |
| RANELAGH TAVERN | ------ | RESIDENTIAL |
| ------ | GUYS HOTEL | RESIDENTIAL |
| ------ | SHIP | CLEARED & SEALED SPACE |
| YATES WINE LODGE | ------ | DUKE |
| ------ | COOPERS ARMS | HOPE TAVERN |
| ------ | ------ | RESIDENTIAL [AGED CARE] |
| ------ | GLOUCESTER TAVERN | ASIAN COMMUNITY EQUALITY CTR. |
| ------ | ------ | EIGHT |
| BARNIES | BEDFORD | PART OF 'LOUNGE' [130, PARADE] |
| ROYAL EXCHANGE | UNDER GRADUATE | UNDER GRADUATE |
| ------ | ------ | RETAIL |
| COVENTRY ARMS [2] | ------ | FAT PUG |
| PHOENIX | WILLOUGHBY | SITE REDEVELOPED - RESIDENTIAL |
| ------ | ------ | INDUSTRIAL UNIT |
| THREE GRACES | CROSS KEYS [2] | MAD HATTERS |
| ------ | ------ | SITE REDEVELOPED - RESIDENTIAL |
| ------ | RAILWAY INN | RAILWAY INN |
| SLUG & LETTUCE @ FOX & VIVIAN | BAROQUE | FOX & VIVIAN |
| BAROQUE | FOX & VIVIAN | FOX & VIVIAN |
| ------ | SLUG & LETTUCE [1] | FOX & VIVIAN |
| FOX | ------ | FOX & VIVIAN |
| ------ | ------ | FUSILIER |
| ------ | ------ | EXACT LOCATION UNKNOWN |

411

| NAME | ST. No. | STREET NAME | FROM | TO |
|---|---|---|---|---|
| GARIBALDI INN | 16 | HIGH STREET | 1861 | 1922 |
| GEORGE & DRAGON | 13 | PARK STREET | c1835 | c1838 |
| GEORGE INN | 53 | HIGH STREET | ≤1822 | c2004 |
| GLASSHOUSE | 38-40 | WARWICK STREET | 2011 | OPEN |
| GLOBE INN | 13 | PARK STREET | 1831 c1838 | c1835 1958 |
| GLOUCESTER HOTEL | 11 | CLEMENS STREET | 1828 | ≥1833 |
| GLOUCESTER TAVERN | 8 | GLOUCESTER STREET | 1835 | 1907 |
| GOLD CUP | 10 | TAVISTOCK STREET | 1839 | 1968 |
| GOLDEN LION | 91-93 | REGENT STREET | 1810 | 1988 |
| GRAND UNION BAR & RESTAURANT | 66 | CLEMENS STREET | 1980 | OPEN |
| GRAPES TAVERN | | CLEMENS STREET | 1849 | 1857 |
| GREAT WESTERN HOTEL | 8 | HIGH STREET [CNR WISE ST] | 1874 | 1967 |
| GREAT WESTERN INN | 13 | CLEMENS STREET | 1860 | 1993 |
| GREEN MAN | | GROVE PLACE | 1833 | 1927 |
| GREEN MAN | 114 | TACHBROOK STREET | 1927 | OPEN |
| GREEN TAILED DRAGON | 2 | GEORGE STREET | 1999 | 2001 |
| GREYHOUND [ALSO KNOWN AS 'SINKERS BOARDING HOUSE'] | | HIGH STREET | 1793 | 1813 |
| GREYHOUND | 17 | LANSDOWNE STREET | ≤1837 | 1993 |
| GRIST MILL | | CHESTERTON DRIVE, SYDENHAM | 1985 | OPEN |
| G's BAR | 27 | AUGUSTA PLACE | 2011 | 2011 |
| GUARDS INN | 45 | HIGH STREET | 1857 | c1994 |
| GUERNSEY COMMERCIAL INN | 29 | CHURCH STREET | 1856 | c1864 |
| GUY TAVERN | 1 | GUY STREET | 1833 | 1929 |
| GUY'S HOTEL | 2-4 | KENILWORTH ROAD | 1964 | 1972 |
| HALF MOON | 36 | SATCHWELL STREET | 1813 | 1845 |
| HALF MOON [CONTIN] | 36 | SATCHWELL STREET | 1859 | 1898 |
| HALF NELSON | | WINSTON CRESCENT / NEWLAND ROAD, LILLINGTON | 1992 | 1996 |
| HARE & HOUNDS | 113 | REGENT STREET | 1831 | 1952 |
| HAUNCH OF VENISON | 130 | PARADE | ≤1895 | 1999 |

| RENAMED FROM | RENAMED TO | CURRENT BUSINESS |
|---|---|---|
| COOPERS WINE VAULTS | ------ | INDIAN TAKEAWAY FOOD |
| GLOBE INN | GLOBE INN | RETAIL |
| ------ | ------ | RESIDENTIAL |
| SLUG & LETTUCE [2] | ------ | GLASSHOUSE |
| ------ <br> GEORGE & DRAGON | GEORGE & DRAGON <br> ------ | RETAIL |
| ------ | ------ | RETAIL |
| EARL GREY ARMS | ------ | ASIAN COMMUNITY EQUALITY CTR. |
| ------ | ------ | CAR PARK |
| ------ | ------ | BANK [RBS] |
| ------ | ------ | GRAND UNION BAR & REST. |
| ------ | ------ | EXACT LOCATION UNKNOWN |
| ALBION HOTEL | ------ | EIGHT [BAR & BISTRO] |
| APOLLO VAULTS | ------ | TAKEAWAY FOOD OUTLET |
| ------ | ------ | SITE REDEVELOPED - RESIDENTIAL |
| ------ | ------ | GREEN MAN |
| TOWN HOUSE | TOWN HOUSE TAVERN | TOWN HOUSE TAVERN |
| BLACK DOG INN | BECAME PART OF [COPPS] ROYAL HOTEL | SITE REDEVELOPED - RETAIL |
| ------ | CASK & BOTTLE | CASK & BOTTLE |
| ------ | ------ | GRIST MILL |
| CAINES | ------ | VACANT & 'TO LET' [END 2013] |
| BUTCHERS ARMS | PIG & FIDDLE | QUEEN VICTORIA |
| BOWLING GREEN INN [2] | GUERNSEY TEMP. HOTEL | RESIDENTIAL |
| ------ | ------ | CAR PARK |
| DESMOND HOTEL | BERNI ROYAL HOTEL | RESIDENTIAL |
| ------ | TURF INN | ENTRANCE TO ROYAL PRIORS |
| TURF INN | PALACE INN | ENTRANCE TO ROYAL PRIORS |
| JACK & JILL | ------ | RESIDENTIAL |
| ------ | ------ | RETAIL |
| ------ | LOUNGE | LOUNGE |

| NAME | ST. No. | STREET NAME | FROM | TO |
|---|---|---|---|---|
| HEATHCOTE INN | | TACHBROOK ROAD, WHITNASH | 1945 | OPEN |
| HINTONS | 27-31 | AUGUSTA PLACE | 1974 | 1989 |
| HOB NOBS | 27 | AUGUSTA PLACE | 1989 | 1993 |
| HOD CARRIER | 102 | COPPICE ROAD, WHITNASH | 1983 | OPEN |
| HOGSHEAD | 41-43 | WARWICK STREET | 1997 | 2004 |
| HOLLY BUSH [OLD] | 89 | KING STREET | ≤1842 | 1974 |
| HOLLY BUSH [NEW] | | HOLLY STREET [CNR EARL STREET] | 1974 | OPEN |
| HOPE & ANCHOR [1] | 30 | OXFORD STREET | ≤1838 | ≥1839 |
| HOPE & ANCHOR | 41 | HILL STREET | 1852 | OPEN |
| HOPE TAVERN | 2 | COURT STREET | c1840 | OPEN |
| HUDDY'S CAFÉ BAR | 24 | VICTORIA TERRACE | 1996 | 1996 |
| IMPERIAL [PH] | | CORNER REGENT & BEDFORD STREETS | 1880 | 1901 |
| IMPERIAL HOTEL | | LANSDOWNE PLACE | 1836 | 1843 |
| IVY TREE | 8 | QUEEN STREET | 1848 | 1907 |
| JACK & JILL | | WINSTON CRESCENT / NEWLAND ROAD, LILLINGTON | 1966 | 1992 |
| JAM BAR & BRASSERIE | 102 | WARWICK STREET | 2009 | 2011 |
| JEKYLL & HYDE | 44-46 | CLARENDON AVENUE | 1986 | 1992 |
| JET | 67 | BRUNSWICK STREET | 2003 | OPEN |
| JET & WHITTLE | 67 | BRUNSWICK STREET | 1964 | 1998 |
| JOINERS ARMS [1] | 59-61 | SHRUBLAND STREET | ≤1856 | 1943 |
| JOINERS ARMS [2] | 63-67 | SHRUBLAND STREET | 1943 | OPEN |
| JOLLY BOATMAN | 1 | ALBION ROW | 1835 | 1836 |
| JOLLY BREWER | 21 | GUY STREET | 1833 | 1981 |
| JUG & JESTER | 13 | BATH STREET | 1997 | OPEN |
| KA BAR | 44 | CLARENDON STREET | 1984 | 1986 |
| KASA BAR | 27 | AUGUSTA PLACE | c1999 | ≥2004 |
| KELLYS | 7 | COURT STREET | 1983 | 2007 |
| KELSEYS | 15-17 | HIGH STREET | ≤2002 | OPEN |
| KINGS ARMS [1] | 1 | WARWICK STREET | 1825 | c1868 |

| RENAMED FROM | RENAMED TO | CURRENT BUSINESS |
|---|---|---|
| ------ | ------ | HEATHCOTE INN |
| ------ | HOB NOBS | VACANT & 'TO LET' [END 2013] |
| HINTONS | KASA BAR | VACANT & 'TO LET' [END 2013] |
| ------ | ------ | HODCARRIER |
| ------ | OLD BUTCHERS | COPPER POT |
| ------ | ------ | SHRUBS & BUSHES |
| ------ | ------ | HOLLY BUSH |
| ------ | ANCHOR TAVERN | RESIDENTIAL |
| ------ | ------ | HOPE & ANCHOR |
| COOPERS ARMS | ------ | HOPE TAVERN |
| ------ | ------ | FAST FOOD OUTLET |
| WINE VAULTS [ROYAL ASSEMBLY ROOMS] | ------ | ART GALLERY |
| ------ | ------ | EXACT LOCATION UNKNOWN |
| ------ | ------ | SITE REDEVELOPED - RESIDENTIAL |
| ------ | HALF NELSON | RESIDENTIAL |
| WHALE BAR | ------ | CREPERIE / RESTAURANT |
| TOP OF TOWN | WINSTONS | CLARENDON |
| BRUNSWICK | ------ | JET |
| ------ | BRUNSWICK | JET |
| SPRINGFIELD INN | ------ | GRASSED AREA |
| ------ | ------ | JOINERS ARMS |
| ------ | PLASTERERS ARMS | SITE REDEVELOPED - INDUSTRIAL |
| ------ | ------ | CHANDOS ST. CAR PARK |
| CHAIR & ROCKET | ------ | JUG & JESTER |
| KINGS ARMS [2] | KINGS ARMS [CONTIN] | MAD HATTERS |
| HOB NOBS | BAR CODE | VACANT & 'TO LET' [END 2013] |
| LEOPARD | ------ | NIGHT CLUB |
| MIDLAND RED CLUB | ------ | KELSEY'S |
| ------ | ------ | RETAIL CLOTHES STORE |

| NAME | ST. No. | STREET NAME | FROM | TO |
|------|---------|-------------|------|-----|
| KINGS ARMS [2] | 44 | CLARENDON STREET | c1868 | 1984 |
| KINGS ARMS [CONTIN] | 44 | CLARENDON STREET | 1986 | 1994 |
| KINGS HEAD | 6 | SQUARE ST, COVENT GARDEN MKT | 1835 | 1871 |
| KO KO's | 45 | WARWICK STREET | ≥2004 | 2012 |
| LAMB | 33 | PARK STREET | 1832 | 1834 |
| LANSDOWNE HOTEL | | CNR PARADE & WARWICK STREET | 1834 | 1860 |
| LANSDOWNE TAVERN | 38 | LANSDOWNE STREET | 1866 | c1972 |
| LEAMINGTON TAVERN | 28-30 | TAVISTOCK STREET | 1830 | 1966 |
| LEEKY JOE'S | 29 | AUGUSTA PLACE | c1991 | c1993 |
| LEICESTER TAVERN | 1 | LEICESTER STREET | 1837 | c1862 |
| LEIF [TEAROOMS & PIANO BAR] | 116 | WARWICK STREET | 2012 | OPEN |
| LEOPARD INN | 7 | COURT STREET | ≤1848 | 1982 |
| LOCK, DOCK & BARREL | 7 | BRUNSWICK STREET | 2000 | 2010 |
| LONDON TAVERN | | HIGH STREET | 1837 | 1838-40 |
| LONDON TAVERN | 12 | SATCHWELL STREET | 1856 | 1961 |
| LOOSE BOX | 4 | BEDFORD STREET | 2011 | OPEN |
| LOUNGE | 130 | PARADE | 1999 | OPEN |
| MACKY'S BAR & RESTAURANT | 40 | WARWICK STREET | 2004 | 2007 |
| MAD HATTERS | 128 | WARWICK STREET | 2014 | OPEN |
| MANOR HOUSE HOTEL | | AVENUE ROAD | 1847 | 2004 |
| MARLBOROUGH HOTEL | 48 | BRANDON PARADE | 1947 | 1963 |
| MASONS ARMS | 31 | RUGBY ROAD | 1837 | 1960 |
| MERRIE LION | 11 | BROOK STREET | 1833 | 1834 |
| MOO | 24 | RUSSELL STREET | 2001 | OPEN |
| MOORINGS | | MYTON ROAD | 1995 | OPEN |
| MOR BAR | 116 | WARWICK STREET | c2009 | ≥2009 |
| MUMBAI BLUU | 4 | BEDFORD STREET | 2004 | 2011 |
| MURPHY'S BAR | 33 | REGENT STREET | 1991 | OPEN |
| MUSWELLS WINE BAR | 9 | PARADE | 1989 | c1994 |

| RENAMED FROM | RENAMED TO | CURRENT BUSINESS |
|---|---|---|
| ------ | KA BAR | MAD HATTERS |
| K A BAR | BAR 44 | MAD HATTERS |
| SHIP | ------ | CLEARED & SEALED SPACE |
| ZEST | ALTORIA | ALTORIA |
| ------ | UNION TAVERN | EXACT LOCATION UNKNOWN |
| ------ | ------ | RETAIL ['BOOTS' CHEMIST] |
| ------ | BUILDERS ARMS | BUILDERS ARMS |
| ------ | ------ | CAR PARKING |
| ------ | ------ | VACANT & 'TO LET' [END 2013] |
| ------ | ------ | RESIDENTIAL |
| PRINCE OF WALES | ------ | LEIF [TEAROOMS & PIANO BAR] |
| ------ | KELLYS | NIGHT CLUB |
| BRIDGE | ----- | RESIDENTIAL |
| ------ | ----- | EXACT LOCATION UNKNOWN |
| PAUL PRY | ------ | ROYAL PRIORS S/CENTRE |
| MUMBAI BLUU | ------ | LOOSE BOX |
| HAUNCH OF VENISON | ------ | LOUNGE |
| ALASTAIR'S | SAINT BAR | SAINT BAR |
| CROSS KEYS | ------ | MAD HATTERS |
| ------ | ------ | RESIDENTIAL |
| ------ | ------ | REDEVELOPED - COMMERCIAL [MARLBOROUGH HOUSE] |
| ------ | ------ | RESIDENTIAL |
| ------ | WHITE LION | BROOK STREET REBUILT |
| ------ | ------ | MOO |
| ------ | ------ | MOORINGS |
| SWEENEYS | TRYST | LEIF [TEAROOMS & PIANO BAR] |
| COACH & HORSES | LOOSE BOX | LOOSE BOX |
| BAKER'S | ------ | MURPHY'S BAR |
| ------ | ------ | CHINESE RESTAURANT |

| NAME | ST. No. | STREET NAME | FROM | TO |
|---|---|---|---|---|
| NEGRO | | BROOK STREET | 1838 | 1839 |
| NELSON INN | 42-44 | BRUNSWICK STREET | 1832 | 1833-34 |
| NEW BINSWOOD TAVERN | | RUGBY ROAD | 1962 | 2010 |
| NEW INN | 32 | BATH STREET | 1793 | 1814 |
| NEW INN | 195-197 | LEAM TERRACE | c1860 | OPEN |
| NEW KINGS ARMS | 69 | WARWICK STREET | 1870 | 1959 |
| NEWBOLD | 18 | NEWBOLD STREET | 2001 | 2012 |
| NEWBOLD COMYN ARMS | | NEWBOLD TERRACE EAST, NEWBOLD COMYN | 1984 | OPEN |
| NEWBOLD INN | 18 | NEWBOLD STREET | 1835 | >1966 |
| NEWBOLD TAVERN | 18 | NEWBOLD STREET | >1966 | 1999 |
| NEWMARKET INN | 50 | TAVISTOCK STREET | ≥1827 | 1883 |
| NOAH'S ARK | 106 | REGENT STREET | 1832 | 1907 |
| OAK INN / HOTEL | 89 | RADFORD ROAD | 1837 | 2010 |
| OAK TAVERN | | COURT STREET | 1880 | 1891-92 |
| OCEAN BAR / OCEAN REEF | 44 | OXFORD STREET | ≤1998 | 2011 |
| ODDFELLOWS HALL INN | 22 | KENILWORTH STREET | 1880 | 1888 |
| OLD BUTCHERS | 41-43 | WARWICK STREET | 2004 | 2005 |
| OLD WHITE LION | 26 | BROOK STREET | c1863 | 1925 |
| ORANGE HOTEL | | CLEMENS STREET | 1812 | ≤1817 |
| OTHER PLACE | 116 | WARWICK STREET | 1998 | 2001 |
| OXFORD TAVERN | 10 | OXFORD STREET | 1835 | 1922 |
| OXYGEN | 44-46 | CLARENDON AVENUE | 2002 | 2008 |
| PACIFIC RIM | 75 | BEDFORD STREET | ≥1998 | 2006 |
| PALACE INN | 36 | SATCHWELL STREET | 1898 | 1976 |
| PAUL PRY | 12 | SATCHWELL STREET | 1832 | 1856 |
| PHOENIX | 12 | AUGUSTA PLACE | ≥1994 | ≥1997 |
| PIG & FIDDLE | 45 | HIGH STREET | c1994 | 2010 |
| PLASTERER'S ARMS | 1 | ALBION ROW | 1836 | 1871-72 |
| PLOUGH & HARROW | | WHITNASH ROAD, WHITNASH | ≤1845 | OPEN |

| RENAMED FROM | RENAMED TO | CURRENT BUSINESS |
|---|---|---|
| ------ | ------ | EXACT LOCATION UNKNOWN |
| ------ | ------ | SITE REDEVELOPED - RESIDENTIAL |
| BINSWOOD TAVERN | VENEW @ THE BINSWOOD | RESIDENTIAL [COMPLETION LATE 2014] |
| ------ | BATH HOTEL | SITE REDEVELOPED - RETAIL |
| ------ | ------ | NEW INN |
| ------ | ------ | SITE REDEVELOPED - RETAIL |
| NEWBOLD TAVERN | REGENCY ARMS | REGENCY ARMS |
| ------ | ------ | NEWBOLD COMYN ARMS |
| ------ | NEWBOLD TAVERN | REGENCY ARMS |
| NEWBOLD INN | NEWBOLD | REGENCY ARMS |
| ------ | TAVISTOCK INN | TAVISTOCK INN |
| ------ | ------ | RETAIL |
| ------ | ------ | CONVENIENCE STORE - WORK IN PROGRESS [JANUARY 2014] |
| ------ | ------ | EXACT LOCATION UNKNOWN |
| ------ | ------ | VACANT [DECEMBER 2013] |
| ROSE & CROWN | ROSE & CROWN | CAR PARK |
| HOGSHEAD | COPPER POT | COPPER POT |
| WHITE LION | ------ | BROOK STREET REBUILT |
| ------ | ------ | EXACT LOCATION UNKNOWN |
| PRINCE OF WALES | CUBA | LEIF [TEAROOMS & PIANO BAR] |
| ------ | ------ | RETAIL |
| WINSTONS | CLARENDON | CLARENDON |
| BEDFORD INN | BARNIES | PART OF 'LOUNGE' [130, PARADE] |
| HALF MOON | SILVER JUBILEE | ENTRANCE TO ROYAL PRIORS |
| ------ | LONDON TAVERN | ROYAL PRIORS S/CENTRE |
| STYLES APART | FLANAGANS | SITE REDEVELOPED - RESIDENTIAL |
| GUARDS INN | QUEEN VICTORIA | QUEEN VICTORIA |
| JOLLY BOATMAN | ------ | SITE REDEVELOPED - INDUSTRIAL |
| ------ | ------ | PLOUGH & HARROW |

| NAME | ST. No. | STREET NAME | FROM | TO |
|---|---|---|---|---|
| POST OFFICE COMMERCIAL HOTEL | 27-28 | BATH STREET | ≤1860 | c1867 |
| PRINCE OF WALES | 116 | WARWICK STREET | 1849 | ≥1994 |
| PRINCE OF WALES [CONTIN] | 116 | WARWICK STREET | 2010 | 2012 |
| PRIORY TAVERN / ARMS | 10 | PRIORY STREET | ≤1838 | ≥1897 |
| PRIORY WAY WINE BAR | 26 | PARK STREET | 1988 | 1996 |
| QUEEN VICTORIA | 45 | HIGH STREET | 2011 | OPEN |
| QUEENS ARMS | 82 | QUEEN STREET | ≤1861 | 1978 |
| QUEENS CROSS INN | 1 | LIVERY STREET | c1835 | 1907 |
| QUEENS HEAD | 7 | BRUNSWICK STREET | 1832 | 1990 |
| RAILROAD INN | | SIDNEY TERRACE, RUGBY ROAD | ≤1843 | 1843-44 |
| RAILWAY INN | 12 | CLEMENS STREET | 1859 | OPEN |
| RAILWAY TAVERN | 10 | CLEMENS STREET | ≤1848 | c1857 |
| RAILWAY TAVERN | 187 | LEAM TERRACE [EAST] | c1849 | c1860 |
| RANELAGH TAVERN | 2-4 | RANELAGH STREET | 1826 | 1988 |
| RED HOUSE | 113 | RADFORD ROAD | ≤1856 | 2012 |
| RED LION | 7 | PARK STREET | ≤1817 | 1908 |
| REGENCY ARMS | 18 | NEWBOLD STREET | 2013 | OPEN |
| REGENT HOTEL | 77 | PARADE | 1819 | 1998 |
| REGENT WINE BAR | 33 | REGENT STREET | ≤1977 | 1983 |
| REINDEER | 66 | CLEMENS STREET | ≤1865 | 1907 |
| RICK'S BAR | 33 | REGENT STREET | 1983 | 1984 |
| RISING SUN | 34 | BEDFORD STREET | 1833 | 1907 |
| ROB ROY | 16 | BROOK STREET | ≤1841 | 1958 |
| ROBBIN'S WELL | 2A | VICTORIA TERRACE | 1998 | OPEN |
| ROSE & CROWN | 22 | KENILWORTH STREET | 1831 | 1963 |
| ROYAL | 2-4 | KENILWORTH ROAD | 1991 | ≥1996 |
| ROYAL EXCHANGE | 2 | HIGH STREET | 1865 | 2008 |
| [COPP's] ROYAL HOTEL | | HIGH STREET | 1816 | 1845 |
| ROYAL HOTEL TAP | | CLEMENS STREET | 1829 | 1841 |

| RENAMED FROM | RENAMED TO | CURRENT BUSINESS |
|---|---|---|
| ------ | ------ | RETAIL |
| ------ | OTHER PLACE | LEIF [TEAROOMS & PIANO BAR] |
| TRYST | LEIF | LEIF [TEAROOMS & PIANO BAR] |
| ------ | ------ | RESIDENTIAL |
| ------ | WIG & PEN | RESTAURANT |
| PIG & FIDDLE | ------ | QUEEN VICTORIA |
| ------ | ------ | RESIDENTIAL |
| ------ | ------ | SITE REDEVELOPED - REGENT COURT SHOPPING MALL |
| ------ | BRIDGE | RESIDENTIAL |
| ------ | COVENTRY ARMS [2] | FAT PUG |
| FOUNTAIN | ------ | RAILWAY INN |
| ------ | ------ | RETAIL |
| ------ | ------ | RESIDENTIAL |
| ------ | DEBONAIR | RESIDENTIAL |
| ------ | ------ | APPROVED 'CHANGE OF USE' TO RESIDENTIAL [JANUARY 2014] |
| ------ | ------ | RETAIL |
| NEWBOLD | ------ | REGENCY ARMS |
| WILLIAMS HOTEL | ------ | RESIDENTIAL/ HOTEL/ RETAIL |
| ------ | RICK'S BAR | MURPHY'S BAR |
| ------ | ------ | GRAND UNION RESTAURANT |
| REGENT WINE BAR | BAKERS | MURPHY'S BAR |
| ------ | ------ | SITE REDEVELOPED - RETAIL |
| ------ | ------ | FRONTAGE/ ENTRANCE TO FLATS |
| COLONNADE (THE) | ------ | ROBBIN'S WELL |
| ------ | ------ | CAR PARK |
| BERNI ROYAL HOTEL | ------ | RESIDENTIAL |
| ------ | EXCHANGE | UNDER GRADUATE |
| ------ | ------ | SITE REDEVELOPED |
| ------ | ------ | SITE REDEVELOPED - RAILWAY BRIDGE |

| NAME | ST. No. | STREET NAME | FROM | TO |
|------|---------|-------------|------|-----|
| ROYAL OAK | 37 | PARK STREET | 1825 | 1884 |
| RUGBY ARMS | | GUYS CLIFFE ROAD | 1875 | 1879-80 |
| RUGBY TAVERN [OLD] | 51 | RUGBY ROAD [CUBBINGTON] | ≤1839 | 1935 |
| RUGBY TAVERN [NEW] | 43 | RUGBY ROAD [CUBBINGTON] | 1935 | OPEN |
| SAINT BAR | 40 | WARWICK STREET | 2007 | OPEN |
| SAUSAGE | 141 | REGENT STREET | 2005 | 2008 |
| SAWYERS ARMS | | MILVERTON | 1837 | c1838 |
| SHAKESPEARE | | TAVISTOCK STREET | 2010 | 2012 |
| SHAKESPEARE INN | 2 | GEORGE STREET | 1853 | 1995 |
| SHAKESPEARE INN / TAVERN | 12 | REGENT STREET | 1827 | c1870 |
| SHIP | | SQUARE ST, COVENT GARDEN MKT. | 1834 | 1835 |
| SILVER JUBILEE | 36 | SATCHWELL STREET | 1977 | 1985 |
| SINKER'S BOARDING HOUSE [ALSO KNOWN AS 'GREYHOUND'] | | HIGH STREET | 1793 | 1813 |
| SIP BAR | 56A | REGENT STREET | ≤2004 | ≥2004 |
| SLUG & LETTUCE [1] | 32 | CLARENDON AVENUE | 1988 | 1989 |
| SLUG & LETTUCE [2] | 38-40 | WARWICK STREET | c2003 | 2010 |
| SLUG & LETTUCE @ THE FOX & VIVIAN | 32 | CLARENDON AVENUE | 1989 | 1995 |
| SOMERVILLE ARMS | 4 | CAMPION TERRACE | ≤1864 | OPEN |
| SOZZLED SAUSAGE | 141 | REGENT STREET | 1997 | 2005 |
| SOZZLED SAUSAGE [CONTIN] | 141 | REGENT STREET | 2008 | 2013 |
| SPRINGFIELD INN | 16 | SPRINGFIELD STREET | 1835 | ≤1856 |
| ST. GEORGES ROAD [54] | 54 | ST GEORGES ROAD | ≤1875 | 1889 |
| STAG & PHEASANT | 138 | WARWICK STREET | 1838 | 1857-59 |
| STAMFORD & WARRINGTON ARMS | 20 | RUGBY ROAD | 1833 | 1908 |
| STAR & GARTER | 4-6 | WARWICK STREET | ≤1808 | OPEN |
| STAR INN | 10 | WISE STREET | 1832 | 1956 |
| STATION INN | | MILVERTON | ≤1845 | 1845 |
| STONELEIGH ARMS | 31 | CLEMENS STREET | ≤1833 | 2001 |
| STONELEIGH HOTEL | | CLEMENS STREET | 1833 | 1834-38 |

| RENAMED FROM | RENAMED TO | CURRENT BUSINESS |
|---|---|---|
| ------ | ------ | RETAIL |
| ------ | ------ | EXACT LOCATION UNKNOWN |
| ------ | ------ | SITE REDEVELOPED - RESIDENTIAL |
| ------ | ------ | RUGBY TAVERN |
| MACKY'S BAR | ------ | SAINT BAR |
| SOZZLED SAUSAGE | SOZZLED SAUSAGE | WARWICK ARMS |
| ------ | ------ | LOCATION UNKNOWN |
| ------ | ALTORIA | ALTORIA |
| ------ | TOWN HOUSE | TOWN HOUSE TAVERN |
| ------ | ------ | EXACT LOCATION UNKNOWN |
| DOG & DUCK | KING'S HEAD | CLEARED & SEALED SPACE |
| PALACE INN | ------ | ENTRANCE TO ROYAL PRIORS |
| BLACK DOG [1] | BECAME PART OF [COPPS] ROYAL HOTEL | SITE REDEVELOPED - RETAIL |
| ------ | ------ | BAKERY / CAFÉ |
| FOX & VIVIAN | SLUG & LETTUCE @ FOX & VIVIAN | FOX & VIVIAN |
| ------ | GLASSHOUSE | GLASSHOUSE |
| SLUG & LETTUCE [1] | FOX | FOX & VIVIAN |
| ------ | ------ | SOMERVILLE ARMS |
| WARWICK ARMS | SAUSAGE | WARWICK ARMS |
| SAUSAGE | WARWICK ARMS | WARWICK ARMS |
| ------ | JOINERS ARMS [1] | GRASSED AREA |
| ------ | ------ | SITE REDEVELOPED - RESIDENTIAL |
| ------ | ------ | RESTAURANT |
| ------ | ------ | RESIDENTIAL |
| ------ | ------ | STAR & GARTER |
| ------ | ------ | SITE REDEVELOPED - KHALSA HOCKEY CLUB |
| ------ | ------ | EXACT LOCATION UNKNOWN |
| ------ | ------ | DERELICT [DECEMBER 2013] |
| BLENHEIM HOTEL | ------ | RETAIL |

| NAME | ST. No. | STREET NAME | FROM | TO |
|---|---|---|---|---|
| STRESA BAR | 86 | REGENT STREET | ≤2006 | ≤2008 |
| STYLES APART | 12 | AUGUSTA PLACE | 1990 | 1994 |
| SUGAR LOAF | | LEAMINGTON PRIORS | 1817 | c1825 |
| SUN | | TACHBROOK ROAD | 2006 | OPEN |
| SUN IN SPLENDOUR | | TACHBROOK ROAD | 1956 | 2006 |
| SWAN [ALSO KNOWN AS 'WHITE SWAN'] | | CLEMENS STREET | 1810 | c1823 |
| SWAN INN | | KENILWORTH STREET | 1833 | 1833-34 |
| SWAN INN | | CNR CLARENDON & SWAN STS | 1835 | 1959 |
| SWAN INN | | ALTHORPE STREET | 1884 | 1888-89 |
| SWEENEY'S | 116 | WARWICK STREET | 2006 | 2007 |
| SYD'S BAR [REGENT HOTEL] | 77 | PARADE | 1960 | ≤1980 |
| TALBOT INN | 34 | RUSHMORE STREET | 1880 | OPEN |
| TAVISTOCK INN | 50 | TAVISTOCK STREET | 1883 | OPEN |
| THREE GRACES | 44 | CLARENDON STREET | 2010 | 2011 |
| THREE TUNS | 60 | CLEMENS STREET | ≤1856 | 1879 |
| TILLER PIN | | QUEENSWAY | 1994 | OPEN |
| TJ'S | 45-47 | BATH STREET | 2002 | OPEN |
| TOP OF TOWN | 44-46 | CLARENDON AVENUE | 1984 | 1986 |
| TOWN HOUSE | 2 | GEORGE STREET | 1995 | 1999 |
| TOWN HOUSE TAVERN | 2 | GEORGE STREET | 2001 | OPEN |
| TOYK BAR | 102 | WARWICK STREET | ≤2004 | ≥2006 |
| TRYST | 116 | WARWICK STREET | ≥2009 | 2010 |
| TURF INN | 36 | SATCHWELL STREET | 1845 | 1859 |
| TURTLE INN | 71 | PARADE | ≤1854 | 1915 |
| UNDER GRADUATE | 2 | HIGH STREET | 2013 | OPEN |
| UNICORN INN | | LEAM TERRACE EAST | ≤1846 | ≥1846 |
| UNION & COMMERCIAL INN | | CHURCH STREET | 1829 | 1830 |
| UNION TAVERN | 33 | PARK STREET | 1835 | 1836 |
| VAULTS [PH] | 13 | BATH STREET | 1831 | 1957 |

| RENAMED FROM | RENAMED TO | CURRENT BUSINESS |
|---|---|---|
| V-BAR | ------ | RESTAURANT |
| CASSIS | PHOENIX | SITE REDEVELOPED - RESIDENTIAL |
| ------ | ------ | LOCATION UNKNOWN |
| SUN IN SPLENDOUR | ------ | SUN |
| ------ | SUN | SUN |
| ------ | ------ | LOCATION UNKNOWN |
| ------ | ------ | EXACT LOCATION UNKNOWN |
| ------ | ------ | RETAIL |
| ------ | ------ | EXACT LOCATION UNKNOWN |
| CUBA | MOR BAR | LEIF [TEAROOMS & PIANO BAR] |
| ------ | CORK AND FORK | ENTRANCE TO TRAVELODGE |
| ------ | ------ | TALBOT INN |
| NEWMARKET INN | ------ | TAVISTOCK INN |
| BAR 44 | FORTY FOUR | MAD HATTERS |
| ------ | ALBATROSS | RETAIL |
| ------ | ------ | TILLER PIN |
| ------ | ------ | TJ'S |
| WINSTONS | JEKYLL & HYDE | CLARENDON |
| SHAKESPEARE INN | GREEN TAILED DRAGON | TOWN HOUSE TAVERN |
| GREEN TAILED DRAGON | ------ | TOWN HOUSE TAVERN |
| ------ | WHALE BAR | CREPERIE / RESTAURANT |
| MOR BAR | PRINCE OF WALES | LEIF [TEAROOMS & PIANO BAR] |
| HALF MOON | HALF MOON | ENTRANCE TO ROYAL PRIORS |
| ------ | ------ | RETAIL |
| EXCHANGE | UNDER GRADUATE | UNDER GRADUATE |
| ------ | ------ | EXACT LOCATION UNKNOWN |
| BOWLING GREEN INN [1] | ------ | SITE REDEVELOPED - RESIDENTIAL |
| LAMB | ------ | EXACT LOCATION UNKNOWN |
| WINE, SPIRITS & ALE MERCHANTS | CHAIR & ROCKET | JUG & JESTER |

| NAME | ST. No. | STREET NAME | FROM | TO |
|------|---------|-------------|------|-----|
| V-BAR | 86 | REGENT STREET | c2001 | ≥2004 |
| VENEW @ THE BINSWOOD | | RUGBY ROAD | 2010 | 2012 |
| VICTORIA ARMS | | QUEEN STREET | ≤1841 | 1841 |
| VICTORIA VAULTS | 44 | TAVISTOCK STREET | c1870 | 1905 |
| VOLUNTEER ARMS | 46 | COMYN STREET | ≤1865 | 1950 |
| VOODOO BAR | 35 | REGENT STREET | 1999 | OPEN |
| WALNUT TREE | | CROWN WAY, LILLINGTON | 1958 | 2009 |
| WARNEFORD ARMS | 36 | CHARLES STREET | 1871 | 1906 |
| WARWICK ARMS | 141 | REGENT STREET | 1844 | 1997 |
| WARWICK ARMS [CONTIN] | 141 | REGENT STREET | 2013 | OPEN |
| WARWICK HOTEL | 35 | REGENT STREET | 1904 | 1984 |
| WARWICK TAVERN | 35 | REGENT STREET | 1823 | 1904 |
| WELLINGTON TAVERN | 9 | WELLINGTON STREET | 1828 | 1860 |
| WHALE BAR | 102 | WARWICK STREET | ≥2006 | ≤2009 |
| WHEATSHEAF INN | 163 | TACHBROOK ROAD | ≤1834 | OPEN |
| WHEELERS ARMS | | KENILWORTH STREET | 1835 | 1839-40 |
| WHITE HART INN | 7 | WINDSOR STREET | ≤1849 | 1966 |
| WHITE HORSE | 4-6 | CLARENDON AVENUE | 1833 | OPEN |
| WHITE LION | 5 | ALTHORPE STREET | 1838 | 1961 |
| WHITE LION | 26 | BROOK STREET | 1835 | c1863 |
| WHITNASH TAVERN | | ST. MARGARETS ROAD, WHITNASH | 1994 | OPEN |
| WIG & PEN | 26 | PARK STREET | 1996 | 2001 |
| WILDE'S | 7 | PARADE | 1976 | OPEN |
| WILLIAM THE FOURTH | | QUEEN STREET | ≤1837 | c1840 |
| WILLIAMS HOTEL | | UNION PARADE | 1819 | 1819 |
| WILLOUGHBY | 12 | AUGUSTA PLACE | ≥1997 | c2009 |
| WILLOUGHBY [CONTIN] | 12 | AUGUSTA PLACE | 2011 | 2013 |
| WILLOUGHBY ARMS | 12 | AUGUSTA PLACE | 1875 | 1983 |
| WINDMILL INN | 209 | TACHBROOK ROAD, WHITNASH | 1861 | OPEN |

| RENAMED FROM | RENAMED TO | CURRENT BUSINESS |
|---|---|---|
| GLASNOST VODKA BAR | STRESA BAR | RESTAURANT |
| NEW BINSWOOD TAVERN | ------ | RESIDENTIAL [COMPLETION LATE 2014] |
| ------ | ------ | EXACT LOCATION UNKNOWN |
| CROSS KEYS [1] | ------ | NIGHT CLUB |
| ------ | ------ | RESIDENTIAL |
| BIRCH TREE | ------ | VOODOO BAR |
| ------ | ------ | SITE REDEVELOPED - RETAIL |
| ------ | ------ | ALTHORPE INDUSTRIAL ESTATE |
| COVENTRY ARMS [1] | SOZZLED SAUSAGE | WARWICK ARMS |
| SOZZLED SAUSAGE | ------ | WARWICK ARMS |
| WARWICK TAVERN | BIRCH & BILLYCOCK | VOODOO BAR |
| ------ | WARWICK HOTEL | VOODOO BAR |
| ------ | ------ | RETAIL |
| TOYK BAR | JAM BAR & BRASSERIE | CREPERIE / RESTAURANT |
| ------ | ------ | WHEATSHEAF INN |
| ------ | ------ | EXACT LOCATION UNKNOWN |
| ------ | ------ | TELEPHONE EXCHANGE |
| ------ | ------ | WHITE HORSE |
| ------ | ------ | ALTHORPE INDUSTRIAL ESTATE |
| MERRIE LION | OLD WHITE LION | BROOK STREET REBUILT |
| BULLDOG | ------ | WHITNASH TAVERN |
| PRIORY WAY WINE BAR | BAR CITRUS | RESTAURANT |
| ------ | ------ | WILDE'S |
| ------ | ------ | EXACT LOCATION UNKNOWN |
| ------ | REGENT HOTEL | RESIDENTIAL/ HOTEL/ RETAIL |
| FLANAGAN'S | BOHEMIA @ WILLOUGHBY | SITE REDEVELOPED - RESIDENTIAL |
| BOHEMIA @ WILLOUGHBY | ------ | SITE REDEVELOPED - RESIDENTIAL |
| AUGUSTA TAVERN | CASSIS | SITE REDEVELOPED - RESIDENTIAL |
| ------ | ------ | WINDMILL INN |

| NAME | ST. No. | STREET NAME | FROM | TO |
|---|---|---|---|---|
| WINE VAULTS | 25-27 | BEDFORD STREET | 1832 | 1952 |
| WINE VAULTS | 56 | BEDFORD STREET | ≤1851 | ≥1974 |
| WINE VAULTS | 58 | WARWICK STREET | ≤1893 | 1961 |
| WINE VAULTS [ASSEMBLY ROOMS] | | REGENT STREET | ≤1849 | 1880 |
| WINSTON'S | 44-46 | CLARENDON AVENUE | 1975-76 | 1984 |
| WINSTONS [CONTIN] | 44-46 | CLARENDON AVENUE | 1992 | 2002 |
| WOODLAND TAVERN | 3 | REGENT STREET | 1833 | OPEN |
| WOODMAN INN | 24 | BEDFORD STREET | 1828 | 1966 |
| WOOLPACK | 77 | REGENT STREET | 1838-40 | c1845 |
| YATES WINE LODGE | 44-46 | WARWICK STREET | 1996 | c2007 |
| ZEST | 45 | WARWICK STREET | ≤2004 | ≥2004 |

| RENAMED FROM | RENAMED TO | CURRENT BUSINESS |
|---|---|---|
| ------ | ------ | EXACT LOCATION UNKNOWN |
| ------ | ------ | RETAIL |
| ------ | ------ | SITE REDEVELOPED - RETAIL |
| ------ | IMPERIAL [PH] | ART GALLERY |
| ------ | TOP OF TOWN | CLARENDON |
| JEKYLL & HYDE | OXYGEN | CLARENDON |
| ------ | ------ | WOODLAND TAVERN |
| ------ | ------ | CAR PARKING |
| BULL & BUTCHER | ------ | EXACT LOCATION UNKNOWN |
| ------ | DUKE | DUKE |
| ------ | KO KO's | ALTORIA |